D0946107

THE
DIMENSIONS
OF
PUBLIC
ADMINISTRATION

Consulting Editor

John C. Bollens

*university of california,
los angeles*

THE DIMENSIONS OF PUBLIC ADMINISTRATION

SECOND EDITION

Joseph A. Uveges, Jr.
western kentucky university

HOLBROOK PRESS, INC.　　　　BOSTON

Library - St. Joseph's College
222 Clinton Avenue
Brooklyn, N. Y. 11205

Fourth printing . . . June 1977

© Copyright 1975 by Holbrook Press, Inc.

© Copyright 1971 by Holbrook Press, Inc., 470 Atlantic Avenue, Boston. All rights reserved. No part of the material protected by this copyright notice may be reproduced or utilized in any form or by any means, electronic or mechanical, including photocopying, recording, or by any informational storage and retrieval system, without written permission from the copyright owner.

Printed in the United States of America.

Library of Congress Cataloging in Publication Data

Uveges, Joseph Andrew, comp.
  The dimensions of public administration.

  Includes bibliographies.
  1. Public administration—Addresses, essays, lectures. 2. United States—Executive departments—Management—Addresses, essays, lectures. I. Title.
JF1351.U63   1975   350   74-28445
ISBN   0-205-04667-3

CONTENTS

96780

PART THREE / ORGANIZATIONAL DYNAMICS AND ADMINISTRATIVE LEADERSHIP

PART FOUR / PUBLIC PERSONNEL MANAGEMENT IN A TIME OF CHANGE

PART FIVE / CHANGING TRENDS IN THE BUDGETARY PROCESS

PART SIX / THE PROBLEMS AND PROSPECTS OF ADMINISTRATIVE RESPONSIBILITY

PREFACE TO THE SECOND EDITION

Much has transpired in the study and practice of public administration since the printing of the first edition. Paramount among these has been the tremendous increase in the interest of students in public sector careers and the proliferation of programs aimed at serving that interest. Along with increased enrollments in public administration courses, there is a renewed concern for the discipline of public administration. A reflection of this growing awareness of identity is the greater effort of academicians and practitioners to research and publish in the public administration journals that have also grown in number. A further reflection of a renewed disciplinary zeal is the adoption by NASPAA of a statement on *Guidelines and Standards for Professional Master's Degree Programs in Public Affairs/Public Administration* in early 1974 and the creation of a section within NASPAA for the purpose of looking closely at undergraduate programs in public administration. Furthermore, since the first edition was published, many new or updated textbooks in public administration have been published, as well as several collections of readings. As I note the growing list of publications I cannot help but be pleased that *The Dimensions of Public Administration* has been so well received and used across the colleges and universities of this nation.

Nevertheless, along with the many supportive comments came many criticisms as well. Writing for a rapidly growing and awakening academic community carries with it the assurance that criticism will be forthcoming. But it is from such inputs that change and improvement can be attained and it is to such a task that the second edition is directed.

Four major concerns should be noted. First, there was evidence of the need to devote more space and time to the policy process aspects of public administration. Secondly, suggestions were made that more attention be given to the application side of administration as well as the theoretical dimensions. Thirdly, as is the case with all anthologies, selections had a tendency to become dated and, more importantly, the state of American society and government was changing so rap-

idly that newer and more relevant topics needed to be included
Finally, as the interest in public administration programs continued
an interest developed also among practitioners in the manner in
which public administration courses were taught and the subject matter handled. Thus this edition offers materials that are relevant and
pertinent to the present administrator as well as the undergraduate
student.

This edition differs greatly from the first. Only seven of the original
thirty-seven selections in the first edition remain. An effort has been
made to synthesize topic materials so that the number of parts has
been reduced from eight to six, a new section on public policy processes has been added, and the section on comparative administration
has been deleted. In light of the recent developments in public attitudes about governmental policies and officials, this edition focuses
on efforts being made in the practice of public administration to
mitigate disputes and to promote greater involvement in the administrative process by not only those within the government, but also
those upon whom government operates. Evidence of this may be
most readily seen in discussions about the effect of executive staff
functions and Watergate upon executive-legislative relations and
presidential leadership; in the ongoing debate over labor-management relations and political activity in the public personnel sector; in
the apparent movement to downgrade PPBS at the national level and
to accelerate revenue-sharing programs as an integral part of the
"new federalism;" and in the growing desire to have public administrators more reflective of the society at large and more representative
of community views in their day to day activities.

Unfortunately, events in the public sector do not run their course
according to the publication schedule of any publisher. Much has
transpired on the national governmental scene since this edition was
submitted for publication. A President who received the highest
popular vote majority has resigned his office under extreme pressure
of the administrative and political nightmare called Watergate to be
replaced by the first President ever to attain that office without a
popular vote mandate. Major questions have arisen regarding the
administrative style of the former President which some blame in
part for the rather narrow awareness evidenced for the public attitude on Watergate and related matters. The events of Watergate
clearly show how personal styles of leadership and administrative
structures may affect the motives and activities of administrative officials whether they be elected or appointed. The manner and style of
the new administration with regard to leadership and management of

executive functions have been and will continue to be substantially affected by the "fall-out" from Watergate and its related events. Legislative-executive relations may be substantially altered depending, in part, on the new President's ability to bring about a working relationship with the Congress and the willingness of Congress to assert itself in the policy vacuum which resulted from the Watergate period. In the final analysis, however, the real impact is yet to be felt and can only be evaluated in the succeeding events and in analysis yet to be written and evaluated.

Not enough can be said to express my sincere appreciation to the many colleagues who offered me support and advice over the past four years since the first edition was published. Not surprisingly, my students deserve to be mentioned since their needs were the stimulus for the first edition and their comments a source of input for the second edition. Having now worked on this project twice, I have gained a high regard for the authors and publishers whose materials are the backbone of the book and for the staff personnel from innumerable publications, without whose assistance and suggestions this project could never have been completed. Finally, I am extremely grateful to Ms. Dianna Simpson, Mrs. Rhonda Ashley, and Ms. Melissa McKenney for their able assistance in the preparation of the manuscript and in the many other tasks they so willingly and expertly carried out.

J. A. U.

PREFACE TO THE FIRST EDITION

The organization of this book rests on the assumption that the reader will gain an awareness of the relationship between administrative theory and administrative reality. That is, he will understand that theory and practice are intimately related, for much of the reality of modern administration is rooted in the administrative theories of the past. In addition, the reader should become aware of the behavior of the administrator as an individual operating within a system. Finally, he will see present efforts to adapt modern administration to the necessities of today's democratic, technological state.

The objectives, then, are threefold:

1. To present the premises of administrative theory, the values they represent, and their application to modern administrative situations. These objectives are met in Parts 1, 2, and 3 of the book.
2. To introduce the ideas of administrative leadership and the modern administrator—his roles and the tools available to him. Part 4 accomplishes this objective.
3. To indicate the variety of functions included in public administration and the dynamic possibilities for change in these areas. These are the objectives of Parts 5, 6, 7, and 8.

This book approaches public administration from the perspective that administration in the United States is a dynamic, everchanging process. Far too often, administration has been viewed as a "nuts and bolts" process devoid of any real relationship to the world of politics. The administrator has been viewed as a technician in a world closed off from the many, often conflicting demands that bear on decision-making. To be sure, public administration in the United States has always resulted from the complex interplay of such diverse elements as culture, values, institutions, processes, and behavior.

Public administration, like all the subfields of political science, has been undergoing vast changes of a conceptual nature. The "traditionalist-behavioralist" controversy had a marked impact on our understanding of public administration. Beliefs and assumptions that were for some time held inviolate are now being questioned. Administrative systems conceived on the values of the early 1900s have been attacked, and new concepts now explain administrative behavior. This conflict of approaches to administration lends a dynamic character to the discipline.

The organizational framework for this collection stems from these conflicting approaches to public administration. Each substantive part of the book includes selections that illustrate the major conceptual questions in public administration. Furthermore, although the articles selected tend to be biased in favor of the behavioral approach, an effort is made to provide a link between the traditional and behavioral emphases.

Perhaps the critical question to be raised at this point might be: What makes public administration so important? The answer to such a question is obvious. Not only have the functions of government expanded markedly in recent years, both on the foreign and domestic scene, but more important, the administrative process is a vital element of the political process. The administrator must be responsive to many forces: Congress, the executive branch, and the public. At the same time, he must apply the law, in many cases, to the very public to which he responds.

The traditions of administration confront the administrator with large numbers of formal regulations, procedures and processes that limit the flexibility available to him. Yet actual administrative practices may force him to bypass certain rules by exercising discretionary judgments. Finally, the fact that he is an individual dealing with other individuals may compel the administrator to act in a manner not clearly prescribed by the structure of his administrative unit.

What makes the study of public administration all the more important is that we live in a highly urban, industrial society where the "administrative state" plays a significant role in allocating advantages and disadvantages. The United States' expanding role as a world power and the increasing demands of a pluralistic, technological society have produced a myriad of new governmental programs. Increasing external and internal demands on the political system have led to an increase in governmental control, particularly in the economic sector as large private organizations are brought more closely under governmental scrutiny. Even so, greater efforts toward control in this sector are sought today. And, if recent history is any guide, government programs and controls in matters of social concern will also be vastly expanded. Certainly, as problems pertaining to welfare, hunger, and race relations obtain higher national priorities, and as state and local governments find themselves unable or unwilling to provide these services and rights, the roles of the national government will grow.

Finally, as the power of the federal government increases in scope and scale, we must be increasingly aware that the traditional democratic processes may only partially control the actions of administrators. If we expect government "of the people, by the people, and for the people," the administrator as a neutral may well be caught on the horns of a dilemma. We must be able to grasp the importance of expertise and neutrality for administrative actions while at the same time find newer, more effective ways to control official acts without destroying administrative initiative. We must be able to use the newest techniques to achieve optimum public satisfaction while maintaining the individual's faith in his government.

The selections in this book can in no way be construed to cover all the diverse writings in public administration in recent years. The readings chosen for publication do, however, express some of the best and most readable contributions available. An effort was made to include up-to-date opinions and data in regard to the major administrative theories and functions.

Most of the articles are reprinted unabridged. In other instances, some repetitious or extraneous material is deleted. While the grouping of selections is mostly based on conventional topics of administration, many individual selections may apply to several of the general topics.

The introductory essays to each Part serve several critical functions. First, they explain the central theme of each Part. Second, they briefly summarize the individual selections and relate them to the general topic under consideration. Finally, the introductions provide a base of departure from which the reader may develop his own interpretation and understanding of the subject.

I would like to express my gratitude to the many people who have been instrumental in the preparation of this book. Of special note in this regard are Professors George Masannat, Thomas Madron, and Hugh Thompson, whose critical comments and suggestions were invaluable. Special thanks are also due the many secretaries and student assistants who carried out many mechanical duties of preparing and proofing the manuscript. I am also grateful to Western Kentucky University for its continued encouragement and support. Last, but most important, I must acknowledge the support of my wife, Joyce, and my children, Michael, Stephen, and Dana Jill, who have suffered long and weathered well the many moods of a struggling author.

It should remain clear that the ultimate responsibility for the introductory essays, the choice of selections, and the suggested readings rests entirely upon the author.

J. A. U.

ONE

FOUNDATIONS FOR THE STUDY OF PUBLIC ADMINISTRATION

The study of public administration is in part a quest for identity. Part One explores this quest by presenting the roles theory played in the development of public administration, the forces at work bringing about changes in administration theory, and the critical roles for theory building as a means to bring about a unified understanding of public administration.

For many, public administration appears to have a "split personality." Some argue that public administration is concerned with how to systematically apply laws faithfully, honestly, economically, and efficiently. Implicit in this definition is the separation of policy making (politics) from policy execution (administration). Others contend that public administration is concerned with the processes through which public administrators participate in the creation, interpretation, and execution of the law, thus combining the policy-making and policy-execution phases. In addition, less than a consensus exists as to whether public administration is an art or a science; both positions have strong supporters.

Administrative theory has played a vital role in the development of a multifaceted public administration. Each of the positions above, among others, has a solid foothold in the theory of public administration. Administrative practices which are based upon these theories abound. In effect, complementary relationships exist between theory and practice in public administration.

In order to understand this complementary relationship between theory and practice we must define our terms. *Theory* is a proposition or set of propositions systematically arranged to explain the relationships in observed phenomena or to explain interrelationships among data not directly observed or otherwise manifest. Theory may be applied in order to communicate actual practices and to prescribe practices based upon observed data. This theoretical approach is consistent with the empirical, behavior-oriented, explanatory approach to public administration commonly referred to as the *behavioral approach.* This conception of public administration has considerable support among scholars of administration at the present time. In addition, theory may communicate assumptive data and prescribe future practices based on such assumptions. This approach is consistent with the normative, value-oriented, prescriptive focus of public administration usually referred to as the *traditional approach.* This "traditional" emphasis was dominant within the profession until the late 1940s, received diminished support during the 1950s and 1960s, and now appears to be gaining renewed interest within the profession.

The selections in this chapter represent a composite of the interaction that exists between theory and practice in the study of public administration. Professor Sharma considers the study of administration as an ongoing process. He suggests that administrative theory has passed through three stages in its evolution: scientific management, organizations and systems, and the administrative process. He identifies the major elements of each of these stages, showing how theories, as tools for analysis and understanding, have tended to interact to bring about a greater awareness of the workings of administration. Although he emphasizes that the administrative process approach represents the current emphasis in administrative theory, he points out that the evolutionary process continues unabated. He proposes that an eclectic approach, with the administrative process school as the core, may well be the newest stage in the evolutionary cycle.

Theory not only leads the way for future practices, but also may reflect practical changes. Herbert Simon analyzes the relationships between developments in administrative structures and the changes taking place in political and social realities. He identifies four domestic and two international dimensions of significant change in administrative institutions and relates these to changes in attitudes and behaviors within our society.

Most important for us as students of administration, is the link which Simon establishes between normative values in administration and certain "decisional-premises." He proposes that we view administration as a decision-making system—a system in which an information flow to achieve political goals and effective service and regulation is all-important. He suggests that administrators are not neutral in the roles they play. However, he contends that their actions are still predictable. In so doing, he helps us to understand what part of theory is normative and what part is descriptive. At the same time, he focuses our attention upon the effective roles played by such theories as they help to expand our understanding of the realities of public administration.

More traditional roles for administrative theory are called into question by recent challenges raised by the "new public administration." H. George Frederickson's selection stresses that the new public administration is nothing more than a reweaving of the fabric of administration so that a new design becomes more readily apparent. According to Frederickson, the "new" emphasis is concerned not only with the efficient and effective management of administrative resources, but is committed also to developing the means to achieve social equity and a better quality of life. The administrator is directed to be more public, prescriptive, client-oriented, and normative in his awareness of and actions toward the administrative state.

New public administration theory would support these roles. Such theory would be developed around four processes: the distributive process, the integrative process, the boundary exchange process, and the socioemotional process. Frederickson suggests that the result of such a shift in emphasis would be: a shift of support for administration from the business-middle class groups to the disadvantaged minorities; an increase in the level of opposition to the administrative state from the legislatures; and the advent of a governmental system in which elected officials speak for the majority and the privileged minorities, while the courts and the administrators speak for the disadvantaged minorities. Although the risks are great, he sees the outcomes as making the bureaucracy more responsive and responsible.

Although the potential for conflict between the traditional and new approaches to public administration exists, not all writers see such conflict as inevitable or disruptive. Orion White, Jr. speaks to the question of how one might bring about the effective merger of theory and practice for the benefit of both the academician and the practitioner. Inherent in this question is the traditional-contemporary theory problem discussed earlier.

White explains that the main intent of all schools of administrative thought and practice has been to create and maintain administrative authority and that the dominant thought at any particular time carries with it a concept of orthodoxy as the basis for action. He counters this "positive science" model with the model of "symbolic exchange" which, by definition, entails tension rather than stability.

By using two examples, he demonstrates that the two models stand not as contradictions, but as reference points for different emphases which interact dialectically. Thus, a synthesis would be effected in which the concept of rationality takes on an element of intuition and feeling heretofore excluded.

White suggests that, regardless of the institutional nature of the administrative unit, all action is still personal and that the ultimate responsibility remains with the individual. At the same time, he takes the position that the administrative man is more humane than the positive science model assumes him to be, thereby reducing the need to encumber the administrator with a variety of control mechanisms.

His call for "administrative praxis" is a call for the administrative theorist and practitioner to work together to modify their particular roles. The theorist should acknowledge that he deals in values and the practitioner should be willing to commit himself to bringing values into a situation and to assume the political risks which might follow.

It should be obvious that the identity crisis has not been ended. Nor is it likely to do so in the near future, especially in the light of the "new public administration." Any effort to build identity upon a floating system of values and their outcomes will tend to reduce the areas of agreement to the more procedural reference points and away from the more substantive (policy) references. Only where substantive policy and procedural factors merge will agreement exist. Nevertheless, if administration is a dynamic process which remains subject to the whims of the academician, the professional, and the public, to seek anything more might be presumptuous.

1

c.l. sharma

ADMINISTRATION AS A FIELD OF STUDY

Administration is a way of conceptual thinking for attaining predetermined goals through group effort. As a concept, it is of universal application. It emerged with the human race and will continue to be employed as long as mankind survives. It is an indispensable ingredient of group effort and is characteristic of all types of undertakings in which people engage to achieve objectives collectively. It may vary in form with the nature of the enterprise but, in substance, it remains the same. Its rudiments are discernible even in the most primitive and simple society, but it becomes increasingly sophisticated in its structure and application as the society becomes more advanced and complex. This becomes readily evident as one compares the administration of the Greek city states with that of the large industrial complexes and continental governments of our time.

THE NATURE OF ADMINISTRATION

The following observations can be made about the nature of administration:

1. Administration is a process consisting of a number of subprocesses. Principally, the subprocesses are planning, organizing, staffing, directing, coordinating, and controlling. These subprocesses are interrelated and interdependent

C. L. Sharma, "Administration as a Field of Study," *International Review of Administrative Science*, vol. 32, no. 4 (1966), pp. 287-300. Reprinted by permission.

and are usually, but not necessarily, carried out simultaneously and continuously in an ongoing enterprise.

2. Administration presupposes a formally organized group of people working together as members of an enterprise. Without group activity, there is no opportunity for the operation of administration. The group may be composed of as few as two persons. The activities of an individual working by himself, which are not complementary to those of any other person, do not lend themselves to the application of administration. People work in groups to attain goals which ordinarily are beyond the possibility of individual accomplishment. It is inconceivable that the group effort would be productive without the assistance of administration, but it is also axiomatic that in the absence of the former the latter would simply be inoperative.

3. For administration to operate, the group of people must be working toward a specific objective or a set of objectives. A group which does not seek to attain an objective or a set of objectives is not the concern of administration. For example, administration is inapplicable to a crowd which has no group goals.

4. Usually, administration is provided with broad objectives, but it is the responsibility of administration to refine them, define them, and render them attainable.

5. Administration seeks to achieve the enterprise objectives by intelligently utilizing the efforts of a group of people, and its success is measured in terms of the accomplishment of predetermined objectives.

6. Administration implies getting the things done through subordinates. An efficient administrator is one who gets the work done through the efforts of his subordinates rather than doing it himself.

7. As administration implies the ability to get the work done through subordinates, it is a distinct skill, different from specialized technical expertness. An administrator may possess some technical skill, but it would be of no use to him in the discharge of his administrative responsibilities.

8. Administrative skill is not a technical skill in the sense of engineering skill or skill in medicine. Yet it is a specialized skill which would significantly determine the achievement of enterprise goals.

9. Administration has emerged as a distinct and identifiable discipline that can be studied, taught, learned, and practiced, and has universal application.

10. The discipline of administration has accumulated some principles concerning the administration of certain aspects of enterprise, and more are in the process of identification. These principles are reasonably well-established, generally accepted, and widely practiced. However, because of the preponderance of human element in administration, the principles are not absolute and infallible and need to be used as guides with great caution.

11. Administration is intangible and invisible. However, orderliness in work, achievement of objectives, and satisfaction of employees are indices of its efficient and continuous operation.

12. Provision of resources, human and material, falls within the purview of administration. It is the responsibility of administration to provide for them in quantity, quality, and variety necessary to attain the objectives of the enterprise.

13. Although administration is ultimately responsible for the provision of resources, both human and material, for the enterprise, primarily it is concerned with the efficient direction of human effort in the manipulation of non-human resources to accomplish the enterprise goals. People are the subject of administration, not land, capital, building, or raw materials.

14. Administration embraces the total enterprise and permeates all parts of it, with varied emphases on its subprocesses at different levels of the organizational structure.

15. Administration is employed at all levels of the organizational structure of an enterprise. At higher levels of the structure it is characterized by more policy formulation, and at lower levels, by more policy execution.

16. Since administration is an inseparable feature of organized activity, the principles of administration would apply to all types of enterprises irrespective of the nature of activities they may be engaged in. The pervasive character of administration can be judged from the fact that no enterprise can be initiated and have a continued existence, without its operation, in any society at any time.

17. The universality of the principles of administration also makes them transferable. Administrative skill is different

from technical skill in the sense that it is basically the same regardless of the nature of the enterprise to which it may be applied. Therefore, able executives can change enterprises, diverse in nature, without any loss in efficiency.

18. Administrative skill is conditioned by the cultural advancement of a society. Such factors as social discipline, scientific knowledge, technical know-how, communication system, industrial achievements, and legal provisions would set a limit on the competency of administrators.

19. Administration is chiefly a mental activity. It may, and usually it does, involve some manual work, but that is not sufficient enough to negate its dominant characteristic.

20. Administration is not an end in itself; it is only a means to accomplish the enterprise objectives.

THE PURPOSE OF ADMINISTRATION

Administration has emerged out of the necessity of man to cooperate. Man has learned the value of cooperation from the realization that through collective effort he can accomplish what he individually can not. Cooperation presupposes some kind of work division among the participating individuals. The division of work is necessitated by human limitations—the inability of the individual to be at two places at the same time, to do two things at the same time, to master more than a small fraction of the vast accumulation of knowledge and skill, and to perform all tasks equally well, as men differ in nature, capacity, and skill. The technological advance has accentuated the imperativeness of the division of work and has substantially reduced the significance of the individual in modern gigantic enterprises. The logical method of dividing work among members of a group is according to their differing abilities attributable to heredity and environment. This results in efficient utilization of individuals with diverse capabilities, and leads to specialization in skills.

Thus, group effort has come to be an irrefutable fact of our time and an indispensable instrument for satisfying most of the human needs. Now, the question arises: Who should guide the group effort? This challenge has been met by administration which provides for the acquisition and integration of human and material resources necessary to attain the predetermined objectives of the enterprise. . . . Therefore, it is administration which leads the group effort to fruition. Without administration, the enterprise would disintegrate and dissolve, if it ever originates.

Administration is a means and not an end in itself. Therefore, the ultimate goals of administration cannot be different from those of the enterprise. Administration comes into being to serve the enterprise and cannot justify its existence otherwise. However, in order to attain the goals of the enterprise, the administration must seek the fulfillment of numerous immediate and intermediate goals. These would include orderliness in activities performed, supply and intelligent utilization of human and material resources, elimination of waste and inefficiency, economy in operations, welfare of employees, satisfaction of clientele, anticipation and resolution of problems, provision of guidance, and others. Effectuation of these subordinate goals is requisite to the realization of enterprise goals, which administration alone can bring about.

No enterprise can succeed in attaining its objectives that does not employ effective administration to its service. To a large extent, the accomplishment of goals of economic, social, political, military, or religious enterprises depends upon the application of efficient administration. Group effort is responsible for the material advancement of a society, which, in turn, is buttressed by continuous and diligent administration. Satisfaction of varied and multiplying human needs will continue to require a greater degree of group effort, which will place unprecedented demand on administration. Efficient administration contributes significantly to the success of an enterprise, and, thereby, cumulatively leads to the prosperity of a society.

ADMINISTRATION—A SCIENCE OR AN ART?

The controversy concerning the classification of the discipline of administration—a science or an art—has not been settled. Admittedly, such a discussion is of academic interest only and does not serve any useful purpose. However, whether administration be classified as a science or an art will depend upon the definition of these terms.

If by science is meant a discipline in which principles can be established through experimentation, administration can not qualify to be called a science because the human element in administration would defy the conducting of rigorous scientific experiments. On the other hand, if by science is meant a systematically organized body of knowledge in a subject field in contrast with a mere collection of traditions, practices, or personal reminiscences, administration would be considered a science just as much as political science or military science. Administration has evolved into a discipline which is now taught in professional schools and which provides a field for fruitful research.

Art is a skill in the application of which the possessor brings to bear his distinctiveness and individuality. The term "art" is used in two senses: First, it may refer to a skill as that of a poet, playwright, or a creative painter. It is commonly understood that such a skill is a gift of nature and can not be acquired through training. Administration is not an art in this sense. Secondly, the term "art" may refer to a skill which can be acquired through training, e.g., the skill of a violinist or that of a teacher. Administration would be considered an art in this sense because administrative skill can be learned, and its use affords an opportunity for the application of individual judgment.

Thus, administration may be considered a science as well as an art because it partakes the characteristics of both. It is a science because it has a well-organized and evolving body of subject matter. To be more exact, it is an applied science because it makes use of the basic sciences, both exact and inexact, drawing rather heavily on the latter. At the same time, it is an art because the administrator would use his skill in the application of his knowledge of administration, which would inevitably reflect his individuality.

THE PROFESSIONAL STATUS OF ADMINISTRATION

A profession is considered to be an occupational group that possesses the following characteristics: (a) Existence of an esoteric body of knowledge, (b) rigorous formal training, (c) formation of a representative association, (d) development of a code of ethics to guide the behavior of its members, (e) insistence on social service as the dominant motive, (f) considerable autonomy in its practice, and (g) establishment of criteria for admission into the profession.

When the professional status of administration is examined against these characteristics, it becomes obvious that it falls far short of the well-established professions of theology, law, or medicine, in all respects, but particularly with respect to the development and enforcement of a code of ethics governing the behavior of its members and the criteria for entry into the profession. Administration, at present, also varies in the degree of sophistication in its application to the various types of enterprises in different societies. Nevertheless, remarkable progress has been made toward professionalization during the last three decades, which is very encouraging in view of the fact that administration, as a discipline, is still in its infancy. Therefore, it would be appropriate to conclude that administration is in the process of acquiring the status of a profession, but it can not claim to have attained it yet.

THE SCHOOLS OF THOUGHT IN ADMINISTRATION

Administration has emerged as a phenomenon of unusual significance during the last three decades and has attracted the attention of scholars engaged in the various fields of study. These scholars have attempted to formulate a conceptual framework to explain the phenomenon of administration, but the diversity of their vantage points has impeded the formation of a consensus. Their explanation of it is analogous to the description of an elephant given by six blind persons. Each point of view contains some grain of truth, but does not encompass the phenomenon in its entirety. These intellectual exercises may, at best, be regarded as different approaches to develop a comprehensive and systematic theory of administration. Among the more significant ones are the following:

1. The administrative process school.
2. The empirical school.
3. The human behavior school.
4. The social system school.
5. The mathematics school.
6. The decision theory school.

The Administrative Process School

This school considers administration as a work process for achieving the objectives of an enterprise. This approach has evolved from the logical analysis of the mental activities essential in the utilization of human and material resources to attain the desired results. These activities have been identified, analyzed, refined, and organized, and constitute the subprocesses of the administrative process. This conceptual framework is of universal application discernible in every group activity, and can be employed for the achievement of objectives of an enterprise as a whole or any constituent part of it. Although there exist some differences among authorities with respect to the nomenclature and classification of the subprocesses, the basic ideas are very similar. The concept of administration, according to this school, involves the accomplishment of predetermined enterprise objectives through the intelligent use of human and material resources.

The approach used by this school may also be designated as "operational" because, essentially, it attempts to analyze the numerous activities of administrators in order to identify the basic functions of administration, and then to deduce the fundamental principles governing these basic functions. Practitioners and scholars in the field of business have been primarily responsible for developing and expounding the administrative process thought, and Henri Fayol, Oliver Sheldon, and Ralph C. Davis would be considered as original contributors to it. The proponents of this school, while cognizant of the value of other disciplines to their approach, refrain from drawing upon them liberally in the development of their theory lest this might make it intellectually cumbersome, and further because of their belief in the segmentation of knowledge as a prerequisite to progress in any field. They fervently hope that verification of the theory through research would bring about improvement in administrative practices.

The administrative process school lately has been criticized severely and parallel concepts have been offered as replacements. These concepts form the subject of discussion in the succeeding paragraphs in this section.

The Empirical School

This school seeks to develop a theory of administration by analyzing the past experiences of successful administrators. The assumption is that an insight into the successful administrative practices would equip the prospective administrator with the competency to administer effectively in comparable situations. This school employs the case study method and the comparative approach expounded by Ernest Dale. The proponents of this school, from the study of cases, have drawn certain generalizations which tend to substantiate the concepts of the administrative process school of thought. However, the experiences of the past should serve only as useful guides and should not be applied slavishly and indiscriminately, as the problems of the future are not likely to be similar to those of the past. This school is also known as the "experience" school because its advocates concentrate on the study of experiences to understand and explain the phenomenon of administration. From the procedures of this school, it can reasonably be inferred that, in the last analysis, there would be very little difference, if any, between the process and the empirical schools of thought, or between the operational and comparative approaches of investigation employed.

The Human Behavior School

This school believes that human beings are the prime movers in an organized activity and, therefore, a grasp of human behavior should constitute the nucleus of administration. The behavioral sciences, especially individual and social psychology, by lending their theories, methods, techniques, and orientation, have contributed to the development of this school. They have brought forth the understanding that maximum individual and group effort toward the realization of enterprise goals is possible only when psychological principles are applied to the administration of the enterprise. The proponents of this school vary in their position from advocating an understanding of human behavior as an essential element of administration to considering human behavior as identical with administration. Some recommend human relations as an art to be mastered by the administrator, others regard leadership and administration as synonymous, and still others view administration as coterminous with the field of social psychology.

This school, by giving prominence to the human aspect as an important element of administration in realizing enterprise goals, has made a significant contribution to our knowledge of administration. The concepts of human relations, motivation, and leadership have been firmly established in the theory of administration, and their importance can not be discounted in successful culmination of group activity. However, the assertion that human behavior is inclusive enough to be co-extensive with administration is tantamount to an exaggeration of one element beyond all proportions.

The Social System School

This school considers administration as a social system, that is, a system of cultural interrelationships. Utilizing the sociological concepts, this school seeks to identify the various social groups in the enterprise, discover their cultural relationships, and integrate them into a social system. This school believes that man and his environment suffer from a number of biological, physical, and social limitations which can be surmounted only through cooperation. A formal organization in which people can communicate with each other and are willing to contribute to the realization of enterprise goals offers the best opportunity for cooperation.

This school is often confused with the human behavior school. This may be because both of these schools draw inspiration from the research in behavioral sciences. Present research and publications in the area of organization theory or in the social systems stem from the conceptual framework of this school.

The significant contributions of this school include recognition of enterprise as a social organism, awareness of the institutional foundations of administrative authority, the role of informal organization in realizing enterprise goals, the knowledge of factors that sustain an organization, an understanding of group behavior in the social systems, and an insight into the social obligations of administration. Admittedly, sociological findings have contributed measurably to administrative effectiveness, but it would be a mistake to consider administration and sociology as one and the same thing.

The Mathematics School

This school believes that administration is a logical process and, therefore, can be expressed in terms of mathematical symbols and relationships. Its proponents consider the function of administration to establish mathematical models and processes that can be employed to predict the outcome in advance. The measurements of known variables can be substituted in the formulas and the information about the unknown can be obtained for the varied situations.

This school has made a significant contribution to the field of industrial administration, especially by way of operations research and linear programming. Its usefulness can further be assessed from its demand for an orderly thinking, its requirement of precisely defining the problem, its insistence on systematic use of logical methodology, its concern for measurability of results, its ability to handle complex problems with ease, and its partial success in reducing the element of subjectivity in administration.

Notwithstanding its great value in administration, mathematics would be regarded only as a tool of administration rather than a school of administration. Mathematics serves most by providing the skills and techniques to improve the administrative practices and its significance can not be disputed. However, despite its impressive sophistication, it can not encompass the total field of administration. It can, at the most, be applied to the physical aspects of administration, but the intangible, intricate, and often baffling human aspects would surely elude its grasp.

The Decision Theory School

This school considers decision-making as the real function of administration—decision being the rational method of choosing, from among possible alternatives, a course of action. Just what the decision theory is concerned with is not definite because some theorists concentrate their attention on the decision itself, others include in their consideration those who make the decision, and still others analyze the decision-making process as well. Further, some study the decision in terms of its economic rationale, others examine the forces operative within the enterprise that might effect the decision, and still others would evaluate even the factors external to the enterprise that might have a bearing on the decision.

The decision theory school has grown out of the area of economics and clearly exhibits the impact of economic theorists on its development when it employs such concepts as marginal utility and economic behavior under uncertainties. Similarly, the influence of the mathematics school is discernible in the use of models and equations in decision-making.

Initially, the decision theory school merely evaluated the alternatives in selecting a course of action. But lately it has begun to examine all the activities of the enterprise through the decision-making approach. This obviously has expanded the scope of the school which now encompasses the total enterprise.

Decision-making is characteristic of administration and is a vitally important function in an enterprise, but it is difficult to conceive of administration as only decision-making without some provision for implementation. No one would deny the contributions of decision theory to administrative thought, but, by itself, it can not explain all the aspects of administration.

Concluding Comments on the Schools of Thought in Administration

1. The schools of thought discussed above represent major approaches to the development of a theory of administra-

tion and are indicative of the keen interest shown in the discipline by scholars in the related disciplines.

2. Some schools of thought have conceived of administration in narrow terms whereas others have taken a broader view of it. The range of perspective is conditioned by the attitude of the theorists. Those who have a predilection for one aspect of administration over others or those who employ a particular technique for analyzing administration which tends to restrict their vision, fail to comprehend the phenomenon of administration in its totality.

3. By and large, the schools of thought are not contradictory but complementary to one another. The differences in their positions stem from the specialized backgrounds of their exponents.

THE ADMINISTRATIVE PROCESS

For the exposition of the field to administration in this paper, the approach recommended by the school of thought which considers administration as a process has been utilized with some modifications. However, before presenting the reasons for the choice, it is necessary to examine the process itself in detail.

The administrative process is not merely a theoretical concept, it is also a technique of administering enterprises, currently in use. As a technique of administration, it represents the third stage in the process of evolution, being preceded by two other stages—the "scientific management" stage and the "organization and system" stage. The evolution of these stages in administration has also been associated with the evolution of the predominant types of administrators. These stages have been characteristic of the business and industrial enterprises in the United States and owe their development to scholars and practitioners in business and industry.

Until the beginning of the twentieth century, there prevailed an economy that was simple and undeveloped. During this period there was little need for a theory of administration because the enterprises were small and almost all the administrative functions were performed by the owner. The owner operated the enterprise, made all decisions for it, possessed absolute authority over its destiny, and was accountable to none. During the last two decades of the nineteenth century, some of the owner-managers were very forceful and dynamic. They stimulated unprecedented progress in the economy of

Library - St. Joseph's College
222 Clinton Avenue
Brooklyn, N. Y. 11205

the country and established a firm industrial base. Being prompted by the concepts of Social Darwinism and the Protestant ethic, they employed all the means, ethical and otherwise, to further their own interests. By their spectacular successes, they augmented the position of the owner-manager in power, prestige, and influence. By 1905, they faded away because of death, retirement, public opinion, and the anti-trust action.

Early in the twentieth century the economy advanced and became more complex. The corporate form of business enterprises began to emerge with capital requirements often exceeding the resources of the individual entrepreneur and thereby rendering the public sale of stock inevitable. The increasing size and complexity of corporate enterprises necessitated the separation of ownership from administration. Thus, a new type of business administrators appeared who operated and controlled the enterprises which they did not own. While they were interested in the prosperity of the enterprises they administered, they were also keen in accumulating personal wealth by using the resources of the enterprises. They were unscrupulous about using others' capital and their sole objective was quick profit. They contributed to the pace of the economy, but their influence waned after 1930 as a result of loss of public confidence in them.

It was during this period that the "scientific management" movement started and exerted a forceful influence on industry. "Scientific management" was an intellectual approach to the practice of administration. It sought to eliminate waste and inefficiency in industry. "The conceptual framework of scientific management, based on Taylor's principles, was: (a) Science, not rule of thumb; (b) harmony, not discord; (c) cooperation, not individualism; (d) maximum output in place of restricted output; and (e) the development of each man to his greatest efficiency and prosperity." The "scientific management" represented the *first* stage in administrative thought. It advanced concepts that could be identified, taught, learned, and practiced, and dealt a severe blow to the position of craftsmanship.

During the 1930's, the *second* stage in administrative thought emerged which may be labeled as "organization and system" stage. An organization was established for the enterprise to serve as a mechanism, and a system of operating and control procedures was instituted to facilitate the workflow. "Scientific management" methods continued to be employed to eliminate waste and inefficiency in operations. Different connotations came to be attached to the terms "administration" and "management." "Administration" represented the ownership point of view and performed the functions of setting goals, formulating policies, establishing organization, and exercising general control for the enterprise. "Management," on the other hand, was responsible for the performance of work within the enterprise.

It was during this period that the professional or career administrators made their appearance; they have been dominant since. The professional administrators neither own the enterprises they operate, nor do they use their resources for their personal interests. They serve as trustees of other people's money, make efficient use of human and material resources for the enterprise, have a sense of responsibility to the investors, employees, consumers, and the public, and are paid for their services. The corporate form of enterprise with a team of administrators has almost replaced the one-man-management enterprise.

During the 1940's, the administrative thought passed into the *third* stage of its evolution, which is designated as "administrative process" stage and which is in vogue today. This approach considered administration as a process rather than an event or a set of procedures and techniques. Scholars endeavored to identify the administrative process, refine it, and analyze it into subprocesses. Further professionalization of administration led to the elimination of the distinction between the terms "administration" and "management," which are now interchangeable. It is interesting to note that the "administrative process" stage in administrative thought evolved in England, France, and the United States independently about the same time and under similar conditions.

Administrative process as a conceptual framework is a composite of a number of subprocesses which are interrelated and interdependent and are usually, but not necessarily, carried out simultaneously and continuously for the attainment of enterprise objectives. The subprocesses are: planning, organizing, staffing, directing, and controlling. In addition, there are two more subprocesses—decision-making and coordinating—which are different from the preceding ones in that they do not fall on the same continuum but are inherent in each one of them. Their pervasive character manifests itself in the fact that regardless of what the administrator does, he essentially makes decisions and seeks to establish and maintain coordination. Some authorities subsume them under other subprocesses, but their cruciality warrants a separate treatment of them on the basis of equality. Further, the administrator would not be able to carry out the subprocesses effectively unless he is assisted by the authority of his position and the communication system of the enterprise. Therefore, authority and communication may be considered as indispensable tools of administration and inalienable elements of the administrative process. Differences of opinion exist with respect to the classification and the nomenclature of the subprocesses, but the concept of administration as a process seems to have met general agreement.

Planning

Planning means determining what shall be done. It comprises a wide range of activities including investigating, forecasting, setting objectives, formulating policies, developing programs, and deciding procedures. These activities need to be carried on for the total enterprise as well as its various segments. Generally speaking, planning consumes more time of executives at the higher levels than it does at the lower levels of the organizational structure, and planning at the higher levels acts as a constraint to all the activities of the enterprise.

Organizing

Organizing means dividing the work of the enterprise into a number of activities, grouping them in a meaningful way, and determining their assignment to employees. In order to obtain coordinated effort, it involves tying them together vertically through delegation of authority and responsibility, and binding them together horizontally through certain administrative devices. This would result in an organizational structure indicating the arrangement of all the activities to be performed, and depicting the authority relationships within the enterprise.

Staffing

It is the responsibility of administration to see that the human and material resources are made available in quantity, quality, and variety appropriate for attaining the enterprise goals. It means procurement of personnel according to the organizational structure and the provision of material resources which they will need to work with in the discharge of their responsibilities. However, administration basically deals with people and seeks to achieve the enterprise goals through them. Thus, people are the subject of administration and not material resources. Therefore, administration's primary responsibility is to ensure continued supply of manpower, that is, staffing, which includes selection, training, evaluation, promotion, compensation, and separation of employees.

Directing

Directing means guiding the activities of the subordinates to pre-determined goals. In directing, the administrator would use such devices as command, suggestion, request, instructions, coaching, re-ward, penalty, and others. Directing subsumes motivating and super-vising of the subordinates as well.

Controlling

Controlling involves measuring performance against the plan, as-certaining if there exists any discrepancy, and adopting corrective measures to ensure the realization of predetermined objectives. Con-trolling also includes innovating which means devising ways to bring about improvement in the setting of goals and their attainment.

Decision-making

Decision-making means selecting a course of action from a number of alternatives. Decision-making pervades the entire administration be-cause, essentially, the administrator makes a series of decisions in his application of the administrative process to the enterprise. Decision-making permeates all parts of the enterprise and deals with every possible subject. Some authorities treat decision-making under plan-ning, which gives the impression that decision-making is part of plan-ning only. However, decision-making can be perceived intertwined equally intimately with other subprocesses as well.

Coordinating

Coordinating implies synchronizing individual and group efforts for the harmonious operation of the enterprise. Coordinated activities are essential for the attainment of enterprise goals. Some authorities do not consider coordination as a separate subprocess of administra-tion. They maintain that coordination is the essence of administration and that each of the administrative subprocesses is an exercise in coordination. However, although it may be difficult to conceive of coordination as a distinct subprocess, or it may appear highly plausi-ble that coordination will accrue from the exercise of other adminis-trative subprocesses, it is unrealistic to assume that it will obtain without assiduously striving for it. The fact that coordination inheres in all the administrative subprocesses is a vindication of its pervasiveness and a manifestation of its indispensability.

No administrator can succeed in the exercise of the administrative process necessary for materializing the goals of the enterprise unless he has the necessary authority vested in him and a system of communication available to him. Without authority and communication, organized activity can neither be initiated nor sustained, and the group would disintegrate into an aggregate. Thus, authority and communication may be viewed as tools the administrator needs to work with to accomplish his tasks.

Authority

Administrative authority is the power of the superordinate to require the subordinate to act in consonance with the achievement of the enterprise goals. Administrative authority entitles the superordinate to make decisions within the limits of his authority and to see that they are implemented. The concept of administrative authority includes compliance on the part of the subordinate. This compliance, however, can be secured in a number of ways: through request, suggestion, persuasion, command, coercion, or sanction. The present trend is toward increased use of request, suggestion, and persuasion, but they are always fortified with authority, should the subordinate find them unacceptable. Administrative authority also carries with it commensurate administrative responsibility as a corollary lest it might degenerate into a license.

Communication

Communication is a means through which the administrator conveys his requests, suggestions, instructions, or commands to his subordinates for their action, and receives suggestions, grievances, and complaints from them for his consideration and action. The channels of communication—upward, downward, or sideways—provide a network of communication connecting all the members of an enterprise, and constitute a system which is co-extensive with the size of the enterprise. The communication system, however, would not be deemed adequate unless it also links the enterprise with the external world. Efficient communication facilitates the dissemination of ideas, acceptance of policies, securing of cooperation, and the attaining of enterprise goals. Communication sustains the organizational structure of the enterprise and renders the operation of the administrative process feasible. The administrator has a wide variety of media and techniques to choose from to communicate with his subordinates.

The Contributions of the Administrative Process School of Thought

The administrative process school of thought has dominated the scene for almost three decades and its impact is discernible in the writings of the scholars and the administrative behavior of the practitioners. It has made significant contributions to the theory and practice of administration, some of which are as follows:

1. The process school of thought has provided the foundation for present day education in administration. Henri Fayol first presented his concepts in 1916 in France; Oliver Sheldon, in 1923 in England; and Ralph C. Davis, in 1935 in the United States. There is a striking similarity among the ideas of these scholars although they developed them independently, being unaware of the contributions of the others. The concepts of these scholars and their successors form the core of the administrative process school of thought and the nucleus of the discipline of administration.

2. The process school of thought considers administration as a process rather than an event or a cluster of techniques, and its concepts are being utilized by all types of enterprises, public or private, large or small, in their operation. Although some concepts from other schools of thought have now been incorporated in the theory of administration, it can not be denied that the concepts from the process school of thought, by far, constitute the bulk and are difficult to replace. The successful operation of huge industrial complexes, continental governments, and intercontinental enterprises may, in a substantial measure, be attributed to the application of the concepts of the administrative process school of thought.

3. The process school of thought has furnished a conceptual framework for the administration of enterprises. It has contributed to the development of administration as a separate and distinct discipline that can be studied, taught, learned, and practiced. Thus, it has refuted the claim of charismatic leadership to indispensability for the administration of enterprises.

4. The process school of thought has led scholars to think of administration in terms of objectives, processes, and guiding principles instead of descriptions of procedures, tech-

niques, and methods. Thus, it enables the administrator to change the varied types of enterprises without any loss in efficiency.

5. The process school of thought enables administration to be operative for the total enterprise or any functional part of it. Formerly, only certain activities of the enterprise were considered to fall within the purview of administration—for example, production and personnel in the case of business administration—but the administrative process approach encompasses all the activities of the enterprise.

6. The process school of thought has provided a conceptual framework of administration which is inclusive, understandable, and time-proven. The concepts of this school of thought are the outcome of mature judgment of scholars and practitioners. Some of them have been analyzed, modified, and improved upon by the later scholars. The process school is at present firmly established as the third stage in the evolution of the administrative thought.

The Weaknesses of the Administrative Process School of Thought

The administrative process school of thought has lately been subjected to severe criticism. Some critics have suggested drastic revision of it, while others have recommended its complete abandonment. The following are pointed out as its notable weaknesses:

1. One of the problems that constantly puzzle the administrators is how to secure maximum contribution of efforts from the employees toward the attainment of enterprise goals. The process school of thought recommends motivational methods based on the concept of economic man. Research in organizational behavior has demonstrated the inadequacy of these measures as motivating devices because man does not always respond to economic stimuli. The social codes, conventions, and traditions prevalent within the enterprise tend to encourage conformity among members even at the cost of personal sacrifice. Factors like varied preference scales of values, taxation, job security, technological advance, and unionization of labor render the problem of employee motivation increasingly complex. Thus, the administrative process conceptual framework fails to furnish satisfactory answers to problems inherent in the proper ways and means to provide for necessary employee motivation.

2. The process school of thought requires the administrator to seek the attainment of enterprise goals with maximum efficiency and at minimum cost. Because of its preoccupation with efficiency and elimination of waste, the administration often forgets its real purpose of service and becomes an end in itself. In business enterprises, it particularly feels obligated to protect the interests of the investors only and has been oblivious of the interests of employees, consumers, and the general public. The conceptual framework of the process school of thought does not include such concepts as human relations, public relations, and employee satisfaction. This provides an opportune ground for the clashes of interests which sporadically explode into conflicts and strifes in enterprises.

3. The process school of thought has treated labor as a commodity. This old commodity concept of labor is incompatible with the present or future values in our society. Labor can no longer be slighted as an inert, passive, and docile "commodity"; it is a vigorous, aggressive, and paralyzing force to be reckoned with. Labor will have to be viewed as an invaluable asset, the intelligent use of which is indispensable for the attainment of the enterprise goals. This changed concept of labor would necessitate modification in the conceptual framework of the process school of thought.

4. The process school of thought utilizes the concepts of the Protestant ethic and Social Darwinism which have stimulated the growth of the economy but which also have provided justification for the exploitation of the many in the interest of the few. However, the emergence of the egalitarian society with its concepts of equality, liberty, and justice has challenged the concepts of the old social order. Administration can not continue to operate in a world of its own creation, and, if it wants to be effective, it has no alternative but to readjust its conceptual framework to make it consistent with the realities of the changing society.

5. Being efficiency oriented, the process school of thought is meticulous in planning, rigorous in execution, and exact in evaluation, all geared to the attainment of the predetermined enterprise goals. Such an administration is not likely to provide an opportunity for the exercise of initiative, creativity, and discretion on the part of the employees because they are required to coordinate their efforts according to the predetermined plan. Under the circumstances, the individual is reduced to the level of a mechanical gadget—

passive, subservient, and dependent—and is debarred from making full contribution of his total potentialities. Further, since the administration is passionately devoted to the attainment of the enterprise goals, the satisfactions and needs of the employees are likely to go unheeded, which may result in the creation of a dissatisfied, disgruntled, and revengeful work force, and which may cause bitterness, suspicion, and distrust between them and the administration. The administrative process conceptual framework needs to be modified so that the individual worker is viewed as a human being with self-esteem, dignity, and pride, and not just a cog in the wheel.

PROSPECTS FOR THE FUTURE

Dissatisfaction with the weaknesses of the administrative process school of thought has impelled scholars to look for a theory of administration in other directions. The outcome of their intensive search has been the appearance of a number of parallel schools of thought, referred to earlier, each one of which claims to offer an acceptable and workable theory of administration. These schools of thought are the fruits of the labor of scholars engaged in diverse, but related, disciplines—psychology, sociology, anthropology, mathematics, and others. That these schools of thought, in themselves, possess the potentiality of dislodging or replacing the administrative process school of thought is beyond the range of probability, because they suffer from a number of serious limitations, too difficult to surmount. Therefore, some kind of synthesis in which the process school of thought would incorporate the needed and useful concepts from other schools of thought to eradicate its deficiencies and to expand its scope so as to make it inclusive portends the direction for the development of a new theory of administration. That a beginning has been made on these lines is evidenced by the inclusion of a number of concepts—e.g., employee satisfaction, public relations, decision-making—within the conceptual framework of the process school of thought. The eclectic approach, with the process school of thought as a core, capable of dealing with all the problems of an enterprise may very well mark the *fourth* stage in the process of evolution of the administrative thought.

2

herbert a. simon

THE CHANGING THEORY AND CHANGING PRACTICE OF PUBLIC ADMINISTRATION

If a science has been culture bound—and public administration certainly has been through most of its history—it becomes difficult to distinguish between progress in the science, on the one hand, and changes in the social institutions it purports to describe, on the other. The difficulties are compounded if the science is normative in intent, because changes in an applied science may reflect either progress in fundamental knowledge or shifts in the relative importance of the various real-world problems that come within its scope. Thus, if the contents of biology textbooks change, we may reasonably conclude that there have been advances in our knowledge of living organisms; whereas if a medical textbook adds a new chapter on gerontology, this is likely to mean that the age profile of the population has changed.

My main thesis, then, is that the developments taking place in public administration theory and practice are, to a considerable extent, consequences of modifications of the social environment of governmental organizations. To sort matters out, I shall devote the first part of my remarks to the changing characteristics of rulers and bureaucrats and of the social and political environment of their work. Then I shall turn to the trends in public administration theory that, in part, record these institutional changes, and in part, represent a steady deepening in our understanding of human social behavior.

From *Contemporary Political Science: Toward Empirical Theory* by the American Political Science Association. Copyright © 1967 by McGraw-Hill, Inc. Used with permission of McGraw-Hill Book Company.

THE CHANGING INSTITUTIONS

As is traditional, we may take Woodrow Wilson's "The Study of Administration," published in 1887, as our jumping-off place. Wilson laid down the postulates, later reinforced by Goodnow and hardly questioned for fifty years, that politics and administration are separate studies: "The field of administration is a field of business. It is removed from the hurry and strife of politics. . . . It is a part of political life only as the methods of the counting-house are a part of the life of society; only as machinery is part of the manufactured product. . . ."

We know now that, taken as a description of American administrative institutions, Wilson's postulate simply is (and was) wrong. The empirical evidence is overwhelming: I need only allude to such classics as Pendleton Herring's *Public Administration and the Public Interest*, published in 1936, or the Stone-Price-Stone study of *City Manager Government in the United States*, published in 1940. A large part of the analytic and descriptive (as distinguished from normative) post-World War II literature of public administration is preoccupied with the administrator's relation to the political process.[1]

It would be gratifying to attribute this correction of false belief to advances in empirical research, but that attribution would be wrong, or at least oversimple. Woodrow Wilson, a contemporary of the muckrakers and himself a major political beneficiary of the rise of reform sentiment, was well aware that most American public administrators were up to their necks in politics. The reasonable—and full idiomatic—interpretation of his postulate is that by "is" he meant "ought to be": "The field of administration *ought to be* a field of business, removed from the hurry and strife of politics."

The whole context of this postulate in Wilson's essay shows his intent to be normative and not descriptive. He is urging the study of administration as a means of improving the operation of the state: "The object of administrative study is to rescue executive methods from the confusion and costliness of empirical experiment and set them upon foundations laid deep in stable principle." He is concerned, as were most of his successors in public administration for the next fifty years, with the applied, practical science of administration; with organizational medicine, not with biology.

Professionalizing the Public Service

Even interpreted normatively, Wilson's postulate is not one to which most of us would subscribe today. But this, too, is criticism out of historical context. The central problems facing American public administration in 1887 were not subtle problems. They were problems of replacing spoils and blatant corruption with at least a modicum of honesty and competence. As the leaders of reform saw then, and as history has confirmed, this called for neutralization of public administration *relative* to its involvement in the political process at that time, and it called for the recruitment of intelligence and the training of skill in that neutralized service.

When these goals had been achieved to a considerable degree, especially at the Federal level, we could put this central issue aside and consider the second-order problems—just as doctors have put aside the problem of polio to concern themselves with that of rheumatic fever. We then discovered that a *complete* separation of policy and administration was impossible, and if possible, would probably be considered undesirable.[2] I shall have more to say later about the empirical facts and their explanation. I wish to make a different point now: What has changed in the policy-administration relation is the actual character of our political institutions and hence the nature of the practical, normative problems they pose.

Decline of Authoritarianism

As a second example of the intermingling of institutional change with change in the practical science of administration, I cite shifts in attitudes toward authority and in the behavior of persons holding authority. By any measure, the human relations movement has been a major scientific contributor to the practice of management. Its message is both normative and factual: It says, "Be nice to people!" and "If you're nice, you get what you want." In thus both holding up certain models of behavior as good and promising good things from them, it mirrors most successful religions.[3]

The evidence is satisfactory, if not overwhelming, that applying good human relations principles in management generally does pay off.[4] Managers can increase the effectiveness of their organizations, and the satisfactions of employees, by avoiding the arbitrary exercise of authority, by securing participation in decision making, by taking into account the values that are important to employees. The question I should like to raise is whether this would have been equally true, say, in 1880. How far is the effectiveness of modern human relations due to waning of the acceptance of authoritarian behavior and a shift toward less authoritarian personality structures in the general populace?

A social historian would have to note that at the same time that modern human relations doctrines were beginning to have some currency in administrative theory and in management, the American family was becoming less authoritarian, and social attitudes toward racial equality and the treatment of criminals and the insane were shifting strongly in a nonauthoritarian direction. The rapid collapse of the colonial system in our generation (and specifically the inability of the colonial powers to continue to defend it morally) would remind him that these changes are not merely American, or even Western, but worldwide. Confronted by these interrelated facts, he would be cautious in drawing the causal arrow, or in treating the human relations movement as much more than a symptom—possibly an accelerator—of powerful existing trends.

Bigness

How much and what kinds of power shall be entrusted to government and how far that power shall be centralized in the Federal bureaucracy are continuing focal themes in debate about American political institutions, although with perhaps decreased intensity as compared with the 1930s. Outside learned journals, the term "bureaucracy" finds its almost sole use as a pejorative in that debate.

While the struggle continues, its front lines move fairly steadily in the direction of "big government." Federalism has lost much of its political appeal, except in the defense of specific interests—Southern white segregationists, suburbanites fighting off the metropolis, and state and local employees. Perhaps its appeal has always been confined largely to such groups, in which case they have become weaker in strength and numbers.

The significance of this trend for public administration is twofold. First, there is a steady erosion of those checks and balances that have limited the hierarchic control of the chief executive over the bureaucracy (although the increase in size of the bureaucracy has had the contrary effect of weakening the day-to-day controls). Second, decentralization in management is more and more regarded as a human relations tool—a means for securing the participation and commitment of subordinates—and as a tool for reducing delays and red tape in decision making, rather than an essential mechanism for maintaining the constitutional balance of political forces.

Again, it would be tempting—but probably erroneous—to attribute these movements to changes in public administration theory. Support from the scholarly literature for the strong manager-execu-

tive probably reached its peak in the thirties—the 1937 reorganization fight will serve as a convenient marker—when the doctrine of
separation of administration from politics was still orthodoxy. Professional opinion has moved to a more "realistic" position regarding the
political role of the bureaucracy, while the internal structures of private and public bureaucracies continue to converge in pattern and
both sets of bureaucracies continue to grow in size.[5]

Bigness and centralized control have not, of course, become
positive values. As many have observed, government grows and
"managerial" values thrive because people want specific services
from government. Bigness and centralization are simply the unintended—perhaps not unanticipated—byproducts of the successful pursuit
of numbers of these specific demands through the political process.
Opposition to bureaucracy has probably always been in considerable
part opposition to such specific demands; it loses its wider political
appeal if the population does not have direct personal experience of
frequent bureaucratic interference with valued freedoms.

Science in Government

In dubbing science an "estate" (warning that only a loose analogy is
intended), Don Price[6] has provided us with a useful label for another
trend that has reached salience—a new form and urgency of the
longstanding problem of bringing expert and generalist into effective
relation. The problem has become salient not only because the experts have arrived in unprecedented numbers and because their expertness is unprecedently esoteric, but for three other reasons as
well.

First, in the Federal case, the experts have been particularly
prominent in the sphere of military affairs; hence scientist-generalist
relations have become intertwined with military-civilian relations, always a touchy topic. Second, some of the experts—those in operations research and management science—claim to have expertness
about the executive process itself, a new form of lese majesty. Third,
the scientists are not only experts advising government, but also
claimants on the resources of government. In this latter role they are
more appropriately called an "interest group"—a familiar term of
political analysis—than an estate. To be sure, they claim that they
have special knowledge and experience for understanding their interest, but that is not a novel claim from an interest group.[7]

Leaving aside the interest-group issue . . . the new prominence of science, then, calls for renewed attention from applied administrative science to the expert-generalist relation and raises relatively novel questions with respect to expertness in the administrative process. We shall put these on our agenda for later consideration.

The Communist Bureaucracies

Even though, as I urged earlier, administrative theory has been culture bound, certain large-scale world phenomena have always been so visible as to invite at least casual comparison of institutions. Thus, in an earlier era, observable similarities among the public bureaucracies of Bismarck's autocratic Germany, Victoria's gentlemanly Britain, and Teddy Roosevelt's brassy America placed an upper bound on speculation about constitutional influences on bureaucratic form. *Differences* among them established a lower bound. In the thirties, comparisons of Germany with the democracies played a similarly useful role.

Today the Communist bureaucracies provide most valuable objects for comparison with Western public—and private—bureaucracies. Their value is greatly enhanced for this purpose by the close convergence of technologies. The question, "Is communism possible?" asked in a multitude of forms both by Western observers and the Communists themselves, has provided fruitful foci for research on administration. It has provided new evidence—about whose interpretation there is not always agreement—on the relation of bureaucracy to personal freedom, on the relation of economic incentives to productivity, and on the behavior of planning and pricing mechanisms as coordinating instruments.[8]

Administration in the Developing Countries

The new nations of Africa and Asia are having an even greater impact on applied administrative science than is Eastern Europe. The reason is plain: In these new countries, American political scientists are not just observers, but have frequently been advisers. Unawareness of ethnocentrism—a major deterrent to losing it—can sometimes survive a two-week consulting trip to a foreign land, but less easily a year's immersion in its affairs. (Some hard data on this point would be extremely valuable for the applied science of administration.)

The new nations have given a great impetus to studies in comparative administration, but have also posed severe methodological problems. Here no easy assumption can be made that "all other things are equal." Almost no other things are equal, and tracing cause-and-effect relations is correspondingly difficult.[9]

As with other institutional changes we have mentioned, the emergence of the new nations emphasizes new facets of administration. Here, if there is little talk of the "scientific estate," there is much of the "technical estate." The presence in a society of military and development experts as almost the only trained cadres makes the problem of political responsibility of the specialists focal and gives the problem a special flavor. Balanced against the difficulties of political control are the urgent needs to acquire technical and managerial competence where none has existed before.[10]

In Summary

I have pointed to six dimensions—four domestic and two international—of significant change in administrative institutions. The American public service has reached a relatively high degree of professionalism; attitudes and behaviors in our society have become progressively less authoritarian; bigness has become a fact, and a more or less accepted fact, of the American bureaucracy; science has acquired a vital and visible role in governmental institutions; Communist bureaucracies have grown up to manage modern technologies; and new nations on three continents seek to leapfrog centuries into industrialization and bureaucratization. I suppose I could easily have listed more such dimensions, but these were the most visible to a general survey.

Because the study of public administration has always had a predominately normative concern, it has responded to these institutional changes with important changes in its own interests and emphases. In the next sections I shall try to relate the institutional shifts to our growing knowledge of the administrative process.

INFLUENCE BY AND OVER THE BUREAUCRACY

If institutions change, and the specific focal problems of public policy change with them, nevertheless the broad problem areas remain impressively stable. We can explain this stability by pointing to certain functional requisites that bureaucracy must satisfy, at least in any culture that we would describe as "modern" or that aspires to be modern.

A bureaucracy—even a fairly small-scale bureaucracy managing a town or a newborn nation—is a complex decision-making, information-processing system. It takes in varieties of information from its environment: the environment of streets to be paved, or streams to be bridged; the environment summarized in the statistics of income, or seen and smelled in the concrete reality of slums; the environment of a street-corner gang, a village school; the environment of a civil-rights rally, a delegation of pet lovers, a legislative committee hearing, an election, a request for a zoning variance.

Filtering this information through its previous beliefs and expectations, interpreting it in the light of legislative mandates and policies, in the light of the values held in the social strata from which its members are drawn, the bureaucracy translates and transforms the incoming information flow into actions (and inactions). It provides services, it regulates, and it exercises its influence on the other governmental organs in the policy-making process.

This is the setting that defines the functional requisites of a government bureaucracy. Two of these requisites stand out: It must develop an appropriate role in the political process and in relation to the other participants in that process. It must maintain an acceptable level of competence in service and regulation.[11] To understand how a bureaucracy satisfies these requirements, we must examine its information flows—we must understand it as a decision-making system.

Birthright Decision Premises

To discover how the bureaucracy is controlled is to discover the sources of the premises that enter into its decisions, especially the value premises that set its goals and that place constraints of due process on its actions.[12] The study of decision premises begins, in turn, with the processes for selecting the members of the bureaucracy. Studies of the origins of the higher American civil service show that recruitment mirrors the open structure of the society—with some bias, to be sure, toward overrepresentation of the higher strata.[13] Similar studies in Britain have shown the gradual decline in political power of the nineteenth-century aristocracy reflected, with some lag, in its decline within the bureaucracy.[14] The Soviet Union reveals a picture of gradual replacement of an elite legitimized by participation in the Revolution by a "managerial" and technical elite whose relation to the political process has become increasingly ambiguous.[15]

Recruitment of the bureaucracy is regarded by a society as a "problem" whenever the recruits fail to represent the prevailing political values—or when, during a period of struggle between opposing values, they overrepresent one set and underrepresent another. Thus the high-water mark of belief in the neutrality of the American bureaucracy occurred during an era of "tweedledum-tweedledee" politics; and challenges to that belief have always been associated with challenges to belief in the "classlessness" of American society. For example, the "good government" movement in American cities has always appealed to essentially middle-class values. The failure of the city-manager plan to capture the large cities can almost certainly be attributed to working-class disinterest in the efficiency goals emphasized by the plan's advocates.[16]

The judiciary and the police are the two parts of the American bureaucracy whose neutrality is most often challenged. The connections between the social origins of judges and their legal views is a topic that has been much studied, with mixed findings. Since it lies outside my jurisdiction here, I will not try to assess the evidence.

Sociologists have given us some valuable insights into the neutrality issue as it impinges on the work of the police. The matter is not simple. On the one hand, we have the observation that particular behavior may be "juvenile delinquency" if the juvenile comes from the slum, but may not be if the juvenile comes from a high-status family. When this happens, we see a regulatory process adapting to differentials in social status and power. (In fact, an alternative analysis is possible: the society may regard the family as a potentially effective mechanism of social control in the latter case but not in the former. When this is true, the discrimination, however much it may violate our notions of "fairness," is functional.) This is the problem, more familiar in an aristocratic society than in ours, of the relation of the workingclass bureaucrat to the gentleman.

On the other hand, the working-class origin of the policeman may lead him to arrange crimes, certain sex offenses for example, in a different order of seriousness than would middle-class or upper-class persons. Different classes may hold different views of due process: polls of public opinion in this country show consistently that regard for personal freedoms is more firmly anchored in the upper than the lower strata.

With strong public attention focused on public education— both its general quality and the access to it of disadvantaged groups— we have discovered that the schools are also not quite neutral purveyors of the common values of the society, as we may have supposed. The significant gulf between the middle-class values of teachers and the working-class values of their pupils is now recognized as one source of the learning and discipline problems of slum schools. The controversy over "client" participation in managing the poverty program reveals another facet of the same problem—this time involving social workers and other "service" professions in the bureaucracy.

The particular problems of neutrality arising from recruitment have been relatively minor problems in the American bureaucracy, though the civil-rights movement has revived them. We would expect them to be far more severe in developing countries, where requirements of technical competence, and sometimes even of literacy, lead to vast overrepresentation of upper-class strata. Where class is also closely related to special forms of economic interest (e.g., landholding), as it is in many developing countries, the class composition of the bureaucracy is a central, not a peripheral, issue. This is reflected in the emphasis placed on this issue in the growing literature of comparative administration.[17]

Profession as a Source of Premises

Victor Thompson (in his *Modern Organization*) built his drama of organization largely around the competing claims of profession and hierarchy. The professional and the specialist come into modern organization because the organization's ability to provide the services demanded of it depend on their technical knowledge and skills. But the professional and specialist bring to the organization not only these skills, but values as well—values that are acquired during professional training and enforced by the desire for professional approval and esteem.

The bureaucrat's choice between identifying with his organization or his profession is the basis, also, of Robert Merton's dichotomy between the local and the cosmopolitan. A number of studies of public bureaucracies[18] and of research organizations[19] have provided concrete evidence for the reality and importance of the choice.

The scientist in an industrial research laboratory, for example, who is a "local" finds no conflict between the applied research goals set by the needs of the business organization in which the laboratory resides and his own scientific activity. The "cosmopolitan" experiences genuine—and often severe—conflict unless the work of the laboratory can qualify as having genuine scientific importance as well as industrial utility.

In his study of *The Forest Ranger*, Herbert Kaufman has offered further evidence of professional controls over value premises. In the forest service, however, the claims of profession and organization are generally reinforcing, rather than conflicting. The forest service and the schools of forestry belong to a single social group that is responsible for forming the values of the future forest ranger during his training as well as supervising his application of those values on the job.

In this kind of social structure, we would predict, and Kaufman finds, that the "interface" between conflicting value systems occurs at the boundaries of the bureaucracy (more accurately, the boundaries of the profession) rather than within it. In the forest service, the professional values of the ranger, supported by the supervisory hierarchy, resist the sometimes conflicting values of local cattle growers or farmers, while the upper levels of the forest service bureaucracy resist interference from other parts of the Federal government.

Findings quite like Kaufman's could be made, no doubt, within the military services, with their service academies, the U.S. Public Health Service, or a municipal library. A quite different picture, of internal professional conflict and accommodation, emerges from those organizations that employ a wide variety of specialists—for example, a social work agency employing accountants, lawyers, and professional social workers.

Thus the interaction of professionalism with hierarchic authority in a bureaucracy varies with the social structure. When the grain of professional specialization runs across the main organizational boundaries, the system experiences the internal competition of specialty with hierarchy noticed by Thompson. When the grain runs parallel with the boundaries, the professions take on much more the character of "estates"—each seeking an area of action within which it is sovereign and not subject to the imposition of value premises from without.

Bureaucratic Neutrality

Through the mechanisms described in the last two sections, the decision makers in a bureaucracy come into their roles already plentifully provided with value premises. In what sense, and to what extent, can they be regarded as neutral agents of the state? How does politics govern administration? Don Price summarizes what he perceives to be the contemporary American norms for bounding the freedom of a professional "estate" (*The Scientific Estate*, p. 137):

> (1) The closer the estate is to the end of the spectrum that is concerned solely with truth, the more it is entitled to freedom

and self-government; and (2) the closer it gets to the exercise of power, the less it is permitted to organize itself as a corporate entity, and the more it is required to submit to the test of political responsibility. . . .

I think this summary captures truth, but not the whole truth. Any profession engaged in administration necessarily exercises power. It applies its knowledge and technique, but it applies them to some end. The forest ranger is not simply someone who knows about the growth and harvesting of trees and how to extinguish forest fires. He *fosters* the growth and orderly harvesting of trees, and he *fights* forest fires. His specialized knowledge is perhaps a necessary condition to society's granting him a measure of autonomy, but it is not a sufficient condition. He will enjoy freedom only to the extent that the values he serves are noncontroversial. The forest ranger's autonomy rests not on his being a *neutral* instrument, but on his being a *reliable* instrument whose values are pretty well known and widely accepted. Thus I grant great autonomy to the operation of my house thermostat, not because it is neutral (it shows a tenacious preference for temperatures of 70 degrees), but because it works persistently and reliably toward a goal of which I approve. I seldom interfere with it.[20]

For this reason, the military service, during time of peace, enjoys no such autonomy as the forest service, although both employ highly technical means toward the realization of social goals. In time of peace there is seldom such consensus as to the conditions under which military force might be employed as there is on the conditions under which forest service resources are used. Once a definite commitment is made to war, we see a great enlargement of the autonomy of the military, although even then its impingement on the whole spectrum of social values is so great, and the balance of priorities so controversial, that it never achieves any great degree of insulation from political control.

The medical estate provides another instructive example of the dependence of autonomy, not on goal neutrality, but on goal consensus. A city health department normally enjoys a considerable measure of professional autonomy; the Food and Drug Administration very much less. The point is not simply that, in the latter case, economic "interests" are involved; they are in both cases. But in regulating the pharmaceutical industry, we are still far from a consensus as to who is protecting whom against what. When and if such a consensus is reached, the agency will be no more "neutral" than it now is; but it will be far more autonomous.

Thus, in explaining the freedom granted to technical, professional groups in the bureaucracy, we must think of them not as neutral, but as predictable in the values they will implement.[21] If the professions did not indoctrinate their members with their values, if professionals really were neutral "guns for hire," then professional groups in the bureaucracy would have less, not more, autonomy than they now enjoy.

Corruption

Our analysis of professional values also helps us understand some phenomena relating to corruption that would otherwise be rather paradoxical. It has been observed that one factor accounting for the rise to power of the "neutral" technicians and even the military in many of the new nations is their relative incorruptibility in environments where corruption is a main enemy of bureaucratic effectiveness. Similarly, there is a strong negative correlation between professionalization and corruptibility among the various segments of the American public service. It might be difficult to prove causality, but the historical association is close and undeniable.

A neutral, value-free professional corps should be the most corruptible of all bodies—a force of janissaries. A corps, on the other hand, deeply indoctrinated with values as well as techniques, would resist demands to use their skills to defeat their values. Thus a military elite, committed to the development of a state powerful enough to defeat its enemies, or an engineering corps, devoted, as engineers generally are, to physiocratic values of growth in productivity, may impose a professional discipline that is highly resistive to corruption. This does not mean that such a group would be politically neutral— if the society were divided on goals or indecisive, the professionals might well seek to impose their dictatorial power on it.[22]

Political Control of Values: Attention

This brings us back to the central problem of politics and administration: to what extent and by what means do the political bodies control the bureaucracy; and in a normative vein, to what extent and by what means should they?

The difficulties in designing a system of political controls center around two distinct problems: the scarcity of attention and the incommensurability of goals.

Time is a scarce resource, for a polity as for a person. A single human being is a serial information-processing system. He can attend to only one, or a very few, things at a time; hence among his most crucial decisions are his decisions to allocate time and attention to one goal rather than another.

A society comprises many human beings who can work in "parallel." Collectively, they can put out fires while they raise corn and teach school. But when consensus is thought to be necessary, when some expression of a "public will" or a legitimizing laying-on of hands is called for, then either the society as a whole must coordinate its attention on the question before it, or the task must be performed by one or more of its repositories of political power. Whether we are talking about a town meeting, a national election, a sitting of a legislature or a legislative committee, or a decision by a political boss, dictator, or bureaucratic executive, these acts require the persons involved, many or few, to attend to that topic and not to another.

Thus the body politic behaves like a parallel information-processing system when it comes to performing its daily routine functions (its heart-beat and breathing, if we stick to the metaphor). But in settling those issues we call "political," it shifts toward a serial, one-at-a-time mode of action. As the volume of political matters grows with the expansion of size and scope of the bureaucracy, the central organs of political decision become choked with work, and deliberately or by force of circumstance, seek means of reconciling responsibility with delegation.

If our analysis of professions is correct, delegation to a profession is one way for the political bodies to influence policy predictably. By selecting the profession, where there is some choice, the political body can influence the values that will be implemented. A number of examples can be cited of the self-conscious use of this technique: the power granted by Congress to the General Accounting Office fluctuates with the level of approval for the "economizing" values that are associated with the profession of accountancy; a liberal state administration broadens the role of social workers, vis-à-vis accountants and lawyers in a welfare agency; the "banking" experts represented through the Federal Reserve Board are counterbalanced by a Council of Economic Advisors.[23]

Notice that delegation of certain functions to a profession is distinguishable from, if not always entirely independent of, representation of "interests." The profession may or may not be an interested party, in the usual sense. Thus staffing a welfare agency with professional social workers is different from appointing representatives of the poor to the agency's board.

Second, the political bodies may seek to increase their capacity for parallel action by operating through committees (in the case of a legislature) or through political ministers (in the case of a chief executive). A legislative committee can serve as a surrogate for the legislature to the extent that it is *not* professional and to the extent that it does represent some of the main competing values relevant to the area it supervises. A similar statement may be made about cabinet officers in relation to a chief executive.

An individual human being survives in spite of his limited capacity for parallel action because, although he can only attend to one thing at a time, there is no restriction as to what that one thing may be. All that is required is that it may be important enough and urgent enough to be placed at the top of the agenda.

A political system overcomes its information-processing limitations in exactly the same way. Congress can act deliberately on only a few matters in each session—everything else must be left to its committees, to the executive and his department heads, or to the bureaucracy. But there is no matter, large or small, to which Congress cannot direct its attention if that matter comes to the top of the agenda; hence there is no matter that is "in principle" exempt from political control.

In a general sense, awareness that limits of attention are important has been with us for a long time, at least since Walter Lippmann's *Public Opinion* (1922). But attention is only now beginning to be a central variable of political analysis—either rivaling the concept of power or requiring radical reinterpretation of the meaning of power.[24] I can indicate only a few of the areas of political analysis where "attention" is beginning to attract the attention it deserves.

Voting behavior lies outside my jurisdiction, but I must mention it briefly anyway. We are acquiring a realistic view of what the role of a citizen in a democracy can and should be, by learning that (1) for most people most of the time, politics is a peripheral interest, (2) "public opinion" is a meaningful and important concept when applied to the small number of issues (and elections) that reach the focus of public attention, and (3) significant attention can also be attracted from particular groups that are specifically and intensively affected by particular issues.

The same kind of analysis applied to political professionals illuminates their behavior as well. If a "citizen" is someone who, to take a round number, attends to politics one hour a day, a congressman is someone who attends to politics ten hours a day. Therefore Congress, as an assembled deliberative body, can apply one order of magnitude more attention to political issues than can the general public; hence,

Congress can behave deliberately with respect to about ten times as many issues—but not one hundred times as many nor one thousand times as many.

Hence, any study of Congressional power or Congressional control over administration must seek to understand how congressmen budget their attention. It must identify the characteristics of an issue that place it at the top of the agenda for many or some congressmen. The prizewinning study by Bauer, Pool, and Dexter, *American Business and Public Policy*, (Prentice-Hall, Inc., Englewood Cliffs, N.J., 1963), has made a major contribution to the unraveling of the relations of attention to influence in the political decision-making process. They say (p. 405):

> What we actually found was that the most important part of the legislative decision-process was the decision about which decisions to consider. A Congressman must decide what to make of his job. The decisions most constantly on his mind are not how to vote, but what to do with his time, how to allocate his resources, and where to put his energy. There are far more issues before Congress than he can possibly cope with. There are very few of them which he does not have the freedom to disregard or redefine.

If attention is a scarce resource for legislators, it is equally so for presidents, governors, and mayors, and only relatively less so for the executives at successive levels of the bureaucracy. From voters to fire fighters, the same mechanisms operate to make each level more or less responsive to the ones above: (1) relative predictability of the values that will be applied to decisions below and (2) in-principle reviewability of any matter that attracts attention and hence becomes "political."

To say that all matters are potentially political is not to assert that some are not more likely than others to become so in fact. To mention three obvious discriminators: small matters are less likely, other things equal, to rise to attention than large matters; matters involving values on which there is consensus, less likely than those involving controversial values; matters where technical complexity hides the value issues, less likely than matters readily accessible to "common sense."[25]

The recent debate over "Who rules?" in the city and the empirical evidence that has been brought to bear on municipal decision making provide further support for the emphasis placed here on attention variables. It is clear from that evidence that the various participants in city politics do not simply "exercise power" but turn their attention in varying degrees to various issues.

Particularly interesting is a recent finding that professional administrators, as compared with other participants, tend to participate only in decisions relating to their professional specialties.[26] By hindsight, the finding, like most observations of human behavior, is not surprising, but it provides a useful empirical corrective, supplementing James March's theoretical one, to oversimplified parallelogram-of-forces views of power. More specifically, it confirms our earlier view of the professional administrator not as a "neutral" but as a predictable proponent and implementer of specific ranges of values identified with his profession.

Political Control of Values: Commensurability

Since the services of modern government consume large resources, the allocation of funds to services represents an important set of policy decisions. But the services of government are exceedingly diverse, and most of them do not lend themselves to evaluation by market criteria or in any other ways that would provide a common denominator for comparison.

Among the most puzzling normative questions facing government today is to provide a rationale for budgeting, and a descriptive question, only slightly less puzzling, is to explain how, in the absence of such a rationale, the budget allocation is in fact accomplished. Some headway has been made in answering the second question at least.

In considerable part, public budgets can be explained as the product of precedent. In first approximation, this year's budget is equal to last year's.[27] However trivial such an explanation appears, we should not discount its significance, for it serves to limit the problem of comparing incommensurable goals to a small fraction of the total budget. If the tax structure remains unchanged, income will change only slowly with the state and size of the economy. Services, then, can all maintain the *status quo,* providing salary increases roughly commensurate with the general movement of the standard of living and increasing in overall size in jurisdictions that are growing but not in others. One study of three large city governments concludes that little more than the mechanisms just described is needed to explain the budget decisions over the last decade or so in those cities.[28]

Change in budgets does occur, however, especially in the Federal government. To take a second step toward an explanation, we call on the concept of "need." The only concept of need in classical economics is a relative one—dollars are to be allocated so that the last, or marginal, dollar allocated to any one purpose achieves as much as the marginal dollar allocated to every other purpose. But "need," as it is actually used in budget conversations, is an absolute, not a relative, term. It involves—at least at the explicit level—no comparison among alternative uses. For example, several years ago a Congressional committee invited the National Academy of Sciences to submit to it a report on the needs of science for Federal support. A report was prepared in response to the request, but instead of providing actual numbers, it consisted largely of a series of philosophic essays about the nature of the questions being asked. The essays, particularly two prepared by economists Harry G. Johnson and Karl Kaysen, were sophisticated but not responsive to the question.[29]

On the other hand, the National Academy has shown no corresponding reluctance to provide estimates of the "needs" of particular branches of science—high-energy physics, chemistry, and university computing facilities, for example. These reports do not require to the same degree comparisons among the sciences. No adequate analysis has yet been made of the kinds of reasoning that go into such reports or of the processes by which the dollar figures are arrived at. From participation on one such study, and observation of others, I can make some casual remarks and then, as with earlier topics, commend the matter to the attention of doctoral candidates looking for dissertation topics.[30]

One way in which "needs" are estimated is by taking a current expenditure figure and applying to it an annual rate of growth. This estimation procedure shifts the problem from estimating dollars to estimating growth rates. The growth rate is not, of course, a predictive rate, but a normative rate—the rate at which the activity "ought" to grow. One way, in turn, of "estimating" the growth is to set an upper bound on the reasonable. For example, it might be "unreasonable" to increase demands for support of scientific research at a rate much more rapid than the population of researchers can be made to grow.

Comparative figures, not between functions but between jurisdictions, provide a second kind of anchor for "needs." Thus the military budget (and more recently the high-energy physics and space budgets) is traditionally made with an eye to what it takes to meet the competition. (Surprisingly, Crecine, in his study of three large-city budget processes, found little or no evidence of such comparisons.)

In an earlier section I argued that a main consequence of professionalization is to increase, rather than decrease, political control over the bureaucracy. This follows not because the professionals are neutral—they are not—but because the values they implement can be predicted from their professional identifications. Their technical competence itself increases the reliability of the connections between their decisions and those values.

Now we must qualify this conclusion. To the extent that professional decision making involves not merely implementing values, but also estimating the resources "needed" for that implementation, the relation between professional and politician becomes stickier. The appropriations subcommittee dealing with the forest service budget cannot make use of or rely on the expertness of the professionals to nearly the same extent that the corresponding policy subcommittee can, for the professional appears before the appropriations subcommittee not as an expert but as a claimant on scarce resources. He can presumably state how he will use the resources, if they are granted, but he cannot state how valuable that use will be in comparison with other potential uses.

Again, I can only commend to researchers a problem that, so far as I know, has not been studied in detail: Would analysis of committee hearings reveal fundamental differences between the expert-politician relations in budget matters and other deliberations, respectively?[31]

The Bureaucrat as Initiator

We have seen that the fact that the legislature and the Chief Executive are serial, rather than parallel, processors has important consequences for the control of the bureaucracies. Their serial character has yet another set of consequences for governmental innovation. An existing governmental activity can go on with only occasional attention from the central political bodies. As we have just seen, even its budget may be a routine matter as long as its level remains constant.

A new governmental activity, even a significant new program within an existing agency, can generally come into existence only after it has received an explicit political blessing. Someone must generate the proposal, and someone must secure for it a place on the crowded agenda. Traditional theory emphasizing the politics-administration distinction would locate the initiatory activities in the political organs—the legislature, the Chief Executive, or interest groups. In fact, the bureaucracy is often a major source of proposals for new programs and of activity to get them placed on the legislative agenda.[32]

To understand the bureaucratic role in initiation, it is necessary to say a few words about the nature of the process. New activities are not simply chosen from existing alternatives; they must be invented or at least developed and adapted from alternatives that existed at previous times or in other jurisdictions. As with mousetraps, governmental innovations must be timely as well as better to get attention. During wartime, to take an extreme example, the political system has relatively little time or patience to consider domestic reforms. But improvements have to be devised before they can be added to the agenda.

There are several reasons why many program proposals originate with technical groups in the bureaucracy and with their associated professions. For the professional, activities contributing to relevant values are always high on the agenda. The professional has a stake in innovations in his specialty that gives them claim on his attention. Second, the professional attends to the parts of his environment from which innovations may emerge that can be adopted or adapted; he is a principal channel of cultural diffusion within his specialty from other jurisdictions and from the sources of new research and development. Third, the professional wants the esteem of fellow professionals—hence he is motivated to innovate for their approval. Fourth, the professional has the technical knowledge and skill that enable him to devise, recognize, adapt, and evaluate potential innovations.

In a highly technical society, and particularly in one that is receptive to innovation, the technicians will be a main source of innovation—and for government this means the bureaucracy and associated professions and often the two of them in concert. The "power" to innovate—even subject to political approval— does not fit the classical categories of power or influence, but is power nonetheless. It is probably the principal power of the bureaucracy in the realm of policy and value. Observation of the exercise of this power is a major reason, in turn, why we today regard the sharp separation of administration from policy as both infeasible and undesirable.

We must take care at this point not to romanticize the technician. To say that the technicians are a main source of innovation is not to say that all or most innovations will be embraced enthusiastically by the technicians. A new idea—an invention—that originates somewhere within the social system of a profession must gain legitimate status within this social system before the profession will become a positive force for diffusing and applying it. The status of the inventor as a legitimate member of the profession is important for the legitimacy of his invention. Inventions that are consistent with, or expand, the goals and role of the profession can expect more prompt acceptance than inventions that imply radical modification or constriction of goals (e.g., the Air Force position on piloted versus pilotless weapons). An innovation may meet stiff resistance if, after an initial rebuff, the innovator turns to groups outside the profession for support (the Billy Mitchell syndrome). Many of the stock examples of professional resistance to change are of this kind—where the inventor was in the profession, but because of his low or marginal status or the potential consequences of his idea for professional goals, the invention was not easily legitimized.

The point is not, then, that professions welcome all changes—this they certainly do not. Acceptance of an invention is almost always a complex, time-consuming, social process. Rather, the point is that on those occasions when change takes place, the locus of invention will more often than not be found within one or another of the technical specialties involved, and the professions will more often serve as channels than as boundaries of diffusion.

The power to initiate—to direct the attention of society to particular possibilities of action—is of greatest importance in the societies undergoing most rapid change. Hence, we would expect an especially great involvement of a professionalized technically trained bureaucracy in the political process in the developing countries. This, indeed, appears to be the case, whether for this reason or for others.

SUMMARY

In this section I have reviewed the old questions of the relation of the bureaucracy to the formation of policy, in the light of contemporary evidence and present-day institutions. Perhaps the main novelty—and most controversial aspect—of the analysis is its interpretation of the meaning of professionalism. If I read the evidence rightly, it leads me to a somewhat different result from the usual one as to the relation between specialty and hierarchy.

The professionals, far from being neutral, identify with characteristic professional values; and this identification increases their predictability and reliability as instruments of policy—hence the feasibility of delegation to them. The power of professionals over policy relates less to their possession of esoteric knowledge that protects them from lay scrutiny than it does to their advantageous position for innovating and initiating new programs.

The exercise of power through initiation rests, in turn, on the fact that influence over the direction of attention of the political organs is a principal means for affecting action. The notion of power as a tug of war among fixed alternatives yields to a notion of power as influence on a sequential decision process, in which actions must be generated as well as chosen and in which attention is a scarce resource.

Finally, the allocation of public resources through budgeting remains one of the murkiest corners of the political process. In the absence of a consistent rationale for comparing the incommensurable, the relation between politician and bureaucrat is more ambiguous in budgeting than perhaps in any other kind of governmental decision making.

ENDNOTES

I am grateful to Herbert Kaufman, Ithiel Pool, Don K. Price, and Donald W. Smithburg for valuable comments on an earlier draft of this chapter.

1. In order not to stir up again the cloud of confusion that surrounded the fact-value question for a generation, let me distinguish unequivocally among three aspects of that question: (1) Do administrators, in fact, participate in establishing the value premises that enter into decisions? (2) Should they so participate? (3) Are the logical bases for establishing value premises of the same nature as those for establishing factual premises? The answer to the first question, which is a purely empirical matter, is, "Yes, in all political systems that have been observed." The answer usually given in the second question nowadays, which is a normative matter involving value premises for its decision, is a qualified "Yes." The answer to the third question, which is a technical matter in formal logic, is definitely "No." In comparing this analysis with the one given in Herbert A. Simon, *Administrative Behavior*, The Macmillan Company, New York, 1947, pp. 45-58, the reader will discover that I have forgotten nothing and learned nothing in the past quarter century. As far as the present chapter is concerned, I shall assume (in spite of my previous experiences with political philosophers who have commented on my works) that a perceptive reader will be able to tell when I am writing declaratively (i.e., in the role of scientist) and when normatively (i.e., as a social engineer who shares democratic values with his compatriots).

2. Few responsible persons advocate a return to pre-civil-service conditions. When John Fischer wrote "Let's Go Back to the Spoils System," in the 1945 *Harper's,* he merely wanted to warn the personnel administrators that they had become paper shufflers and were impeding the development of an effective merit system.

3. On rereading, this sounds cynical, but that was not my intention. A central problem of effective social architecture is to arrange institutions so that doing good will pay off. To say that man should be changed to *want* the good simply transfers the architectural problem to the design of child-rearing institutions. On this point I find myself in agreement with B. F. Skinner.

4. For a recent excellent summary of the evidence, see Daniel Katz and Robert L. Kahn, *The Social Psychology of Organizations*, John Wiley & Sons, Inc., New York, 1966, especially chaps. 8 and 11–13.

5. "Realistic" is in quotes to emphasize that we are examining the normative side of things. In descriptive science, "realistic" means veridical, descriptive of reality; in normative science, it means less demanding of change from existing institutions, nonutopian.

6. Don Price, *The Scientific Estate*, Harvard University Press, Cambridge, Mass., 1965.

7. On the scientist's reaction to being evaluated by nonscientists, see Alan T. Waterman's fascinating review of *Scientist and National Policy-Making in Science*, vol. 144, pp. 1438–1439, June 19, 1964.

8. Instances of informal comparative observation abound in the literature. For a contemporary example, see the entries under "USSR" in the index of Robert A. Dahl and Charles E. Lindblom, *Politics, Economics, and Welfare*, Harper & Row, Publishers, Incorporated, New York, 1953, and especially the discussion on pp. 393–402.

9. For a broad survey of the new comparative research, with emphasis on bureaucratic-political relations, see David E. Apter, *The Politics of Modernization*, The University of Chicago Press, Chicago, 1965.

10. The emergence of military elites as "modernizing" forces, most dramatically in the Moslem nations (beginning with Turkey in the 1920s), has led to some reexamination of the political bases for military dictatorship. For an example, see P. J. Vatikiotis, "Dilemmas of Political Leadership in the Arab Middle East," *American Political Science Review*, vol. 55, pp. 103–111, March, 1961. Apter, *op. cit.*, discusses at length both military and technical elites, but his analysis of the latter (pp. 434–450) is blemished by a confusion between the scientist and the technician and a consequent overemphasis on freedom of information, so highly valued by the former.

11. These are central requisites of bureaucracy in any political system. Within a specific setting, other requirements follow from them, which vary from one kind of political system to another. On functionalism, see Almond, "A Functional Approach to Comparative Politics," in Gabriel A. Almond and James S. Coleman, *The Politics of the Developing Areas*, Princeton University Press, Princeton, N.J., 1960. For a further discussion of functional analysis, references to its literature, and an application to modernization processes, see Apter, *op. cit.*, chap. 7, "The Requisites of Government." The two requisites I have mentioned are closely parallel to Apter's "consummatory legitimacy" and "instrumental legitimacy," respectively. They are, of course, known by many other names in the literature of political theory.

12. This is an application of the basic thesis of my *Administrative Behavior* (e.g., as stated on pp. 220–228). James G. March has recently explored with great insight the circumstances under which understanding pro-

cess is likely to be a more fruitful approach to the study of political systems than measuring power. See "The Power of Power" in David Easton (ed.), *Varieties of Political Theory*, Prentice-Hall, Inc., Englewood Cliffs, N.J., 1966, chap. 3.

13. W. Lloyd Warner *et al.*, *The American Federal Executive*, Yale University Press, New Haven, Conn., 1963.

14. W. L. Guttsman, *The British Political Elite*, MacGibbon & Kee, London, 1963.

15. M. Djilas, *The New Class*, Frederick A. Praeger, Inc., New York, 1957.

16. Edward C. Banfield and James Q. Wilson, *City Politics*, Harvard University Press and The M.I.T. Press, Cambridge, Mass., 1963, pp. 182–185 and chap. 13 generally. Ithiel Pool, in his chapter in this volume, exhibits the other side of this coin: that the identification of citizen with the polity depends in part on the citizen's belief that there are among the rulers (and I would add also the bureaucrats) "people like himself." Surely this is one component in the theory of representation that Heinz Eulau calls for in his chapter in this volume.

17. Apter, *op. cit.*, chaps. 4 and 5.

18. Dwaine Marvick, *Career Perspectives in a Bureaucratic Setting*, Institute of Public Administration, The University of Michigan Press, Ann Arbor, Mich., 1954.

19. H. A. Shepard, "Patterns of Organization for Applied Research and Development," *Journal of Business*, vol. 29, pp. 261–267, 1956; and D. C. Pelz, "Some Social Factors Related to Performance in a Research Organization," *Administrative Science Quarterly*, vol. 1, pp. 310–325, 1956.

20. From other passages in Don Price's *The Scientific Estate*, I conclude that the author probably would not disagree with this qualification of his summary statement. See particularly pp. 122–124, 133, and 148–149.

21. Samuel P. Huntington, "Interservice Competition and the Political Roles of the Armed Services," *American Political Science Review*, vol. 55, pp. 40–52, March, 1961, points out (p. 48):
The armed services differ from most civilian groups . . . in the extent to which the bureau philosophy becomes . . . explicit. . . . The importance of doctrine stems from the extent to which the military groups are perceived to be and perceive themselves to be simply the instruments of a higher national policy . . . and each activity . . . is justified only by its contribution to the realization of the prescribed hierarchy of values and purposes.

22. I find, to my embarrassment, no ready references to empirical evidence supporting the strong statements of this section. Studies of the sociology of the professions are relevant, however. See, for example, Doctor X, *Intern*, Harper & Row, Publishers, Incorporated, New York, 1965.

23. H. A. Simon *et al.*, *Public Administration*, Alfred A. Knopf, Inc., New York, 1950, pp. 166–172.

24. James G. March, *op. cit.*, pp. 66–67. See also Ithiel Pool's chapter in this volume. The attention variable provides another crucial building block in the new theory of representation that Heinz Eulau calls for in his contribution to this volume. The representative can be held responsible

for anything to which citizens attend, hence potentially for anything—but not for everything!

25. See Ira Sharkansky, "An Appropriations Subcommittee and Its Client Agencies," *American Political Science Review*, vol. 59, pp. 622-628, September, 1965:

    . . . the legislators . . . devote more than the average amount of supervisory and control efforts to the agencies that spend the most money, whose requests have increased most rapidly, and whose behavior toward the subcommittee has deviated most frequently from subcommittee desires.

26. Kent Jennings, "Public Administrators and Community Decision Making," *Administrative Science Quarterly*, vol. 8, pp. 18-43, June, 1963.

27. See Aaron Wildavsky, *The Politics of the Budgetary Process*, Little, Brown and Company, Boston, 1964.

28. John P. Crecine, "A Computer Simulation Model of Municipal Resource Allocation," unpublished doctoral dissertation, Carnegie Institute of Technology, Pittsburgh, Pa., 1966.

29. *Basic Research and National Goals*, a report to the Committee on Science and Astronautics, U.S. House of Representatives, by the National Academy of Sciences, March, 1965. See especially the summary and chapters by Johnson and Kaysen. For the background of the report and the others mentioned here, see Kenneth Kofmehl, "COSPUP, Congress, and Scientific Advice," *Journal of Politics*, vol. 28, pp. 100-120, 1966.

30. See, for example, *Digital Computer Needs in Universities and Colleges*, Publication no. 1233, National Academy of Sciences-National Research Council, Washington, 1966; and the chapter by Revelle in *Basic Research and National Goals, op. cit.*

31. I.e., we need studies that can be compared with Sharkansky's data, mentioned earlier.

32. The literature on the relation of the bureaucracy to change is voluminous and somewhat contradictory. For samples, see Simon *et al., op cit.*, chap. 2; Peter M. Blau, *The Dynamics of Bureaucracy*, The University of Chicago Press, Chicago, 1955, chap. 12; James Q. Wilson, "Innovation in Organization," in James D. Thompson (ed.), *Approaches to Organizational Design*, The University of Pittsburgh Press, Pittsburgh, Pa., 1966; James G. March and Herbert A. Simon, *Organizations*, John Wiley & Sons, Inc., New York, 1958, chap. 7.

3

h. george frederickson

TOWARD A NEW PUBLIC ADMINISTRATION

In full recognition of the risks, this is an essay on new Public Administration. Its first purpose is to present my interpretation and synthesis of new Public Administration as it emerged at the Minnowbrook Conference on New Public Administration. Its second purpose is to describe how this interpretation and synthesis of new Public Administration relates to the wider world of administrative thought and practice. And its third purpose is to interpret what new Public Administration means for organization theory and *vice versa.*

To affix the label "new" to anything is risky business. The risk is doubled when newness is attributed to ideas, thoughts, concepts, paradigms, theories. Those who claim new thinking tend to regard previous thought as old or jejune or both. In response, the authors of previous thought are defensive and inclined to suggest that, "aside from having packaged earlier thinking in a new vocabulary there is little that is really new in so-called new thinking." Accept, therefore, this caveat: Parts of new Public Administration would be recognized by Plato, Hobbes, Machiavelli, Hamilton, and Jefferson as well as many modern behavioral theorists. The newness is in the way the fabric is woven, not necessarily in the threads that are used, and in arguments as to the proper use of the fabric—however threadbare.

The threads of the Public Administration fabric are well known. Herbert Kaufman describes them simply as the pursuit of these basic values: representativeness, politically neutral compe-

Copyright © 1971 by Chandler Publishing Company. Reprinted from *Toward A New Public Administration: The Minnowbrook Perspective.* Edited by Frank Marini by permission of Chandler Publishing Company, an Intext publisher.

tence, and executive leadership.[1] In different times, one or the other of these values receives the greatest emphasis. Representativeness was preeminent in the Jacksonian era. The eventual reaction was the reform movement emphasizing neutral competence and executive leadership. Now we are witnessing a revolt against these values accompanied by a search for new modes of representativeness.

Others have argued that changes in Public Administration resemble a zero-sum game between administrative efficiency and political responsiveness. Any increase in efficiency results *a priori* in a decrease in responsiveness. We are simply entering a period during which political responsiveness is to be purchased at a cost in administrative efficiency.

Both the dichotomous and trichotomous value models of Public Administration just described are correct as gross generalizations. But they suffer the weakness of gross generalizations: They fail to account for the wide, often rich, and sometimes subtle variation that rests within. Moreover, the generalization does not explain those parts of Public Administration that are beyond its sweep. Describing what new Public Administration means for organization theory is a process by which these generalizations can be given substance. But first it is necessary to briefly sketch what this student means by new Public Administration.

WHAT IS NEW PUBLIC ADMINISTRATION?

Educators have as their basic objective, and most convenient rationale, expanding and transmitting knowledge. The police are enforcing the law. Public-health agencies lengthen life by fighting disease. Then there are firemen, sanitation men, welfare workers, diplomats, the military, and so forth. All are employed by public agencies and each specialization or profession has its own substantive set of objectives and therefore its rationale.

What, then, is Public Administration?[2] What are its objectives and its rationale?

The classic answer has always been the efficient, economical, and coordinated management of the services listed above. The focus has been on top-level management (city management as an example) or the basic auxiliary staff services (budgeting, organization and management, systems analysis, planning, personnel, purchasing). The rationale for Public Administration is almost always better (more efficient or economical) management. New Public Administration adds *social equity* to the classic objectives and rationale. Conventional or classic Public Administration seeks to answer either of these questions: (1) How can we order more or better services with available resources (efficiency)? or (2) How can we maintain our level of services while spending less money (economy)? New Public Administration adds this question: Does this service enhance social equity?

The phrase social equity is used here to summarize the following set of value premises. Pluralistic government systematically discriminates in favor of established stable bureaucracies and their specialized minority clientele (the Department of Agriculture and large farmers as an example) and against those minorities (farm laborers, both migrant and permanent, as an example) who lack political and economic resources. The continuation of widespread unemployment, poverty, disease, ignorance, and hopelessness in an era of unprecedented economic growth is the result. This condition is morally reprehensible and if left unchanged constitutes a fundamental, if long-range, threat to the viability of this or any political system. Continued deprivation amid plenty breeds widespread militancy. Militancy is followed by repression, which is followed by greater militancy, and so forth. A Public Administration which fails to work for changes which try to redress the deprivation of minorities will likely be eventually used to repress those minorities.

For a variety of reasons—probably the most important being committee legislatures, seniority legislatures, entrenched bureaucracies, nondemocratized political-party procedures, inequitable revenue-raising capacity in the lesser governments of the federal system—the procedures of representative democracy presently operate in a way that either fails or only very gradually attempts to reverse systematic discrimination against disadvantaged minorities. Social equity, then, includes activities designed to enhance the political power and economic well-being of these minorities.

A fundamental commitment to social equity means that new Public Administration attempts to come to grips with Dwight Waldo's contention that the field has never satisfactorily accommodated the theoretical implications of involvement in "politics" and policy making.[3] The policy-administration dichotomy lacks an empirical warrant, for it is abundantly clear that administrators both execute and make policy. The policy-administration continuum is more accurate empirically but simply begs the theoretical question. New Public Administration attempts to answer it in this way: *Administrators are not neutral. They should be committed to both good management and social equity as values, things to be achieved, or rationales.*

A fundamental commitment to social equity means that new Public Administration is anxiously engaged in change. *Simply put, new Public Administration seeks to change those policies and structures that systematically inhibit social equity.* This is not seeking change for change's sake nor is it advocating alterations in the relative roles of administrators, executives, legislators, or the courts in our basic constitutional forms. Educators, agriculturists, police, and the like can work for changes which enhance their objectives and resist those that threaten those objectives, all within the framework of our governmental system. New Public Administration works in the same way to seek the changes which would enhance its objectives—good management, efficiency, economy, and social equity.

A commitment to social equity not only involves the pursuit of change but attempts to find organizational and political forms which exhibit a capacity for continued flexibility or routinized change. Traditional bureaucracy has a demonstrated capacity for stability, indeed, ultrastability.[4] New Public Administration, in its search for changeable structures, tends therefore to experiment with or advocate modified bureaucratic-organizational forms. Decentralization, devolution, projects, contrasts, sensitivity training, organization development, responsibility expansion, confrontation, and client involvement are all essentially counterbureaucratic notions that characterize new Public Administration.[5] These concepts are designed to enhance both bureaucratic and policy change and thus to increase possibilities for social equity. Indeed, an important faculty member in one of the best-known and largest Master in Public Administration programs in the country described that degree program as "designed to produce change agents or specialists in organizational development."

Other organizational notions such as programming-planning-budgeting systems, executive inventories, and social indicators can be seen as enhancing change in the direction of social equity. They are almost always presented in terms of good management (witness McNamara and PPB) as a basic strategy, because it is unwise to frontally advocate change.[6] In point of fact, however, PPB can be used as a basic device for change (in McNamara's case to attempt to wrest control from the uniformed services, but in the name of efficiency and economy). The executive inventory can be used to alter the character of the top levels of a particular bureaucracy, thereby enhancing change possibilities. Social indicators are designed to show variation in socioeconomic circumstances in the hope that attempts will be made to improve the conditions of those who are shown to be disadvantaged.[7] All three of these notions have only a surface neutrality or good-management character. Under the surface they are devices by which administrators and executives try to bring about change. It is no wonder they are so widely favored in Public Administration circles. And it should not be surprising that economists and political scientists in the "pluralist" camp regard devices such as PPB as fundamentally threatening to their conception of democratic government.[8] Although they are more subtle in terms of change, PPB, executive inventories, and social indicators are of the same genre as more frontal change techniques such as sensitivity training, projects, contracts, decentralization, and the like. All enhance change, and *change is basic to new Public Administration.*

New Public Administration's commitment to social equity implies a strong administrative or executive government—what Hamilton called "energy in the executive." The policy-making powers of the administrative parts of government are increasingly recognized. In addition, a fundamentally new form of political access and representativeness is now occurring in the administration of government and it may be that this access and representativeness is as critical to major policy decisions as is legislative access or representativeness. *New Public Administration seeks not only to carry out legislative mandates as efficiently and economically as possible, but to both influence and execute policies which more generally improve the quality of life for all.* Forthright policy advocacy on the part of the public servant is essential if administrative agencies are basic policy battlefields. New Public Administrationists are likely to be forthright advocates for social equity and will doubtless seek a supporting clientele.

Classic Public Administration emphasizes developing and strengthening institutions which have been designed to deal with social problems. The Public Administration focus, however, has tended to drift from the problem to the institution.[9] New Public Administration attempts to refocus on the problem and to consider alternative possible institutional approaches to confronting problems. The intractable character of many public problems such as urban poverty, widespread narcotics use, high crime rates, and the like lead Public Administrators to seriously question the investment of ever more money and manpower in institutions which seem only to worsen the problems. They seek, therefore, either to modify these institutions or develop new and more easily changed ones designed to achieve more proximate solutions. *New Public Administration is concerned less with the Defense Department than with defense, less with civil-service commissions than with the manpower needs of administrative agen-*

cies on the one hand and the employment needs of the society on the other, less with building institutions and more with designing alternate means of solving public problems. These alternatives will no doubt have some recognizable organizational characteristics and they will need to be built and maintained, but will seek to avoid becoming entrenched, nonresponsible bureaucracies that become greater public problems than the social situations they were originally designed to improve.

The movement from an emphasis on institution building and maintenance to an emphasis on social anomalies has an important analogue in the study of Public Administration. The last generation of students of Public Administration generally accept both Simon's logical positivism and his call for an empirically based organization theory. They focus on generic concepts such as decision, role, and group theory to develop a generalizable body of organization theory. The search is for commonalities of behavior in all organizational settings.[10] The organization and the people within it are the empirical referent. The product is usually description, not prescription, and if it is prescription it prescribes how to better manage the organization internally. The subject matter is first *organization* and second the type of organization—private, public, voluntary.[11] The two main bodies of theory emerging from this generation of work are decision theory and human-relation theory. Both are regarded as behavioral and positivist. Both are at least as heavily influenced by sociology, social psychology, and economics as they are by political science.

New Public Administration advocates what could be best described as "second-generation behavioralism." Unlike his progenitor, the second-generation behavioralist emphasizes the *public* part of Public Administration. He accepts the importance of understanding as scientifically as possible how and why organizations behave as they do but he tends to be rather more interested in the impact of that organization on its clientele and *vice versa.* He is not antipositivist nor antiscientific although he is probably less than sanguine about the applicability of the natural-science model to social phenomena. He is not likely to use his behavioralism as a rationale for simply trying to describe how public organizations behave.[12] Nor is he inclined to use his behavioralism as a facade for so-called neutrality, being more than a little skeptical of the objectivity of those who claim to be doing science. He attempts to use his scientific skills to aid his analysis, experimentation, and evaluation of alternative policies and administrative modes. *In sum, then, the second-generation behavioralist is less "generic" and more "public" than his forebear, less "descriptive" and more "prescriptive," less "institution oriented" and more "client-impact oriented," less "neutral" and more "normative," and, it is hoped, no less scientific.*

This has been a brief and admittedly surface description of new Public Administration from the perspective of one analyst. If the description is even partially accurate it is patently clear that there are fundamental changes occurring in Public Administration which have salient implications for both its study and practice as well as for the general conduct of government. The final purpose of this chapter is a consideration of the likely impact of new Public Administration on organization theory particularly and the study of administration generally. (The term "theory" is used here in its loose sense, as abstract thought.)

ORGANIZATION THEORY AND NEW PUBLIC ADMINISTRATION

Understanding of any phenomenon requires separating that phenomenon into parts and examining each part in detail. In understanding government this separation can reflect institutions such as the traditional "fields" in political science—Public Administration, legislative behavior, public law, and so forth. Or this separation can be primarily conceptual or theoretical such as systems theory, decision theory, role theory, group theory—all of which cut across institutions.

Public Administration has never had either an agreed upon or a satisfactory set of subfields. The "budgeting," "personnel administration," "organization and management" categories are too limiting, too "inside-organization" oriented, and too theoretically vacant. The middle-range theories—decisions, roles, groups, and the like—are stronger theoretically and have yielded more empirically, but still tend to focus almost exclusively on the internal dynamics of public organizations. The new Public Administration calls for a different way of subdividing the phenomenon so as to better understand it. This analyst suggests that there are four basic processes at work in public organizations and further suggests that these processes are suitable for both understanding and improving Public Administration. The four suggested processes are: the distributive process; the integrative process; the boundary-exchange process; and the socioemotional process.

The Distributive Process

New Public Administration is vitally concerned with patterns of distribution. This concern has to do first with the *external* distribution of goods and services to particular categories of persons, in terms of the benefits that result from the operation of publicly administered programs.

Cost-utility, or cost-benefit, analysis is the chief technique for attempting to understand the results of the distributive process. This form of analysis presumes to measure the utility to individuals of particular public programs. Because it attempts to project the likely costs and benefits of alternative programs it is a very central part of new Public Administration. It is central primarily because it provides a scientific or quasi-scientific means for attempting to "get at" the question of equity. It also provides a convenient or classic Public Administration rationale for redistribution. Take, for example, McNamara's justifications for decisions based on cost-utility analysis in the Department of Defense. These justifications were generally urged on the basis of substantive military criteria.

Because of the emergence of "program-planning-budgeting systems" we are beginning to see, in the policy advocacy of the various bureaus and departments of government, their attempts to demonstrate their impact on society in terms of utility. Wildavsky and Lindblom have argued that rational or cost-utility analysis is difficult if not impossible to do. Further, they contend, rational decision making fundamentally alters or changes our political system by dealing with basic political questions within the arena of the administrator. To date they are essentially correct, empirically. Normatively they are apologists for pluralism. Cost-benefit analysis can be an effective means by which inequities can be demonstrated. It is a tool by which legislatures and entrenched bureaucracies can be caused to defend publicly their distributive decisions. The inference is that a public informed of glaring inequities will demand change.

Like the executive budget, rational or cost-benefit decision systems (PPB) enhance the power of executives and administrators and are, again, a part of new Public Administration. Because PPB is being widely adopted in cities and states, as well as in the national government, it seems clear that new Public Administration will be highly visible simply by a look at the distributive processes of government over the next decade or two. The extent to which PPB will result in a redistribution which enhances social equity remains to be seen.

Benefit or utility analysis in its less prescriptive and more descriptive form, known in political science as "policy-outcomes analysis," attempts to determine the basic factors that influence or determine policy variation. [13] For example, "outcomes analysts" sketch the relationship between variations in public spending (quantity) and the quality of nonspending policy outcomes. The policy-outcomes analyst attempts to determine the relationship between the levels of spending in education and the IQ's, employability, college admissibility, and the like of the products of the educational process. This analysis is essentially after the fact, and indeed is commonly based on relatively out-of-date census data. It is, therefore, useful to new Public Administration, but only as a foundation or background.

A newer form of distributive analysis is emerging. This approach focuses on equity in the distribution of government services within a jurisdiction and asks questions such as: Does a school board distribute its funds equitably to schools and to the school children in its jurisdiction, and if not is inequity in the direction of the advantaged or disadvantaged? Are sanitation services distributed equitably to all neighborhoods in the city, and if not in what direction does inequity move and how is it justified? Is state and federal aid distributed equitably, and if not how are inequities justified? [14]

Patterns of internal-organization distribution are a traditional part of organization theory. The internal competition for money, manpower, status, space, and priorities is a staple in organization theory as any reading of the *Administrative Science Quarterly* indicates. We learn from this literature the extent to which many of the functions of government are in essence controlled by particular bodies of professionals—educators, physicians, attorneys, social workers, and the like. We learn how agencies age and become rigid and devote much of their energies to competing for survival purposes. We learn the extent to which distribution becomes what Wildavsky calls a triangulation between bureaus, legislatures (particularly legislative committees), and elected executives and their auxiliary staffs. [15] Finally, we have whole volumes of aggregated and disaggregated hypotheses which account for or attempt to explain the decision patterns involved in the internal distributive process. [16]

In new Public Administration the internal distributive process is likely to involve somewhat less readiness to make incremental compromises or "bargain" and somewhat more "administrative confrontation." If new Public Administrators are located in the staff agencies of the executive, which is highly likely, they will doubtless be considerably more tenacious than their predecessors. The spokesman for an established agency might have learned to pad his budget, to overstaff, to control public access to records, and to expand his space in preparation for the compromises he has learned to expect. He might now encounter a zealot armed with data which describe in detail padding, overstaffing, and suppressed records. Therefore an organization theory based primarily on the traditional administrative bargaining process is likely to be woefully inadequate. There is a need to develop a theory which accounts for the presence of public administrators considerably less willing to bargain and more willing to take political and administrative risks.

It is difficult to predict the possible consequences of having generalist public administrators who are prepared to rationalize their positions and decisions on the basis of social equity. Administrative theory explains relatively well the results of the use of efficiency, economy, or good management as rationale. We know, for instance, that these arguments are especially persuasive in years in which legislatures and elected executives do not wish to raise taxes. But we also know that virtually anything can be justified under the rubric "good management." When public administrators leave the safe harbor of this rhetoric, what might occur? The best guess is a more open conflict on basic issues of goals or purposes. Some administrators will triumph, but the majority will not; for the system tends to work against the man seeking change and willing to take risks for it. The result is likely to be a highly mobile and relatively unstable middle-level civil service. Still, actual withdrawal or removal from the system after a major setback is likely to be preferred by new public administrators to the psychic withdrawal which is now common among administrators.

One can imagine, for instance, a city personnel director prepared to confront the chief of police and the police bureaucracy on the question of eligibility standards for new patrolmen. He might argue, backed with considerable data, that patrolman height and weight regulations are unrealistic and systematically discriminate against deprived minorities. He might also argue that misdemeanor convictions by minors should not prohibit adults from becoming patrolmen. If this were an open conflict, it would likely array deprived minorities against the majority of the city council, possibly against the mayor, and certainly against the chief and his men (and no doubt the Police Benevolent Association). While the new public administrator might be perfectly willing to take the risks involved in such a confrontation, present theory does not accommodate well what this means for the political system generally.

The Integrative Process

Authority hierarchies are the primary means by which the work of persons in publicly administrated organizations is coordinated. The formal hierarchy is the most obvious and easiest-to-identify part of the permanent and on-going organization. Administrators are seen as persons taking roles in the hierarchy and performing tasks that are integrated through the hierarchies to constitute a cohesive goal-seeking whole. The public administrator has customarily been regarded as the one who builds and maintains the organization through the hierarchy. He attempts to understand formal-informal relationships, status, politics, and power in authority hierarchies. The hierarchy is at once an ideal design and a hospitable environment for the person who wishes to manage, control, or direct the work of large numbers of people.

The counterproductive characteristics of hierarchies are well known.[17] New Public Administration is probably best understood as advocating modified hierarchic systems. Several means both in theory and practice are utilized to modify traditional hierarchies. The first and perhaps the best known is the project or matrix technique.[18] The project is, by definition, temporary. The project manager and his staff are a team which attempts to utilize the services of regularly established hierarchies in an on-going organization. For the duration of the project, the manager must get his technical services from the technical hierarchy of the organization, his personnel services from the personnel agency, his budgeting services from the budget department, and so forth. Obviously the project technique would not be effective were it not for considerable top-level support for the project. When there are conflicts between the needs of the project and the survival needs of established hierarchies, top management must consistently decide in favor of the projects. The chief advantage of projects are of course their collapsible nature. While bureaucracies do not disestablish or self-destruct, projects do. The project concept is especially useful when associated with "one time" hardware or research and development, or capital improvement efforts. The concept is highly sophisticated in engineering circles and theoretically could be applied to a large number of less technical and more social problems.[19] The project technique is also useful as a device by which government contracts with industry can be monitored and coordinated.

Other procedures for modifying hierarchies are well known and include the group-decision-making model, the link-pin function, and the so-called dialectical organization.[20] And, of course, true decentralization is a fundamental modification hierarchy.[21]

Exploration and experimentation with these various techniques is a basic part of new Public Administration. The search for less structured, less formal, and less authoritative integrative techniques in publicly administered organizations is only beginning. The preference for these types of organizational modes implies first a relatively high tolerance for variation. This includes variations in administrative performance and variations in procedures and applications based upon differences in clients or client groups. It also implies great tolerance for the possibilities of inefficiency and diseconomy. In a very general sense this preference constitutes a willingness to trade increases in involvement and commitment to the organization for possible decreases in efficiency and economy, particularly in the short run. In the long run, less formal and less authoritative integrative techniques may prove to be more efficient and economical.

There are two serious problems with the advocacy by new Public Administration of less formal integrative processes. First, there may develop a lack of Public Administration specialists who are essentially program builders. The new Public Administration man who is trained as a change agent and an advocate of informal, decentralized, integrative processes may not be capable of building and maintaining large, permanent organizations. This problem may not be serious, however, because administrators in the several professions (education, law enforcement, welfare and the like) are often capable organization builders, or at least protectors, so a Public Administration specialist can concentrate on the change or modification of hierarchies built by others.

The second problem is the inherent conflict between higher- and lower-level administrators in less formal, integrative systems. While describing the distributive process in Public Administration it was quite clear that top-level public administrators were to be strong and assertive. In this description of the integrative process there is a marked preference for large degrees of autonomy at the base of the organization. The only way to theoretically accommodate this contradiction is through an organizational design in which top-level public administrators are regarded as policy advocates and general-policy reviewers. If they have a rather high tolerance for the variations in policy application then it can be presumed that intermediate and lower levels in the organization can apply wide interpretive license in program application. This accommodation is a feeble one, to be sure, but lighter-lower-level administrative relations are a continuing problem in Public Administration, and the resolution of these problems in the past has tended to be in the direction of the interests of upper levels of the hierarchy in combination with subdivisions of the legislative body and potent interest groups. New Public Administration searches for a means by which lower levels of the organization and less potent minorities can be favored.

The Boundary-Exchange Process

The boundary-exchange process describes the general relationship between the publicly administered organization and its reference groups and clients. These include legislatures, elected executives, auxiliary staff organizations, clients (both organized and individual), and organized interest groups. The boundary-exchange process also accounts for the relationship between levels of government in a federal system. Because publicly administered organizations find themselves in a competitive political, social, and economic environment, they tend to seek support. This is done by first finding a clientele which can play a strong advocacy role with the legislature, then by developing a symbiotic relationship between the agency and key committees or members of the legislature, followed by building and maintaining as permanent an organization as is possible.

The distributive and integrative processes which have just been described call for vastly altered concepts of how to conduct boundary exchange in new Public Administration.[22] Future organization theory will have to accommodate the following pattern of boundary exchange. First, a considerably higher client involvement is necessary on the part of those minorities who have not heretofore been involved. (It is unfair to assume that minorities are not already involved as clients; farmers, bankers, and heavy industries are minorities and they are highly involved clients. In this sense all public organizations are "client" oriented.) This change probably spells a different kind of involvement. A version of this kind of involvement is now being seen in some of our cities as a result of militancy and community-action programs, and on the campuses of some universities. A preferred form of deprived-minority-client involvement would be routinized patterns of communication with decentralized organizations capable of making distributive decisions that support the interests of deprived minorities, even if these decisions are difficult to justify in terms of either efficiency or economy.

In a very general way, this kind of decision making occurs in time of war with respect to military decision making. It also characterizes decision patterns in the Apollo program of the National Aeronautics and Space Administration. These two examples characterize crash programs designed to solve problems that are viewed as immediate and pressing. They involve a kind of backward budgeting in which large blocks of funds are made available for the project and wide latitude in expenditures is tolerated. The detailed accounting occurs after the spending, not before, hence backward budgeting. Under these conditions what to do and what materials are needed are decided at low levels of the organization. These decisions are made on the presumption that they will be supported and the necessary resources will be made available and accounted for by upper levels of the organization. This same logic could clearly be applied to the ghetto. A temporary project could be established in which the project manager and his staff work with the permanently established bureaucracies in a city in a crash program designed to solve the employment, housing, health, education, and transportation needs of the residents of that ghetto. The decisions and procedures of one project would likely vary widely from those of another, based on the differences in the circumstances of the clientele involved and the political-administrative environments encountered. The central project director would tolerate the variations both in decisions and patterns of expenditures in the same way that the Department of Defense and NASA cover their expenditures in times of crisis.

The danger will be in the tendency of decentralized projects to be taken over by local pluralist elites. The United States Selective Service is an example of this kind of take-over. High levels of disadvantaged-minority-client involvement are necessary to offset this tendency. Still, it will be difficult to prevent the new controlling minorities from systematic discrimination against the old controlling minorities.

From this description of a boundary-exchange relationship, it is probably safe to predict that administrative agencies, particularly those that are decentralized, will increasingly become the primary means by which particular minorities find their basic form of political representation. This situation exists now in the case of the highly advantaged minorities and may very well become the case with the disadvantaged.

The means by which high client involvement is to be secured is problematic. The maximum-feasible-participation notion, although given a very bad press, was probably more successful than most analysts are prepared to admit. Maximum feasible participation certainly did not enhance the efficency or economy of OEO activities, but, and perhaps most important, it gave the residents of the ghetto at least the impression that they had the capacity to influence publicly made decisions that affected their well-being. High client involvement probably means, first, the employment of the disadvantaged where feasible; second, the use of client review boards or review agencies; and third, decentralized legislatures such as the kind sought by the Brownhill School District in the New York City Board of Education decentralization controversy.

The development of this pattern of boundary exchange spells the probable development of new forms of intergovernmental relations, particularly fiscal relations. Federal grants-in-aid to states and cities, and state grants-in-aid to cities will no doubt be expanded, and probably better equalized.[23] In addition, some form of tax sharing is probably called for. The fundamental weakness of the local governments' revenue capacity must be alleviated.

The use of the distributive and integrative processes described above probably also means the development of new means by which administrators relate to their legislatures. The elected official will probably always hold continuance in office as his number-one objective. This means that a Public Administration using less formal integrative processes must find means by which it can enhance the re-election probabilities of supporting incumbents. Established centralized bureaucracies do this in a variety of ways, the best known being building and maintaining of roads or other capital facilities in the legislators' district, establishing high-employment facilities, such as federal office buildings, county courthouses, police precincts, and the like, and distributing public-relations materials favorable to the incumbent legislator. The decentralized organization seems especially suited for the provision of this kind of service for legislators. As a consequence it is entirely possible to imagine legislators becoming strong spokesmen for less hierarchic and less authoritative bureaucracies.

The Socioemotional Process

The Public Administration described herein will require both individual and group characteristics that differ from those presently seen. The widespread use of sensitivity training, T techniques, or "organizational development" is compatible with new Public Administration.[24] These techniques include lowering an individual's reliance on hierarchy, enabling him to tolerate conflicts and emotions, and indeed under certain circumstances to welcome them, and to prepare him to take greater risks. From the preceding discussion it is clear that sensitizing techniques are parallel to the distributive, integrative, and boundary-exchange processes just described.

Socioemotional-training techniques are fundamental devices for administrative change. These techniques have thus far been used primarily to strengthen or redirect on-going and established bureaucracies. In the future it is expected that the same techniques will be utilized to aid in the development of decentralized and possibly project-oriented organizational modes.

A recent assessment of the United States Department of State by Chris Argyris is highly illustrative of the possible impact of new Public Administration on organizational socioemotional processes.[25] Argyris concluded that "State" is a social system characterized by individual withdrawal from interpersonal difficulties and conflict; minimum interpersonal openness, leveling, and trust; a withdrawal from aggressiveness and fighting; the view that being emotional is being ineffective or irrational; leaders' domination of subordinates; an unawareness of leaders' personal impact on others; and very high levels of conformity coupled with low levels of risk taking or responsibility taking. To correct these organizational "pathologies" Argyris recommended that:

1. A long-range change program should be defined with the target being to change the living system of the State Department.

2. The first stage of the change program should focus on the behavior and leadership style of the most senior participants within the Department of State.

3. Simultaneously with the involvement of the top, similar change activities should be initiated in any subpart which shows signs of being ready for change.

4. The processes of organizational change and development that are created should require the same behavior and attitudes as those we wish to inculcate into the system (take more initiative, enlarge responsibilities, take risks).

5. As the organizational development activities produce a higher level of leadership skills and begin to reduce the system's defenses in the area of interpersonal relations, the participants should be helped to begin to reexamine some of the formal policies and activities of the State Department that presently may act as inhibitors to organizational

effectiveness (employee evaluations and ratings, promotion process, inspections). The reexamination should be conducted under the direction of line executives with the help of inside or outside consultants.

6. The similarities and interdependencies between administration and substance need to be made more explicit and more widely accepted.

7. The State Department's internal capacity in the new areas of behavioral-science-based knowledge should be increased immediately.

8. Long-range research programs should be developed, exploring the possible value of the behavioral disciplines to the conduct of diplomacy.

The characteristics of the State Department are, sad to say, common in publicly administered organizations. While Argyris' recommendations are particular to "State," they are relevant to all highly authoritative hierarchy-based organizations.

While new Public Administration is committed to wider social equity, the foregoing should make it clear that a more nearly equitable internal organization is also an objective.

CONCLUSIONS

The search for social equity provides Public Administration with a real normative base. Like many value premises, social equity has the ring of flag, country, mother, and apple pie. But surely the pursuit of social equity in Public Administration is no more a holy grail than the objectives of educators, medical doctors, and so forth. Still, it appears that new Public Administration is an alignment with good, or possibly God.

What are the likely results for a *practicing* public administration working from such a normative base? *First,* classic public administration on the basis of its expressed objectives commonly had the support of businessmen and the articulate and educated upper and upper-middle classes. The phenomenal success of the municipal-reform movement is testament to this. If new Public Administration attempts to justify or rationalize its stance on the basis of social equity, it might have to trade support from its traditional sources for support from the disadvantaged minorities. It might be possible for new Public Administration to continue to receive support from the educated and articulate if we assume that this social class is becoming increasingly committed to those public programs that are equity enhancing and less committed to those that are not. Nevertheless, it appears that new Public Administration should be prepared to take the risks involved in such a trade, if it is necessary to do so.

Second, new Public Administration, in its quest for social equity, might encounter the kinds of opposition that the Supreme Court has experienced in the last decade. That is to say, substantial opposition from elected officials for its fundamental involvement in shaping social policy. The Court, because of its independence, is less vulnerable than administration. We might expect, therefore, greater legislative controls over administrative agencies and particularly the distributive patterns of such agencies.

Third, new Public Administration might well foster a political system in which elected officials speak basically for the majority and for the privileged minorities while courts and the administrators are spokesmen for disadvantaged minorities. As administrators work in behalf of the equitable distribution of public and private goods, courts are increasingly interpreting the Constitution in the same direction. Legislative hostility to this activity might be directed at administration simply because it is most vulnerable.

What of new Public Administration and academia? First let us consider the theory, then the academy.

Organization theory will be influenced by new Public Administration in a variety of ways. The uniqueness of *public* organization will be stressed. Internal administrative behavior—the forte of the generic administration school and the foundation of much of what is now known as organization theory—will be a part of scholarly Public Administration, but will be less central. Its center position in Public Administration will be taken by a strong emphasis on the distributive and boundary-exchange processes described above.

Quantitatively inclined public-organization theorists are likely to drift toward or at least read widely in welfare economics. Indeed it is possible to imagine these theorists executing a model or paradigm of social equity fully as robust as the economist's market model. With social equity elevated to the supreme objective, in much the way profit is treated in economics, model building is relatively simple. We might, for example, develop theories of equity maximization, long- and short-range equity, equity elasticity, and so on. The theory and research being reported in the journal *Public Choice* provides a glimpse of this probable development. This work is presently being done primarily by economists who are, in the main, attempting to develop variations on the market model or notions of individual-utility maximization. Public organization theorists with social-equity commitments could contribute greatly by the creation of models less fixed on market environments or individual-utility maximization and more on the equitable distribution of and access to both public and private goods by different groups or categories of people. If a full-blown equity model were developed it might be possible to assess rather precisely the likely outcomes of alternative policies in terms of whether the alternative does or does not enhance equity. Schemes for guaranteed annual income, negative income tax, Head Start, Job Corps, and the like could be evaluated in terms of their potential for equity maximization.

The less quantitatively but still behaviorally inclined public-organization theorists are likely to move in the direction of Kirkhart's "consociated model." They would move in the direction of sociology, anthropology, and psychology, particularly in their existential versions, while the quantitatively inclined will likely move toward economics, as described above. And, of course, many public-organization theorists will stay with the middle-range theories—role, group, communications, decisions, and the like—and not step under the roof of the grand theories such as the consociated model, the social-equity model, or the so-called systems model.

What does new Public Administration mean for the academy? One thing is starkly clear: We now know the gigantic difference between "public administration" and "the public service." The former is made up of public-management generalists and some auxiliary staff people (systems analysis, budgeting, personnel, and so on) while the latter is made up of the professionals who man the schools, the police, the courts, the military, welfare agencies, and so forth. Progressive Public Administration programs in the academy will build firm and permanent bridges to the professional schools where most public servants are trained. In some schools the notion of Public Administration as the "second profession" for publicly employed attorneys, teachers, welfare workers will become a reality.

Some Public Administration programs will likely get considerably more philosophic and normative while others will move more to quantitative management techniques. Both are needed and both will contribute.

The return of policy analysis is certain in both kinds of schools. Good management for its own sake is less and less important to today's student. Policy analysis, both logically and analytically "hard-nosed," will be the order of the day.

Academic Public Administration programs have not commonly been regarded as especially exciting. New public administration has an opportunity to change that. Programs that openly seek to attract and produce "change agents" or "short-haired radicals" are light years away from the POSDCORB image. And many of us are grateful for that.

ENDNOTES

1. Herbert Kaufman, "Administrative Decentralization and Political Power," *Public Administration Review* (January-February, 1969), pp. 3-15.
2. Frederick Mosher and John C. Honey wrestle with the question of the relative role of professional specialists as against the generalist administrator in public organizations. See Frederick Mosher, *Democracy and the Public Service* (New York: Oxford University Press, 1968), pp. 99-133. See also John C. Honey, "A Report: Higher Education for the Public Service," *Public Administration Review* (November, 1967).
3. Dwight Waldo, "Scope of the Theory of Public Administration," James C. Charlesworth (ed.), *Theory and Practice of Public Administration: Scope, Objectives and Methods* (Philadelphia: The American Academy of Political and Social Sciences, October, 1968), pp. 1-26.
4. Anthony Downs, *Inside Bureaucracy* (Boston: Little, Brown, 1967).
5. In a very general way most of these are characteristics of what Larry Kirkham (see Chap. 5 above) calls the consociated model.
6. See especially Charles L. Schultze, *The Politics and Economics of Public Spending* (Washington, D.C.: The Brookings Institution, 1969).
7. The general "social equity" concern expressed in the essays in Raymond A. Bauer, *Social Indicators* (Cambridge, Mass.: MIT Press, 1967) is clearly indicative of this.
8. Aaron Wildavsky, *The Politics of the Budgetary Process* (Boston: Little, Brown, 1964) and Charles Lindblom, *The Intelligence of Democracy* (New York: Glencoe Free Press, 1966).
9. See especially Orion White's essay in this volume (Chap. 3) on this point.
10. See especially James March and Herbert Simon, *Organizations* (New York: John Wiley and Sons, 1963).
11. See especially Amitai Etzioni, *A Comparative Analysis of Complex Organizations* (New York: Glencoe Free Press, 1961).
12. An exchange occurring at an informal rump session of the Minnowbrook Conference is especially illustrative of this. Several conferees were discussing errors in strategy and policy in the operations of the United States Office of Economic Opportunity. They were generalizing in an attempt to determine how organizations like O.E.O. could be made more effective. Several plausible causal assertions were advanced and vigorously supported. Then a young but well-established political scientist commented that causal assertions could not be supported by

only one case. True correlations of statistical significance required an 'N" or "number of cases" of at least thirty. The reply was, "Has Public Administration nothing to suggest until we have had thirty O.E.O.'s? Can we afford thirty O.E.O.'s before we learn what went wrong with the first one? By ducking into our analytical and quantitative shelters aren't we abdicating our responsibilities to suggest ways to make the second O.E.O or its equivalent an improvement on the first?"

13. For a good bibliographic essay on this subject see John H. Fenton and Donald W. Chamberlayne, "The Literature Dealing with the Relationships Between Political Process, Socioeconomic Conditions and Public Policies in the American States: A Bibliographic Essay," *Polity* (Spring, 1969), pp. 388-404. See also Chap. 9 above.

14. Equity is now a major question in the courts. Citizens are bringing suit against governments at all levels under the "equal protection of the laws" clause claiming inequities in distribution. Thus far the courts have taken a moderate equity stance in education and welfare. See John E. Coons, William H. Clune, and Stephen D. Sugerman, "Educational Opportunity: A Workable Constitutional Test for State Structures," *California Law Review* (April, 1969), pp. 305-421.

15. Aaron Wildavsky, *op. cit.*

16. March and Simon, *op. cit.;* Downs, *op. cit.;* and James L. Price, *Organizational Effectiveness* (Homewood, Ill.: Irwin, 1968).

17. See Victor Thompson, *Modern Organization* (New York: Knopf, 1961); Robert V. Presthus, *The Organizational Society* (New York: Knopf, 1962); and Downs, *op. cit.*

18. David I. Cleland and William R. King, *Systems Analysis and Project Management* (New York: McGraw-Hill, 1968); David I. Cleland and William R. King, *Systems Organizations, Analysis, Management: A Book of Readings* (New York: McGraw-Hill, 1969); George A. Steiner and William G. Ryan, *Industrial Project Management* (New York: Macmillan, 1968); John Stanley Baumgartner, *Project Management* (Homewood, Ill.: Irwin, 1963).

19. H. George Frederickson and Henry J. Anna, "Bureaucracy and the Urban Poor," mimeographed.

20. See Rensis Likert, *New Patterns of Management* (New York: McGraw-Hill, 1961); and Orion White, "The Dialectical Organization: An Alternative to Bureaucracy," *Public Administration Review* (January-February, 1969), pp. 32-42.

21. Kaufman, *op. cit.*

22. James Thompson, *Organizations in Action* (New York: McGraw-Hill, 1967).

23. Deil S. Wright, *Federal Grants-In-Aid: Perspectives and Alternatives* (Washington, D.C.: American Enterprise Institute for Public Policy Research, 1968).

24. See especially the essays of Larry Kirkhart (Chap. 5) and Orion White (Chap. 3) above.

25. Chris Argyris, "Some Causes of Organizational Ineffectiveness Within the Department of State" (Washington, D.C.; U.S. Government Printing Office [Center for International Systems Research, Occasional Paper No. 2], November, 1966).

4

orion white, jr.

THE CONCEPT OF ADMINISTRATIVE PRAXIS

The problem of defining the proper relation of theory to practice has been the traditional bane of public administration. Much has been said on the issue, but the need for a redefinition of the relationship seems imperative. This article will present a review of the issue, state the imperatives which make it urgent to rethink the question, and present a conceptualization of the theory-practice nexus based on critical analysis of the view that seems traditional to the field.

A BACKGROUND VIEW OF THE ISSUE

One way of conceptualizing the history of the field of academic public administration is to see its literature as an evolving set of statements concerning four interrelated questions: (1) what theory of knowledge best fits the reality of the administrative world; (2) what is the proper concept of human nature in organizations; (3) what is the most effective model of professionalism—as the dominant role set of the administrative actor; and (4) what is the most productive way to relate "theory" (or, synonymously, "principle," "analysis," "research," and the like) to the pragmatics of government organization (White and Marini, 1971). As is indicated by the key value words in these questions ("best fits," "proper," "most effective," "most productive"), the answers to these problems were and are seen as relating necessarily to a superordinate framework which imparts meaning

Reprinted from the *Journal of Comparative Administration* Vol. V, No. 1 (May 1973) pp. 55–85 by permission of the Publisher, Sage Publications, Inc.

or "rightness and wrongness" to the proposed answers. That is, the question for administrative theory is not "what is the nature of man" but rather, "what is the best way of conceptualizing man in order to affect or optimize the goals, mission, or purpose of government administrative agencies?" Even more implicit and more important than this sort of bias in the questions is the relation of the answer to the context of the question itself—namely, government administration. That is, it would seem that what one would consider proper answers to the questions would change if and when the nature of the governmental process within which the administrative agencies functioned changed. Relating even philosophical analysis to a concrete context can thus be seen as one of the rather novel intellectual tasks faced by those interested in developing a theory of government administration.

Early or "classical" public administration legitimated itself by embracing "science" as a metaphor and symbol and at the same time addressing the problems of the day (mainly, how to manage the cities). However, in those days, the field was not scientific or theoretical in any strict sense. Its principles were based on the lowest level of abstraction from existing reality organized by rather obvious categories. Hence, there was no theory-practice gap because the "theory" of the time was simply a set of crude, practical principles. These were useful not only because they were so conceptually immediate but because they also fitted the emerging political, class, and institutional power configurations of the day (White, 1971).

When the field split into its bifurcated form in the 1940s, however, theory and practice were separated. The "Traditionalists," holding to the classical principles of, for example, Gulick and Urwick, yet following Herring and Appleby in asserting the political nature of administration, in effect suppressed theory. Normative concerns became paramount, and the idea of the "public interest" ascended as the main "theoretical" concept of this approach. However, the public interest notion came to be a basis for the assertion on the part of the practitioner of a gap in *ideal* and practice. The public interest was seen as impracticable in most parts of the "real world." (Hence the famous claim from the experienced administrator to the novice: "The professors told you how it *ought* to be; I'll show you how it is.")

On the other hand, with Simon and the various "modern" offshoots which grew in the literature of public administration as a result of his work, the problem was quite different. In the fields of "organization theory," "decision theory," and "comparative" or "development administration," which have all been substantially influenced by Simon, the desired relation between theory and practice was rather explicitly that of applied science. From the point of view of the practitioner, this approach carried to the classroom and the field produced a true "theory-practice gap." Models, concepts, hypotheses, and data all proliferated to such an extent that an esoteric confusion set in (Wilcox, 1968; Leavitt, 1963; Golembiewski, 1965; Likert, 1967). Hypotheses were substantiated, qualified, disputed; models went in and out of fashion.[1] Perhaps the major practical consequence, taking the broad view of the real world of administrative practice, was that the human relations tradition was amended and furthered in a humanistic direction, while at the same time the technology of administrative processes became more sophisticated and automated.

There are some exceptions to this general pattern, however. Certainly a radically different view seems to be implicit in the so-called "new public administration" (Kirkhart, 1971). The departure point in this "new" school seems to be versions of a phenomenological view of knowledge. It does not seem clear at this point what this will mean for the linkage of theory to action. One analysis in this vein is Bjur's work on "contextual modeling," which posits that theory can effectively guide action when it stems from an awareness of the contextual (relative) nature of theoretical generalizations themselves (Bjur, 1970).

For decades, practitioners as well as academicians concerned with the relevance of the field have complained about the lack of integration of theory and practice. To the practitioner, the academician is abstract, esoteric, idealistic—of little or no help in the everyday affairs of government. The academician sees the practitioner as demanding that he violate his professorial role to become a consultant and that the university become a research arm of administrative agencies—in solving specific problems that ought to be the worry of the administrator. Yet, current policy failures—as illustrated in the policy errors entailed in the U.S. involvement in Vietnam, inability to predict or control the costs of our defense program, and the apparent failure of many of our domestic social programs—make it imperative that we make some attempt to solve this problem.

The field of public administration (as well as the social sciences generally) seems to be finally beginning the struggle to integrate theory and practice under the paradigm "policy analysis." The popularity of the move toward policy analysis thus provides an excellent arena for discussion of the theory/practice problem (Archibald, 1970). Moreover, the movement of some nations such as the United States toward a "postindustrial" condition seems to hold rather profound implications for the manner in which we can best view the connection of theory with practice. Just as a substantial part of the useful rationale for viewing theory and practice from the classical, traditional, and modern perspectives lay in their relevance to the contexts within which they flourished, so must the move to postindustrialism serve as a powerful light in defining what relevant definition of the theory-practice nexus can be struck.

Before examining the implications of postindustrialism for theory-practice, however, we should first look to the present situation. Only by doing so can we see what type of reconceptualization seems in order.

THE POSITIVE SCIENCE MODEL OF THEORY AND ACTION

In spite of the differences in perspective among the classical, traditional, and modern schools of public administration theory, one common theme related them. A remarkable yet persistent aspect of public administration is that it has seldom dwelled on management technique in and of itself. Instead, the main intent in all phases has been to *create and maintain administrative authority.* Public administration has consistently justified the establishment of an administrative form of command. Hence, lying under the disagreements of various approaches, one can see that all versions of public administration theory support *orthodoxy* as the basis of action, since it is when orthodoxy is achieved that, in principle, administration begins.

We can see this pattern in the historical development of the issue of theory and practice. In the classical phase, theory consisted of practical principles drawn from existing reality at the first order of abstraction and hence was embedded in the existing authority pattern of American society. And while traditionalists prescribed that the most expert view be applied to every problem in a diligent pursuit of the public interest, existing patterns of social disadvantage remained the same or worsened. The modernists, of course, produced the tradition on which the orthodoxy of "rigorous irrelevance" stands.

The unanimity of public administration theory on the basic issue of the basis of administrative authority can be explained by the dominance of a common underlying model of theory and action—or more specifically a common manner of approaching human reality and experience. One descriptive name for this approach is the "positive science model." Though it is deeply embedded in our culture and, through the culture, in our social institutions, its aspects are obvious and simple. Through this model, time is viewed as a linear phenomenon. Hence, action is seen as occurring through time from the present into the future, which then becomes the past—i.e., a frame for an evaluational retrospect. Space is perceived through perception of boundaries, as distinguished from a concept of space as field or process. Relationship (between bounded entities) is seen almost totally as causal, where one event is necessarily the product of another or other events. Experience is assimilated through the process of reification, where sense impressions are evaluated and objectified. Underpinning all of this is an ontology or stasis, which shows the "natural order" as a condition of rest—and, as a corollary, movement, change, process, as aberrational conditions begging explanation. The force of this view can perhaps be traced to a dichotomy of self and experience—the separation of self from experience. The effect of this view is to present "reality" to the individual as real in a compelling sense. Hence, reality becomes the base point of action and guides it through the device of "analysis" designed to produce the "facts."

The world view implies an equally simple and obvious schema for the theory-action relation. The motive of action becomes a "problem." What this means is that action is seen from this view as always remedial to some disequilibrium in the natural order of things. Problems, in this sense, demand action. Before action can occur, however, the problem must be analyzed. Again, from the positive science model, the nature of this analysis is predetermined. First a theory (or at least a set of concepts) must be formulated which defines the variables relevant to the problem and which, indeed, give the problem its analytical (as opposed to its social and political) definition. This conceptualization, of course, emerges from the initial experience with the perceived problem and from the institutional theories which define the existing status quo. To illustrate, the problem of maladaptive social behavior on the part of blacks in the United States manifests itself in excessive use of drugs, sexual promiscuity and consequent illegitimacy, and so on. The analysis which is then carried out as a possible guide to the solution defines the relevant variables in terms of a causal pattern within the black family itself. This occurs in spite of the fact that the problematic behavior is itself being evaluated from a relativistic framework (i.e., it is not mind-altering drugs nor illegitimate sex per se which are problematic, but certain drugs taken by certain people and particular types of sex behavior engaged in by particular people). From this, it appears that the behavior is being *analyzed* from a relativistic perspective. There are other, broader views from which to define the etiological pattern behind the problem that would minimize the role of black family structure and highlight other aspects of the total picture—in white middle-class society, for example. Such illustrations indicate that the true basis of problem definition and analysis is political.

Moreover, this is a politics which involves the producers of knowledge and the process of knowledge production. This comes about because, in spite of the power of the positive science model as a cultural force, popular intuition eventually reveals the problem-solution schema as working the reverse of the way it pretends to work—i.e., that it objectively arrives at solution to objectively defined problems. As James Q. Wilson (1968) puts this point:

> Theories of social change are often suspect in my eyes because they seem to lead automatically to the policy conclusion favored by their author. It is as if one decided what program one wanted adopted and then decided what "caused" an event in order to justify that remedial program.

Such delegitimation tends to produce a paradox. As knowledge comes to be increasingly tied to institutional action, knowledge producers are likely to begin competing for the rewards entailed by acceptance of their theories (or solutions). The effect is an opening up of the knowledge community. Indeed, more- or less-indigenous theories and theorists (e.g., blacks and women analyzing their own condition from nonacademic base points) are likely to arise. This development, however, instead of producing a true pluralism in the arena of theory and action, tends instead to lead to suppression of those theories that imply solutions that are outside the current parameters of the system. The knowledge community has a stake in this suppression, as such pluralism threatens both its legitimacy in the society at large and the integrity of its own internal rules of knowledge production. The practitioners have a stake in such suppression because this pluralism will imply lines of action that may involve taking risks that they are not willing to take.

It is in the problem definition (or pronouncement) stage and the stage of analysis which follows where the powerful conservative tendencies of the positive science approach to theory and action can be seen most clearly. The tendency to draw conceptual premises from the existing context virtually ensures that the subsequent research will end in conclusions that reify the problem and imply solutions that reinforce rather than eliminate it. Herbert Gans' (1971) analysis of our welfare programs is a case in point.

But more pertinent to our concerns here is the nature of the "solution" itself, as the final outcome of the positive science model of theory and action. Solution can be seen in its generic form to be made up of elements analogous to the model which underlies it. The analogue to linear time is *prior commitment* or *plan.* One decides now what is to be done then as a solution. Seeing space as defined by boundaries inclines the action to be an attempt to control—which is to say, to maintain or alter patterns of boundary. Where relationship is seen as causal, action will be seen as rational, where the objects of analysis (things or people) are seen as instruments for the realization of (distinct) goals and objectives. Since experience is assimilated through the process of reification, one will look more and more to "data" (the more quantified the better) as the means of defining and evaluating the action. Hence, action becomes data. From an ontology of stasis, of course, solution will be seen as action which returns or tends to return the system to a state of equilibrium. So, a summary view of solution as action shows it to be a planned attempt to control, objectively, so that defined ends are realized—ends which are expressed as data and which are tied to the reassertion of the equilibrium of the system at which the solution is directed (Gouldner, 1957; Greenwood, 1961). It can be seen from this sketch of the nature of solution and the way in which the problem-solution schema operate that orthodoxy must be the basis of administration action. The process of problem-solution itself is oriented toward ensuring stability of existing societal patterns. The concept of solution (and the nature of action implied under it) is monistic and unilateral—which is to say, administrative. Plans must be agreed upon, and acted out through time to an objective that all share: stability. Where in this process can heterodoxy enter?

THE POSITIVE SCIENCE MODEL IN POSTINDUSTRIAL SOCIETY

In order to see the positive science model and its schema of theory and action as it relates to the emergence of postindustrial society, we must examine the underlying psychocultural value which it entails. It is at this level, the level of basic value, that the implications of the move to postindustrialism can be seen the clearest.

At this level, the positive science model and the problem-solution schema can be seen as interrelated to a system of *meaning*. This, of course, is not a new idea. It has long been recognized that the philosophical and theoretical systems of science are tied closely to the social, political, cultural, even theological realms. Put in its simplest form, the meaning of life in the positive science view is solution. Under this model, life becomes a process of moving from one solution to the next. *Action is the essence of existence.* In broader terms, solution implies that the meaning of existence is security. That is, life poses problems (that are known as the phenomenon of insecurity) which are to be solved, and solutions are known by the reduction of insecurity.

What postindustrial society means structurally is a shift to a service economy, where the organic relationships of human existence are more and more the subject of intervention or substitution by social institutions. In the advanced stages of postindustrialism, we can imagine that the concern of social institutions would become maintenance of social processes that formerly were handled by organic units such as the family, friendship groups, and the like. This of course is already happening. One's attitude toward work traditionally was gained through family socialization. Increasingly we are viewing this key aspect of socialization as the duty of formal social institutions such as schools, the media, various counseling agencies for youth and adults, and so on. Herein lies the paradox of social development: When security is a problem, in the earlier stages of development, problems of social relationship are dealt with organically. As security becomes assured through development, the very mechanism through which security is ensured (productive capacity) seems to vitiate the organic processes which handle the key problems of relationship. We simply trade one problem for another.

The implication of this change toward postindustrialism at the level of our concern here is that solution as the basis for meaning becomes obsolete. Action, since it comes to be taken over by machines and machine-like processes, becomes automatic. Tensions are reduced as they arise; hence, problems in the traditional sense do not "happen." To continue to focus on action under the problem solution schema means that individuals and social institutions become simply aspects of the system, following its logic even to the level of personal life.

THE DIALECTIC AS AN ALTERNATIVE TO POSITIVE SCIENCE

In drawing a counter-model to positive science, we can begin where we left off. That is, we can see from the above analysis that a counter-model must ultimately imply a different basis for the meaning of existence. It therefore seems best to begin describing the counter-model in terms of the different concept of meaning which it entails.

Under the positive science model, society can be seen either as a system of symbiotic economic exchanges (which ensures security) or a consensual organization based on an overriding normative order which in its way ensures security. Stasis in these views is implied as a proper condition—i.e., undisrupted exchange and no dissent from the social value system. An alternative view of society would posit it to be a system of *symbolic exchanges*—generally of words (Dreitzel, 1970; Berger and Luckman, 1966; Friere, 1972). It is necessary to stress that *symbolic exchange, by definition, entails tension.* That is, to exchange a symbol (for example, a word), none of the parties to the exchange must either hold or posit a complete definition of the symbol. In order for the symbol to possess a socially proper meaning, it must hold content that is tension-laden—that is, that exists somewhere between the poles of complete ambiguity and complete perspicuity. This is only to say, of course, that the symbol must be interesting. If the symbol is interesting, it will hold something to receive and will allow for something (other words) to be given back. Hence, meaning derives from the tension between ambiguity and perspicuity in social symbols.

How does this relate to postindustrialism? We can see that the response of industrial society to the breakdown of organic social processes is going to be the provision of greater "social services" to replace these processes. It follows that since it is the positive science model that creates this problem, it probably cannot serve effectively as a basis for its solution.

Taking the dimensions along which we described the positive science model earlier, an alternative can be sketched. In such an alternative, time would be viewed as a holistic phenomenon—i.e., as existing only in what we now call the present. Space would be seen as diffuse—as a field where there is interaction, but between more loosely defined categories (e.g., as in viewing matter in terms of waves instead of particles). Relationship would be seen as synchronous rather than causal; that is, events would be seen as explainable only in the context of a single moment, and where everything which occurs in that moment is seen as potentially meaningful for understanding the event. That is, the moment is made up of events which occur together rather than as a result of each other. Experience would not be reified, but would be seen in much more subjective terms, as essentially personal and hence best transferable through empathy. The ontology of this view would be movement and change rather than stasis.

It must be emphasized that the relation of the positive science model to the counter-model sketched above is dialectical, which is to say that it stands not as a contradiction but as a reference point for a different emphasis. The emphasis of the positive science model is totally on thinking and sensing (data gathering) as the conceptual frame for action. By standing between this model and the alternative described here, the policy actor would in a particular moment attempt to synthesize (in a synthesis which cannot be specified beforehand) the two models. What is intended by the alternative is not replacement of the positive science model and rejection of the concept of rationality which follows from it. Rather, the objective here is to seek a broader notion of rationality than is possible under the positive science model, a notion of rationality which comprehends all human psychic functions. This means that, in addition to thinking and sensing, the elements of intuition and feeling would be brought into the picture.

In order for intuition and feeling to complement positive science analysis, the tension between them and the processes of thinking and sensing *must be accepted*. Thinking and sensing, taken alone, tend to produce a "double bind" type of policy analysis, where two contradictory alternatives (usually both undesirable to some extent) result from the analysis. Hence, "People in the underdeveloped world are starving, therefore, we must *either* let them starve or feed them." Or "The communists are afoot in Southeast Asia, therefore, we must *either* let them have the whole area or defeat them." While these illustrations seem grossly oversimplifed, the massive interventions which we characteristically tend to take to solve problems seem to indicate that basically the reasoning behind our policies must be tragically stark and simplified. Only through processes of intuition, which supplement causal reasoning, and through effective processes which bring the element of moral judgment into the picture, can policy makers act through such dilemmas instead of, as we characteristically do, making the "agonizing decision" to force ourselves over one or the other of the horns of the dilemma.

In a model of dialectical action, then, we would see policy actors synthesizing *all* the human psychic processes in their rationality, emphasizing the present situation as the real context of the analysis and of the act. Past and future would be brought in as meaningful artifacts, to be emphasized differently in different situations. The objective of action would be creation rather than control, so that the intent would be to move beyond the present situation rather than to prevent the recurrence of a "problem." The idea derived from the concept of synchronicity would be encounter rather than rational instrumentality. By the same line of reasoning, the notion of retrospective evaluation through data analysis would be qualified by a concept of commitment to the idea that the basic quality of human experience must be responsibility. Last, as is implied by the above, the outcome of the act would be evolution beyond the pattern which currently defines the system within which the action is taking place. It is clear from this summary picture that this view of action stresses relating, both to self and to the other, rather than doing. *Action is seen as interaction.*

Why is this model of action more appropriate to the task of providing services in postindustrial society? In a postindustrial services economy (hypothetically, where survival problems are dealt with through automation), we each will, in a sense, pay each other for relating to each other. The extreme form of this picture will probably never come to pass, of course, so the question we face amounts to: In what form can we provide services which will tend to preserve as much of the organic aspects of human life as possible? It seems clear that the positive science model would aggravate this problem and tend to destroy these organic aspects if we used it as the guide for providing services. Since action (i.e., "doing something to") is what is stressed in the positive science model of solution, its prescription for services must be to define the client as a problem, intervene toward the client so as to produce some alteration in "it," and send "it" back in altered, "adapted" form to the social order. We need not dwell here on the apparently destructive nature of this prescription. In the field of psychological therapy, we can see evidence of the effects already with the growing advocacy of drastic psychological interventions such as behavior modification, chemotherapy, and now therapeutic sexual intercourse between therapist and patient (Shepard, 1971). It takes little imagination to become horrified at the picture of a society full of manipulated, doped, and professionally seduced "human beings." We can expect that this bizarre pattern may be carried into every area of service as long as the emphasis in service provision is upon *action*—i.e., causally producing an effect upon the client. If services can properly replace organic human processes at all, it must be through a realization that services are relationships and, as such, action must be a subordinate aspect of the matter.

We can briefly illustrate this point in two contrasting examples, one drawn from internal processes of advanced industrial society and the other involving an advanced society providing development services to less-developed countries.

The case of the policeman in the ghetto. Police service is perhaps the area other than psychological therapy in which the difficulty of the positive science model carried into social services is clearest and most immediate (Perry, 1971). The implications of the positive science model have been drawn out rather explicitly in the policeman's role. Police service is perhaps the epitome of the planned (i.e., formally defined), rationally implemented, and quantitatively evaluated social service designed to maintain the equilibrium of the existing social order. What has gone wrong as we have applied the model to this case? The first difficulty lies in the principle of planned action. In the attempt to grant the policeman authority to uphold the law and rationally to circumscribe this authority, we soon totally confuse both the situation and the policeman. The average policeman must uphold approximately 30,000 federal, state, and local enactments. The impossibility of his doing so means that he actually bases his behavior on a politicized and personalized discretion. What the policeman does is attempt to "keep the peace" under a façade of objectivity and rationality that covers his own professional role stresses, his personal and socially induced biases, and the deeper political motivations on which the entire concept of police service as social control is based. The result, of course, is a progressive delegitimation of the policeman in the eyes of those in the community who encounter him most—the disadvantaged—since it is here that intuition will have the greatest opportunity to see through the façade. Hence we have the situation of the policeman in the ghetto coming under attack for his very existence.

The positive science model solution to this problem is to rationally plan and implement a response. We have seen this already. The solution to the problem is, first, to set up internal inspection offices to investigate charges of racial bias and brutality—that is, to reinforce system controls with more controls. The effect of this move has been to create or aggravate internal dissension within the departments. A second type of response, now in widespread use, is the "community relations unit." These units are planned as a special attempt to control ill feeling in the community through special programs such as educational lectures, youth programs neighborhood centers, and the like.

This response to the perceived problem makes perfect sense as a *planned solution.* It does not, however, alter the situation and probably makes it worse. The clientele of the community relations unit can certainly get along with and agree with the policemen in it—yet not find their feelings changed about the patrolman they encounter when they next engage the police department in the context of a conflict. Also, patrolmen tend to have little respect or use for the community relations "cops" whom they tend to regard as "panty-waists" and "softies" who do not known how to be policemen. Further, the special community relations unit arrangement tends to establish an invidious distinction between patrolmen and unit officers. The community relations policemen are "good guys"; the patrolmen are "bad guys." In such a case, the patrolmen feel even less responsibility for community relations than previously. The effect of the whole program is to remove responsibility to the client, as the patrolman on the beat feels that the relationship aspects of police work are to be dealt with through the community relations unit, while the community relations unit does not feel it can be responsible for the behavior of the patrolman on the street. In effect, the solution has institutionalized the problem.

What the alternative model sketched here would prescribe in the case of police services might be quite different.[2] It follows from the description of the model outlined above that, to begin with, the "problem" would not be specific charges such as racism, brutality, and the like. Rather, the focus would be on the establishment of a process of interaction between police and community, where each group attempted to behave in such a way as to ensure that the relation would be maintained. This simple objective entails powerful constraints and, in effect, implies a wholly different concept of police service. What is implied in a relational situation is that each side attempt to see the other in progressively unobjectified terms. At the level of interaction, this means training policemen to see clients not as categories, but as part of a common situation with the policeman. Perhaps the most powerful beginning for this would be in training the policeman to see himself as an individual rather than as part of a paramilitary, homogeneous unit of professionals. Throughout, the point would be made that effective police work means maintaining a sense of openness between the client and the policeman. Change would mean a shift to helping rather than controlling as the dominant concern of the policeman. This does not mean, of course, that violence would be eliminated from the interaction with the client. As always, violence (in some cases) would be an essential part of the policeman's behavior. But the problem with the use of violence often lies not so much in the act of violence itself as in the relational context (or lack of one) within which the act occurs.

It is impossible in this short space to outline fully the implications of the alternative model sketched here for the work of the policeman. In sum, what this alternative implies is placing responsi-bility for the relational aspects of the policeman's role *on the police-man,* rather than attempting to plan rationally for and institutionalize these aspects.

The case of the technical assistant in less-developed countries. The problem of the positive science model applied to technical aid to less-developed countries is different from but related to that of the police-man. In the case of the policeman, the rationalism which follows from the model leads to lines of action which remove responsibility and institutionalize the problem. In the case of aid to developing countries, it leads us to institutionalization of the problem through the assumption of too much "responsibility" on the part of the policy actors.

The implications of the positive science model for development are clear. The problem is "underdevelopment," and it is manifest in such indicators as malnutrition, low gross national product, high rates of ill health, and so on. The solution has been to bring about develop-ment by manipulation of the variables considered most powerful in producing it—e.g., agricultural output, education, basic industry, and so on. The scale of the intervention prescribed has characteristically been large and unilateral (from the top down), or, as critics would say, elitist. This is not the forum for debating the effectiveness of various approaches to development; it suffices here to note that con-troversy exists as to the effectiveness of development efforts (Lyman, 1970; Cohn, 1971; Daly, 1971).

We can say, however, that unintended consequences can be expected to occur from *any* "development" intervention aimed at the ecosystem. The question is not so much how can they be elimi-nated as how can they be minimized. One answer is to broaden the analysis of possible consequences of various lines of action. The diffi-culty with this approach is that it is likely to lead to larger and larger interventions, as the basic principle of the matter must be that the more variables one wishes to control, the larger one's action has to be. And the larger the action, the larger the unintended conse-quences are likely to be.

The approach indicated by the alternative model sketched here would be to deemphasize action and stress the development of rela-tionships between the persons providing aid and the persons in the host country who are affected by a policy under consideration or being implemented. The usual term for this is to allow participation in the matter. Less may seem to be accomplished, but perhaps more would be accomplished relative to unintended secondary and tertiary effects and external diseconomies than through a policy of rationally designed and implemented action. Also, a major consequence of policy built and implemented through a participatory relationship would be drastic revision of the evaluational categories by which policy outcomes are assessed. The most dramatic illustration of this is perhaps Paulo Freire's (1972) concept of literacy in the area of education in less-developed countries.

THE PROBLEM OF INSTITUTIONAL REFORM

A major area of concern still to be addressed here is the matter of how to change administrative organizations in a way that will allow us to move beyond the positive science model. As a beginning point in addressing this issue, it should be noted that what is being attacked here is not *science and scientific rationality*. Indeed, the classical model of science, which stresses disproof rather than positive proof, openendedness, and community, is both the metaphor for the counter-model proposed here and has been used as a model for organizational change toward increased openness and participation (Bennis, 1966). Nor is what is being attacked here a particular epistemological position that has dominated in universities and in policy formation arenas. No epistemological position of any respectability is as simplistic as the positive science model sketched here. Rather, what is being discussed is a deeply rooted psychocultural pattern of long standing and great power (Geiger, 1967). The ideal image of scientific community and scientific knowledge was no match for this force at the cultural level. It was the cultural pattern of positive science which shaped the institutions in which scientists came to work, and through role rewards and stresses imposed in these institutions, this cultural pattern came to be the normative structure of the scientific community itself. It was not a scientific community that received Velikovsky, but rather a group of scientists working under the cultural orthodoxy of the positive science model (Juergens, 1963).

Hence, the task of institutional reform is not one that begins in the delegitimation of an epistemological position, but must go to a deeper level. An epistemology *can* be extracted from the positive science model and effectively attacked, but as convincing as all the charges are that could be cast against the positive science model at this level, its true appeal lies on other, more pragmatic, grounds.

The defense of the model at this level often goes something like this: "We all know that there is no absolute truth and that facts are relative. But we have to act as if facts are binding and absolute. How else could men communicate with each other? How could we have a common world? Wouldn't everything fall apart? Wouldn't all knowledge become totally political and chaos ensue? Wouldn't science become the servant of the state?"

The basis of this retort lies in the attractive fact that, in the positive science model, one man's assertions are held *accountable* to an "objective" or "external" criterion of experience. Hence, no man is a law unto himself; all men must justify themselves to the "truth." On this a predictable social order can be built, and man can escape the jungle of all against all. The ultimate appeal of the positive science model is like that of the Constitution: We all know it is not absolute and contains no positive, clear rules—but we feel we must *act* as if it contains the absolute truth of our way of government. When two men disagree under the positive science model, they will both appeal to an objective standard. However, as we saw earlier, all such disputes are essentially political. If the men are of equal power, neither will be able to define the standard in a way that will make him the winner in the dispute. In this case the standard will be "partly right" and a compromise will be struck. Each goes his way, saying to the other, "Well, that's true too." If power is unequal, the more powerful will define the standard in such a way as to show himself to have "the truth." He will then be able to subordinate the other. Each will go his way, the one feeling resentful and oppressed, the other saying. "Well, that's the way things are."

The point is that, in the dispute, the focus is on the external standard, not on the other person. Hence, the standard attains a compelling reality and structures the outcome. A more important effect, however, is that the human beings involved do not see or acknowledge each other as persons because the standard intervenes. They compromise, and, with compromise, human alienation begins. With alienation, in turn, comes fear of other men, and fear of other men reinforces the need for the imposition of external standards in the social world. Herein lies the set of forces supporting the positive science model.

Roughly the same pattern holds within the person. As one reifies theory and makes it objective, he accepts it as a force determining his own behavior and destiny. If he is a professional, the effect is magnified as he interjects codes and prevailing theories. The dominant theories of his profession and his society become explanations for his own behavior. He does not experience his life, he explains it.

He denies his experience. He does what he does because "he has to"—his professional analysis compels him to. Responsibility becomes applying the analysis. Eventually he sees himself doing things he does not intend to do. He is now self-estranged. He needs the positive science model more than ever.

Hence, the positive science model can be seen as valid only in terms of the psychological preconditions that it brings about. It is a negatively reinforcing philosophical-psychological tautology. It must, therefore, be rejected on the grounds of its practicality as an external control since in effect, it creates the problem it solves.

If we reject the positive science model, we are placed in a position that depicts man as a free, responsible actor. In his discourse with other men, he must rely basically on his commitment of the other as a fellow human being and plausibility as the communication device whereby he builds a common world with his fellows.

What seems threatening about giving up the positive science model is losing external standards for ascertaining truth and trading for this a reliance on and trust in people. This is a trust that people can communicate directly to *each other*, can agree with each other, can trust each other and live together on the basis of this trust.

Before an alternative to the positive science model can seem anything but impossible, therefore, we must make plausible a view of man that will show him capable of living together in society without ultimate reliance on the external standards that the positive science model supplies.

The model of man underlying the positive science model. It will cause little contention to assert that in our culture the dominant model of man is composed of a curious mixture of Freudian and behavioralist psychology. It is this model which helps make the myth of the positive science model seem essential to man's social life.

In the Freudian-behaviorist model, roughly construed, man is made up of four parts. He possesses, first, a biological element—a body—with a fixed set of "drives." At the psychic level, closely related to the drives, is the "id," a set of unstructured, capricious, seething needs. The id feeds the drives, motivating the individual in the direction of the need-drive which is dominant at the moment. This drive, because it is seen as rapacious, will lead to the destruction of the individual if it is given full vent in the social world, however, Hence, it must be mediated—by the "reality principle" or "ego." This is where social roles and behavioralism come in. The ego satisfies the drive at least partially by having the body perform social roles which are acceptable manifestations of the drives. A traditional carry-over from learning these roles (mainly from the parents) is the super-ego, where the individual's "character or principles reside. These stand in a dynamic relation to the ego and act as the person's moral conscience.

In this model, therefore, the basic element of the person is the id, and its biological counterpart, the drives. This is the "motivational structure" of the human. The necessity for external control appears obvious. The ego must look to reality, the superego must look to tradition—or the person will "go wild" in pursuit of his drives.

It is this anxiety about being or existence which provides the basis for the plausibility of an alternative model of man—one that would not need as a corollary the positive science model of knowledge.

Though here we can only give this alternative model an adumbration, we can show clearly how it contrasts with the Freudian-behaviorist model. We begin in this model with the assertion that biological drives are *not* dominant motivators to the individual—that drives are subordinate to something else (Tomkins, 1967). This "something else"—the dominant motivator—is the individual's search for "identity" or "self." What people are "up to" by this view is the construction of a coherent, acceptable, and permanent definition of themselves. In this view, man is a natural organism, integrated in his feeling and intellect (Perls, 1969a, 1969b; Fagan and Shepherd, 1970). Moreover, if healthy and attuned to the situation, man is able to focus on that aspect of the total "gestalt" of his existence which is most in need of repair or completion. He is self-curative and grows naturally in a psychic as well as physical sense. In short, he knows the right thing to do and does not need external control or guidance. Man's unconscious would not be seen as terrible and terrifying, but highly structured and a central locus for the psychodynamics of finding one's identity.

In sum, this view of man sees him as centered in his unconscious, where his mechanism of individuation resides (Jung, 1968, 1964, 1958). The unconscious "feeds into" "consciousness," where "projects" are formulated (e.g., falling in love) which when pursued further lead to the discovery of one's identity. The projects are set up initially through roles (where partners on the project are encountered), and acted out through the bodily drives (so that, for example, sexual intercourse becomes "lovemaking").

As noted above, the plausibility of this model is based on the fact that its central element is the *being* of the person: his identity. But its practical effect is just as important. In the Freudian-behaviorist model, man's motives are seen as intrinsically conflicting because they stem from biological drives which demand scarce resources for their reduction. Hence, an external source of control—built on the positive science model—must be established for society to be possible. The alternative model shows man's motives to be synergistic or mutually reinforcing. One needs others for the discovery of his identity. And the other must be a partner, not an object. Hence, dominance relations (where the subordinate becomes a projection of the superordinate) do not further finding one's self. It is in this sense that the existentialist assertion "My being, my freedom, are inextricably tied to the being and freedom of the other" makes sense.

The point of the foregoing section is this: There is a model of man, at least somewhat plausible in our age, which does not have as a corollary the positive science model of knowledge. It is through acceptance of this model of man that the individual can find a dialectical position between the positive science model and the alternative model, so that each becomes a reference point or context for his action in a particular situation. Once freed from a view of man which entails *reliance* on the positive science model alone as a controlling mechanism, the human actor can see and accept the incomplete and thereby biased quality of his thinking and sensing, taken alone. With this perspective and in the tension of the moment, he can synthesize both types of capacity in action—rational action (Royce, 1964).

The nature of practice: personal versus institutional action.   Up to this point an attempt has been made to provide a basis for the rejection of the positive science model from its position of dominance and briefly to sketch an alternative to it. Before we can fully understand the alternative, however, we must reexamine the concept of action in another light.

Action can be described in terms of two generic types, one real, the other apparent. These are personal and institutional action. The personal action model derives from the notion of man as a natural organism who does what he needs to do when he needs to do it. Personal action is naturally motivated. Further, one acts without anxiety and responsibility because he acts through only his own personal resources. The use of these resources in action can easily be "covered" by the sense of motivation and responsibility which pursuance of the gestalt provides.

A person acting in an institutional setting apparently finds other elements impinging upon him. First, his actions must be temporally phased and meshed with the actions of others and with the "system." He has to do things "on time." Second, he is objectified. The institution assumes that, because objective, not personal, goals are being pursued, the person must be externally motivated. Third, actions are to be oriented to external criteria of performance, or "standards." Finally, in addition to timing, objectification, and standards, anxiety is added to the institutional actor's situation. This anxiety stems from the fact that the individual must act with extrapersonal resources, "authority." His feelings cannot adequately cover the use of power other than his own, and he experiences anxiety in acting as a result.

If we examine these institutional impingements, however, we see that they are but artifacts and that personal action is the only true form of the human act. Timing, for example, has its counterpart at the personal level in "interaction"—the simple acknowledgement of the other. Timed coordination for the achievement of a common purpose is personally sensible. It is only when timing is imposed beyond the needs of interaction that it becomes an institutional artifact. Second, as the previous analysis of models of man indicates, objectification is an artifact consequent to a view of man that is not undeniable. We can assert that it is an artifact by asserting an alternative view of man. Third, "standards" are an artifact on the same grounds as objectification. Compelling standards depend on a model of knowledge which shows knowledge to be compelling. A plausible model which shows knowledge not to be compelling can be outlined as was done here.

The problem of anxiety over the use of extrapersonal resources is more problematic—because such anxiety is palpable. But it must be asserted that this anxiety is not institutionally caused and is rather a personal phenomenon. Institutions do not positively exist. They are but concrete manifestations of the biased theory that results from the positive science model. They are an attempt to control the individual by limiting him to the thinking-sensing functions which are dominant in this model. It is this reality—that the individual exists alone, with no true external guidance, and must act in the face of this condition—which causes the anxiety of the institutional actor. The anxiety comes from knowing that he is not really compelled, even though the institution says he is. Theories (for example, of the "best therapy" for a client) and professional codes only obscure the reality that when the administrator acts toward a client it must be, it necessarily is, a personal act. In fact, then, what exists in what we call "institutions" is a network of social relationships between people, as people. We have no alternative but to place trust and responsibility in the people who make up the network. In this light, the problem of the institutional actor becomes that of overcoming his anxiety and *acting* in response to his personal situation in the institution.

How impossible an idea is this? We can answer by looking at the system of institutional action which exists under the positive science model. First, as Victor Thompson (1965) has noted, institutional controls usually do not work as they are supposed to. When something goes wrong, the weakest person who can be linked to the wrongdoing is blamed, and that is usually the end of it. In institutions, in a quite real sense, might makes right—only this fact is more difficult to see there. Second, and worse, we can see that institutional controls can quite easily lead to atrocities. The order to "kill," given at the top, is separated from the actual killing done at the bottom. Institutional controls link the two. Neither level feels responsible: the bottom because it only followed orders; the top because it had no control over what *actually* happened. Responsibility evaporates: "The institution did it."

In sum, the argument here is that all action is personal and ought to be seen as such. But there are two senses in which the structure of the institutional actor's situation can truly impede his ability to act personally. One structural factor is size. Things can get so large that they are incomprehensible in personal terms—which is to say, simply, that they are incomprehensible. The actor can rightfully demand decentralization to a human level if he is to assume personal responsibility for his acts. Another structural factor is the system for evaluating action. By the positive science model and its institutional counterpart, performance review is usually spaced over rather lengthy periods of time—so that the "facts can accumulate." Then a ritual of evaluation occurs (e.g., an audit, performance review, and so on), and a positive or negative emotion will be great. If something has gone wrong, something great must be done to dispel the emotion, which is essentially aggressive. Hence, blame is assessed, guilt (a self-aggressive, destructive emotion) is felt, and punishment is inflicted. The principle is: Two wrongs make a right. For action to be personal and responsible, a different system of evaluation must be used. It must be based on an evaluative feedback loop of a very short time frame. Negative feedback would result in shame on the part of all members of the system, since in this view all members of a social network are linked some way to everything that happens within it. Shame is a positive emotion, where one faces not an external standard, but oneself. This leads to the feeling of responsibility ("This is what I did"), which in turn leads to remedy ("This is what I can do about it now."). In sum, we can see that institutions do possess a negative, if not a positive, reality. They thereby destroy responsibility in two ways: by taking it from the individual through a deception, and by putting blame where responsibility should be.

THE CONCEPT OF ADMINISTRATIVE PRAXIS

The argument to this point can be quite simply summarized. Theory (conventionally thought of) is a statement of relative truth based upon and biased by the fact that it stems from partial psychic functioning. Hence, institutions, which must be based on a theory of one sort or another, have no "objective" reality. As such, institutions cannot properly determine human action. When a human being within an institution acts, it is necessarily a personal choice to act consistently or inconsistently with the artifact of the institution and the theory upon which it is based.

At this point, it is possible to see how theory relates to action and to determine how the administrator may link theory to action.

The administrator is seen as facing, first, a moral choice. The problem in making this choice is to have *alternative values* available for selection. This is where theory comes in: Values are not truly "available" when put in the form of ideals. Availability means that the value seems practicable. And for practicability, a theory, replete with data, must be attached to the value. Theory is valuable for its mobilizing effect—it makes a value coherent. It helps the administrator secure the cooperation of others he needs to implement the value. (This mobilizing effect is similar to that of the "framing effect" of a piece of art—which mobilizes aesthetic affect [Polanyi, 1970].) In turn, as the theory makes the value coherent, research makes the theory and its action implications plausible. Research is necessarily oriented toward action.

However, to view theory and research as such is not to achieve "praxis," which is the integration of theory with action (Lefebre, 1969). No matter how coherent a theory, no matter how appealing the data make it, it cannot be brought into action without a *commitment* to do so. This commitment is acted out through the use of intuition and feeling, which overcome the bias of theory as it applies to a specific situation. It is the use of intuition and feeling which we tend to call the assumption of responsibility. Responsibility means, in this sense, moving beyond the safety of the cognitive thinking-sensing theory and acting in the dark of the moment, where we know that outcomes are not totally predictable and that justice is not knowable. It is intuition and feeling that guide us, mysteriously, through this darkness.

Responsibility, then, is the missing link between theory and action. To bring theory to practice, the administrator must be willing to commit himself to bringing *values* into a situation—values that can only be communicated and justified in his actions. In the past, the practitioner wanted the theoretician to "get into his shoes" and see his situation through his eyes so as to ensure that "relevant" answers to the practitioner's problems would be generated. The difficulty with this approach is that, by taking the same view, the same answers will appear to the academic (now a consultant) as appeared to the practitioner. Fresh answers come only from fresh perspectives. This means, however, that the answers will not "fit" the situation. Novel answers represent novel value frameworks.

Hence, for the theoretician and the practitioner to be able to work together, each must modify his stance. The practitioner must commit himself to risking the implementation of new value orientations in his situation. The theoretician, on the other hand, must become more honest about what he is attempting to sell to the practitioner. In being offered a theory, the working administrator is being asked to take a political risk. This must be acknowledged. If the theoretician would acknowledge that he deals in values, he might better be able to develop workable strategies for the implementation of his theories by the practitioner.

CONCLUSION: HOW PRACTICAL IS PRAXIS?

This analysis appears to violate the orthodoxy of thinking about theory, institutions, responsibility, and practice in public administration. However, it should be remembered that several decades ago many of the distinguished intellectual leaders in the field of public administration rejected the "politics-administration dichotomy" and the "fact-value" distinction that went with it. The argument made here is really a restatement, in positive form, of the rejection of a distinction between facts and values—i.e., an attempt to "live up to" that classical premise.

ENDNOTES

1. Perhaps the clearest illustration of this is the still lively controversy over the role of hierarchical authority in achieving organizational effectiveness. The issue is multifaceted, with (at least) the behavioralists such as Simon, the traditionalists—who still argue essentially the Taylor position—and the humanists taking different and contending positions.
2. The Perry paper cited here was prepared specifically as an illustration of the concept of administrative praxis.

REFERENCES

ARCHIBALD, D. A. (1970) "Three views of the experts' role in policymaking: systems analysis, incrementalism, and the clinical approach." Policy Sciences 1: 73–86.

BENNIS, W. G. (1966) Changing Organizations. New York: McGraw-Hill.

BERGER, P. L. and T. LUCKMAN (1966) The Social Construction of Reality. Garden City, N.Y.: Doubleday.

BJUR, W. G. (1970) "On contextual modeling." University of Southern California. (mimeo)

COHN, E. J. (1971) "Social criteria for project and sector lending." U.S. Department of State Agency for International Development, June. (mimeo)

DALY, H. E. (1971) "Toward a stationary economy," in J. Harte and R. H. Socolow (eds.) Patient Earth. New York: Holt, Rinehart & Winston.

DREITZEL, H. P. (1970) Recent Sociology No. 2. New York: Macmillan.

FAGAN, J. and I. L. SHEPHERD (1970) Gestalt Therapy Now. Palo Alto: Science and Behavior Books.

FREIRE, P. (1972) Pedagogy of the Oppressed. New York: Herder & Herder.

GANS, H. (1971) "The uses of poverty: the poor pay all." Social Policy 2 (May/June): 20–24.

GEIGER, T. (1967) The Conflicted Relationship. New York: McGraw-Hill.

GOLEMBIEWSKI, R. T. (1965) Men, Management, and Morality. New York: McGraw-Hill.

GOULDNER, A. (1957) "Theoretical requirements of the applied social sciences." Amer. Soc. Rev. 22 (February): 92–102.

GREENWOOD, E. (1961) "The practice of science and the science of practice," pp. 73–82 in W. G. Bennis et al. (eds.) the Planning of Change. New York: Holt, Rinehart & Winston.

JUERGENS, R. G. (1963) "Minds in chaos: a recital of the Velikovsky story." Amer. Behavioral Scientist 7 (September): 4–17.

JUNG, C. G. (1968) Analytical Psychology: Its Theory and Practice. New York: Random House.

JUNG, C. G. (1964) Man and His Symbols. Garden City, N.Y.: Doubleday.

JUNG, C. G. (1958) The Undiscovered Self. Boston: Little, Brown.

KIRKHART, L. (1971) "Toward a theory of public administration," pp. 127-164 in F. Marini (ed.) Toward a New Public Administration: The Minnowbrook Perspective. San Francisco: Chandler.

LEAVITT, H. [ed.] (1963) The Social Science of Organizations. Englewood Cliffs, N.J.: Prentice-Hall.

LEFEBRE, H. (1969) The Sociology of Karl Marx. New York: Random House.

LIKERT, R. (1967) The Human Organization. New York: McGraw-Hill.

LYMAN, P. (1970) "Building a political-economic approach to development." Prepared for delivery at the American Political Science Association Meeting, Los Angeles, September.

PERLS, F. (1969a) Gestalt Therapy Verbatim. Lafayette, Calif.: Real People Press.

PERLS, F. (1969b) Ego, Hunger, and Aggression. New York: Random House.

PERRY, D. C. (1971) "Police-community relations: training for street level praxis," Prepared for delivery at the American Society for Public Administration Meeting in Denver, April.

POLANYI, M. (1970) "What is a painting?" Amer. Scholar 39 (Autumn): 655-669.

ROYCE, J. R. (1964) The Encapsulated Man. Princeton: D. Van Nostrand.

SHEPARD, M. (1971) The Love Treatment: Sexual Intimacy Between Patients and Psychotherapists. New York: Wyden.

THOMPSON, V. (1965) Modern Organization. New York: Alfred A. Knopf.

TOMKINS, S. S. (1967) "Homo patients: a reexamination of the concept of drive," in J.F.T. Bugental (ed.) Challenge of Humanistic Psychology. New York: McGraw-Hill.

WHITE, O., JR. (1971) "Organization and administration for new technological and social imperatives," in D. Waldo (ed.) Public Administration in a Time of Turbulence. San Francisco: Chandler.

WHITE, O., JR. and F. MARINI (1971) "Toward a new public administration— theory and politics." Syracuse University Maxwell School of Citizenship and Public Affairs. (mimeo)

WILCOX, H. G. (1968) "The culture trait of hierarchy in middle class children." Public Administration Rev. 28 (May/June): 222-235.

WILSON, J. Q. (1968) "Why we are having a wave of violence." New York Times Magazine (May 19): 23-24.

FURTHER READINGS

ALTSHULER, ALAN. "The Study of Public Administration." Alan Altshuler ed. The Politics of the Federal Bureaucracy. New York: Dodd, Mead & Co., 1968, pp. 55-72.

ARNOLD, PERI. "Re-Organization and Politics: A Reflection on the Adequacy of Administrative Theory." *Public Administration Review.* 34: 3 (May–June, 1974), 204–211.

BAKER, RICHARD J. S. *Administrative Theory and Public Administration.* London: Hutchinson & Co., Ltd., 1972.

CAIDEN, GERALD E. *The Dynamics of Public Administration.* New York: Holt, Rinehart and Winston, Inc., 1971.

CHARLESWORTH, JAMES C. ed. *Theory and Practice of Public Administration: Scope, Objectives, and Methods.* Philadelphia: The American Academy of Political and Social Science, 1968.

DUNSIRE, A. *Administration: The Word and the Science.* New York: John Wiley & Sons, 1973.

DVORIN, EUGENE P. and ROBERT H. SIMMONS. *From Amoral to Humane Bureaucracy.* San Francisco: Canfield Press, Inc., 1972.

GAUS, JOHN M. *Reflections on Public Administration.* University: University of Alabama Press, 1947.

HART, DAVID K. "Social Equity, Justice, and the Equitable Administrator." *Public Administration Review,* vol. 34, no. 1 (Jan.–Feb., 1974), 3–11.

KAUFMAN, HERBERT. "Administrative Decentralization and Political Power." *Public Administration Review,* vol. 29, no. 1 (Jan.–Feb., 1969), 3–15.

KAUFMAN HERBERT. "Emerging Conflicts in the Doctrines of Public Administration." *American Political Science Review,* vol. 50 (December 1956), pp. 1057–1073.

MARINI, FRANK. ed. *Toward a New Public Administration.* San Francisco: Chandler, 1971.

MARTIN, ROSCOE C. *Public Administration and Democracy.* Syracuse: Syracuse University Press, 1965.

MOSHER, FREDERICK C. *Democracy and the Public Service.* New York: Oxford University Press, 1968.

PRESTHUS, ROBERT. *Behavioral Approaches to Public Administration.* University: University of Alabama Press, 1965.

REDFORD, EMMETTE S. *Democracy in the Administrative State.* New York: Oxford University Press, 1969.

REDFORD, EMMETTE S. *Ideal and Practice in Public Administration.* University: University of Alabama Press, 1966.

WALDO, DWIGHT. *The Administrative State: A Study of the Political Theory of American Public Administration.* New York: The Ronald Press Company, 1948.

WALDO, DWIGHT. *Perspective on Administration.* University: University of Alabama Press. 1956.

WALDO, DWIGHT. *Public Administration in a Time of Turbulence.* Scranton, Pa.: Chandler, 1971.

WALDO, DWIGHT. *The Study of Public Administration.* New York: Doubleday & Company, Inc., 1955.

WU, CHI-YUEN. "Public Administration in the 1970's." *International Review of Administrative Science.* vol. 37, no. 3 (1971), 161–170.

YARWOOD, DEAN L. ed. *The National Administrative System.* New York: John Wiley and Sons, 1971.

TWO

THE INTERFACE BETWEEN PUBLIC ADMINISTRATION AND PUBLIC POLICY

Political science has traditionally considered public administration to be a subfield of that discipline. The significance of political phenomena to public administration has, however, increased or decreased according to the dominant emphases in the profession. Since the advent of the reform era of politics with its attendant call for less politics and more management in public administration, public administration became more and more related to the professional management context. This had the effect of reducing the significance of the political science school in public administration and increasing the managerial quantitative influence.

Recent developments would indicate, however, that an increasing number of academicians and practitioners in the public administration field are becoming aware once again of the importance of politics to the administrative process. One indication of this is the rapid increase in the number of policy studies found in the learned public administration journals. A second indication is the number of texts in public administration which now pursue a "policy process" approach to administration. A third example of this reawakening to the political dimension of public administration is seen in the growth of student awareness of the administrative process as part of a larger political system and therefore subject to the forces operating from within.

Public policy results from the interplay of a variety of forces at work in the political system to bring about certain types of outcomes through the actions taken by actors within decisional units. It sees public policy as being shaped by a systematic process of interaction among individual and group preferences, governmental institutions, and decisional actors. This model would be equally applicable to the manner in which major policy decisions were made, whether by Congress or in the administrative branch on the one hand, or by individuals vested with decisional powers within the agencies themselves on the other. In effect this approach broadens the boundaries of public administration to encompass the larger political system. It makes the student aware that the administrative process includes identifying policy needs, promoting policy objectives for action by other actors in the process, interpreting policy directives received from the legislative, executive, and/or judicial branches, as well as the variety of management processes necessary for successfully implementating policy choices.

Perhaps the most obvious facet of the policy-making process is that decisions must be made. How we arrive at decisions and for what purpose they are to be used becomes vitally important. Carl Friedrich speaks to this point when he explores the interactions which exist between political decision making, public policy, and planning. He points out that we may distinguish three types of political decisions: individual, group, and public. Since decisions reflect choices among alternatives, he proposes that all decisions are problem related and thus demand the greatest amount of information in order to generate more adequate choices.

In public policy questions, this process takes on additional importance. According to Friedrich, it is essential that some goal, objective, or purpose exists toward which policies can be directed. For this reason he suggests that *planning,* the collection and coordination of information which experts can use to solve problems that a given goal presents, take a central role. Public policy and planning are thus linked in the expectation that better political decisions will be made. Friedrich concludes that democracy and freedom provide a more suitable condition for this to occur.

Can this policy process be described? Does it have any identity which can be used for the purpose of analyzing the public administrative world? John Straayer proposes a systematic model around which one may base an analysis of public policy decisions. He divides the process into five distinct parts: 1) the production of demands; 2) the formation of the policy system; 3) the generation of outputs; 4) the formation of a policy implementation system; and 5) the application of the plan to the environment. His model would suggest that the actors and roles in any given policy question might vary and/ or be completely different. By viewing his model we can easily see that the ability to receive information and to use it effectively is dependent upon all the segments of the system operating in a manner in which they are receiving and sending the required information.

Straayer illustrates this by identifying the relationships between political resources and policy outputs. Those individuals and groups who possess the ability—political, organizational, or economic—to amass political resources tend to evoke the most favorable responses from the policy system. Those who are less fortunate (in his article, those with ghetto or poverty problems) tend to lack sufficient political resources to be effective; that is, they are normally unable to activate the informational processes in a manner to achieve their policy goals. In concluding, Straayer suggests the paradox that the policy processes appear to preclude effective remedial policy due to an imbalance of political resources in the larger political system.

The policy process at work might best illustrate the complexities of public policy making. Environmental quality has emerged as a major issue in American politics. Lynton Caldwell discusses environmental quality as an administrative problem. He explains that the purpose of administration is to obtain a synthesis of artificial (political or man-made) and natural systems that will at the same time serve man's needs and values and still maintain the life-support systems of the planet.

He brings out the problems associated with defining policy objectives, finding appropriate structures, and developing affective procedures. Of major importance for all of the three mentioned is the continuing interaction of input factors (political, scientific, structural, and personal) which tend to limit or preclude the taking of certain actions. He suggests that any solution to the policy problems in environmental areas rests on the ability of decision makers (administrators) to extract a synthesis from among the many variables at work in the policy system, based upon a holistic or systems approach to the problem.

A second example of the changing images of the policy process is found in Herman Mertins' article in which he discusses the impact of changes in value orientations about the nature of the federal system upon national transportation policy. He contends that the *new Federalism,* decentralized power and responsibility, changes the character of the inputs that affect transportation policy by emphasizing the community of local level as opposed to the national level of government. He contends that by reorganizing Federal government agencies and departments, greater opportunities are afforded to inputs which will tend to maximize the local view over the national or even regional.

Mertins points out that previous transportation policy came into being due to a variety of input factors: a general lack of effective, long-term pressure by a well-coordinated "lobby" to bring about the necessary policy support through funding; the pressures to reduce the inflationary trend which were reflected in executive actions to impound funds, including those for transportation; questions in regard to the efficacy of having a "single urban fund" as opposed to the normal fragmented approach; and conflicts which arose between the transportation needs on the one hand and the environmental and energy crises on the other.

He further raises some questions about the future of federal transportation policy. Can an adequate transportation policy reflecting a planned and coordinated approach to the nation's transportation dilemma be developed with such a decentralized system as envisaged by the new Federalism? Who would take the role of leadership to develop such a policy if one could be forthcoming? Thus a shift in the basic approach to the federal-state-local governmental roles which is represented in the concept of the new Federalism very substantially affects the nature of the policy process and its outcomes.

Of course, what is attempted in Part Two is to illustrate the fascinating, interactive processes which operate in the formation, maintenance, and application of public policy. So long as relatively democratic processes prevail in such a way that participants in the political process have access to the decisional units and so long as the actors within the system remain more or less responsive to these inputs, policy decisions in the public sector will remain subject to question, review, and adaptation. The real significance of the public policy process approach is its ability to describe this ongoing process.

5

carl j. friedrich

the w. clifford clark memorial lecture, 1970

POLITICAL DECISION-MAKING, PUBLIC
POLICY AND PLANNING

Decision is a central concept of existentialism, and since existential-ism is the dominant philosophy of our century, it is not surprising that decision-making should have become a major pre-occupation of po-litical scientists. Sartre, the leading French existentialist, has written: 'Man first of all exists . . . and what one calls my will is probably the expression of a former and more spontaneous decision . . . When we say that a man chooses himself, we mean that each of us not only chooses himself but that in doing so he chooses all men.' Existential-ism stresses the sudden, the spontaneous, indeed the exceptional, in decision-making. The maturing of a decision, the often slow process of reaching a decision, that is of the separating of the several possibili-ties which must precede a decision, is not sufficiently brought out ('decide' comes from the Latin *decidere* which is related to *caedere* which means 'to cut'). In politics the process of reaching a decision is crucial and efforts have been made for some years to clarify and describe this process. Seen in the perspective of these inquiries, the choosing of oneself which existentialism stresses is no true decision at all because there are no alternatives; for the alternative of not choos-ing oneself does not in fact exist.

From *Canadian Public Administration*. Spring 1971. Volume XIV, No. 1. Reprinted by permission of The Institute of Public Administration of Canada and the author.

Even so, it is true that man is confronted by the inexorable necessity of constantly deciding, and this necessity is man's freedom and responsibility. This viewpoint has often been echoed by writers in politics and law. One of the most radical wrote at one point: 'Sovereign is he who decides on the state of emergency.' Such an assertion is characteristic in stressing the marginal situation of an emergency. This kind of decisionist outlook is much inclined to interpret a decision as more or less arbitrary; that is to say, not derived from reasons, principles, or norms. It is 'free' in the sense of being 'without law': it intuitively springs from the human being who exists and who cannot go on existing without choosing, deciding, acting. In the Christian perspective, the ultimate source of such thinking is pride, the arrogance which the Greeks called *hybris*.

In recent parlance it has become fashionable to talk of operations in the field of policy. This leads to an inclination to stress, in the realm of politics, arbitrary will rather than right and law as the ultimate reference. Even a bad decision is better than no decision, it is said, and a decision is seen as an 'intuition' out of nothing. No proposition could be further from the truth. Man does not only choose from available alternatives, but he invents new ones. He selects that course of action which his preliminary exploration suggests as likely of success. The tendency of decisionist theory to overstress its suddenness has, incidentally, the consequence that a decision cannot be discussed. It is, as people now like to say, 'non-negotiable.'

In truth, this way of looking at decisions is superficial; for in the making of decisions it is always a matter of choosing between alternative courses of action. Very sudden 'decisions' are either decisions which really reflect a previous decision or correspond to established custom. Let me illustrate by an example: if a man in authority at a moment of danger calls in the police, that decision may be right or wrong. But when he is reproached for not having consulted with others, as happened to the president of Harvard University a year ago, the answer must be that there was danger in delay. The answer implies that when there is danger in delay, a less good decision is preferable to no decision. The stress here is on the contingency of the evaluation and therefore that the decision might indeed be the best. This example shows how crucial is the *process* of deciding. Much depends upon it.

It is easy to over-estimate the element of decision-making in political action; for whenever an order is highly rationalized, that is to say when it is an order in which many actions are repeated in accordance with fully rationalized methods and rules, not many genuine decisions are made. The continental European view of the judge as a man who authoritatively subsumes concrete cases under established rules is perhaps the most distinctive expression of a rationalized bureaucracy wherein discretion is reduced to an absolute minimum. Very different are the instances of great historical decisions, especially in war. Decisive battles were fought because a commander decided to go into battle. But even in these instances, there may be objection.

Tolstoy has, in a famous passage of his great novel *War and Peace,* made mocking remarks about Napoleon because he believed, and his historians with him, that he made a decision when he became involved in war against Russia in 1812. Wars are, according to Tolstoy, the product of the womb of history; and he even calls rulers and generals 'the slaves of history.' When discussing the outbreak of the war of 1812, he asks:

> What produced this extraordinary occurrence? What were its causes? The historians tell us with naïve assurance that its causes were the wrongs inflicted on the Duke of Oldenburg, the non-observance of the Continental System, the ambition of Napoleon, the firmness of Alexander, the mistakes of the diplomats, and so forth and so on . . . To us, their descendants who are not historians and who can therefore regard the event with unclouded common sense, an incalculable number of causes present themselves. The deeper we delve in search of these causes, the more of them we find; and each separate cause, or whole series of causes, appears to us equally valid in itself and equally false by its insignificance compared to the magnitude of the events, and by its importance to occasion the event. To us the wish or objection of this or that French corporal to serve a second term appears as much a cause as Napoleon's refusal to withdraw his troops beyond the Vistula and to restore the Duchy of Oldenburg; for had he not wished to serve, and had a second, a third and a thousandth corporal and private also refused, there would have been so many less men in Napoleon's army and the war could not have occurred . . . And there was no one cause for that occurrence . . .

In other words, Tolstoy believes that a decision may be possible, but is highly improbably in many instances in which it is believed to have occurred. Men act in accordance with their social situation. It is not necessary to go as far as Tolstoy in order to perceive that what seems to be a decision need not be one; thus we are once more in face of the question, wherein does the process of decision consist? What happens when one decides? How do political decisions come about?

It is apparent that every decision is a response to a change in the environment of the decision-maker. This is especially true in politics. If everything remains the same, no decision is necessary. One attempt to sketch the process of political decision-making puts it as follows: 'Decision-making is a process which results in the selection from a socially defined limited number of problematical alternative projects, the one project intended to bring about the particular state of affairs envisioned by the decision-maker. This definition is too rationalist and too teleological, and so are many others like it. It neglects or gainsays the situational aspects. It may also be questionable whether there is always a 'future state' that is being envisaged by the decision-maker. It may be just a vague notion or a sense of direction that guides him. But before we can empirically define the phenomenon of decision-making, it seems to me necessary to distinguish several types of political decisions.

Broadly speaking, three types of political decisions may be distinguished in accordance with the different patterns of 'reaching' a decision. I suggest that we distinguish individual decisions, group decisions, and public decisions. Our distinction is only approximately right, for individual and group decisions may be public as well. How do these three types look specifically, and when do they occur? Individual decisions are particularly characteristic of the administrator and the citizen. They may be further subdivided by whether consultations precede the decision or not. Most citizens are likely to decide without much advice for whom to vote in an election or what alternative to select in a referendum, whether to write to their representative, whether to subscribe to one newspaper or another, whether to go to an election meeting or to read a book about the candidates. To these random examples of individual private decision by the individual citizen correspond decisions by the administrator, such as which subordinate to criticize, what reply to make to a complaint, how to phrase a memorandum to his superior, and so forth. All these decisions may be made with advice, and whether to seek such advice may itself be part of the individual's decision-making, though it may be obligatory. Custom, office rule, or even a constitutional provision may require it—for example, the 'advise and consent' rule of the US Constitution. But even so, the decision of whether or what to propose is often made without prior advice; and whether to seek advice or what to propose is decided by the individual office holder. To illustrate, President Nixon's decision to propose Judge Carswell for the US Supreme Court was presumably reached after extensive consultations and inquiries, and his own statements can be taken at face value.

The second kind of decision is arrived at by the joint-action of a group. Such a decision may require unanimity or some kind of majority. It may be reached after the members of the group have more or less extensively consulted with each other. Courts, commissions, legislative committees, and other public bodies acting without public participation utilize this kind of procedure. Such group decisions carry greater authority and are usually employed for matters of some moment. Hence we find in judicial systems that the higher courts make group decisions while the lower courts act through individual judges. It is worth noting that there are no general rules about the procedure in such groups, but there may be very elaborate specific rules for particular groups. Civil and criminal procedure are illustrations for that.

If a decision requires a public discussion, as is the case with legislation, a particularly important kind of decision, it deserves to be recognized as a distinctive type even though it is also a group decision. The rules of procedure are typically very carefully elaborated. Every modern parliament has its own rules of procedure and these must be co-ordinated with the role of the parliament in the political system. The history of procedure in the House of Commons is the history of freedom. A very general survey of even one such body of rules of procedure shows how complicated the process of decision-making has become in the public realm and how difficult it is to abstract from the specific in order to construct a general model of political decision-making. The situation is further complicated by the fact that such public decisions are, on account of their publicity, so difficult to reach that the true decision-making is transferred to party conclaves or even more restricted groups—groups which meet in secrecy or at least allow only limited publicity. Experience has taught people that this is the usual thing.

We now return to the question of which general traits can be identified in all political decisions. We can state the following: in all three types it is a question of what action is required to meet a problem; hence, decisions are problem-related. And, since political problems are typically communal, they cannot be gainsaid or escaped; for even the refusal to make a decision is a kind of decision and, in fact, a very frequent one—things are permitted to stay as they are.

Decisions are, as we said, always decisions between alternatives, but these alternatives are not always very precisely stated. One of the most important results of recent research is the conclusion that we must presuppose that all possibilities, in other words all manageable alternatives, have been considered in the process of making a decision. It has been suggested that instead of such radical rationality, we should assume that in reality a limited rationality prevails. Instead of seeking an optimal solution, people are content with a minimal solution which suffices under the circumstances without claiming to allow for all possible alternatives. This is an overstatement, but it makes an important point. Solutions may also remain somewhere between the optimal and the minimal solution.

In any case, decisions can be made only between alternatives; yet the opinion which is sometimes expressed that there could be only two alternative decisions is unsound. Such dichotomic decisions are, as a matter of fact, often the most difficult and vexing. Hamlet's cry, 'To be or not to be,' is perhaps the most basic of these decisions and, in a sense, all other decisions can even be traced back to it. In politics the decision between peace and war illustrates the 'either-or' decision in its most unhappy inescapability. Often decisions are put into this form when, actually, several alternatives are available. Even peace or war may be a decision of that kind and the same is even more true of other seemingly dichotomic decisions. One should be ever alert against the oratorical tendency to make problems appear in the form of such an 'either-or' decision. 'Better dead than Red' is a contemporary example of this type of obfuscation. In the viable representation of concrete political problems the possibilities of mistaking the complex reality combining numerous alternatives for a simple 'either-or' are very great; and it is frequently an important part of political skill to discover and reveal hidden alternatives. We shall return to this problem of the hidden alternatives later, but one thing is certain and that is until the alternatives are brought out and clearly defined, a decision will be inadequate, if not impossible.

And yet, any vote has to be taken upon the 'either-or' question of accepting or rejecting a proposal. Elaborate rules such as those about putting forward and seconding a motion seek to ensure that this happens. Yet the dichotomy is often deceptive: the 'ayes' and 'nays' in many votes may often stand for very different reasons. If a faculty group is confronted with a motion to propose a certain candidate for appointment, the 'nays' may include not only persons who do not favour the particular candidate but also others who favour one of the other candidates, though they would be quite willing to accept this one if their special preferences are not eligible. The same possibility is even more frequently found in cases where alternative policies are involved. Tentatively we may sum up what has so far been said regarding political decisions by defining such a decision as the choice of one of several alternative courses of action suggested by a problem situation.

The fact that political decisions are problem-related, and the further fact that all possible alternatives need to be explored, is the basis of the need for decentralization. The need is often the ground for federalizing a political order. But it is not necessary to go as far as federation, with its rigidities. The need for decentralization is also the justification for local self-government. Students of public administration have given a good deal of thought to and have carried on research on the problems of top-heavy organization and the desirable 'span' of decision-making authority. How great a load can be carried by a central office? When do communications break down? The Soviet Union has found itself obliged to explore the possibilities of decentralization. It has been an important issue in the arguments over reform in Czechoslovakia and Yugoslavia.

I wish now to turn to a kind of decision which has been of particular importance in modern politics and to which we usually refer as a 'policy.' Policy is one of the magic words of the contemporary world, as it was in the sixteenth and seventeenth centuries. Policy means a proposed course of action of a person, group, or government within a given government that contains obstacles and opportunities which the policy as proposed intends to utilize and overcome in an effort to reach a goal, or realize an objective, or achieve a purpose. Policy is important in all organizations, but the most important is public policy: a proposed course of action of the government or one of its subdivisions. I am, of course, in this lecture concerned with public policy, but the policy of other groups deserves serious attention. As our definition shows, I consider it essential for public policy that there be a goal, objective, or purpose. Furthermore, public policy is not some chance course of action proposed by a heedless or reckless person, but rather it presupposes a deliberate effort on the part of qualified men to assess the pros and cons of alternative courses of action and a decision in favour of the one seen as most likely to succeed. It is obvious then that the policy-maker should know as many of the conditions as might affect the proposed action. This is easier in domestic than in foreign policy. In the domestic sphere policy obviously calls for a thorough knowledge, not only of the technical and such like conditions, but also of the institutional setting. Many well-intentioned initiatives on the part of reformers come to nothing because these several conditions, but more particularly the institutional setting, are overlooked. There is no sense in proposing that an official do things which in the nature of his office he is unable to do. This general proposition is interestingly illustrated in the field of foreign policy where there are constant demands that countries like the United States should have a different foreign policy, or indeed any foreign policy. It is very doubtful whether within the democratic context an integrated foreign policy is possible. The recent valiant endeavour by President Nixon to state such a policy illustrates this difficulty. A thoughtful student of these matters might well ask whether what is thus publicly stated is not intended rather to mislead domestic and world opinion than to inform it. In a policy field as complicated as the foreign policy of a world power, even a partial decision in a particular sector is apt sooner or later to affect all other fields and the range of alternatives is therefore very broad and extremely difficult to assess. The problem of the hidden alternatives, already mentioned above, is particularly perplexing here. Such hidden alternatives may be due to the fact that a particular power is not adequately informed about the intentions and policies of other powers and great opportunities may be missed. Such a situation arose before the First World War, and the secrecy by which Lord Grey, the British Foreign Minister, had preserved information concerning his commitments to France and Russia misled the Imperial German government. This danger of misleading an adversary may in turn become a very strong reason for disclosing policy objectives. In his policy paper, Nixon's aside to the effect that an effort of the Soviet Union to increase its power in the Middle East would be a matter of grave concern to the United States is a characteristic instance.

These brief reflections which could be expanded readily in various directions, which I do not have time to explore, lead to the problem of planning, for planning is a policy of very great complexity. Planning seeks to link and inter-relate various aspects of a field of public policy or maybe several aspects, an obvious example being economic and social planning. Therefore planning is closely linked to the question of the role of the expert — a question of special urgency in a highly industrialized democratic society. For what planning implies most of the time is the collection and effective co-ordination of the knowledge which such experts can bring to the solution of the problems which a particular goal presents. This fact produces great difficulties, for the expert, possessing a certain special knowledge, is usually not prepared to make the solution of objective tasks dependent upon the will or the opinion of an inexpert majority. It has therefore often been asserted that democracy and planning are incompatible and cannot be combined, a question to be taken up later. Suffice it to say here that, if this were true, the future chances of democracy would be poor, for planning is essential for many matters which must be decided in an advanced, modern society. Likewise, the task of modernization in an underdeveloped country cannot be fulfilled without comprehensive planning.

Many believe that planning is a phenomenon of the twentieth

century, but monarchical absolutism had already practised planning on a considerable scale; mercantilism and cameralism were really theories of planning for an economy. Hence the development of statistics in the seventeenth century, for information is for planning of absolutely vital importance. Later on liberalism urged, against all such planning, that it was much better to allow 'natural' forces free play. Adam Smith stressed, in his famous critique of mercantilism,[28] how dubious all planning is. And, contrary to prevailing notions, socialism, or rather socialists, including Karl Marx, did not at first develop the idea of planning, but the almost diametrically opposed notion of a nearly anarchic social order of free co-operation. This, their original outlook, is often forgotten now, because socialism and communism found themselves, after the socialization of the means of production, faced with the task of effectively co-ordinating production. Thus what happened in the Soviet Union after the revolution occurred in England and France after the Second World War: an over-all planning of the economy is undertaken. These efforts at planning within a democratic context had, however, a different form than that prevailing in the Soviet Union. Such planning occurred rather pragmatically and without ideological justifications; it parallels the spread of planning in smaller organizations. The story of the spread of PPB (programming, planning and budgeting) is relevant here. Enterprises and communities find themselves confronted today by the need for planning. Such planning is being done with increasingly refined methods since the development of the computer, for the computer facilitates the handling of ever larger amounts of informational data and thus provides a chance to prepare increasingly complex decisions.

These technical improvements often veil or obscure the basic problems; for all planning presupposes a basic decision as to what is to be the result of the plan. Thus industrialization has been the main task in the Soviet Union, and the stress on heavy and armament industry resulted from the notions of Stalin concerning the problems of Soviet domestic and foreign policy. The kind of planning consequent upon these goals seemed to presuppose and to imply that there must be an authoritative person or collective who could decide what goal the planning was to serve. For a democracy in the western sense of a constitutional democracy, it is characteristic that such basic decisions are made by the people, especially in the English tradition in which elections are linked to policy decisions. Thus, for example, the priority to be given to economic, social, military and other goals must be settled; there may be frequent changes. Germany recently decided to put educational development ahead of all other demands, In the US the *Reports* of the Council of Economic Advisers are full of discussions of these difficult issues of priorities. Planning has been implemented effectively in more limited fields, such as water resources, but the problem of interrelation with other goals remains. Changes, then, are hard to combine with an orderly planning process.

It has been suggested that the budget involves planning for one year, but such planning is of course restricted to the government and its activities and within the wider context such as a modern economy presents, a one-year plan is inadequate. On the other hand, a five-year plan, or whatever may be the number of years, means that the responsibility of government toward the people is, for this period, jeopardized. To cope with this issue, Puerto Rico, a developing country, has adopted a procedure which resembles budgetary practice. A plan for several years, developed by the Planning Office, is submitted and resubmitted to the legislature every year together with a report about the progress of development, and changes are made in the plan on the basis of popular criticism. Puerto Rico has, therefore, a plan for several years, but it is altered from year to year. Puerto Rico has made unbelievable progress under this system during the last twenty years, and the per capita income has become more than ten times what it was. But unfortunately there are no special studies in detail about the extent to which this is due to planning. In any case, this system has lately deteriorated, though it worked very well during the fifties, at the beginning of the Commonwealth. This deterioration is due, I am told, to the breakdown of relations between the Planning Board and the chief executive.

In all economic planning of this kind, it is necessary that three viewpoints are continually adapted to each other, at least in relatively free countries. There is first the satisfaction of the consumer, second the advance in production, and finally exceptional achievements. The sense of achievement, which is closely linked to a sense of craftsmanship, introduces into all these fields of activity a dynamic element.

The responsibility of a planning office must extend to all three of these issues. At the same time and as a part of it, it has been found that the planning staff, or at least its head, must be closely linked to those authorities that are making the important political decisions, and they should be integrated into the top echelon of decision-makers. If this is not done, the result is likely to be that planning becomes an academic exercise. Besides the above mentioned troubles in Puerto Rico, we might refer here to a similar experience with the planning staff in the American Department of State where the inability of Dulles to use such a staff effectively led to its disintegration. Similar experiences have been made in the Soviet Union where likewise it appeared that planning can only be successful if it prepares and indeed occasions the decisions of the top decision-makers. In this sense a planning office reinforces hierarchical tendencies in government and elsewhere. But this need not be the consequence, as such a tendency can be combatted by suitable procedures.

The responsibility of a planning authority can be toward the higher-ups in the official hierarchy or toward the electorate at large. If a planning staff assists a chief executive, as is nowadays often the case, such a staff will usually be responsible towards the executive. If the planning staff is instead responsible to parliament or a community council, the responsibility toward the people will be reinforced. Nowadays, many talk about planning as if it were possible to escape such responsibility through planning. Staffs of experts are praised or denounced as 'technocrats' who are not accountable. Such a view is often embodied in the vision of a managerial society. But these notions imply too narrow a basis of legitimacy: the rulers are believed to be legitimized by technical achievement. Achievement has always been an important factor in legitimacy, but rarely the only one. The clamour for planning, misunderstood as technicalization of value-related decisions and policies, is ill-conceived. *Planning only makes sense, to repeat it once more, within the context of rational decision-making based upon prevailing, in other words communal, values and beliefs.*

These facts and notions have brought it about that many believe democracy, or a free society, and planning mutually exclude each other and that is is therefore necessary to avoid all arrangements that involve planning. Hayek is the best known representative of this view. In his famous book he developed the proposition that socialism would lead, via a planned economy, to an enslavement of man. That this may be the result, is undeniable in light of twentieth century experience. But the dangers inherent in the concentration of economic power can be effectively combatted only by 'planning' a free enterprise economy—by coordinating the separate decisions of the entrepreneurs through an effective body such as the *Commisariat du Plan* at Paris. In France the *Commisariat du Plan* is by law required to be keenly interested in the position of the representatives of business and labour, but the basic decision, which is to modernize and industrialize France, was never an issue. It is important in this connection to remember that the Rome Treaties for the formation of a European economic union also contained such a basic decision and that therefore the work directed toward the establishment of a Common Market brought with it planning on a larger scale. In view of recent developments, notably the experience of the Federal Republic of Germany in overcoming the recessions of the sixties, it may even be permissible to risk the assertion that a democracy cannot, in a highly industrialized society, survive without comprehensive planning; for industrial progress, even the avoidance of major crisis, is no longer possible without planning. Puerto Rico is an interesting case in point.

We might recall in this connection that each constitution, at least as far as it affects the economy, contains a plan, and the American Constitution of 1787 may be thus considered. Soon after the adoption of the Constitution, Alexander Hamilton supplemented it by his famous 'Report of Manufactures' of 1791. This report has become a sort of Magna Carta of American economic development. The argument of the report about 'infant industries' which one must develop through customs duties is a central planning thought, and the decision in its favour has had far reaching consequences. Many today look upon the American economic development as a 'natural' process, and people forget that human beings who had to make decisions and sketch plans had to act to bring about this development.

Along with what has just been said, it is important to realize, as I already hinted, that a detailed budget which all modern states have is a plan for one year. Everyone knows how important for the development of constitutional democracy has been this 'power of the purse,' the decision concerning the budget. Only in recent times have people come to realize how many economic policy decisions are implied in a decision about fiscal policy. Likewise, only in more recent years has it been more clearly recognized and studied that certain kinds of taxation favour particular economic developments while others inhibit them. John Maynard Keynes has placed these aspects in the centre of all thought on economic policy. The government's finances now appear as a means for steering economic development. Thus the budget was recognized as a plan, especially when extended over several years, for such an extension does not imply any alteration in principle. It is therefore difficult to see why it should be impossible to employ procedures comparable to budgetary ones, for subjecting the planning process to democratic controls.

Even so, the question remains whether over-all planning can be organized in a way compatible with freedom. The rise of totalitarian dictatorships has actualized this problem. Comprehensive planning had played a considerable role in the First World War and much more in the Second World War. In these cases, the basic decision about the planning goal was provided by the circumstances: the war must be won. And after a war the basic decision was likewise fixed in favour of reconstruction. This can be generalized to say that such crises produce a fixation of popular will and facilitate or even fixed planning, especially within the framework of a democracy. Furthermore, economic progress and the improvement in the standard of living have today become almost universally accepted as in the public interest and therefore can serve as a basis for planning. But for the many additional decisions with which planning confronts us, more particularly the question of priorities such as armament and security versus the fight against poverty and pollution, a participation of the public and its representatives cannot be avoided. Hence only a responsible planning staff can be accepted.

Therefore, a centrally planned and directed economy nonetheless raises once more the issue of totalitarian rule, for only such rule seems to make an integrated direction possible. It is obvious that in a totalitarian dictatorship a dictator or a politburo will make the basic decisions upon which planning is based. It is less obvious how the mistakes made in planning can be corrected. If the basic decision is, as in the case of the Soviet Union above delineated, unsound, mistakes in planning may be a consequence of the original basic decision. It is inevitable that very extended conflicts and controversies will be the consequence. All in all, we can say that totalitarian planning is based upon goals which are in part determined by the ideology. Hence such planning is in its very nature totalist, and will therefore not recoil from radical transformation of the social structure. Thus economic planning cannot be separated from social planning. Therefore it cannot be limited in time. Total planning is so much a necessary part of a totalitarian regime that without it a process of disintegration would soon commence.

The situation is very different in the case of the attempts at planning which have been made in relatively open societies. Such planning is mostly partial planning of particular fields of activity which seem to require particular attention. Planning is, under these circumstances, the steering and co-ordination of the activities of a particular commitment or program for the economy and its resources, for social improvement, for educational development, and so forth. But it is a mistake to think that planning as such has any particular importance. Many people talk as if planning were a panacea which could solve difficult problems. Such an opinion is very misleading, for planning presupposes a notion concerning the solution that is to be sought by way of planning. Planning of a university reform, for example, presupposes that a decision has been made as to what kind of university is to be brought into being. All planning in a vacuum which could get along without such decisions is bound to fail, for only when the basic decision has been made can the many partial decisions, which an attempt at planning projects, be made. Oftentimes however, the call for planning asks for much less and embodies merely the desire to collect information which is needed for a reform. We have seen that in every process of decision-making such information constitutes the first step which must be made toward a decision. But even the gathering of such information presupposes that a pre-decision has been made so as to provide a standard for selecting the useful from the very voluminous materials. European states had to discover this in a painful way when, without any adequate preparation, they undertook to socialize important branches of the economy. The participation of the people as producers and consumers has proved itself an ineluctable condition of successful planning. It has since been institutionalized.

By way of summary and conclusion, let me say that decision-making, policy and planning are closely tied and that under contemporary conditions of advanced industrial society, as well as in underdeveloped countries, these three processes cannot be considered in isolation. All depend upon a considerable measure of rationality, but it seems important not to over-estimate this aspect. Whether it is a matter of individual decisions or group decisions, and whether they are public decisions or not, decisions are related to known alternatives, and tend in the last analysis to become dichotomic. Still, it is incorrect to say, as is sometimes done, that all decisions are dichotomic. Planning procedures are, of course, particularly striking evidence of the complex character of nondichotomic decision-making. Public policy also is usually adopted in facing a multi-faceted reality in which a number of alternative ways of dealing with environmental challenges are handled. Planning is often involved in effective policy-making as the very process of sorting out such alternatives. And the opinion which sees an insoluble conflict between planning and democracy is untenable. Experience has shown further that the voters have a sense of appreciation for objective achievements. The electorate at the same time recognizes that there are other than technical problems, and it reacts sharply when the values and beliefs of the community are at stake. If the often-heard claim that planning is incompatible with democracy or with a free society is therefore untenable, contemporary evidence suggests that they both presuppose planning under contemporary conditions. Hence planning and public policy are least likely to be defective under such conditions as only democracy and freedom can provide.

6

john adrian straayer

THE AMERICAN POLICY PROCESS AND THE
PROBLEMS OF POVERTY AND THE GHETTO

As is apparent to even the most casual observer there is a fairly substantial gap between certain articulated American values and the living conditions of millions of U.S. citizens. Equality of opportunity and a minimal level of decency for all constitute a part of the American creed. Political speeches are full of demands for good health, education, housing, recreation, and employment for all; and, at least in the abstract, most Americans voice their support. But the conditions in which millions of people find themselves fall far short of these articulated values. Many Americans remain discriminated against, unemployed, ill-housed and ill-fed. The purpose of this paper is to try to explain through an examination of the policy process why the American political system fails to generate policy designed to realize articulated American values.

THE AMERICAN POLICY PROCESS

The American policy process can be aptly conceptualized by employing an adaptation of David Easton's systemic "input-output model"[1]—an adaptation which is similar as well to the structure-functional model of Almond and Coleman.[2] All systemic models are, of course, both static and dynamic. The terms "system" and "process" imply motion—a continuously moving phenomenon. For purposes of analysis however, a systemic model can allow one artificially to stop

From *Western Political Quarterly*, xxiv, #1 (March 1971). Reprinted by Permission of the University of Utah, Copyright Holder.

an ongoing, or dynamic, process. This is what has been done to the model which is employed here and illustrated in Figure 1. It is essentially static in nature and artificially segments the policy process into five stages: (1) the production of demands; (2) the formation of a policy system; (3) the generation of outputs; (4) the formation of a policy implementation system; and (5) the application of a plan (policy) to the environment.

The production of demands involves the organization of an aware and concerned public around a particular set of environmental conditions which are perceived to be problematic in nature. This "interested" or "relevant" public, then, will employ all the resources at its disposal so as to put the perceived problem on the agenda of government and generate remedial public policy.

The human environment contains an innumerable number of conditions and sets of conditions from which demands emerge. There are slums, jobs of all types, good housing, bad housing, suburbs, core cities, taxes of all sorts, (and with all sorts of implications), transportation systems and so forth. Additionally, the environment contains numerous individuals and groups of individuals who, because of wide variations in family, church, school and peer group backgrounds, vary greatly in terms of values, knowledge, wants and skills. The combination of these innumerable and various sets of environmental conditions with the values, knowledge, wants, and skills of innumerable individuals and groups of individuals with varying backgrounds and perceptions, results in the production of a wide and diverse variety of personal and group wants and places a wide variety of demands upon government.

Having perceived certain conditions as problematic in nature, groups and clusters of groups bring to the government their demands for change. As students of group politics have long pointed out, in petitioning government to envoke public policy so as to change the environment and eliminate conditions perceived as problematic, groups rely on such political resources as unity, size, organization, cohesiveness and money. Further, they employ various lobby tactics, such as propagandizing to the public at large, testifying before various committees, and assisting or opposing certain candidates in election campaigns.[3]

As an example of this phenomenon, a group or cluster of groups may perceive a certain level of unemployment as undesirable and may then call upon the government for whatever action is necessary to lower the unemployment level. A lowering of the unemployment level, however, may necessitate certain changes in the national tax structure; changes which, when operationalized, may generate dissatisfaction on the part of some group or cluster of groups. Or secondly, a group or cluster of groups may perceive the amount of money spent at the state, local, and federal levels for education to be insufficient and may consider this to constitute a public problem. This cluster of groups, then, may demand that the government take action so as to increase its expenditures in that area. To some other group or cluster of groups, however, the level of funding of American education may not appear to constitute a public problem. This difference of opinion clearly results from varying perceptions of the environment—a variation generated by variations in values.

Once a problem appears on the agenda of government, a policy formation system will form around it.[4] A combination of individuals, interest groups, agencies of the executive, legislative committees or sub-committees, and others will come together based upon their common interest in the problem.[5] They will form a "policy system." Obviously, the components of policy systems will vary with the problem involved. Not all agencies and interest groups are interested in each and every one of the problems that are placed upon the agenda of government. The American Medical Association, for example, will be interested in the problems of health care and will be involved in the formation of health care policy. Additionally, the A.M.A. may have a mild interest in certain other problems—but it probably will have little interest in, and will not be active in, an area such as agricultural problems and policy.

We might look at one specific example—that of education. The interested publics which will collectively form the educational policy system will, in all likelihood, include the U.S. Department of Health, Education, and Welfare generally, the U.S. Office of Education specifically, the National Education Association, certain Catholic, Jewish, and Protestant church organizations, various labor groups, state and local education associations, individual and collective groupings of colleges and universities, and certain committees on both the Senate and House side—including most likely, committees having to do with education and finance. These groups, committees, and agencies will interact, employing their various political resources in efforts to control the content of policy output. They will interact in conflict and compromise situations, and will collectively hammer out public policy. This policy will be, quite simply, a system response to demands generated by the earlier perception of the existence, in the environment, of problem conditions.

The interaction described above, which results in the generation of policy output involves interaction among various portions of

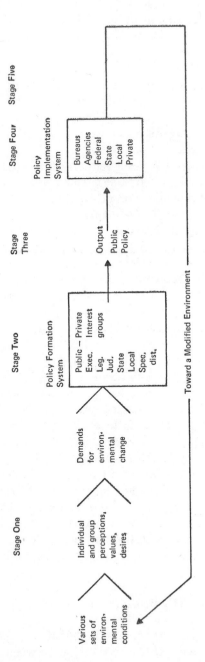

Stage 1: Production of demands for environmental change
2: Formation of a policy system
3: Generation of public policy
4: Formation of a policy implementation system
5: Application of intendedly remedial policy to the environment

FIGURE 1   A model of the American Policy System

the relevant public. It is a game of conflict and compromise played by the rules of the political game and within the accepted ideological context. It involves the employment of all sorts of lobbying techniques; it involves articulation by interest groups of their demands and desires; it involves action on the part of political parties; it involves interaction within committtees and within the full Congress; and it involves executive, legislative, and judicial interaction. The result is public policy—a statement of a "preferred state of affairs." It is a plan, a compromise plan probably, to change the environment and recast it according to the values of the individuals and groups who were the most successful in the earlier bargaining stages of the policy formation process.

Once public policy has been formulated it must be administered—applied to problem conditions. This nearly always involves efforts at cooperation by public and private agencies at various levels of government. Also, in some cases it involves the adoption of new activities by an existing organization. It may involve the assumption by the U.S. Office of Education, for example, of the duties of administering a new aid-to-education program. Or, it may involve the assumption by the U.S. Department of Transportation of new duties having to do with the control of air traffic. In some cases, however, new policy implementation systems must be created. This generally occurs when the problem at hand has to do with an activity heretofore not dealt with by the government. So, for example, the first public policy dealing with the Social Security System necessitated the formation of a largely new administrative system. Of course, totally new administrative systems are seldom formulated. What generally happens instead is that some components of existing administrative systems are pulled together so as to create a "quasi-new" system.

The final stage, and one suggested above, involves the application of the public policy to the environment. It has to do with the entire processes of public administration and involves collecting, ordering and mobilizing physical and human resources so as to alter the environment and recast it in a form more like the preferred state of affairs articulated in public policy. It involves, in short, bureaucratic utilization of information, expertise and materials in the drive for administrative rationality—in the attempt to fulfill public goals.[6]

IMPLICATIONS OF THE POLICY PROCESS

Perhaps the most salient of the points implied by the above description of the policy process is the relationship between political resources and policy output. The character of public policy is most significantly influenced, as group theorists point out, by the individuals and groups most successful at amassing and mobilizing resources. There is, at each stage of the policy process, considerable conflict, as a multiplicity of factions seek to direct the determination of policy content.

Who gets what, when, and how, as Harold Lasswell has aptly stated, is determined neither by accident or change, but by the skillful employment of political power. Political power is relevant at all stages of the policy process as it is needed to gain access to government and to be effective once access is achieved. Political resources are necessary to influence political parties and successfully place questions on their agenda. It is needed to influence congressional committees, to influence public opinion and in turn place pressure on decision-makers, to affect the formation of administrative systems, to influence administrative appointments, and to influence the behavior of administrative units. Thus, groups like AFL-CIO, the Chamber of Commerce, the steel industry, the auto industry, the education lobby, the farmers, and others, all seek access to decision-makers by amassing for themselves such political resources as money, voting numbers, organization and leadership skill.

The nature of most American public policy substantiates the above thesis. We constantly pass aid-to-education bills, agricultural policy bills, full employment bills, minimum wage bills, highway bills, veteran bills, foreign policy programs, labor and business legislation, and so forth—all of which reinforce the point that public policy tends to be produced in those problem areas around which interested and politically powerful publics form. Thus, the veterans are able to mobilize political resources and pressure the government into creation and administration of aid-to-veterans policy. The farm lobby has organized around what they perceive to be farm problems and they have been able to generate policy which guarantees some of them a very high level of government support. The same is true in the areas of labor, education, business, and others.

It is clear now, that there are certain requisites for success in the American policy process; and it is clear that for groups to be successful in generating public policy favorable to them they must amass and employ political resources and lobby effectively.

But what does this mean for ghetto and poverty problems? First of all, it is clear that there are environmental conditions which invoke negative responses from individuals. Few people actually "like" slums, unemployment, poor education, family disorganization, crime, poverty, poor housing, poor dietary conditions, and so forth. Individuals within the ghetto, depending upon their level of awareness and their expectations, react negatively to their environment. They would like jobs, good housing, good food, and good conditions generally. Further, many people outside the ghetto also react negatively to these conditions. Many politically aware and concerned individuals and groups, while they may not live in poverty or ghetto conditions, see a need for change simply because ghetto conditions violate their perceptions of traditional American values. Both those within and outside of the ghetto, then, who view these conditions negatively, desire remedial public policy designed to alter conditions.

There is, however, less of a propensity for a public to form around ghetto and poverty problems and lobby effectively. There are several reasons for this. First of all, the poor lack solidarity, both socially and politically. Some are white, some are black, many are children or women, most are uneducated, and many are unemployed.[7] Conglomerations of people in the ghetto are just that—conglomerations. Such groupings tend to lack leadership, and political awareness and concern. Ghetto dwellers and poor people generally, while they have values and desires, while they can identify conditions as undesirable, and while they may individually have demands, tend not to aggregate in such a way as to articulate successfully these demands to government. In short, they lack the political power and resources, the skill, the ingenuity, the vote, and the access to government generally, which groups like the AMA, AFL-CIO, NEA, Chamber of Commerce, and the VFW possess. While these latter groups have organized and classified demands, have mobilized resources so as to place demands on the agenda of government, and have been successful in achieving many of their goals, the poor have had less success. Given the structures and processes of American government, the poor simply cannot win. They lack the requisite resources.

Occasionally, however, some successful attempts are made to organize and articulate the demands of the poor, and thus the problems of the ghetto and of poverty reach the agenda of government. This is evidenced by the passage in 1965 of President Johnson's povery program and by such continued program efforts as Head Start. However, poverty and ghetto-related public policy tends to be both minimal and poorly funded. Whereas the military-industrial complex is extremely strong, articulate, and successful in terms of influencing policy, as evidenced by the size of defense budgets, only about 12 percent of the federal budget in 1968 was allocated to domestic health, education and welfare programs. This suggests that, even if poverty and ghetto problems reach the agenda of government, strong, forceful and innovative public policy, supported by high levels of fundings, is not likely to be the common output of the system. Further, what is true in terms of policy formation is true also of policy administration. As the political power and the political resources of the affected public in the area of poverty and ghetto problems are minimal, likewise their success in generating remedial action is minimal.

The picture facing the poor is not an optimistic one. American values seem to call for the elimination of ghettos and poverty. But the nature of the public policy process is such that highly effective remedial policy is not likely to be forthcoming. Those affected by the poverty and ghetto problems are not in possession of the resources necessary to form an effective, articulate and resourceful public around the problem. This seems to mean, then, that the nature of the American policy process is such that it precludes the maximization of articulated American values. Those most in need of help, those most affected by the ghetto and by poverty, those most deprived of the promises of American ideology, are also the least able to structure conditions so as to be able to achieve these promises. Those who need to use government the most so as to regulate the environment, are the least able to do so.

ENDNOTES

1. A good brief description of Easton's model can be found in David Easton, "An Approach to the Analysis of Political Systems," *World Politics*, 9 (April 1957), 383–400.
2. Gabriel Almond and James S. Coleman, *The Politics of Developing Areas* (Princeton University Press, 1963); see the Introduction especially.
3. See, as examples, David Truman's *The Governmental Process* (New York: Knopf, 1964), and Harmon Zeigler's *Interest Groups in American Society* (Englewood Cliffs: Prentice-Hall, 1964).
4. Charles O. Jones, among others, has wrestled with the question of "when is a problem?" or "when does a given set of environmental conditions constitute a "public problem?" He offers us one very simple and useful answer to the question, namely, "when it reaches the agenda of government."
5. John Dewey, in *The Public and Its Problems*, suggests that the formation of a "public" around a problem constitutes one of the crucial aspects of politics. In fact, he suggests that the public's major problem is one of "discovering" itself.
6. It remains true, of course, that the implementation of public policy, that public administration, involves much more than simple, mechanical and automatic alteration of the environment. The preferred state of affairs

will seldom be fully realized. As Norton Long in the *Public Administration Review,* 9 (1949), 257-64, Robert Presthus in *The Organizational Society* (New York: Knopf, 1962), and others have long pointed out, there are numerous hurdles in the search for "administrative rationality."

7. See Anthony Downs, *Who Are the Urban Poor* (New York: Committee for Economic Development, 1968).

7

lynton k. caldwell

ENVIRONMENTAL QUALITY AS AN
ADMINISTRATIVE PROBLEM

The advent of environmental quality as a public issue has presented government with a problem of organization and management that, if not entirely new, is unprecedented in its scope and complexity. Although some of its components are traditional functions of government—water supply, for example—it differs in the aggregate from most other public services. Unlike many regulatory and client-centered programs, the environmental issue is concerned with the impact of everyone upon the environment.

This "everyone" is more abstract than the usual objects of governmental action: as, for example, farmers, airlines, veterans, or the unemployed. It includes the total range of human activities that significantly affect man's environment. But it does not deal with the totality of these activities—only with those aspects that relate to the quality or condition of the environment. It must also deal with these activities in a time context uncongenial to practical politics; it must consider long-term and accumulative consequences. In order to act effectively on many environmental issues, government must act *before* the issue becomes acute, and this often means before the public generally is aware of the need for or receptive to taking public action.

Despite their breadth and complexity, it is easier to define environmental issues than it is to specify the content of even more ab-

Reprinted from Caldwell, Lynton K. "Environmental Quality as an Administrative Problem" in volume no. 400 of *The Annals* of the American Academy of Political and Social Science. Copyright © 1972, by the American Academy of Political and Social Science. All rights reserved.

stract concepts such as social justice, equal opportunity, or national security. The environment itself is tangible and measurable, even though some of the values perceived or sought in it are not. Many people, however, find environmental concepts difficult to comprehend; these concepts often require a way of thinking about man-environment relationships that are contrary to or absent from conventional assumptions. Governments have consequently found it difficult to define environmental issues adequately. Our discussion will be focused largely upon the United States, which has taken a lead among nations in specifying the meaning of environmental quality in a public statute: Public Law 91-190, the National Environmental Policy Act of 1969.

DEFINING POLICY OBJECTIVES

The origin of environmental policy, and hence of its administration, is to be found in the political movement that made environmental quality a public issue. Although the environmental issue relates to everyone, all are not equally concerned. Some are more interested and informed than others, some are more directly affected by the administration of environmental policies. The tasks of the administrator are obviously influenced by who is concerned, how, and with what intensity.

In the United States, environmental policy has developed from the "grass roots," as a popular movement. But its leaders and more influential followers have come from the upper levels of society as measured by income and education. More than perhaps any other issue, the environment has become an object of concern among the professional occupations, especially among scientists, engineers, and physicians. Organized groups, such as the Scientists Institute for Public Information, the National Sanitation Foundation, and various civic and professional associations, have campaigned for public awareness of environmental issues and for enactment of protective legislation and its effective implementation by public agencies.

The environmental administrator therefore faces an active sector of the public that is exceptionally knowledgeable about the issues with which he is concerned—some members of which may be better informed on substantive matters than the administrator himself. This activist group, moreover, possesses the information, skills, and relationships necessary to get policies adopted and administered in a complex technological society. Its influence may be disproportionate to its numbers, but it represents the kind of politics that may become more common as issues increasingly involve scientific knowledge and methods of analysis that depend upon more than the average amount of formal education.

Foresight with respect to possible futures is more often a characteristic of the highly educated man and the scientist than it is of people generally. The environmental issue is especially dependent upon calculations of trends and projections of probable futures. But actual determination of the kind of future toward which public policies are directed is a form of political action. Long-range and comprehensive national planning is implied in the solution of many environmental problems. Yet this type of planning has not generally been acceptable to any major sector of American politics. The search for market mechanisms (such as effluent charges) or technological fixes (such as bio-degradable containers) is, in part, motivated by dislike and distrust of comprehensive environmental planning and administration.

It seems improbable, however, that "the invisible hand" of economic self-interest or the inventive ingenuity of technologists can resolve all of modern societies' environmental problems. They do not afford means for defining policy objectives, and are to some extent advocated by persons who dislike the idea of government having other than the most general objectives in relation to the environment. But, contrary to the opinions of some skeptics, environmental quality is not merely a transient enthusiasm that will wane when the costs of environmental amenities are confronted. The problems that man faces in his environment, and especially those that he has created for himself, will not diminish or disappear without human intervention. Enthusiasm may diminish, but the problems can be expected to remain and often to intensify. Honest and comprehensive analyses of environmental problems and their possible solutions, free from preconceived assumptions, are needed as bases for choice among identified, alternative courses of action. Unfortunately, this approach to policy-making is as yet very imperfectly developed in government anywhere.

Environmental problems are seldom of the kind that yield to the adversary procedures characteristic of American politics and litigation. Environmental issues are characteristically manifest in the form of problems and so require a problem-focused approach. Their tests of truth tend to be those of science rather than those of conventional politics. To the extent that verifiable tests of science can be applied to practical problems of the environment, the conventional ground rules of politics and administration may possibly be changed. The scope and direction of public administration would to this extent be channeled by the demonstrable facts of issues. The personal latitude of the politician and administrator would be reduced as the parameters of a decision became more restricted through clarification of the problem. But, conversely, environmental problems are often amenable to alternative solutions, each of which entails its own set of consequences. The public official may thus have his latitude for judgment simultaneously narrowed with respect to the problem and broadened with respect to solutions, but not necessarily for action.

The technical feasibility of a "solution" carries no promise of political feasibility. The environmental administrator may therefore find that his problems are increasingly defined for him by scientists, beyond his jurisdiction and control, and that the available solutions cannot be implemented without inter-agency or inter-governmental coöperation, also beyond his control. Regulatory policies and procedures are of uncertain life expectancy; they are subject to unpredictable changes in knowledge or technology. In the United States, for example, air and water pollution policies have been in an almost continuous state of change. Regulation of foam and phosphates in household detergents offers a familiar illustration of a much larger number of unstable policy issues. Clearly, environmental quality objectives pose organizational and procedural problems with which public administration, as we have known it, has not been well prepared to cope.

In the necessity for interrelating policy and procedure, structure and strategy, environmental administration is not unique; but, for effective results, there is no area of public affairs in which the necessity is more compelling. Even military operations may not be more exacting, for national strategy need only be more effective than that of a fallible enemy that may be subverted or may make mistakes. But the processes of the natural world cannot be propagandized, nor does "nature" make what men call "mistakes." And, in addition, environmental policy requires for its successful implementation that which men have always found most difficult—collective self-control.

Defining policies with respect to man's future environment is, therefore, a very large, complex, and continuing process, It is an integrative process that must transcend the compartmentalization of governmental functions and jurisdications and must provide continuing communication among all sectors of society having significant environmental concerns. Governments have nowhere attempted to do this and, accordingly, have not been structured to do it. As they now attempt to cope with environmental problems, they are certain to encounter difficulties presented by unsuitable structures for the formulation and administration of effective environmental policies.

FINDING APPROPRIATE STRUCTURES

The unsuitability of the present governmental structure for the formulation and administration of environmental policy is a consequence of its ad hoc historical evolution. The committees of the United States Congress and the bureaus of the Executive Branch are largely client-centered or process-oriented. At all governmental levels, functions have been added one at a time, in response to specific needs or importunities. Very little attention has been given to the broad purposes or missions of government at different levels. Aphorisms or "practical" assumptions have largely guided reorganization efforts. There is nothing wrong with being practical, but there is danger in the uncritical acceptance of assumptions in relation to their probable effect upon the outcome of reorganization efforts.

Present-day understanding of organizational problems and possibilities is more sophisticated than one might conclude from an examination of the recommendations of reorganization committees and commissions. Their scope of inquiry has often been narrowed in the definition of their task. As with the Hoover and Knestenbaum Commissions, the organizational task usually has been to make the present system work better. In a rapidly changing world, this bias of "practical" men may have no more than a superficial, short-term practicality. In fact, the strengthening of inappropriate arrangements and institutions may reduce the ability of the nation to cope with emergent problems.

The unsuitability of existing governmental structure for environmental purposes lies in its tendency to make for exclusiveness among its specialized divisions and for legalized inflexibility in the administration of its programs. Under Section 102 of the National Environmental Policy Act,

> The Congress authorizes and directs that all agencies of the Federal Government shall—(A) utilize a systematic, interdisciplinary approach which will insure the integrated use of the natural and social sciences and the environmental design arts in planning and decisionmaking which may have an impact on man's environment.

In actual fact, implementation of this directive is impeded by the way in which the federal agencies are organized and the way in which their missions have been defined by law and historical experience. On the highly theoretical assumption that the Office of Management and Budget or the congressional appropriations committees would authorize funds specifically to implement this statutory provision, it is nevertheless, doubtful that many agencies will voluntarily modify their procedures in this direction.

In some cases, of which the Bureau of Reclamation may offer an example, the agency mission may have been so conceived and so defined that the principal effect of "a systematic, interdisciplinary approach" could be to call the agency's mission into question. Perhaps this was a possibility foreseen in the drafting of the statute, but it is not to be expected that any human organization, including any outside of government, is likely to carry self-examination to this "extreme." But, even if the agency's mission is confirmed by broad environmental considerations, application of "a systematic, interdisciplinary approach" is likely to intrude into areas that have been assigned by law to other agencies. Given the specialized basis of administrative organization in the United States, interdisciplinary approaches are likely to imply inter-agency conclusions.

Governmental administration, for all its complexity, tends to be simplistic in relation to its problems. It ie especially deficient in the skills of policy synthesis and administrative adaptation. These skills have not traditionally been encouraged in the American public service. They run counter to the Jeffersonian antipathy to "discretion in government;" and, in the words of the Saint Thomas of democracy, the all-important objective of holding the public official to account was to "bind him down from mischief by the chains of the Constitution."[1]

But, to cope with the problems of a rapidly changing world, governments need powers that have traditionally been perceived as dangerous. Qualities of flexibility and adaptability in administration suggest discretion and unpredictability. A traditional method of enforcing accountability is through a precise and invariant specification of rules and procedures. If, however, an administrator is held accountable primarily for specified results, it becomes contradictory to bind him too tightly in choice of means.

Traditional precepts and methods of enforcing accountability are products of a simpler age, when the functions of government were few, easily defined, and seldom mutually interrelating. The historical assumptions, doctrines, and institutions of American government took shape at the end of the eighteenth century during a period of minimal dependence of individuals upon government or upon social institutions. The biases that crystalized during the periods of colonization and pioneering have continued to persist, but often in juxtaposition with popular demand that government "do something" about specific problems that disturb people. Paradoxically, public attitudes, notably on environmental issues, have frustrated public action on the very matters about which there is widespread public complaint.

It is not, in principle, a popular fear of abuse of power that is inappropriate; it is its misapplication under now prevailing circumstances. Modern society has inadvertently assumed a much more difficult task of self-direction and control than it has ever previously undertaken to perform. Because former methods of enforcing accountability may no longer be consistent with society's need for positive results, it does not follow that the principle of public accountability should be abandoned. The logic of present circumstances is that more appropriate methods of obtaining accountability, both as to ends and to means, should be developed. If the structure of public decision-making is now obstructing a fully responsible exercise of public powers, an appropriate restructuring should be sought. Restructuring, merely in a technical sense, is no panacea for coping with public problems. But nothing can be accomplished without organization, and all forms of organization are not equally good for any given purpose.

Finding a structure appropriate to effective performance and accountability is not a one-time effort; it is a continuing task in a changing world. High among the qualities of such a structure must be flexibility and adaptability. Implementation of these qualities depends not only upon statutory and executive authorization on substantive matters, but also upon consistent budgetary and personnel policies. For example, realistic phase-out of redundant agencies and programs cannot be accomplished without workable plans for the transfer and reassignment of personnel. Program and performance budgeting are in principle the right approaches to fiscal flexibility. But statutory authorization to spend continues to be viewed in some agencies, and by some Congressmen, as an indefinite mandate for continuing implementation. For example, proposals to de-authorize water resource projects approved by Congress, many years before the enactment of a national environmental policy, are hardly more easily entertained by the Bureau of Reclamation or the Corps of Engineers than proposals to repeal the Ten Commandments would be among Jews and Christians.

The reorganization of the Executive Branch proposed by President Richard Nixon on March 25, 1971[2] seems in some respects to be a step in a direction that would better serve a national policy for environmental quality. His recommendation for a super-department of natural resources provides a more logical grouping of related functions than that now prevailing. It could facilitate coördination among environmental impact programs and might tend to force policy decisions, both in the Congress and the Executive Branch, into a broader, longer-range context. The President has surely been right in calling for a reconstituting of executive agencies to serve the broad ends or purposes of government. It is a welcome corrective to the ad hoc and incremental approach that has long been the almost unquestioned formula for "practicality" in governmental reorganization.

Nevertheless, the President's proposal has some serious weaknesses. Both his message to the Congress and the Memorandum of the President's Advisory Council on Executive Organization[3] (Ash Council) upon which it was based gave less than adequate consideration to the criteria underlying executive reorganization. Some criteria were identified, but more attention should have been given to their implications in a proposal of such far reaching importance and effect. It would have been especially useful to have accompanied the proposed restructuring with plans and procedures for the subsequent evaluation of its effectiveness and for modifying and correcting its arrangements in the light of experience and of specified criteria, not only for effectiveness but for responsiveness and responsibility. Some important questions regarding the implications of the reorganization for the exercise of public initiative and authority do not appear to have been considered. They are likely to be asked, however, in such congressional hearings as may eventually be held on the reorganization bills.

Finding an appropriate structure for environmental policy and administration is not feasible unless a broader range of public purposes is considered. Environmental considerations obviously affect almost every governmental program, in some degree. And the present distribution of environment-relating activities among different departments and independent agencies would necessitate changes in their structure, should environmental activities be removed. For these reasons, and to this extent, the President's comprehensive approach to reorganization has been correct. But, should changes in the structure of government of this magnitude and this importance be treated primarily as a technical, and largely as a presidential, function?

The President has obviously expected the Congress to share in the final decision regarding his proposals. But public interest and the probability of congressional acceptance might have been increased had the President's advisory committee been a broader representative body, with congressional participation. Developing a better organizational plan is only the first half of the reorganization task. Obtaining acceptance may be as difficult. Public understanding of the proposal is needed, not only to obtain legislative acceptance but to facilitate implementation of the plan once it is put into effect. A greater measure of openness in planning and in review of proposals could have this important educative benefit.

Restructuring the Executive Branch is not a suitable task for a coalition of special-interest horse traders, or a national town meeting: but the Ash Council, drawn almost exclusively from the nongovernmental business community, was too narrowly based for the task. Nevertheless, its recommendations may be taken as an important first step toward a reorganization of the Executive Branch that is long overdue. What is needed, above all and was notably missing from the Ash Council Report, is a carefully thought-out rationale for functional/structural relationships in the federal government. There is a philosophy of government and of public priorities implicit in both the council's report and the President's proposals. The President was more articulate regarding underlying values and was less committed to a predominant economic orientation for public affairs than his advisory council. But much more is implied in this exercise than any of its published output has revealed.

Restructuring for environmental administration, other than through specific incremental improvements, belongs to a much larger effort to redefine the purposes and functions of the federal government. For this great task, nothing less than a joint presidential-congressional national commission seems appropriate. Its membership should consist of individuals whose experience, thoughtfulness, and ability to transcend parochial and special-interest representation has been attested by past performance. The President's reorganization plan could constitute an appropriate point of departure for this commission.

It is possible that the proposals for structural change growing out of this broader-based review might not differ greatly in form and function from those recommended by the Ash Council. The very important difference should be in the philosophy of federal public service and rationale for executive reorganization that the President and his advisers did not adequately provide. For it is not enough to know how agencies are to be brought together functionally. It is equally, if not more, important to know how this relationship is to affect goals and strategies.

The Council on Environmental Quality (CEQ), for example, has been established as a statutory agency in the Executive Office of the President. Its history during the first two years of its existence has been primarily the administration of Section 102 of the National Environmental Policy Act of 1969. Its situation in the Executive Office has been a source of both strength and limitation. Implicit in its statutory organization is a leadership role in the formulation of national environmental policy. But constitutional prerogative in policy definition rests with the President and the Congress. The council's influence on policy must therefore be indirect and persuasive. It possesses the structure and mandate needed for policy leadership, but its political base is less adequate. Unlike the Council of Economic Advisers, it has no specific joint committee in the Congress to receive and consider its reports. It may not be able to differ greatly from predominant viewpoints in the Executive Branch. Thus, the mere existence of a high-level advisory body on environmental policy issues is no guarantee that its views will be considered or that it will even formulate policy positions to recommend to the President and the Congress. Changes in its political milieu would be required if it were to become a major independent force for policy formulation.

The environmental issue implies a new outlook and emphasis in American government, in many respects contradictory to hitherto prevailing assumptions. Past assumptions are reflected in the present structure. Unless a new structure facilitates the new purpose—consistent with other major objectives—the results will be frustration, disappointment, and a continuing decline of public confidence in government. Much more is at stake than government's handling of environmental issues, important as they may be.

DEVELOPING EFFECTIVE PROCEDURES

Whatever the structure, a variety of methods are available to give effect to environmental policies. These methods, or approaches, to policy objectives fall into four general sets. They are not, however, fully comparable or alternative. No single approach leads to all desirable objectives. They are, in brief:

1. Self-executory; for example, the pricing of pollution and other forms of environmental degradation through taxes, licenses, and rebates.

2. Self-helping; for example, establishment of "environmental rights" which may be enforced through judicial action.

3. Technological: for instance, specifications regarding applications of technology; assistance for development of ameliorating technological innovations.

4. Administrative; for instance, air and water quality standards; controls over emissions, land use, waste disposal, and other environment-affecting behaviors.

All these approaches have been undergoing rapid change. It would not be useful to dwell upon them in any great detail. Because no one of them answers all purposes and each has certain advantages, their use in combination offers optimal implementation of environmental policies.

Self-Executory Approach

The self-executory approach minimizes governmental regulation, and through taxes or other fiscal devices is designed to cause polluters to adopt environmental protection measures in their own economic self-interest. The effectiveness of this approach depends on the availability of effective protective technologies and the pricing of the so-called "right to pollute" to discourage as much pollution as is economically feasible. This method is most readily applicable to those aspects of environmental policy having to do with pollution and consumption. Simplicity and economy of administrative costs are in its favor. It deserves to be used more extensively—for example, to reduce redundant outdoor advertising.

Self-Help Approach

The self-help approach also reflects a reluctance to depend upon public administration for environmental protection. Its advocacy has often been premised on the unwillingness of the public agencies to protect the environmental "rights" of the individual citizen. The tendency of regulatory agencies to become symbiotically associated with the interests regulated is cited as a reason for preferring a tangible court order to the will-o'-the-wisp of administrative action. "Sue the bastards" has been the motto of the more determined environmentalists, but litigation is a method also available to environmental protection agencies in government, and it has also been used. The law permitting, self-help remains the ultimate resort when all other methods fail.

The class-action suit has rapidly become the major method by which individual citizens have collectively challenged governmental action on environmental issues. This remedy, however, was sharply attacked by Solicitor General of the United States Erwin N. Griswold, in defending the government against a suit brought by the Sierra Club to enjoin the departments of Agriculture and the Interior from permitting a multimillion dollar tourist and commercial recreation facility to be developed in a national forest and wildlife refuge area in Mineral King Valley in California. In argument before the Supreme Court, the Solicitor General declared that if environmental class-action suits continued to be permitted and to be carried to the Supreme Court, he would " . . . find it very difficult to think of any legal issue arising in government which will not have to await one or more decisions in court before the administration charged with enforcing the law can take action."[4]

Technological Approach

Technological solutions are also sought, in part, to obviate a need for regulatory action. If technology can be employed to solve the environmental problem without inducing unwanted side-effects, it is the ideal protective approach. For example, since low-voltage power lines can be economically placed underground, esthetic and safety regulations regarding their overhead placement are becoming less important. Recycling and recovery technologies could greatly reduce enforcement costs of air and water pollution control. Government assistance for research and development in environmental protection technology should, therefore, be understood as a method of administering environmental protection policy.

Administrative Approach

Administrative regulation implies surveillance and control of environment-affecting behavior. It extends from standard setting and quality control enforcement, as administered by the Environmental Protection Agency, to the outright management of environmental services, chiefly at state or local levels of government. In part, regulation is evidence of the inadequacy, or inadequate use, of the aforementioned procedures. For example, total elimination of internal combustion automobile engines or of factory stack emissions would remove the need for their regulation—but might create a new need in some other aspect.

Public Ownership

Public initiative and direct management are often more effective approaches to environmental objectives than attempts to regulate. For example, public planning of urban growth and of land use could hardly be less effective than attempts to regulate the private interest performance of these activities. Public ownership of land could—not inevitably would—greatly facilitate the reshaping of America's urban and rural environments. Popular prejudice against extensive public ownership and direct management of land has become increasingly irrational, as the great mass of Americans would tend to benefit from it and only the relatively few who are successful speculators and developers would be disadvantaged.

Rational choice among administrative procedures cannot be made without considering the institutional and political setting in which action is to occur. In the United States, the complexity and uncertainty of this setting argues in favor of a pluralistic or multi-instrumental approach. If no single method or group of methods appears clearly to be the answer to an administrative need, the course of wisdom may be to try anything that has any plausible possibility of success. In any case, as we have noted, the problems of the human environment differ to a degree that precludes any "best method" as a panacea for dealing with them collectively.

A Task of Synthesis

The task of environmental administration may most realistically be understood as a part of the price that man must pay for taking control of evolution from natural forces. Since the beginning of history, man has progressively substituted artificial systems of his own contrivance for direct dependence on natural systems. Nature, however, maintains her own systems, but not man's. Human technologies are not self-renewing; all eventually run down or wear out, and all are ultimately dependent upon the continuing operation of the natural systems of the biosphere from which they derive their energy or substance. The survival of civilized man is thus contingent upon maintaining his own contrived systems and their essential bases of support in the natural world. Environmental administration has now become necessary, because the unprecedented expansion of human population and technology has imposed stresses upon all systems, natural and artificial; these stresses threaten the survival of the systems, and hence the survival of civilized man.

Reduced to essential terms, the task of environmental administration may be defined as integrating the operation of man's artificial systems with those of the natural world. The objective of this task is the satisfaction of human needs and values, qualitative as well as quantitative, psychological as well as material, esthetic as well as economic. The environmental crisis is a consequence of maladjustments among the systems of man and those of nature, and resource depletion, pollution, and qualitative deterioration of the environment are consequences. In most cases, the human error is to extract from the environment more than natural systems can renew or to overwhelm their capacity to absorb and recycle the residual products of man's activities.

To optimize relations between artificial and natural systems it is chiefly necessary to avoid constructing man-made systems in places and in ways that unnecessarily destroy benefits that man is receiving from natural systems. Wherever natural systems are, in effect, working for man—producing effects beneficial to human welfare—artificial systems should intrude only after a careful weighing of probable gains and losses. Examples of need for better systems articulation may be found in human developments affecting coastal, estuarial, and inland marshlands, in the practices of surface mining, in highway and airport construction, and in the sub-division of land for residential and industrial purposes. Not all natural systems operate to human advantage, but environmental disorders result more often from human interference with those that are beneficial than from adverse effects—for instance, climatic change or continental subsidence—attributable primarily to "nature."

The tasks of systems articulation are too varied, complex, and dynamic to be dealt with solely through automatic or self-executory means. Engineering and administration based on verifiable scientific research are unavoidable tools of public policy directed toward simultaneous advancement of civilized conditions and the maintenance of man's natural life-support systems.

The task of environmental administration, therefore, implies a systems or holistic approach to its mission. For example, the organization of the Environmental Protection Agency was strongly influenced by the interconnections among the forms and manifestations of pollution, and the flow and transformation of pollutants through the various media of the biosphere. The structure of the EPA should enhance the possibility of its effectively integrating environmental protection measures with the operations of man-made and natural systems.

The emerging recognition of need for international institutional arrangements for environmental protection and control has stimulated serious examination of the kinds of administrative structures and procedures that might be feasible and effective within the present configuration of world politics. Illustrative of one of the more detailed and carefully thought out analyses of the problem of international environmental administration is a report to the United States Department of State by the Committee on International Environmental Programs of the National Academy of Sciences.[5] It is becoming increasingly clear that effective control over man's impact upon his environment will require concerted action at all political levels, from local to global. Administrative regulation for environmental protection and control will, in the nature of the problems encountered, increasingly be seen as an intergovernmental and transnational problem for which new institutional arrangements and administrative procedures will be required. To those familiar with past failures of international control efforts, this prospect may seem utopian. But it may be even more utopian to believe that nations can continue indefinitely to serve their perceived short-range, exclusive interests without regard for the ultimate consequences of environmental degradation. National action on environmental issues in the future seems certain to take place against a background of international concern to a degree seldom found with regard to more clearly localized domestic issues.

The ultimate task of environmental quality agencies at all political levels, and especially at the top of each administrative hierarchy, is a task of synthesis. This consideration implies a structure and a criterion for personnel selection that will facilitate the integrative synthesizing functions of the work to be done. To achieve their intended effects, and to avoid unintended consequences, administrative regulations for environmental control should be developed within a general strategy for reaching a specified state of future environment. Such a strategy would require consideration of such basic issues as the numbers and distributions of future populations, the emphasis of the economic system, the role of science in society, and the suitability of institutional arrangements for accomplishing agreed-upon purposes. At whatever political level these tasks are undertaken, their relationship to action at other levels must be considered if effective results are to be obtained.

Attention to the technical and tactical aspects of environmental administration will always be required. It is important to monitor their effects, not only upon the specific environmental problem with which they are concerned, but also upon the operations of the relevant socio-ecological system as a whole, and this may, in some instances, imply international surveillance. Administrative policy and organization should provide for this need, as they do in the separation of the policy and surveillance functions of the Council for Environmental Quality from the operational functions of the EPA and other environment-related control agencies. It would accordingly be a major strategic error to remove the CEQ from the Executive Office of the President to a "line operation" in a department of natural resources or environment—a possibility implied in the Ash Council Report. The only feasible move would be a lateral move into a national planning agency, independent of personal control by the President and equally answerable to the Congress. This development would be improbable unless presidential government were to be modified, perhaps informally, in the direction of cabinet responsibility. An executive branch of hardly more than seven super-departments would seem to increase the feasibility of such a possibility.

If the growing problems of the environment are as serious as even moderate observers believe, major changes in the structure and procedures of public administration are unavoidable. These changes can be avoided only if the problems spontaneously disappear, or society proves unable or unwilling to cope with them. Each of these eventualities seems less probable than the probability of institutional change.

ENDNOTES

1. Paul Leicester Ford, ed., *Kentucky Resolutions* (1798); *Works*, vol. 8, p. 475.
2. *Weekly Compilation of Presidential Documents*, vol. 7, no. 13, pp. 541–545.
3. *Memoranda for the President of the United States: Establishment of a Department of Natural Resources; Organization for Economic and Social Programs.* February 5, 1971. Submitted by the President's Advisory

Council on Executive Organization, this document was intended for consideration within the Executive Office and was not generally published.
4. Note comment in *The Washington Post,* November 18, 1971; *The Evening Star* (Washington, D.C.), November 17, 1971; and *The New York Times,* November 18, 1971.
5. *The Institutional Implications of International Environmental Coöperation.* A Report to the Department of State by the Committee for International Environmental Programs (Washington, D.C.: National Academy of Sciences, November 1, 1971).

8

herman mertins, jr.

THE "NEW FEDERALISM" AND FEDERAL TRANSPORTATION POLICY

The character of federal transportation policy making is undergoing a significant transformation. To some, the current period reflects little more than uncertainty and hesitancy about the roles that federal leadership should play, or not play, in responding to the enormous challenges of providing for national mobility in all of its forms. But the currents of change run far deeper than the surface waters indicate. Indeed, what appears to be taking place represents a fundamental reorientation of the Executive Branch. The specific form is the application of the "New Federalism"—with its emphasis on decentralized responsibility and power—to transportation policy making.

Present ferment is not without its disturbing contradictions and unanticipated consequences. These range from the problems produced by specific outputs of applied policy, which are experienced at state and local levels, to the growing number of dilemmas faced by top-level organizational entities, which play vital parts in evolving the substance of national transportation policies.

But this is not to imply that the fruits of change within the federal establishment can be assessed meaningfully by focusing solely on the impacts of applying a different "philosophy of government." For while these transpire, the *policy environment* of planning for transportation continues its own metamorphosis. New and modified

Reprinted from the *Public Administration Review*, journal of the American Society for Public Administration. Volume XXXIII, #3 (May-June, 1973). ©Copyright 1973 by the American Society for Public Administration.

patterns of need and response, encompassing both the public and private sectors, are constantly generated.

Transportation policy making involves highly complex, interactive processes. Even if no conscious policy framework exists at the federal level, planning for transportation adjusts and evolves in some form or other. The functions of transportation are that fundamental.

This article will examine the interaction of the New Federalism with several major features of transportation policy making, as well as with policy areas impacting directly on transportation policy. No pretenses are made to suggest that facets discussed constitute the bulk of important variables now influencing federal policy activities. In fact, most of the article's attention will be devoted to one major aspect of emerging changes—that which affects the movement of passengers in ground transportation. Even here, treatment of interactions must be oversimplified.

Of the elements of federal transportation policy making being influenced by the New Federalism, the following appear most prominent: (1) the policy setting, including the Executive structure most responsible for evolving policy; (2) present federal financial aids for transportation; (3) the impact of impoundments as they have been applied to transportation; (4) plans for new financing schemes, particularly general and special revenue sharing; (5) national policies, or the lack of such policies, governing environment, energy, and land use; and (6) proposals for Executive Branch reorganization. In practice, these factors defy indivisibility; they perform as highly interactive elements in a much more elaborated network.

THE POLICY SETTING

In its earliest period, federal transportation inputs were made on an ad hoc basis with little attention to interrelationships among modes of transportation. The overriding drive was to encourage development of all facilities of transportation. Growth in capacity—whatever its form—was considered a "good." Another early concern involved the cost of transportation; this encouraged developments which would provide "ready substitutes" for the various modes.[1]

Matching these piecemeal actions was the fragmented nature of the federal organization concerned with transportation policy making. In fact, it was not until the mid-1960s that the Department of Transportation was established.[2] The Department thus inherited a legacy of transportation development within individual modes; each occupied a unique "policy compartment."

The spirit of the legislation and hearings surrounding creation of DOT was that it would function as a "holding company" for most of the components of federal structure concerned with transportation. Transportation development was viewed primarily as a *functional* policy goal to be pursued on its own merits, rather than as a facilitator or ingredient in processes designed to serve other ends. In this way, DOT assumed the posture of providing "one roof" under which the Executive Branch could coordinate and consolidate the fragmented pieces of "national transportation policy."

One further point concerning the Department of Transportation deserves explication—the matter of leadership and initiative. In spite of the restrictions placed by Congress on the freedom of action of the Secretary of Transportation, so encompassing was its legislative charge that opportunities for exercising initiatives proved numerous.[3]

As the first Secretary of DOT noted, up to then the national transportation system was left with a minimum of interference by government; competition was depended on to resolve conflicts. But the new DOT created, for the first time, a centralized mechanism for national transportation planning. And this capacity intensified as planning gained renewed respectability in the late 1960s. In a number of ways, growth of the reputation of DOT initiatives was enhanced during the first Nixon Administration under the leadership of John A. Volpe.

However, a new brand of policy yeast in the transportation "cake"—New Federalism—now signals a sharp turn, even reversal, in direction. Specifically, it espouses return of policy initiatives to state and local governments, the "grass roots." Nor is this change in emphasis simply a matter of rhetoric. As will be discussed shortly, the programmatic contents of virtually all major planning and funding programs, as well as federal organizations with transportation policy-making capacities, stand to be substantially reoriented.

FEDERAL FUNDING FOR TRANSPORTATION—THE CHANGING SCENE

Certainly the most critical elements of federal transportation policy making are the level, and character, of federal financial support. One aspect of the total financial picture illustrating the nature of emerging federal policy making, particularly as it begins to take on the imprint of the New Federalism, is aid devoted to urban transportation.

Significant federal involvement in dealing with urban transportation problems is relatively recent. It started in a limited way with the Housing Act of 1961 which initially authorized $50 million for federal loans to be used to acquire and improve mass transportation facilities in urban areas and $25 million for transit demonstration grants.

But perhaps the greatest single impetus for reorienting federal policy toward more direct, meaningful involvement was the Transportation Message of President John F. Kennedy, delivered in 1962.[4] It paved the way for subsequent legislation by outlining the needs for continuing demonstration grants, comprehensive planning in urban areas (as a qualification for receiving aid), and other programs.

One of the products of the Kennedy approach was the Urban Mass Transportation Act of 1964; it has served as the primary instrument for rendering such federal assistance since its passage. The Act initially authorized a $375 million program.

Recent Approaches

The year 1970 witnessed the emergence of a more sweeping approach to urban transportation problems in the form of the Urban Mass Transportation Assistance Act.[5] Developed within the Nixon Administration by DOT, the Act was to provide for a federal program of assistance that was to amount to $10 billion over a 12-year period. Further, it authorized the incurrence of obligations amounting to $3.1 billion in the first five years.

Assessed in terms of their responsiveness to national urban needs, these programs appear more significant in intent than commitment. This appears most obvious in capital grant activity which has as its objectives:

1. Providing mobility for urban residents who cannot use autos.

2. Improving peak hour travel in urban regions.

3. Achieving land use patterns and environmental conditions that enhance urban living.

The record of performance from February 1965 up to 1972 shows that federal funding provided through the Urban Mass Transportation Administration totaled a little over $1 billion for 279 projects.[6]

Why this relatively low level of performance, given the magnitude of the problems extant? Several factors account for the situation. First, except for the last two fiscal years, the level of requests for funding in both the Johnson and Nixon Administrations was limited. Second, Congress has been wary of committing substantial resources, a reaction closely related to the amorphous nature of the clientele to be served—narrowly conceived as the *users* of urban transportation—not the entire urban population. As a consequence, requested levels of funding authorization have been consistently and substantially reduced. Third, UMTA has encountered continuing problems in allocating authorized funds. These have been blamed on delays in securing final budgetary authorizations and in qualifying applicant projects. Fourth, until very recently no effective mass transportation lobby existed that could wield sufficient political clout, in comparison to that fielded by the "established" modes of transporation. And most recently affecting the flow of assistance has been the practice of impounding funds.

Impounded Funds

The interaction of anti-inflation measures, the goals of the New Federalism, and the capacity of federal policy making to be responsive to national transportation needs is well illustrated by the results of impounding funds authorized for mass transportation purposes.

This practice was initiated by the Executive Office of the President and was *first* applied to transportation expenditures. In fiscal 1971, Congress authorized UMTA to obligate $600 million. Subsequently, the Office of Management and Budget limited the amount that could be utilized to a level of $400 million. Of this amount, only $283.7 million was ultimately designated for capital grants. The balance was consumed by UMTA expenses, including R & D and administrative costs.[7] Thus, fiscal 1971, which started out as a "good" year for mass transportation, concluded by looking very much like its predecessors.

Expenditure levels for fiscal 1972 encountered a similar fate. Congress authorized a limit of $900 million; OMB subsequently limited obligations to $600 million and $510 million was ultimately spent.

Yet unclear is what will happen in fiscal 1973. It is estimated that $863.7 million will be spent. If such occurs, effects of impoundments in the previous two years may be eased somewhat, but they cannot be erased.

Executive impoundments of funds are not new; they have been employed for a variety of reasons over the years. Standing in back of such practices are the provisions of the Anti-Deficiency Act[8] that provide for temporary deferrals and control of funds in excess of immediate needs, awaiting congressional action affecting their use, or held in accordance with congressional action.

However, the nature of current practices differs from the past. Its rationale rests on the desire to control the level of *total* federal spending, not on the basis of limiting expenditures because of programs that have encountered technological, administrative, or implementation problems.

Current impoundment practices are not without their defenders. Even DOT pronouncements have provided ready explanations for the policies adopted. The following is typical:

> ... It is not considered as being "withheld" because its planned use is consistent with congressional intent. The Congress provided a total of $3.1 billion of contract authority for the 5-year period 1971–1975. Executive branch apportionments will result in $1 billion of this amount having been used by June 30, 1972, for fiscal 1973, leaving $1.1 billion, or $550 million per year for fiscal years 1974 and 1975.[9]

Questions about Impoundments

Why have these practices been employed to govern allocation of funding or capital grants for urban mass transportation projects? Why has up to one-third of the available grant money been impounded? It could well be that the Administration has serious reservations about the efficacy of the program. It is difficult to tell. No specific basis has been established to justify withholding of federal expenditures for urban mass transportation.

One clue may be the backlog of capital projects awaiting federal matching funds in urban mass transportation. It is staggering— and growing continuously. Indeed, as of this writing, UMTA had over $4 billion of such applications pending. What bases should be used to decide upon the allocation of limited funds? Indeed, in view of the spirit of the New Federalism, the Administration might have concluded that specific decisions of this nature should not be made in Washington and, therefore, have decided to slow the process. Such would then build further pressure for revenue sharing, an approach much more compatible with New Federalism.

Whatever the case, the annual testimony rendered by DOT officials in support of capital grants creates some anomalies. These appear replete with elaborate justifications for authorizing agency funding at levels that, almost without exception, exceed those finally approved by Congress. Virtually all programs recommended fall into the category of "vitally needed." Yet when the matter of budgetary performance is evaluated, one might conclude that numerous new activities, or extensions of existing programs, apparently are not so "vital" after all.

On the surface, at least, the withholding of one-third of UMTA capital grants reflects a lack of federal commitment to continuing past funding practices.[10] But that should not be interpreted as a lack of concern about the need for governmental action. The more basic question may be *which* government should decide and act. Under New Federalism, the expected answer would be "state and local."

The Issue of Operating Subsidies

Also intimately involved with the impact of New Federalism is the growing concern about the need for operating subsidies for mass transportation.

The year 1972 produced a growing tide of pressure for such federal assistance which took form in the proposed Housing and Urban Development Act of 1972. Chapter 6 of the bill included authority for DOT to provide $400 million per year to assist in maintaining urban transport services, Further, under its proposed capital grant program, requirements for local matching grants would have decreased from one-third to 10 per cent.[11]

These provisions ultimately failed to survive in the House. Similar measures included in the 1972 Federal-Aid Highway Act also failed of enactment when the entire piece of legislation died at the close of the 92nd Congress.

How has the Nixon Administration responded to these suggested approaches? Clearly, operating subsidies are most controversial because of the inherent magnitude of funding involved. But just as much of an issue is the problem of determining state and local vs. federal responsibilities. Here, again, the point of contention is not only financial but philosophical.

On the financial side, analyses conducted by DOT concede that there is a "severe problem," that the federal government has some responsibility to help solve it, and that past policies have probably contributed to making it as bad as it is.

One general conclusion reached is that *all* major urban transit systems are faced with a self-defeating cycle of increasing costs, spiraling fares, and a huge drop in ridership.[12] All lead to a decrease in service which, in turn, perpetuates and intensifies the process. Paradoxically, in spite of the implications of this cycle, there is general agreement that mass transit systems must not be allowed to go out of existence because of the drastic effects this would have on the remainder of the transportation system. Nevertheless, this raises the question about whether operating subsidies treat the symptom or the cause.

Then there is the philosophical side of the question. If the New Federalism is to become a reality, what mechanisms should be utilized to transfer not only the power of decision making back to those governmental units closest to the problems but also resources as well? State and local governments already allocate more than $400 million annually for transit operating assistance.

Aside from these problems, operating subsidies present other difficulties. Foremost is the challenge of designing an incentive system that would lead to improved service and more efficient operations. How could the allocation of subsidies be effectively controlled so as not simply to intensify demands for higher wages for transit workers? How could increased use of off-peak capacities be related to incentives? How could varying requirements for subsidies be equitably resolved? How could subsidies be allocated effectively between public and private mass transit carriers, particularly in areas in which they compete for ridership?[13]

It has been proposed that operating subsidies be provided on the basis of passengers carried at, for example, eight cents per trip. But this incentive system, as all others conjured up so far, presents serious problems. In this case, the subsidy would rise as the level of utilization and, presumably, efficiency rose. This would mean that the amount of subsidy would increase when, if anything, the need for it decreased. On the other hand, those operations in difficulty because of decreased ridership would receive less of a subsidy. In some respects, this would be counter to the normal rationale for determining subsidy needs and justifying their continuation.

A Single Urban Fund?

Another facet of the evolving approaches that could affect both the character and composition of urban transportation financing and, consequently, the policy-making framework, is the DOT proposal to establish a single urban fund. This concept grew out of the 1972 Highway Needs Report[14] and reflects a basic component of the New Federalism—discretionary use of the funds exercised by state and local officials rather than federal authorities. Under its provisions, choices on the allocation of funds between highway and mass transit needs would be made on a *decentralized* basis.

If the proposal were adopted, a single urban fund would be authorized at $1 billion in fiscal 1974 and $1.85 billion in fiscal 1975. Such monies would become available for use on *any* public capital transportation project. Forty per cent of the fund would be distributed to the nation's standard metropolitan statistical areas on the basis of their share of the total national SMSA population. A second 40 per cent would be allocated to the states on the basis of their share of the national SMSA population. The remaining 20 per cent would be retained for discretionary use by the Secretary of DOT. All funds would be allocated on a 70 per cent federal and 30 per cent state and local matching basis.[15]

One of the primary goals of the proposal would be to force the 268 major urban areas to develop organizational and administrative mechanisms to deal with their *total* transportation problem on a coordinated basis. This strategy recognizes that most metropolitan areas now lack such consortia. The consortia to be formed would be structured to assure proportional representation, to prepare long-range comprehensive plans, and to take responsibility for the administration of programs.

The nature of this proposal again is consistent with other aspects of federal transportation policy now evolving. The aim is to shift responsibilities for *initiatives* in urban mass transportation away from Washington and to the "scene of action."

Impacts of Revenue Sharing

Of all the financing measures introduced by the Nixon Administration, revenue sharing represents the most fundamental and sweeping departure from past policies. It would drastically alter the character of federal influence in transportation policy making.

Indeed, the impact of "General Revenue Sharing" is already being felt. Under this program,[16] funds amounting to about $30 billion are to be shared with state and local governments over a five-year period. Made available with few stipulations, some of the money has already been used by localities to bolster existing transit systems. In these circumstances, transportation funding has been placed in the position of competing for priority consideration against other pressing state and local needs.

Still pending before Congress is the "Special Revenue Sharing Program For Transportation."[17] It was first proposed by President Nixon in March of 1971; this program would be distilled from 23 existing federal grant-in-aid programs in urban mass transit, airport grants, highway construction, safety, and beautification. Funding to support the allocation structure would be drawn from general revenues, the Highway Trust Fund, and the Airport and Airway Trust Fund. The initial annual level of funding would be $2.6 billion.

The avowed purpose of the program is to *shift downward* the focus of transportation policy making. Of course, an important by-product would also be the passing down of the "hassles" that surround mobilization and allocation of federal funds for transportation purposes.

Many questions surround the efficacy of the revenue sharing approach. As Congressman John J. McFall has noted, it appears to be a simple answer to a complex problem.[18] And he questions the capacity of the states, without direction, to implement *national* policy without federal leadership.

There is also the question of how needs for future development of existing and emerging national *systems*—highways, aviation, rail, high speed ground transportation—can be met by state and local officials.

In addition, concern exists about advancement of the states-of-the-art in transportation. How will advanced technology be fostered and applied under these circumstances? Are traditional political jurisdictions—states, urban areas, counties, towns—capable of dealing with the complexities of transportation policy making in an age characterized by intertwined, interlocked dependencies and relationships?

All of these concerns must be traded off against the potential advantages of encouraging decentralization of policy making.

OTHER INTERLOCKING POLICY CONCERNS

Closely associated with the content of federal transportation policy making, and often integral parts of it, are plans and programs to govern management of the environment, provide for energy needs, and determine land use. Each of these will be analyzed briefly in terms of implications of the New Federalism and their interfaces with transportation policy.

Environmental Policy

In general terms, the relationships of environment to transporation have been provided for within the federal transportation policy framework.

In DOT, the position of Assistant Secretary for Environment and Urban Systems was established in fiscal 1969 to deal with the problem of achieving a balance between human values and engineering values in the development of transportation systems. Both under the provisions of the Transportation Act of 1966 and the National Environmental Act of 1969, measures have been taken to safeguard parks, recreational facilities and other public lands, public water supplies, urban and rural aesthetics, historical sites, and the like. All projects subject to NEPA must be accompanied by an environmental impact statement. Indeed, numerous projects have been stopped or modified, even retroactively, in the past three years.

Energy Policy

Unlike the approach taken to deal with environmental problems related to transportation, little has been accomplished to cope with the implications of the "energy crisis" as it affects federal transportation policy making. In part, this is explained by the lack of federal commitment to *national* planning for energy needs. The result has been a piecemeal focus on the narrow band of needs that affect the immediate future.[19]

Within DOT, research has been undertaken on obtaining new sources of petroleum, increasing efficiency of its use, and developing new power sources. However, one senses neither a mood of urgency nor commitment of substantial resources to these endeavors. This, in spite of the fact that national transportation is 98 per cent highway dominated and, therefore, petroleum dominated. Will such systems be able to perform under the conditions and constraints of 1990 and beyond? Can such questions be coped with by state and local government?

Land Use Policy

The development of a national land use policy still awaits formulation and implementation sometime far into the future. Indeed, the needs for such policy are only dimly perceived. The most recent, proposed legislation to give serious attention to the problem was the Land Use Policy and Assistance Act of 1972.

This legislation was not adopted by Congress. It would have stimulated the first significant federal involvement in land use regulation, emphasizing state programs for areas of critical environmental concern, key facilities, regional and large-scale developments, and coastal zones.

According to federal projections, the land use challenges to be met are overwhelming. These include needs to build as many homes, schools, hospitals, and other public facilities before the year 2000 as were built in the past 300 years.

The vastness of this problem of appreciating the interaction of transportation policy and land use policy has been recognized, at least in one respect. In a statement submitted to Congress in 1972, DOT called for a redefinition of the *role* of transportation, particularly in urban areas. It noted that transportation should be viewed as a subsystem within an overall urban system of interrelated parts.[20] The suggested DOT strategy called for rational definitions of broad community goals. From these would stem the suggested means for governing orderly growth and the respective roles that the modes of transportation might perform in accomplishing them.

Most significant in these pronouncements, as they suggest the silhouettes of future policy, is the view that the substantial responsibility for determining future *national* land use patterns ought to be lodged with the states and local governments. Again, the dominant theme of the New Federalism is decentralized prerogatives. But one must ask: Are these sufficient?

ORGANIZATIONAL CHANGE AND FEDERAL POLICY

As part of his State of the Union Message of January 22, 1971, President Nixon called for a sweeping reform of the federal Executive structure, including those elements charged with the responsibility for formulating and implementing federal transportation policies. As

Figure 1 demonstrates, one of its effects, if enacted, would be to eliminate the existing Department of Transportation.

Of the numerous changes involved, the most significant would be the shearing away of federal highway programs and urban mass transportation programs, which would be located in the Department of Community Development, from the balance of existing transportation programs, which would shift to the Department of Economic Affairs.

While the organizational implications are important, the underlying philosophy is even more so. Essentially, the change would result in approaching the planning of highways and mass transportation not in terms of *national* sub-systems of transportation but rather as integral parts of *community*, or local planning.[21] Thus, transportation, as a function, would no longer be considered a viable organizing concept.

Numerous concerns have been voiced about the proposal; however, a thorough review of them is beyond the scope of this article. Only several related to transportation policy making can be touched upon here.

First, the proposed reshuffling of transportation responsibilities would occur just when DOT, created in 1966, was reaching a reasonable degree of efficiency. In effect, the case for changes that would "put like functions under one roof" follows within only a few years a similar rationale used in the strong case made to create DOT.[22] A related point is that the reorganization would once again relocate UMTA; the agency moved from HUD to DOT only four years ago.

A second objection centers on its impact on achieving coordinated *systems* of transportation. How would the new organizations cope with national intermodal planning?

A third objection notes that about 80 per cent of the federal-aid highway mileage lies outside of towns and cities and that the programs are predominantly national in impact. It asks: How could such systems be planned and controlled effectively if state and local prerogatives predominate?

A fourth objection relates to the organizing concept of the Department of Community Development, particularly its amorphous character. Would not any federal program qualify for inclusion, since all have some direct or indirect bearing on community development?

While prospects for approval of this proposal for reorganization appear dim, its contents remain important to understanding emerging emphases of federal transportation policy making.

As noted in the analyses of other factors interacting with and

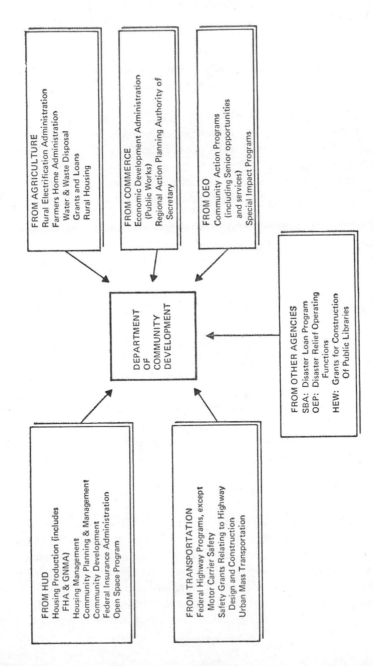

FIGURE 1 Transfers to the proposed department of community development.

reshaping federal transportation policy making, the plan represents yet another of the concerted steps taken to reorient the federal role in transportation policy making. It reflects the movement toward increasing state and local prerogatives in the planning process, setting goals and relative priorities, and securing and determining the disposition of federal funding.

Assertiveness and leadership in federal transportation policy making are being systematically de-emphasized. In their place, roles emphasizing technical assistance, facilitation, and low-key influence appear to be emerging.

The nature of the New Federalism is not necessarily to withdraw from the many battles of forging viable policies; however, movement of the federal forces out of the "front lines" has become increasingly evident.

The question remains whether other governmental jurisdictions will have the human, financial, and technical capacities, as well as the political courage, to cope successfully with the challenges now being shifted to them. An equally basic question is whether successful approaches to national transportation problems can be formulated by the individual or confederated actions of state and local government.

CONCLUDING COMMENTS

As this brief examination of federal transportation policy making concludes, I should note that the definition of a comprehensive national transportation policy has been an elusive goal pursued by both the Executive Branch and Congress over the past five decades. The present Administration, following past practice, has avoided formulating such a policy statement, although voluminous data bearing on it have been collected. Of course, the real possibility exists that such a policy statement is not desired. Certainly the formality of a plan or compendium of guides is not a prerequisite of policy.

Future federal transportation policy may well continue to eschew formal statements and elaborations in favor of specific actions within substantive program fields. Moreover, during the remainder of the Nixon Administration, policy will probably be elaborated in terms of the desires and requirements of state and local governments.

This would represent the New Federalism in action. Presumably, the strategy would be to somehow amalgamate these into a coherent national tapestry. If such indeed becomes the goal, it remains to be seen how the design is chosen and who performs the weaving.

ENDNOTES

1. Herman Mertins, Jr., *National Transportation Policy in Transition* (Lexington, Mass.: D.C. Heath and Company, 1972), pp. 3-20.
2. *Ibid.*, pp. 77-103.
3. *Ibid.*, pp. 91-103.
4. "The Transportation System of Our Nation," Message from the President of the United States, House of Representatives, Document No. 384, 87th Congress, 2nd Session, April 5, 1962.
5. Public Law 91-453.
6. *Department of Transportation and Related Agencies Appropriations for 1973*, Hearings Before a Subcommittee of the Committee on Appropriations, House of Representatives, 92nd Congress, 2nd Session, Part 2 (Washington, D.C.: U.S. Government Printing Office, 1972), pp. 751-752.
7. *Urban Mass Transportation*, Hearing Before the Subcommittee on Housing of the Committee on Banking and Currency, House of Representatives, 92nd Congress, 2nd Session (Washington, D.C.: U.S. Government Printing Office, February 23, 1972), p. 44.
8. 31 U.S. Code 665.
9. *Department of Transportation and Related Appropriations for 1973, op. cit.*, Part 1, pp. 74-75.
10. The one-third cutback is also justified by the Nixon Administration on the grounds that even though "reserve limits" have been imposed, the amount of federal spending devoted to capital grants is greater than ever before. See the testimony of then Secretary of Transportation John A. Volpe, *ibid.*, p. 72.
11. Mertins, *op. cit.*, p. 170.
12. *Urban Mass Transportation, op. cit.*, p. 79.
13. *Department of Transportation and Related Appropriations for 1973, op. cit.*, Part 2, pp. 613-614; Part 3, pp. 12-13.
14. *1972 National Highway Needs Report*, Federal Highway Administration, U.S. Department of Transportation (Washington, D.C., March 1972).
15. *Department of Transportation and Related Appropriations for 1973, op. cit.*, Part 2, pp. 647-648.
16. The program was established by Public Law 92-000.
17. "Revenue Sharing for Transportation," Message from the President of the United States, House of Representatives, Document No. 71, 92nd Congress, 1st Session, March, 18, 1971.
18. *Department of Transportation and Related Appropriations for 1973, op. cit.*, Part 3, p. 277.
19. *Ibid.*, p. 11.
20. *Ibid.*, p. 115.
21. *Department of Community Development Act*, Report of the Committee on Government Operations, No. 92-1096, House of Representatives, 92nd Congress, 2nd Session (Washington, D.C.: U.S. Government Printing Office, May 25, 1972), pp. 2-65.
22. Mertins, *op. cit.*, pp. 77-80.

FURTHER READINGS

BISH, ROBERT L. *The Public Economy of Metropolitan Areas.* Chicago: Markham, 1971.

CALDWELL, LYNTON K. "Environment: A New Focus for Public Policy." *Public Administration Review,* vol. 23 (September 1963), pp. 132–139.

CALDWELL, LYNTON K. "Environmental Policy as a Catalyst of Institutional Change." *American Behavioral Scientist,* vol. 17, no. 5 (May–June, 1974), 711–730.

GILMOUR, ROBERT S. "Political Barriers to a National Policy." *Proceedings of the Academy of Political Science, The National Energy Problem.* 31: 2 (December, 1973), 183–194.

GREEN, EDITH. "The Educational Entrepreneur—A Portrait." *Public Interest,* no. 28 (Summer, 1972), 12–25.

HART, JOHN. "Executive Reorganization in the USA and the Growth of Presidential Power." *Public Administration,* vol. 52 (Summer, 1974), 179–191.

HOLTZMAN, ABRAHAM. *Legislative Liaison: Executive Leadership in Congress.* Chicago: Rand McNally, 1970.

LEVINE, ROBERT A. *Public Planning.* New York: Basic Books, 1972.

LINDBLOM, CHARLES E., *The Policy-Making Process,* Englewood Cliffs, N.J.: Prentice-Hall, 1968.

LOWI, THEODORE J. "Four Systems of Policy, Politics, and Choice." *Public Administration Review,* vol. 32, no. 4 (July–Aug., 1972), 298–310.

MCCONNELL, GRANT. *Private Power and American Democracy.* New York: Alfred A. Knopf, 1966.

MOLLENKOPF, JOHN and JON PYNOS. "Property, Politics, and Local Housing Policy." *Politics and Society,* vol. 2, no. 4 (Summer, 1972), 407–432.

NADEL, MARK. "Economic Power and Public Policy: The Case of Consumer Protection." *Politics and Society,* vol. 1, no. 3 (May, 1971), 313–326.

PORTER, DOUGLAS R. "Regions and Federal Policy: The Orphan Annie of the New Federalism." *The Bureaucrat,* vol. 2, no. 1 (Spring, 1973), 36–44.

PRICE, DON K. "Money and Influence: The Links of Science to Public Policy." *Daedalus,* vol. 103, no. 3 (Summer, 1974), 97–114.

RANNEY, AUSTIN. *Political Science and Public Policy.* Chicago: Markham Publishing Co., 1968.

ROURKE, FRANCIS E. ed. *Bureaucratic Power in National Politics.* 2nd ed. Boston: Little, Brown, 1972.

SANTOS, C. R. "Public Administration as Politics." *Canadian Public Administration,* vol. 12, no 2 (Summer 1969), pp. 213–223.

SEIDMAN, HAROLD. *Politics, Position, & Power, The Dynamics of Federal Organization.* New York: Oxford University Press, 1970.

SHANI, MOSHE. "US Federal Government Reorganization: Executive Branch Structure and Central Domestic Policy-making Staff." *Public Administration,* vol. 52 (Summer, 1974), 193–208.

SHARKANSKY, IRA. *The Maligned States: Policy Accomplishments, Problems, and Opportunities.* New York: McGraw-Hill, 1972.

SHNEIDER, JERROLD E. "Making Government Work." *American Behavioral Scientist,* vol. 17, no. 4 (March–April, 1974), 585–608.

SULZNER, GEORGE T. "The Policy Process and the Uses of National Governmental Study Commission." *Western Political Quarterly,* vol. 24, no. 3 (Sept., 1971), 438–448.

SUNDQUIST, JAMES L., with DAVID W. DAVIS. *Making Federalism Work, A Study of Program Coordination at the Community Level.* Washington, D.C.: Brookings, 1969.

THAYER, FREDERICK C. "Presidential Policy Processes and 'New Administration': A Search for Revised Paradigms." *Public Administration Review,* vol. 31, no. 5 (Sept. - Oct., 1971), 552–561.

WADE, LARRY L. *The Elements of Public Policy.* Columbus: Charles E. Merrill Publishing Co., Inc., 1972.

WADE, L. L. and CURRY, R. L. *A Logic of Public Policy: Aspects of Political Economy.* Belmont, Calif.: Wadsworth, 1970.

WAMSLEY, GARY and MEYER ZALD. "The Political Economy of Public Organizations." *Public Administration Review,* vol, 33, no. 1 (Jan. - Feb., 1973), 62–73.

WHITE, ORION and BRUCE L. GATES. "Statistical Theory and Equity in the Delivery of Social Services." *Public Administration Review,* vol 34, no. 1 (Jan. - Feb., 1974), 43-51.

WOLL, PETER. *Public Policy.* Cambridge: Winthrop Publishers, Inc., 1974.

WOLMAN, HAROLD. "Organization Theory and Community Action Agencies." *Public Administration Review,* vol. 32, no. 1 (Jan. - Feb., 1972), 33-42.

THREE

ORGANIZATIONAL DYNAMICS AND ADMINISTRATIVE LEADERSHIP

The administrative setting is an organizational setting. Much of our awareness of the administrative world is derived from our knowledge about the workings of administrative organizations. Part Three presents several facets of organization and management theory as that theory has evolved, especially in terms of administrative leadership and processes.

Traditionally, organization theory has provided structural frameworks within which the administrative unit would operate most efficiently. Prescriptive organization charts were drawn based on assumptions about the nature of man in an organizational setting. The focus of these charts tended to be on the tasks that the individual performed in an administrative setting. The emphasis was on recommending practical administrative structures under which man would work most effectively to accomplish the administrative goal. The processes of leadership—indeed, leadership itself—were believed to be identifiable and leadership was viewed as dependent on the person following those roles prescribed by the organization chart.

More recently, new attitudes towards administrative organizations have arisen. Contemporary organization and management theories have expanded the range of considerations for understanding the operations of administrative units. These more interdisciplinary, contemporary theories recognize the influences of personal attitudes and behaviors on the administrative organization. They focus on the individual and his environment, emphasizing that administrative man is an individual who is part of a group setting while he works within a broader social environment. The emphasis has shifted from prescribing how people *should* behave toward more accurately describing how people in organizations *do* behave. In addition, they are concerned with how such behavior affects the ability of the administrative unit to complete its given task as well as the extent to which executive leadership is affected by behavioral and environmental factors.

Contemporary organization and management theories utilize the behavioral mode in an attempt to establish meaningful generalizations about administrative activity. They assume that regularities of human behavior can be identified by means of systematic and scientific investigation. Furthermore, they contend that these regularities may be applied to specific adminstrative situations to explain behavior therein. However, in contrast to traditional theory, these approaches are open-ended; as each aspect of human behavior is identified and recorded, there is a great likelihood that additional questions may arise leading to further study.

The development of organizational theories is linked to varying concepts about the nature of administration and the men who administer. Professor James L. Gibson discusses the relationships between assumptions about the nature of man in an organizational setting and the philosophies of organizational theorists that arise from these assumptions. He designates three trends in organization theory: a "traditional-mechanistic focus," a "humanistic, person-oriented trend," and a "realistic-synthesis" in which man and his environment interact.

Gibson describes the traditional focus as a prescriptive attempt to create organizational patterns based on the assumption that man is an inert instrument performing certain given tasks. Man's role is seen as being a *constant*, not a *variable,* in the operation of the organization. Counter to this view, the humanistic approach questions the traditional assumptions and suggests they be replaced by the view that man in the organization is socially oriented and directed. This orientation of man implies that he may at times act in an unpredictable fashion and that certain "unanticipated consequences" may be incompatible with organizational needs.

According to Gibson, the synthesis of these two positions is found in the systems approach where the emphasis is shared among environmental factors and the individual's unique personality. The synthesis occurs as organizational processes are developed that link together these complex patterns of interaction and provide the base for growth, stability, and social interaction beneficial to the organizational unit. By assuming that interpersonal conflict is a regularly occurring organizational characteristic, the realistic synthesis trend utilizes a dimension of organizational reality which, up until now, was considered to be dysfunctional and subject to control.

The objective of administrative organization is to successfully carry out an assigned task or reach a predetermined goal. Effective administration depends largely on the leadership capabilities of those administrators charged with the responsibility of carrying out organizational tasks. However, leadership in administration is far more than a role played by an executive. Rather, it is a process in which the executive, among others, plays a determinant part. As a process, it is dependent upon the interplay of many—and often conflicting—forces. For this reason, leadership has traditionally been viewed as the ability to unite people (groups) within or related to the organization for the purpose of attaining the sought after goal.

Leadership may be reflected in the degree to which the executive influences policy making. However, the student should be aware that policy making may be directed toward either change or the maintenance of the status quo, whichever the goal may be. Under the demands of a changing political and social environment, the administrative leader is likely to face policy-making decisions that will require change. Such change may necessitate new and unique methods for its resolution. Thus a degree of innovation and experimentation becomes part of the leadership role.

There are many prescriptions for effective leadership—from Max Weber's charismatic leader and the bureaucratic system to Richard Neustadt's picture of the President as a "pursuader." Some writers have defined leadership in terms of "traits" or "characteristics," on the assumption that leadership would be more effective if the leader possessed these traits. Others have seen leadership as related to the "situation" and conclude that certain situations demand more of one trait than of another.

Leadership tends to be exemplified through the actions of individuals. The administrative leader is often identified by the position he holds in the organization. We often expect leadership to be exercised by those who possess administrative authority. However, leadership is not restricted to this rather formal context. The leader not only must be in a position to command action and determine policy, but also must be in a manipulator of men and things. He must be willing to take the initiative, to innovate, to compromise, and even to take a "stand on principles" in order to achieve the organizational goal. His success will be determined partly by his personality, character, and ability to sell himself and his program. In addition, he must have access to the necessary information on which he can base his judgments. And increasingly he must have available means that will enable him to effectively utilize and communicate such information. In a practical sense, the process of leadership is to effectively use men and materials, by means of command, persuasion, or both, in order to attain a given task, goal, or policy decision.

Leadership patterns are by no means static. Professors Robert Tannenbaum and Warren H. Schmidt discuss leadership patterns in terms of changing societal and organizational pressures. They view leadership in the context of group dynamics, asserting that leadership is very much affected by the manner in which the leader relates himself to his subordinates. They propose a continuum of possible leadership behaviors with each type related to the degree of authority used by the leader and the amount of freedom available to his subordinates.

They emphasize the leader's need not only to consider what his subordinates are interested in or how they look at things, but also to consider the personal, group, and situational factors which condition his ability to lead in an organizational setting. They conclude that the successful leader may not be viewed primarily as either authoritarian or democratic, but rather sensitive enough to the organizational climate to determine the most appropriate behavior for the given situation.

Their awareness of the variability of leadership patterns is evident in a "retrospective commentary" in which they call for more attention to be given to the interdependence of the managerial, subordinate, and situational forces found in the organization. They recognize the need to be more aware of the forces outside the organization (environmental forces) and the relevant interdependencies between the organization and its environment—a view that is significant to the public leader.

One attribute normally associated with the administrative leader is his ability to make policy or decisions. Organizational research shows, however, that the administrative decision, while perhaps made by an individual, is seldom the result of that one person's knowledge or activity to the exclusion of others. Rather, organizational decisions made by administrative leaders tend to be group related. That is, information generation, analysis, and utilization in the decisional processes come, in part, from groups of individuals working in concert under a variety of influencing factors, only one of which being the superior administrator who requests the information and/or recommendation.

Professor Andre L. Delbecq's paper presents a theoretical model dealing with the decisional processes of organizations, in which he links particular decisional processes to the group structures within the organization. He identifies the task-oriented nature of administrative organizations and suggests that the administrative task not only is the goal of the organization, but also is a variable element affecting organizational operations. He proposes three decision-making strategies which explain the affect of task variances upon organizational decision making: routine (programmed), creative, and negotiated. His models suggests that within each of these strategies, differences in group structures and task identification bring about variations in the context and content of decision making.

Delbecq examines how variances in group structures, roles, processes, styles, and norms affect the types of decision-making strategies utilized and the types of decisions reached. He contends that formal organizations are structured in terms of the predominant task determined by the organization. He adds, however, that if *task* is defined by one organizational member subjectively, (a position that he favors), the role expectations and behaviors, influenced by this definition, may inhibit the processes of decision making. His models suggest that the management of these processes must include accepting variations in task identification and weighing such differences.

The best example of the interrelatedness of leadership and organizational dynamics is the ongoing debate about the nature of Presidential power. Thomas E. Cronin's selection pinpoints the relationship between the "Presidential Establishment" and the nature of the national executive role in policy making. Cronin points out that the "swelling of the presidency" is not necessarily a new phenomenon; sustained growth has been evident in the Executive branch since the early 1900s. However, he shows clearly how the Nixon administration has vastly expanded its staff membership through newly authorized institutions (Council on Environmental Quality, Office of Consumer Affairs, Federal Energy Office, etc.) and has increased its policy impact by dispersing previous domestic policy staff assistants throughout the Cabinet departments.

Cronin suggests that these developments have tended to isolate the executive decision-making procedures from the traditional checks and balances (such as the electoral selection processes and/or congressional oversight) and has tended to reduce the contributions of Cabinet members and executive departments (those most identifiable to the general public) to a minimum. The vacuum left has been filled rather quickly by the influences of anonymous, unelected, and unratified aides whose positions tend to be dependent upon executive approval.

The impact on governmental policy and leadership has been to create an unwieldy, overspecialized, uncoordinated bureaucracy. Cronin contends furthermore that the increased reliance of a President upon his own enlarged staff leads to a loss of the detachment and objectivity so necessary for effective leadership. With this type of organizational structure the temptation to trust a smaller number of close associates in order to reduce the chance of "security leaks" or "special interest pressures" contrary to administration desires increases.

The corrective, according to Cronin, is for Congress to counter the trend of executive expansion by: 1) curbing its own impulse to create new executive agencies; 2) increasing its watchdog role over executive activities; 3) promoting greater coverage by the media of the "establishment;" and 4) reversing the trend of diminishing the importance of the executive departments.

If Professor Cronin's thesis needs testing, what better time for such testing than now, in the midst of the Watergate controversy? Arthur Schlesinger's paper, the "Runaway Presidency," is a clarion call for a renewed analysis of the role of the executive in policy making in the United States. Using Watergate as a backdrop, Schlesinger discusses the crisis of the presidency from an historical, institutional, and political perspective. Noting that in other times there were cries for a diminished executive role, he goes on to discuss suggestions for change ranging from the "plural executive" or the six-year single term restriction on executive power to a call for moving closer to the parliamentary form of government.

He presents the arguments of Senator Ervin to restore the so-called constitutional balance between the executive and legislative branches, as best exemplified by Ervin's role on the Senate Select Committee on Watergate. He points out, however, that Ervin's position runs the risk of creating a generation of weak presidents at a time when domestic crises appear to demand a strong cohesive national presidency.

Rather than any of the preceding, Schlesinger calls for a greater emphasis on making the important decisions of government "shared decisions" based on mutual respect and comity. In effect, this is a call to reopen the executive decisional process and diminish the influence of close associates who are not directly responsible to the public. He suggests that the real effectiveness of control over the presidency lies not in laws, but rather in politics. This would require a decline in the "reverence" for the "institution of the President" and an increase in the more healthy skepticism of earlier days. Finally—almost reluctantly, it appears—Schlesinger concludes that if these mechanisms fail to impede the runaway presidency then the rehabilitation of impeachment will be essential to contain the presidency and preserve the Constitution.

From the two preceding selections, the conclusion might easily be drawn that only a reassertion of political controls over the executive branch head will suffice in creating a more responsible and responsive executive leader. This assumption implies the belief that management or organizational structures cannot be trusted to provide effective checks upon the power of supervisory (executive) personnel. William Eddy suggests that this may not be the case at all. He proposes instead that theories and processes exist in the management sector that may be used to guarantee greater executive effectiveness within the organizational setting without the attendant "political" consequences that might result from a reassertion of political controls over the executive.

Eddy proposes two relatively new approaches to organizational effectiveness. One of these would be technologically based approaches to management control such as PPBS (Planning, Programming, Budgeting Systems) and a second, newer approach would be that of OD (Organizational Development). He contends that the OD model offers the best possibility for retaining the necessary organizational control mechanisms while still providing greater access to and control over behavior which might be dysfunctional.

OD seeks to bring about change and improvement by involving members of the organization in problem analysis and planning. It proposes an alternative normative model for human behavior in organizations based on interpersonal competence, collaboration, and teamwork, and group dynamics and skills. It assumes that increased effectiveness and adaptability will result when analysis is freed from the limitations and restrictions of highly structured and formal organizations.

The application of OD to public organizations has been rather slow to materialize and Eddy suggests several reasons for this delay. He submits that it may appear to some people that OD conflicts with the more traditional bureaucratic structures in its effort to effectively use organizational personnel in order to attain organizational tasks or goals. He proposes that administrators in the public sector should review their own personal values as well as the values inherent in their administrative organizations. They might then find that OD processes could be used more effectively in information gathering and evaluation and prevent the continuing of a "closed system" psychology in public management.

It should be obvious at this time that administrative leadership and organizational dynamics are interrelated processes. Furthermore, leadership cannot be viewed apart from organizational structures and functions nor from the questions arising from external political forces. Any effort to evaluate the leadership abilities or successes of any public official— elected or appointed—will be in a large part linked to the normative perspectives of the evaluators. Nevertheless, research and analysis continues for the purpose of better indentifying and using data that may be helpful in achieving organizational goals. Most likely, those data and processes which best fit our normative "mind-set" will be viewed as being successful; those which do not will likely be criticized.

9

james l. gibson

ORGANIZATION THEORY AND THE NATURE
OF MAN

A recent contribution to the literature of organization theory raises serious questions about the nature of men who participate in organizations.[1]

If Anthony Downs' hypotheses are correct, William H. Whyte's quietly-conservative, status-conscious and security-seeking organization man has been replaced by a new variety whose characteristics are even less admirable than those of his predecessor. If Downs is correct, the organization man of today is suspicious, distrustful, jealous, deceitful, self-centered, apathetic, and immature. He is intolerant of differences, unable to communicate in depth with his fellows, and short-sighted. In short, here is a man whose integrity and moral fiber should be seriously questioned.[2]

Downs, however, is not the only writer to introduce some interesting organizational characters. Robert Presthus developed three personality types to be found in organizations which he called the upward-mobiles, the indifferents, and the ambivalents.[3] Victor A. Thompson and others suggest similarly evocative concepts to describe some of the more irrational behavior of organizations (bureaupathology) and to portray the behavior of some individuals in organizations (bureausis).[4]

If the views of these writers are correct, there is need for a great deal of research and study directed at finding ways of mak-

James L. Gibson, "Organization Theory and the Nature of Man," *Academy of Management Journal*, vol. 9, no. 3 (September 1966), pp. 233-244. Reprinted by permission.

ing life in modern organizations more meaningful. I share the value system of those who believe "that work which permits autonomy, responsibility, social connection, and self-actualization furthers the dignity of the human individual, whereas work without these characteristics limits the development of personal potential and is therefore to be negatively valued."[5] And I value negatively the behavior of organization members who "inevitably distort information which they relay upwards to their superiors or downward to their subordinates,"[6] or who "distort the orders they receive from their superiors, interpreting them to their own benefit . . . as they develop the implications of those orders for their subordinates."[7]

To say the least, the conclusion from the above statements is simply that some organization men are dishonest; to the extent that organizations create conditions which encourage and reward such behavior, to that extent, organization theorists should be concerned.

In the remainder of this article, I outline the development of organization theory in terms of its underlying assumptions regarding the nature of man. My purpose is to stimulate thought and action on two fronts:

1.   To urge organization theorists and practitioners to express explicitly their assumptions about the nature of man; and,

2.   To urge more analysis of ongoing organizations to determine the causes of behavior which Downs, Presthus, and Thompson describe.

This discussion seeks to add to the literature on the philosophy of organizations by emphasizing the value premises which underlie some of the major strands of thought.

The vehicle used to develop the literature is a classification system of three categories: the *mechanistic tradition*; the *humanistic challenge*; and, the *realistic synthesis*. An essential feature of the literature classified in the mechanistic tradition category is the view of man as a constant without peculiar features and malleable without incident into the organization structure; man is characterized as a machine—predictable, repairable, and replaceable. The literature of the humanistic challenge is characterized by an awareness of man as a unique element in the organization structure; man is viewed as having a need structure and individual differences are tolerated. The literature of the realistic synthesis is not easily characterized, but its essential feature is to treat man as one of a number of variables in the organization all of which are interdependent and interacting. Man is seen as being acted upon and as acting on the organization environment.

THE MECHANISTIC TRADITION

The writers of the mechanistic tradition focused on *two* aspects of organization theory.

At *one level*, Frederick W. Taylor and others analyzed the basic tasks of the individual members. The objective of Taylor and his followers was to reduce the contributions of each workman to the smallest, most specialized unit of work possible and to eliminate any uncertainty about the expected outcome. Elementary to such analysis were (and are) work simplification studies which break down manual labor tasks into definite repetitive movements and motion and time studies which establish time standards for the accomplishment of each movement. As Taylor himself said:

> Perhaps the most prominent single element in modern scientific management is the task idea. The work of every workman is fully planned out by the management at least one day in advance, and each man receives in most cases complete written instructions, describing in detail the task which he is to accomplish, as well as the means to be used in doing the work. And the work planned in advance in this way constitutes a task which is to be solved, as explained above, not by the workman alone, but in almost all cases by the joint effort of the workman and the management. This task specifies not only what is to be done but how it is to be done and the exact time allowed for doing it.[8]

To assure that each task is performed according to the plan, the worker is paid on an incentive basis which rewards him for meeting the expectations of the organization and punishes him if he does not. The application of scientism tended to reduce the skills of craftsmen to routine, procedural predictable sequences of movement; workers were to be as interchangeable as the cogs in Eli Whitney's cotton gin.

Underlying the procedural prescriptions of scientific management were definite assumptions about the nature of man. Taylor said:

> A reward, if it is to be effective in stimulating men to do their best work, must come soon after the work has been done. But few men are able to look forward for more than a week or perhaps at most a month, and work hard for a reward which they are to receive at the end of this time.[9]

Later, in discussing the reasons for the failure of profit sharing schemes, he said: "Personal ambition always has been and will remain a more powerful incentive to exertion than a desire for the general welfare."[10] The view that man is motivated solely and predictably by economic considerations and is an isolated factor of production independent of social and group pressures guided the development of scientific management theories and practices.

The postulates of scientific management were quite appealing to those who were concerned with administrative aspects of organizations—the *second level* of analysis.

Wolin suggests that Saint-Simon[11] laid the foundations of organization theory "with the conscious intent of establishing a defense against political instability and social disorder" in the aftermath of the French Revolution.[12] However, it was one hundred years later before a theory of organization structuring was articulated.

The most prominent writers of what is often called "Classical Organization Theory" were Luther Gulick,[13] Henri Fayol,[14] James D. Mooney and A. C. Reiley,[15] and L. Urwick[16] all of whom wrote from the perspective of business or military organizations. These writers owe an intellectual debt to Max Weber who provided the "ideal type" of administrative organization which he called a bureaucracy.[17] Even though Weber's model is based primarily on the European methods of organizing the civil servants (chiefly the Prussian experience), the characteristics of his "ideal type" are illustrative of the main features of classical organization theory.

According to Weber, the essential characteristics of the "ideal type" are as follows:[18]

1. All tasks necessary for the accomplishment of the goals are broken down into the smallest possible unit; the division of labor is carried out to the extent that specialized experts are responsible for the successful performance of specified duties.

2. Each task is performed according to a "consistent system of abstract rules"[19] to assure uniformity and coordination of different tasks. This uncertainty in the performance of tasks due to individual differences is theoretically eliminated.

3. Each member or office of an organization is accountable to a superior for his or its decisions as well as for his or its subordinates. The authority is based on expert knowledge and is sanctioned and made legitimate by the ultimate source of authority—the chief official at the top of the hierarchial pyramid.

4. Each official in the organization conducts the business of his office in an impersonal, formalistic manner. He maintains a social distance between himself and his subordinates and between himself and the clients of the organization. The purpose of this impersonal detachment is to assure that personalities do not interfere with the efficient accomplishment of the mission.

5. "Employment in the bureaucratic organization is based on technical qualifications and is protected against arbitrary dismissal."[20] Promotions are based on seniority and achievement. Because employment is considered a career and the vagaries of making a living are eliminated, a high degree of loyalty for the organization is engendered in the members.

The inherent logic of the bureaucratic structure led Weber to believe that the bureaucratic form of administration is "superior to any other form in precision, in stability, in the stringency of its discipline, and in its reliability. It thus makes possible a particularly high degree of calculability of results for the heads of the organization and for those acting in relation to it."[21] Thus Weber presented the case for bureaucratic administration on precisely the same grounds that the Taylorites presented the case for Scientific Management. In fact Weber himself drew the analogy: "The fully developed bureaucratic mechanism compares with other organizations exactly as does the machine with nonmechanical modes of production."[22]

The bureaucratic form of organization was (and is) prominent in business practice. The proponents of its use in this context formulated "principles" which are obviously in the Weberian tradition. Haynes and Massie have codified these principles as follows:[23]

1. The Unity of Command principle: No member of an organization should report to more than one superior.

2. The Span of Control principle: No superior should have responsibility for the activities of more than five to eight subordinates.

3. The Exception principle: A superior should delegate responsibility for routine matters to subordinates.

4. The Scalar principle: Every organization should have a well defined hierarchial structure.

One is struck by the prescriptive nature of these principles, by their similarity to the characteristics of Weber's ideal type, and by their concern for order and certainty in carrying on the activities of the organization.

The evidence supplied in the foregoing discussion suggests the assumptions regarding the nature of man underlying scientific management and classical organization theory. March and Simon observe that two "views" of organization members are pervasive: "First, in general there is a tendency to view the employee as an inert instrument performing the tasks assigned to him. Second, there is a tendency to view personnel as a given rather than as a variable in the system."[24] Mason Haire has been less polite: "These are the implicit assumptions about man on which classical organization theory seems to me to be based: He is lazy, short-sighted, selfish, liable to make mistakes, has poor judgment, and may even be a little dishonest."[25]

From another perspective, William F. Whyte argues that there are three assumptions underlying the theory: First, it is assumed that "man is a rational animal concerned with maximizing his economic gains," second, "each individual responds to economic incentives as an isolated individual," and third, "men, like machines, can be treated in a standardized fashion."[26]

THE HUMANISTIC CHALLENGE

It was only in the 1930's that these assumptions and their implications for organization theory and practice were seriously challenged. The body of concepts that developed during the initial thrust of the industrial revolution and which I have characterized as mechanistic was soon confronted with evidence that seriously challenged its validity. This challenge (which I call the humanistic challenge) came from two sources:

1. There were those who questioned the basic assumptions of the scientific management approach regarding the motivation of men; and,

2. There were those who questioned the efficiency of the bureaucratic form of organization.

Although the two sources of challenge were seemingly unrelated, the emphasis of both was the same, namely: the participants of organizations are not constants and cannot be regarded as givens; and, a large mass of empirical evidence was soon available to show that participants adjust the environment to meet their individual and group needs. And part of this adjustment process is related to motivations, as some industrial engineers were to discover.

In 1924, engineers at the Hawthorne Works, a division of the Western Electric Company in Chicago, began a series of tests to determine the relationship between certain variables and the rate of production.[27] A number of frustrating experiments caused the scientists to reject their original hypothesis (that a high and positive correlation exists between working conditions and the rate of output) and they formulated alternative hypotheses. The major sources of data for testing the revised hypotheses were the voluminous recordings of interpersonal conversations that the experimenters had accumulated. These conversations between workers and the scientists revealed that the workers were members of closely knit work groups and that these work groups had established acceptable patterns of behavior for the members. These patterns of behavior, in turn, were based on the sentiments of the members of the group, but these sentiments were easily disguised and difficult to isolate. Nevertheless, the scientists discarded their statistical techniques and "denuded of their elaborate logical equipment"[28] they went into the shop to learn the things that were important to the workers.

The findings of the Hawthorne studies challenged the basic assumptions of earlier organization theory, namely the social isolation of the worker and the primacy of economic incentives. For these two assumptions, the human relations school substituted the view that man desires "first, a method living in social relationship with other people, and, second, as part of this an economic function for and value to the group."[29] Thus man (according to Mayo and his followers) "is a uniquely social animal who can achieve complete 'freedom' only by fully submerging himself in the group."[30] Based on the notion of man as a gregarious animal, the human relations school included in their ideology a view of a society in which man could best achieve his freedom. But the industrial society is not such a society and in fact the process of industrialization destroys the cultural traditions of former times which had enhanced social solidarity. The results of industrialization are social disorganization and unhappy individuals.

According to Mayo the responsibility for restoring the bases for social stability belongs to administrators of large industrial firms. With leadership that is human-oriented rather than production-oriented the prospects for social stability and its concomitant, a meaningful life for the individual, are enhanced. In fact Mayo has said: "If our social skills (that is, our ability to secure cooperation between people) had advanced step by step with our technical skill, there would not have been another European war."[31] Thus the ideology of the founders of the "human relations" approach consisted of three parts: (1) a view of man as a social animal, (2) a view of industrial society as incompatible with the basic nature of man, and (3) a view of the solution to man's dilemma as resting with industrial leaders.

The findings of the Hawthorne experiments were exceedingly important to those members of society primarily concerned with rational industrial supervision.[32] It had long been a mystery why workers would restrict output and produce far below standards established by exacting analyses. The Hawthorne studies provided both diagnosis and prescription. The practical application of human relations theory required careful consideration of the informal organization, work teams, and symbols that evoke worker response. Unions were viewed in a new dimension and were seen as making a contribution to effective organization rather than as the consequence of malfunctions in the organization.[33] Participative management, employee education, junior executive boards, group decisions and industrial counseling became important means for improving the performance of workers in the organization. Industrial leaders were spurred on by researchers whose findings indicated that "every human being earnestly seeks a secure, friendly, and supportive relationship and one that gives him a sense of personal worth in the face-to-face groups most important to him."[34] Thus, in practice, the "herd hypothesis" replaced the "rabble hypothesis."

The research methodology, the ideology, and the practice of human relations have been attacked on several points. The methodology of the supporting research is criticized for dealing with only immediate variables and for ignoring the external environment; the work is viewed as static and subject to little change over time. The findings of single case studies do not provide sufficient data for the construction of a rigorous theory of man and his organizations. But at a more fundamental level, the ideological view of man is attacked. "They (the human relations advocates) begin by saying that man dislikes isolation and end by consigning him to the care of the managerial elite for his own salvation."[35] Thus by losing his identity man becomes free or so assert the Mayo-ites.[36]

Critics of the practice of human relations have pointed to a number of defects. Most vehemently criticized has been the use of human relations techniques as means of manipulating workers to accept the superior's view of reality. Indeed, one has said: "I am totally unable to associate the *conscious practice of human relations skill* (in the sense of making people happy in spite of themselves or getting them to do something they don't think they want to do) with the *dignity of an individual person created in God's image.*"[37]

This tendency toward manipulation is, at least in part, due to a misunderstanding of the purpose of the social sciences, "to the belief that the function of the social sciences is the same as that of the physical sciences, namely, to gain control of something outside."[38]

A second misunderstanding, and one springing directly from the ideology of human relations, is the belief that the business firm is a total institution which provides for all the needs of its members and that such an institution has the "right" to demand total loyalty. The attempt to gain total loyalty underlies much of personnel and human relations work; administrators frequently use the tags "loyal service" and "loyal employee" to describe the record of a retiring organization member. On this point Peter Drucker has said: "It is not only not compatible with the dignity of man, but it is not permissible to believe that the dignity of man can or should be realized totally in a partial institution."[39] The present state of human relations theory might be expressed as follows: "Let's treat people like people, but let's not make a big production of it."[40]

The findings of post-Weber studies of bureaucratic behavior are similar to the findings of the Hawthorne studies—the reaction of individuals to organizational factors is not always predictable.[41] Merton,[42] Selznick,[43] and Gouldner[44] suggest that treating people as machines not only leads to unforeseen consequences but can actually reinforce the use of the "machine model." Each researcher studied some form of procedure designed to control the activities of the members of the organization.

Merton analyzed the organizational need for control and the consequent concern for reliability of members' behavior. In order to get the desired results, the organization implements standard rules and procedures. Control is achieved by assuring that the members are following the rules. Merton points out three consequences that result from concern for reliability of behavior: (1) officials react to individuals as representative of positions having certain specified rights and privileges; (2) rules assume a positive value as ends rather than as means to ends; and, (3) decision-making becomes routine application of tried and proven approaches and little attention is given to alternatives not previously experienced.[45] The organization becomes committed to activities that insure the status quo at the expense of greater success in achieving organization objectives.

Selznick studied the consequences of a second technique for achieving control and reliability—the delegation of authority. As in-

tended, the specialized competence required to carry out the delegate tasks has the positive effect of achieving organization goals, but
there are unintended consequences. Delegation of authority "results
in departmentalization and an increase in the *bifurcation of interests*
among the subunits in the organization."[46] Members of the organization become increasingly dependent upon the maintenance of subunits and there is a growing disparity between the goals of the subunit
and the goals of the organization. The content of decisions is increasingly concerned with subunit objectives and decreasingly concerned
with organization goals, except that there must not be too great a
disparity between the two. Subunit officials seek to make legitimate
their activities by squaring their decisions with precedent. Again
there seems to be an inherent tendency in the bureaucratic structure
toward conservatism and the maintenance of the status quo.[47]

Gouldner gives additional support to the thesis that organizational techniques designed to implement control often entail unanticipated results. In his study of industrial organization he found, among
other things, that the improvisation of rules to assure control results
in the knowledge of *minimum acceptable levels of behavior* and that
members of organizations gear their activities to these minimum levels of behavior if there is a high level of bifurcation of interest. As
officials perceive this low performance, they react by increasing the
closeness of supervision and by enacting additional rules and procedures. Again, the unintended consequences are increasing tension
among members, increasing nonacceptance of organization goals, and
increasing the use of rules to correct matters.[48]

To summarize, the essence of the humanistic challenge is that
man in organizations is socially oriented and directed. He has multiple needs which affect and are affected by the work environment; he
reacts unpredictably, yet predictably, to stimuli encountered in the
organization. The "unintended consequences" of bureaucratic methods imply that man may be incompatible with organization needs.
The scene is set, then, for contemporary organization theorists to
devise a synthesis of the two polar positions.

THE REALISTIC SYNTHESIS[49]

An important feature of modern organization theory[50] is the systems
approach which treats organizations as complex sets of mutually dependent and interacting variables. In this framework the participants
are one set of variables which act on all other variables. Because this

paper is concerned only with the place of man in organization theory, I will outline the features of the systems approach (which I term the realistic synthesis) and then return to the discussion of man as a variable in the system.

The systems approach to organization theory presents the opportunity to view the organization as a totality. The emphasis is on the parts of the system, the nature of interaction among the parts, the processes which link the parts, and the goals of the system.[51] The key parts are the individual and his unique personality, the formal structure of jobs, the informal groups, the status and role patterns within the groups, and the physical environment. Relating these parts are complex patterns of interactions which modify the behavior and expectations of each. The basic parts are linked together by certain organizational processes including structured roles, channels of communication, and decision-making. These processes provide means for overcoming the centrifugal tendency of the parts[52] and for directing the parts toward the ultimate goals of the organization—growth, stability and social interaction.[53]

The systems approach is a realistic synthesis because it views the individual as only one of many parts, because it allows for modification of the parts, because it views conflict within the organization as a natural byproduct of group endeavor, and because it anticipates dynamic rather than static patterns of interaction.

The realistic view of man in the organization acknowledges the contributions of the Hawthorne experiments, but it has added certain ideas that go beyond "human relations." The basic premise seems to be that man's needs and the organization's needs are inconsistent.[54] Man's behavior is seen to be motivated by a hierarchy of needs and once the most basic needs are satisfied, the individual turns to the ultimate source of satisfaction—self-actualization. But to achieve self-actualization requires that the healthy individual be "independent, creative . . . exercise autonomy and discretion, and . . . develop and express . . . unique personality with freedom."[55] The organization, however, presents barriers to this development of self-actualization and requires that the individual be dependent upon others for goal-setting and direction and conform to norms far below the level of his ability or expectations. The results of this conflict are immature behavior and frustration-oriented activites, the overt expression being determined by the unique personality of the individual. Argyris' studies indicate that an organization member experiencing frustration and conflict may behave in any one of the following ways.[56]

a. He may leave the organization.

b. He may work hard and become president.

c. He may adapt through the use of defense mechanisms.

d. He may adapt by lowering his work standards and by becoming apathetic.

Other students of organizational behavior also perceive basic conflicts between the organization and the individual. Presthus argues that the reactions of members can be characterized by three bureaucratic types: the upward-mobiles; the indifferents; and, the ambivalents. The upwardmobiles are those who react positively to the organizational requirements and by adopting the sanctioned behavioral patterns succeed in it.[57] The indifferents are the great majority who view their jobs as means to secure off-work satisfactions and who neither seek nor expect on-job satisfaction.[58] The ambivalents are a small minority who are unable to play the organizationally defined role which would enable them to realize their ambitions.[59] The similarity between these three patterns of behavior and the adaptive responses which Argyris lists is evident.

Thus, the contemporary view of the nature of man in organizations recognizes the essential conflict that exists. Whereas: the mechanistic tradition considered conflict to be dysfunctional to organizational purposes and felt that it could be neutralized by monetary payments; and, the humanist challenge viewed conflict as dysfunctional but believed that human relations techniques could control it; the realistic synthesis assumes that conflict is a normal aspect of organization life.

The problem posed then is how to harness the energies of conflict such that both organizational and individual needs are realized. Given the problem, we can accept at the outset that neither will be met perfectly—this being the essence of the conflict.[60] And whether conflict or cooperation is the *essential* nature of man does not seem to be relevant,[61] since research indicates that many organization members are *in fact in conflict* with the requirements of the organization.

ASSUMPTIONS HAVE CONSEQUENCES

I offer no final conclusions as to where recent efforts in organization theory and organization structuring will lead us;[62] all the evidence is not in and final arguments have not been heard. However, it is not difficult to concur with Haire's statement:

> Whenever we try to plan what an organization should be like, it is necessarily based on an implicit concept of man. If we look . . . at the outline of a "classical" organization theory and some more modern alternatives, we begin to see the change in the concept of man.[63]

Of course, to point out the importance of the assumptions which underlie organization theory is my major purpose. Anthony Downs would, perhaps, argue that these modern alternatives are not being tried since his findings indicate that much of classical organization theory is still with us. Perhaps again, the reason for its continued use is that those of us who study organizations have not given sufficient attention to questions that are value-laden.

Specifically, in what kinds of organizations do men behave in the very unattractive ways which Downs depicts? Or more basically, do we consider such behavior to be unattractive? What are the particular features of ongoing organizations that create the climate for such behavior? What variables are controlling and controllable? Or can we dismiss the problem by suggesting that the pressure-packed and anxiety-ridden culture of the times is the real culprit? But if it is concluded that such behavior is a necessary concomitant of organizations, I for one will count it a cost.

ENDNOTES

1. Anthony Downs, "A Theory of Bureaucracy," *American Economic Review, Papers and Proceedings* (May, 1965), pp. 439–446.
2. Downs does not make such harsh indictments of the nature of man; he states only that officials distort information and orders, fear investigations of their activities, champion the status quo, seek consensus of goals, and perform acts that would be embarrassing if publicly known. The adjectives that I use to describe the behavior are my own. The reader is invited to study Downs' paper and draw his own conclusions.
3. Robert Presthus, *The Organizational Society* (New York: Alfred A. Knopf, 1962).
4. Victor A. Thompson, *Modern Organization* (New York: Alfred A. Knopf, 1961) and Marshall E. Dimock, *Administrative Vitality* (New York: Harper and Brothers, 1959).
5. Robert Blauner, *Alienation and Freedom* (Chicago: The University of Chicago Press, 1964), p. 15. fn. 1.

6. Downs, *op. cit.*, p. 443.
7. *Ibid.*, pp. 443-444.
8. Frederick W. Taylor, *Scientific Management* (New York: Harper and Brothers, 1911), p. 39.
9. *Ibid.*, p. 94.
10. *Ibid.*, p. 95.
11. See Henri de Saint-Simon, *Social Organization, The Science of Man, and other Writings*, edited and translated by Felix Markham (New York: Harper and Row, 1965).
12. Sheldon S. Wolin, *Politics and Vision* (Boston: Little, Brown and Co., 1960), p. 376.
13. Luther Gulick and L. Urwick (eds.), *Papers on the Science of Administration* (New York: Institute of Public Administration, 1937).
14. Henri Fayol, *General and Industrial Management* (London: Sir Isaac Pitman and Sons, 1949).
15. J. D. Mooney and A. C. Reiley, *Principles of Organization* (New York: Harper and Brothers, 1939).
16. L. Urwick, *The Elements of Administration* (New York: Harper and Brothers, 1943).
17. Max Weber, *The Theory of Social and Economic Organization*, translated by A. M. Henderson and Talcott Parsons (New York: Oxford University Press, 1947). Michel Crozier in *The Bureaucratic Phenomenon* (Chicago: University of Chicago Press, 1964), a study of the French experience in organization of the civil service, points out three usages of the term bureaucracy: (1) the "traditional usage" is the political science concept of government by bureaus but without participation by the governed; (2) The Weberian usage is the sociological concept of rationalization of collective activities; and, (3) the vulgar usage is the laymen's concept which implies the dysfunctional nature of "bureaucratic" organizations, i.e., red tape, procedural delays, frustrations of agents and clients, p. 3.
18. Weber, *ibid.*, pp. 329-340. For more reflective analyses of the "ideal type" see Peter M. Blau, *Bureaucracy in Modern Society* (Chicago: University of Chicago Press, 1956), pp. 27-56 and Victor A. Thompson, *op. cit.*, pp. 12-21.
19. Weber, *ibid.*, p. 330.
20. Blau, *op. cit.*, p. 30.
21. Weber, *op. cit.*, p. 334.
22. *From Max Weber: Essays in Sociology*, translated by H. H. Gerth and C. Wright Mills (New York: Oxford University Press, 1946), p. 214 and quoted in Blau, *op. cit.*, p. 31.
23. W. Warren Haynes and Joseph L. Massie, *Management* (Englewood Cliffs, N.J.: Prentice-Hall, Inc., 1961), pp. 39-43. Other writers, notably L. Urwick, *op. cit.*, pp. 119-129 have lengthened the list, but the four here seem to be primary. Herbert A. Simon refers to such principles as "proverbs" in *Administrative Behavior* (New York: The Macmillan Co., 1945), pp. 20-36 because they have neither empirical verification nor universality of application.
24. James G. March and Herbert A. Simon, *Organizations* (New York: John Wiley and Sons, 1958), p. 29.

25. George B. Strother (ed.), *Social Science Approaches to Business Behavior* (Homewood, Illinois: The Dorsey Press, Inc., 1962), p. 175. And lest one think that contemporary organizations are free of such assumptions, consider this statement by E. F. Scoutten, Vice-President, Personnel, Maytag Company: "Operating management has long since known what academic experts appear to reject. Many people, perhaps the majority, prefer to accept instruction, direction, and order without question, and in fact are uncomfortable and, therefore, resist being placed in situations where they are required to evaluate or otherwise exercise independent thought." Mason Haire, (ed.), *Organization Theory in Industrial Practice* (New York: John Wiley and Sons, 1962), p. 86.

26. William F. Whyte, *Money and Motivation* (New York: Harper and Brothers, 1955), pp. 2-3.

27. The Hawthorne Studies are reported in T. N. Whitehead, *The Industrial Worker*, 2 volumes (Cambridge, Massachusetts: Harvard University Press, 1938), Fritz J. Roethlisberger and William J. Dickson, *Management and the Worker* (Cambridge, Massachusetts: Harvard University Press, 1947), Fritz J. Roethlisberger, *Management and Morale* (Cambridge, Massachusetts: Harvard University Press, 1941), and Elton Mayo, *The Human Problems of an Industrial Civilization* (New York: The Macmillan Co., 1933).

28. F. J. Roethlisberger, *ibid.*, p. 16.

29. Mayo, *op. cit.*, p. 18.

30. Clark Kerr, *Labor and Management in Industrial Society* (Garden City, New York: Doubleday and Co., Inc., 1964), p. 54.

31. Elton Mayo, *The Social Problems of an Industrial Civilization* (Boston: Division of Research, Graduate School of Business Administration, Harvard University, 1947), p. 33.

32. Burleigh B. Gardner, *Human Relations in Industry* (Chicago: Richard D. Irwin, Inc., 1945) is a "classic" of this tradition.

33. See William F. Whyte, *Pattern for Industrial Peace* (New York: Harper and Brothers, 1951).

34. Rensis Likert, *Motivation: The Core of Management* (New York: American Management Association, 1953). Reprinted in Harry Knudson, *Human Elements of Administration* (New York: Holt, Rinehart, and Winston, 1963), p. 81.

35. Kerr, *op. cit.*, p. 57.

36. It is not quite fair to say that Mayo "asserts" in this connection. In *Human Problems of an Industrial Civilization, op. cit.*, he analyzes various traditional cultures and presents as evidence of the social nature of man the many practices designed to achieve social integration, e.g., ritual custom, codes, family and tribal instincts.

37. Malcolm P. McNair. "Thinking Ahead: What Price Human Relations?" *Harvard Business Review* (March-April, 1957), pp. 15-23. Reprinted in Harold Koontz and Cyril O'Donnell, *Readings in Management* (New York: McGraw-Hill Book Co., Inc., 1959), p. 279.

38. Peter Drucker, "Human Relations: Where Do We Stand Today?" in Knudson, *op. cit.*, p. 264. The purpose of the social sciences is to gain understanding of one's self as Drucker explains.

39. *Ibid.*, p. 364.

40. McNair, *op. cit.*, p. 285.
41. This discussion is based on March and Simon, *op. cit.*, pp. 36-47.
42. Robert K. Merton, "Bureaucratic Structure and Personality," *Social Forces*, Vol. 18, (1940), pp. 560-568.
43. Philip Selznick, *TVA and the Grass Roots* (Berkeley: The University of California Press, 1949).
44. Alvin W. Gouldner, *Patterns of Industrial Bureaucracy* (New York: The Free Press of Glencoe, 1954).
45. March and Simon, *op. cit.*, pp. 38-39.
46. *Ibid.*, p. 41.
47. Such is the thesis of Robert Michels, *Political Parties* (Glencoe, Illinois: The Free Press, 1949), whose concept of the "iron law of oligarchy" is a classic description of the tendency of organizations to become conservative as the demands for more specialized competence intensify.
48. March and Simon, *op. cit.*, p. 45. Those studies are classics in the development of our knowledge of organizational behavior. It is obvious that many of Downs' hypotheses are suggested by this literature, particularly the hypotheses that organizations value status quo solutions and consensus and that the content of decisions is limited to precedents.
49. Some third dimension as a basis for synthesis and the criteria for its selection are a concern to many students of organization theory. The work of Warren B. Bennis and many others could be cited. The focus of this paper, however, is on *values* more than the whole panorama.
50. Some presentations of modern organization theory are March and Simon, *op. cit.;* Mason Haire (ed.), *Modern Organization Theory* (New York: John Wiley and Sons, 1959); Albert H. Rubenstein and Chadwick J. Haberstroh, *Some Theories of Organization* (Homewood Illinois: The Dorsey Press, Inc., 1960); Joseph A. Litterer, *The Analysis of Organizations* (New York: John Wiley and Sons, 1965); and Theodore Caplow, *Principles of Organizations* (New York: Harcourt, Brace and World, Inc., 1964).
51. William G. Scott, "Organization Theory: An Overview and an Appraisal," *Academy of Management Journal* (April, 1961), pp. 7-26. Reprinted in Joseph A. Litterer (ed.), *Organizations: Structure and Behavior* (New York: John Wiley and Sons, 1963), p. 19.
52. John M. Pfiffner and Frank P. Sherwood, *Administrative Organization* (Englewood Cliffs, N.J.: Prentice-Hall, Inc., 1960), pp. 116-117.
53. Scott, *op. cit.*, p. 22.
54. This view is developed by Chris Argyris in *Personality and Organization* (New York: Harper and Brothers, 1957) and more recently in *Integrating the Individual and the Organization* (New York: John Wiley and Sons, 1964).
55. George Strauss, "Some Notes on Power-Equalization" in Harold J. Leavitt, editor, *The Social Science of Organization* (Englewood Cliffs, N.J.: Prentice-Hall, Inc., 1963), p. 46.
56. *Personality and Organization* . . . pp. 78-79.
57. Robert Presthus, *op. cit.*, pp. 164-204.
58. *Ibid.*, pp. 205-256.
59. *Ibid.*, pp. 257-285.
60. Conflict and struggle for power in organizations lead to patterns of

behavior that are political in nature. Melville Dalton in *Men Who Manage* (New York: John Wiley and Sons, 1959) analyzes organizational politics.

61. Nor is there a final answer since some men (e.g. Thomas Hobbes) have viewed the essence of man to be conflict while others (e.g. John Locke) have viewed man as essentially cooperative. Realization of the individual through the group is not characteristic of Rousseau.

62. See William W. Cooper, Harold J. Leavitt, and Maynard W. Shelly, *New Perspectives in Organization Research* (New York: John Wiley and Sons, Inc., 1964) for some indications.

63. Strother, *op. cit.*, pp. 170–171.

10

robert tannenbaum
warren h. schmidt

HOW TO CHOOSE A LEADERSHIP PATTERN

- "I put most problems into my group's hands and leave it to them to carry the ball from there. I serve merely as a catalyst, mirroring back the people's thoughts and feelings so that they can better understand them."
- "It's foolish to make decisions oneself on matters that affect people. I always talk things over with my subordinates, but I make it clear to them that I'm the one who has to have the final say."
- "Once I have decided on a course of action I do my best to sell my ideas to my employees."
- "I'm being paid to lead. If I let a lot of other people make the decisions I should be making, then I'm not worth my salt."
- "I believe in getting things done. I can't waste time calling meetings. Someone has to call the shots around here, and I think it should be me."

Each of these statements represents a point of view about "good leadership." Considerable experience, factual data, and theoretical principles could be cited to support each statement, even though they seem to be inconsistent when placed together. Such contradictions point up the dilemma in which the modern manager frequently finds himself.

From Robert Tannenbaum and Warren H. Schmidt, "How to Choose a Leadership Pattern and A Retrospective Comment," *Harvard Business Review,* Vol. 51, (May-June, 1973). © 1973 by the President and Fellows of Harvard College; all rights reserved.

NEW PROBLEM

The problem of how the modern manager can be "democratic" in his relations with subordinates and at the same time maintain the necessary authority and control in the organization for which he is responsible has come into focus increasingly in recent years.

Earlier in the century this problem was not so acutely felt. The successful executive was generally pictured as possessing intelligence, imagination, initiative, the capacity to make rapid (and generally wise) decisions, and the ability to inspire subordinates. People tended to think of the world as being divided into "leaders" and "followers."

New Focus

Gradually, however, from the social sciences emerged the concept of "group dynamics" with its focus on *members* of the group rather than solely on the leader. Research efforts of social scientists underscored the importance of employee involvement and participation in decision making. Evidence began to challenge the efficiency of highly directive leadership, and increasing attention was paid to problems of motivation and human relations.

Through training laboratories in group development that sprang up across the country, many of the newer notions of leadership began to exert an impact. These training laboratories were carefully designed to give people a firsthand experience in full participation and decision making. The designated "leaders" deliberately attempted to reduce their own power and to make group members as responsible as possible for setting their own goals and methods within the laboratory experience.

It was perhaps inevitable that some of the people who attended the training laboratories regarded this kind of leadership as being truly "democratic" and went home with the determination to build fully participative decision making into their own organizations. Whenever their bosses made a decision without convening a staff meeting, they tended to perceive this as authoritarian behavior. The true symbol of democratic leadership to some was the meeting—and the less directed from the top, the more democratic it was.

Some of the more enthusiastic alumni of these training laboratories began to get the habit of categorizing leader behavior as "democratic" or "authoritarian." The boss who made too many decisions himself was thought of as an authoritarian, and his directive behavior was often attributed solely to his personality.

New Need

The net result of the research findings and of the human relations training based upon them has been to call into question the stereotype of an effective leader. Consequently, the modern manager often finds himself in an uncomfortable state of mind.

Often he is not quite sure how to behave; there are times when he is torn between exerting "strong" leadership and "permissive" leadership. Sometimes new knowledge pushes him in one direction ("I should really get the group to help make this decision"), but at the same time his experience pushes him in another direction ("I really understand the problem better than the group and therefore I should make the decision"). He is not sure when a group decision is really appropriate or when holding a staff meeting serves merely as a device for avoiding his own decision-making responsibility.

The purpose of our article is to suggest a framework which managers may find useful in grappling with this dilemma. First, we shall look at the different patterns of leadership behavior that the manager can choose from in relating himself to his subordinates. Then, we shall turn to some of the questions suggested by this range of patterns. For instance, how important is it for a manager's subordinates to know what type of leadership he is using in a situation? What factors should be consider in deciding on a leadership pattern? What difference do his long-run objectives make as compared to his immediate objectives?

RANGE OF BEHAVIOR

Exhibit I presents the continuum or range of possible leadership behavior available to a manager. Each type of action is related to the degree of authority used by the boss and to the amount of freedom available to his subordinates in reaching decisions. The actions seen on the extreme left characterize the manager who maintains a high degree of control while those seen on the extreme right characterize the manager who releases a high degree of control. Neither extreme is absolute; authority and freedom are never without their limitations.

Now let us look more closely at each of the behavior points occurring along this continuum.

The Manager Makes the Decision and Announces It.

In this case the boss identifies a problem, considers alternative solutions, chooses one of them, and then reports this decision to his subordinates for implementation. He may or may not give consideration to what he believes his subordinates will think or feel about his decision; in any case, he provides no opportunity for them to participate directly in the decision-making process. Coercion may or may not be used or implied.

The Manager "Sells" His Decision.

Here the manager, as before, takes responsibility for identifying the problem and arriving at a decision. However, rather than simply announcing it, he takes the additional step of persuading his subordinates to accept it. In doing so, he recognizes the possibility of some resistance among those who will be faced with the decision, and seeks to reduce this resistance by indicating, for example, what the employees have to gain from his decision.

The Manager Presents His Ideas, Invites Questions.

Here the boss who has arrived at a decision and who seeks acceptance of his ideas provides an opportunity for his subordinates to get a fuller explanation of thinking and his intentions. After presenting the ideas, he invites questions so that his associates can better understand what he is trying to accomplish. This "give and take" also enables the manager and the subordinates to explore more fully the implications of the decision.

The Manager Presents a Tentative Decision Subject to Change.

This kind of behavior permits the subordinates to exert some influence on the decision. The initiative for identifying and diagnosing the problem remains with the boss. Before meeting with his staff, he has thought the problem through and arrived at a decision—but only a tentative one. Before finalizing it, he presents his proposed solution for the reaction of those who will be affected by it. He says in effect, "I'd like to hear what you have to say about this plan that I have developed. I'll appreciate your frank reactions, but will reserve for myself the final decision."

The Manager Presents the Problem, Gets Suggestions, and then Makes His Decision.

Up to this point the boss has come before the group with a solution of his own. Not so in this case. The subordinates now get the first chance to suggest solutions. The manager's initial role involves identifying the problem. He might, for example, say something of this sort: "We are faced with a number of complaints from newspapers and the general public on our service policy. What is wrong here? What ideas do you have to coming to grips with this problem?"

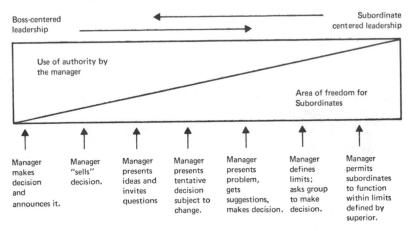

Boss-centered leadership

Subordinate centered leadership

Use of authority by the manager

Area of freedom for Subordinates

| Manager makes decision and announces it. | Manager "sells" decision. | Manager presents ideas and invites questions | Manager presents tentative decision subject to change. | Manager presents problem, gets suggestions, makes decision. | Manager defines limits; asks group to make decision. | Manager permits subordinates to function within limits defined by superior. |

EXHIBIT I.   Continuum of leadership behavior.

The function of the group becomes one of increasing the manager's repertory of possible solutions to the problem. The purpose is to capitalize on the knowledge and experience of those who are on the "firing line." From the expanded list of alternatives developed by the manager and his subordinates, the manager then selects the solution that he regards as most promising.[1]

The Manager Defines the Limits and Requests the Group to Make a Decision.

At this point the manager passes to the group (possibly including himself as a member) the right to make decisions. Before doing so, however, he defines the problem to be solved and the boundaries within which the decision must be made.

An example might be the handling of a parking problem at a plant. The boss decides that this is something that should be worked on by the people involved, so he calls them together and points up the existence of the problem. Then he tells them:

"There is the open field just north of the main plant which has been designated for additional employee parking. We can build underground or surface multilevel facilities as long as the cost does not exceed $100,000. Within these limits we are free to work out whatever solution makes sense to us. After we decide on a specific plan, the company will spend the available money in whatever way we indicate."

The Manager Permits the Group to make Decisions within Prescribed Limits.

This represents an extreme degree of group freedom only occasionally encountered in formal organizations, as, for instance, in many research groups. Here the team of managers or engineers undertakes the identification and diagnosis of the problem, develops alternative procedures for solving it, and decides on one or more of these alternative solutions. The only limits directly imposed on the group by the organization are those specified by the superior of the team's boss. If the boss participates in the decision-making process, he attempts to do so with no more authority than any other member of the group. He commits himself in advance to assist in implementing whatever decision the group makes.

Key Questions

As the continuum in *Exhibit I* demonstrates, there are a number of alternative ways in which a manager can relate himself to the group or individuals he is supervising. At the extreme left of the range, the emphasis is on the manager—on what *he* is interested in, how *he* sees things, how *he* feels about them. As we move toward the subordinate-centered end of the continuum, however, the focus is increasingly on the subordinates—on what *they* are intersted in, how *they* look at things, how *they* feel about them.

When business leadership is regarded in this way, a number of questions arise. Let us take four of especial importance:

Can a Boss Ever Relinquish His Responsibility by Delegating It to Someone Else?

Our view is that the manager must expect to be held responsible by his superior for the quality of the decisions made, even though operationally these decisions may have been made on a group basis. He should, therefore, be ready to accept whatever risk is involved whenever he delegates decision-making power to his subordinates. Delegation is not a way of "passing the buck." Also, it should be emphasized that the amount of freedom the boss gives to his subordinates cannot be greater than the freedom which he himself has been given by his own superior.

Should the Manager Participate with His Subordinates Once He Has Delegated Responsibility to Them?

The manager should carefully think over this question and decide on his role prior to involving the subordinate group. He should ask if his presence will inhibit or facilitate the problem-solving process. There may be some instances when he should leave the group to let it solve the problem for itself. Typically, however, the boss has useful ideas to contribute, and should function as an additional member of the group. In the latter instance, it is important that he indicate clearly to the group that he sees himself in a *member* role rather than in an authority role.

How Important Is It for the Group to Recognize What Kind of Leadership Behavior the Boss Is Using?

It makes a great deal of difference. Many relationship problems between boss and subordinate occur because the boss fails to make clear how he plans to use his authority. If, for example, he actually intends to make a certain decision himself, but the subordinate group gets the impression that he has delegated this authority, considerable confusion and resentment are likely to follow. Problems may also occur when the boss uses a "democratic" facade to conceal the fact that he has already made a decision which he hopes the group will accept as its own. The attempt to "make them think it was their idea in the first place" is a risky one. We believe that it is highly important for the manager to be honest and clear in describing what authority he is keeping and what role he is asking his subordinates to assume in solving a particular problem.

Can You Tell How "Democratic" a Manager Is by the Number of Decisions His Subordinates Make?

The sheer *number* of decisions is not an accurate index of the amount of freedom that a subordinate group enjoys. More important is the *significance* of the decisions which the boss entrusts to his subordinates. Obviously a decision on how to arrange desks is of an entirely different order from a decision involving the introduction of new electronic data-processing equipment. Even though the widest possible limits are given in dealing with the first issue, the group will sense no particular degree of responsibility. For a boss to permit the group to decide equipment policy, even within rather narrow limits, would reflect a greater degree of confidence in them on his part.

Deciding How to Lead

Now let us turn from the types of leadership which are possible in a company situation to the question of what types are *practical* and *desirable*. What factors or forces should a manager consider in deciding how to manage? Three are of particular importance:

- Forces in the manager.
- Forces in the subordinates.
- Forces in the situation.

We should like briefly to describe these elements and indicate how they might influence a manager's action in a decision-making situation.[2] The strength of each of them will, of course, vary from instance to instance, but the manager who is sensitive to them can better assess the problems which face him and determine which mode of leadership behavior is most appropriate for him.

Forces in the manager.   The manager's behavior in any given instance will be influenced greatly by the many forces operating within his own personality. He will, of course, perceive his leadership problems in a unique way on the basis of his background, knowledge, and experience. Among the important internal forces affecting him will be the following:

1. His *value system.* How strongly does he feel that individuals should have a share in making the decisions which affect them? Or, how convinced is he that the official who is paid to assume responsibility should personally carry the burden of decision making? The strength of his convictions on questions like these will tend to move the manager to one end or the other of the continuum shown in *Exhibit I.* His behavior will also be influenced by the relative impor-

tance that he attaches to organizational efficiency, personal growth of subordinates, and company profits.[3]

2. *His confidence in his subordinates.* Managers differ greatly in the amount of trust they have in other people generally, and this carries over to the particular employees they supervise at a given time. In viewing his particular group of subordinates, the manager is likely to consider their knowledge and competence with respect to the problem. A central question he might ask himself is: "Who is best qualified to deal with this problem?" Often he may, justifiably or not, have more confidence in his own capabilities than in those of his subordinates.

3. *His own leadership inclinations.* There are some managers who seem to function more comfortably and naturally as highly directive leaders. Resolving problems and issuing orders come easily to them. Other managers seem to operate more comfortably in a team role, where they are continually sharing many of their functions with their subordinates.

4. *His feelings of security in an uncertain situation.* The manager who releases control over the decision-making process thereby reduces the predictability of the outcome. Some managers have a greater need than others for predictability and stability in their environment. This "tolerance for ambiguity" is being viewed increasingly by psychologists as a key variable in a person's manner of dealing with problems.

The manager brings these and other highly personal variables to each situation he faces. If he can see them as forces which, consciously or unconsciously, influence his behavior, he can better understand what makes him prefer to act in a given way. And understanding this, he can often make himself more effective.

Forces in the subordinate. Before deciding how to lead a certain group, the manager will also want to consider a number of forces affecting his subordinates' behavior. He will want to remember that each employee, like himself, is influenced by many personality variables. In addition, each subordinate has a set of expectations about how the boss should act in relation to him (the phrase "expected behavior" is one we hear more and more often these days at discussions of leadership and teaching). The better the manager understands these factors, the more accurately he can determine what kind of behavior on his part will enable his subordinates to act most effectively.

Generally speaking, the manager can permit his subordinates greater freedom if the following essential conditions exist:

- If the subordinates have relatively high needs for independence. (As we all know, people differ greatly in the amount of direction that they desire.)
- If the subordinates have a readiness to assume responsibility for decision making. (Some see additional responsibility as a tribute to their ability; others see it as "passing the buck.")
- If they have a relatively high tolerance for ambiguity. (Some employees prefer to have clear-cut directives given to them; others prefer a wider area of freedom.)
- If they are interested in the problem and feel that it is important.
- If they understand and identify with the goals of the organization.
- If they have the necessary knowledge and experience to deal with the problem.
- If they have learned to expect to share in decision making. (Persons who have come to expect strong leadership and are then suddenly confronted with the request to share more fully in decision making are often upset by this new experience. On the other hand, persons who have enjoyed a considerable amount of freedom resent the boss who begins to make all the decisions himself.)

The manager will probably tend to make fuller use of his own authority if the above conditions do *not* exist; at times there may be no realistic alternative to running a "one-man show."

The restrictive effect of many of the forces will, of course, be greatly modified by the general feeling of confidence which subordinates have in the boss. Where they have learned to respect and trust him, he is free to vary his behavior. He will feel certain that he will not be perceived as an authoritarian boss on those occasions when he makes decisions by himself. Similarly, he will not be seen as using staff meetings to avoid his decision making responsibility. In a climate of mutual confidence and respect, people tend to feel less threatened by deviations from normal practice, which in turn makes possible a higher degree of flexibility in the whole relationship.

Forces in the situation. In addition to the forces which exist in the manager himself and in his subordinates, certain characteristics of the general situation will also affect the manager's behavior. Among the more critical environmental pressures that surround him are those which stem from the organization, the work group, the nature of the problem, and the pressures of time. Let us look briefly at each of these:

Type of organization—Like individuals, organizations have values and traditions which inevitably influence the behavior of the people who work in them. The manager who is a newcomer to a company quickly discovers that certain kinds of behavior are approved while others are not. He also discovers that to deviate radically from what is generally accepted is likely to create problems for him.

These values and traditions are communicated in numerous ways—through job descriptions, policy pronouncements, and public statements by top executives. Some organizations, for example, hold to the notion that the desirable executive is one who is dynamic, imaginative, decisive, and persuasive. Other organizations put more emphasis upon the importance of the executive's ability to work effectively with people—his human relations skills. The fact that his superiors have a defined concept of what the good executive should be will very likely push the manager toward one end or the other of the behavioral range.

In addition to the above, the amount of employee participation is influenced by such variables as the size of the working units, their geographical distribution, and the degree of inter- and intra-organizational security required to attain company goals. For example, the wide geographical dispersion of an organization may preclude a practical system of participative decision making, even though this would otherwise be desirable. Similarly, the size of the working units or the need for keeping plans confidential may make it necessary for the boss to exercise more control than would otherwise be the case. Factors like these may limit considerably the manager's ability to function flexibly on the continuum.

Group effectiveness—Before turning decision-making responsibility over to a subordinate group, the boss should consider how effectively its members work together as a unit.

One of the relevant factors here is the experience the group has had in working together. It can generally be expected that a group which has functioned for some time will have developed habits of cooperation and thus be able to tackle a problem more effectively than a new group. It can also be expected that a group of people with similar backgrounds and interests will work more quickly and easily than people with dissimilar backgrounds, because the communication problems are likely to be less complex.

The degree of confidence that the members have in their ability to solve problems as a group is also a key consideration. Finally, such group variables as cohesiveness, permissiveness, mutual acceptance, and commonality of purpose will exert subtle but powerful influence on the group's functioning.

The problem itself—The nature of the problem may determine what degree of authority should be delegated by the manager to his subordinates. Obviously he will ask himself whether they have the kind of knowledge which is needed. It is possible to do them a real disservice by assigning a problem that their experience does not equip them to handle.

Since the problems faced in large or growing industries increasingly require knowledge of specialists from many different fields, it might be inferred that the more complex a problem, the more anxious a manager will be to get some assistance in solving it. However, this is not always the case. There will be times when the very complexity of the problem calls for one person to work it out. For example, if the manager has most of the background and factual data relevant to a given issue, it may be easier for him to think it through himself than to take the time to fill in his staff on all the pertinent background information.

The key question to ask, of course, is: "Have I heard the ideas of everyone who has the necessary knowledge to make a significant contribution to the solution of this problem?"

The pressure of time—This is perhaps the most clearly felt pressure on the manager (in spite of the fact that it may sometimes be imagined). The more that he feels the need for an immediate decision, the more difficult it is to involve other people. In organizations which are in a constant state of "crisis" and "crash programming" one is likely to find managers personally using a high degree of authority with relatively little delegation to subordinates. When the time pressure is less intense, however, it becomes much more possible to bring subordinates in on the decision-making process.

These, then, are the principal forces that impinge on the manager in any given instance and that tend to determine his tactical behavior in relation to his subordinates. In each case his behavior ideally will be that which makes possible the most effective attainment of his immediate goal within the limits facing him.

Long-run Strategy

As the manager works with his organization on the problems that come up day by day, his choice of a leadership pattern is usually limited. He must take account of the forces just described and, within the restrictions they impose on him, do the best that he can. But as he looks ahead months or even years, he can shift his thinking from tactics to large-scale strategy. No longer need he be fettered by all of the forces mentioned, for he can view many of them as variables over which he has some control. He can, for example, gain new insights or skills for himself, supply training for individual subordinates, and provide participative experiences for his employee group.

In trying to bring about a change in these variables, however, he is faced with a challenging question: At which point along the continuum *should* he act?

Attaining objectives.   The answer depends largely on what he wants to accomplish. Let us suppose that he is interested in the same objectives that most modern managers seek to attain when they can shift their attention from the pressure of immediate assignments:

1.   To raise the level of employee motivation.

2.   To increase the readiness of subordinates to accept change.

3.   To improve the quality of all managerial decisions.

4.   To develop teamwork and morale.

5.   To further the individual development of employees.

In recent years the manager has been deluged with a flow of advice on how best to achieve these longer-run objectives. It is little wonder that he is often both bewildered and annoyed. However, there are some guidelines which he can usefully follow in making a decision.

Most research and much of the experience of recent years give a strong factual basis to the theory that a fairly high degree of subordinate-centered behavior is associated with the accomplishment of the five purposes mentioned.[4] This does not mean that a manager should always leave all decisions to his assistants. To provide the individual or the group with greater freedom than they are ready for at any given time may very well tend to generate anxieties and therefore inhibit rather than facilitate the attainment of desired objectives. But this should not keep the manager from making a continuing effort to confront his subordinates with the challenge of freedom.

CONCLUSION

In summary, there are two implications in the basic thesis that we have been developing. The first is that the successful leader is one who is keenly aware of those forces which are most relevant to his behavior at any given time. He accurately understands himself, the individuals and group he is dealing with, and the company and broader social environment in which he operates. And certainly he is able to assess the present readiness for growth of his subordinates.

But this sensitivity or understanding is not enough, which brings us to the second implication. The successful leader is one who is able to behave appropriately in the light of these perceptions. If direction is in order, he is able to direct; if considerable participative freedom is called for, he is able to provide such freedom.

Thus, the successful manager of men can be primarily characterized neither as a strong leader nor as a permissive one. Rather, he is one who maintains a high batting average in accurately assessing the forces that determine what his most appropriate behavior at any given time should be and in actually being able to behave accordingly. Being both insightful and flexible, he is less likely to see the problems of leadership as a dilemma.

RETROSPECTIVE COMMENTARY

Since this HBR Classic was first published in 1958, there have been many changes in organizations and in the world that have affected leadership patterns. While the article's continued popularity attests to its essential validity, we believe it can be reconsidered and updated to reflect subsequent societal changes and new management concepts.

The reasons for the article's continued relevance can be summarized briefly:

- The article contains insights and perspectives which mesh well with, and help clarify, the experiences of managers, other leaders, and students of leadership. Thus it is useful to individuals in a wide variety of organizations—industrial, governmental, educational, religious, and community.
- The concept of leadership the article defines is reflected in a continuum of leadership behavior (see *Exhibit I* in original article). Rather than offering a choice between two styles of leadership, democratic or authoritarian, it sanctions a range of behavior.
- The concept does not dictate to managers but helps them to analyze their own behavior. The continuum permits

them to review their behavior within a context of other alternatives, without any style being labeled right or wrong.

(We have sometimes wondered if we have, perhaps, made it too easy for anyone to justify his or her style of leadership. It may be a small step between being nonjudgmental and giving the impression that all behavior is equally valid and useful. The latter was not our intention. Indeed, the thrust of our endorsement was for the manager who is insightful in assessing relevant forces within himself, others, and the situation, and who can be flexible in responding to these forces.)

In recognizing that our article can be updated, we are acknowledging that organizations do not exist in a vacuum but are affected by changes that occur in society. Consider, for example, the implications for organizations of these recent social developments:

- The youth revolution that expresses distrust and even contempt for organizations identified with the establishment.
- The civil rights movement that demands all minority groups be given a greater opportunity for participation and influence in the organizational processes.
- The ecology and consumer movements that challenge the right of managers to make decisions without considering the interest of people outside the organization.
- The increasing national concern with the quality of working life and its relationship to worker productivity, participation, and satisfaction.

These and other societal changes make effective leadership in this decade a more challenging task, requiring even greater sensitivity and flexibility than was needed in the 1950's. Today's manager is more likely to deal with employees who resent being treated as subordinates, who may be highly critical of any organizational system, who expect to be consulted and to exert influence, and who often stand on the edge of alienation from the institution that needs their loyalty and commitment. In addition, he is frequently confronted by a highly turbulent, unpredictable environment.

In response to these social pressures, new concepts of management have emerged in organizations. Open-system theory, with its emphasis on subsystems' interdependency *and* on the interaction of an organization with its environment, has made a powerful impact on managers' approach to problems. Organization development has emerged as a new behavioral science approach to the improvement of individual, group, organizational, and interorganizational performance. New research has added to our understanding of motivation in the work situation. More and more executives have become concerned with social responsibility and have explored the feasibility of social audits. And a growing number of organizations, in Europe and in the United States, have conducted experiments in industrial democracy.

In light of these developments, we submit the following thoughts on how we would rewrite certain points in our original article.

The article described forces in the manager, subordinates, and the situation as givens, with the leadership pattern a resultant of these forces. We would now give more attention to the *interdependency* of these forces. For example, such interdependency occurs in: (a) the interplay between the manager's confidence in his subordinates, their readiness to assume responsibility, and the level of group effectiveness; and (b) the impact of the behavior of the manager on that of his subordinates, and vice versa.

In discussing the forces in the situation, we primarily identified organizational phenomena. We would now include forces lying outside the organization, and would explore the relevant interdependencies between the organization and its environment.

In the original article, we presented the size of the rectangle in *Exhibit I* as a given, with its boundaries already determined by external forces—in effect, a closed system. We would now recognize the possibility of the manager and/or his subordinates taking the initiative to change those boundaries through interaction with relevant external forces—both within their own organization and in the larger society.

The article portrayed the manager as the principal and almost unilateral actor. He initiated and determined group functions, assumed responsibility, and exercised control. Subordinates made inputs and assumed power only at the will of the manager. Although the manager might have taken into account forces outside himself, it was *he* who decided where to operate on the continuum—that is, whether to announce a decision instead of trying to sell his idea to his subordinates, whether to invite questions, to let subordinates decide an issue, and so on. While the manager has retained this clear prerogative in many organizations, it has been challenged in others. Even in situations where he has retained it, however, the balance in the relationship between manager and subordinates at any given time is arrived at by interaction—direct or indirect—between the two parties.

Although power and its use by the manager played a role in our article, we now realize that our concern with cooperation and collaboration, common goals, commitment, trust, and mutual caring limited our vision with respect to the realities of power. We did not attempt to deal with unions, other forms of joint worker action, or

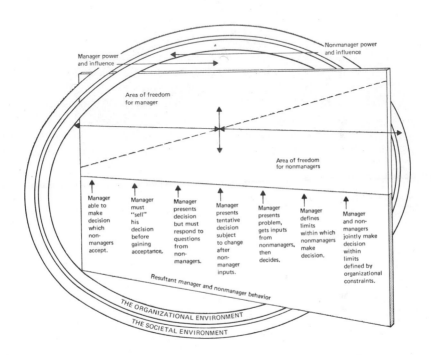

Manager power and influence

Nonmanager power and influence

Area of freedom for manager

Area of freedom for nonmanagers

| Manager able to make decision which non-managers accept. | Manager must "sell" his decision before gaining acceptance. | Manager presents decision but must respond to questions from non-managers. | Manager presents tentative decision subject to change after non-manager inputs. | Manager presents problem, gets inputs from nonmanagers, then decides. | Manager defines limits within which nonmanagers make decision. | Manager and non-managers jointly make decision within limits defined by organizational constraints. |

Resultant manager and nonmanager behavior

THE ORGANIZATIONAL ENVIRONMENT

THE SOCIETAL ENVIRONMENT

EXHIBIT II.   Continuum of manager-nonmanager behavior.

with individual workers' expressions of resistance. Today, we would recognize much more clearly the power available to *all* parties, and the factors that underlie the interrelated decisions on whether to use it.

In the original article, we used the terms "manager" and "subordinate." We are now uncomfortable with "subordinate" because of its demeaning, dependency-laden connotations and prefer "nonmanager." The titles "manager" and "nonmanager" make the terminological difference functional rather than hierarchical.

We assumed fairly traditional organizational structures in our original article. Now we would alter our formulation to reflect newer organizational modes which are slowly emerging, such as industrial democracy, intentional communities, and "phenomenarchy."* These new modes are based on observations such as the following:

● Both manager and nonmanagers may be governing forces in their group's environment, contributing to the definition of the total area of freedom.
● A group can function without a manager, with managerial functions being shared by a group members.
● A group, as a unit, can be delegated authority and can assume responsibility within a larger organizational context.

Our thoughts on the question of leadership have prompted us to design a new behavior continuum (see *Exhibit II*) in which the total area of freedom shared by manager and nonmanagers is constantly redefined by interactions between them and the forces in the environment.

The arrows in the exhibit indicate the continual flow of interdependent influence among systems and people. The points on the continuum designate the types of manager and nonmanager behavior that become possible with any given amount of freedom available to each. The new continuum is both more complex and more dynamic than the 1958 version, reflecting the organizational and societal realities of 1973.

ENDNOTES

1. For a fuller explanation of this approach, see Leo Moore, "Too Much Management, Too Little Change," HBR January-February 1956, p. 41.
2. See also Robert Tannenbaum and Fred Massarik, "Participation by Subordinates in the Managerial Decision-Making Process," *Canadian Journal of Economics and Political Science*, August 1950, p. 413.
3. See Chris Argyris, "Top Management Dilemma: Company Needs vs. Individual Development," *Personnel*, September 1955, pp. 123–134.
4. For example, see Warren H. Schmidt and Paul C. Buchanan, *Techniques that Produce Teamwork* (New London, Arthur C. Croft Publications, 1954), and Morris S. Viteles, *Motivation and Morale in Industry* (New York, W. W. Norton & Company, Inc., 1953).

* For a description of phenomenarchy, see Will McWhinney, "Phenomenarchy: A Suggestion for Social Redesign," *Journal of Applied Behavioral Science*, May 1973.

11

andre l. delbecq

THE MANAGEMENT OF DECISION-MAKING
WITHIN THE FIRM: THREE STRATEGIES
FOR THREE TYPES OF DECISION-MAKING[*]

Recent theory concerned with group problem-solving suggests that different types of decision making require different group structures and processes. The administrator who "manages" the decision-making process must, therefore, organize the executive team in different ways as he deals with the variety of decision-making situations within the firm.

Every practicing administrator is well aware of these qualitative differences in the problem-solving situations which he and his management team face. Further, even without conscious effort on his part, the management group will often change its pattern of communication and individual managers will adjust their roles, as the management team faces different tasks. Research evidence shows that over time, problem-solving groups tend to adjust their behavior in keeping with changes in the nature of group problem-solving.[1]

On the other hand, the process of adjustment to new decision-making situations is often slow, usually incomplete, and occasionally nonexistent. Managers develop expectations about appropriate behavior in decision-making meetings with their superiors, so that their behavior falls into a pattern with limited variability which may be appropriate for some types of decision making, but highly inappropriate for other decision-making situations.[2] However, if the manager is

Andre L. Delbecq, "The Management of Decision-Making Within the Firm: Three Strategies for Three Types of Decision-Making," *Academy of Management Journal*, vol. 10, no. 4 (December 1967), pp. 329–339.

highly sensitive to differences in the decision-making tasks faced by the management team, and can verbally redefine both his own and his subordinates roles in a fashion congruent with the new decision-making situation, research indicates that the management group can much more readily change its behavior as the result of such role redefinition in order to adjust to a new decision-making situation.[3]

The purpose of this article is to set forth three decision-making strategies, each of which is tailored to a different type of problem-solving situation encountered within the firm. Further, each strategy will be examined to determine the degree to which it differs from the logic of classical organization models. It is hoped that this examination of the three different strategies will fullfill the following purposes:

1. The administrator will become more sensitive to the kind of group structure and process which each of the three problem-solving tasks demands,

2. The problems of implementing the strategies within a traditional formal organization culture will be clearer, and

3. The implications for the redesign of traditional formal organization models to facilitate greater flexibility for problem-solving can be suggested.

THE RELEVANCE OF "TASK" FOR GROUP STRUCTURE

Since the body of this article proposes that managers should reorganize group structure and process as they face different types of decision tasks, a word about the relevance of task as a variable around which to construct "organization" is appropriate. It is axiomatic to say that individual behavior is goal directed,[4] and that group behavior is purposeful or goal directed as well.[5] The task of a group is normally thought of, however, only in terms of the stated goal of the group's activity. Thus, there are familiar typologies of groups based on stated goals. For example, Wolman classifies groups as being Instrumental Groups (which individuals join for the satisfaction of "to take" needs, e.g., business associations), Mutual Acceptance Groups (in which "give" and "take" motives are important, e.g., friendship relations), and Vectorial Groups (which people join for the purpose of serving a lofty goal).[6]

Another typology dealing with organizations as macro-groups is that of Scott and Blau who speak of Mutual Benefit Associations (where the prime beneficiary is the membership), Business Concerns (where the owner is the prime beneficiary), Service Organizations (where the client group is the prime beneficiary), and Commonweal Organizations (where the prime beneficiary is the public at large.)[7]

What is not immediately apparent in each of these descriptive typologies is that task, as a variable, affects several dimensions of the system (regardless of whether one is referring to a small group or a large organization) including:

1. *Group structure:* In terms of the relationship between the individual members,

2. *Group roles:* In terms of the behavior required of individual group members which are necessary to facilitate task accomplishment.

3. *Group process:* In terms of the manner of proceeding toward goal accomplishment,

4. *Group style:* In terms of the social-emotional tone of interpersonal relationships (e.g., the amount of stress on individual members, the congeniality of interpersonal relations, the perceived consequences of individual and group success or failure),

5. *Group norms:* Relative to each of the preceding four dimensions.

Thus, in treating task as merely the end goal, many of the theoretical as well as the practical implications of the group's or organization's tasks are not made explicit. For example, when mutual benefit organizations are compared with business concerns, one would expect the former to be characterized by greater dispersion of power (structure), broader membership participation in goal setting (roles and process), greater emotional support of individual members (style), and stronger egalitarianism (norms).

In a similar fashion, the problem-solving "task" faced by a particular managerial team, within a particular organization, at a particular point of time, likewise must affect the structure, roles, process, style, and norms of the management team if the group is to optimally organize itself to deal with its tasks.[8]

STRATEGIES FOR GROUP PROBLEM SOLVING

Against this background, we can now proceed directly to classify decision situations as found in groups and organizations and to specify group strategies implied in behaviorally oriented group and organization studies appropriate for dealing with each of the situations.[9]

Strategy One: Routine Decision Making

The first decision situation with which we will deal is the routine decision-making situation. In Simon's terminology, this is the "programmed" decision-situation; in Thompson's terminology, the "computational" decision.[10] Here, the organization or group agrees upon the desired goal, and technologies exist to achieve the goal. In such a situation the following strategy can be specified as consistent with behavioral models:

1. *Group structure:* The group is composed of specialists, with a coordinator (leader).

2. *Group roles:* Behavior is characterized by independent effort, with each specialist contributing expertise relative to his own specialty, including the coordinator (leader) who specializes in coordination across task phases.

3. *Group process:* At the beginning of the planning period, specialists, with the coordinator, specify the productivity objectives. Subsequently, excepting occasional joint meetings to review progress, coordination of specialist endeavors is generally obtained by means of dyadic (two-person) communication between individual specialists and their coordinator, or through horizontal communication between specialists.

4. *Group style:* Relatively high stress is characteristic. Stress is achieved through quality and quantity commitments and time constraints, agreed upon in joint consultation at the beginning of the planning period. Responsibility is decentralized within areas of specialization, but coordination is centralized in the coordinator.

5. *Group norms:* Norms are characterized by professionalism (high sense of individual responsibility and craftsmanship); commitment to shared team objectives relative to quantity and quality of output; economy and efficiency.

The above strategy evidences both similarity and dissimilarity when compared with classical organizational models. It is similar in that there is a clear division of labor, functional and structural specialization (specialization in work, and between work and coordination), and centralized coordination.

On the other hand, this "optimal" model is dissimilar in several significant ways. To begin with, responsibility is obtained primarily through team commitments to group objectives, dealing with both the quantity and quality of the output. This commitment, elicited through joint discussion between the specialists and the coordinator at the beginning of the planning period, places responsibility on both the team members and the coordinator, rather than locating responsibility solely in the coordinator.

Control is obtained in two ways. First, the coordinator provides the feedback mechanism for the team by monitoring the progress of individual specialists to assure conformity to shared productivity and time objectives. Situations where actual performance deviated from prior commitments are brought to the shared attention of the team, which institutes appropriate correction measures. Thus, discipline rests upon joint commitments rather than upon superordinate sanctions.[11] Second, because motivation is task-intrinsic, specialists are "normatively" expected to be "self-controlled" through professional, reference-group standards. Authority is likewise decentralized, based upon specialist expertise and shared norms.

Since responsibility, authority, and discipline are shared within the management team, there is less status disparity between the coordinator and the specialist than is the case between supervisor and subordinates in traditional organization models. Indeed, coordination is seen as a type of specialization, rather than as a function of superior personal attributes, or positional status. As a consequence, there is a propensity for fluid changes in group personnel; different task experts bring to bear their differentiated competences at different points of time as the group encounters various phases of decision making in the completion of a project. Further, the role of the coordinator may shift between the specialists on occasions, as the coordination requirements demand different admixtures of skills at various phases of project management.

Admittedly, the strategy assumes high quality personnel in terms of both task skills and interpersonal skills. Further, it requires a degree of autonomy for both individual specialists and each specialist team, an autonomy which must be predicated on personal and organizational maturity. It also assumes that the objectives of the organization and each group can be integrated into a meaningful, internally consistent ends-means chain, where, at each level and between each area, objectives can be translated in terms of appropriate technologies.

Nonetheless, although a "pure" strategy (best approximated in project management, matrix management, or task-force groups), movement towards such a model for structuring groups dealing with "routine" tasks appears capable of avoiding many of the dysfunctions of classical organizational models, while captivating the advantages of division of labor, specialization, centralized coordination, and task-intrinsic motivation.

Strategy Two: Creative Decision Making

The second decision situation with which we will deal is the creative decision-making situation. Here we are talking about decision making which in Simon's terminology is "heuristic" and in Thompson's terminology is "judgmental."[12] The central element in the decision making is the lack of an agreed-upon method of dealing with the problem; this lack of certitude may relate to incomplete knowledge of causation, or lack of an appropriate solution strategy. In such a situation, the following strategy can be specified as consistent with behavioral models.[13]

1. *Group structure:* The group is composed of heterogeneous, generally competent personnel, who bring to bear on the problem diverse frames of reference, representing channels to each relevant body of knowledge (including contact with outside resource personnel who offer expertise not encompassed by the organization), with a leader who facilitates creative (heuristic) processes.

2. *Group roles:* Behavior is characterized by each individual, exploring with the entire group all ideas (no matter how intuitively and roughly formed) which bear on the problem.

3. *Group processes:* The problem-solving process is characterized by:
    a. spontaneous communication between members (not focused in the leader)
    b. full participation from each member
    c. separation of idea generation from idea evaluation
    d. separation of problem definition from generation of solution strategies
    e. shifting of roles, so that interaction which mediates problem solving (particularly search activities and clarification by means of constant questioning directed both to individual members and the whole group) is not the sole responsibility of the leader

    f. suspension of judgment and avoidance of early concern with solutions, so that emphasis is on analysis and exploration, rather than on early solution commitment.

4. *Group style:* The social-emotional tone of the group is characterized by:
   a. a relaxed, nonstressful environment
   b. ego-supportive interaction, where open give-and-take between members is at the same time courteous
   c. behavior which is motivated by interest in the problem, rather than concern with short-run payoff
   d. absence of penalties attached to any espoused idea or position.

5. *Group norms:*
   a. are supportive of originality, and unusual ideas, and allow for eccentricity
   b. seek behavior which separates source from content in evaluating information and ideas
   c. stress a nonauthoritarian view, with a relativistic view of life and independence of judgment
   d. support humor and undisciplined exploration of viewpoints
   e. seek openness in communication, where mature, self-confident individuals offer "crude" ideas to the group for mutual exploration without threat to the individual for "exposing" himself
   f. deliberately avoid credence to short-run results, or short-run decisiveness
   g. seek consensus, but accept majority rule when consensus is unobtainable.[14]

Obviously, the above prescription for a strategy to deal with creativity does not easily compliment classical organization theory. Structural differentiation and status inequality (other than achieved status within the group) are deemphasized. The decisive, energetic, action-oriented executive is a normative misfit. Decisions evolve quite outside the expected frame of reference of the "pure" task specialist. Communication is dispersed, rather than focused in a superior or even a coordinator. Motivation is totally task-intrinsic, the pleasure being much more in the exploration than in an immediately useful outcome. Indeed, the very personnel who thrive by excellent application and execution of complex technologies in the first strategy, find the optimal decision rules for the second strategy unnatural, unrealistic, idealistic, and slow.

Nonetheless, although all members of any organization will not find both of the strategies equally comfortable, it can be expected that most organizational members can approximate the strategy given appropriate role definitions. The point, here, is that the group structure and process which is called for to facilitate creativity is intrinsically different from our first strategy. While the first strategy called for an internally consistent team of complementary specialists who are "action" oriented, the second strategy calls for a heterogeneous collection of generalists (or at least generically wise specialists not restricted to the boundaries of their own specialized frame of reference, and even, not necessarily of the immediate group or organization) who are deliberately and diagnostically patient in remaining problem-centered. The membership, roles, processes, style, and norms of strategy two are more natural to the scientific community (or a small sub-set thereof) than to the practicing executive. The general implications, however, must await the exposition of the third strategy.

Strategy Three: Negotiated Decision Making

The third decision situation with which we will deal is the negotiated decision-making strategy. In this instance, we are concerned with a strategy for dealing with opposing factions which, because of differences in norms, values, or vested interests, stand in opposition to each other, concerning either ends or means, or both.[15] Organization theory has never given much attention to groups in conflict, since several elements of classical models precluded such open conflict. One element was, of course, the existence of monocratic authority. At some level in the hierarchical system, authority to "decide" was to be found. Parties representing various opinions might be given a hearing, but ultimately Manager X was to make the decision. Another element in classical thought which precluded open conflict was the conviction, however utopian, that conflict was merely symptomatic of inadequate analysis. Adequate problem solving would surely show that the conflict was artificial and that an integrative decision could be reached. Thus, the study of mechanisms for negotiation between groups in conflict was left to the student of political science and social conflict and was excluded from organizational models.

Nonetheless, the realities of conflict have been ubiquitous. Present models encourage the sublimation of conflict, veiling it in portended rationality. As one wag expressed the matter, "If people don't agree with me, it isn't that I am wrong, or that they are right, but merely that I haven't been clear." In spite of Trojan efforts at "clear communication," the elimination of all conflict through analysis is, indeed, a utopian desire. There have been, and will be, instances where the organization finds itself encompassing two "camps," each supported by acceptable values and logic, and each committed to a different course of action, relative to either means, ends, or both. The question remains, then, as to what would be an appropriate strategy in those cases where "analysis" cannot provide an acceptable solution to both parties since the disparate opinion or positions are based on assumptions and premises not subject to total decision integration.

The following strategy can be specified:

1. *Group structure:* The group is composed of proportional representation of each faction (but with the minority never represented by less than two persons), with an impartial formal chairman.[16]

2. *Group roles:* Each individual sees himself as a representative of his faction, seeking to articulate and protect dominant concerns of the group he represents, while at the same time negotiating for an acceptable compromise solution.

3. *Group processes:* The problem-solving process is characterized by:
    a. orderly communication mediated by the chairman, providing opportunity for each faction to speak, but avoidance of factional domination
    b. formalized procedures providing for an orderly handling of disputation
    c. formalized voting procedure
    d. possession of veto power by each faction
    e. analytical approaches to seeking compromise, rather than mere reliance on power attempts.

4. *Group style:* Group style is characterized by:
    a. frankness and candor in presenting opposing viewpoints
    b. acceptance of due process in seeking resolution to conflicts
    c. openness to rethinking, and to mediation attempts
    d. avoidance of emotional hostility and aggression

5. *Group norms:* Group norms are characterized by:
    a. desire on the part of all factions to reach agreement
    b. the perception of conflict and disagreement as healthy and natural, rather than pathological

    c. acceptance of individual freedom and group freedom to disagree

    d. openness to new analytical approaches in seeking acceptable compromise

    e. acceptance of the necessity of partial agreement as an acceptable, legitimate, and realistic basis for decision making.

There is, obviously, no parallel in either structure or norms to the above strategy in classical organizational models. The acceptance of open conflict; provision for due process between conflicting groups; openness to compromise; evolution of policy and objectives through negotiation; and "representative groups" while found in the "underworld" in most organizations, are outside the general organizational model. Indeed, managers involved in "negotiations," either in the personnel (labor relations) or marketing (customer relations) areas, find it difficult to articulate the legitimacy of many of their decisions except through rationalizations.

CONCLUSIONS AND IMPLICATIONS

Both the propensities for groups to change the nature of their interaction as they change task, and/or task phases, and the prescriptions for group strategies dealing with differentiated decision situations as set forth above, indicate that the structure and processes of groups must be related to changes in the characteristics of the decision-making tasks. Whether one agrees with each proposition in each of the decision strategy models set forth in this article or not, the fact that each of the decision-making situations is endemically different is difficult to refute.

On the other hand, formal organizations as conceived in present organizational models are presumably structured in terms of the predominant type of task encountered by the system. (Thus, the "bureaucratic" model is based on facilitating "routine" decision making; the labor union council is structured to deal with negotiated decision making; etc.). Since task is, in the most pertinent sense, what members of the organization subjectively define it to be as they respond to the situation in which they find themselves, the internal features of a decision group within the organization will generally be conditioned by the predominant structured roles created to deal with the "typical" decisions encountered in day-to-day organizational tasks. As a result, role expectations and behaviors conditioned in the central organizational system (the formal organization) may inhibit the decision task performance in the subsystem (the decision-making committee, conference, or task force).

Since there are several types of decisions to be made within complex organizations, with each general type calling for a different group structure and process, a major role of the manager in such a system is the evoking of appropriate changes in behaviors on the part of the managerial team as it moves across task types by means of role redefinition. This assumes that the manager can classify decision tasks according to the models presented here, or some other conceptual scheme, and that the managerial team can respond with congruent role flexibility. Earlier pilot research by the author indicates that such flexibility seems to be within the capacities of a large portion of the population, given appropriate role redefinition by the superior.[17]

In a real sense, then, management of the decision-making process is management of the structure and functioning of decision groups, so that these decision-making processes become congruent with changes in the nature of the decision-making task being undertaken at a particular point of time within the organization.

Finally, we spent considerable time delineating the "taskforce," "systems management" or "matrix organizational" approach (strategy one)[18] as the appropriate strategy for routine decision making purposefully, since it seems to provide a mechanism for integrating various types of decision making at various phases of project management within a flexible structure. It is felt that strategy one avoids the structural rigidity of formal organization models such as "bureaucracy." There is no reason, for instance, why "creative" or "negotiated" strategies cannot be incorporated into the objectives and standards-setting decision sessions at the beginning of the planning period. Further, there is no reason why personnel other than the "task specialists" cannot mediate the decision making by participation in these early decision phases. Thus, by dropping the assumption of "agreed upon technologies" and "agreed upon objectives," and incorporating strategies two and three into these early planning sessions, or intermittently juxtaposing these strategies with strategy one, the possibility for incorporating decision-making flexibility into the "project management" context of strategy one seems not only feasible, but a desirable movement in the direction of fluid group structures and processes. Such a movement toward organizational fluidness is more congruent with the need for role flexibility as the management team moves across decision strategies at various phases of project planning and implementation.

ENDNOTES

1. Harold Guetzkow and Herbert A. Simon, "The Impact of Certain Communication Nets Upon Organization and Performance in Task Oriented Groups," *Management Science*, I (1955), 233-250; Rocco Carzo, Jr., "Organization Structure and Group Effectiveness," *Administrative Science Quarterly* (March, 1963), pp. 393-425.

2. Leonard Berkowitz, "Sharing Leadership in Small, Decision-Making Groups," *Journal of Abnormal and Social Psychology* (1953), pp. 231-238; Andre L. Delbecq, "Managerial Leadership Styles in Problem-Solving Conferences," *Academy of Management Journal*, VII, No. 4 (Dec., 1964), 255-268.

3. Andre L. Delbecq, "Managerial Leadership Styles in Problem-Solving Conferences: Research Findings on Role Flexibility," *Academy of Management Journal*, VIII, No. 1 (March, 1965), 32-43.

4. Harold J. Leavitt and Ronald A. H. Mueller, *Managerial Psychology* (Chicago: University of Chicago Press, 1964), pp. 8-9.

5. Robert T. Golembiewski, *The Small Group* (Chicago: University of Chicago Press, 1962), p. 181.

6. Benjamin Wolman, "Instrumental, Mutual Acceptance and Vectorial Groups." Paper read at the Annual Meeting of the American Sociological Association, August 1953.

7. Peter M. Blau and W. Richard Scott, *Organizations, A Comparative Approach* (San Francisco: Chandler Publishing Company, 1962).

8. W. C. Schutz, "Some Theoretical Considerations for Group Behavior," *Symposium on Techniques for the Measurement of Group Performance* (Washington, D.C.: U.S. Government Research and Development Board, 1952), pp. 27-36.

9. The reader should be clearly forewarned that each of the strategies is the author's own conceptualization. While an extensive review of the literature, both theoretical and empirical, underlies each strategy, it is not meant to be implied that the strategy represents a model about which scholars universally agree. Rather, the strategies represent the theoretical position of the author which is consistent with much of the literature, but is admittedly open to question and refinement.

10. J. Thompson and Arthur Tuden, "Strategies, Structures, and Processes of Organizational Decision," *Comparative Studies in Administration*, ed. Thompson, *et al.* (Pittsburgh, Pa.: University of Pittsburgh Press, 1959), pp. 198-199; H. Simon, *The New Science of Management Decisions* (New York: Harper Brothers, 1960), Chapters 2, 3.

11. For a treatment of the manner in which group norms control individual behavior, see Andre L. Delbecqu and Fremont A. Shull, "Norms, A Feature of Symbolic Culture: A Major Linkage Between the Individual, The Small Group and Administrative Organization," *The Making of Decisions*, ed. W. J. Gore and J. W. Dyson (N.Y.: The Free Press of Glencoe, 1964), pp. 213-242.

12. Herbert A. Simon and Allen Newell, "Heuristic Problem Solving: The Next Advance in Operations Research," *Operations Research Journal* (Jan.-Feb., 1958); Thompson and Tuden, *op. cit.*

13. Particularly useful models dealing with individual and group creativity

can be found in William E. Scott, "The Creative Individual," *Journal of Management* (Sept., 1965); Larry Cummings, "Organizational Climates for Creativity." *Journal of the Academy of Management* (Sept., 1965): Victor A. Thompson, "Bureaucracy and Innovation," *Administrative Science Quarterly* (June, 1965): Gary Steiner, *The Creative Organization* (Chicago: University of Chicago Press, 1965); and Norman R. F. Maier, *Problem-Solving Discussions and Conferences* (New York: McGraw-Hill, 1963).

14. In development of the above model, we have consciously avoided the issue of "nominal" groups (where members work without verbal interaction in generalizing solution strategies) vs. "interacting" groups. While preliminary evidence favors "nominal" groups in generating ideas, the question as to the appropriateness of the nominal group strategy for the total decision process (i.e., evaluation as well as idea generation) remains in question.

Further, the experimental tasks used in the studies may be different in kind from organizational decision making. In any event, the above model seems quite adaptable to separation into nominal and interacting processes at various phases, using modifications which do not vitiate the general tenor of the model. For a discussion of nominal vs. interacting groups, see Alan H. Leader, "Creativity in Management," Paper read at the Midwest Division of the Academy of Management, April 8, 1967; P. W. Taylor, P. C. Berry, and C. H. Block. "Does Group Participation When Using Brainstorming Facilitate or Inhibit Creative Thinking?" *Administrative Science Quarterly*, III (1958), 23–47.

15. In this respect, we assume a position different from that of Thompson and Tuden in their earlier model who posit that "compromise" decision making is predicted on disagreement about ends. Thompson and Tuden, *op. cit.*

16. The justification for the minority never being represented by less than two persons is that it is difficult for one person to represent his group across the boundary and that a minority of one is easy prey for a majority coalition of two members, let alone more than two.

17. Andre L. Delbecq (March, 1965). We agree that some individuals will find it impossible to assume flexible roles due to their particular developmental history which results in a fixated behavior pattern. We also agree that some roles will be more natural than others for individuals due to their developmental history. We disagree, however, with the notion that the normal population cannot assume at least functionally relevant roles in accordance with the various strategies, a point which appears to be the position of some theorists. A more conservative viewpoint than ours is assumed by Abraham Zaleznic in *Human Dilemmas of Leadership* (New York: Harper & Row. 1965).

18. For an elaborated treatment of "Matrix Organization" see Fremont A. Shull, *Matrix Structure and Project Authority for Optimizing Capacity* (Monograph, Business Research Bureau, Southern Illinois University, Carbondale, Illinois, 1965); Warren Bennis, "Beyond Bureaucracy," *Transactions* (Summer, 1965); John F. Mee, "Ideational Items: Matrix Organization," *Business Horizons* (Summer, 1964), pp. 70–72; and Carl R. Praktish, "Evolution of Project Management." Paper read at Midwest Academy of Management, April, 1967.

12

thomas l. cronin

THE SWELLING OF THE PRESIDENCY

The advent of Richard Nixon's second term in the White House is marked by an uncommon amount of concern, in Congress and elsewhere, about the expansion of presidential power and manpower. Even the President himself is ostensibly among those who are troubled. Soon after his reelection, Mr. Nixon announced that he was planning to pare back the presidential staff. And in recent days, the President has said he is taking action to cut the presidential workfore in half and to "substantially" reduce the number of organizations that now come under the White House. Mr. Nixon's announcements have no doubt been prompted in part by a desire to add drama and an aura of change to the commencement of his second term. But he also seems genuinely worried that the presidency may have grown so large and top-heavy that it now weakens rather than strengthens his ability to manage the federal government. His fears are justified.

The presidency has, in fact, grown a full 20 per cent in the last four years alone in terms of the number of people who are employed directly under the President. It has swelled to the point where it is now only a little short of the State Departments' sprawling domestic bureaucracy in size.

This burgeoning growth of the presidency has, in the process, made the traditional civics textbook picture of the executive branch of our government nearly obsolete. According to this view, the executive branch is more or less neatly divided into Cabinet departments

From Thomas E. Cronin, "The Swelling of the Presidency," *Saturday Review of the Society*, January 20, 1973. © Copyright 1973 by Saturday Review.

and their secretaries, agencies and their heads, and the President. A more contemporary view takes note of a few prominent presidential aides and refers to them as the "White House staff." But neither view adequately recognizes the large and growing coterie that surrounds the President and is made up of dozens of assistants, hundreds of presidential advisers, and thousands of members of an institutional amalgam called the Executive Office of the President. While the men and women in these categories all fall directly under the President in the organizational charts, there is no generally used term for their common terrain. But it has swelled so much in size and scope in recent years, and has become such an important part of the federal government that it deserves its own designation. Most apt perhaps is the Presidential Establishment.

The Presidential Establishment today embraces more than twenty support staffs (the White House Office, National Security Council, and Office of Management and Budget, etc.) and advisory offices (Council of Economic Advisers, Office of Science and Technology, and Office of Telecommunications Policy, etc.). It has spawned a vast proliferation of ranks and titles to go with its proliferation of functions (Counsel to the President, Assistant to the President, Special Counselor, Special Assistant, Special Consultant, Director, Staff Director, etc.). "The White House now has enough people with fancy titles to populate a Gilbert and Sullivan comic opera," Congressman Morris Udall has reasonably enough observed.

There are no official figures on the size of the Presidential Establishment, and standard body counts vary widely depending on who is and who is not included in the count, but by one frequently used reckoning, between five and six thousand people work for the President of the United States. Payroll and maintenance costs for this staff run between $100 million and $150 million a year. (These figures include the Office of Economic Opportunity (OEO), which is Executive Office agency and employs two thousand people, but not the roughly fifteen thousand-man Central Intelligence Agency, although that, too, is directly responsible to the Chief Executive.) These "White House" workers have long since outgrown the White House itself and now occupy not only two wings of the executive mansion but three nearby high-rise office buildings as well.

The expansion of the Presidential Establishment, it should be emphasized, is by no means only a phenomenon of the Nixon years. The number of employees under the President has been growing steadily since the early 1900s when only a few dozen people served in the White House entourage, at a cost of less than a few hundred thousand dollars annually. Congress's research arm, the Congressional Research Service, has compiled a count that underlines in particular the accelerated increase in the last two decades. This compilation shows that between 1954 and 1971 the number of presidential advisers has grown from 25 to 45, the White House staff from 266 to 600, and the Executive Office staff from 1,175 to 5,395.

But if the growth of the Presidential Establishment antedates the current administration, it is curious at least that one of the largest expansions ever, in both relative and absolute terms, has taken place during the first term of a conservative, management-minded President who has often voiced his objection to any expansion of the federal government and its bureaucracy.

Under President Nixon, in fact, there has been an almost systematic bureaucratization of the Presidential Establishment, in which more new councils and offices have been established, more specialization and division of labor and layers of staffing have been added, than at any time except during World War II. Among the major Nixonian additions are the Council on Environmental Quality, Council on International Economic Policy, Domestic Council, and Office of Consumer Affairs.

The numbers in the White House entourage may have decreased somewhat since November when the President announced his intention to make certain staff cuts. They may shrink still more if, as expected, the OEO is shifted from White House supervision to Cabinet control, mainly under the Department of Health, Education, and Welfare. Also, in the months ahead, the President will probably offer specific legislative proposals, as he has done before, to reprogram or repackage the upper reaches of the executive.

Even so, any diminution of the Presidential Establishment has so far been more apparent than real, or more incidental than substantial. Some aides, such as former presidential counselor Robert Finch, who have wanted to leave anyway, have done so. Others, serving as scapegoats on the altar of Watergate, are also departing.

In addition, the President has officially removed a number of trusted domestic-policy staff assistants from the White House rolls and dispersed them to key sub-Cabinet posts across the span of government. But this dispersal can be viewed as not so much reducing as creating yet another expansion—a virtual setting up of White House outposts (or little White Houses?) throughout the Cabinet departments. The aides that are being sent forth are notable for their intimacy with the President, and they will surely maintain direct links to the White House, even though these links do not appear on the official organizational charts.

Then, too, one of the most important of the President's recent shifts of executive branch members involves an unequivocal addition to the Presidential Establishment. This is the formal setting up of a second office—with space and a staff in the White House—for Treasury Secretary George Shultz as chairman of yet another new presidential body, the Council on Economic Policy. This move makes Shultz a member of a White House inner cabinet. He will now be over-secretary of economic affairs alongside Henry Kissinger, over-secretary for national security affairs, and John Ehrlichman, over-secretary for domestic affairs.

In other words, however the names and numbers have changed recently or may be shifted about in the near future, the Presidential Establishment does not seem to be declining in terms of function, power, or prerogative; in fact, it may be continuing to grow as rapidly as ever.

Does it matter? A number of political analysts have argued recently that it does, and I agree with them. Perhaps the most disturbing aspect of the expansion of the Presidential Establishment is that it has become a powerful inner sanctum of government, isolated from traditional, constitutional checks and balances. It is common practice today for anonymous, unelected, and unratified aides to negotiate sensitive international commitments by means of executive agreements that are free from congressional oversight. Other aides in the Presidential Establishment wield fiscal authority over billions of dollars in funds that Congress has appropriated, yet the President refuses to spend, or that Congress has assigned to one purpose and the administration routinely redirects to another—all with no semblance of public scrutiny. Such exercises of power pose an important, perhaps vital, question of governmental philosophy: Should a political system that has made a virtue of periodic electoral accountability accord an ever-increasing policy-making role to White House counselors who neither are confirmed by the U.S. Senate nor, because of the doctrine of "executive privilege," are subject to questioning by Congress?

Another disquieting aspect of the growth of the Presidential Establishment is that the increase of its powers has been largely at the expense of the traditional sources of executive power and policy-making—the Cabinet members and their departments. When I asked a former Kennedy-Johnson Cabinet member a while ago what he would like to do if he ever returned to government, he said he would rather be a presidential assistant than a Cabinet member. And this is an increasingly familiar assessment of the relative influence of the two levels of the executive branch. The Presidential Establishment has become, in effect, a whole layer of government between the President and the Cabinet, and it often stands above the Cabinet in terms of influence with the President. In spite of the exalted position that Cabinet members hold in textbooks and protocol, a number of Cabinet members in recent administrations have complained that they could not even get the President's ear except through an assistant. In his book *Who Owns America?*, former Secretary of the Interior Walter Hickel recounts his combat with a dozen different presidential functionaries and tells how he needed clearance from them before he could get to talk to the President, or how he frequently had to deal with the assistants themselves because the President was "too busy." During an earlier administration, President Eisenhower's chief assistant, Sherman Adams, was said to have told two Cabinet members who could not resolve a matter of mutual concern: "Either make up your mind or else tell me and I will do it. We must not bother the President with this. He is trying to keep the world from war." Several of President Kennedy's Cabinet members regularly battled with White House aides who blocked them from seeing the President. And McGeorge Bundy, as Kennedy's chief assistant for national security affairs, simply sidestepped the State Department in one major area of department communications. He had all important incoming State Department cables transmitted simultaneously to his office in the White House, part of an absorption of traditional State Department functions that visibly continues to this day with presidential assistant Henry Kissinger. Indeed, we recently witnessed the bizarre and telling spectacle of Secretary of State William Rogers insisting the he *did* have a role in making foreign policy.

In a speech in 1971, Sen. Ernest Hollings of South Carolina plaintively noted the lowering of Cabinet status. "It used to be," he said, "that if I had a problem with food stamps, I went to see the Secretary of Agriculture, whose department had jurisdiction over that problem. Not anymore. Now, if I want to learn the policy, I must go to the White House to consult John Price [a special assistant]. If I want the latest on textiles, I won't get it from the Secretary of Commerce, who has the authority and responsibility. No, I am forced to go to the White House and see Mr. Peter Flanigan. I shouldn't feel too badly, Secretary Stans [Maurice Stans, then Secretary of Commerce] has to do the same thing."

If Cabinet members individually have been downgraded in influence, the Cabinet itself as a council of government has become somewhat of a relic, replaced by more specialized comminglings that as often as not are presided over by White House staffers. The Cabinet's decline has taken place over several administrations. John Kennedy started out his term declaring his intentions of using the Cabinet as a major policy-making body, but his change of mind was swift, as his Postmaster General, J. Edward Day, has noted. "After the first two or three meetings," Day has written, "one had the distinct impression that the President felt that decisions on major matters were not made—or even influenced—at Cabinet sessions, and that discussion there was a waste of time . . . . When members spoke up to suggest or to discuss major administration policy, the President would listen with thinly disguised impatience and then postpone or otherwise bypass the question."

Lyndon Johnson was equally disenchanted with the Cabinet as a body and characteristically held Cabinet sessions only when articles appeared in the press talking about how the Cabinet was withering away. Under Nixon, the Cabinet is almost never convened at all.

Not only has the Presidential Establishment taken over many policy-making functions from the Cabinet and its members, it has also absorbed some of the operational functions. White House aides often feel they should handle any matters that they regard as ineptly administered, and they tend to intervene in internal departmental operations at lower and lower levels. They often feel underemployed, too, and so are inclined to reach out into the departments to find work and exercise authority for themselves.

The result is a continuous undercutting of Cabinet departments—and the cost is heavy. These intrusions can cripple the capacity of Cabinet officials to present policy alternatives, and they diminish self-confidence, morale, and initiative within the departments. George Ball, a former undersecretary of state, noted the effects on the State Department: "Able men, with proper pride in their professional skills, will not long tolerate such votes of no-confidence, so it should be no surprise that they are leaving the career service, and making way for mediocrity with the result that, as time goes on it may be hopelessly difficult to restore the Department . . . . "

The irony of this accretion of numbers and functions to the Presidential Establishment is that the presidency is finding itself increasingly afflicted with the very ills of the traditional departments that the expansions were often intended to remedy. The presidency has become a large, complex bureaucracy itself, rapidly acquiring many dubious characteristics of large bureaucracies in the process: layering, overspecialization, communication gaps, interoffice rivalries, inadequate coordination, and an impulse to become consumed with short-term, urgent operational concerns at the expense of thinking systematically about the consequences of varying sets of policies and priorities and about important long-range problems. It takes so much of the President's time to deal with the members of his own bureaucracy that it is little wonder he has little time to hear counsel from Cabinet officials.

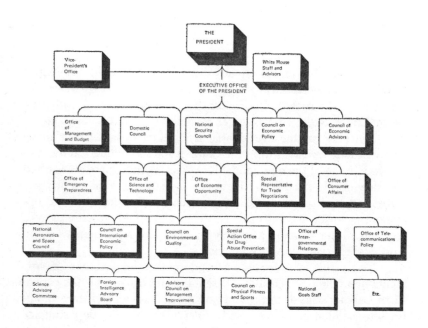

FIGURE 3.1 The presidential establishment.

Another toll of the burgeoning Presidential Establishment is that White House aides, in assuming more and more responsibility for the management of government programs, inevitably lose the detachment and objectivity that is so essential for evaluating new ideas. Can a lieutenant vigorously engaged in implementing the presidential will admit the possibility that what the President wants is wrong or not working? Yet a President is increasingly dependent on the judgment of these same staff members, since he seldom sees his Cabinet members.

Why has the presidency grown bigger and bigger? There is no single villain or systematically organized conspiracy promoting this expansion. A variety of factors is at work. The most significant is the expansion of the role of the presidency itself—an expansion that for the most part has taken place during national emergencies. The reason for this is that the public and Congress in recent decades have both tended to look to the President for the decisive responses that were needed in those emergencies. The Great Depression and World War II in particular brought sizable increases in presidential staffs. And once in place, many stayed on, even after the emergencies that brought them had faded. Smaller national crises have occasioned expansion in the White House entourage, too. After the Russians successfully orbited *Sputnik* in 1957, President Eisenhower added several science advisers. After the Bay of Pigs, President Kennedy enlarged his national security staff.

Considerable growth in the Presidential Establishment, especially in the post-World War II years, stems directly from the belief that critical societal problems require that wise men be assigned to the White House to alert the President to appropriate solutions and to serve as the agents for implementing these solutions. Congress has frequently acted on the basis of this belief, legislating the creation of the National Security Council, the Council of Economic Advisers, and the Council on Environmental Quality, among others. Congress has also increased the chores of the presidency by making it a statutory responsibility for the President to prepare more and more reports associated with what are regarded as critical social areas— annual economic and manpower reports, a biennial report on national growth, etc.

Most recently, President Nixon responded to a number of troublesome problems that defy easy relegation to any one department— problems like international trade and drug abuse—by setting up special offices in the Executive Office with sweeping authority and sizable staffs. Once established, these units rarely get dislodged. And an era of permanent crisis ensures a continuing accumulation of such bodies.

Another reason for the growth of the Presidential Establishment is that occupants of the White House frequently distrust members of the permanent government. Nixon aides, for example, have viewed most civil servants not only as Democratic but as wholly unsympathetic to such objectives of the Nixon administration as decentralization, revenue sharing, and the curtailment of several Great Society programs. Departmental bureaucracies are viewed from the White House as independent, unresponsive, unfamiliar, and inaccessible. They are suspected again and again of placing their own, congressional, or special-interest priorities ahead of those communicated to them from the White House. Even the President's own Cabinet members soon become viewed in the same light; one of the strengths of Cabinet members, namely their capacity to make a compelling case for their programs, has proved to be their chief liability with Presidents.

Presidents may want this type of advocacy initially, but they soon grow weary and wary of it. Not long ago, one White House aide accused a former Labor Secretary of trying to "out-Meany Meany." Efforts by former Interior Secretary Hickel to advance certain environmental programs and by departing Housing and Urban Development Secretary George Romney to promote innovative housing construction methods not only were unwelcome but after a while were viewed with considerable displeasure and suspicion at the White House.

Hickel writes poignantly of coming to this recognition during his final meeting with President Nixon, in the course of which the President frequently referred to him as an "adversary." "Initially," writes Hickel, "I considered that a compliment because, to me, an adversary is a valuable asset. It was only after the President had used the term many times and with a disapproving inflection that I realized he considered an adversary an enemy. I could not understand why he would consider me an enemy."

Not only have recent Presidents been suspicious about the depth of the loyalty of those in their Cabinets, but they also invariably become concerned about the possibility that sensitive administration secrets may leak out through the departmental bureaucracies, and this is another reason why Presidents have come to rely more on their own personal groups, such as task forces and advisory commissions.

Still another reason that more and more portfolios have been given to the presidency is that new federal programs frequently concern more than one federal agency, and it seems reasonable that someone at a higher level is required to fashion a consistent policy and to reconcile conflicts. Attempts by Cabinet members themselves to solve sensitive jurisdictional questions frequently result in bitter squabbling. At times, too, Cabinet members themselves have recommended that these multi-departmental issues be settled at the White House. Sometimes new presidential appointees insist that new offices for program coordination be assigned directly under the President. Ironically, such was the plea of George McGovern, for example, when President Kennedy offered him the post of director of the Food-for-Peace program in 1961. McGovern attacked the buildup of the Presidential Establishment in his campaign against Nixon, but back in 1961 he wanted visibility (and no doubt celebrity status) and he successfully argued against his being located outside the White House—either in the State or Agriculture departments. President Kennedy and his then campaign manager Robert Kennedy felt indebted to McGovern because of his efforts in assisting the Kennedy presidential campaign in South Dakota. Accordingly, McGovern was granted not only a berth in the Executive Office of the President but also the much-coveted title of special assistant to the President.

The Presidential Establishment has also been enlarged by the representation of interest groups within its fold. Even a partial listing of staff specializations that have been grafted onto the White House in recent years reveals how interest-group brokerage has become added to the more traditional staff activities of counseling and administration. These specializations form a veritable index of American society:

Budget and management, national security, economics, congressional matters, science and technology, drug abuse prevention, telecommunications, consumers, national goals, intergovernmental relations, environment, domestic policy, international economics, military affairs, civil rights, disarmament, labor relations, District of Columbia, cultural affairs, education, foreign trade and tariffs, past Presidents, the aged, health and nutrition, physical fitness, volunteerism, intellectuals, blacks, youth, women, "the Jewish community," Wall Street, governors, mayors, "ethnics," regulatory agencies and related industry, state party chairmen, Mexican-Americans.

It is as if interest groups and professions no longer settle for lobbying Congress, or having one of their number appointed to departmental advisory boards or sub-Cabinet positions. It now appears essential to "have your own man right there in the White House," Once this foothold is established, of course, interest groups can play upon the potential political backlash that could arise should their representation be discontinued.

One of the more disturbing elements in the growth of the Presidential Establishment is the development, particularly under the current administration, of a huge public-relations apparatus. More than 100 presidential aides are now engaged in various forms of press-agentry or public relations, busily selling and reselling the President. This activity is devoted to the particular occupant of the White House, but inevitably it affects the presidency itself, by projecting or reinforcing images of the presidency that are almost imperial in their suggestions of omnipotence and omniscience. Thus the public-relations apparatus not only has directly enlarged the presidential work-force but has expanded public expectations about the presidency at the same time.

Last, but by no means least, Congress, which has grown increasingly critical of the burgeoning power of the presidency, must take some blame itself for the expansion of the White House. Divided within itself and ill-equipped, or simply disinclined to make some of the nation's toughest political decisions in recent decades, Congress has abdicated more and more authority to the presidency. The fact that the recent massive bombing of North Vietnam was ordered by the President without even a pretense of consultation with Congress buried what little was left of the semblance of that body's war-making power. Another recent instance of Congress's tendency to surrender authority to the presidency, an extraordinary instance, was the passage by the House (though not the Senate) of a grant to the President that would give him the right to determine which programs are to be cut whenever the budget goes beyond a $250 billion ceiling limit—a bill which, in effect, would hand over to the President some of Congress's long-cherished "power of the purse."

What can be done to bring the Presidential Establishment back down to size? What can be done to bring it to a size that both lightens the heavy accumulation of functions that it has absorbed and allows the Presidential Establishment to perform its most important functions more effectively and wisely?

First, Congress should curb its own impulse to establish new presidential agencies and to ask for yet additional reports and studies from the President. In the past Congress has been a too willing partner in the enlargement of the presidency. If Congress genuinely wants a leaner presidency, it should ask more of itself. For instance, it could well make better use of its own General Accounting Office and Congressional Research Service for chores that are now often assigned to the President.

Congress should also establish in each of its houses special committees on Executive Office operations. Most congressional committees are organized to deal with areas such as labor, agriculture, armed services, or education, paralleling the organization of the Cabinet. What we need now are committees designed explicitly to oversee the White House. No longer can the task of overseeing presidential operations be dispersed among dozens of committees and subcommittees, each of which can look at only small segments of the Presidential Establishment.

Some will complain that adding yet another committee to the already overburdened congressional system is just like adding another council to the overstuffed Presidential Establishment. But the central importance of what the presidency does (and does not do) must rank among the most critical tasks of the contemporary Congress. As things are organized now, the presidency escapes with grievously inadequate scrutiny. Equally important, Congress needs these committees to help protect itself from its own tendency to relinquish to the presidency its diminishing resources and prerogatives. Since Truman, Presidents have had staffs to oversee Congress; it is time Congress reciprocated.

Similar efforts to let the salutary light of public attention shine more brightly on the presidency should be inaugurated by the serious journals and newspapers of the nation. For too long, publishers and editors have believed that covering the presidency means assigning a reporter to the White House press corps. Unfortunately, however, those who follow the President around on his travels are rarely in a position to do investigative reporting on what is going on inside the Presidential Establishment. Covering the Executive Office of the President requires more than a President watcher; it needs a specialist who understands the arcane language and highly complex practices that have grown up in the Presidential Establishment.

Finally, it is time to reverse the downgrading of the Cabinet. President Nixon ostensibly moved in this direction with his designation several days ago of three Cabinet heads—HEW's Caspar W. Weinberger, Agriculture's Earl L. Butz, and HUD's James T. Lynn—as, in effect, super-secretaries of "human resources," "natural resources," and "community development" respectively. The move was expressly made in the name of Cabinet consolidation, plans for which Mr. Nixon put forward in 1971 but which Congress has so far spurned.

The three men will hold onto their Cabinet posts, but they have been given White House offices as well—as presidential counselors—and so it may be that the most direct effect of the appointments is a further expansion of the Presidential Establishment, rather than a counter-bolstering of the Cabinet. But if the move does, in fact, lead to Cabinet consolidation under broader divisions, it will be a step in the right direction.

Reducing the present number of departments would strengthen the hand of Cabinet members vis-à-vis special interests, and might enable them to serve as advisers, as well as advocates, to the President. Cabinet consolidation would also have another very desirable effect: it would be a move toward reducing the accumulation of power within the Presidential Establishment. For much of the power of budget directors and other senior White House aides comes from their roles as penultimate referees of interdepartmental jurisdictional disputes. Under consolidated departments, a small number of strengthened Cabinet officers with closer ties to the President would resolve these conflicts instead. With fewer but broader Cabinet departments, there would be less need for many of the interest-group brokers and special councils that now constitute so much of the excessive baggage in the overburdened presidency.

Meantime, the presidency remains sorely overburdened—with both functions and functionaries—and needs very much to be cut back in both. Certainly, the number of presidential workers can and should be reduced. Harry Truman put it best, perhaps, when he said with characteristic succinctness: "I do not like this present trend toward a huge White House staff. . . . Mostly these aides get in each other's way." But while the number of functionaries is the most tangible and dramatic measure of the White House's expansion, its increasing absorption of governmental functions is more profoundly disturbing. The current White House occupant may regard cutting down (or transferring) a number of his staff members as a way of mollifying critics who charge that the American presidency has grown too big and bloated, but it is yet another thing to reduce the President's authority or his accumulated prerogatives. As the nation's number-one critic of the swelling of government, President Nixon will, it is hoped, move—or will continue to move if he has truly already started—to substantially deflate this swelling in one of the areas where it most needs to be deflated—at home, in the White House.

13

arthur m. schlesinger, jr.

THE RUNAWAY PRESIDENCY

I

"The tyranny of the legislature is really the danger most to be feared, and will continue to be so for many years to come," Jefferson wrote Madison six weeks before Washington's first inauguration. "The tyranny of the executive power will come in its turn, but at a more distant period." On the eve of the second centennial of independence, Jefferson's prophecy appears almost on the verge of fulfillment. The imperial presidency, created by wars abroad, has made a bold bid for power at home. The belief of the Nixon Administration in its own mandate and in its own virtue, compounded by its conviction that the republic has been in mortal danger from internal enemies, has produced an unprecedented concentration of power in the White House and an unprecedented attempt to transform the presidency of the Constitution into a plebiscitary presidency. If this transformation is carried through, the President, instead of being accountable every day to Congress and public opinion, will be accountable every four years to the electorate. Between elections, the President will be accountable only through impeachment and will govern, as much as he can, by decree. The expansion and abuse of presidential power constitute the underlying issue, the issue that Watergate has raised to the surface, dramatized, and made politically accessible.

From Arthur M. Schlesinger, Jr., *The Imperial Presidency*, chapter eleven, pp. 377–419. Boston: Houghton Mifflin Company. Copyright© 1973 by Arthur M. Schlesinger, Jr. Reprinted by permission of the publisher, Houghton Mifflin Company, and the author.

In giving great power to Presidents, Americans have declared their faith in the winnowing processes of politics. They have assumed that these processes, whether operating through the electoral college or later through the congressional caucus or still later through the party conventions, will eliminate aspirants to the presidency who reject the written restraints of the Constitution and the unwritten restraints of the republican ethos.

Through most of American history that assumption has been justified. "Not many Presidents have been brilliant," James Bryce observed in 1921, "some have not risen to the full moral height of the position. But none has been base or unfaithful to his trust, none has tarnished the honour of the nation." Even as Bryce wrote, however, his observation was falling out of date—Warren G. Harding had just been inaugurated—and half a century later his optimism appears as much the function of luck as of any necessity in the constitutional order. Today the pessimism of the Supreme Court in an 1866 decision, *ex parte Milligan*, seems a good deal more prescient. The nation, as Justice Davis wrote for the Court then, has "no right to expect that it will always have wise and humane rulers, sincerely attached to the principles of the Constitution. Wicked men, ambitious of power, with hatred of liberty and contempt of law, may fill the place once occupied by Washington and Lincoln."

The presidency has been in crisis before; but the constitutional offense that led to the impeachment of Andrew Johnson was trivial compared to the charges now accumulating around the Nixon Administration. There are, indeed, constitutional offenses here too—the abuse of impoundment and executive privilege, for example; or the secret air war against Cambodia in 1969-1970, unauthorized by and unknown to Congress; or the prosecution of the war in Vietnam after the repeal of the Tonkin Gulf Resolution; or the air war against Cambodia after the total withdrawal of American troops from Vietnam. But these, like Andrew Johnson's far less consequential defiance of the Tenure of Office Act, are questions that a President may more or less plausibly insist lie within a range of executive discretion. The Johnson case has discredited impeachment as a means of resolving arguable disagreements over the interpretation of the Constitution in advance of final judgment by the Supreme Court.

What is unique in the history of the presidency is the long list of potential *criminal* charges against the Nixon Administration. The investigations in process suggest that Nixon's appointees were engaged in a multitude of indictable activities: at the very least, in burglary; in forgery; in illegal wiretapping; in illegal electronic surveillance; in perjury; in subornation of perjury; in obstruction of justice; in destruction of evidence; in tampering with witnesses; in misprision of felony; in bribery (of the Watergate defendants); in acceptance of bribes (from Vesco and ITT); in conspiracy to involve government agencies (the FBI, the CIA, the Secret Service, the IRS, the Securities and Exchange Commission) in illegal action.

As for the President himself, he has denied that he knew either about the warfare of espionage and sabotage waged by his agents against his opponents or about the subsequent cover-up. If Nixon knew about these things, he obviously conspired against the basic processes of democracy. If he really did not know and for nine months did not bother to find out, he is surely an irresponsible and incompetent executive. For, if he did not know, it can only be because he did not want to know. He had all the facilities in the world for discovering the facts. The courts and posterity will have to decide whether the *Spectator* of London is right in its harsh judgment that in two centuries American history has come full circle "from George Washington, who could not tell a lie, to Richard Nixon, who cannot tell the truth."

Whether Nixon himself was witting or unwitting, what is clearly beyond dispute is his responsibility for the moral atmosphere within his official family. White House aides do not often do things they know their principal would not wish them to do—a proposition which I and dozens of other former White House aides can certify from experience. It is the President who both sets the example and picks the men. What standards did Nixon establish for his White House? He himself has admitted that in 1970, till J. Edgar Hoover forced him to change his mind, he authorized a series of criminal actions in knowing violation of the laws and the Constitution—authorization that would appear to be in transgression both of his presidential oath to preserve the Constitution and of his constitutional duty to see that the laws are faithfully executed. In 1971, as he has also admitted, he commissioned the White House plumbers, who set out so soon thereafter on their career of burglary, wiretapping, and forgery. "From the time when the break-in occurred," he said of the Watergate affair in August, 1973, "I pressed repeatedly to know the facts, and particularly whether there was any involvement of anyone in the White House"; but two obvious sources—John Mitchell, his intimate friend, former law partner, former Attorney General, head of the Committee for the Re-Election of the President, and Patrick Gray, acting director of the FBI itself—have both testified under oath that he never got around to pressing them. He even, through John

Ehrlichman, asked the Ellsberg judge in the midst of the trial whether he would not like to be head of the FBI. And he continues to hold up Ehrlichman and Haldeman as models to the nation—"two of the finest public servants it has been my privilege to know."

Nixon, in short, created the Nixon White House. "There was no independent sense of morality there," said Hugh Sloan, who served in the Nixon White House for two years. ". . . If you worked for someone, he was God, and whatever the orders were, you did it. . . . It was all so narrow, so closed. . . . There emerged some kind of separate morality about things." "Because of a certain atmosphere that had developed in my working at the White House," said Jeb Stuart Magruder, "I was not as concerned about its illegality as I should have been." "The White House is another world," said John Dean. "Expediency is everything." "No one who had been in the White House," said Tom Charles Huston, "could help but feel he was in a state of siege." "On my first or second day in the White House," said Herbert Porter, "Dwight Chapin [the President's appointments secretary] said to me, 'One thing you should realize early on, we are practically an island here.' That was the way the world was viewed." The "original sin," Porter felt, was the "misuse" of young people "through the whole White House system. They were not criminals by birth or design. Left to their own devices, they wouldn't engage in this sort of thing. Someone had to be telling them to do it." Gordon Strachan told of his excitement at "being twenty-seven years old and walking into the White House and seeing the President"; but, when asked what word he had for other young men who wanted to come to Washington and enter the public service, he said grimly, "My advice would be to stay away."

This is not the White House we have known—those of us, Democrats or Republicans, who served other Presidents in other years. Appointment to the White House of Roosevelt or Truman or Eisenhower or Kennedy or Johnson seemed the highest responsibility one could expect and therefore required higher standards of behavior than most of us had recognized before. And most of us look back at our White House experience, not with shame and incredulity, as the Nixon young men do, but as the most exhilarating time in our lives. Government, as Clark Clifford says, is a chameleon, taking its color from the character and personality of the President.

Moreover, Nixon's responsibility for the White House ethos goes beyond strictly moral considerations. In the First Congress, Madison, arguing that the power to remove government officials must belong to the President, added, "We have in him the security for the good behavior of the officer." This makes "the President responsible to the public for the conduct of the person he has nominated and appointed." If the President suffers executive officials to perpetrate crimes or neglects to superintend their conduct so as to check excesses, he himself, Madison said, is subject to "the decisive engine of impeachment."

II

The crisis of the presidency has led some critics to advocate a reconstruction of the institution itself. For a long time people have felt that the job was becoming too much for one man to handle. "Men of ordinary physique and discretion," Woodrow Wilson wrote as long ago as 1908, "cannot be Presidents and live, if the strain be not somehow relieved. We shall be obliged always to be picking our chief magistrate from among wise and prudent athletes,—a small class."

But what was seen until the late 1950s as too exhausting physically is now seen, after Vietnam and Watergate, as too dizzying psychologically. In 1968 Eugene McCarthy, the first liberal presidential aspirant in the century to run against the presidency, called for the depersonalization and decentralization of the office. The White House, he thought, should be turned into a museum. Instead of trying to lead the nation, the President should become "a kind of channel" for popular desires and aspirations. Watergate has made the point irresistible. "The office has become too complex and its reach too extended," writes Barbara Tuchman, "to be trusted to the fallible judgment of any one individual." "A man with poor judgment, an impetuous man, a sick man, a power-mad man," adds Max Learner, "each would be dangerous in the post. Even an able, sensitive man needs stronger safeguards around him than exist today."

The result is a new wave of proposals to transform the presidency into a collegial institution Mr. Tuchman suggests a six-man directorate with a rotating chairman, each member to serve for a year, as in Switzerland. Lerner wants to give the President a Council of State, a body that he would be bound by law to consult and that, because half its members would be from Congress and some from the opposite party, would presumably give him independent advice. Both proposals were, in fact, considered and rejected at the Constitutional Convention.

Hamilton and Jefferson disagreed on many things, but they agreed that the convention had been right in deciding on a one-man presidency. A plural executive, Hamilton contended, if divided within itself, would lead the country into factionalism and anarchy and, if united, could lead it into tyranny. When power was placed in the hands of a group small enough to admit "of their interests and views being easily combined in a common enterprise, by an artful leader," Hamilton thought, "it becomes more liable to abuse, and more dangerous when abused, than if it be lodged in the hands of one man, who, from the very circumstances of his being alone, will be more narrowly watched and more readily suspected." With a single executive it was possible to fix accountability. But a directorate "would serve to destroy, or would greatly diminish, the intended and necessary responsibility of the Chief Magistrate himself."

Jefferson had favored a plural executive under the Articles of Confederation, and, as an American in Paris, he watched with sympathy the Directoire of the French Revolution. But these experiments left him no doubt that plurality was a mistake. As he later observed, if Washington's Cabinet, in which he had served with Hamilton, had been a directorate, "the opposing wills would have balanced each other and produced a state of absolute inaction." But Washington, after listening to both sides, acted on his own, providing the "regulating power which would keep the machine in steady movement." History, moreover, furnished "as many examples of a single usurper arising out of a government by a plurality, as of temporary trusts of power in a single hand rendered permanent by usurpation."

The question remains whether the world has changed enough in two centuries to make these objections obsolete. There is, of course, the burden-of-the-presidency argument. But is the presidential burden so much heavier than ever before? The scope of the national government has expanded beyond imagination, but so too have the facilities for presidential management. The only President who clearly died of overwork was Polk, and that was a long time ago. Hoover, who worked intensely and humorlessly as President, lived for more than thirty years after the White House: Truman, who worked intensely and gaily, lived for twenty. The contemporary President is really not all that overworked. Eisenhower managed more golf than most corporation officials or college presidents; Kennedy always seemed unhurried and relaxed; Nixon spends almost as much time in Florida and California as in Washington, or so it appears. Johnson's former press secretary, George Reedy, has dealt with the myth of the presidential work load in terms that rejoice anyone who has ever served in the White House. "There is far less to the presidency, in terms of essential activity," Reedy correctly says, "than meets the eye." The President can fill his hours with as much motion as he desires; but he also can delegate as much "work" as he desires. "A president moves through his days surrounded by literally hundreds of people whose relationship to him is that of a doting mother to a spoiled child. Whatever he wants is brought to him immediately—food, drink, helicopters, airplanes, people, in fact, everything but relief from his political problems."

As for the moral and psychological weight of these political problems, this is real enough. All major presidential decisions are taken in conditions of what General Marshall, speaking of battle, used to call "chronic obscurity"—that is, on the basis of incomplete and probably inaccurate intelligence, with no sure knowledge where the enemy is or even where one's own men are. This can be profoundly anguishing for reasonably sensitive Presidents, especially when decisions determine people's livelihoods or end their lives. It was this, and not the work load, that did in Wilson and the second Roosevelt. But is the sheer moral weight of decision greater today than ever before? Greater for Johnson and Nixon than for Washington and Lincoln or Wilson or FDR? I doubt it very much.

If there is an argument for a plural executive, it is not the alleged burden of the presidency. The serious argument is simply to keep one man from wielding too much power. But here the points of Hamilton and Jefferson still have validity. The Council of Ten in Venice was surely as cruel as any doge. One wonders whether a six-man presidency would have prevented the war in Vietnam. It might well, however, have prevented the New Deal. The single-man presidency, with the right man as President, has its uses; and historically Americans have as often as not chosen the right man.

The idea of a Council of State has more plausibility. But it works better for foreign than for domestic policy. A prudent President is well advised to convoke ad hoc Councils of State on issues of war and peace. Kennedy added outsiders to his Executive Committee during the Cuban missile crisis; and it was an ad hoc Council of State in March, 1968, that persuaded Johnson to cease and desist in Vietnam. But, as an institutionalized body, with membership the ex officio perquisite of the senior leadership of House and Senate—that is, of the men in Congress who in the past have always been inclined to go along with Presidents—it could easily become simply one more weapon for a strong President. As Gouverneur Morris said at the Constitutional Convention, the President "by persuading his Council . . . to concur in his wrong measures would acquire their protection for them."

Above all, both the plural executive and the Council of State are open to the objection that most concerned the Founding Fathers—the problem of fixing accountability. In the case of high crimes and misdemeanors, who, to put it bluntly, is to be impeached? The solution surely lies not in blurring responsibility for the actions of the executive but in making that responsibility categorical and in finding ways of holding Presidents to it.

III

The other change in the institution of the presidency under discussion runs in the opposite direction. The idea of a single six-year presidential term is obviously designed not to reduce but to increase the independence of the presidency. This idea naturally appeals to the imperial ethos. Lyndon Johnson advocated it; Nixon has commended it to his Commission on Federal Election Reform for particular study. What is more puzzling is that it also has the support of two eminent senators, both unsympathetic to the imperial presidency. Mike Mansfield of Montana and George Aiken of Vermont—support that gives it a hearing it would not otherwise have had.

It is not a new idea. Andrew Jackson recommended to Congress an amendment limiting Presidents to a single term of four to six years; Andrew Johnson did the same; the Confederate Constitution provided for a single six-year term. Mansfield and Aiken now press their version on the ground, as Mansfield says, that a six-year term would "place the Office of the Presidency in a position that transcends as much as possible partisan political considerations." The amendment, says Aiken, "would allow a President to devote himself entirely to the problems of the Nation and would free him from the millstone of partisan politics."

This argument has a certain old-fashioned good-government plausibility. How nice it would be if Presidents could be liberated from politics for six years and set free to do only what is best for the country! But the argument assumes that Presidents know better than anyone else what is best for the country and that the democratic process is an obstacle to wise decisions. It assumes that Presidents are so generally right and the people so generally wrong that the President has to be protected against political pressures. It is, in short, a profoundly antidemocratic position. It is also profoundly unrealistic to think that any constitutional amendment could transport a President to some higher and more immaculate realm and still leave the United States a democracy. As Thomas Corcoran told the Senate

Judiciary Committee during hearings on the Mansfield-Aiken amendment, "It is impossible to take politics out of politics."

But, even if it were possible to take the presidency out of politics, is there reason to suppose this desirable? The electorate often knows things that Presidents do not know; and the nation has already paid a considerable price for presidential isolation and ignorance. Few things are more likely to make Presidents sensitive to public opinion than worrying about their own political future. Moreover, if public opinion is at times a baneful influence, what else is democracy all about? The need to persuade the nation of the soundness of a proposed policy is the heart of democracy. "A President immunized from political considerations," Clark Clifford told the Senate Judiciary Committee, "is a President who need not listen to the people, respond to majority sentiment, or pay attention to views that may be diverse, intense and perhaps at variance with his own."

The Mansfield-Aiken amendment expresses distrust of the democratic process in still another way—by its bar against re-eligibility. If anything is of the essence of democracy, it is surely that the voters should have an unconstrained choice of their leaders. "I can see no propriety." George Washington wrote the year after the adoption of the Constitution, "in precluding ourselves from the service of any man, who on some great emergency shall be deemed universally most capable of serving the public."

IV

Oddly, the crisis of the imperial presidency has not elicited much support for what at other times has been a favored theory of constitutional reform: movement in the direction of the British parliamentary system. This is particularly odd because, whatever the general balance of advantage between the parliamentary and presidential modes, the parliamentary system has one feature the presidential system badly needs now—the requirement that the head of government be compelled at regular intervals to explain and defend his policies in face-to-face sessions with the political opposition. Few devices, it would seem, are better calculated both to break down the real isolation of the latter-day presidency and to dispel the spurious reverence that has come to envelop the office.

In a diminished version, applying only to members of the Cabinet, the idea is nearly as old as the republic itself. The proposal that Cabinet members should go on to the floor of Congress to answer questions and take part in debate, "far from raising any constitutional difficulties," as E. S. Corwin once observed, "has the countenance of early practice under the Constitution." The Confederate Constitution authorized Congress to grant the head of each executive department "a seat upon the floor of either House, with the privilege of discussing any measures appertaining to his department," and Congressman George H. Pendleton of Ohio, with the support of Congressman James A. Garfield, argued for a similar proposal in the Union Congress in 1864. In his last annual message, President William Howard Taft suggested that Cabinet members be given access to the floor in order, as he later put it, "to introduce measures, to advocate their passage, to answer questions, and to enter into debate as if they were members, without of course the right to vote. . . . The time lost in Congress over useless discussion of issues that might be disposed of by a single statement from the head of a department, no one can appreciate unless he has filled such a place."

In the meantime, the young Woodrow Wilson carried the idea a good deal further toward the British model, arguing that Cabinet members should not just sit voteless in Congress but should be actually chosen "from the ranks of the legislative majority." Instead of the chaotic and irresponsible system of government by congressional committees, the republic would then have Cabinet government and ministerial responsibility. Though Wilson did not renew this specific proposal in later years, it very likely lingered in the back of his mind. On the eve of his first inauguration he noted that the position of the presidency was "quite abnormal, and most lead eventually to something very different." "Sooner or later," the President must be made "answerable to opinion in a somewhat more informal and intimate fashion—answerable, it may be, to the Houses whom he seeks to lead, either personally or through a cabinet, as well as to the people for whom they speak. But that is a matter to be worked out."

Wilson never found time to work it out. Today there appears to be little interest in reforms that squint at parliamentarianism. This may be in part because the parliamentary regimes best known in America—the British and French—have themselves moved in the direction of prime-ministerial or presidential government and offer few guarantees against the Vietnam-Watergate effect.

V

The problem of reining in the runaway presidency centers a good deal more at the moment on substantive than on structural solutions. Congress, in other words, has decided it can best restrain the presidency by enacting specific legislation in the conspicuous fields of presidential abuse. The main author of this comprehensive congressional attack on presidential supremacy, well before he assumed the chairmanship of the Senate Select Committee investigating Watergate, has been Senator Sam Ervin of North Carolina.

The republic owes a great deal to Sam Ervin. No one for a long time has done so much to educate the American people in the meaning and majesty of the Constitution (though his Constitution seems to stop with the ten amendments adopted in 1791; at least he does not show the same fervor about the Fourteenth and Fifteenth Amendments as he does about the First and Fourth). For most Americans the Constitution has become a hazy document, cited like the Bible on ceremonial occasions but forgotten in the daily transactions of life. For Ervin the Constitution, like the Bible, is superbly alive and fresh. He quotes it as if it had been written the day before; the Founding Fathers seem his contemporaries; it is almost as if he has ambled over from the Convention at Philadelphia. He is a true believer who endows his faith with abundant charm, decency, sagacity, and toughness. The old-fashioned Constitution—"the very finest document ever to come from the mind of men"—could have no more fitting champion in the battle against the imperial presidency.

But Ervin is concerned with more than the vindication of the Constitution. His larger design is to establish a new balance of constitutional power. Congress itself, Ervin thinks, has negligently become "the chief aggrandizer of the Executive." The restoration of the Constitution, he believes, requires the systematic recovery by Congress of powers appropriated by the presidency. The bills designed to constrain presidential war powers are, in his view, a confused and sloppy application of this strategy; he has little use for them. His own approach, direct and unequivocal, is expressed in the bill in which he proposes to give Congress absolute authority to veto executive agreements within sixty days. Congress never had, or even seriously sought, such authority before. While the provocation is real enough, the bill, if enacted, would give Congress unprecedented control over the presidential conduct of foreign affairs.

A leading item on Ervin's domestic agenda is executive privilege. This question has been historically one of conflicting and unresolved constitutional claims. In the nineteenth century, while insisting on a general congressional right to executive information. Congress acknowledged a right, or at least a power, of presidential denial in specific areas. It acquiesced in these reservations because they seemed reasonable and because responsible opinion saw them as reasonable. But what Congress saw as an expression of constitutional comity. Presidents in the later twentieth century—Nixon above all—have come to see as their inherent and unreviewable constitutional right.

Ervin, in response, has introduced a bill requiring members of the executive branch summoned by a committee of Congress to appear in person, even if they intend to claim executive privilege. Only a personal letter from the President could warrant the claim; and the bill gives the committee the power to decide whether the presidential plea is justified. In the words of Senator William Fulbright, it places "the final responsibility for judging the validity of a claim of executive privilege in the Congress, where it belongs."

A presidential thesis in violation of the traditional comity between the two branches has thus produced a congressional answer that would itself do away with what has been not only a historic but a healthy ambiguity. For one hundred and eighty years the arbiter in this question has been neither Congress nor the President nor the courts but the political context and process, with responsible opinion considering each case more or less on merit and turning against whichever side appears to be overreaching itself. The system is not tidy, but it encourages a measure of restraint on both sides and has avoided a constitutional showdown. Now absolute presidential claims have provoked an absolute congressional response. Would this really be an improvement? Would Ervin and Fulbright themselves twenty years earlier have wanted to give Joe McCarthy and his committee "the final responsibility" to judge whether executive testimony could be properly withheld?

Next on the Ervin agenda stands the restoration of congressional control over something it has thought it had anyway—the power of the purse. This means a solution of the problem of presidential impoundment. Impoundment existed before Nixon, but no previous President used it to overturn statutes and abolish programs against congressional will. For Nixon, impoundment is a means of taking from Congress the determination of national priorities.

The courts have been more willing to grasp the nettle of impoundment than they were, at least at the start, in the case of executive privilege. In decision after decision this year, judges have declared one aspect after another of the impoundment policy illegal. No judge has accepted Nixon's claim that he has a "constitutional right" not to spend money voted by Congress. One judge calls his use of impoundment "a flagrant abuse of executive discretion." "It is not within the discretion of the Executive," says another, "to refuse to execute laws passed by Congress but with which the Executive presently disagrees." The decisions are, however, as they should be, constructions of specific statutes and stop short of proposing a general solution to the impoundment controversy.

Though the courts have rallied splendidly, it is not really very satisfactory to have to sue the executive branch in every case in order to make it carry out programs duly enacted by Congress. But Congress itself has found it hard to make a stand on the Constitution. For Nixon has changed the issue with some success from a constitutional to a budgetary question. Impoundment, in other words, is alleged as the only answer a fiscally responsible President can make to insensate congressional extravagance. Sam Ervin derides this proposition. "Congress," he says, "is not composed of wild-eyed spenders, nor is the President the embattled crusader against wasteful spending that he would have you believe." The figures bear Ervin out. Congress, for example, cut more than $20 billion from Administration appropriation requests in Nixon's first term. Congress and the presidency roughly agree on the amount of money government should spend but disagree, as Ervin puts it, "over spending priorities and [the President's] authority to pick and choose what programs he will fund." Impoundment, says Ervin, has to do not with the budget but with the separation of powers.

It is a political fact, fully recognized by Ervin, that anti-impoundment legislation will have to be accompanied by new evidences of congressional self-control in spending. Ervin is personally a budget-balancer anyway. So his impoundment bill includes a spending ceiling. The bill, as passed by the Senate in 1973, also has certain eccentricities for a constitutional fundamentalist. After a clear statement in Section 1 that impoundment is unconstitutional, subsequent sections say that nevertheless the President is authorized to commit this unconstitutional act for periods up to seventy days. Thereafter impoundments not covered by the antideficiency acts (which permit the executive to impound funds not required to achieve the purpose of a statute) must cease unless Congress specifically approves them by concurrent resolution. The House, on the other hand, is quite willing to let impoundments stand unless specifically disapproved by one house of Congress. Both bills legitimize impoundment; but, where the House would place the burden on Congress in each case to stop impoundment, Ervin would place the burden on the President in each case to justify impoundment.

VI

In one area after another, with the concealed passion and will of a deceptively relaxed personality, Ervin is moving to restore the balance of the Constitution by cutting the presidency down to constitutional size. However, his is the Constitution not of Abraham Lincoln but of *ex parte Milligan.* "What the framers intended," he says, "was that the President . . . should be merely the executor of a power of decision that rests elsewhere; that is, in the Congress. This was the balance of power between the President and Congress intended by the Constitution." The "ultimate power," Ervin says, is "legislative."

It is hard to know how literally to take the Ervin scheme. If it sounds at times like an effort to replace presidential government by congressional government, it must be remembered that the Ervin proposals have been provoked by an attempt to alter the nature of the system. Ervin and his colleagues are fighting to protect Congress from the plebiscitary presidency, not to frustrate the leadership of a President who recognizes his accountability to Congress and the Constitution. Yet, if taken literally, the Ervin scheme is a scheme of presidential subordination. Where presidential abuse of particular powers has harmed the country, those powers are now to be vested in Congress. Pursued to the end, the Ervin scheme could produce a national polity which would be almost as overbalanced in the direction of congressional supremacy as the Nixon scheme is in the direction of presidential supremacy.

The Ervin counterattack thus runs the risk of creating a generation of weak Presidents in an age when the turbulence of race, poverty, inflation, crime, and urban decay is straining the delicate bonds of national cohesion and demanding, quite as much as in the 1930s, a strong domestic presidency to hold the country together. For Sam Ervin is of the pure Jeffersonian school, like the old Tertium Quids who felt that Jefferson and Madison, in building up the presidency and seeing the national government as an instrument of the general welfare, had deserted the true faith.

The pure Jeffersonian doctrine was a witness rather than a policy, which is why Jefferson and Madison themselves abandoned it. The pure Jeffersonian idea of decentralized power receded in the course of American history because local government simply did not offer the means to attain Jeffersonian ends. In practice, pure Jeffersonianism meant a system under which the strongest local interests, whether planters, landlords, merchants, bankers, or industrialists, consolidated their control and oppressed the rest; it meant all power to the neighborhood oligarchs. Theodore Roosevelt explained at the start of the twentieth century why Hamiltonian means had become necessary to achieve Jeffersonian ends, how national authority was the only effective means of correcting injustice in a national society.

"If Jefferson were living in our day," said Wilson in 1912, "he would see what we see: that the individual is caught in a great confused nexus of complicated circumstances, and that . . . without the watchful interference . . . of the government there can be no fair play." And, for the first Roosevelt and for Wilson, as for their joint heir, the second Roosevelt, national authority was embodied in the presidency.

This has not been a bad thing for the republic. It is presidential leadership, after all, that brought the country into the twentieth century, that civilized American industry, secured the rights of labor organization, defended the livelihood of the farmer. It is presidential leadership that has protected the Bill of Rights against local vigilantism and natural resources against local greed. It is presidential leadership, spurred on by the Supreme Court, that has sought to vindicate racial justice against local bigotry. Congress would have done few of these things on its own: local government even fewer. It would be a mistake to cripple the presidency at home because of presidential excesses abroad. History has shown the presidency to be the most effective instrumentality of government for justice and progress. Even Calvin Coolidge, hardly one of the more assertive of Presidents, said, "It is because in their hours of timidity the Congress becomes subservient to the importunities of organized minorities that the President comes more and more to stand as the champion of the rights of the whole country."

The scheme of presidential subordination can easily be pressed to the point of national folly. But it is important to contend not for a strong presidency in general but for a strong presidency within the Constitution. The presidency deserves to be defended on serious and not on stupid points. Watergate has produced flurries of near hysteria about the life expectancy of the institution. Thus Charles L. Black, Jr., Luce Professor of Jurisprudence at the Yale Law School, argues that, if Nixon turned over his White House tapes to Congress or the courts, it would mean the "danger of degrading or even destroying the Presidency" and constitute a betrayal of his "successors for all time to come." The republic, Black says, cannot even risk diluting the "symbolism" of the office lest that disturb "in the most dangerous way the balance of the best government yet devised on earth"; and it almost seems that he would rather suppress the truth than jeopardize the symbolism.

Executive privilege is not the issue. No Presidents cherished the presidency more than, say, Jackson or Polk; but both readily conceded to Congress the right in cases of malversation to penetrate into the most secret recesses of the executive department. Nor, in the longer run, does either Ervin's hope of presidential subordination or Black's fantasy of presidential collapse have real substance. For the presidency, though its wings can be clipped for a time, is an exceedingly tough institution. Its primacy is founded in the necessities of the American political order. It has endured many challenges and survived many vicissitudes. It is nonsense to suppose that its fate as an institution is bound up with the fate of the particular man who happens to be President at any given time. In the end power in the American order is bound to flow back to the presidency.

Congress has a marvelous, if generally unfulfilled, capacity for oversight, for advice, for constraint, for chastening the presidency and informing the people. When it really wants to say no to a President, it has ample means of doing so; and in due course the President will have no choice but to acquiesce. But it is inherently incapable of conducting government and providing national leadership. Its fragmentation, its chronic fear of responsibility, its habitual dependence on the executive for ideas, information, and favors—this is life insurance for the presidency.

Both Nixon and Ervin are wrong in supposing that the matter can be settled by shifting the balance of power in a decisive way to one branch or the other. The answer lies rather in preserving fluidity and re-establishing comity. Indeed, for most people—here Ervin is a distinguished exception—the constitutional and institutional issues are make-believe. It is largely a matter, as Averell Harriman says, "of whose ox is getting gored: who is in or out of power, and what actions either side may want." When Nixon was in the opposition, there was no more earnest critic of presidential presumption. Each side dresses its arguments in grand constitutional and institutional terms, but their contention is like that of the two drunken men described long ago by Lincoln who got into a fight with their greatcoats on until each fought himself out of his own coat and into the coat of the other.[1]

VII

What is required is, in Herbert Wechsler's phrase, a set of neutral principles—principles, that is, that are not shaped in response to a particular situation but work all the time, transcending any particular result involved. The supreme neutral principle, as vital in domestic policy as in foreign policy, is that all great decisions of the government must be shared decisions. The subsidiary principle is that if the presidency tries to transform what the Constitution sees as concurrent into exclusive authority, it must be stopped; and if Congress tries to transform concurrent into exclusive authority, it must be stopped too. If either the presidency or Congress turns against the complex balance of constitutional powers that has left room over many generations for mutual accommodation, then the ensuing collision will harm both branches of government and the republic as well. Even together, Congress and the presidency are by no means infallible; but their decisions, wise or foolish, at least meet the standards of democracy. And, taken together, the decisions are more likely to be wise than foolish.

All Presidents affect a belief in common counsel, but most after a time prefer to make other arrangements. Still, the idea is right, and the process of accountability has to begin inside the President himself. A constitutional President can do many things, but he has to believe in the discipline of consent. It is not enough that he personally thinks the country is in trouble and genuinely believes he alone knows how to save it. In all but the most extreme cases, action has to be accompanied by public explanation and tested by public acceptance. A constitutional President has to be aware of what Whitman called "the never-ending audacity of elected persons" and has to understand the legitimacy of challenges to his own judgment and authority. He has to be sensitive directly to the diversity of concern and conviction in the nation, sensitive prospectively to the verdict of history, sensitive always to the decent respect pledged in the Declaration of Independence to the opinions of mankind.

Yet Presidents chosen as open and modest men are not sure to remain so amid the intoxications of the office; and the office has grown steadily more intoxicating in recent years. A wise President, having read George Reedy and observed the fates of Johnson and Nixon, will take care to provide himself, while there still is time, with antidotes to intoxication. Presidents in the last quarter of the twentieth century might, as a beginning, plan to rehabilitate (I use the word in almost the Soviet sense) the executive branch of government. This does not mean the capitulation of the presidency to the permanent government; nor should anyone forget that it was the unresponsiveness of the permanent government that gave rise to the aggressive White House of the twentieth century. But it does mean a reduction in the size and power of the White House staff and the restoration of the access and prestige of the executive departments. The President will always need a small and alert personal staff to serve as his eyes and ears and one lobe of his brain, but he must avoid a vast and possessive staff ambitious to make all the decisions of government.

Above all, he must not make himself the prisoner of a single information system. No sensible President will give one man control of all the channels of communication: any man sufficiently wise to exercise such control properly ought to be President himself.

As for the Cabinet, while no President in American history has found it a very satisfactory instrument of government, it has served Presidents best when it has contained men strong and independent in their own right, strong enough to make the permanent government responsive to presidential policy and independent enough to carry honest dissents into the Oval Office. Franklin Roosevelt, who is fashionably regarded these days as the cause of it all, is really a model of how a strong President can operate within the constitutional order. While no President wants to create the impression that his Administration is out of control, FDR showed how a masterful President could maintain the most divergent range of contacts, surround himself with the most articulate and positive colleagues, and use debate within the executive branch as a means of clarifying issues and trying out people and policies. Or perhaps FDR is in a way the cause of it all, because he alone had the vitality, flair, and cunning to be clearly on top without repressing everything underneath. In a joke that Henry Wallace, not usually a humorous man, told in my hearing in 1943, FDR could keep all the balls in the air without losing his own. Some of his successors tried to imitate his mastery without understanding the sources of his strength.

But not every President is an FDR, and FDR himself, though his better instincts generally won out in the end, was a flawed, willful, and, with time, increasingly arbitrary man. When Presidents begin to succumb to delusions of grandeur, when the checks and balances inside themselves stop operating, external checks and balances may well become necessary to save the republic. The nature of an activist President in any case, in Samuel Lubell's phrase, is to run with the ball until he is tackled. As conditions abroad and at home have nourished the imperial presidency, tacklers have had to be more than usually sturdy and intrepid.

How to make external checks effective? Congress can tie the presidency down by a thousand small legal strings; but, like Gulliver, the President can always break loose. The effective means of controlling the presidency lie not in law but in politics. For the American President rules by influence; and the withdrawal of consent, by Congress, by the press, by public opinion, can bring any President down. The great Presidents have understood this. The President, said Andrew Jackson, must be "accountable at the bar of public opinion for every act of his Administration." "I have a very definite philosophy about the Presidency," said Theodore Roosevelt. "I think it should be a very powerful office, and I think the President should be a very strong man who uses without hesitation every power that the position yields; but because of this fact I believe that he should be sharply watched by the people [and] held to a strict accountability by them."

Holding a President to strict accountability requires, first of all, a new attitude on the part of the American people toward their Presidents, or rather a return to the more skeptical attitude of earlier times: it requires, specifically, a decline in reverence. An insistent theme in Nixon's public discourse is the necessity of maintaining due respect for the presidency. The possibility that such respect might be achieved simply by being a good President evidently does not reassure him. He is preoccupied with "respect for the office" as an entity in itself. Can one imagine Washington or Lincoln or the Roosevelts or Truman or Kennedy going on in public, as Nixon repeatedly does, about how important it is to do this or that in order to maintain "respect for the office"? But the age of the imperial presidency has produced the idea that run-of-the-mill politicians, brought by fortuity to the White House, must be treated thereafter as if they have become superior and perhaps godlike beings.

The Nixon theoreticians even try to transform reverence into an ideology, propagating the doctrine, rather novel in the United States, that institutions of authority are entitled to respect per se, whether or not they have done anything to earn respect. If authority is denied respect, the syllogism ran, the whole social order will be in danger. "Your task, then, is clear," Pat Moynihan charged his President in 1969: "To restore the authority of American institutions." But should institutions expect obedience that they do not, on their record of performance, deserve? To this question the Nixon ideologues apparently answer yes. An older American tradition would say no, incredulous that anyone would see this as a question. In that spirit I would argue that what the country needs today is a little serious disrespect for the office of the presidency; a refusal to give any more weight to a President's words than the intelligence of the utterance, if spoken by anyone else, would command; an understanding of the point made so aptly by Montaigne: "Sits he on never so high a throne, a man still sits on his bottom."

But what if men not open and modest, even at the start, but from the start ambitious of power and contemptuous of law, reach the place once occupied by Washington and Lincoln? What if neither personal character, nor the play of politics, nor the Constitution itself avail to hold a President to strict accountability? In the end, the way to control the presidency may have to be not in many little ways but in one large way. In the end, there remains, as Madison said, the decisive engine of impeachment.

VIII

This is, of course, the instrument provided by the Constitution. But it is an exceedingly blunt instrument. Only once has a President been impeached, and there is no great national desire to go through the experience again. Yet, for the first time in a century, Americans in the 1970s have to think hard about impeachment, which means that, because most of us flinch from the prospect, we begin to think hard about alternatives to impeachment.

One alternative is the censure of the President by the Congress. That was tried once in American history—in 1834 when the Senate censured Andrew Jackson on the ground that, in removing the government deposits from the Second Bank of the United States, he had "assumed upon himself authority and power not conferred by the Constitution and laws, but in derogation of both." Jackson's "protest" to the Senate was eloquent and conclusive. The Senate resolution, he said, charged him with having committed a "high crime." It was therefore "in substance an impeachment of the President." If Congress really meant this, Jackson said, let it be serious about it: let the House impeach him and the Senate try him. Jackson was plainly right. The slap-on-the-wrist approach to presidential delinquency makes little sense, constitutional or otherwise. There is no halfway house in censure. If a President has committed high crimes and misdemeanors, he should not stay in office. This does not mean, of course, that a fainthearted Congress may not pass a resolution of censure and claim to have done its duty. But, unless the terms of the resolution make it clear why the President is merely censurable and not impeachable, the action is a cop-out and a betrayal of Congress' constitutional responsibility.

Are there other halfway houses? Another proposal seems worth consideration: that is, the removal of an offending President by some means short of impeachment. A resolution calling on the President to resign and passed by an overwhelming vote in each house could have a powerful effect on a President who cares about the Constitution and the country. If either the President or the Vice President then resigned, the President, old or new, could, under the Twenty-fifth

Amendment, nominate a new Vice President, who would take office upon confirmation by both houses of Congress. "Admirable," said Cardinal Fleury after he read the Abbé de Saint-Pierre's *Project de Paix Perpétuelle*, "save for one omission: I find no provision for sending missionaries to convert the hearts of princes." Alas, Presidents who succeed in provoking a long-suffering Congress into a resolution calling for their resignation are not likely to be deeply moved by congressional disapproval nor inclined to cooperate in their own liquidation.

If Presidents will not resign of their own volition, can they be forced out without the personal and national ordeal of impeachment and conviction?

A proposal advanced in various forms by leading members of the House of Representatives this year contemplates giving Congress authority by constitutional amendment to call for a new presidential election when it finds that the President can no longer perform the functions of his office (Representative Bingham) or that the President has violated the Constitution (Representatives Edith Green and Morris Udall).

The possibility of dissolution and new elections at times of hopeless stalemate or blasted confidence has serious appeal. Dissolution would give a rigid electoral system flexibility and responsiveness. It would permit, in Bagehot's phrase, the timely replacement of the pilot of the calm by the pilot of the storm. It would remind intractable Congresses that they cannot block Presidents with immunity, as it would remind high-flying Presidents that there are other ways of being shot down besides impeachment. But my instinct is somehow against it. One congressman observes of the Green-Udall amendment that it "would, in effect, take one-half of the parliamentary process and not the entire parliamentary process." This is certainly the direction and logic of dissolution. The result might well be to alter the balance of the Constitution in unforeseeable and perilous ways. It might, in particular, strengthen the movement against the separation of powers and toward a plebiscitary presidency. "The republican principle," said the 71st Federalist, "demands that the deliberate sense of the community should govern the conduct of those to whom they intrust the management of their affairs; but it does not require an unqualified complaisance to every sudden breeze of passion, or to every transient impulse which the people may receive from the arts of men, who flatter their prejudices to betray their interests."

I think that the possibility of inserting dissolution into the American system is worth careful examination. But digging into the foundations of the state, as Burke said, is always a dangerous adventure.

IX

Impeachment, on the other hand, is part of the original foundation of the American state. The Founding Fathers placed the blunt instrument in the Constitution with the expectation that it would be used, and used most especially against Presidents. "No point is of more importance," George Mason told the Convention, "than that the right of impeachment should be continued. Shall any man be above Justice? Above all shall that man be above it, who [as President] can commit the most extensive injustice?" Benjamin Franklin pointed out that, if there were no provision for impeachment, the only recourse would be assassination, in which case a President would be "not only deprived of his life but of the opportunity of vindicating his character." Corruption or loss of capacity in a President, said Madison, was "within the compass of probable events. . . . Either of them might be fatal to the Republic."

The genius of impeachment lies in the fact that it can punish the man without punishing the office. For, in the presidency, as elsewhere, power is ambiguous: the power to do good means also the power to do harm, the power to serve the republic also the power to demean and defile it. The trick is to preserve presidential power but to deter Presidents from abusing that power. Shall any man be above justice? George Mason asked. Obviously not; not even a President of the United States. But bringing Presidents to justice is not all that simple.

History has turned impeachment into a weapon of last resort—more so probably than the Founding Fathers anticipated. Still, it is possible to exaggerate its impact on the country. It took less than three months to impeach and try Andrew Johnson, and the nation—in a favorite apprehension of 1868 as well as of 1973—was not torn apart in the process. Three months of surgery might be better than three years of paralysis. Yet impeachment presents legal as well as political problems. There is broad agreement, among scholars at least, on doctrine. Impeachment is a proceeding of a political nature, by no means restricted to indictable crimes. On the other hand, it plainly is not to be applied to cases of honest disagreement over national policy or over constitutional interpretation, especially when a President refuses to obey a law that he believes strikes directly at the presidential prerogative. Impeachment is to be reserved, in Ma-

son's phrase at the Constitutional Convention, for "great and dangerous offenses."

The Senate, in trying impeachment cases, is better equipped to
be the judge of the law than of the facts. When Andrew Johnson was
impeached, there had been no dispute about the fact that he had
removed Stanton. When Andrew Jackson was censured, there had
been no dispute about the fact that he had removed the deposits. The
issue was not whether they had done something but whether what
they had done constituted a transgression of the laws and the Constitution. But in the Nixon case the facts themselves remain at issue—
the facts, that is, of presidential complicity—and the effort of a hundred senators to determine those facts might well lead to chaos. The
record here may be one of negligence, irresponsibility, and even deception, but it is not necessarily one of knowing violation of the
Constitution or of knowing involvement in the obstruction of justice.
While impeachment is in the Constitution to be used, there is no
point in lowering the threshold so that it will be used casually. All this
argues for the determination of facts before the consideration of impeachment. There are two obvious ways to determine the facts. One
is through the House of Representatives, which has the sole power to
initiate impeachment. The House could, for example, instruct the
Judiciary Committee to ascertain whether there were grounds for
impeachment, or it could establish a select committee to conduct
such an inquiry. The other road is through the courts. If the Special
Prosecutor establishes incriminating facts, these can serve as the basis
for impeachment.

But what if a President himself withholds evidence—for example, Nixon's tapes—deemed essential to the ascertainment of facts? If
a President says "the time has come to turn Watergate over to the
courts, where the questions of guilt and innocence belong," and then
denies the courts the evidence they need to decide on innocence or
guilt, what recourse remains to the republic except impeachment?
Apart from the courts, President Polk said quite explicitly that the
House, if it were looking into impeachment, could command testimony and papers, public and private, official or unofficial, of every
agent of the government. If a President declines for whatever reason
to yield material evidence in his possession, whether to the courts or
to the House, this itself might provide clear grounds for impeachment.

All these things are obscure in the early autumn of 1973. It is
possible that Nixon may conclude that the Watergate problems are
not after all (as he told the Prime Minister of Japan) "murky, small,
unimportant, vicious little things," but are, rather, evidence of a pro-

found and grievous imbalance between the presidency and the Constitution. Perhaps he may, by an honest display of candor and contrition, regain a measure of popular confidence, re-establish constitutional comity and recover presidential effectiveness. But full recovery seems unlikely unless the President himself recognizes why his presidency has fallen into such difficulties. Nixon's continued invocation, after Watergate, of national security as the excuse for presidential excess, his defense to the end of unreviewable executive privilege, his defiant assertion that, if he had it to do over again, he would still deceive Congress and the people about the secret air war in Cambodia—such unrepentant reactions suggest that he still has no clue as to what his trouble was, still fails to understand that the sickness of his presidency is caused not by the overzealousness of his friends or by the malice of his enemies, but by the expansion and abuse of presidential power itself.

X

For the issue is more than whether Congress and the people wish to deal with the particular iniquities of the Nixon Administration. It is whether they wish to rein in the runaway presidency. Nixon's presidency is not an aberration but a culmination. It carries to reckless extremes a compulsion toward presidential power rising out of deeprunning changes in the foundations of society. In a time of the acceleration of history and the decay of traditional institutions and values, a strong presidency is both a greater necessity than ever before and a greater risk—necessary to hold a spinning and distracted society together, necessary to make the separation of powers work, risky because of the awful temptation held out to override the separation of powers and burst the bonds of the Constitution. The nation requires both a strong presidency for leadership *and* the separation of powers for liberty. It may well be that, if continuing structural compulsions are likely to propel future Presidents in the direction of government by decree, the rehabilitation of impeachment will be essential to contain the presidency and preserve the Constitution.

Watergate is potentially the best thing to have happened to the presidency in a long time. If the trails are followed to their end, many, many years will pass before another White House staff dares take the liberties with the Constitution and the laws the Nixon White House has taken. If the nation wants to work its way back to a constitutional presidency, there is only one way to begin. That is by showing Presidents that, when their closest associates place themselves above the law and the Constitution, such transgressions will be not forgiven or forgotten for the sake of the presidency, but exposed and punished for the sake of the presidency.

If the Nixon White House escapes the legal consequences of its illegal behavior, why will future Presidents and their associates not suppose themselves entitled to do what the Nixon White House has done? Only condign punishment will restore popular faith in the presidency and deter future Presidents from illegal conduct—so long, at least, as Watergate remains a vivid memory. Corruption appears to visit the White House in fifty-year cycles. This suggests that exposure and retribution inoculate the presidency against its latent criminal impulses for about half a century. Around the year 2023 the American people will be well advised to go on the alert and start nailing down everything in sight.

A constitutional presidency, as the great Presidents have shown, can be a very strong presidency indeed. But what keeps a strong President constitutional, in addition to checks and balances incorporated within his own breast, is the vigilance of the people. The Constitution cannot hold the nation to ideals it is determined to betray. The reinvigoration of the written checks in the American Constitution depends on the re-invigoration of the unwritten checks in American society. The great institutions—Congress, the courts, the executive establishment, the press, the universities, public opinion—have to reclaim their own dignity and meet their own responsibilities. As Madison said long ago, the country cannot trust to "parchment barriers" to halt the encroaching spirit of power. In the end, the Constitution will live only if it embodies the spirit of the American people.

"There is no week nor day nor hour," wrote Walt Whitman, "when tyranny may not enter upon this country, if the people lose their supreme confidence in themselves,—and lose their roughness and spirit of defiance—Tyranny may always enter—there is no charm, no bar against it—the only bar against it is a large resolute breed of men."

ENDNOTE

1. Lincoln to H. L. Pierce et al., April 6, 1859. Lincoln, *Collected Works,* ed. R. P. Basler (New Brunswick, 1953), III, 375. Lincoln was amused by the fact that the Democrats of his day had stopped mentioning Jefferson while the Republicans constantly invoked him. "If the two leading parties of this day are really identical with the two in the days of Jefferson and Adams, they have performed about the same feat as the two drunken men."

14

william b. eddy

BEYOND BEHAVIORALISM? ORGANIZATION DEVELOPMENT IN PUBLIC MANAGEMENT

Professional public administrators and their academic cohorts have traditionally gleaned through developments in the field of organization and management in search of approaches to greater effectiveness. This search has encompassed business as well as public management techniques and has reached into the disciplines of social science and various new technologies. Of course, several significant developments have occurred within public management itself. A relatively new approach labeled "organizational development" or "OD" is now available. There is evidence that the new approach holds promise for helping cope with some of the perennial problems of government institutions. However, OD is based on a somewhat different model of organization and a different value system than those under which many agencies presently operate. Thus it would seem to require rather careful examination.

Most of the earlier approaches to organizational effectiveness were related to the bureaucracy and administrative management models. They were based on a legal-rational philosophy and utilized "principles of management." These approaches have as their main focus the regularizing of organizational behaviors and procedures in order to achieve greater reliability. It is assumed that the organization will operate most effectively if all requisite performances are planned, organized, and programmed according to an established set of procedures, and enforced by a hierarchy of authority.

From *Public Personnel Review,* 31:3, July, 1970. Reprinted by permission of the International Personnel Management Association.

This approach has been described by contemporary theorists as being primarily a "command" or "compliance" system. There is no question about the considerable utility of this approach to government institutions as well as other organizations. Other approaches related to administrative management, or at least consonant with it, include the development of the professional administrative function, the search for talented manpower, and the civil service merit system.

NEW MANAGEMENT APPROACHES

Two new, or at least newly visible, approaches to organization effectiveness are now becoming available. One of these is the set of technologically based approaches to management control which involve such techniques as systems analysis, operations research, program budgeting, and other methods facilitated by the computer. This collection of methodologies has clearly caught the fancy of many of those in public administration and is beginning to prove its usefulness in a variety of settings.

The other newer approach, which has been utilized to a lesser degree in government, is not as clearly defined. It sometimes goes by the name of "applied behavioral science," sometimes "planned change," and sometimes "organization development" or "OD." It is based on the social sciences and focuses particularly upon utilizing more effectively the human resources of the organization. It involves the kinds of concepts referred to by political scientists as "behavioralism." However OD puts the social scientist in a new role in dealing with organizations.

Social scientists and others with behavioral orientations have previously spent considerable time describing, judging, and frequently upbraiding bureaucracy. The works of Merton and Thompson are examples of this position. Even those who were concerned with application of behavioral science remained somewhat distant from the basic fiber and day-to-day operation. The social science literature on application has tended to fall into the following categories:

1. Training programs in which information and principles regarding human behavior are presented to managers in order to help them understand their peers and subordinates, and practice "better human relations," i.e., to humanize the organization.

2. Attitude and morale surveys in which employee responses are gathered, summarized, and sometimes made available to management as well as incorporated into scholarly articles. (For example, Delbert C. Miller, "Using Behavioral Science to Solve Organization Problems," *Personnel Administration,* Jan.-Feb. 1968, pp. 21-29.)

3. Descriptive research studies which bear generalizations about various aspects of the operation. For example, employee response to change, problems of role conflict, leadership characteristics, etc. (As in Robert Presthus, *Behavioral Approaches to Public Administration,* University of Alabama Press, 1965.)

4. The technology of personnel psychology has been applied in such areas as testing, performance appraisal, employee relations, and placement.

Additionally, some consulting firms have utilized social science knowledge in their analyses and recommendations.

Recently a new thrust involving much more direct *intervention* into the ongoing process of the organization has been evolving, and is being applied in some private businesses and a few public agencies.

This new approach is a result of two major developments in the field of organizational behavior. The first is the accumulation of data leading to more sophisticated theories of organizational behavior with major emphasis on developing the human potential of an organization. Antecedents to this current approach include the Hawthorne studies; the work of Lewin, Lippitt, and others on planned change; the adult education movement in the United States; the motivationally oriented management theories of McGregor, Argyris, Likert and others; and the focus on interpersonal process developed by the National Training Laboratories. These approaches tend to deemphasize the aspects of technical competence and substantive knowledge and to pay close attention to the *process* whereby people interact in organizations. They view the organization as a social system and focus upon interpersonal and intergroup relationships.

The second development is a set of skills and techniques involving the application of behavioral science. These skill areas have come out of such sources as management consulting, sensitivity training, the role and techniques of the change agent, action research, and counseling psychology. The organization development approach leads the practitioner considerably beyond the earlier approaches to the utilization of social science. The process is much more than the "expert" analyzing the situation from the point of view of his discipline and providing generalizations about what he sees occurring. OD involves injecting the social science practitioner with his knowledge and skills into the mainstream of the organization. It involves him as a person as well as a storehouse of knowledge in the risks and responsibilities of organizational life.

Although many of the concepts of behavioral science are several decades old, they have not been consolidated into a single point of view. Their sum and substance however is considerably more than the old position that organizations, and thus organizational behavior, consists of nonrational people who are influenced to deviate from the prescribed organizational procedures by a variety of social and emotional factors. The purpose of this paper is to explore the meaning of some of these developments in applied behavioral science and to examine the possible value of this approach in public administration.

THE ORGANIZATION DEVELOPMENT MODEL

Before doing this however, it may be useful to spell out more clearly what is meant by the current practitioners who use and operate within the concept of organizational development.

Organizational development is an organic, process-oriented approach to organizational change and management effectiveness. It seeks to bring about change and improvement by involving members of the organization in problem analysis and planning. It builds on the Theory Y assumptions of Douglas McGregor, and proposes an alternative normative model for human behavior in organization. It stresses interpersonal competence, collaboration and teamwork, and group dynamics skills. It counts on gaining increased effectiveness and adaptability by helping free employees from the limitations and restrictions of highly structured organizations. It seeks to build more employee participation and more collaborative decisionmaking and problem-solving. It is first cousin to other recently developed approaches such as management by objectives, job enlargement, action research, and the Scanlon profit-sharing and participation plan.

The theoretical basis of organization development is anchored in the contemporary writings of Argyris, Beckhard, Likert, Bennis and Blake, to name a few. Current publications on organization development efforts include those in the Weldon Manufacturing Company (Morrow, et al.), TRW Systems Group (Davis), and Esso Standard Oil Company (Foundation for Research on Human Behavior). Behavioral scientists and trainers in universities, companies, and consulting firms have formed an "OD network" for the purpose of sharing ideas and experiences.

A SAMPLE EFFORT

Although there is no single formalized set of procedures, a typical organization development effort might include the following stages:

1. A problem recognition stage in which the organization recognizes the fact that its productivity is being hampered by ineffective interpersonal relations or other kinds of socially related variables, and calls in outside consultants or addresses its own members to exploring these problems.

2. A data gathering stage in which interviews, observations, meeting analysis techniques, or other approaches are utilized to pinpoint difficulties involved in the organization's operation and provide suggestions for reasons for these difficulties.

3. A data analysis and feedback stage in which members of management are brought together and involved in reviewing the findings, diagnosing problem areas, and planning strategies for improvement and change.

4. The intervention programs which are designed to bring about desired changes may include meetings (on-site or at retreats) at which organizational members are helped to participate in developing new programs or new approaches to existing situations.

5. The responsibility for helping the organization come to grips with change problems and to work its way through the difficulties encountered is often assigned to someone in a "change agent role" who is either a member of the organization or an outside consultant. This individual usually does not play the role of the expert advisor, but rather uses his clinical skills as well as his knowledge to help facilitate the problem-solving process of the group.

6. Members of the organization collaboratively develop procedures, policies, and norms which reinforce and implement the new ways of operating developed in the previous change efforts.

7. Training is an important component of OD. Ongoing programs integrated into the change process are made avail-

able to employees. Training methods tend to be participatory and experience-based. The laboratory approach of the National Training Laboratories (T-Groups or sensitivity training) is frequently used to help employees develop interpersonal competence and teamwork skills such as group problem-solving and decision-making.

It is important to emphasize that organization development involves more than simply teaching good human relations and going off on week-end retreats for cathartic purposes. One of the central concepts in the process is that of "confrontation." Emphasis is placed on helping organizational members recognize and come to grips with organizational problems at the human interaction level which are often ignored or swept under the rug under the assumption that conflict is to be avoided at all costs. Structural and procedural change, often the beginning points of the more traditional approaches, may be the end result of involvement in an organizational development program.

APPLICATIONS IN PUBLIC MANAGEMENT

Experience indicates that OD has enough promise that professional public administrators might well wish to examine it for possible usefulness in government. Organizational development and the kinds of variables with which it deals may help agencies come to grips with some of the problems that plague them. Long standing problems that do not seem to be amenable to solution by traditional administrative approaches include the following.

Difficulty in attracting, holding, and developing competent, committed employees. A more meaningful and stimulating working environment, with more opportunity for participation in agency planning and decisionmaking, and with greater possibility for personal growth and development, may be required to help government compete with private industry for employees.

Overcoming rigidity and resistance to change. Collaborative models of preparation for and implementation of change are needed to help facilitate change while reducing some of the traditional difficulties and resistances encountered in change programs.

Overemphasis on structure and compliance to the neglect of goal-orientation and innovation. Ways need to be found to enhance rather than restrict the potential contributions of employees.

Another set of difficulties has been complicated by attempts of government to deal with urban life. These include:

Intergroup cooperation. The increasing complexity of the urban society and the developing technologies make it mandatory that units of government as well as subunits within the agency be able to communicate and collaborate effectively as they take on highly related projects. Yet it is very difficult to legislate cooperation. Organizational development approaches focus on clearing away some of the barriers to collaboration and helping people to learn how to work more effectively together.

Operation in arenas in which there is a lack of traditional hierarchical power. Government administrators at a variety of levels find themselves in situations in which it is important to influence others or to bring about collaborative action, but there are no mechanisms for *requiring* that things be done. They are finding that they need greater skills in facilitating cooperative action among volunteers, community groups, etc., utilizing mechanisms other than power.

Temporary systems. Much of the work of problem-solving at the local government level occurs within the context of groups formed outside or at the perimeter of traditional governmental agencies (Model Cities groups, citizens task forces, community action programs, intergovernmental organizations, etc.). It is no secret that these kinds of organizations have often floundered in their attempts to "get organized" and fulfill their missions. Yet knowledge currently available about how to build and maintain temporary social systems should be able to increase the probability of success.

There are beginning to be a few examples of organization development activities in public management. These include Project ACORD in the State Department (reported by Marrow), the work of Golembiewski, and activities with the City of Kansas City (reported by F. Gerald Brown). A few communities and federal agencies are using some of the components of organization development—particularly laboratory training techniques.

DOES OD FIT PUBLIC ADMINISTRATION?

Several possible reasons for the minimal utilization of organization development in government are suggested below as hypotheses for consideration.

1. The older methods for improving organizational performance (O&M, systems and procedures, etc.) are more conso-

nant with, and supplement, the legal-rational bureaucratic approach in which most government units have been built. Although the traditional approach has been changed in several respects by some of the new methodologies, the basic tenets of the "command system" have usually not been questioned or challenged. The older methodologies have instead been largely ways of shoring up, protecting, and increasing the efficiency of the traditional approach. Utilization of organizational development may require a more drastic change in focus than would other techniques.

2. Applied behavioral science and organization development have "natural enemies" in the fields of political science and public administration. Some political scientists have viewed with suspicion the "behavioral" view of the organization. They have often seen its value, if any, as suggesting difficulties or limitations to the existing system rather than proposing alternative ways of managing. Additionally, it seems to the present writer that some in the field of political science and public administration are somewhat fixated on the Machiavellian concept of authority. They tend to react against any approach which suggests decreasing the amount of direct and unilateral authority held by individuals in top level positions.

3. There is the feeling, shared by some in business, that the behavioral sciences are proposing a "tender-minded approach" to organization which overplays the need to have workers happy and satisfied and underplays the emphasis on productivity (the "human relations" approach of the 1940–50 period).

4. There is a certain degree of misunderstanding and lack of information regarding some of the basic ideas involved in participative management. There is suspicion that this approach courts the disaster of turning the organization over to the employees, abdicating leadership and authority, and establishing management by committee. Supporters contend that an emphasis on the people process does not necessarily require a deemphasis on production and that greater involvement of organizational members in decisionmaking does not decrease the authority of the manager.

5. The basic assumptions and values of organization development may be inappropriate in public organizations. The behavioral science that supports the OD approach is more than a set of techniques or ways of improving the efficiency of the traditional form of organization. It questions some of

the basic operational assumptions underlying bureaucracy, and raises possibilities of changing not so much the *structure* as the *process* and *philosophy* of organizations. Some of the assumptions and values about human behavior in contemporary organizations which the OD approach supports are the following:

Openness of communication and authenticity of human expression are appropriate behaviors. They not only help people perform more effectively as individuals but they make for more effective work relations. Individuals should be encouraged to "level" with each other regarding feelings and ideas.

Conflict is an inherent part of organizational operation. It should not be covered up or compromised away, but should be acknowledged and dealt with openly. It is possible to learn how to "manage" conflict and turn it to productive use.

Wider participation in decisionmaking and planning and wider sharing of information are valuable. They not only help motivate employees through greater involvement, but also bring about greater utilization of human resources and more efficient problem-solving.

A climate of mutual trust is an important factor in organizations. It minimizes defensiveness, opens communications, allows people to take more creative risks and thus be more innovative.

Organizations can operate more effectively if there is less reliance on formal structure, rules, regulations, red tape, and procedures. People can be counted on to behave more responsibly rather than less responsibly if they are partially freed from organizational control. Self-direction, rather than external direction, is a distinct possibility, granting acceptance of the organization's goals.

Concepts of power and authority need to be revised. Unilateral authority is not necessary for organizational effectiveness. Managers who delegate and in other ways share a good deal of the decision-making will, in the end, build more productive work units.

An important value in organizations involves the development of the employees as people to greater degrees of commitment, responsibility, and personal awareness. Many in the field of OD are committed to the humanistically-oriented psychology of Carl Rogers, Abraham Maslow, and others.

There is an emphasis on change. It is assumed that continual receptivity and adaptability to change are important organizational values.

Public administrators considering the possible utilization of organizational development will have to review these values and decide whether or not they are antithetical to the particular values and needs of their own organizations, and whether they would pose too much difficulty for the existing form. For example, some may assert that political competition and public accountability via the press mitigate against openness of communication and objective problem-solving. Costello has identified several points of contrast between public and private organizations relevant to the question of how change takes place in city government. Some of the unique characteristics of public agencies—such as sudden and drastic leadership changes, high visibility of decision-making and extreme difficulty in cutting existing functions and services—may place conditions upon the application of OD in some situations.

CONCLUSION

The implementation of the behavioral science approach to organization development is not quick and cheap, nor is it a panacea. More is needed than speeches, policy statements, and short-term training programs. A decision to try organization development must be a decision to commit time and money over a relatively extended period of time to the development of people and of the organization. Development activities cannot be routinized and written into the procedures to be handled by a staff assistant. Indoctrination training must be replaced with training approaches which tie the individual's learning needs and experiences directly into his organizational performance. Risks must be taken and the possibility of feedback which is uncomfortable for those in power has to be anticipated.

TRW Systems, a fast-moving aerospace contracting firm, is a heavy consumer of applied behavioral science and advocate of the OD model. "Based on what we know today," says an executive of another firm, "TRW Systems may turn out to be one of the earliest complete models of the American business—industrial organization of the future." (See John Poppy, "New Era in Industry: It's OK to Cry in the Office," *Look*, July 9, 1968, p. 66.)

Public administrators may or may not be making similar statements in a few years. But it is likely that they will be called upon to make decisions about the potential value of organizational development programs to their organizations.

The author is indebted to Robert Saunders, F. Gerald Brown, and Thomas P. Murphy for their comments and suggestions.

FURTHER READINGS

ALLISON, GRAHAM T. *Essence of Decision.* Boston: Little, Brown and Company, 1971.

AMERICAN SOCIETY FOR PUBLIC ADMINISTRATION. *Automation in Government.* Washington, D.C.: The Society, 1963.

ANDERSON, PATRICK. *The President's Men.* Garden City: Doubleday & Company, Inc., 1968.

ARGYRIS, CHRIS. *Executive Leadership: An Appraisal of a Manager in Action.* New York: Harper & Row, Publishers, 1953.

ARGYRIS, CHRIS. *Personality and Organization.* New York: Harper & Row, Publishers, 1957.

ARGYRIS, CHRIS. *Understanding Organizational Behavior.* Homewood: Dorsey Press, 1960.

ART, ROBERT J. *The TFX Decision: McNamara and the Military.* Boston: Little, Brown and Company, 1968.

BARNARD, CHESTER I. *The Functions of the Executive.* Cambridge: Harvard University Press, 1938.

BLAU, PETER. *Bureaucracy in Modern Society.* New York: Random House, Inc., 1956.

BLAU, PETER and RICHARD SCOTT et al. *Formal Organizations.* New York: John Wiley & Sons, Inc., 1958.

BURSK, EDWARD C., and JOHN F. CHEFMAN. *New Decision-Making Tools for Managers.* New York: Harper & Row, Publishers, 1965.

CLEVELAND, HARLAN. "Systems, Purposes, and the Watergate." *The Bureaucrat,* vol. 2, no. 4 (Winter, 1973), 452–457.

COLEMAN, JAMES. "Games as Vehicles for Social Theory." *American Behavioral Scientist,* vol. 12, no. 6 (July-August 1969), pp. 2–6.

CORNOG, GEOFFREY Y. et al. eds. *EDP Systems in Public Management.* Chicago: Rand McNally & Co., 1968.

CORNWELL, ELMER E., JR. *Presidential Leadership of Public Opinion.* Bloomington: Indiana University Press, 1965.

CORSON, JOHN J., and R. SHALE PAUL. *Men Near the Top: Filling Posts in the Federal Service.* Baltimore: The Johns Hopkins Press, 1966.

CRECINE, JOHN P. *Government Problem-Solving: A Computer*

Simulation of Muncipal Budgeting. Chicago: Rand Mc-Nally, 1969.

CRONIN, THOMAS E. "Everybody Believes in Democracy Until He Gets to the White House . . . An Examination of White House Department Relations." *Law and Contemporary Problems,* vol. 35, no. 3, Summer 1970, pp. 573–625.

CRONIN, THOMAS E. and SANFORD D. GREENBERG. *The Presidential Advisory System.* New York: Harper & Row, Publishers, 1969.

DENHARDT, ROBERT B. "Bureaucratic Socialization and Organizational Accommodation." *Administrative Science Quarterly,* vol. 13, no. 3 (December 1968), pp. 441–450.

DIAL, O. E. ed. "Forum on Computers: To Dedicate or Not to Dedicate, That Is the Question." *The Bureaucrat,* vol. 1, no. 4 (Winter, 1972), 305–378.

DIMOCK, MARSHALL E. *The Executive in Action.* New York: Harper & Row, Publishers, 1954.

DOWNS, ANTHONY. *Inside Bureaucracy.* New York: Little, Brown and Company, 1967.

DROR, YEHEZEKEL. *Public Policymaking Reexamined.* San Francisco: Chandler Publishing Company, 1969.

ETZIONI, AMITAI. *A Comparative Analysis of Complex Organizations.* New York: The Free Press, 1961.

ETZIONI, AMITAI. *Complex Organizations.* New York: Holt, Rinehart & Winston, Inc., 1961.

ETZIONI, AMITAI. "Mixed Scanning: A Third Approach to Decision-Making." *Public Administration Review,* vol. 27, no. 4 (December 1967), 385–392.

ETZIONI, AMITAI. *Readings on Modern Organizations,* Englewood Cliffs, N.J.: Prentice-Hall, Inc., 1969.

FENNO, RICHARD. *The President's Cabinet.* Cambridge: Harvard University Press, 1959.

GAWTHROP, LOUIS C. *Bureaucratic Behavior in the Executive Branch.* New York: The Free Press, 1969.

GOLEMBIEWSKI, ROBERT T. *Behavior and Organization: O & M and the Small Group.* Chicago: Rand McNally & Co., 1962.

GOLEMBIEWSKI, ROBERT T. *Organizing Men and Power: Patterns of Behavior and Line-Staff Models.* Chicago: Rand Mc-Nally & Co., 1967.

GOLEMBIEWSKI, ROBERT T. and FRANK GIBSON. eds. *Managerial Behavior and Organization Demands.* Chicago: Rand McNally & Co., 1967.

GULICK, LUTHER, and L. URWICK. *Papers on the Science of Administration.* New York: Institute of Public Administration, 1937.

HALAL, WILLIAM E. "Toward a General Theory of Leadership." *Human Relations,* vol. 27, no. 4 (April, 1974), 401–416.

HARE, A. P., et al. eds. *Small Groups: Studies in Social Interaction.* New York: Alfred A. Knopf, Inc., 1965.

HARGROVE, ERWIN C. *Presidential Leadership: Personality and Political Style.* New York: The Macmillan Company, 1966.

HARMON, MICHAEL M. "Social Equity and Organizational Man: Motivation and Organizational Democracy." *Public Administration Review,* vol. 34, no. 1 (January-February 1974), 11–18.

HEIN, LEONARD W. *Quantitative Approach to Managerial Decisions.* Englewood Cliffs: Prentice-Hall, Inc., 1967.

HERSHEY, CARY. "Responses of Federal Agencies to Employee Risk-Taking." *The Bureaucrat,* vol. 2, no. 3 (Fall, 1973), 285–293.

HOLLOMAN, CHARLES and HAL HENDRICK. "Adequacy of Group Decisions as a Function of the Decision-Making Process." *Academy of Management Journal,* vol. 15, no. 2 (June, 1972), 175–184.

JACOB, CHARLES E. *Policy and Bureaucracy.* Princeton: D. Van Nostrand Company, 1966.

JAMES, DOROTHY BUCKTON. *The Contemporary Presidency.* New York: Pegasus, 1969.

KATZ, ROBERT L. "Skills of an Effective Administrator and A Retrospective Commentary." *Harvard Business Review,* vol. 52, no. 5 (Sept.–Oct., 1974), 90–102.

KIRKHART, LARRY and NEELY GARDNER. eds. "Symposium: Organization Development." *Public Administration Review.* 34: 2 (March-April, 1974), 97–140.

KOENIG, LOUIS W. *The Chief Executive.* New York: Harcourt, Brace & World, Inc., 1964.

LACY, ALEX B., JR. "The White House Staff Bureaucracy." *Transaction,* vol. 6, no. 3 (January 1968), pp. 50–56.

LA PORTE, TODD R. "The Context of Technology Assessment: A Changing Perspective for Public Organizations." *Public Administration Review,* vol. 31, no. 1 (January-February 1971), 63–73.

LINDBLOM, CHARLES. "The Science of Muddling Through." *Public Administration Review,* vol. 19, no. 1 (1959), 79–88.

MAILICK, SIDNEY and EDWARD H. VAN NESS. *Concepts and Issues in Administrative Behavior.* Englewood Cliffs: Prentice-Hall, Inc., 1962.

MANN, DEAN E., and JAMESON W. DOIG. *The Assistant Secretaries: Problems and Processes of Appointment.* Washington: The Brookings Institution, 1965.

MARCH, JAMES G. *Handbook of Organizations.* Chicago: Rand McNally & Co., 1965.

MARCH, JAMES G., and HERBERT SIMON. *Organizations.* New York: John Wiley & Sons, Inc., 1958.

MERTON, ROBERT K., *et al.* eds. *Reader in Bureaucracy.* New York: The Free Press, 1952.

MEYER, MARSHALL W. *Bureaucratic Structure and Authority Coordination and Control in 254 Government Agencies.* New York: Harper & Row, 1972.

MEYER, MARSHALL W. "Two Authority Structures of Bureaucratic Organization." *Administrative Science Quarterly,* vol. 13, no. 2 (September, 1968), 211–228.

MOUZELIS, NICOS P. *Organization and Bureaucracy.* Chicago: Aldine Publishing Co., 1968.

MURPHY, JOHN F. *The Pinnacle: The Contemporary American Presidency.* Philadelphia: J. B. Lippincott Co., 1974.

MURPHY, THOMAS. "Congressional Liaison: The NASA Case." *Western Political Quarterly,* vol. 25, no. 2 (June, 1972), 192–214.

NEUSTADT, RICHARD. *Presidential Power.* New York: John Wiley & Sons, Inc., 1960.

NEWLAND, CHESTER A. ed. "Forum on Management by Objectives in the Federal Government." *The Bureaucrat,* vol. 2, no. 4 (Winter, 1973), 351–426.

O'BRIEN, GORDON E. "Leadership in Organization Settings." *The Journal of Applied Behavioral Science,* vol. 5, no. 1 (January–March, 1969), 45–63.

PASCHAL, JOEL F. ed. "The Presidential Office." *Law and Contemporary Problems,* vol. 21 (Fall 1956), 609–752.

PEABODY, ROBERT. *Organizational Authority.* New York: Atherton Press, Inc., 1964.

PRESS, CHARLES, and ALAN ARIAN. *Empathy and Ideology: Aspects of Administrative Innovation.* Chicago: Rand McNally & Co., 1966.

PRESTHUS, ROBERT V. *The Organizational Society.* New York: Vintage Books, 1965.

PRESTON, LEE E. and JAMES POST. "The Third Managerial Revolution." *Academy of Management Journal,* vol. 17, no. 3 (September, 1974), 476–486.

ROSENBLOOM, RICHARD S. "The Role of Analysis." *New Tools for Urban Management: Studies in Systems and Organizational Analysis.* Boston: Harvard University, Div. of Research, Graduate School of Business Administration, 1971, 221–252.

SAYLES, LEONARD R., and MARGARET CHANDLER. *Managing Large Systems: Organizations for the Future.* New York: Harper & Row, 1971.

SELIGMAN, LESTER G. "Presidential Leadership: The Inner Circle and Institutionalism." *Journal of Politics,* vol. 58, no. 3 (August 1956), 410–426.

SELZNICK, PHILIP. *TVA and the Grass Roots: A Study in the Sociology of Formal Organizations.* Berkeley: University of California Press, 1949.

SIMON, HERBERT A. *The Shape of Automation for Men and Management.* New York: Harper & Row, Publishers, 1965.

SJOBERG, GIDEON, *et al.* "Bureaucracy and the Lower Class." *Sociology and Social Research,* vol. 50, no. 3 (April, 1966), 325–337.

SORENSEN, THEODORE. *Decision-Making in the White House.* New York: Columbia University Press, 1963.

STANLEY, DAVID T. *Changing Administrations: The 1961 and 1964 Transitions in Six Departments.* Washington, D.C.: The Brookings Institution, 1965.

SULLIVAN, ROBERT R. "The Role of the President in Shaping Lower Level Policy-Making Processes." *Polity,* vol. 3, no. 2 (Winter, 1970), 201–221.

SUNDQUIST, JAMES L. *Politics and Policy: The Eisenhower, Kennedy, and Johnson Years.* Washington, D.C.: The Brookings Institution, 1968.

SWEENEY, STEPHEN B., and JAMES C. CHARLESWORTH. *Governing Urban Society: New Scientific Approaches.* Philadelphia: American Academy of Political and Social Science, 1967.

THOMAS, NORMAN C. and HAROLD L. WOLMAN. "The Presidency and Policy Formulation: The Task Force Device." *Public Administration Review.* vol. 29, no. 5 (September-October, 1969), 459–471.

THOMPSON, JAMES D. *Organizations in Action.* New York: McGraw-Hill Book Company, 1967.

THOMPSON, VICTOR A. *Modern Organization.* New York: Alfred A. Knopf, Inc., 1961.

U.S. BUREAU OF THE BUDGET. *Report to the President on the Management of Automatic Data Processing in the Federal Government.* 89th Congress, 1st Session, Sen. Doc. No. 15. Washington, D.C.: U.S. Government Printing Office, 1965.

WANN, A. J. *The President as Chief Administrator: A Study of Franklin D. Roosevelt.* Washington, D.C.: Public Affairs Press, 1968.

"THE WHITE HOUSE STAFF v. THE CABINET." *The Washington Monthly,* Feb., 1969.

WHITE, ORION F., JR. "The Dialectical Organization: An Alternative to Bureaucracy." *Public Administration Review,* vol. 29, no. 1 (January-February 1969), 32–42.

WHYTE, WILLIAM H., JR. *The Organization Man.* New York: Simon & Schuster, Inc., 1956.

WILDAVSKY, AARON. "The Self-Evaluating Organization." *Public Administration Review,* vol. 32, no. 5 (September-October, 1972), 509–520.

WILSON, H. T. "Rationality and Decision in Administrative Science." *Canadian Journal of Political Science,* vol. 6, no. 2 (June, 1973), 271–294.

FOUR

PUBLIC PERSONNEL MANAGEMENT IN A TIME OF CHANGE

The management of administrative personnel is a major component in the machinery of public administration. Students of administration have traditionally been concerned with the selection, evaluation, and discipline of administrative personnel. Part Four explores the personnel management function within a contemporary framework. The chapter's objective is to view personnel administration as part of a changing administrative world, subject to the same influences and pressures as other administrative functions.

The theories of personnel administration exhibit many of the same assumptions about the nature of man made by traditionalist and behavioralist organization theories. Prescriptions for the recruitment, examination, classification, evaluation, promotion, and training of governmental personnel dominate the early literature. The inadequacies of the spoils system, based largely upon its decentralized, political base of power, were highlighted by the administrative reformers of the 1870s. In protest of the existing system, they called for a centralized, nonpolitical, efficient system of personnel management—assuming that if the political aspects of personnel administration could be removed, effective administration could occur. Little, if any, regard was evident for the human dimensions of administrative personnel.

As governmental functions increased, became more complex, and the need for greater numbers of personnel arose, administrators simply expanded the routine, traditional, nonpolitical procedures for recruitment and evaluation. Nevertheless, social changes in recent years, coupled with advances in our knowledge about the human elements of administration, help give rise to new questions about the personnel function in administration. Recent trends indicate a desire to review the effectiveness of an objective, routine, impersonal approach to the management of personnel—to explore the relationships between traditional selection methods and the satisfactory performance of administrative tasks. In addition, questions have been raised about the relationship between personnel achievement and morale. Furthermore, questions are being asked about the political isolation of public personnel and the advisability of public personnel organizations for the purpose of collectively representing the interest of public personnel in their relationships with public managers.

Professor David H. Rosenbloom discusses the development of the public personnel administration process, explaining the basic assumptions and values underlying its evolution as well as questioning its ability to effectively serve a changing public environment. He states that the field must develop a greater degree of self-awareness and methodological sophistication and that it should act to adopt a perspective that tends to be more analytical of political relationships in personnel processes and behavior. He calls for greater attention to be given to differentiating more clearly among public and private administrative processes. Only then, he believes, may elements of personnel administration in the public sector which have political significance be identified and used for the development of a more effective public personnel system.

Rosenbloom suggests four areas of political importance that contemporary public personnel administration should confront: 1) bureaucratic representation; 2) the relationships between public personnel practices and the development of agency cultures and patterns of behavior; 3) the relationships between public personnel practices and the general political participation and orientation of civil servants; and 4) a new approach to the topic of labor relations in the public sector. In each of the above areas, Rosenbloom outlines dominant trends that need to be reevaluated and proposes alternatives to correct obvious problem areas.

The selections in Part Three which follow Rosenbloom's article deal with questions related to his four topical areas. Regarding bureaucratic representation, Earl Reeves examines the question in historical perspective and attempts to demonstrate how changing attitudes toward bureaucratic representativeness have governed the public personnel selection process. He focuses on recent attempts of Blacks to achieve equal employment opportunity, suggesting that their problems are similar to those faced by other minorities and women.

The question at hand, according to Reeves, is how minorities can effectively express themselves and shape the manner in which government responds to their needs. He explains that minorities turn increasingly to the bureaucracy as a result of the ongoing buildup of policy-making power in administrative units apart from the more traditionally representative areas such as the Congress or the Presidency. He suggests a link between bureaucracy as an avenue to power and an instrument for control and a greater degree of acceptance of the bureaucratic role for society at large.

He contends that the civil service system is inherently nonrepresentative, since the established qualifications are not representative of the broader society. More flexible standards are required in the qualification stages of civil service and greater attention should be given to "compensatory employment." A further suggestion Reeves makes is that programs for job training and job identification be developed so that minorities may not only learn the necessary skills, but may also be aware of job availability and mobility.

Many efforts have been made to bring about more equitable representation in the public sector. Although great attention has been given to the Civil Rights Act of 1964 as the keystone for equal opportunity programs, Harry Grossman suggests that the Equal Employment Opportunity Act of 1972 has equally far-reaching consequences for the public sector, especially at the state and local level.

Grossman carefully examines the provisions of the EEO Act of 1972 and compares them with previous provisions from the 1964 Civil Rights Act. He discusses the problems which appear to have arisen regarding providing for equal opportunity under a merit system. Noteworthy among these is a concern for open competition versus selection processes and a general apprehension of the possibility of quotas being used to determine selection of personnel. Within these topics Grossman refers to relevant court decisions which have attempted to clarify the relationships between quotas, hiring tests and practices, and the location of burden of proof.

Grossman concludes that while quotas and proportional representation have no place in merit system employment practices, goals and timetables are different. The question is, however, whether goals and timetables become semantic substitutes for quotas. He counsels that the selection process should be followed judiciously so that government agencies will, if challenged, be able to show to the satisfaction of the courts a rational nexus between qualification standards and duties to be performed.

In an addendum, he shows that recent administrative and judicial decisions have not completely cleared the air or removed questions about the applicability of EEO standards. Furthermore, he presents questions for future reference for state and local managers as they attempt to cope with EEO provisions.

Governmental employees are not only becoming more representative of ethnic and/or racial diversity, but they are also beginning to pursue more effective voices in matters relating to working conditions, salary, fringe benefits, and many other traditionally labor-management type questions. Richard Murphy outlines the evolution of public labor-management relations in the decade, 1960–1970. He points out that the changes have been dramatic in terms of governmental recognition of unions, the involvement of third parties in some agency judgments, the development of appeals and grievance procedures, and an upgrading of labor-management relations in public personnel to a "high level of attention" in administrative decision making.

Murphy shows how a series of executive orders and public employee pressures (especially the postal workers' "work stoppage" and the similar activities of the air traffic controllers) aided in the movement's efforts to gain a degree of cohesiveness and the acceptance, by government, of collective bargaining and grievance procedures.

Some problems still remain, according to Murphy. Legislation prohibiting strikes and the remaining limitations on the processes of representation and negotiation in the bargaining process are two good examples. Nevertheless, Murphy predicts greater political activity by governmental employee unions, a degree of conflict among public employees over "social action" programs in the merit process, and an increase in the use of private sector precedents and procedures in the governmental labor-management sector. To effectively adapt to these suggested trends, Murphy submits that centralized personnel management power as seen through the Civil Service Commission, Office of Management and Budget, and Congress will have to be diminished and replaced by more flexible procedures.

What are the long-range implications for public administration as the trend toward collective bargaining continues? Felix Nigro outlines eight ways in which public administration has been affected, considers the resulting changes in levels of influence of participants in the public policy process, discusses a concern for the role of the public interest, and presents an evaluative balance sheet.

Nigro suggests the following effects of collective bargaining upon public personnel administration: 1) bilateral determination of the conditions of work; 2) the policing of public officials through binding grievance arbitration clauses; 3) widening participation of unions in program policy making; 4) an intensification of the political activities of unions; 5) an increase in the fiscal crises of government due to collective bargaining settlements; 6) a recognition that public collective bargaining differs significantly from bargaining in the private sector; 7) a continuing decline in the power of civil service commissions; and 8) changes in the budgetary processes.

After discussing the effects of collective bargaining, Nigro suggests a list of relative roles of participants both before and after collective bargaining, pinpointing how the decisional processes regarding personnel as well as policy questions may have been changed. He suggests that the public interest has not been ignored, since collective bargaining decisions have not wiped out laws or regulations which reflect legislative preferences. In fact, he states that much of the concern for the public interest may now be found in the process of collective bargaining itself. However, Nigro calls for the public to be made more readily aware of the full costs of settlements since they ultimately will have to pay the bill.

As a balance, Nigro concludes that collective bargaining has proved itself by reducing public employer arbitrariness and paternalism and is an effective antidote for bureaucratic excesses. Factors which need further attention, according to Nigro, include some curbs on excessive union power, tax reform to enable the adequate financing of contract settlements, and a greater interest and role played by both the legislative sector and civic groups and individuals, all of whom possess real stakes in the outcome of professional negotiations.

One of the major concerns regarding labor-management relations in the public sector is the efficacy of public employee strikes. Robert Booth Fowler examines the legal and philosophical aspects of public employee strikes against a background of the democratic system.

Fowler explores five points of dispute over public employee strikes: 1) Are public employee strikes compatible with the concept of sovereignty? 2) Can public employee work stoppages be reconciled with democratic government? 3) How will strikes affect the preservation of the merit system and decent relations? 4) Is legalization of public employee strikes necessary to guarantee full rights for public workers? and 5) Is the legal right to strike justifiable in terms of current demands for political reality?

Professor Fowler concludes that within certain limitations, especially those regarding the balance between democratic equality and the potential for spurning the public will, government workers ought to have the legal right to strike.

An additional matter of concern for a changing public personnel sector is the question of greater political activities of members of the nonelective civil service. Philip Martin explains recent trends in this area by first explaining in detail how the Pendleton Act of 1883 began the movement toward political neutrality for civil servants, with additional refinements taking place through executive orders, Civil Service Commission actions, legislation, and court decisions. Secondly, he focuses on recent efforts to have this narrow view, as exemplified in the Hatch Act of 1939, broadened or declared unconstitutional.

Many changes in the personnel process led to the belief that changes might also be in the offing in regard to political activity by public employees. Unionization, collective bargaining, and "affirmative action programs" all seemed to indicate the personnel process was open to greater individuality. Martin believes the courts enhanced this view through several narrow decisions on the lower federal level that tended to place higher priority upon the exercise of free speech found in political activity than upon laws prohibiting political activity. Such decisions first overturned state political neutrality statutes and later did the same for the federal Hatch Act.

The Supreme Court, however, rejected lower federal court interpretations and ruled that the Hatch Act was indeed valid. The Supreme Court decision held that such restrictions are consistent with job security and advancement apart from political activities. Furthermore, the Court stated that the Hatch Act prohibitions applied to all federal merit employees in the restriction of all political activity. It appears, therefore, that the Hatch Act will not be questioned in the courts unless some invidious discrimination were to be established. In conclusion, Martin suggests that if reform is to come it will have to come through legislation either at the state or federal level. The appropriate remedy, it appears, seems to be political rather than judicial.

Having considered the problem of adaptation and

change in the public personnel sector in reference to questions of representation, labor-management relations, and political activity, some attention should be given to the attitudes of bureaucrats toward certain democratic principles. Since career bureaucrats are involved in a great many of the day-to-day operational as well as broader policy decisions, their attitudes about democratic principles are important indicators of the effective functioning of democratic administration.

Robert L. Wynia's selection presents data from a study of the attitudes of federal career bureaucrats toward certain democratic principles. From the data, he concludes that: 1) the type of agency with which the bureaucrat is affiliated is an important determinant of his attitude toward democratic values; 2) "defense-oriented agency" bureaucrats tend to be more antidemocratic in their attitudes; 3) the greater the longevity in any agency, the greater the likelihood of an increase in antidemocratic attitudes; and 4) the more formal education the bureaucrat has, the stronger his democratic beliefs and attitudes.

Much remains to be understood about the changing nature of personnel administration. Demands for change and innovation in the procedures of personnel recruitment and management reflect, in part, changes in the American society and political life. In addition, the governmental recruiter, it appears, will have to meet the same standards in recruitment of minorities and women as does his counterpart in the private sector. Furthermore, inequities in working conditions and salary, coupled with an increasingly organized and vocal civil servant, provide critical questions about the future of public personnel management practices. Finally, increasing attention will need to be given to the long-range effects of merit system protections on the attitudes that bureaucrats possess toward democratic values.

In this part only a few contemporary problems have been explored. Some suggestions for dealing with them have also been made, but only the future will provide evidence of the ability of the public personnel system to successfully deal with them.

15

david h. rosenbloom

PUBLIC PERSONNEL ADMINISTRATION AND POLITICS: TOWARD A NEW PUBLIC PERSONNEL ADMINISTRATION

Public personnel administration, as an academic field, is currently lacking in appeal for the vast majority of political scientists and even for many public policy oriented public administrationists. It has, as a recent introductory political science text noted, become little more than a "specialty 'tool,'" which is ". . . generally taught as a technical specialty, revolving around such topics as position classification . . . and methods of recruitment and selection for the civil service."[1] This is true despite the fact that many have recognized that within the field there are several topics having widespread political ramifications.[2] The purpose of this article is to explicate the reasons for the current status of public personnel administration and to suggest a path which could be followed in order to develop a new and more useful public personnel administration.

I

The current status of public personnel administration is related to intellectual developments which have taken place in the related areas of political science and public administration. Public personnel administration is a profession as well as a discipline, and as such, it has

Reprinted by permission from the *Midwest Review of Public Administration*, Vol. 7, No. 2 (April 1973), pp. 98–110. Copyright 1973 by the Midwest Review of Public Administration, Inc.

always had a practical and prescriptive bias. Its literature is formalistic and highly value-laden, with the standard goals being greater efficiency, economy, and procedural regularity. In the years since World War II, however, the major intellectual developments in political science and public administration have been in an opposite direction. Both have become less prescriptive, less formalistic, more value-free, and more behaviorally oriented. In addition, public administration, in particular, has undergone changes which have placed public personnel administration on tenuous intellectual grounds. Public administration, as a field, has come to recognize that to a large extent its focus must be on "public" rather than on "administration," if it is to make a *special* contribution. It is partly in this connection that public administration rejected a portion of the core of its former body of theory (or framework of "proverbs," if the reader prefers) and became far more concerned with decision making and public policy-making. As a result, some areas which were more central to public administration in the past have largely now become the preserves of other fields, including sociology and business administration. Thus, Waldo observed: "There is over-all a wide gap between the interests and activities of the scholars identified with Theory of Organization and the interests and activities of scholars trained in and identified with political science and the related or subdiscipline of public administration."[3] In terms of public personnel administration, it is especially important that there are now few, if any, who argue that the general behavioral patterns of individuals in organizations are significantly related per se to whether the organizations are public or private by definition. If behavioral patterns in public and private organizations are similar, however, *public* personnel administration, as it is now constituted, is largely without a viable rationale.[4]

The current status of public personnel administration is also related to its self-imposed narrowness of scope. Although public personnel administrationists are sometimes sweeping in their generalizations pertaining to the importance of the field, they nevertheless fail to address themselves fully to its public or political aspects, despite the fact that these might be the only legitimate basis for a *public* personnel administration. For example, O. Glenn Stahl, one of the most influential American public personnel administrationists, has concluded that, "There is no single activity which will net such economy or promote such performance as may be realized through continued improvements in the quality and the motivation of public personnel."[5] His concepts of economy and performance, however, are almost totally apolitical. Public personnel administration, as a whole, has also failed to address itself to the fact that all public personnel systems are primarily political products and therefore, that terms such as "economy," "efficiency," "performance," and "best qualified" cannot be, and have not been, defined without reference to political values.

Perhaps the most important factor in public personnel administration's rejection of an approach more oriented toward politics has been its simultaneous commitment to the "merit system" and its failure to understand correctly the nature of that system. In the minds of most public personnel administrationists, the merit system is associated with efficiency, economy, procedural justice, quality, and political neutrality. It has been treated as something upon which, as a whole, there can be no legitimate disagreement, and therefore as something which is inherently apolitical. Thus, the slogan "only the best shall serve the state" became the rallying cry of public personnel administrationists, as though it were akin to a natural law, rather than a legitimizing proposition for a particular set of political arrangements.[6] Merit systems, however, were often introduced at least as much in connection with demands for a redistribution of political power, authority, and influence among members of political communities, as to secure better economy and efficiency. Civil service reform in the United States, Great Britain, and sixth-tenth century China present just three such examples.

In the United States, the civil service reformers thought that, in the words of Carl Schurz, "The question whether the Departments at Washington are managed well or badly is, in proportion to the whole problem, an insignificant question."[7] What they wanted, as they clearly stated, was to make it possible for a new class of politicians to emerge, or, "To restore ability, high character, and true public spirit once more to their legitimate spheres in our public life, and to make active politics once more attractive to men of self-respect and high patriotic aspirations."[8] In short, nothing less than a fundamental change in political leadership. In Great Britain, as J. D. Kingsley observed, ". . . the debate occasioned by the Northcote-Trevelyan recommendations ran clearly along class lines"[9] and the overall issue was the distribution of political power, authority, and influence, rather than more efficient administration. In China, "After several centuries of division, the Sui (589–618) and the T'ang (618–906) dynasties saw in the training and recruitment of a centralized civil service the best means of overcoming the powers of regionalism and of the hereditary aristocracy."[10] Although there is some doubt as to whether "the rise of this aristocracy of merit . . . definitely freed the dynasty from its dependence on an older, hereditary aristocracy,"[11] there is little doubt that personnel administrative reforms were introduced with this prospect in mind.

The historical relationship between merit systems and the distribution of political power, authority, and influence suggests that merit values such as selection of the best qualified, efficiency, and economy, which historically have been predominantly political values cannot be defined fully and legitimately without reference to other political values. It should be noted, in this context, that some now consider all major public administrative values to be political values as well. It is here, perhaps, that public personnel administration currently leaves the most to be desired from the point of view of political science. The field has devoted itself almost entirely to attempting to discover the principles and practices through which public personnel systems can assure the highest degree of economy and efficiency in an apolitical sense, and it has almost completely ignored the impact of these principles and practices on such politically relevant factors as bureaucratic representativeness and individual, group, and organizational political behavior. It should be noted in passing that this shortcoming of public personnel administration has itself become politically relevant in the U.S. today as members of some minority groups and women have been increasingly arguing that procedures designed to obtain the "best" civil servants tend to be racially, ethnically, and/or sexually discriminatory and, therefore, that they are inherently not the best procedures.

A final reason for the current lack of interest in public personnel administration among political scientists and many public administrationists is a more technical one: the field as a whole has failed to develop satisfactorily as either a science or an art, even within its excessively narrow confines. For example, "The cornerstone of the public personnel program is the process of selection by means of competitive examinations . . ."[12] but, ". . . hundreds of public jurisdictions have probably never done a validity study"[13] and there are many major barriers to such studies. First, there is the difficulty of determining what constitutes "job success." "A 'success rating' usually amounts to a kind of 'report card' which is made out by the employees' supervisor," and, ". . . such ratings are inevitably limited in reliability—particularly when different *supervisors are rating different people*,"[14] as is the case in the vast majority of large jurisdictions. A second limitation is that ". . . generally only a limited portion of the test-taking group ever get the chance to perform on the job."[15] Third, those appointed often have very similar scores, thereby limiting the amount of variation likely to be explained by those scores. Finally, public jurisdictions tend to be forced to give examinations having "face validity," but face validity does not necessarily coincide with content validity. As a result of these barriers, civil service examination validity coefficients are typically at about the .25 level and seldom greater than .50.[16] In other words, performance on civil service examinations usually explains only about 6 per cent of the variance in job performance and rarely more than 25 per cent. What then of the cornerstone, not to mention the rest of the structure? The problem would not be so acute if public personnel administration were less value-laden and less ideological, and had sought to explain the remainder of the variance in some other ways. By and large, however, it has not. It is this defect in particular which has led some to conclude that the merit system and public personnel administration in general contribute little more than a means of keeping "undesirables" out of the civil service in an inexpensive and relatively neutral fashion,[17] and that therefore public personnel administration, as an intellectual endeavor, has made little contribution apart from rationalizing the political status quo.

II

If public personnel administration is to progress and develop more toward its full potential, at least two of its current limitations must be overcome. First, the field must develop a greater degree of self-awareness and methodological sophistication. It must seek to define its sphere of interest with a greater degree of consciousness and do more to assert an existence independent of governmental practices and practitioners, just as political science has an existence apart from law and politicians. In this connection, public personnel administration must seek to understand more fully its own development and explore further the extent to which public personnel practices and theories have been related to political variables. At the same time that the field must become less value-laden and less ideological, it must make greater efforts to become more methodologically sophisticated. It must, for example, seek to explain a far greater share of the variance in on-the-job performance, and in other personnel factors. In this regard, the field might find it useful to adopt a more experimental approach, where possible. In short, public personnel administration must seek to discover true relationships rather than presumed ones. In addition to developing greater methodological sophistication to deal with its traditional concerns, public personnel administration should also do the same with regard to what should become its new concerns. This, then, relates to the second limitation to be overcome.

In order to overcome its current excessively narrow scope, public personnel administration must adopt a perspective which is more analytic of political relationships and political behavior. It must go beyond the value constraints of its understanding of the merit system and attempt to develop an understanding of the impact of public personnel administration on political variables, and vice-versa, rather than simply on efficiency and economy in a technical sense. At least for the time being, however, this political perspective should probably be a limited one. The field, by the very nature of its concerns, must retain some of its applied and prescriptive bias. If it is to remain, or more accurately, to become *public* personnel administration, it must also avoid following the path of modern organization theory, or of duplicating it, in rejecting a meaningful distinction between public and private organizations. Thus, in addition to normal limitations based on the relevance of public personnel administrative theory, hypotheses, principles, and practices to political variables, public personnel administration should not concern itself with political behavior which is not oriented toward or highly relevant to macro-politics. That is to say, that, at least for the present, public personnel administration should not seek to develop further understanding of individual political behavior which is essentially intra-organizationally oriented, unless such behavior is believed to be relevant to macro-politics.

The justification for the above approach, and indeed for *public* personnel administration itself is related ultimately to Weber's conception of the state as being distinguished from other organizations on the basis of its " . . . monopoly of the legitimate use of physical force within a given territory."[18] Despite the problems sometimes incurred in attempting to distinguish public from private organizations, it is always the case that central national administrative apparatuses and the people who are responsible for their functioning have a degree of direct or primary political power which is not available to the vast majority of private organizations[19] and administrators. Therefore, it is not necessary to consider whether the intra-organizationally oriented behavior of public employees differs from that of private employees, or whether the overall organizationally oriented behavior of structurally similar public and private organizations differs, as to recognize that, in general, the political outputs of each are fundamentally different in terms of their "authoritative" or binding qualities. In addition, it is probably true that civil servants employed by central administrative organizations tend to possess more political authority and influence in their extra-organizationally oriented political behavior, directly and indirectly by virtue of their association with these organizations, than do people doing similar types of tasks in private organizations.[20] On the basis of this distinction between the general political characteristics of public and private organizations, many areas into which public personnel administration could and should legitimately expand can be identified. Perhaps it will eventually prove possible to develop a general theory of public personnel administration on this basis. For the time being, however, rather than attempting to build a framework from the top down, public personnel administration would probably be better off by developing a sounder foundation. In this regard, there are at least four areas of political importance which appear to be significantly related to public personnel administrative practices, and which also appear to be fundamental to the development of a more useful public personnel administration.

III

The first of these areas, and perhaps the most important, is that of bureaucratic representation. In an age in which much of the policy of all governments is formulated in public bureaucracies, the potential importance of their representativeness is hard to overestimate. It can hardly be much less important, and might even be more, for example, than the representativeness of legislatures. For the most part, however, public personnel administration, which, at least in theory, has always been concerned with the relationship between the input of manpower and the quality of bureaucratic outputs, has in practice avoided any serious consideration of whether either these "inputs" or outputs do have a representative quality, whether they have any relationship to one another in this regard, or whether the outputs are related to any other than technical efficiency. In fact, public personnel administration has been largely oblivious to the major questions posed by the concept of representative bureaucracy, which, incidentally, has been developed almost entirely by political scientists rather than by public personnel administrationists. To understand more fully exactly what is involved here, it is necessary to briefly identify the major aspect of that concept.

The concept of representative bureaucracy has now been in the literature of political science for some time, and has received considerable attention. It was perhaps most comprehensively defined by Krislov, who concluded that it had "four intertwined meanings:"

> The most obvious is the simple representational notion that all social groups have a right to political participation and to influence. The second can be labeled the functional aspect; the wider the range of talents, types, and regional and family contacts found in a bureaucracy, the more likely it is to be able to fulfill its functions, with respect to both internal efficiency and social setting. Bureaucracies also symbolize values and power realities and are thus representational in both a political and an analytic sense. Therefore, finally, social conduct and future behavior in a society may be channelized and encouraged through the mere constitution of the bureaucracy.[21]

In addition, Mosher has provided a note of clarity by distinguishing between passive (or sociological) and active (or responsible) representation. The former ". . . concerns the source of origin of individuals and the degree to which, collectively, they mirror the total society." In active representation, on the other hand. ". . . an individual (or administrator) is expected to press for the interests and desires of those whom he is presumed to represent, whether they be the whole people or some segment of the people"[22]

It is logically a task of public personnel administration to attempt to answer many of the questions posed by the concept of representative bureaucracy. Public personnel administration's sole concern with efficiency and economy might have been appropriate at an earlier time when public bureaucracies did not have important policy functions, but it is certainly inappropriate today. Broad questions, such as the following, for instance, must be approached in a far more adequate fashion: What is the relationship between active and passive representation? What is the political and administrative importance of each? And with what does it vary? What factors serve to encourage or discourage a strong relationship between the two? What personnel practices, such as examinations and protections against discriminatory treatment, serve to foster or to limit passive and active representation? What are the political and administrative effects of using personnel procedures, such as quotas for minority group hiring and promotion, which either limit or increase passive representation? Until public personnel administration deals reasonably effectively with such questions, it will remain highly underdeveloped and continue to be concerned with much that is less important.

A second and related area into which public personnel administration could profitably expand concerns the relationship between public personnel administrative practices and the development of agency cultures and patterns of behavior. The latter, of course, are inherently political and of political interest because they are directly related to public policy outputs. Although there is a considerable overlap between this area and that of representative bureaucracy, there is also a significant difference of focus. Here the concern is with the agency as a whole, its general outlook and the development of institutionalized behavioral patterns, rather than with the individual and his contribution to passive or active representation. As Seidman has observed, "Each agency has its own culture and internal set of loyalties and values which are likely to guide its actions and influence its policies."[23] He has also noted that,

> ... because people believe what they are doing is important and the way they have been taught to do is right, they are slow to accept change. Institutional responses are highly predictable, particularly to new ideas which conflict with institutional values and may pose a potential threat to organizational power and survival. Knowledgeable Budget Bureau officials estimate that agency positions on any major policy issue can be forecast with nearly 100 per cent accuracy, regardless of the administration in power.[24]

Although Seidman argues that culture and behavior are largely products of structural and organizational arrangements, personnel practices, as Downs has argued, probably also play an important role. Firstly, the development of agency cultures must depend heavily on internal socialization processes and methods of treating deviant behavior (disciplinary procedures). Both of these, of course, are largely questions for personnelists. Secondly, Downs has hypothesized that such personnel concerns as agency rates of growth and methods of promotion are important in determining agency behavior: "Fast-growing bureaus experience a rising proportion of climbers and a declining proportion of conservers," and, "if most of the officials occupying key positions in a bureau are of one type, then the bureau and its behavior will be dominated by the traits typical of that type."[25] In addition, if Downs is correct, such personnel procedures as promotion by seniority would tend to increase the proportion of "conservers" in an agency, give the total agency a conserver culture and increase the importance of bureau pathologies perculiar to that group. Other personnel practices, including recruitment and selection, position classification, status gradations, the nature and use of authority, and so forth, would also seem to be relevant here as they make agencies more or less attractive to different types of "organizational men" and therefore, presumably are also related to different kinds of organizational behavior and public policy outputs. The task of public personnel administration is, of course, to analyze the relationships between such practices, their development, and the development of organizational cultures and behavioral patterns. Again, focusing only on individual ability and proper placement of individuals in a technical sense does not seem to explain adequately agency performance and behavior, and again variables of political importance, rather than simply economy and efficiency are involved.

Another area in which public personnel administration could make an important contribution concerns the relationship between public personnel administrative practices and the general political participation and orientation of civil servants. Public personnel administration has, of course, addressed itself to a part of this subject area in its traditional concern with regulations concerning political neutrality, conflicts of interest, and adverse actions. In general, however, the treatment of these subjects has been technical, legal, and largely from a narrow administrative perspective. Little systematic effort has been made to understand the impact of these features on politics and political variables.[26] Political neutrality regulations, for example, range from almost no restrictions on the part of Scandinavian civil servants, through substantial limitations on the partisan political activities of U.S. civil servants, to an almost complete denial of political rights to some civil servants in Japan. But the consequences of these regulations for political systems is largely unknown, as is the relative commonness and importance of the political activities of civil servants where such activity is permitted. Yet without a better understanding of these activities, the consequences, and necessity, desirability, or sensibility of regulations in this area cannot be known, despite the wealth of opinion expressed upon them. The same applies with respect to conflicts of interest. In some countries civil servants cannot join a private firm for two years after they have retired from the service, if they have had official dealings with that firm. In other countries no such regulation exists. Although it could be assumed that policy formulation and the development of relationships or complexes involving public agencies and private firms or groups could be influenced by these differences, in fact very little is known about their consequences. The protections afforded civil servants against adverse actions present another case in point. These usually have been developed for administrative reasons or as a result of collective bargaining, rather than for political reasons, and they vary widely among political systems. It is reasonable to assume that they have political consequences because they largely remove sanctions against civil servants for engaging in legitimate, but disfavored political activity. Public personnel administration, however, has failed to approach this subject from this point of view and consequently very little is known about it.

Each of the above categories of public personnel regulations, and perhaps others as well, appear, on their face, to be related to the potential political behavior of civil servants and therefore, of course, to the political importance and consequences of that behavior. Developments concerning the legal-constitutional position and political participation of civil servants in the U.S. in the last decade provide a good illustration that such a relationship can exist and have significant consequences. Beginning in the 1960s and continuing to the present time, the legal-constitutional position of U.S. civil servants has undergone major changes in the direction of providing them with greater constitutional protections, including those of free speech and association, and greater due process in removals and adverse actions.[27] At the same time, a significant number of them, with at least a general awareness of their greater security, began to engage in permissible, but decidedly disfavored political activities including the signing of rather strongly worded anti-war petitions, the petitioning of departmental secretaries for changes in national policies, the organization of political pressure groups within the Federal service, and related activities.[28] These forms of political participation raise numerous questions which are legitimately the concern of public personnel administrationists and should at least be addressed, if not fully answered. For example, how direct is the relationship between a strengthening of civil servants' legal-constitutional position and their proclivity to take part in political activities? To what entent is this proclivity also related to their positions in agencies? How does the public at large react to such activities and with what does this reaction vary? How do administrative officials and politicians react to the activities and to the civil servants taking part in them? What effect does greater political participation have on internal administrative arrangements, behavior, and policy outputs? And, more normatively, how desirable is it from the point of view of various aspects of the political system?

A final area in which public personnel administration should adopt a new approach involves labor relations. Regulations and practices pertaining to employee organization and collective bargaining have long been considered an important aspect of public personnel administration, but, in general, public personnel administrationists have failed in this area, as in the others, to develop an adequate political focus. The overall political relevance of public employee unionization has, perhaps, best been conveyed by Chapman in his study of public personnel practices in Western Europe: "The truth is that people employed in government service are tending to become not only self-governing but also self employed. All the evidence . . . points in this direction. The drift towards the syndical state machine is one of the unnoticed oddities of the last fifty years."[29] With regard to the power position of civil service unions, he concluded:

> Their power now lies in their numerical strength and its potential electoral importance to politicians. This is reinforced by the fact that they are the accepted spokesmen for those employed by the state. Their aim is to protect the interests of the state in so far as those interests coincide with the interests of their members. Indeed, some extremists have held that the body of civil servants is the state.[30]

The fact that Chapman perceived this development as having been a "drift" is significant because it speaks directly to public personnel administration's apolitical approach in an area in which politics is of fundamental importance. Although it is probably too late to drastically affect the power positions of public service unions, if that should be desirable, there are many questions which are still worth analyzing. For example, What are the public personnel administrative and political causes and effects of administrative systems in which civil service *unions* are engaged in the administration of public services? What are the public personnel administrative, general administrative, and political roots of different styles of union leadership, growth, and relative power? What happens, and under what conditions, when employee organizations seek to recast public personnel practices in a way more suitable to themselves? How do all of these affect popular control, representative bureaucracy, and other general aspects of public service?

In conclusion, public personnel administration has more or less fallen by the intellectual wayside in recent years as a result of its failure to keep up with developments in related areas in political science and public administration, its overly narrow scope, and its inability to develop satisfactorily as an art or a science within its limited realm. The field has the potential to make significant contributions in both political science and public administration and it may be able to revive itself by becoming more self-conscious and methodologically sophisticated, and by adopting a more political focus.

Hopefully, this article will serve as a meaningful step toward the development of a new, and far more useful, public personnel administration.

ENDNOTES

1. Stephen Wasby, *Political Science—The Discipline and Its Dimensions* New York: Charles Scribner's Sons, 1970), pp. 425-426.
2. *Ibid.*, p. 427.
3. Dwight Waldo, "Theory of Organization: Status and Problems," in Amitai Etzioni, ed., *Readings on Modern Organizations* (Englewood Cliffs: Prentice-Hall, 1969), p. 22.
4. Thus, there are really two principal courses open to public personnel administration. It must either develop a distinctive focus by more adequately addressing the public (especially the political and public policymaking) aspects of governmental personnel administration, or essentially merge with personnel administration in general. Remaining in its current state, as I will argue below, amounts to little more than serving to place a veneer of professional legitimacy in a peculiar set of political arrangements.
5. O. Glenn Stahl, *Public Personnel Administration* (New York: Harper and Row, 1962), p. 480.
6. See Norman Sharpless, Jr., "Public Personnel Selection—An Overview," in J. Donovan, ed., *Recruitment and Selection in the Public Service* (Chicago: Public Personnel Association, 1968), pp. 8-9.
7. Carl Schurz, *Speeches, Correspondence, and Political Papers of Carl Schurz*, ed. by F. Bancroft (New York: G. P. Putnam's Sons, 1913), II, p. 123.
8. Editorial in *Harper's Weekly*, XXXVII (July 1, 1893), p. 614.
9. J. Donald Kingsley, *Representative Bureaucracy* (Yellow Springs: Antioch Press, 1944), p. 63.
10. See *The Chinese Civil Service*, ed. by Johanna Menzel (Boston: D. C. Heath and Co., 1963), p. vii.
11. *Ibid.*, p. viii.
12. Stahl, *Public Personnel Administration*, p. 67.
13. Kenneth Wentworth, "The Use of Commercial Tests," in Donovan, ed., *Recruitment and Selection*, p. 155.
14. Glenn McClung, "Statistical Techniques in Testing," *ibid.*, pp. 339-340.
15. *Ibid.*, p. 340.
16. *Ibid.*, Table 2.
17. See, for example, Samuel Krislov, *The Negro in Federal Employment* (Minneapolis: University of Minnesota Press, 1967), p. 55.
18. *From Max Weber: Essays in Sociology*, ed. by H. H. Garth and C. W. Mills (New York: Oxford University Press, 1958), p. 78.
19. Note that one could make the same argument with regard to what might be called "non-central" public organizations, such as public corporations and state farms, which are more analogous to private firms in many ways than to public administrative and public policymaking organizations in the usual sense.

20. The term "task" is intended to distinguish the nature of the work activity from its specific substance.

21. Krislov, *The Negro*, p. 64.

22. Frederick C. Mosher, *Democracy and the Public Service* (New York: Oxford University Press, 1968), p. 12. On representative bureaucracy see also V. Subramanian "Representative Bureaucracy: A Reassessment," *61 American Political Science Review* (December 1967), pp. 1010–19.

23. Harold Seidman, *Politics, Position, and Power* (New York: Oxford University Press, 1970), p. 18.

24. *Ibid.* See also Louis Gawthorp, *Bureaucratic Behavior in the Executive Branch* (New York: The Free Press, 1969), esp. chaps. vii–ix. Gawthorp argues that agencies fall into one of two main categories, innovative or consolidative.

25. Anthony Downs, *Inside Bureaucracy* (Boston: Little, Brown and Co., 1967), p. 263, numbers 7, 6.

26. My own *Federal Service and the Constitution* (Ithaca: Cornell University Press, 1971) is an attempt to deal with this area as a whole from a political perspective.

27. See *ibid.*, chaps. vii–viii.

28. See D. Rosenbloom, "Some Political Implications of the Drift Toward a Liberation of Federal Employees," *31 Public Administration Review* (July/August 1971), pp. 420–426.

29. Brian Chapman, *The Profession of Government* (London: Unwin University Books, 1959), p. 297.

30. *Ibid.*, p. 296.

16

earl j. reeves

EQUAL EMPLOYMENT AND THE CONCEPT
OF THE BUREAUCRACY AS A
REPRESENTATIVE INSTITUTION

The problem of maintaining, or in some cases creating for the first time, confidence in the institutions of government is one of the basic challenges facing the United States today. Rarely in the history of the nation has there been such widespread and bitter disenchantment with the political system.

Anti-war protests, student unrest and violence and the eruption of violence in the streets of our cities have forced the government to face the realitics of alienation and frustration. In particular the emergence of the black power movement with its overtone of black nationalism and separatism has combined with the smell of smoke and the sound of gunfire to confront us with the fact of black disillusionment with the American political system.

This paper focuses primarily on the attempts to gain equal employment opportunities for blacks because this has been the main focus of national attention in recent years. But the basic problems that are examined here also confront members of other minority groups and they are also the basis of much of the current movement for women's liberation.

The old mood which maintained a facade of patient accommodation has been replaced by a spirit of militant impatience. No longer is the black man willing to come hat in hand to beg crumbs from the

Reprinted by permission from the *Midwest Review of Public Administration*, Vol. 6, No. 1 (February 1972), pp. 3–13. Copyright 1972 by the Midwest Review of Public Administration, Inc.

white man's table. Now he demands not only an opportunity to sit at the table, but also a voice in determining the menu.

Blacks are therefore searching for ways in which they can express themselves politically and shape the ways in which government responds to the urban crisis in which they are so intimately involved. The American political system is a complex, decentralized system, with elaborate checks and balances designed to prevent rapid or radical change. The question now is not only whether the system can change, but in which direction will it go and to what extent blacks can participate in directing those changes.

There has been a substantial increase in black representation in state legislatures and the United States Congress (although the number is still disproportionately low). And there has been a flood of legislative enactments dealing with health, poverty, transportation, civil rights and other urban problems. But there is often a large gap between legislative promise and administrative performance. As a result, many blacks have come to view the legislation as mere shadow action designed to pacify the cities without really dealing with the problem.

It is both reasonable and necessary, therefore, to examine the relationship between blacks and the bureaucracy. In particular this paper seeks to examine the bureaucracy as a representative institution and the possibility that with the new emphasis on equal employment opportunities it may provide a channel through which blacks can obtain real access to political power.

The role of the bureaucracy in our society has been greatly expanded. It is now intimately involved in the policy making process and in fact the bureaucracy is likely, day in and day out, to be a major source of policy initiative. It has become a medium for registering the diverse wills that make up the people's will and as such it is a significant part of the representative process.

Furthermore, this increased policy role of the bureaucracy makes it the subject of considerable attention by the various interest groups. These groups recognize that whatever action may be taken by the President and Congress the bureaucracy will play a major role in determining the pro-program's success or failure. The bureaucracy becomes in fact

> the institutionalized embodiment of policy, an enduring organization actually or potentially capable of mobilizing power behind policy. The survival interest and creative drives of administrative organizations combine with clientele pressures to compel such mobilization. The party system provides no enduring insti-

tutional representation for group interests at all comparable to that of bureaus of the Department of Agriculture. Even the subject matter committees of Congress function in the shadow of agency permanency.[1]

This expanded role in the policy making process increases the importance of the representative function of the bureaucracy; if the bureaucracy is going to make basic decisions it must in some way be responsive to the society as a whole. Norton Long contends that as a result of the Jacksonian conception of the civil service as the preserve of the common man the bureaucracy actually provides a democratic or popular balance to the oligarchie tendencies of Congress.[2]

Representation, however, is a two way street. In addition to providing the represented with access to power it also tends to bind him to political system. And in fact the tendency for representation to promote a commitment to the political system has been one of the major justifications for expanding its scope. Samuel Krislov, for example, urges the necessity for increasing the employment of minority persons in the bureaucracy because

> the incorporation of representatives of different social groups into the enforcement machinery involves these groups with the policy itself and commits them to its maintenance. Participation, even if only in the implementation of policy on the part of lower-rung officeholders, makes less salient and less risky the role of top office holders. Lower-rung officeholders feel some commitment to a policy over which they have a measure of control and transmit that sense of responsibility to the groups in which they are socially anchored.[3]

This motivation for extending the base of representation may be offensive to blacks because it reflects a desire to co-opt or buy-off blacks to keep them from revolting against the existing structure. But the representative function of the bureaucracy also provides a channel for the exercise of power. And this power can become black power when it is exercised by black men. Charles Silberman emphasizes this point when he comments that

> Sooner, or later, Negro militants will have to face up to the dilemma posed by their desire, on the one hand, to become a part of the "power structure," and their determination, on the other, to remain free of white control. For if Negroes are to be elected and appointed to high office—if they are, in fact to enter the "power structure" and help shape the decisions that count—they will have to give up a good deal of their freedom to criticize and protest, this is the price of power.[4]

It can be seen, therefore, that the bureaucracy has a significant representative function, and that this function served both as an avenue to power and an instrument of control. But there is a need for a further definition of the role of the representative within the bureaucracy.

After an exhaustive survey of the various definitions and nuances which the term has acquired Hannah Pitkin sets forth the following general definition.

> Political representation is primarily a public, institutionalized arrangement involving many people and groups, and operating in the complex ways of large-scale social arrangements. What makes it representation is not any single action by any one participant, but the over-all structure and functioning of the system, the patterns emerging from the multiple activities of many people. It is representation if people (or constituency) are present in governmental action even though they do not literally act for themselves.[5]

Perhaps more appropriate to the subject of this paper, however, is her discussion of "descriptive representation" which appears to be the basic idea underlying most discussion of the representative role of the bureaucracy. This conception of representation holds that the only genuinely representative body is one whose composition corresponds accurately to that of the whole society.

In this conception of representation the emphasis is not on the method of selection, the formal authorization, or the means of holding the representative accountable.

> Rather it depends on the representative's characteristics, on what he *is* or is *like*, on being something rather than doing something. The representative does not act for others, he "stands for" them, by virtue of a correspondence or connection between them, a resemblance or reflection.[6]

If we accept this conception of representation then the representativeness of the bureaucracy depends primarily on the extent to which it accurately reflects the composition of our society. And while the federal bureaucracy in the United States has been broadly democratic in its recruiting it has been grossly unrepresentative of minority groups and especially of blacks.

In the earliest days of the Republic governmental employment was regarded as the prerogative of the upper class and, following British practice, was essentially open only to gentlemen. In case there might have been any doubt that blacks were thereby excluded, the United States Congress passed a law in the 1820's explicitly prohibiting the employment of blacks in the United States Post Office Department.

The democratization of the civil service in the Jacksonian era made the bureaucracy more representative of the white population but provided little if any change for blacks. Even after the Civil War, employment of blacks was very limited and only rarely were blacks allowed to rise to even token positions of representability such as diplomatic assignments to Haiti, Liberia and Santo Domingo.

The creation of the classified civil service in 1883 opened the door slightly but it was not until 1940 that racial discrimination was actually prohibited in federal employment. Systematic efforts to enforce the law emerged only in the 1950's and not until the 1960's was there any significant positive effort to recruit blacks and members of other minority groups for federal employment.[7]

But while the quest for equal employment is essential if the bureaucracy is to be representative, it raises certain questions about the traditional operation of the merit system. In particular, administrators may find it difficult to reconcile equality of opportunity with their traditional, and supposedly color-blind, search for the "best qualified" applicants.

If minority groups were equal in all respects except employment, if all those competing under the merit system really started from an equal beginning, there would be no problem. But everyone does not start equally; some, especially blacks from inner-city ghettos, start under a series of handicaps. Many begin with the handicaps of limited education, limited experience, low motivation and poor work habits which have placed them in the unemployable category.

Others may have completed their formal education at least through high school and perhaps even college and yet because of the inadequacy of their schools may find themselves at a distinct disadvantage in competing with their suburban counterparts. And this disadvantage may be increased even further by the existence of "cultural bias" in the examinations that are used to screen applicants.

The excessive failure rate for black college students who take the Federal Service Entrance Examination, for example, raises suspicions that the test may reflect a person's background rather than ability. The U. S. Supreme Court has taken note of this problem and has recently prohibited the use of even apparently neutral tests if they result in discrimination.[8]

Samuel Krislov asserts that the current emphasis on equal employment presents a two-fold challenge to the traditional operation of the merit system. The first challenge comes from the demand for a re-evaluation of the traditional educational and experience require-ments for federal employment. The great American fetish for formal education has effectively restricted job opportunities for many able and otherwise competent persons, especially those from low income or minority families.

It becomes essential, therefore, to develop more flexible stan-dards of evaluation which put more emphasis on basic ability and potential and less on the mere attainment of certain formal standards. Employers must be able to take into consideration the limited educa-tional and employment opportunities which were available to a per-son.

The second challenge is the call for "compensatory employ-ment" or "reverse discrimination." This is not a new idea. Veterans have benefited from the compensatory bonus points which are added to their score on civil service examinations. But there is probably much less public support for extending this concept to blacks than there was for providing it to veterans. Even Krislov reacts rather vigorously against the idea. He rejects it as unworkable because it is not sufficiently "self-containing and self-defining to be satisfied with-out continuous social strife." For him in fact "the remedy is worse than the disease."[9]

Silberman, however, contends that compensatory programs are essential and even insists that it may be necessary to temporarily impose quotas in order to force real compliance with the objectives of equal employment opportunities.

> The object is not compensation. . . . it is to overcome the ten-dencies to exclude the Negro which are built into the very mar-row of American society. . . . A formal policy of nondiscrimina-tion, of employing people "regardless of race, color, or creed," however estimable, usually works out in practice to be a policy of employing whites only. Hence, Negroes demand for quotas represents a necessary tactical attempt to fix the responsibility for increasing employment of Negroes on those who do the hir-ing. . . . Not to use numbers as a yardstick for measuring per-formance is, in effect, to revert to "tokenism." The point is not whether there is some "eight" number of Negroes to be em-ployed—obviously there is not—but simply that there is no meaningful measure of change other than numbers.[10]

The Federal bureaucracy has made some progress in eliminat-ing barriers which hinder the opportunities of the "qualified" black man. And at the other end of the spectrum some attention has been given to developing programs to reach those who did not meet traditional job standards.

To be effective in drawing blacks into the civil service in sufficient numbers and to avoid simply creating a black bureaucratic elite, it is necessary to recognize, however, that many blacks have had neither the opportunity nor the desire to acquire the qualifications now in demand. The only solution, therefore, may be to hire "unqualified" blacks and train them on the job.[11]

On the basis of this realization a two-pronged approach to the problems of employing the disadvantaged has emerged. One prong has been the development of various job training programs related to the war on poverty. These programs are aimed at preparing the disadvantaged for the general job market but they create a pool of workers who can be tapped by the bureaucracy. Among these programs are the Job Corps, the Neighborhood Youth Corps, the New Careers Program, and the Manpower Development Training Act.

The other, and by far the most difficult, part of the problem is the necessity to provide jobs for those who have received training. One approach has been the attempt to redesign jobs to eliminate routine, lower-level duties from middle and high level jobs and to collect these duties in new groupings to open new job opportunities for the disadvantaged. This effort to obtain Maximum Utilization of the Skills and Training of employees (MUST) is intended to redesign entry level positions to permit the hiring of people of lower skill levels who have a potential for learning.

Even if the application of MUST opens up new employment opportunities for the disadvantaged, it is still necessary to devise methods by which those disadvantaged persons who have received training can be connected with the available jobs.

In a normal open competitive examination the disadvantaged are normally too far down on the register of eligibles to be available for employment. The MUST program, however, creates entry level jobs that can and should be filled by a person with limited education or experience. These jobs may involve work that is hard, dirty and unpleasant such as working in a laundry, loading and unloading heavy loads, shoveling snow, etc., and, therefore, these jobs are not very appealing to a person who is qualified for some higher position. In order to prevent the register from being cluttered up with overqualified applicants and to open opportunities for unskilled persons who need a job and are willing to work at almost anything, the Civil Service Commission has developed a new method of rating applicants for Maintenance and Service Worker positions and for certain clerical positions.

This plan screens out those who are overqualified and creates a special Worker-Trainee register for those who are unskilled but who rate high on willingness to work, reliability, ability to follow instructions and ability to perform hard labor.

Part of the rationalization of this program has been the assertion that it will reduce employee turnover in these less desirable jobs. This emphasis, however, is likely to produce a suspicious response from blacks who feel that it is just another indication that employers want to exploit blacks and want to keep them limited to jobs that "keep them in their place."

Therefore, if this program is to be effective it must be part of a total package which not only permits entry to low level jobs but also provides a chance to advance. The Civil Service Commission itself recognizes this and has contended that

> A potential value of these jobs is that an eligible hired for one job will often be entering the work-force for the first time and may be using this job as a springboard to higher level work. This employment will allow him to demonstrate reliability, dependability, safety, etc., and help to provide him with a marketable employment record. [12]

These efforts to expand the opportunities for blacks, especially those who do not meet traditional job qualifications, may present problems.

> Efficiency may be lowered by the costs of hiring unqualified Negroes and training them on the job. Even more damage to efficiency may be done by the blow to the morale (and consequently to the productivity) of white employees when firms begin to discriminate in favor of Negroes. To be sure, no corporation is completely consistent in its adherence to the principle of merit; all kinds of subjective and irrational judgments enter in to the selection and promotion of employees. But deliberately departing from the merit principle is something else again, and there is no point in pretending the corporation will not pay a heavy price for doing so. [13]

In spite of the difficulties, this program is not as much of a departure from merit principles as it may seem at first. The development of the MUST concept provides job opportunities which are not only available to unskilled, inexperienced workers but which are too simple and, therefore, unattractive to those with greater qualifications. The use of the "Worker-Trainee" designation to limit these jobs to persons with limited education and experience represents a genuine effort to match the right person with the right job.

In fact the most significant feature of this effort is that instead of treating merit as a static concept which judges an individual only by his past, there is now an attempt to develop a dynamic concept of merit in which motivation, dependability and the intangible quality of potential create a more flexible and more humane standard of judgment.

Thus, some progress has been made in promoting equality of employment opportunities which in turn makes the bureaucracy more representative in the descriptive sense. But there still remain certain problems. In the first place, the bureaucracy cannot be considered genuinely representative simply because it includes a certain proportion of black and minority employees if they are all, or primarily, employed in the lowest echelons of the hierarchy.

We have noted that genuine employment opportunities must include the possibility of career development leading to positions of responsibility and influence. And just as it has been necessary to actively recruit blacks for initial entry into the bureaucracy it will also be necessary to make a special effort to seek out, train and promote blacks. Any attempt to operate on a "color-blind." "business as usual" basis will in reality continue to discriminate against blacks. This is, in fact, the very essence of the black's charge that the system is racist. The accumulated patterns of discrimination have created a stacked deck which automatically, even without malice aforethought, restricts blacks unless positive measures are taken to overcome the system.

And the problem is so complex that even the promotion of certain quotas of people with black skin will not achieve the necessary breakthrough if in the process they are whitewashed or professionalized right out of their skin. The typical white response to the question of equality has been, in effect, to tell the black person that the way to succeed is to conform to the image of the white middle class.

This approach fails to recognize that blacks are not just "white men with black skin." There is a cultural heritage of alienation and powerlessness that has been a major factor in the "unemployability" of many residents of the ghetto. The lack of power has been especially destructive to black men. In order to avoid the attacks on the ego and self-respect which come from powerlessness blacks have often simply withdrawn from the system.

But even the person with real drive and motivation becomes discouraged when advancement must be achieved by the sacrifice of his own identity. Over sixty years ago. W. E. B. DuBois wrote movingly of the inner struggle of the black American.

> One ever feels his two-ness,—an American, a Negro; two souls, two thoughts, two unreconciled strivings; two warring ideals in one dark body, whose dogged strength alone keeps it from being torn asunder.
>
> The history of the American Negro is the history of this strife,— this longing to attain self-conscious manhood, to merge his double self into a better and truer self. In this merging he wishes neither of the older selves to be lost. He would not Africanize America, for America has too much to teach the world and Africa. He would not bleach his Negro soul in a flood of white Americanism, for he knows that Negro blood has a message for the world. He simply wishes to make it possible for a man to be both a Negro and an American, without being cursed and spit upon by his fellows, without having the door of Opportunity closed roughly in his face. [14]

The rise of group identity and self-respect which is symbolized by the black power concept is an important and essential sign that blacks are beginning to throw off their shackles and achieve political maturity. As part of the process it is essential that they be able to "believe in their hearts that they are *men, men* who can stand on their own feet and control their own destinies." [15]

In order to do this blacks must be in a position to make or at least influence the decisions that affect them. And if they cannot do it in person they must at *least* be represented in the political process. This representation must be provided by fellow blacks because only blacks can understand the full impact of the systematic racism of our society. Only blacks can be adequately sensitive to the intricate, almost invisible, nuances of discrimination that pervade the implementation of even the most progressive government programs.

The representative role of the black bureaucrat is extremely difficult and tenuous. On the one hand, he is likely to face a certain ambivalence in the attitudes of his white colleagues, who may "respect" him but who wish he was not "quite so sensitive" about racial issues. And the very act of becoming part of the "white establishment" as a bureaucrat makes him suspect among many blacks as one who has "sold out to whitey" and become an Uncle Tom.

Therefore, white administrators must be aware of these cross-pressures and be prepared to understand and deal equitably with black members of the bureaucracy and not be "turned off" by their rhetoric or by certain other manifestations of their "blackness." If they fail to do this, and attempt to promote and listen only to those blacks who have been coopted into the system, they will deny genuine representation to blacks.

In the final analysis, a genuinely representative bureaucracy must be representative in its own internal composition. And this representativeness must extend through all levels of the hierarchy. This requires an opportunity for blacks and other minorities to pursue a career with real opportunities for advancement to positions of decision making, even if this requires the use of quotas and compensatory hiring, training and promotion programs.

It is not sufficient to conceive of the representative function of the bureaucracy simply as a device for social control—a means of keeping the natives from becoming too restless. White Americans must recognize that, while being black is no guarantee of omniscience, the experience of being black in American and living along the raw edge of the political system can produce a special sensitivity to the impact of governmental action and inaction on the individual. And in our highly organized, technological, depersonalized society this sensitivity is a resource we cannot afford to waste.

ENDNOTES

Note: This paper is in part an outgrowth of and elaboration on certain themes that were first developed in the author's article "Making Equality of Employment Opportunity a Reality in the Federal Service," 30 *Public Administration Review* (January/February, 1970), pp. 43-49.

1. Norton Long, *The Polity* (Chicago: Rand McNally and Co., 1962), p. 52.
2. *Ibid.*, p. 70.
3. Samuel Krislov, *The Negro in Federal Employment: The Quest for Equal Opportunity* (Minneapolis: University of Minnesota Press, 1967), p. 51.
4. Charles Silberman, *Crisis in Black and White* (New York: Vintage Books, 1964), p. 211.
5. Hannah Pitkin, *The Concept of Representation* (Berkeley: University of California Press, 1967), pp. 221-222. Originally published by the University of California Press; reprinted by permission of The Regents of the University of California.
6. *Ibid.*, p. 61.
7. Samuel Krislov, *op. cit.*, p. 32.
8. *Wall Street Journal*, March 9, 1971.
9. Samuel Krislov, *op. cit.*, p. 79.
10. Charles Silberman, *op. cit.*, p. 241.
11. *Ibid.*, p. 245.
12. U. S. Civil Service Commission: CSC Operations Letter No. 337-555.
13. Charles Silberman, *op. cit.*, pp. 245-246.
14. W. E. B. DuBois, *The Souls of Black Folk* (New York: Fawcett Publications, Inc., 1961), p. 17.
15. Charles Silberman, *op. cit.*, p. 116.

17

harry grossman

THE EQUAL EMPLOYMENT OPPORTUNITY ACT OF 1972, ITS IMPLICATIONS FOR THE STATE AND LOCAL GOVERNMENT MANAGER

On March 24, 1972, H.R. 1746, 92nd Congress, became law, enacted as Public Law 92-261, the Equal Employment Opportunity Act of 1972, amending Title VII of the Civil Rights Act of 1964 (78 Stat. 253; 42 U.S. Code 2000e).[1] While the 1972 statute did not receive the same attention in the communications media given to the 1964 Act, for the public section, that is, federal, state and local government agencies, including school systems, it was as important a piece of legislation as the parent 1964 law was to the private sector at whom it was directed.

The purpose of this article is to examine the more significant provisions of the 1972 law and their implications for the managers of units of state and local governments. In addition to strengthening the powers of the United States Equal Employment Opportunity Commission (EEOC) established by the Civil Rights Act of 1964 over discriminatory employment practices in the private sector, the 1972 amendments brought state and local "governments, governmental agencies, political subdivisions" and "any governmental industry, business, or activity" within its coverage under the definitions of "person" and "employer" in Section 701 of the basic statute.

Similarly, Section 701 was amended so as to include within the term "employment agency" activities of states and political subdivisions which regularly undertake to procure employees for an em-

Reprinted from *Public Personnel Management, II,* #5 (Sept.-Oct., 1973). Used by permission of the International Personnel Management Association.

ployer or job opportunities for employees. State agencies, previously covered by the 1964 Civil Rights Act, Title VII, by references to the United States Employment Service and the system of state employment services which receive federal assistance continue to be covered under the term "employment agency."

"Employee" was redefined to accommodate the exclusion of elected public officials of states and political subdivisions and persons chosen by them for their personal staffs or in policy making levels or as immediate advisers in the exercise of the constitutional or legal powers of the office.[2] The 1972 statute makes it perfectly clear that this exemption does not apply to state and local government employees who are subject to civil service laws.[3]

The key provisions of Title VII of the Civil Rights Act of 1964 as they affect state and local government agencies are in Sections 703 (a), (b), (c), (d) and (e) which delineate unlawful employment practices. Briefly, discrimination in hiring, firing, pay, or other terms or conditions of employment because of race, color, religion, sex or national origin is made an unlawful employment practice, as is any employer's limiting, segregating or classifying employees in any way which would tend to deprive any employee of employment opportunities or otherwise adversely affect his status as an employee because of his race, color, and so forth. Discriminatory practices on the part of employment agencies and labor organizations were similarly outlawed. An important amendment to Section 701 of the 1964 Act was the addition of a subsection in the 1972 Act concerning religion as used in the statute. Henceforth, religion includes all aspects of observance and practice as well as belief, "unless an employer demonstrates that he is unable to reasonably accommodate" such observance or practice by an employee or prospective employee "without undue hardship on the conduct of the employer's business."

COMMISSION STRENGTHENED

Section 704 of the 1964 Act created the Equal Employment Opportunity Commission (EEOC) but its powers under that statute were extremely limited. The intent of the 1964 law was for the Commission to seek voluntary compliance and to try to eliminate discriminatory practices through conferences, conciliation, or persuasion, and it was without power to enforce the provisions of the Act through legal process.[4] All that, however, was changed by the 1972 Amendment, Section 4.

The Commission henceforth is empowered by law to prevent any person, which includes state and local governmental agencies, from engaging "in any unlawful employment practice." While still retaining the original provision of the Act for the Commission to first endeavor to resolve a complaint through informal methods of conference, conciliation and persuasion, the Commission now can bring a civil action in a United States District Court against a non-governmental employer where it is unable to secure a satisfactory conciliation agreement. In the case of a state or local governmental employer, the Commission is directed to refer the case to the Attorney General of the United States who may bring such an action in the appropriate federal district court. The 1964 Act only provided that with respect to persons included in that statute, the Commission was required to notify an aggrieved party that it was unable to obtain voluntary compliance whereupon such aggrieved party could bring a civil action against the respondent named in the charge. The Attorney General could and still can intervene in such suit in the discretion of the court if he certifies that "the case is of general public importance."

Provisions in the 1964 law for deferring to state or local authority where such authority exists to grant or seek relief or institute criminal proceedings with respect to discriminatory employment practices were carried forward into the 1972 Amendments.[5]

Another important amendment to the 1964 statute is in Section 7 of the 1972 Act. By this section the provisions of Section 11 of the National Labor Relations Act, 49 Stat. 455; 29 United States Code 161, are made applicable to all hearings and investigations conducted by the Equal Employment Opportunity Commission. This section covers such things as issuance of subpoenas requiring attendance and testimony of witnesses, provisions relating to witnesses' privileges and immunities, fees, and so forth.

TIME LIMITS EXTENDED

Time limits for filing charges of discrimination were extended by the 1972 Amendment from 90 days to 180 days after the alleged unlawful practice, and where an aggrieved party first sought redress from a state or local authority for equal employment opportunity, from 210 days to 300 days or within 30 days after notice that the state or local agency has terminated proceedings, whichever is earlier.

Where preliminary investigation of a charge filed with EEOC indicates a need, the Attorney General may bring an action against a state or political subdivision for preliminary or temporary relief pending final disposition. Such cases must be assigned for hearing in the appropriate federal court at the earliest practical date and expedited in every way. Remedies provided by the 1972 law include injunction and such affirmative action as hiring with or without back pay or any other equitable relief as the court deems appropriate.[6]

States and political subdivisions will now have to keep records they may not have had to keep before concerning the racial, religious, ethnic or sex classification of applicants for jobs and of persons hired and will have to be prepared to furnish data as the EEOC shall prescribe by regulation. If a state or local government finds that such recordkeeping or reporting creates an "undue hardship," it must prepare a case for exemption by EEOC, and if denied, to seek relief therefrom by petition to the appropriate federal district court.

Two years after the date of enactment, March 24, 1972, the functions of the Attorney General in cases of "patterns or practice" of discrimination, vested in it under the Title VII, Civil Rights Act of 1964 are scheduled for transfer to EEOC unless the President chooses to submit a different reorganization plan which is not vetoed by the Congress.

The lesson for the state and local government agency manager from the EEO Act of 1972 is that examination and employment practices which result in discrimination in hiring, assignment, training opportunities, promotion pay classification or other benefits or conditions of employment will be stopped. This will come to pass by affirmative action programs prepared and adopted by the states and political subdivisions with guidance and assistance from EEOC, the United States Civil Service Commission in the exercise of its responsibilities under the Intergovernmental Personnel Act of 1970[7] or by provisions of applicable state or local law, or, in the alternative, by EEOC's exercising its newly given enforcement powers through the office of the Attorney General and the United States courts. In short, equality of employment opportunity in all levels of government will be achieved, preferably by recognition, voluntary acceptance and application of the moral imperative, or through persuasion, conference, withholding of federal money and the like, otherwise by order of the courts.

OPEN COMPETITION VS. SELECTIVE PRACTICES

Merit systems, if they are truly founded on sound, job related, competitive examination principles, need not be sacrificed or compromised in the quest for equality of opportunity for government jobs. There is nothing in the EEO Act of 1972 that calls for such things as quotas, proportional representation, or compensatory hiring, to make up for past discrimination or that requires abandonment of valid standards in favor of any particular segment of our population. Chairman Robert E. Hampton of the United States Civil Service Commission expressed it this way upon the occasion of his acceptance of the 1972 Stockberger Award for outstanding contributions to the advancement of public personnel management. "The most significant progress made in equal opportunity has been made under personnel systems applying sound merit principles where personnel decisions are made on an objective basis rather than on a subjective basis—a basis under which rank discriminatory practices would thrive. . . . To capitulate to those forces who would inject chaos into the personnel system under the guise of compensation for past social injustice would in reality defeat the goals we are all so desirous of achieving."

In a memorandum to heads of federal departments and agencies on EEO, dated May 11, 1972, Chairman Hampton also stated, "A 'goal' is a realistic objective which an agency endeavors to achieve on a time basis, within the context of the merit system of employment. A 'quota,' on the other hand, would restrict employment or development opportunities to members of the particular groups by establishing a required number or proportionate representation. . . . 'Quotas' are incompatible with merit principles. . . . Goals and timetables must not be interpreted by managers and supervisors as quotas. Agency action plans and instructions involving goals and timetables must state that all actions to achieve goals must be in full compliance with merit system requirements."

APPREHENSION OVER QUOTAS

Following hard on the heels of Chairman Hampton's statement, President Nixon replied to an inquiry from the American Jewish Committee expressing apprehension over the prospects of quotas and proportional representation in federal hiring. Wrote the President, "I have sought and will continue to seek to enlarge opportunities for men and women of all religious, ethnic, and racial backgrounds to serve in responsible positions, but the criteria for selection that I have employed and will continue to employ will be based on merit. . . . I agree that numerical goals, although an important and useful tool to measure progress which remedies the effect of past discrimination, must not be allowed to be applied in such a fashion as to, in fact, result in the imposition of quotas, nor should they be predicated upon or directed toward a concept of proportional representation."[8]

Yet the quota concept is neither dead nor has it been laid to rest. President Nixon and Chairman Hampton may have spoken out clearly on the subject as far as federal employment is concerned and the Civil Service Commission has the responsibility for enforcement of equal opportunity in that sector under Section 717 of the EEO Act of 1972.[9] However, the courts will probably have the last say on this both with respect to federal as well as state and local government agencies. This question was raised but not decided with respect to government employment in *Commonwealth of Pennsylvania et al.* v. *O'Neill et al.*[10] While refusing to impose quotas for other reasons, the court clearly stated that its refusal was not to suggest that such a remedy for discrimination was unconstitutional. Said the court, "Although expressing no opinion on this issue at the present time, we do note that American progress in its attempt to eradicate racial discrimination is due largely to the generally held belief that individuals, regardless of their race, creed, religion, sex or national origin should be accorded an equal chance to compete . . . on the basis of individual ability. In our democracy, rights are accorded primarily to individuals, as distinguished from groups. Opening the doors long shut to minorities is imperative, but in so doing, we must be careful not to close them in the face of others, lest we abandon the basic principle of nondiscrimination that sparked the effort to pry open those doors in the first place."

There are, however, a few cases decided since Title VII of the Civil Rights Act involving the private sector where the courts refused to reject the idea of compensatory practices and quotas.

In *Contractors Ass'n. of Eastern Pa.* v. *Secretary of Labor,* 442 F. 2d 159 (1971) involving the famous "Philadelphia Plan" for increasing minority employees in the construction trades on federally funded projects, the contractors argued that the plan, "by imposing remedial quotas, violated the EEO Act of 1964, Section 703(a) in that they would have to refuse to hire some white tradesmen and compel them to classify applicants by race." The court rejected this claim as an "overly simple" reading of the plan and the Labor Department's findings which led to its adoption. In essence the court affirmed the legality and constitutionality of executive orders and affirmative action programs which required employers who come within their terms to be color-conscious. The court's rationale was that Congress did not intend Title VII of the Civil Rights Act of 1964 to preempt provisions of executive orders of the President prescribing fair employment practices.

Addressing itself to the claim that the plan provides racial quotas prohibited by the equal protection clause of the Fifth Amendment, the court said that it was not so prohibited because it was a "valid executive action designed to remedy the perceived evil that minority tradesmen have not been included in the labor pool for the performance of construction projects in which the federal government has a cost and performance interest." The Supreme Court denied certiorari October 12, 1971, in 404 U.S. 854.

SPECIFIC PERCENTAGES COULD BE UPHELD

It would seem from this case that where federal money or assistance is involved, affirmative action plans which call for specific numbers or percentages of minorities or women to be hired by states and local governments could be upheld by the courts. It is difficult, however, to reconcile the "Philadelphia Plan" rationale with the view of Title VII expressed by Chief Justice Burger in *Griggs et al.* v. *Duke Power Co.* (1971) 401 U.S. 424 at 430, 91 S.Ct. 849 at 853, when he said, "Congress did not intend by Title VII, however, to guarantee a job to every person regardless of qualifications. In short, the Act does not command that any person be hired simply because he was formerly the subject of discrimination, or because he is a member of a minority group. Discriminatory preference for any group, minority or majority, is precisely and only what Congress has prescribed. What is required by Congress is the removal of artificial, arbitrary, and unnecessary barriers to employment when the barriers operate invidiously to discriminate on the basis of racial or other impermissable classification."

Lower federal courts have spoken in even stronger terms in framing remedies for past discriminatory employment practices. Thus in the Fifth U. S. Circuit, the District Court for the District of Alabama said, "Only by adopting a 'but-for' approach (bumping incumbent junior whites) or by precluding whites from the seniority system (giving preference in future vacancies to blacks with less plant-wide seniority than whites) could blacks be given greater opportunities to gain their rightful place. . . . Such remedies have been rejected in this Circuit." *Buckner* v. *Goodyear Tire and Rubber Co.* 339 F. Supp. 1108 (1972) (N.D. Alabama M.D.), citing *Local 189, United Papermakers and Paperworkers, AFL-CIO CLC* v. *U.S.* 416 F.2d. 980 (1969) Cert. denied, 397 U.S. 919. In the 4th circuit, the U.S. District

Court for the Western District of North Carolina took an opposite view when it ordered as a remedy for discriminatory employment practice hiring ratios which will provide for participation by qualified blacks in traditionally white job classification in order to overcome the effects of past discrimination. *U.S.* v. *Central Motor Lines, Inc.*, 338 F. Supp. 532 (1971) citing a 5th circuit decision as authority, *Local 53, Asbestos Workers* v. *Vogler* 407 F. 2d 1047 (1969). Looking at the cases involving the private sector, it would seem that the issue of quotas or proportional representation of minorities or women in an equal employment situation under Title VII is still quite unsettled, and in terms of state and governmental subdivision employment, the question is still untried.

HIRING TESTS AND PRACTICES

Since examinations and tests of one kind or another are the common and accepted practice in public employment, this aspect of EEO bears close scrutiny. Neither Title VII of the 1964 Act nor the EEO Act of 1972 preclude testing and examining tools and techniques, and such techniques in and of themselves will not be set aside. However, their use in any particular employment setting may be questioned as discriminating if it is shown that they have led to disparate results. If such results are shown statistically, then the validity of the tests or techniques becames a matter for judicial inquiry in a Title VII case. "The Act proscribes not only overt discrimination but also practices that are fair in form, but discriminatory in operation. The touchstone is business necessity. If an employment practice which operates to exclude Negroes cannot be shown to be related to job performance, the practice is prohibited." *U.S.* v. *Jacksonville Terminal Co.* CCA 5th Cir. (1971) 451 F. 2d 418 at 447. (quoting Chief Justice Burger in the *Griggs* case.) Speaking specifically of a pre-employment test, the Supreme Court in *Griggs* v. *Duke Power Co.*, *supra*, called for a "demonstrable relationship" between the test and the successful performance of the job for which the test is used.

In cases arising in the private sector, the U.S. Employment Service's General Aptitude Battery Test used for referral of applicants within a given range of scores on various parts of the test for employment as laboratory assistants, was found by the court not to have been "discriminatorily designed or used," *U.S.* v. *N.L. Industries* (Missouri) 339 F. Supp. 1167 (1972). In *Buckner et al.* v. *Goodyear Tire and Rubber Co. et al, supra,* the United States District

Court (Alabama) upheld the use of tests for qualifying applicants for a 4-year craft apprenticeship program. The tests used were the California Test Bureau Mathematics Test, Otis Mental Ability, Bennett Mechanical Comprehension, Educational Testing Service Reading Comprehension and Expression, and the Minnesota Paper Form Board Tests. These tests had been adopted upon recommendation of an independent, professional consultant in guidance and testing. In applying the measurement of "demonstrable relationship" the court concluded that the tests need not be validated as against job performance in the crafts to which the apprentice program led, but only as against performance in the apprenticeship program, provided that there was also shown a relationship between the apprenticeship and the craft to which it led.

SIMILAR INQUIRIES LIKELY

Similar inquiries into job relatedness can be expected, and in fact have already arisen with respect to tests and practices in hiring for public sector jobs coming within the provisions of either the equal protection clause of the United States Constitution or the executive order of the President for EEO in the federal service. Thus, in a recent case,[11] the Board of Appeals and Review of the United States Civil Service Commission ruled that a minimum physical requirement of five feet, eight inches in height and 145 pounds in weight for appointment as a National Park Police Officer, was not based on a rational and relevant job analysis and therefore discriminated not only against most women but also against many men. It could conceivably be argued that such a requirement is not discrimination because of sex or race or national origin but only against short people and light weight people of all classifications and therefore not a violation of EEO prohibitions involving race, religion, color, sex or national origin. Obviously, however, females, as a group, are predominantly excluded by the practice under question.

As to the degree of job relatedness that needs to be shown in public sector employment practices, the United States Court of Appeals for the First Circuit addressed itself to this question in a case arising under the equal protection clause of the Fourteenth Amendment as it applied to examinations for police jobs in the cities and towns of Massachusetts.[12] "In pursuing an inquiry as to the relationship between each (examination) requirement and successful performance on the job, a court might adopt a relaxed standard of review whereby it would be a sufficient justification that under some reasonable version of the facts, the classification (e.g. height requirements, swim test, written test) is rationally related to a permissible goal. . . ."

BURDEN OF PROOF

As has been the case in the private sector, once a showing has been made that statistically, a public employment practice has resulted in exclusion of a certain group, the burden of justifying the practice is on the challenged governmental activity. This was so held by the First Circuit Court of Appeals when it said, "The public employer must, we think, in order to justify the use of a means of selection shown to have a racially disproportionate impact, demonstrate that the means is in fact substantially related to job performance."[13] To the same effect it was held by the United States District Court for the District of Columbia that where it was shown that (a) the number of black police officers, while substantial, is not proportionate to the population of the city; (b) a higher percentage of blacks fail the test than whites; and (c) the test has not been validated to establish its reliability for measuring subsequent performance, this showing would be sufficient to shift the burden of the inquiry to the government agency.[14] Here, however, as in the *Goodyear Tire and Rubber Co.* case, *supra,* the defendant prevailed when the court was satisfied that the test was shown to be reasonably and directly related to the requirements of the police recruit training program and was neither so designed nor operated to discriminate against otherwise qualified blacks.

CONCLUSION

The Equal Employment Opportunity Act of 1972, bringing state and local employment practices under the federal jurisdiction of EEOC presents a new challenge and writes a new chapter in the history of this nation's advance toward justice for all. Quotas and concepts of proportional representation may be an easy way to compensate for past ills, but it is not the right or the fair way. Those who attack them as reverse discrimination and as a denial of equal opportunity for others are well justified in so doing. Given the posture expressed by President Nixon and Chairman Hampton of the United States Civil

Service Commission, quotas and proportional representation have no place in public employment systems based on merit principles. Goals and timetables are something else. They must, however, be closely scrutinized, completely understood, and carefully used lest they be but a semantic substitute for quotas and reverse discrimination. Ultimately the Supreme Court must rule on this issue.

Objective employment practices and tests if valid, rational and uniformly applied are still among the best techniques for the public sector's quest for equality as well as quality in recruitment and hiring. Broad band or umbrella type examinations which are used to establish lists of eligibles for a wide variety of different kinds of jobs which may call for disparate knowledges, skills and abilities, may have to be used judiciously as well as selectively so that the government agency will, if challenged, be able to show to the satisfaction of the federal courts a rational nexus between the qualification standards used and the duties of the job to be filled, the career ladder that normally follows or the training program for which the applicants have been recruited. Standards, however, should not be dropped to the point where they become meaningless and impair the efficiency, effectiveness and professionalism in the public sector in order to accommodate under the guise of equal opportunity those who are in fact not qualified for the work to be done.

ADDENDUM

The following addendum by the author reflects significant developments in the law dealing with discrimination in public employment which occurred after the above was written.

OPEN COMPETITION VS. SELECTIVE PRACTICES

Notwithstanding the 1972 public statements of the President and the Chairman of the United States Civil Service Commission, *supra*, on the matter of permissible numerical goals and timetables in contrast to prohibited quotas and proportional representation in the recruitment and hiring of minority peoples, differences in views continued to persist among various federal agencies which have some kind of enforcement responsibilities in the area of equal employment in state and local governments.

In an effort to speak with one tongue, the chairmen of the Civil Service Commission, and of the Equal Employment Opportunity

Commission and the assistant attorney general, Civil Rights Division along with the acting director of the Office of Federal Contract Compliance of the Department of Labor issued a memorandum of understanding on March 23, 1973, *Federal Policy on Remedies Concerning Equal Employment Opportunity in State and Local Government Personnel Systems.*

The highlights of the agreement were their recognition that:

"There is no conflict between a true merit selection system and equal employment opportunities laws—because each requires non-discrimination in selection, hiring, promotion . . . based on the person's ability and merit, not on the basis of race, color, national origin, religion or sex.

"Goals and timetables are appropriate as a device to help measure progress in remedying discrimination.

"Where an individual person has been found to be the victim of an unlawful employment practice as defined in the [Equal Employment Opportunity] Act, he or she should be given 'priority consideration' for the next expected vacancy, regardless of his relative 'ability ranking' at the time. . . .

"[There are] basic distinctions between permissible goals on the one hand and impermissible quotas on the other. . . . Use of such goals does not and should not require an employer to select on the basis of race, national origin, or sex, a less qualified person over a person who is better qualified by objective and valid procedures."

Yet, the matter of establishing employment quotas and/or directing absolute or partial preference for minority members as a remedy for past discrimination in public employment continues to plague the courts. In *Harper* v. *Mayor and City Council*, May 2, 1973, 41 U.S. Law Week 2636 (5-29-73), a fire department case, the United States District Court for the District of Maryland noted that the Supreme Court had yet to address the matter and proceeded with a rather detailed analysis of the state of the law in a lengthy footnote, number 69. It ended by finding no sufficiently compelling need for imposing quotas.

Among the cases cited by the Court in footnote 69 was *Bridgeport Guardians, Inc. et al.* v. *Bridgeport Civil Service Commission,* U.S. District Court for the District of Connecticut, January 29, 1973, 354 F. Supp. 778, involving police examinations. In that case the court observed at page 798:

"Much of the controversy . . . has concerned the difference between quota hiring to remedy past discrimination and some arguably less rigid approach involving affirmative action toward a goal. Ultimately the distinction becomes illusory. . . . A quota, for all its unhappy connotations, is simply a recognition of the reality in reaching the desired goal. See U.S. v. Wood, Wire and Metal Lathers International Union, Local 46, 471 F. 2d 408 (2nd Cir. 1973)."

On appeal to the circuit court, the imposition of quotas for appointment to entrance level patrolmen jobs was held to be justified and affirmed because of past exclusionary hiring, but not so for jobs above that rank. *Bridgeport Guardians Inc.* v. *Civil Service Commission,* June 28, 1973 CA2; 42 U.S. Law Week 2059 (7-31-73).

In its most recent order and decision in *Western Addition Community Organization* v. *Alioto,* 70-1335, WTS, May 9, 1973, the District Court for the Northern District of California refused to impose hiring quotas for fire department jobs in San Francisco, even if legal, looking at them as extreme and as a last resort, not considered necessary in that case at that time. Previous decisions in this case are reported in 340 F. Supp 1351 and 330 F. Supp 536.

Uncertainty and perplexity will continue in this area until the Supreme Court speaks directly and on point. It is this writer's view that as a matter of constitutional law, it is extremely difficult to support a proposition that court's equity power is so broad as to enable it to direct a government agency to give preference in employment to some persons over others based on race, color, religion, sex or national origin. See *Mancari* v. *Morton,* U. S. District Court for the District of New Mexico, No. 9626, June 1, 1973, which, relying in part on the EEO Act of 1972, struck down Indian preference statutes for employment with the U. S. Bureau of Indian Affairs of the Department of Interior. See also the dissenting opinion of Senior Circuit Judge VanOosterhout in *Carter* v. *Gallagher,* (1971) 8th Circuit, 452 F. 2d 315 at 332. A court's directing such preference would seem to violate the Constitution's equal protection provisions.

HIRING TESTS AND PRACTICES

One of the principal effects of the EEO Act of 1972 in public employment practices at the state and local levels was to subject them to the guidelines for tests published by the U.S. Equal Employment Opportunity Commission (EEOC) in Title 29, Code of Federal Regulations, (CFR) Part 1607. It was so held in the most recent decision in *Western Addition Community Organization* v. *Alioto,* May 9, 1973, *supra.*

EEOC guidelines for determining the validity of employment tests are predicated on a presumption against their use contained in Section 1607.3 which reads as follows:

"§ 1607.3 Discrimination defined.

The use of any test which adversely affects hiring, promotion, transfer or any other employment or membership opportunity of classes protected by title VII constitutes discrimination unless: (a) the test has been validated and evidences a high degree of utility as hereinafter described, and (b) the person giving or acting upon the results of the particular test can demonstrate that alternative suitable hiring, transfer or promotion procedures are unavailable for his use."

The result of the court's view in the *Western Addition* case, *supra*, appears to be that rather than adopting "a relaxed standard of review" in pursuing an inquiry into the relationship between a test and job performance in cases formerly brought under the Fourteenth Amendment equal protection clause, as the circuit court did in *Castro* v. *Beecher*, 459 F. 2d 725, the courts will now apply the EEOC guidelines. Those guidelines call for rigid and specific methods of test validation and evidence which "positively demonstrates" absence of discrimination (Sec. 1607.4(b)]. "Evidence should consist of empirical data demonstrating that the test is predictive of or significantly correlated with important elements of work behavior which comprise or are relevant to the job. . . ." [Sec. 1607.4(c)]. "Empirical evidence . . . must be based on studies employing generally accepted procedures for determining criterion-related validity, such as those described in *'Standards for Educational and Psychological Tests and Manuals'* published by the American Psychological Association. . ."[15] Personnel specialist responsible for selecting qualifying tests for government positions would be well advised to familiarize themselves thoroughly with those guidelines.

JUDICIAL REVIEW OF EEO COMPLAINTS

On July 13, 1973, the U.S. District Court for the District of Columbia handed down a far reaching decision on the nature of the Court's jurisdiction in discrimination complaint cases. In *Hackley* v. *Johnson et al.* and *Franklin* v. *Laird et al.*, C.A. #1258-72 and 2127-72, the Court held that the complainants were not entitled to a new trial of their complaints in the district court under the EEO Act of 1972, but that the court's role was to review the administrative record of the complaint processing in the employing agency and on appeal, before the U.S. Civil Service Commission. Recognizing that the issue was one of first impression for the Court, meaning that it had no precedent, the Court said, "The trial *de novo* is not required in all cases. The District Court is required by the Act to examine the administrative record with utmost care. If it determines that an absence of discrimination is affirmatively established by the clear weight of the evidence in the record, no new trial is required. If this exacting standard is not met, the Court shall, in its discretion, as appropriate, remand, take testimony to supplement the administrative record, or grant the plaintiff relief on the administrative record."

While *Hackley* and *Franklin* were federal employees, and had had their complaints processed in their own agencies first and then in the Civil Service Commission under Executive Order 11478, *Equal Employment Opportunity in the Federal Government*, there is good reason to believe that the same result would follow in the case of a state or municipal employee who brings suit under the Act after first exhausting the administrative remedies provided by state or local law in accordance with Section 706 (c).

ENDNOTES

1. Effective July 2, 1965, one year after enactment, it prohibits discrimination because of race, color, religion, sex or national origin, in hiring, upgrading and all other conditions of employment in the private sector, e.g., "in industry affecting commerce."
2. "This exemption is intended to be read very narrowly and is in no way intended to establish an overall narrowing of the expanded coverage of State and local governmental employees. . . ." *Report of the Subcommittee on Labor of the Committee on Labor and Public Welfare, U.S. Senate, Legislative History of the Equal Employment Opportunity Act of 1972*, pp. 1771–1772.
3. The 1972 law eliminates the previous exemption for educational institutions so that all except religious educational institutions are now covered by Title VII. Ibid. p. 1770.
4. *American Newspaper Publishers Assn.* v. *Alexander DC:* D. C. (1968) 294 F. Supp. 1100; *Edwards* v. *North American Rockwell Corp.* D.C. Calif. (1968) 291 F. Supp. 199; *EEOC* v. *United Assn. of Journeyman and Apprentices Local 189*, CCA Ohio (1971) 438 F. 2d 408.
5. The first *Annual Report of the Equal Employment Opportunity Commission* for the fiscal year ending June 30, 1966 reported 31 states and the District of Columbia which had fair employment laws governing race, creed, color or national origin to which it would defer action on

complaints and nine states and the District of Columbia to which it would defer action on complaints of discrimination because of sex. At the time of the debate on the Equal Employment Opportunity Act of 1972, at least 33 states were reported as having provisions in their antidiscrimination laws that provide enforceable coverage to state and local government personnel. Actually 28 states specifically covered such employees. These are Arizona, California, Colorado, Connecticut, Delaware, Idaho, Illinois, Indiana, Iowa, Kansas, Kentucky, Massachusetts, Michigan, Minnesota, Missouri, Montana, Nebraska, Nevada, New Hampshire, New Mexico, Ohio, Oklahoma, Oregon. Pennsylvania, Utah, Washington, West Virginia, and Wyoming. Four other states cover such employees either by interpretation of statute (New York, Wisconsin) or by the Governor's Code (Alaska, New Jersey). Eleven states without any fair employment statute or code covering employment practices were listed as Alabama, Arkansas, Georgia, Louisiana, Mississippi, North Dakota, South Carolina, South Dakota, Virginia, Texas. *Legislative History of the Equal Employment Act of 1972*, Committee Print, *supra*, pp. 1153, 1154.

6. The Attorney General in a case involving state or local governmental agencies could secure a three-judge federal court to hear an action under Section 706(f) (2), as amended, "where prompt judicial action is necessary." Decisions of such a court may be appealed directly to the Supreme Court, *Rule 65, Federal Rules of Civil Procedure.*

7. 48 Stat. 1909, 42 U.S.C. 4701. The commission administers a grant in aid program to assist state and local government to improve personnel administration.

8. Letter of August 11, 1972, "I share the views of the American Jewish Committee in opposing the concepts of quotas and proportional representation."

9. The EEO Act of 1972 did not supplant but rather reinforced the EEO program for the federal civil service established under Executive Order 11478 dated August 8, 1969. EEO programs for that sector of government have been in effect under presidential executive orders since the administration of President Franklin D. Roosevelt.

10. CCA, 3rd Circuit No. 72-1614, September 14, 1972, 41 United States Law Week 2162.

11. News item re Shirley Long appearing in *Federal Times* December 6, 1972, Vol. 8 #39.

12. *Castro et al.* v. *Beecher et al.* (1972) 459 F. 2d 725.

13. Ibid at 732.

14. *Davis* v. *Washington,* DC:D.C. (1972) 348 F. Supp. 15.

15. Sec. 1607.5(a).

18

richard j. murphy

THE DIFFERENCE OF A DECADE:
THE FEDERAL GOVERNMENT

When the public administration scholars write the history of federal personnel administration in the decade of the 1960's, they will almost certainly record that the changes which were then set in motion in salary, labor relations, equal opportunity, and appeals reforms—as well as the overall impact of these reforms on government operations—were as profound as any occurring in any single decade since the passage of the Pendleton Act.

At the beginning of the decade, with the exception of the TVA and Bonneville within the Interior Department, there was no union recognition in the federal government (although unions existed, some with large memberships), no exclusive bargaining units, dues checkoff, negotiated agreements, or written contracts. What appeals and grievance systems existed were spotty, lacking in uniform fundamentals, partial in coverage, discriminatory in treatment, unilaterally initiated, completely run by management and largely unused by employees. Federal salaries were universally recognized as lagging well behind private industry, pay bills had been vetoed, and the top salary paid to the highest ranking career employee was well under $20,000. Finally, equal employment opportunity was hardly more than a phrase, with widespread segregation in employee unions, segregated

Reprinted from the *Public Administration Review,* journal of the American Society for Public Administration, vol. 32, no. 2 (March–April, 1972), Copyright 1972 by the American Society for Public Administration. Reprinted by permission.

facilities in virtually every agency, and practically no minority employees in middle- or upper-level jobs throughout the government.

As the decade ended in 1970, union recognition was official policy, and the government was dealing with 134 unions, including 81 national or international ones. Fifty-eight per cent of all federal employees (1,542,000) were covered in 3,010 exclusively recognized units. Forty-six per cent (1,227,235) were covered under 1,509 negotiated agreements (not including 6,000 additional local Post Office agreements). Forty-one federal agencies were dealing with unions exclusively recognized in one or more units, and an estimated 1,200,-000 employees were remitting annually $30 million in dues deductions through their agencies.

Very importantly, agency judgments were now subject to third-party reviews by several other federal agencies or even independent arbitrators, depending on the subject.

Appeals and grievance systems with uniform minimum standards existed in all government agencies; veterans and nonveterans were treated equally; and third-party procedures, many of them negotiated and including arbitration of grievances, existed and were widely used.

Numerous federal salary bills had been signed into law by three Presidents, top career salaries were now at $36,000, and some observers, both in and out of government, were claiming that federal salaries were now ahead of private industry.

Equal employment opportunity was now a top management concern, and several programs existed to achieve progress in this important area.

Most importantly, all of these above-mentioned programs were having a dramatic impact on government operations, as never before, and operating officials were having to recognize, many for the first time, that labor relations and personnel administration had to be given top-level attention. Personnel administration, particularly labor relations expertise, had for the first time become really important in many agencies, and in others, it almost certainly will.

What happened (or didn't happen) in the personnel area could have a substantial impact on costs and productivity. The equal employment program and its problems could have a vital effect on community relations. Operating methods, policy planning, and the time allocation of the top staff could be severely affected by union problems. If these problems were not resolved, the entire operation might be adversely affected by a demonstration, slow-down, or outright work stoppage. Appropriate consultation between unions and management might often be the critical difference between success or failure of important programs. And disciplinary cases, improperly handled, could be lost, morale lowered, and efficiency of operations impaired.

Many agencies found that they simply could not graft the new labor relations responsibility on to their existing personnel structures, and that, indeed, labor relations required a considerable reorganization of operating procedures, if not the personnel structure itself. Still others found that the skills of the traditional personnelists were not adequate to cope with the demanding new responsibilities and that new skills, training, and expertise were needed. Practically all found, some the hardest of ways, that unless the personnel shop enjoyed top-level access, support, and funding, the new responsibilities would at some point overwhelm the agency.

The status of personnel administration and labor relations either has changed or is beginning to change in many federal agencies, usually depending upon the degree of union organization and contract negotiations. While the degree of change, support, and funding is very uneven (in many it is still minute), it is nonetheless very clear in direction—a more important role for the personnel and labor relations function. What a difference a decade can make!

THE HISTORICAL EVOLUTION

How did all this come about? Very briefly, these are the highlights:

Prior to the '60's, employee unions had existed for many decades, particularly in the Navy, Post Office, and Government Printing Office.[1] They were protected by the right given to government employees (by the Lloyd-La Follette Act of 1912) to petition Congress and to join organizations affiliated with outside bodies which do not impose an obligation to engage in, or support, a strike against the United States. To this day, the Lloyd-La Follette Act remains the only positive piece of federal union recognition legislation on the statute books; it was passed in response to several attempts by Postmasters General and Presidents to "gag" federal employees. Postal unions gradually grew and the National Federation of Federal Employees (NFFE), as well as the American Federation of Government Employees (AFGE), AFL-CIO, the two largest nonpostal unions, were formed.

For the most part, government employee unions acted as lobbying groups in attempting to secure wage increases and benefits from Congress, and as petitioners in handling both group and individual grievances with the various agencies. The 1950's saw increased attempts by the unions to secure official union recognition by statute (which had been granted in 1935 to unions in private industry) through the repeated introduction of the Rhodes-Johnston Bill in Congress. One of the senators showing interest in this bill was John F. Kennedy, and, significantly, it was Kennedy who as presidential candidate promised that, if elected, he would give the bill "more sympathetic treatment" than it had received in Congress.

Once elected, Kennedy appointed a task force under Secretary of Labor Arthur Goldberg to recommend to him an appropriate program for labor-management relations in the federal service. Using precedents already established in New York City, Philadelphia, and Wisconsin, the task force recommended a program which President Kennedy signed into Executive Order 19088 in January 1962.[2]

Executive Order 10988: The Breakthrough

This Order, hailed by union officials as the "Magna Carta" of federal employee unionism, for the first time gave unions official recognition in the government, in either exclusive or other form, depending upon their ability to secure votes or memberships of employees. Negotiation of written agreements was specifically authorized, a strong management rights clause was included, and advisory arbitration was permitted for grievances, contract interpretations, and bargaining unit determinations. Negotiation impasses were to be settled by means short of arbitration, and, significantly, the primary responsibility for implementing the Order and rendering final judgments was left to each agency. Wages and fringes were reserved to Congress and excluded from bargaining. A companion Order, 10987, was issued which directed the establishment of an adverse action appeals system within each agency, and accorded both veterans and nonveterans similar treatment.

Under 10988, union membership growth was extensive. The Post Office Department administered the largest collective bargaining election ever held and negotiated four detailed national agreements. Defense, Veterans Administration, Labor, General Services Administration, and Treasury also conducted extensive negotiations, while other agencies engaged mostly in consultations, with some bargaining.

The Next Stage: Executive Order 11491

The subsequent experience growing out of the Order led to an ad hoc group of top officials under the leadership of Civil Service Commission Chairman John W. Macy, Jr., to recommend to President Johnson the appointment of a President's Review Committee on Federal Employee-Management Relations, to evaluate the experience under Executive Order 10988, and to recommend whatever adjustments were needed. Such a group was appointed by President Johnson in 1967 and came up with a comprehensive program of recommendations, built around a central decision-making authority and extensive third-party procedures, which, unfortunately, were never sent to the White House for final approval due to the opposition of the Defense Department.[3] These recommendations were, however, later included, almost entirely, in the report to President Nixon by a study committee under Civil Service Commission Chairman Robert E. Hampton. President Nixon had appointed this committee in 1969, following a campaign promise, reminiscent of President Kennedy's. The Hampton Committee[4] found that Executive Order 10988 had "produced some excellent results," but that several important changes were urgently needed. It recommended, and President Nixon approved, a comprehensive new Executive Order 11491, the principal thrust of which was to provide extensive third-party dispute settling procedures and centralized new administrative machinery, while still excluding wages and fringes from bargaining.

Specifically, the new Order created a Federal Labor Relations Council, consisting of the Chairman of the Civil Service Commission, the Secretary of Labor, and the Director of the Office of Management and Budget, to decide major policy issues; strengthened the exclusive bargaining agents by eliminating other forms of union recognition; gave the Assistant Secretary of Labor for Labor-Management Relations a key role in deciding bargaining unit, representation, and unfair labor practice cases; prohibited union or agency shops; authorized binding arbitration of grievances; and created a Federal Service Impasses Panel to settle negotiation impasses, either by itself or with the assistance of fact-finders or arbitrators. Although it did not meet two of labor's most insistent "demands," union recognition by law (allowing recourse to the courts) and decision-making machinery completely independent of the Executive Branch, for the first time an agency head could be overruled on labor relations issues and a negotiation impasse be resolved by another government agency, with presidential blessing. To many traditionalists, that was indeed astounding!

The Postal Strike: A "First"

Executive Order 11491 had been in effect a few months when two dramatic events occurred, sending shock waves throughout the government and the general public—the strikes of some 200,000 postal workers and of several thousand Federal Aviation Administration (FAA) air traffic controllers. The postal strike—the first and largest national strike in federal history—led to direct emergency negotiations between management and the exclusive national postal unions (represented by AFL-CIO President George Meany) to get the employees back to work. This culminated in an unprecedented agreement in which the unions supported the enactment of postal reform legislation, which they had previously opposed, providing for a government corporation to operate the Postal Service. In return, they received the largest pay raise they had ever obtained, and no retaliatory action was taken against the strikers. All other federal workers were given a 6 per cent increase. The entire agreement (called by the AFL-CIO the largest collective bargaining agreement in history at $2.5 billion) was enacted into law by Congress with certain modifications in August 1970.

The Postal Reorganization Act was precedent-breaking because in removing the Postal Service from the provisions of Executive Order 11491, it conferred upon postal employees virtually all the labor relations benefits, except the right to strike, enjoyed by workers in private industry under the Taft-Hartley Act. The National Labor Relations Board (NLRB) was designated to determine bargaining units, supervise elections, and hear unfair practice cases; full collective bargaining was authorized for wages, with a "comparability with private industry" policy laid down for compensation and benefits. Moreover, an elaborate procedure was set forth, including fact-finding and, ultimately, binding and compulsory arbitration to settle bargaining deadlocks.[5]

As to the air traffic controllers, while their strike was a partial one, did not enlist the public sympathy evoked by the postal strikers, and resulted in the dismissal of quite a few of those participating, still it dramatically revealed the potential widespread work disruption when employees have deeply felt grievances.

The Latest Stage: Executive Order 11616

Executive Order 11491, never satisfactory to some of the union leaders for various reasons, was branded by some of them as obsolete after the postal strike. Now that the right to bargain for wages and fringe benefits had been given postal workers, some argued the same full collective bargaining privileges should be granted to all federal employees. A sore point all along had been that the Order disallowed negotiations by labor representatives on official time, and there were continuous rumbles that the Federal Labor Relations Council was "management-oriented" because of its composition.

In September 1971 President Nixon announced (as an amendment to Executive Order 11491) the issuance of Executive Order 11616, based on hearings held by the Federal Labor Relations Council in October 1970. These amendments, among other things, permitted a limited amount of negotiation by union representatives on the clock, required grievance procedures in all new agreements, strengthened the jurisdiction of the Assistant Secretary of Labor in unfair labor practice cases, and permitted grievance arbitration without the employee's consent but only upon the request of the exclusive union representative.

These changes, however, did not meet some of the strong complaints registered by various groups during the hearings, namely: lack of neutral administrative machinery outside Executive control; no judicial review; unduly limited scope of negotiations; ban on the union and agency shops; and lack of status for professional groups. [6]

THE PICTURE TODAY

While no agency has not experienced some effects from the various executive orders, the impact has been very uneven. [7] The Postal Service is by far the most involved, with negotiations covering over 625,000 employees (or 87 per cent of the Service's work force); it has a master national contract, with some 6,000 supplemental agreements totalling over 250 separate substantive contract items. But other agencies have become more involved each year, and in 1967, for the first time, more employees were covered in exclusive bargaining units outside the Postal Service than in it.

An important point to note is the large number of unions in exclusively recognized units which have not exercised their right to negotiate a contract. There are about 1,500 such units; outside of the Postal Service, only 31 per cent of federal employees are covered by agreements. The AFL-CIO-affiliated unions generally have high percentages of their members covered by agreements, with the independent employee organizations usually lagging considerably behind. Since the federal government is still largely in an organizing phase, this development is not too surprising, but it does mean that both unions and management will undoubtedly be more occupied with contract negotiations in the future. This is particularly true in such agencies as Treasury, the Office of Economic Opportunity, and the FAA, all of which have relatively high percentages of union activity but relatively few contracts.

As to employee desires, in 92 per cent of 624 elections conducted in 1970, they voted for union representation. However, only 61 per cent of those eligible actually voted, which compares with 89 per cent average participation in private sector NLRB elections. Concerning the unions, nearly all have grown substantially since 1962, with the nonpostals growing spectacularly, since the Post Office had long been highly organized. AFGE is now the largest union in the federal service, representing over 530,000 employees, as compared with only 76,000 in 1964. The American Postal Workers Union (APWU), an amalgamation of five formerly separate postal unions, is the second largest federal union, with the National Association of Letter Carriers (NALC), NFFE, and the National Association of Government Employees (NAGE), following in that order. Postal reorganization, with its new bargaining opportunities, has served as a great stimulus to unite many of the formerly warring postal unions. Other postal mergers with undoubtedly follow, but very few mergers have taken place outside the Postal Service.

It should also be mentioned that three of the agencies not covered by Executive Order 11616 are in the process of establishing employee relations programs of their own: the State Department with its components (excluded by decision of President Nixon in 1971), the District of Columbia (following the '70 strike of D.C. sanitation workers), and the Government Printing Office (which has appointed an "umpire" to perform all third-party functions, following the printers' strike of 1970).

As 1971 ended, the federal government's strike future was unclear. What was clear, however, was that the mandatory penalties of dismissals, jail sentences, and fines provided by PL 84-330 are totally unrealistic and unenforceable. The large rewards received by postal employees, printers in the Government Printing Office, and sanitation workers in the District of Columbia, in their 1970 strikes, and the absence of any subsequent discipline against them, certainly will not dampen the increased militancy evident among government workers at all levels, federal, state, and local. The continued large increase in strikes at the local level keeps building the pressure on federal union leaders for similar action.[8]

Yet, the strike avoidance record of the federal government is superb, compared either with state or local government, or with private industry, especially during the latter's organizing phase in the '30's. Surely the fact that FAA has dismissed 68 employees, suspended scores of others, while the Professional Air Traffic Controllers Organization (PATCO) suffered financial disaster and decertification will have some sobering effect on union officials, especially if they estimate that only a small portion of the total agency workforce can be prevailed upon to strike. Still, where a strike is massive, subsequent disciplinary action is very unlikely. The effectiveness of injunctions when finally obtained must be noted, but to date judges have been very reluctant to issue them.

Despite the success of the postal strike, postal workers in New York City did call off their plans for another walkout in July 1971 when they discovered that other postal workers would not join them. The contract provisions about to be agreed upon were considered fairly good by a majority of the postal workers.

President Nixon's six-month postponement of the scheduled January 1972 federal pay increase, and the deferral of the scheduled October 1971 postal salary increase could, under certain conditions, trigger some serious job actions, just as happened with the postal walkout in 1970. There is no guarantee against the occurrence of future strikes, especially wildcats. Actually, as long as a strike threat remains just that, it may help rather than hinder collective negotiations.

SOME CONCLUDING OBSERVATIONS

Politics.   The involvement of government employee unions in politics continues strong, and is growing, particularly among non-postal unions. AFGE has just created a Committee on Federal Employee Political Education, similar in objectives to COPE of the AFL-CIO, while the American Federation of State, County, and Municipal Employees (AFSCME) started a program to financially support its friends for election to Congress. The creation of the Postal Service diminished somewhat postal workers' political activities and spending during the last congressional campaign and during postal negotiations. However, postal union leaders have recently announced the calling of huge Washington rallies to secure from Congress improved retirement benefits and to exert other pressures.

Pay. The government pay picture changed dramatically for the better during the '60's, and the Federal Pay Comparability Act of 1970 provides a significant role for the unions in making recommendations on pay rates. While the President's decision to defer for six months the expected increases in January 1972 had a dampening effect, union participation in federal wage setting can be expected to continue.

Costs. Good labor-management relations programs cost money and cannot be contained within conventional personnel budgets. The federal government is desperately understaffed in labor expertise, and vastly expanded training and staffing in this field are essential. More money simply must be forthcoming from Congress, or the costs will be paid ten times over in labor troubles.

Social Action. An area which bears careful watching is the interaction between social action programs, race relations, and craft unionism. AFGE has been having several problems with its "activist" OEO and HEW locals regarding certain social and political issues, while the National Alliance of Postal and Federal Employees, an overwhelmingly black union, has been blasting both postal management and other postal unions for alleged racial discrimination. The Alliance, an old and sizeable postal union, is moving into other federal agencies in an aggressive fashion, with the help of the Southern Christian Leadership Conference. Most federal unions have paid little real attention to racial issues in the past, but many have acquired minority group officers within the last few years. Moreover, minority hiring programs have generally brought both overt and covert opposition from certain unions to "lowering of standards." Management can be expected to be pulled in both directions by federal unions on racial issues in the immediate future, with more direct action by minority group employees in ever more federal agencies to be expected.

Private Sector Influence. The last few years have witnessed an increasing use of private sector precedents and procedures in the federal government. Wisely, the Department of Labor has ruled that private sector NLRB precedents will be used but will not necessarily be binding in rendering decisions under Executive Order 11616. Private mediators, fact-finders, and arbitrators have been increasingly used, as have the services of the Federal Mediation and Conciliation Service, which increased its assistance to federal agencies (including preventive mediation) fourfold in 1970.

As the Federal Labor Relations Council, Federal Service Impasses Panel, and the Assistant Secretary of Labor for Labor-Management Relations continue to render their decisions, tailored specifically to the federal service, a considerable body of precedent is being created to guide agency officials and all others concerned.

The Future. Beyond any doubt, the scope of federal negotiations will continue to be expanded, and the areas formerly reserved to central direction by the Civil Service Commission, the Office of Management and Budget, and Congress will diminish.

The merit system as we have known it will continue to be under attack, and compromises with union requests will be made in many areas.

The Civil Service Commission will find more and more of its activities cast into a labor-management framework, with major internal reorganization becoming necessary. Its ability to adapt to this formidable challenge—and up to now it has done so very well—will determine its continued existence. The Commission, as the central personnel authority, should play a very prominent role as spokesman for the President in the labor relations area, and, with the help of the Labor Department, as purveyor of helpful and official guidance to agency personnel management on labor relations questions. To do this well will require the dropping of its adjudicatory role; its firm, forthright self-identification as the President's agent for personnel management; and the elevation of the role of its Chairman in dealing with other federal agencies. Above all, it cannot afford to be under the thumb of the Office of Management and Budget in this vital area, or surrender its function to accountants.

Finally, Congress should eventually pass legislation, putting onto the statute books something more positive than the elementary Lloyd-LaFollette Act. We have now had ten years of experience with union recognition in the federal government, and appropriate experimentation has taken place. The trend at both the federal and state levels has been fairly well crystallized, so that legislation is now desirable. Such legislation should repeal PL 84-330, while still prohibiting strikes against the federal government. It should write the majority of provisions of Executive Order 11616 into law, but should broaden the scope of negotiations, allow limited union security arrangements, and create an independent commission, representative of the general public, to administer the program, resolve impasses, and decide the day-to-day operating problems under the law. Moreover, Congress should commit itself adequately to finance and staff the program as it would any other endeavor vital to the national interest.

Few matters rate a higher priority than the continued maintenance of an uninterrupted high level of vital services by the United States government and its employees.

ENDNOTES

1. Wilson R. Hart, *Collective Bargaining in the Federal Civil Service* (New York: Harper & Row, 1961), and William B. Vosloo, *Collective Bargaining in the United States Federal Civil Service* (Chicago: Public Personnel Association, 1966).
2. President's Task Force on Employee-Management Relations in the Federal Service, *A Policy for Employee-Management Cooperation in the Federal Service* (Washington, D.C.: U.S. Government Printing Office, November 1961).
3. See Richard J. Murphy and Morris Sackman, *The Crisis in Public Employee Relations in the Decade of the Seventies* (Washington, D.C.: Bureau of National Affairs, Inc., 1970).
4. See *Report and Recommendations on Labor-Management Relations in the Federal Service* (Washington, D.C.: U.S. Civil Service Commission, October 1969).
5. See *Postal Reorganization Report No. 91-1363*, 91st Congress, Second Session, U.S. House of Representatives, August 3, 1970.
6. See *Labor-Management Relations in the Federal Service* (Washington, D.C.: U.S. Federal Labor Relations Council, 1970).
7. See Anthony F. Ingrassia, "Widening Dimensions of the Federal Bargaining Table," *Civil Service Journal*, Vol. 12, No. 1 (July-September 1971).
8. See Richard J. Murphy, "Public Employee Strikes," in Murphy and Sackman, *op. cit.*, pp. 7-79.

19

felix a. nigro

THE IMPLICATIONS FOR PUBLIC ADMINISTRATION

The four years since publication of the March/April 1968 PAR symposium on "Collective Negotiations in the Public Service" make a big difference. The developments are clearer to identify, although not surprising, and there is more documentation to support predictions about the future. In this article, we will: (1) present in detail *eight* specific ways in which public administration has been affected; (2) consider the resulting changes in the relative influence of different participants in the public policy-making process; (3) discuss the concern about the public interest; and (4) conclude with a final, evaluative balance sheet.

EIGHT SPECIFIC EFFECTS

First, bilateral determination of the conditions of work is now well-established for very large numbers of public employees. Fifty-eight per cent of the federal work force is now represented by unions recognized as exclusive bargaining agents, which is ". . . far greater than the coverage in private employment."[1] Furthermore, contrary to a lingering misconception, 35 per cent of all federal white-collar employees are so represented; indeed, there are now more white-collar than blue-collar workers so represented. Of the more than a

Reprinted from the *Public Administration Review,* journal of the American Society for Public Administration, Vol. 32, No. 2 (March–April, 1972), Copyright 1972 by the American Society for Public Administration. Reprinted by permission.

million state and local government employees in New York, 900,000 are exercising their collective bargaining rights under legislation passed in 1967. In New York City, about 280,000 of the some 370,000 municipal workers are represented by the six major unions. Some education authorities consider that collective bargaining is now the "prevailing decision-making style" in the public school systems.[2]

The rapidly growing membership base justifies employee leaders' optimism about winning representation rights for even higher percentages of the total work force. About one million federal employees are members of employee organizations, while, "Membership in unions and employee associations currently totals about two million, or more than one-third of all non-instructional fulltime employees of states, cities, counties, school districts and other local authorities, as compared with less than 30 per cent organization of nonagricultural workers in the private sector."[3]

Second, public officials are increasingly being policed through binding grievance arbitration clauses in collective contracts. Four years ago such clauses were far less common, and management often resisted them tooth and nail. Executive Order 11616 continues the provision in Executive Order 11491 permitting union-negotiated grievance procedures with binding arbitration; and it also requires *all* new agreements to contain negotiated grievance procedures for resolving disputes over interpretation of contract terms.

The significance of binding grievance arbitration was clear in the recent school teacher strike in Newark, New Jersey. The strike became inevitable when the Newark school board announced it would not agree to a new contract containing the provision for binding arbitration. Teachers who grieve transfers can get them cancelled if the arbitrator agrees that management's action violates the contract or is otherwise unfair. Many teachers fear transfers to slum neighborhoods, and the whites are apprehensive that black-dominated school boards may transfer them out of their jobs. A compromise on this issue was reached as part of the final strike settlement in Newark.[4] While this was a dramatic confrontation, grievance arbitration is now curbing the discretion of numerous public officials in many routine and nonroutine matters, depending on the coverage of the contracts. The truth is that grievance arbitration, based on the principle of fairness guaranteed by final decision making by a neutral third party, is an important part of the "new public administration."

Third, unions are widening their participation in program policy making, whether or not they have this role in the contract. Many public officials are strongly opposed to contract provisions calling for joint management-union determination of program questions, such as class sizes, caseloads, and number of police in patrol cars. While management should not, and legally cannot, abdicate its role in many program areas, it is obvious from recent developments, particularly in state and local government, that strong unions can influence and even determine certain program decisions even though denied such a role in the contract.

The instrument, both simple and blunt, is the "job action," threatened or actual. New York City is a good example; on repeated occasions, Mayor Lindsay and some of his department heads have insisted on their "management prerogatives"—but eventually made decisions which represent important concessions to union demands. Although it is thunderously proclaimed that management alone determines the budget, later it is quietly announced that the number of new positions requested for a particular department has been substantially increased. Management both decided—and listened to the unions!

According to one analysis, the "controversy over the establishment of an independent New York City Health and Hospitals Corporation to take over the city's decaying municipal hospital system remained insoluble until the union representing hospital workers gave its blessing—at a price in increased power for the union and its members that is not yet fully known."[5] Unions have always sought to influence decisions of this kind through lobbying and the political process, but now, despite anti-strike laws, they have added the new wallop of the "job action."

Fourth, the unions have intensified their political activities. Success in collective bargaining, far from causing diminished political activity, has been accompanied by stepped-up political action to capitalize on the power of expanded union memberships and a record of success in contract settlements. Political activity coalitions are constantly forming, with doctrinal differences submerged in the interest of greater impact in lobbying and in rewarding or punishing elective officials at the polls. The alliance between the AFL-CIO-affiliated AFSCME and the NEA, with the latter's history of disdain for "labor," is a strange one, dubbed an "odd-couple" arrangement by the AFT (the NEA's big competitor), which claims that, although it also is AFL-CIO, it was not even consulted on the pact by AFSCME.

Fifth, collective bargaining settlements are substantially increasing the personal service budget and contributing to the financial crisis in government, particularly at the state and local level. While comprehensive research findings in this area are still in the preparation stage,[6] the relationship between contract settlements and soaring budgets is obvious in many places.

With large numbers of public employees, even moderate increases can raise the wage bill by hundreds of thousands of dollars. Wages, pensions, and other "fringes" accounted for 56 per cent of New York City's $7.8 billion budget in one recent fiscal year, with rising labor costs accounting for half of the budget increase. This rise in the wage bill, in a period of declining revenues, has naturally led to increased taxpayer interest in worker productivity, with management now in a better position to insist that the workers put out more. A beneficial result is that management is spurred to give greater attention to methods of evaluating program results and measuring worker productivity, whereas previously it tended to neglect these areas. At the same time, the unions, aware of the taxpayer discontent, know that they cannot expect the productivity question to be overlooked in contract negotiations.[7]

Sixth, the political environment of government makes collective bargaining different in important ways from bargaining in the private sector. While the role of "market discipline" in preventing excessive wage settlements has been exaggerated in the present era of giant companies and lessened competition, it is still true that consumers can elect to buy less expensive, non-union made products, or substitute products, of which many are available. The consumers of public (government) services have no such choice. Companies can move or go out of business; government agencies cannot.[8]

If this argument seems like theoretical economics not applicable today, evidence from the real world is clear, based upon the performance of principal "actors" in the political process—elective officials. When strikes in essential services are threatened or occur, chief executives and other politicians are very sensitive to the angry protests of the inconvenienced public which often hates the strikers, but the inconvenience more. The tendency is to make substantial, relatively quick concessions to the government unions. Walkouts are not very extended, and, as the private sector experience shows, it is the *long* strikes which are the hardest for the unions to win.

Private companies sometimes manage to operate during massive walkouts by using supervisors to provide at least limited service. In some governmental jurisdictions the supervisors have full collective bargaining rights (not permitted supervisors under Taft-Hartley), and they may walk out with the nonsupervisory employees or overlook slowdowns—which means they cannot be counted on to side with the top management during labor disputes.[9]

Public employee leaders like AFSCME President Jerry Wurf insist that many politicians are hostile and that the government unions do not have excessive power. This certainly is true in many parts of the country, particularly in the small towns and the rural areas. It is in the big cities with heavily unionized employees and a record of resort to strikes that the potential for excessive union power appears greatest. Those proposing solutions for public employee disputes sometimes fail to take into account these variations. New York City may be ripe for compulsory arbitration, but countless other jurisdictions do not need this last-ditch machinery.

The different environment in government does not justify denial of collective bargaining rights or even of a limited right to strike. To deny, however, the potential for undue union power in government under certain circumstances is simply to disregard the reality. The search for workable solutions in the public interest proceeds best when that reality is clearly understood and accepted.

Seventh, the decline in the power of civil service commissions, which are buffeted by forces besides the unions anyway, is continuing. The role of the commission, based on the civil service law, in recommending pay plans and revisions does not mean much when, as provided by another law, or on a de facto basis, pay and fringes are negotiated by management and union representatives. For various good reasons, the commissions, with rare exceptions, do not represent management at the bargaining table, and they usually are not in a position to influence the management stands greatly. Suffice it to say that a settlement desired by the chief executive and/or legislators will likely be concurred with by the commission, but it may not even be seriously asked for its opinion.

When collective bargaining agreements provide for final-step binding grievance arbitration, the civil service commission also loses its prestigious role as principal court of appeal for the aggrieved employee. Increasingly, important provisions of the civil service rules and regulations are negotiated along with economic benefits, which reduces the commission's policy-making role. It is not surprising that some labor relations experts, anxious to solidify management strength for dealing with the unions around the chief executive, are happy with the recommendation in the National Civil Service League's new Model Public Personnel Administration Law to abolish civil service commissions.

While the commissions decline, the position of many personnel directors is both clarified and strengthened. Frequently, they are either the chief spokesmen, or members, of the management's negotiating team, which makes it clear that they *are* part of management. The critical nature of labor relations, and their prominent role in it, give them an importance many have not had in the past. Their background for labor relations thus becomes a key consideration in their employment and training.

Eighth, the budgetary process is being affected in several ways. Negotiations and budgetary time tables should be synchronized; this is being attempted, but with not too much success since bargaining deadlocks often extend beyond budget submission and adoption dates. Somehow, chief executives and legislatures must make good estimates of the amounts needed in the budget to finance the labor contracts, so as to eliminate or reduce the need for supplementary appropriations, or for reductions-in-force or other cuts in already funded programs. Contrary to the long-expounded postulate of honesty in budgets, ways must be found to "hide" the estimated funds for the settlements in unsuspected parts of the estimates. The expectation is that the unions, if they knew the maximum amounts management would settle for, would ask for more.

RELATIVE ROLES IN THE POWER GAME

Collective bargaining in government is visibly altering the relative shares of different individuals and groups in the formulation and implementation of public policy. An agenda for research to identify these changes in selected jurisdictions is presented in the table included in this article. Based on this writer's analysis of kinds of changes which have occurred, a scheme of rankings is proposed for verification by researchers in different communities. The rankings show relative roles for different participants *before* and *after* the introduction of collective bargaining (CB). Since there are different phases of policy making influenced by labor relations, the rankings are separate for these phases, as defined in the footnotes in the table.

There is no precise agreement by the participants and observers as to these relative shares, even before CB, and, of course, the picture varies by place, depending upon the extent of unionization, strength of the labor movement in the area, and other factors. While civil service commissions have had important influence in recommending pay and fringe benefit plans, their greatest power has been in recommending and implementing the rules and regulations which cover all aspects of the technical personnel program. Although these rules and regulations usually require the approval of the chief executive and sometimes of the legislative body, such approval without major change is generally much easier to obtain than for recommendations in the economic benefit area. (If this assumption is wrong, its inaccuracy would be revealed by the projected research.) If the investigations in a particular community reveal that the unions have jumped in influence, not only in determinations on economic benefits but also in general personnel policy formulation, this would document one of the "impressions" in the table. Another "impression" to be tested is that the unions also have climbed up several notches in program policy implementation, but not quite as many in program policy formulation.

Undoubtedly, some of the rankings in the table of other participants such as department heads and the general public will look "wrong" to many PAR readers; the idea, however, is to provide a usable guide for launching much-needed research in the volatile, emotion-laden area of labor relations. As to research methodology, interviewing and analysis of recorded decisions and of positions taken by the respective participants, and newspaper and other written accounts of the effective factors in the decisions would be used. While the influence process is obscure in some aspects, there is plenty of information in the hearing and other records of civil service commissions, and in the briefs and published statements of unions and taxpayer and other groups. The collective contracts themselves will provide much of the data. Quite a few insightful public officials are available to contribute opinions to the "before" and "after" comparisons; the "before" is not so long ago.

THE PUBLIC INTEREST QUESTION

When, in the flush of their successes of the 1960's, some public employee leaders proclaimed the doctrine that collective contracts supersede provisions in existing laws and regulations, the "public interest" question came to the fore in an unprecedented way. If the price of bilateralism in determination of employment conditions was to be the shunting aside of the public and its legislative representatives in such decisions, then the net impact would be less democracy in the total political system.

Worries on this score have since lessened; as the result of court decisions, the resistance of appointed and elected officials, and a modification of the unions' own stand on this matter, the agreements generally are not wiping out laws and regulations.[10] It is now the

TABLE 4.1 Public administration and collective bargaining: one impression of changed roles

Policies Governing Pay and Fringes		Other Personnel Policies[1]		Formulation of Program Policy[2]		Implementation of Program Policy[3]	
Before CB	After CB	Before CB	After CB	Before CB	After CB	Before CB	After CB
1. Legislature	1. Unions Chief executive	1. Legislature	1. Legislature	1. Legislature	1. Legislature	1. Chief executive	1. Chief executive
2. Chief executive	2. Legislature	2. Civil service commission	2. Unions Chief executive	2. Pressure groups (excluding unions)	2. Pressure groups (excluding unions)	2. Department heads (including budget director)	2. Department heads (including budget director)
3. Pressure groups (excluding unions)	3. Pressure groups (excluding unions)	3. Chief executive	3. Civil service commission	3. Chief executive	3. Chief executive	3. Pressure groups (excluding unions)	3. Pressure groups (including unions)
4. Unions	4. Budget director and department heads	4. Department heads	4. Department heads	4. Department heads	4. Unions	4. Legislature	4. Legislature
5. Civil service commission and budget director	5. Civil service commission	5. Pressure groups (excluding unions)	5. Pressure groups (excluding unions)	5. Unions	5. Department heads	5. Unions	5. General public
6. Department heads	6. General public	6. Unions	6. General public	6. General public	6. General public	6. General public	
7. General public		7. General public					

1. Recruitment, promotion, transfer, lay-off, reinstatement, service rating, training, disciplinary, and other personnel processes.
2. Determination of the content of legislation dealing with substantive programs of government.
3. Policies made in carrying out substantive program authorized by the legislature.

process of collective bargaining in government which causes much of the concern about the public interest.

In an era of great pressures to reform existing institutions and make them "open," to some people the collective negotiations now taking place in government are unduly secretive. Too often the final "package," announced by management and union representatives after a long "blackout" period during which the press and the public are told very little, represents a very important commitment of community resources about which even legislators have had nothing to say.

Abe Raskin, the labor editor of the *New York Times*, knows that an essential element of private sector collective bargaining is closed negotiating sessions, but he and others believe that the public should be told in detail about management and union stands on proposals by mediators. Since the negotiations continue or resume after mediators intervene and make proposals, Raskin's position basically is that collective bargaining in government is different and requires divulgences to the public. "The people of New York are entitled to know what they are being asked to pay and what increased efficiency they can expect to get in return—before the deal is made, not after." [11]

Raskin may be wrong about making public mediators' recommendations, but his argument that the full costs, present and future, of settlements should be revealed to the public is unassailable. Management has sometimes been able to reduce the unions' demands for increased wages and other benefits by agreeing to liberal increases in pensions, to be funded, and therefore paid for, by the taxpayers at some future time.

Frank P. Zeidler, former mayor of Milwaukee, has suggested the possibility of public referenda on proposed contracts, just as on bond issues. [12] If the Rhode Island court interpretation, cited by Van Asselt above, is accepted, namely, that private arbitrators become public officials when they issue awards fixing government salaries, then it can be argued that there is clear justification for giving the public the opportunity to vote on arbitral awards and proposed settlements.

While collective bargaining in government has in recent years moved closer to the industrial model, there are many unresolved perplexing questions of how to modify that model to meet the special needs of government. The view is spreading that mediators, factfinders, arbitrators, and the personnel of supposedly "neutral" labor relations agencies favor the "private" interests of the unions over those of the general public. The challenge is to create, in all necessary detail, a special kind of collective bargaining for government which will give sufficient protection to the public interest and thus allay these fears.

THE BALANCE SHEET

The tendency is either to be for the unions or against, but the picture is a mixed one, as is so often the case with complicated developments. Our conclusions are:

1. Collective bargaining has proved itself a salutary check on public employer arbitrariness and paternalism. No review group analyzing the experience under existing collective bargaining programs in government has recommended their termination. Whatever the shortcomings found, the desirability of collective bargaining has been upheld by such groups as proved in practice.

2. Collective bargaining is an excellent antidote for the evils of bureaucracy. The employee feels that he counts for something through the strength of his union: now management *must* listen. It is possible that the unions have done more to alleviate the much-discussed conflict between organization and individual needs than any other force or technique.

3. Curbs on excessive union power *are* needed, and, in some places, compulsory arbitration may be the answer.

4. The difficulties in financing contract settlements have made the need for tax reform very clear; indeed, union leaders with vision are pushing efforts for such reform. They have a common interest with local officials in ending the heavy reliance on property taxes which has caused the virtual bankruptcy of so many cities.

5. Legislatures must assert their role, else chief executives and the unions may relegate them to an increasingly minor role in labor relations. Since the collective bargaining process does contribute to executive power, this is another point at which the modern legislature should hold firm against encroachment on its powers.

6. Civic groups and individual citizens can get in the act by developing strong positions in advance on contract negotiations. At present, they are usually silent and inactive while

public management and the unions busily negotiate in private. Surely there is a way for the public to be heard before it is too late; the trouble is that too few people have as yet figured out when and how to inject themselves effectively into the changed decision-making processes.

There is no inexorable force which will make collective bargaining turn out one way or another, nor are the developments so swift as to make it problematic that humans can shape the future picture. Dramatic as the unionism is, its significance has not yet been appreciated by enough of the public or, for that matter, of public management.

ENDNOTES

1. *Labor Management Relations in the Federal Service, Executive Order 11491 As Amended by Executive Order 11616 of August 26, 1971, Reports and Recommendations, United States Federal Labor Relations Council* (Washington, D.C.: The Council, 1971), p. 38.
2. See George R. La Noue and Marvin R. Pilo, "Teacher Unions and Educational Accountability," in Robert H. Connery and William V. Farr (eds.), *Unionization of Municipal Employees* (New York: The Academy of Political Science, Columbia University, 1971), p. 147.
3. Jack Stieber, "State, local unions pass industry and still going," *LMRS Newsletter*, Vol. 2, No. 7 (July 1971), p. 1.
4. See Fox Butterfield, "At Root of Newark Teacher Strike: Race and Power," *New York Times*, April 8, 1971.
5. John M. Leavens *et al*, "City Personnel: The Civil Service and Municipal Unions," in pamphlet published for Institute of Public Administration in New York by Sage Publications, p. 17.
6. The Brookings Institution will publish a monograph on this subject.
7. On educational productivity, see Myron Lieberman, "Professors Unite!" *Harper's Magazine*, Vol. 243, No. 1457 (October 1971), p. 69.
8. See Harry H. Wellington and Ralph K. Winter, Jr., "The Limits of Collective Bargaining in Public Employment," *The Yale Law Journal*, Vol. 78, No. 7 (June 1969); and John F. Burton, Jr., and Charles Krider, "The Role and Consequences of Strikes by Public Employees," and Wellington and Winter, "More on Strikes by Public Employees," *The Yale Law Journal*, Vol. 79, No. 3 (January 1970).
9. See Anthony C. Russo, "Management's View of the New York City Experience," in Connery and Farr, *op. cit.*, pp. 87-88.
10. See Felix A. Nigro, "Collective Bargaining and the Merit System," *ibid.*, pp. 55-67.
11. *New York Times*, editorial page, March 19, 1971.
12. Frank P. Zeidler, *New Roles for Public Officials in Labor Relations*, Public Employee Relations Library, No. 23 (Chicago: Public Personnel Association), p. 20.

20

robert booth fowler

NORMATIVE ASPECTS OF PUBLIC
EMPLOYEE STRIKES

Strikes by public employees should be legal—within certain limitations.

In recent years at all levels of government public employee strikes have been a growing part of political reality in America. Since they are usually illegal, the normative policy question they generate is whether or not public servants should have a right to strike. This article attempts to formulate an answer. After examining the empirical dimensions of the phenomenon of public worker strikes, it will proceed to explore five central points of dispute: (1) Are public employee strikes compatible with the concept of sovereignty? (2) Can public employee work stoppages be reconciled with democratic government? (3) Will they preserve in the civil service the merit system and decent relations? (4) Is legalization of public employee strikes necessary to guarantee public workers full roles as equal citizens? (5) Is the legal right to strike justifiable, due to current demands of political reality? Finally, the article concludes that within certain limitations, government workers ought to have the legal right to strike.

THE PHENOMENON OF PUBLIC WORKER STRIKES

Impressive numbers of public workers are unionized today. Out of two million government employees, almost 20 percent are union

Reprinted from *Public Personnel Management*, III, #2 (March-April, 1974). Used by permission of the International Personnel Management Association.

members. More than half of all federal employees belong to unions. While the proportion of state and local employees who hold union cards is much lower with no more than one-third in any state, there is unmistakable evidence of expansion of union affiliation at these levels. It is significant that the American Federation of State, County and Municipal Employees (AFSCME) is the fastest growing union in the AFL-CIO, with almost 500,000 members by the beginning of this decade.[1]

There is considerable disagreement about whether the expanding union movement in public employment has caused the increased resort to strikes. But there is no doubt about the expansion itself, even though it is often forgotten that strikes occurred in the public service in other times. People also forget that most conflicts are resolved short of strikes. Yet the widespread impression that public strikes are multiplying which was created by the news coverage of the 1970 postal workers' strike, numerous school teacher work stoppages, outbreaks of the blue flu, and strike troubles in New York City in particular, is not a mere media illusion.[2]

The differences between 1958 and 1968 starkly illuminate the trend pattern. The number of work stoppages went from 15 near the end of the 1950s to 254 a decade later; the number of workers involved went from 1700 to 202,000; the number of idle days exploded from 7500 to 2.5 million. All of these figures represent rates of expansion far in excess of developments in private industry in the same period. The situation has been notoriously more serious in New York City: between 1964 and 1968 alone almost 2 million man-hours were lost due to strikes.

After the escalating pattern of the 1960s, there has been some leveling off in the number of idle days and the number of strikers (except for the 1970 postal workers' strike). But the incidence of actual strikes continues to burgeon. By 1970 there were over 400. Experts today seem sure that the future will include more strikes, more idle days, and more people involved.[3]

There has also been a rapid alteration in the official policy stances of government worker organizations. Some still have anti-strike provisions in their constitutions, but others have reversed their traditional no-strike position, including AFSCME, the National Educational Association, and even the firefighters. At the same time expert, academic literature on public employee strikes which was once almost unanimously hostile, is filled today with support for the right of government workers to strike under various stipulations. Though some opposition also remains, the shift is remarkable.[4]

Governments are beginning to look at the strike situation with a fresh eye. Many states are investigating the entire area of collective bargaining and strikes in the public sector. Several state task forces have reported recently. Their conclusions differ considerably, but their very existence is a significant sign of interest on the part of government. The most important development of the last several years, however, has been the passage of laws in several states sanctioning, for the first time in U.S. history, the legal right to strike for the public worker, albeit under substantial limitations.

Hawaii and Pennsylvania pioneered in this area in 1970. The main restriction they attempt to impose is a prohibition of strikes that demonstrably damage the public interest. More limited strike provisions for more limited numbers of public employees now exist in other states, including Vermont and Montana. For example, in Vermont teachers may strike if there is no court finding that they are severely hurting the public weal. Montana has modest strike privileges for public nurses. The trend is clear, and one may safely predict that these states will soon be joined by others. Relaxation of interdictions on public strikes is more and more the order of the day.[5]

STRIKES AND SOVEREIGNTY

Arguments over legalization of public worker strikes traditionally began with the question of whether legal strikes could be reconciled with sovereignty in our political system. It has long been a standard argument that the result of legalization will be public unions gaining so much power through strikes they will compromise the sovereignty, or the ultimate authority, of the American people or their government. Today this old dispute is both far less important and far less frequent in serious normative and empirical argument than in the past. But there remains an important issue of theory here.

Students who fear that public employee strikes may have an adverse effect upon sovereignty have a legitimate fear, in principle. No political community should surrender power to anyone without exploring whether its sovereignty might be sacrificed in the process. Yet there is so far no factual confirmation of this fear with regard to public employee unions. Nor is there much evidence to sustain the thesis that legalization will add to the danger. But little can be said until there is substantial empirical investigation of the effect of present and future strikes.

The current evidence from the United States is only fragmentary; but studies of major strikes, such as the New York teachers' in 1968, the New York transit workers' in 1966, and the Memphis sanitation strike of 1968, do not reveal a collapse of sovereignty. Hundreds of other, less acrimonious work stoppages offer even slighter evidence.

There is also considerable data from several foreign countries in which the right to strike has been sanctioned. Canadian experience suggests no impairment of sovereignty. In Europe, where practice has long allowed public employees to strike whatever the laws, there is no data to support the fears that tacit or explicit legalization will compromise ultimate popular and governmental sovereignty.[6]

The sovereignty argument against legalizing public strikes is often challenged from a second, more indirect, angle. The applicability of the concept of sovereignty to the U.S. political system is in doubt today. Our political order has already so thoroughly delegated its sovereign power that the sovereignty model is as irrelevant as worry about sovereignty is pointless. The pluralist model, not the sovereignty one, is the descriptive model and pluralist government has already led to so much bilateral decision making between governments and group interests that adding another set of bilateral relationships, this time between governments and their employees, scarcely merits a ripple of concern.[7]

In theory, however, the sovereignty model remains applicable to the United States. American ideology continues to confirm what the first words of the Constitution assert, that sovereignty rests in the end with the people of the United States. Moreover, while it may seem that sovereignty has been delegated in many areas, one may argue that what actually has been delegated is some of the authority which flows from sovereignty. This grant often carries specific, legislative authorization and, even when it does not it is theoretically recoverable by the population at large, though with some difficulty. In any case, the evidence from abroad is too optimistic and the evidence from the United States is too modest to justify becoming enmeshed in abstract worries about legal public employee strikes posing a danger to sovereignty.

STRIKES AND DEMOCRATIC GOVERNMENT

A more pressing and more complex argument against legalizing strikes by government employees turns around the possibility of damage to democratic government, regardless of whether or not there is a threat to the idea of final sovereignty. The claim is that all government employee strikes flout majority will. This view identifies two aspects of public employee strikes as potential distortions of public will: the results of strike settlements, and costs *during* the strike, especially the loss of services. Clearly both aspects could easily interfere with public mandates.

The broader issue raised here is whether our democratic government can sustain the tremendous group pressures of pluralism, much less bear the inclusion of so potentially powerful a group as strike-armed government workers, without losing its concern for general interests and majority sentiments. So far this alarm is also only an anticipation of possible, but unsupported evils. Solid empirical evidence is needed before anyone can know how legitimate it is. First, one should examine the possible threat to the public desires that might come out of a strike settlement. By means of a strike, a public union might force either such overwhelming employee benefits as to flout public will and badly skew public budgets, or be granted decision-making power over public policy. Whether either event will happen depends on how effective strikes are as weapons against governments. Some students contend that, compared to a private business, governments are helpless before a strike. A government cannot change locations—it cannot go South; it cannot simply go out of business. If it is a local government, it is often tightly restricted financially by its state government or its property tax base, or both. It is also likely to be under heavy citizen pressure to end any strike, since demand for public services is frequently inelastic. Thus striking unions can quickly place a government in a painful position where its vulnerability is obvious.[8]

The spread of relations governed by collective bargaining between government employers and employees has already altered their relations. Certainly there is mounting unpleasant evidence from New York City, for example, that the results of some public strikes have involved high pay and fringe benefits, as well as important influence over public policy for militant unions, particularly in public education. The public frequently appears to be lost in the process. Probably one may anticipate the disquieting prospect of future settlements which simply ignore public sentiment. The rising incidence of interest in multilateral decision-making in the public employment field partially reflects this recent experience. The multilateral approach seeks to devise mechanisms by which public opinion may be brought to bear in decision-making, including public strike negotiations, an arena in which they are too often absent for the health of a democratic society.[9]

Commonly, however, opponents of public employee strikes go

too far and paint governments as helpless, pathetic entities. In reality, governments are hardly weak. Administrators often cannot give striking employees what they want, even if we grant the unlikely assumption that administrations ever want to do so. They face legislatures, taxpayers, other interest groups, opposing political factions or parties, and various constitutional or statutory boundaries, any and all of which may block convenient resolutions of government worker strikes at the citizenry's cost. Moreover, there are always pressures on strikers, such as lost wages and the possibility governments will dispense with public unions by subcontracting. These forces ordinarily militate against union intransigence and strengthen the hand of governments. By no means is the ordinary situation structured predominantly against governments.

On the other hand, there is a serious danger of becoming too sanguine about government worker strikes and democratic government. One is right to question how the checks and balances will actually work; no one knows at present. All we have is the mixed and partial evidence of case studies. Until the accelerating rate of public employee strikes provides us with enough data either way, however, worry about the anti-democratic possibilities of strike settlements remains legitimate, if unresolvable. In the future, it may become a potent argument against legalizing public employee strikes.

Long before a strike reaches settlement, of course, mandated public services cease to take place and damage to the public occurs. The question is, how much interference, for how long, and with what services, is tolerable? The problem concerns the proper boundary lines. Clearly any strike, or pattern of strikes, that renders impossible democratic government in any society or governmental unit would be unacceptable. But this is not the most likely threat. More probable are public strikes that endanger one or more services highly valued by the general political community. If strikes are to be legalized, one proposed solution has been the establishment of a test of "essentiality." Services "essential" to the democratic community could not be struck, but others could be.

This kind of solution will inevitably suffer from one major flaw. Like most proposed solutions to the public strike dilemma, it will be mechanistic. They often contain the implicit assumption that a law, a formula, or a procedure can be found which by some magic dynamic will dissolve the difficulties, but reality often is not nearly so cooperative. Strikes constantly originate in explosive grievances, which no law or procedure will be able to contain, direct, or end.

There are at least three other notable problems that need to be confronted in employing some standard of essentiality. First, who should decide on the necessity for ordering an end to a strike that intrudes into the realm of essentiality? Second, should the formula apply at all levels of government? And third, should it apply to workers in all types of government services?

Three basic proposals have been made to the first problem. One is that an appropriate executive officer should have the power to invoke a Taft-Hartley-style law to prevent a legal strike which interferes with an "essential" public service and, therefore, the democratic will. Another proposal is that an independent board of some sort should have this power, and a third proposal is that this decision should be a judicial function. The question here is whether there can be any fair arrangement when the executive has control, or whether power should be given to independent bodies or judges.

The second problem, the question of whether a distinction should be made among levels of government employees in considering who may strike, seems open to a more determinate resolution. This issue comes up when it is argued that federal employees are more essential than employees of local or state governments and, therefore, should never be allowed to strike, or not permitted to strike as long or as often. This is a weak argument, however, since many federal employees, such as Pentagon janitors, are far less important than local workers like policemen. Any attempt, therefore, to draw distinctions on the basis of the level of employment is doomed because the boundaries are not useful and ensure nearly endless confusion and anomalies.

The same confusion is likely to ensue if the solution to the third problem (what kinds of employees at any given level should be permitted to strike) is to try again to employ some principle of essentiality. Before the fact it is too hard to discern just how essential most government services are. One suspects that most are far less central than we sometimes let ourselves believe. Police, government hospital employees, and army personnel are highly important. Exactly how, though, does one proceed from there?

Should one place firemen in the special category? Given the widespread practice of volunteer fire companies, need we believe government firemen are essential? Beyond such reasonably controversial cases, lies the vast bulk of government workers, whether blue or white collar. Few of them can legitimately be considered "essential," at least without a practical test.

Rather than applying a theoretical test of essentiality before the fact, surely a better strategy would be to grant the right to all employees across the board and then to stop their strikes if the consequences prove deleterious to essential, mandated public service. Experience may demonstrate to us that some jobs are just too crucial ever to sustain strikes; but we should let experience teach us that, rather than give indiscriminate reign to any assumptions we may have. Under this "consequences test" we can predict that a strike by New York City police would be enjoined far sooner than one by the Oklahoma City public health nurses, but the aim would be to let practice determine empirically what is "essential."[10]

MERIT SYSTEM AND DECENT RELATIONS PRESERVED?

Apart from democratic and sovereignty considerations, there are two further serious objections to legalized public strikes which originate in concerns about the effects of strikes on the public service. Objections are raised that legalizing public worker strikes is incompatible with a merit system and will promote disastrous relations between administrators and their employees.

Proponents of the merit system worry that this dearly won mode of bureaucratic organization will be eliminated by hostile government employee unions. Specifically, their fear is that strike-armed unions may force replacement of open competition for jobs and promotion with union shops and advancement by seniority.

The possible danger here is real only if one accepts the assumptions of much of the literature which deifies the merit system above all else. But despite such a common assumption, it is not patently obvious that sacrifice of part of the merit system would be unacceptable. The value that is attached to the merit system by opponents of public worker strikes needs to be defended *before* anyone should be worried about the consequences of possible loss of some part of the system.

Even if one agrees that this system is worth preserving, its destruction by public worker unions using the legal strike remains to be empirically demonstrated. Speculation on this matter ought to be matched by evidence. Certainly at present there is too little data. The findings from Wisconsin's extensive experience with collective bargaining in the public realm suggest that the fear may be exaggerated, though its collective bargaining settlements were generally accomplished without work stoppages and always without legal strikes. Moreover, the famous New York City teacher's strike, which was partly a strike *for* the merit system, reminds us to be cautious before we assume that the merit system and powerful employee unions will inevitably involve incompatible goals. The suspicions, nonetheless, are understandable. Union shops and seniority advancement are time-honored trade union objectives. The question is whether strike-armed government unions will force their acceptance in the civil service. This remains to be seen in the possibly tumultuous years ahead.[11]

Also troublesome is the question of the possible effects of adversely altered relations in government service that may occur as a result of government unions being permitted to strike. Suspicions may increase, tensions become aggravated, and trust break down between officials and union employees. In a short time, job performance may become the victim, with obvious costs. This is no idle possibility, as anyone who has gone through a government worker strike knows. As I observed personally during the 1970 teaching assistant union work stoppage at the University of Wisconsin, relations between administrators, professors, teaching assistants, and students, deteriorated sharply. Nor did these results pass immediately with the end of the strike.

It may be a great error, however, to stress this potential cost, while ignoring the broader significance of the growing government worker turbulence. Surely the antiauthoritarian revolt of our times is manifesting itself in the union movement, too. The upheavals and dissatisfactions on the assembly line, most recently illuminated by the troubles at Lordstown, have now become common knowledge not only in corporate offices but in the popular press as well. Militant public employee actions, including strikes, are expressing this general trend. Organizational citizenship, like political citizenship, appears to face a precipitous decline. Increasingly, the issue may not be whether relations will be again as pleasant as they were before a public strike, so much as the question of the nature of the proper relationships among men and women in government employ in an era of change.[12]

CITIZENSHIP AND STRIKE RIGHT

Increasingly important in arguments over legalizing public employee strikes is the question of whether guaranteeing the right to strike is necessary to ensure government workers the full equality as citizens they demand increasingly in this anti-authoritarian era. Proponents of public strike legalization insist that full equality requires legalization.

From a normative viewpoint the great advantage gained from legalizing strike opportunities might be that government workers would be admitted at last to fuller membership in the political community. This right to strike exists in law for almost all legally unionized private workers, and is central to their public and private lives. How can it be denied public employees without making them second-class citizens? A part of the citizenry of our community seems to be singled out and forbidden full membership simply because they are public workers.[13]

Such second class citizenship has more than merely formal implications when organized group power counts for so much. Speaking broadly, the evidence is that public employees do tend to fall behind equivalent private employees in wages and other benefits. Yet as Professor Mathew Holden, Jr. suggests, it should be noted that argument at this level can ignore two considerations. First, public workers usually have far greater security in their jobs than do many privately employed union members. Is this security a fair trade-off for second class citizenship? In a democratic system, it is hard to see how such an arrangement is coincident with democratic equality. Perhaps more telling is the suggestion that some government employees already have enormous power in the political community and adding to their strength by allowing them the legal right to strike will not create equal citizenship, but a highly privileged elite. For example, one could ask whether the police are not already so licensed or empowered by society that they are hardly inferior to other citizens because they lack the legal right to strike. Nor will they become less powerful when they gain that right. Their arsenal of influence is sufficiently awesome at present.

This view makes sense for the police, but not for the vast bulk of public workers. Few public employees occupy jobs that involve the actual or potential power of the ordinary policeman. Most public employees have mundane jobs with little, if any, special influence. The army of secretaries, engineers, and clerks who constitute the civil service are not notably influential in their roles. The argument, therefore, generally remains one about equality and democracy. Proponents of legalizing employee strikes challenge American pluralism to admit government workers into the pluralist pie of wealth and power, a pie often celebrated but not so often shared.

Opponents suggest that citizens are at present equal in their formal political rights, whether they are public employees or not. Why should government workers fail to use the normal political means they share with other citizens to advance their status? This view does not recognize sufficiently the agreement reached about the insights of Robert Dahl and David Truman. In American pluralism formal political rights go only a limited way; power in pluralist democracy largely turns around the resources one's group can muster to work in the pluralist, political processes. In this situation government workers without the strike resource are at a great disadvantage. It is in this deeper sense that denying them the opportunity to strike truncates their democratic equality. The issue is not whether they should have a formal right others have; it is whether they should have the potent means of access to the pluralist pie that others have.

This does not mean that it is fair to ignore the most serious argument of opponents, the dangers potentially posed to the public will. The truth is that it is by no means certain that admitting government employees into American pluralism will enhance democracy as a whole. Yet to restrict the public employees' access to American pluralism because of broader doubts about the relationship between popular will and pluralism is to make public employees pay an unfair and unequal price. Of course there will remain a compelling need to reconcile potential conflicts between the objectives of citizen equality and possible damage to the public will. In practice this means that there must be limits to any legal right to strike for public employees. The Taft-Hartley-like proposal aims to accomplish this objective as much as is feasible.[14]

POLITICAL REALITY AND STRIKE RIGHT

Finally, there is a need to explore several pragmatic points in the debate over the legalization of government employee strikes. Is the cost in disrespect for law, shown in the rising number of illegal strikes, worth prohibition? Is the loss of an opportunity to direct and control strikes within a legal framework worth the prohibition? Is the cost of the obvious failure of forbidding strikes worth the prohibition?

First, one might argue that legalization is required in order to increase respect for law by avoiding the escalating hostility that striking unions manifest. As it stands this contention is unconvincing. By its logic one also ought to favor legalizing murder or robbery, since these laws, too, are often disobeyed. It is not clear, moreover, if in any given case legalization would promote greater respect for law. Legalization in the fact of widespread disrespect might only encourage more law violations, since it may seem that lawbreaking works. Evidence necessary to support or reject this argument in the case of government worker unions is missing.

Yet there is a point here, though it is more a point about representation than about law. If large numbers of people who are other-wise generally law-abiding begin to disobey a law, their intense views are not being represented. Perhaps the conclusion should be that in a democratic political system an adjustment in the law ought to be forthcoming. But even this response cannot be easily determined un-til an assessment is made of other groups or persons who may support the present law. They also desire and deserve representation in a democracy.

A better pragmatic argument for legalizing government em-ployee work stoppages may be that this could be a way of controlling social forces which otherwise will operate outside of ordinary legal discipline, direction, and inspection. Law can be the sanction which prevents pluralist forces from tearing society apart when harmony is disrupted. That is, legalizing public employee strikes may be an effec-tive mechanism for controlling a new pluralist force and for assisting it to enter the general community of competing and cooperating forces. A simple illustration of how this might work is the following: one of the problems with illegal government worker strikes is that they often occur sporadically in different bureaucracies, often with-out coordination, and they sometimes involve small and particularist-ic groups. Legalizing strikes might make possible the setting of condi-tions under which strikes could take place, including provision for large-unit strikes only. This might bring some order to the confusion of myriad public employee walkouts. Heavy penalties for striking will not work as a substitute; they have demonstrably failed. More and more strikes can be expected, since public unions contend that being militant and generating strikes is effective. Perhaps the best strategy is to legalize the strikes, so that one may endeavor to guide them.[15]

CONCLUSIONS AND RESERVATIONS

Thinking about public employee strikes and their possible legaliza-tion, and reviewing the evidence appropriate to them, obviously raises many issues. They are not simple, nor are they unambiguous. The conclusion of this article, however, is that the demands of prac-ticality as well as citizen equality lead to support for the legalization of the right to strike for public employees in principle. Yet two reser-vations remain. One is the generalized, but important, point that the issues, already difficult in themselves, are made more problematic by the limitations of evidence. A second is that substantial doubt must remain about the balance between the benefit for democratic equality *versus* the potential for spurning the public will implicit in permitting public worker strikes. The threat to democratic sentiments may turn out to be substantial. The use of a Taft-Hartley-style scheme to minimize the danger is a palliative which sounds attractive, but it remains untested and speculative.

It may well be that a nice balance between fears about a loss of democratic will and arguments for legalizing public work stoppages cannot, or will not, always be achieved in practice. This observation wisely reminds us that we should not assume that passing laws means achieving solutions; indeed, we must not believe that there is going to be any totally desirable solution in this matter of public policy.

My analysis and argument will satisfy neither the strongest advocates nor the most active opponents of legalizing these strikes. There must be some compromise if we have any serious intention of maximizing the often conflicting human values in politics. While it certainly entails grave risks, my proposal is meant as a compromise. Behind my entire argument lies an old-fashioned democratic faith, which believes granting fuller citizenship to public employees will improve our democratic community. Experience may prove it wrong, but we will not know until we try.

ENDNOTES

1. H. Conany and L. Dewey, "Union Membership Among Government Employees," *Monthly Labor Review* (July 1970); C. Stenberg, "Labor Management Relations in State and Local Government: Progress and Prospects," *Public Administration Review* (March/April 1972), pp. 102–107; R. Walsh, *Sorry—No Government Today: Unions vs. City Hall* (Boston: Beacon Press, 1969), ch. 4.
2. D. Ziskind, *One Thousand Strikes of Government Employees* (New York: Columbia University Press, 1940).
3. S. White, "Work Stoppages of Government Employees," *Monthly Labor Review* (December 1969), pp. 29–34.
4. R. Doherty and W. Oberer, *Teachers, School Boards, and Collective Bargaining: A Changing of the Guard* (Ithaca: Cayuga Press, 1967); A. Ross, "Public Employee Unions and the Right to Strike," *Monthly Labor Review* (1969), pp. 14–18; J. Finkelman, "When Bargaining Fails," in K. Warner, ed., *Collective Bargaining in the Public Service, Theory and Practice* (Chicago: Public Personnel Association, 1967); G. Nesvig, "The New Dimensions of the Strike Question," *Public Administration Review* (March/April 1968), pp. 126–132; J. Burton and C. Krider "The Role and Consequences of Strikes by Public Employees," and H. Wellington and R. Winter, Jr., "More on Strikes by Public Employees," *Yale Law Journal* (January 1970), pp. 418–43.

5. J. P. Goldberg, "Changing Policies in Public Employee Labor Relations," Monthly Labor Review (July 1970); M. Moskow, J. J. Loewenberg, and E. C. Koziara, Collective Bargaining in Public Employment (New York: Random House, 1970), p. 282; R. Murphy and M. Sackman, eds., Crisis of Public Employee Relations in the 70's (Washington: Bureau of National Affairs, 1970), pp. 188-193 and 201-211; H. S. Roberts, Labor-Management Relations in the Public Service (Honolulu: University of Hawaii Press, 1970), ch. 7.

6. R. Kelley, "Some Sensational Strikes in the Public Sector," in Murphy and Sackman, ed., Crisis of Public Employee Relations in the 70's, op. cit., ch. 7; M. Somerhausen, "The Right to Strike in the Public Service," in D. Kuger and C. Schmidt, eds., Collective Bargaining in the Public Service (New York: Random House, 1969), pp. 204-214; G. W. Taylor, "Public Employee Strikes, or Procedures," Trial and Labor Relations Review (67), pp. 617-636.

7. See T. Lowi, The End of Liberalism (New York: Norton, 1969); M. Godine, Labor Problem in the Public Service (Cambridge: Harvard University Press, 1951), chs. 3, 7 and 11.

8. K. Warner and M. Hennessy, Public Management at the Bargaining Table (Chicago: Public Personnel Association, 1967), ch. 5.

9. F. Nigro, "The Implication for Public Administration," Public Administration Review (March/April 1972), pp. 120-126; K. McLennan and M. Moskow, "Multilateral Bargaining in the Public Service," Monthly Labor Review (April 1969), pp. 58-60.

10. L. White, "Strikes in the Public Service," Public Personnel Review (January 1949); A. Weisenfeld, "The Philosophy of Bargaining" Arbitration Journal (1967) pp. 44-45.

11. P. Camp and W. Lomax, "Bilateralism and the Merit Principle," Public Administration Review (March/April 1968), pp. 132-137; F. Mosher, Democracy and the Public Service (New York: Oxford University Press, 1968), chs. 6-7.

12. Madison, Wisconsin Capitol Times, 11 April 1972; R. Denhardt, "Organizational Citizenship and Personal Freedom," Public Administration Review (January/February 1968), pp. 47-54.

13. See A. Weisenfeld, "Public Employees Are Still Second Class Citizens," Labor Law Journal (March 1969).

14. W. R. Hart, Collective Bargaining in the Federal Civil Service (New York: Harper, 1961), ch. 4.

15. T. R. Donahue, "The Future of Bargaining in the Federal Government," Monthly Labor Review (July 1969), pp. 67-69; E. W. Bakke, "Reflections on the Future of Bargaining in the Public Sector," Monthly Labor Review (July 1970), pp. 21-25.

21

philip l. martin

THE HATCH ACT IN COURT: SOME RECENT
DEVELOPMENTS

The quest for the political neutrality of nonelective civil servants has been a long-standing objective in American history reaching back as far as the colonial period.[1] Under the Constitution this policy was evidently first urged in 1801 when Thomas Jefferson admonished the handful of federal employees of that time to be nonpartisan in performing their work, but no serious congressional effort was made to establish a nonpolitical public service until after the assassination of President Garfield by a disappointed patronage seeker. This tragic event, of course, led to the passage of the Pendleton Act in 1883, but its principle of neutrality had to be more precisely defined by President Theodore Roosevelt. In 1907 he ordered that Civil Service Rule I, which prohibited involuntary acts such as assessed political contributions or coerced campaign work, be amended to provide that persons "in the competitive classified service, while retaining the right to vote as they please and to express privately their opinions on all political subjects, shall take no active part in political management or in political campaigns."

Applying this blanket prohibition to individual cases, the Civil Service Commission over the next 33 years rendered more than 3,000 decisions which became the precedents for answering requests for advice and for making future rulings.[2] However, Rule I only applied to the 69 per cent of federal employees who constituted the competi-

Reprinted from the *Public Administration Review,* journal of the American Society for Public Administration, Vol. 33, No. 5 (September–October, 1973). Reprinted by permission.

tive civil service. Therefore, in order to include most of the remaining 31 per cent the Hatch Political Activities Act was passed in 1939. One year later it was amended to incorporate all state and local employees working in federally funded programs, and in 1966 its restrictions were extended to the employees of private organizations who work with community action programs funded by the Economic Opportunity Act.

Although it has been expanded by Congress, there has been growing dissatisfaction with the Hatch Act during the past three decades. To begin with, uncertainty has developed in some quarters regarding the congressional intention in passing the original law. The traditional interpretation has been that a comprehensive statute was needed because during the rapid expansion of the federal government in the days of the New Deal, employees of relief agencies such as the Works Progress Administration were being used for political purposes.[3] After examining the debates and other records of the event, it has been concluded on the other hand that while Senator Hatch and the other framers of the act were concerned with protecting more federal employees, they also wanted to liberalize the restrictive policy evolved by the Civil Service Commission and to protect freedom of speech.[4] As a means of achieving these goals they intentionally wrote a broad, loosely worded statement in order to permit liberal interpretation.[5] Agreeing with the second viewpoint, it has thus been argued in Congress that the basic purpose of the law is not being implemented because contrary to expectations the vague language has been narrowly defined to produce even greater restrictions.[6]

A second source of encouragement to the opposition has been the vote of 4-3 by which the Supreme Court in 1947 barely upheld the Hatch proscriptions.[7] In addition, its decision does not rest upon a very firm constitutional foundation. A review of the *Mitchell* case clearly indicates that the justices were divided on the prevailing theory which classified government employment as a privilege not entitled to constitutional protection.[8] According to this distinction, Congress can stipulate for the federal service whatever conditions and policies are deemed necessary to protect the public interest, and the *Mitchell* majority would not abandon nor modify the privilege-right doctrine even though it admittedly deprived individuals of freedom of speech, the guarantee to peaceably assemble, and the right to petition their government. Opposing this view, the three dissenters not only criticized the denial of First Amendment rights but they also raised a counterargument which in essence holds that: "if government employees can be deprived of political participation because they might get involved in a corrupting or at least an unfair influence on public policy, then on the same grounds we logically could prohibit farmers, veterans, businessmen, doctors, union members, and others from engaging in political party activity since they clearly have a large and direct interest in government expenditures, regulations, subsidies, and the like."[9] Despite its logic, this judicial philosophy has not gained currency with very many opponents to the Hatch Act. Instead the opposition's argument has consistently been that government employees should not be deprived of their constitutional rights any more than other citizens who are concerned or involved with government operations and policies.

Since the *Mitchell* decision was made by a sharply divided and incomplete court, the protest against the Hatch Act has persisted, but until 1971 the federal judiciary refused to reopen the issue.[10] In that year the first significant break with precedent came in the case involving a Macon, Georgia, ordinance which barred firemen from "contributing any money to any candidate, soliciting votes, or prominently identifying themselves in a political race with or against any candidate for office." A federal circuit court ruled against this prohibition,[11] and a few months later a federal district court invalidated a Cranston, Rhode Island, statute barring its civil servants from running for elective office while in municipal employment.[12] In both cases it was concluded that *Mitchell* is no longer a valid precedent because in later cases involving freedom of speech the Supreme Court has sought to better protect this right by requiring more tightly defined restrictions than the ones contained in the two local laws against political activity.

Applying this line of reasoning, on July 31, 1972, a three-judge federal court, while excluding the state and local amendments on a technicality, declared the federal provisions of the Hatch Act to be unconstitutional.[13] This was not, however, an unqualified decision against the future enactment of political proscriptions. To the contrary, the court admitted that there is "an obvious, well-established governmental interest" in placing such limitations on its employees, but it was stipulated that "If there are impermissible areas of activity, the overriding government interest must be marked with utmost clarity by the Congress in a form that is obvious to the sophisticated and unsophisticated alike." According to this ruling, only clear definitions will preclude the ridiculous interpretations of the past which have punished federal employees for disparaging the President in private conversation,[14] failing to discourage the political activities of a spouse,[15] and criticizing the treatment of veterans in a closed meeting of the American Legion.[16] These examples were among several the court selected from the case history of enforcement by the Civil Service Commission.

The *Mitchell* precedent was not only set aside for being inconsistent with later rulings involving freedom of speech, but the special court also states that the shift in judicial doctrine "coupled with changes in size and complexity of public service, place *Mitchell* among other decisions outmoded by the passage of time." That the court should be influenced by size is understandable, because the federal work force has increased from 953,891 in 1939 to approximately 2.7 million employees in 1972.

Since there are heavy concentrations of these workers in certain areas, the effect of political prohibitions on local and state politics has been noticeable as in the case of the Washington, D.C., metropolitan region, the home of 291,000 federal and 40,000 District of Columbia employees. Compounding the problem is the fact that the Hatch Act has also been applied to partisan activities by members of a worker's family, thereby neutralizing even more than the aforementioned 331,000 civil servants.

Under these circumstances, it was inevitable that some effort would be made to get around the restrictions. Therefore, in recent years special nonpartisan parties for federal employees have been formed, and these organizations have affected local elections particularly in Arlington County, Virginia, and Montgomery County, Maryland.[17] Similar developments have not been reported at the state level, but using only the 17,000 federal workers employed in Alaska, Representative Begich calculated that 21 per cent of its voting population is forbidden to engage in political activities.[18] Concern with such repressive effects was undoubtedly an imposing factor in the court's decision, and the tenor of its ruling suggests that even if the Supreme Court again approves the present law, it must be revised in order to obviate endless conflict and litigation arising from attempts at circumvention.

SUPREME COURT RULING

On June 25, 1973, the Supreme Court by a vote of 6 to 3 overturned the lower court's decision,[19] and in a companion case Oklahoma's "Little Hatch Act" was upheld.[20] Rejecting the argument that the ban on political activities was "outmoded by the passage of time" and encouraged civil servants to follow the motto, "Don't stick your neck out," the Supreme Court said that such restrictions are necessary if job security and advancement are to depend on meritorious perform- ance instead of political involvement. As for the lack of clear stan- dards, it was pointed out that Congress in passing the Hatch Act intentionally incorporated the over 3,000 precedents[21] in order to deprive the Civil Service Commission of rule-making power in con- nection with political activity.

In sustaining the constitutionality of the political prohibitions of the Hatch Act, the Supreme Court emphasized that there was no violation of individual rights. On this score it was stated that:

> The restrictions so far imposed on federal employees are not aimed at particular groups or points of view, but apply equally to all partisan activities. . . . They discriminate against no racial, ethnic or religious minorities nor do they seek to control politi- cal opinions or beliefs.[22]

Judging by this statement, it seems clear that unless there is some invidious discrimination being practiced, a legislature's power to im- pose restrictions on the political activities of its employees will not be questioned by the judiciary. Therefore, the fairness and impartiality of a "Hatch Act" is evidently more important than the infringement upon individual rights which can result from government employ- ment.

The latest Supreme Court decision is not only out-of-step with its other rulings concerning freedom of speech, but it is not in tune with contemporary developments in public administration. The three-judge court was more accurate with its reference to the changes in size and complexity which have taken place in recent years. While the reference to size has been made clear, it is less obvious what was meant by complexity. Perhaps the court was think- ing in terms of the expanded relationships between federal and state and local governments which have led to extensions of the Hatch Act.

However, there is another aspect to consider, because the court conceivably was referring to Paul Appleby's thesis that administration is an integral and probably the most important part of the political process.[23] On this score, Norton Long has attacked the once sacred policy-administration dichotomy by pointing out that "However at- tractive an administration receiving its values from political policy- makers may be, it has one fatal flaw. It does not accord with the facts of administrative life."[24]

Following these leads, other writers have focused increasing attention on the interrelationship of administration and politics,[25] and unquestionably, public administrators over the last 40 years have become more active in policy making. Much of this greater participation has developed because, after the *Schechter Case* of 1935, the Supreme Court has gradually relaxed its enforcement of the nondelegation doctrine.[26] In fact it has become a mere facade behind which Congress vests more discretionary authority in top-level administrators. Career employees can thus become involved in the political implications of policy making, and they may frequently negotiate with the political branches of the government for support of agency programs.[27] Yet, since these activities of a political nature generally take place in the upper echelons, it is unreasonable on these grounds to apply the Hatch Act to all levels of government employment, but where should the line be drawn?

Assessing its effect 12 years after the law was passed, a former staff officer of the Civil Service Commission, Milton Esman, asserted that the doctrine of political neutrality had been insufficiently debated in this country. He contended that proponents believe it necessary to treat everyone equally, inasmuch as it is administratively impossible to distinguish among categories of employees because "the spoils system may crop up just as virulently among industrial as among administrative and clerical employees."[28] On the other hand, the opponents were accused of being "too busy attacking the principle of political neutrality to draw fine distinctions." In Esman's opinion, the Hatch prohibitions should only apply to white- and not to blue-collar workers. Today, in view of the growth in government employment and of the increase in what should be classified as political responsibility for ranking career administrators, it would seem that a more valid distinction for enforcing political prohibitions should also be drawn between upper and lower GS-grades.

REFORM NEEDED

No matter for which groups, if any, it might be decided to permit voluntary political activity, some reform of the Hatch Act is needed. The current provisions no longer seem enforceable, nor do they command compliance. For example, after the law was declared unconstitutional, the American Postal Workers Union endorsed Senator George McGovern for President.[29] This action was taken with a full awareness that the judicial panel had stayed its decision until the

Supreme Court could review the case. This fact seems to have mattered very little to the union, which was intent upon exercising what it regards as an inviolable constitutional right.

Other instances of noncompliance will probably occur, because there has been a rapid increase in public unions which have become more active and more militant in demanding rights such as collective bargaining and the strike. In municipal government, sanitation workers and school teachers have struck for better salaries and working conditions. At the national level the postal workers conducted a successful strike. In short, the days of breaking the Boston police strike are over, despite the ill-fated air controllers' effort of 1970 against the Federal Aviation Agency. An important reason for this change is that public opinion is not as adverse to public unionism and striking as it was a few decades ago. Likewise, attitudes toward political participation by civil servants appears to be changing as part of the trend which has motivated recent movements such as, for example, those to eliminate racial and sex discrimination.

What are the chances for reform? Several measures are currently being considered, but not much enthusiasm has been generated among congressmen. Over the years a number of alternatives to the Hatch Act have been desultorily debated, but no one has seemed sure of what kind of reform, if any, is needed or is possible. The problem concerning revision is illustrated by the experience of the Commission on Political Activity of Government Personnel, which was created in 1966 to make a full review of the restrictions against political participation.[30] Among other things, its report recommended giving more latitude in voluntary political activity such as holding any local office whose duties are not full-time, but the Commission weakened its case by being unable to delineate between nonpartisan and partisan local government activity.

Not only has Congress found resolution of this kind of question difficult, but in addition the out party is always suspicious that any extension of political rights to the bureaucracy will strengthen the party in power. Opening the door only slightly, it is feared, will lead to political manipulation in the public service. Therefore, Congress has found it easier to agree on extending prohibitions to more government employees, but Congress will probably not be able to ignore the issue much longer because protests against the overly broad provisions of the Political Activities Act will likely continue. After being rebuked by the Supreme Court, government workers and particularly their unions will now have to apply pressure for legislative reform, if there is to be any liberalization of the law.

ENDNOTES

1. For a history of political restrictions on public officeholders in the United States, see H. Eliot Kaplan, "Political Neutrality of the Civil Service," *Public Personnel Review*, Vol. 1 (1940), pp. 10–23.
2. The impact of these decisions is analyzed by Henry Rose, "A Critical Look at the Hatch Act," *Harvard Law Review*, Vol. 75 (1962), pp. 510–526.
3. See John W. Macy, Jr., *Public Service* (New York, Harper and Row, 1971), pp. 159–160.
4. See Dalmas H. Nelson, "Political Expressions Under the Hatch Act and the Problem of Statutory Ambiguity," *Midwest Journal of Political Science*, Vol. 2 (1958), pp. 77–78.
5. *Ibid.*
6. See *Congressional Record*, 92d Congress, 2d Session, (daily edition, March 9, 1972), p. E2297; and *ibid.*, (daily edition, March 28, 1972), p. H2667.
7. *United Public Workers of America* (CIO) *v. Mitchell*, 330 U.S. 75 (1947).
8. See Arch Dotson, "The Emerging Doctrine of Privilege in Public Employment," *Public Administration Review*, Vol. 15 (1955), pp. 78–79.
9. O. Glenn Stahl, *Public Personnel Administration*, (New York: Harper and Row, 1962, fifth edition), p. 363.
10. *Hobbs v. Thompson*, 448 F. 2d 456 (1971).
11. *Mancuso v. Taft*, 341 F. Supp. 574 (1972).
12. *National Association of Letter Carriers v. U.S.*, 346 F. Supp. 578 (1972).
13. United States Civil Service Commission Political Activity Reporter, Vol. 1, 1971, Index #24, Dunham 32 AR144.
14. *Ibid.* Index #17, Brock, 1935 Min. 209.
15. *Ibid.*, Index #25, Davis, 1935 Min. 154.
16. See *Washington Post*, August 1, 1971, pp. A1 and A16.
17. *Congressional Record*, 92d Congress, 2d Session, (daily edition, March 28, 1972), p. H2667.
18. cf. Paul Appleby, *Policy and Administration* (University, Ala: University of Alabama Press, 1949).
19. *U.S. Civil Service Commission v. Letters Carriers*, U.S. (1973).
20. *Broadrick v. Oklahoma State Personnel Board*, U.S. (1973).
21. *Supra*, note 2.
22. *U.S. Civil Service Commission v. Letters Carriers*, *op cit.*
23. Paul Appleby, *Policy and Administration* (University, Ala.: University of Alabama Press, 1949).
24. Norton E. Long, "Public Policy and Administration: The Goals of Rationality and Responsibility," *Public Administration Review*, Vol. 14 (1954), p. 23.
25. See Lewis C. Mainzer, *Political Bureaucracy* (Glenview, Ill.: Scott, Foresman and Co., 1973), and his excellent bibliographical essay on administration and politics, pp. 166–176.
26. Kenneth C. Davis, "A New Approach to Delegation," *Chicago Law Review*, Vol. 36 (1969), pp. 713–714.

27. See J. Leiper Freeman, *The Political Process: Executive Bureau-Legislative Committee Relations* (New York: Random House, 1965, revised edition), and Francis E. Rourke, *Bureaucracy, Politics, and Public Policy* (Boston: Little, Brown and Co., 1969).

28. Milton J. Esman, "The Hatch Act: A Reappraisal," *Yale Law Journal*, Vol. 60 (1951), p. 997.

29. See *Washington Post*, August 17, 1972, p. A6.

30. For an analysis of the Commission's work, see Charles O. Jones, "Re-evaluating the Hatch Act: A Report on the Commission on Political Activity of Government Personnel," *Public Administration Review*, Vol. 29 (1969), pp. 249–254.

22

bob l. wynia

FEDERAL BUREAUCRATS' ATTITUDES
TOWARD A DEMOCRATIC IDEALOGY

In 1964 a prominent political scientist, Dr. Herbert McClosky, published a study on consensus and ideology in American politics.[1] His
study, which focused on popular and elite consensus surrounding
American democratic ideology, demonstrated that considerable variation exists around the values held by two large segments of the
American populace, the "general electorate" and the "political influentials." This intriguing analysis raised a number of legitimate questions which called for further research. This article reports on research that serves as an expansion of the McClosky study in some
respects, but is original in other respects. We chose to apply certain
of the McClosky postulates and apply them to a very unresearched
segment of a "democratic" society, the career bureaucracy. Of principal concern was the attitude bureaucrats or national planners hold
toward certain democratic ideals and principles. Also, what effect, if
any, do the agency affiliations, education levels, and years in the
public service have on their attitudes?

OVERVIEW OF THE FEDERAL BUREAUCRACY

Although often recognized as a "fourth branch" of government, the
federal career bureaucracy and the career bureaucrat in particular is

Reprinted from the *Public Administration Review,* journal of the American Society for Public Administration, Vol. 34, No. 2 (March-April, 1974).
Reprinted by permission.

undoubtly one of the least studied phenomena of present-day American government. The federal bureaucracy is a huge, complex mechanism comprising thousands of government agencies with over three million employees. Many of the most serious decisions which need to be made each day are directly related to policy interpretations arrived at by the career bureaucrat,° protected by the Civil Service system and not elected by the public. What ideological views do these federal executives hold? Is there a common ideology among them? What democratic principles do they espouse? What level of faith do they have in the democratic process? How committed are they to democratic values?

One noted author makes the following premises about public service executives:

1. Governmental decisions and behavior have tremendous influence upon the nature and development of our society, our economy, and our policy;

2. The great bulk of decisions and actions taken by governments are determined or heavily influenced by administrative officials, most of whom are appointed, not elected;

3. The kinds of decisions and actions these officials take depend upon their capabilities, their orientations, and their values; and

4. These attributes depend heavily upon their backgrounds, their training and education, and their current associations.[2]

He went on to make the point that:

> Many political scientists prefer to deal with the concepts and ideas of old thinkers, of whom few were concerned with administration; or with items they can count—citizen votes, legislative votes, or attitudes as measured through surveys. They have given rather little attention to administration and administrators as a significant element in government.[3]

The premise stated by Mosher and the further elaboration that little attention is paid to people who administer and plan government programs seem clear enough. A basic and accepted principle of democratic rule is that *elected* officials set policy which guides the nation, state, city, or school district. Often overlooked is that fact that much of the policy power of a democracy lies not in the hands of those elected officials, but rather is two steps removed from them (some of this power being drained off by political executives) in the personnel who are neither elected nor politically appointed and are protected from removal on political grounds—the career civil service. Mosher says:

> They influence—or make—decisions of great significance for the people, though within an environment of constraints, controls, and pressures which itself varies widely from one jurisdiction to another, from one field or subject to another, and from one time to another.[4]

A most critical need is to recognize to what extent policy decisions are made at the level of the career civil servant, what is policy and what is program (if indeed they are separable), and (the subject of this article) what the attitudes of the individual public executive are. If career executives are important in decision making, then certainly their attitudes are of importance to us. While long advocated (and made law by the Hatch Act) that career people should have no close political relationships, this policy has not recognized the fact that all people hold certain philosophical principles or attitudes which affect their actions. It is to these "principles" or "attitudes" we are addressing ourselves. Like Mosher we found little definitive research and only slightly more subjective reporting aimed at attitudes of public service officials.

No studies we are aware of have dealt with such important areas as attitudes or behavioral characteristics of top level federal civil servants. Warner describes in detail the social, economic, and educational backgrounds of federal executives and their families.[5] Stanley appraises various features of a personnel system for the higher civil service and considers the attractiveness of federal careers through the eyes of present and former federal employees.[6] Kilpatrick was concerned with the image of federal service as held by employees themselves, the business community, college and high school groups, and the public generally.[7]

Thus we may be able to accurately describe a "typical" executive's physical and historical characteristics almost down to hair and eye color, yet we are unable to compile comprehensive data (let alone cite exploratory research) on such gross characteristics as political party or organization affiliations.

For brevity and because the "research" that has been done is only tangentially related to our concern here, we will not review it in any more detail.[8]

For this research, 42 of the attitude scale items were selected from McClosky's research on the basis of those most likely to fit a Guttmann scale. These 42 items fit into six subscales:

1. "Rules of the game," with emphasis on fair play, respect for legal procedures, and consideration for the rights of others;

2. "Support for general statements of free speech and opinion";

3. "Support for specific applications of free speech and procedural rights";

4. "Belief in equality"—broken down into political, social and ethnic, and economic equality;

5. "Political cynicism"—defined as a feeling that the system will not govern justly and for the common good;

6. "Sense of political futility"—defined as a feeling that one cannot reach an influenced system.

Agree-disagree statements covering the six subscales were administered to 405 federal executives representing 52 different federal agencies and all geographic areas of the country. From observation and past research studies we hypothesized that: (1) The career bureaucrat would demonstrate little consensus on democratic principles: (2) The bureaucrat who had worked primarily in a "social agency" would demonstrate a higher degree of agreement on statements relating to a positive attitude toward specific democratic privileges than executives from the other types of agencies ("defense related" and "others"); and (3) Variables, years in the federal service, employing agency, and years of education would affect attitudes on all of the value scales, with significant changes over time.

Standard cross tabulations were run, as was a Guttmann scale. While only one set of items scaled out above .90, this was anticipated since McClosky reported he too had utilized a "modified Guttmann." This is an indication that items within the sets are not amenable to traditional scaling methods but must be looked at in a quasi-scaling manner or in undimensional terms. We resorted strictly to a raw percentage comparison and suggest that more research needs to be done on scaling procedures for this type research.

ANALYSIS AND DISCUSSION

We have focused our analysis on those scales and items where the largest percentages of difference occur. Most of the percentages range from 20–30 per cent agreement. This seems exceedingly significant when one projects these figures over three million federal bureaucrats. While the overall data lend support to the fact that there is extensive agreement with the democratic philosophy within the bureaucracy, there are many areas of grave and undisputed disagreement on specific applications of democratic principles. These are highlighted.

The items in Table 1 when viewed as pertaining to specific applications of the democratic ideology, illustrate the percentage of

TABLE I

Item	Percentage of Bureaucrats Who Agree with Item
There are times when it almost seems better for the people to take the law into their own hands rather than wait for the machinery of government to act.	31.9
We might as well make up our minds that in order to make the world free a lot of innocent people will have to suffer.	31.0
We have to teach children that all men are created equal but almost everyone knows that some are better than others.	37.5

TABLE II

Item	Percentage of Bureaucrats Who Agree with Item
There are times when it almost seems better for the people to take the law into their own hands rather than wait for the machinery of government to act.	31.9
We might as well make up our minds that in order to make the world free a lot of innocent people will have to suffer.	31.0
If congressional committees stuck strictly to the rules and gave every witness his rights, they would never succeed in exposing the many dangerous subversives they have turned up.	28.0
To bring about great changes for the benefit of mankind often requires cruelty and even ruthlessness.	27.0
The true American way of life is disappearing so fast that we may have to use force to save it.	18.6

bureaucrats who agree with democracy in the abstract. The table also points out to the same time that a significant number of bureaucrats (over one-third) do not hold to certain constitutional guarantees.

Over one-fourth of the bureaucrats (28.3 per cent) agreed with all the statements on the 42-item instrument. Since a large number of the items express authoritarian assumptions which oppose many democratic ideals, they were analyzed individually.

For example 24.6 per cent of all bureaucrats agreed that "when the country is in great danger we may have to force people to testify against themselves even if it violated their rights."

A most noticeable and consistent attitude appears in items which advocate or at least accept the use of force, for whatever purpose. There is considerable acceptance of people "taking the law into their own hands," innocent people having to suffer congressional committees breaking rules to explore "dangerous subversives," the use of "cruelty and even ruthlessness" in order to bring about changes for the "benefit of mankind," and using force to save the "American way of life."

Free speech in the abstract is an area where considerable agreement is apparent when analyzing gross percentages for the total subscale. As a basic freedom, bureaucrats want free speech protected; however Table III illustrates how in specific situations some will agree to suspend this basic constitutional right and guarantee.

Once the variables, agency, education, and years in the public service become part of the analysis, a different picture of bureaucrat attitudes emerge. Data collection relating to these variables utilized the following definitions:

1. Social agencies, including the Departments of Health, Education, and Welfare; Labor; Housing and Urban Development; and the Office of Economic Opportunity

TABLE III

Item	Percentage of Bureaucrats Who Agree with Item
A person who hides behind the laws when he is questioned about his actions doesn't deserve much consideration.	24.8
When the country is in great danger, we may have to force people to testify against themselves even if it violates their rights.	24.6

2. Defense-related agencies including all Department of Defense agencies and bureaus; and

3. "Other," including all other departments and independent agencies of the federal government.

Years of education was broken down into three specific groups: high school diploma or below, bachelor's degree, and above the bachelor's degree level.

Years in the public service was divided into four levels: 5 years or less, 6 through 15 years, 16 through 25 years, and people with over 26 years in the public service.

On all items defense agency executives agreed more often than the other two groups. Within each of the tables there are some notable differences in the levels of agreement. It is quite obvious that either defense agencies tend to draw more "anti-democratic" types of individuals to work there, or that attitudes are altered over time. Indeed, there is good evidence in our data to substantiate this change over time theory (see Table IV).

There has been considerable speculation in the literature that time in the bureaucracy is a telling factor in attitude change. Our data seems to suggest the notion that years in the service when linked with years of education and agency type is a critical variable in attitude determination and change. The more years in the federal service, the lower the acceptance of democratic ideals. The more education, the more openness to a democratic philosophy. The less "social" oriented the agency, the more "anti-democratic" the attitude.

Throughout the scale figures, social agency bureaucrats consistently agree less with the items than either defense or other agency bureaucrats. We assume that either the type of person who is drawn to employment in a social agency or the "environment" of that agency plays some important role in determining the attitude of the individual executive. Table V demonstrates the rather divergent view of the "rules of the game" aspect of democratic ideology. These items refer to consideration for the rights of others, respect for legal processes, and general fair play.

On specific items we note that defense agency executives are more inclined toward the use of force, approving the use of any methods to "get the right things done"; are willing to justify unfairness or brutality in order to carry out some "great purpose"; and even accept "cruelty and ruthlessness" in order to bring about great changes for the benefit of mankind.

TABLE IV

Item	Average	Agency			Years of Education			Years in Service			
		Social	Dept. of Defense	Other	0-12	13-15	16+	1-5	6-15	16-25	26+
When the country is in great danger, we may have to force people to testify against themselves even if it violates their rights.	24.6	25.3	30.9	20.4	25.6	26.3	22.5	15.2	23.3	24.6	28.8
Any person who hides behind the laws when he is questioned about his activities doesn't deserve much consideration.	24.8	19.0	29.3	24.4	41.0	26.6	19.1	12.1	16.5	24.6	37.5

Percentage of Agrees

TABLE V

Rules of the Game Scale	
Agency	Average Percentage Agree
Social	21.7
Defense	36.6
Other	24.6

Perhaps the most definitive attitudinal responses are apparent when analyzing a specific item within the scale. One gets a much clearer picture of attitudes both within the bureaucracy as a whole as well as across the boundaries of the variables. Thus, in an item dealing with exposing dangerous subversives, the contrast between social agency executives and defense agency executives takes on added significance when considering the more than two-to-one ratio of difference.

As was pointed out earlier, when we turn to the influence years of schooling tends to play in dveloping or altering bureaucratic atti-

TABLE VI

	Percentage of Agreement	
Item	Social Agencies	Defense Agencies
Almost any unfairness or brutality may have to be justified when some great purpose is being carried out.	19.3	22.0
To bring great changes for the benefit of mankind often requires cruelty and even ruthlessness.	25.0	33.3
The true American way of life is disappearing so fast that we may have to use force to save it.	9.5	29.3

TABLE VII

	Percentage of Agreement	
Item	Social Agencies	Defense Agencies
If congressional committees stuck strictly to the rules and gave every witness his rights, they would never succeed in exposing the many dangerous subversives they have turned up.	17.9	38.5

tudes, we note that the less education the more "antidemocratic" the attitude. The effect of these negative attitudes toward basic human rights, minority peoples, and the American political system on the decision-making process seem obvious. From data in our research it is clear that these attitudes are considerably different depending on how many years he attended school. Table VIII illustrates this phenomenon.

TABLE VIII

Item	Percentage of Agreement		
	Years of Education		
	0-12	*13-15*	*16+*
We might as well make up our minds that in order to make the world better a lot of innocent people will have to suffer.	38.5	33.9	26.2
If congressional committees stuck strictly to the rules and gave every witness his rights, they would never succeed in exposing the many dangerous subversives they have turned up.	48.7	31.9	19.1
I don't mind a politician's methods if he manages to get the right things done.	20.5	15.7	11.0
Almost any unfairness or brutality may have to be justified when some great purpose is being carried out.	20.5	22.4	11.6
The true American way of life is disappearing so fast that we may have to use force to save it.	28.2	20.4	14.5
Any person who hides behind the laws when he is questioned about his activities doesn't deserve much credit or consideration.	41.0	26.6	19.1
Every person should have a good house, even if the government has to build it for him.	10.3	28.8	32.4

The effect of years of education is equally apparent on the final item in Table VIII which calls for a reverse in the agree-disagree pattern to demonstrate democratic values.

Bureaucratic attitudes toward equality of people indicate a rather divergent spread. Defense agency executives, for whatever reasons, consistently demonstrate attitudes of an anti-democratic nature, whenever the issue of racial or social equality are raised. Table IX supports our contention that a large percentage of defense agency executives fail to support basic protections and social guarantees of a democratic system.

TABLE IX

Item	Percentage of Agreement		
	Social	Agency Dept. of Defense	Other
We have to teach children that all men are created equal, but almost everyone knows that some are better than others.	34.6	43.9	34.7
Just as is true of fine race horses, some breeds of people are just naturally better than others.	19.5	28.5	17.3
Regardless of what some people say, there are certain races in the world that just won't mix with Americans.	13.3	26.0	13.8
The trouble with letting certain minority groups into a nice neighborhood is that they gradually give it their own atmosphere.	20.2	27.9	20.3

DISCUSSION

Several observations can be offered by way of summarizing and commenting upon the data. Earlier we discussed the critical role played by career executives in the policy-setting—decision-making process in our constitutional form of government. If we accept the earlier premise that career bureaucrats are vital components of this decision-making process, then clearly additional and extensive research is called for in order to attempt a clarification of some our data. Do nonegalitarian attitudes affect the decision-making process, and how? Would higher-grade (GS 16, 17, 18) executives follow this same pattern? Are the variables interdependent, and if so to what degree?

Perhaps the most perplexing aspect of this inquiry is the social agency-defense agency differences. Both groups seem to indicate a molding of attitudes to fit the particular agency affiliation. The democratic principles and beliefs seem to be learned over time. Within the bureaucracy, it seems safe to suggest that, depending on the agency, these principles will be reinforced, thwarted, supported, or squelched. Our findings certainly support the long-espoused need to have a system for moving federal executives regularly across agency lines, providing for a variety of experiences and environments—thus allowing for the development of a more balanced set of attitudes.

Finally, to what degree is consensus on democratic principles really necessary? Can a "democratic system" stay democratic when a

high percentage of its bureaucrats disagree with many of its fundamentals? Obviously consensus on fundamental principles among this
most influential group is unnecessary if we are willing to accept the
manner in which our present system operates. If on the other hand, as
our evidence suggests, changes in attitude are desirable in order to
provide a *more* "democratic" system, then we anticipate broad acceptance of these findings. Evidence suggests that the active, involved, and articulate classes rather than the public at large are the
ones who serve as the major carriers of the democratic ideology; thus
responsibility for keeping the system going depends heavily on them.
We would certainly include federal career executives in this class.
Yet it is apparent that a large number of them hold attitudes alien to
democratic ideals. One senses that, like most Americans today, federal bureaucrats show little interest in political ideas[9] because they
are more concerned with personal affairs. Yet doesn't this lack of
interest, lack of knowledge of fundamental rights, lack of understanding of basic constitutional guarantees stand out as evidence that many
bureaucrats covertly feel our form of "democracy" by bureaucracy is
failing? The effect of these attitudes, alien to the democratic ideology,
is untested but worthy of much speculation and study.

ENDNOTES

1. Herbert McClosky, "Consensus and Ideology in American Politics," *The
   American Political Science Review*, Vol. 58, No. 2 (June 1964), p. 361.
2. Frederick Mosher, *Democracy and the Public Service* (New York: Oxford
   Press, 1968), p. 1.
3. *Ibid.*, p. 2.
4. *Ibid.*, p. 3.
5. W. L. Warener, *et al., The American Executive* (New Haven: Yale University Press, 1963).
6. David T. Stanley, *The Higher Civil Service* (Washington, D.C.: The
   Brookings Institution, 1964).
7. Cummings Kilpatrick, *et al., The Image of the Federal Service* (Washington, D.C.: The Brookings Institution, 1964).
8. John Macy, "Executive Preparation for Continuing Change," address,
   October 13, 1968, Washington, D.C.; Robert Sherrill, "Rebels on the
   Potomac," *Nation*, February 27, 1967, p. 239; Fritz Marx, "The Mind of
   the Career Man," *Public Administration Review* (Summer 1960), and
   "The Conditions of the Federal Employee and How to Change It,"
   Public Administration Review (July/August 1969), pp. 435–440; David
   Hapgood, "The Right to Speak Out from Within," *Washington Monthly*
   (September 1969), p. 53; Frank Sherwood, unpublished speech to Ex-
   ecutive Seminar Center, 1970; Anders Richter, "The Existentialist Ex-

ecutive," *Public Administration Review* (July/August 1970), p. 415; Samuel Stouffer, *Communism, Conformity and Civil Liberties* (New York: Columbia Press, 1955); Protho and Grigg, "Fundamental Principles of Democracy: Basis of Agreement and Disagreement," *Journal of Politics,* Vol. 22 (1960), p. 276; V. O. Key, "Public Opinion and the Decay of Democracy," *The Virginia Quarterly Review* Vol. 37, No. 4 (Autumn 1961), p. 431; and McClosky, *op. cit.,* p. 376.
9. V. O. Key, *op. cit.,* p. 432.

*The terms career bureaucrat, federal executive, and public service official are used interchangeably throughout this article. All refer to executives of the federal government above the GS 12 level who are protected by Civil Service laws and regulations. This study focuses primarily on the GS 13, 14, and 15.

FURTHER READINGS

American Psychological Association. "Job Testing and the Disadvantaged." *American Psychologist.* vol. 24, no. 7 (July 1969).

BELL, DANIEL. "On Meritocracy and Equality." *Public Interest.* no. 29 (Fall, 1972), 29–68.

BERNSTEIN, MARVER H. *The Job of the Federal Executive.* Washington, D.C.: The Brookings Institution, 1958.

"Collective Bargaining for Public Employees and the Prevention of Strikes in the Public Sector." *Michigan Law Review.* vol. 68, no. 2 (December 1969), 260–302.

CONNERY, ROBERT H., and WILLIAM V. FARR. eds. *Unionization of Municipal Employees.* Proceedings. The Academy of Political Science, Columbia University, New York, vol. 30, no. 2, 1970.

CORSON, JOHN J. "Equipping Men for Career Growth in the Public Service." *Public Administration Review,* vol. 23 (March 1963), pp. 1–9.

CORSON, JOHN J. and R. SHALE PAUL. *Men Near the Top: Filling Key Posts in Federal Service.* Committee for Economic Development. Baltimore: The Johns Hopkins Press, 1966.

COUTURIER, JEAN J. "Crisis Conflict and Change: The Future of Collective Bargaining in Public Service." *Good Government.* vol. 86, no. 1 (Spring, 1969), pp. 7–11.

DEAN, SIR MAURICE. "Accountable Management in the Civil Service." *Public Administration* (London), vol. 47 (Spring 1969), pp. 49–64.

DONOVAN, J. J. *Recruitment and Selection in the Public Service.* Chicago: Public Personnel Association, 1968.

FEIGENBAUM, CHARLES. "Civil Service and Collective Bargaining: Conflict or Compatibility." *Public Personnel Management,* 3:3 (May-June, 1974), 244–252.

GOLEMBIEWSKI, ROBERT T.; and COHEN, MICHAEL. eds. *People in Public Service: A Reader in Public Personnel Administration.* Itasca, Ill.: Peacock, 1970.

GROSSMAN, HARRY. "The Equal Employment Opportunity Act of 1972, Its Implications for the State and Local Government Manager." *Public Personnel Management,* vol. 2, no. 5 (Sept.-Oct., 1973), 370–379.

HELLRIEGEL, DON and LARRY SHORT. "Equal Employment Opportunity in the Federal Government: A Comparative Analysis." *Public Administration Review,* vol. 32, no. 6 (Nov.-Dec., 1972), 851–858.

KATOR, IRVING. "The Federal Merit System and Equal Employment Opportunity." *Good Government.* vol. 89, no. 1 (Spring 1972).

KAUFMAN, HERBERT. *Administrative Feedback: Monitoring Subordinates' Behavior.* Washington, D.C.: The Brookings Institution, 1973.

KIETA, JOSEPH. "The Strike and Its Alternatives in Public Employment." *Public Personnel Review.* vol. 31, no. 4 (Oct., 1970), 226–230.

KILPATRICK, FRANKLIN P., M. C. CUMMINGS, and M. K. JENNINGS. *The Image of the Federal Service.* Washington, D.C.: The Brookings Institution, 1964.

KRISLOV, SAMUEL. *The Negro in Federal Employment: The Quest for Equal Opportunity.* Minneapolis: University of Minnesota Press, 1967.

KRUGER, DANIEL H., and CHARLES T. SCHMIDT, Jr. eds. *Collective Bargaining in the Public Service.* New York: Random House, 1969.

LOEWENBERG, J. JOSEPH, and MICHAEL H. MOSKOW. eds. *Collective Bargaining in Government.* Readings and Cases, Englewood Cliffs, N.J.: Prentice-Hall, Inc. 1972.

MARTIN, PHILIP L. "The Hatch Act: The Current Movement for Reform." *Public Personnel Management.* 3:3 (May–June, 1974), 180–184.

MCGREGOR, EUGENE B., JR. "Social Equity and the Public Service." *Public Administration Review,* vol. 34, no. 1 (Jan.–Feb., 1974), 18–29.

MILLETT, JOHN D. *Organization for the Public Service.* Princeton: D. Van Nostrand Company, Inc., 1966.

MOSHER, FREDERICK C. *Democracy and the Public Service.* New York: Oxford University Press, 1968.

MUSOLF, LLOYD D. "Separate Career Executive Systems: Egalitarianism and Neutrality." *Public Administration Review.* vol. 31, no. 4 (July–Aug., 1971), 409–419.

NIGRO, FELIX. "Collective Bargaining and the Merit System." *Proceedings of the Academy of Political Science,* vol. 30, no. 2 (1971), 55–67.

NIGRO, FELIX. *Management-Employee Relations in the Public Service.* Chicago: Public Personnel Association, 1969.

NIGRO, FELIX. "A Symposium, Collective Bargaining in the Public Service: A Reappraisal," *Public Administration Review,* vol. 32, no. 2 (March–April, 1972).

NIGRO, LLOYD G. ed. *"A Mini-Symposium:* Affirmative Action in Public Employment," *Public Administration Review,* 34:3 (May–June, 1974), 234–246.

President's Task Force on Employee-Management Relations in the Federal Service. *A Policy for Employee-Management Cooperation in the Federal Service.* Washington, D.C.: U.S. Government Printing Office, 1961.

Public Personnel Association. *Public Personnel Administration: Progress and Prospects.* Chicago: Public Personnel Association Report No. 681, 1968.

REHMUS, CHARLES M. "Constraints on Local Governments in Public Employee Bargaining." *Michigan Law Review.* vol. 67, no. 5 (March 1969), 919–930.

ROACH, ED D. and FRANK W. MCCLAIN. "Executive Order 11491: Prospects and Problems." *Public Personnel Review.* vol. 31, no. 3 (July, 1970), 197–202.

ROBERTS, HAROLD S. *Labor-Management Relations in the Public Service.* Honolulu: University of Hawaii, Industrial Relations Center, 1968.

ROBINSON, JAMES B. "The Public Sector Labor Force in 1980." *The Bureaucrat,* vol. 2, no. 4 (Winter, 1973), 442–451.

SAFREN, MARIAN A. "Title VII and Employee Selection Techniques." *Personnel.* vol. 50, no. 1 (Jan.–Feb., 1973), 26–36.

SCHNECK, RODNEY E. "The Responsibilities of Management Toward Its Employees." *Canadian Public Administration.* vol. 12, no. 1 (Spring 1969), 78–88.

SNELL, WILLIAM. "Bargaining in the Public Sector." *Personnel.* vol. 49, no. 5 (Sept.–Oct., 1972), 60–67.

STANLEY, DAVID T. *Managing Local Government Under Union Pressure,* Washington, D.C.: Brookings, 1972.

STANLEY, DAVID T. "What are Unions Doing to Merit Systems?" *Public Personnel Review,* vol. 31, no. 2 (April, 1970), 108–113.

Symposium. "Collective Negotiations in the Public Service." *Public Administration Review.* vol. 28, no. 2 (March/April 1968), 111–147.

"Symposium on Collective Bargaining in the Public Service: A Reappraisal." *Public Administration Review.* vol. 32, no. 2 (March–April, 1972), 97–126.

TAYLOR, VERNON R. *Test Validity in Public Personnel Selection.* Chicago: Public Personnel Association, 1971. Public Employment Practices Bulletin No. 2.

THOMAS, EUGENE M., III. "Collective Bargaining in the Public Interest." *Municipal Finance,* vol. 42, no. 1 (August 1969), 67–70.

U.S. Civil Service Commission. *The Federal Career Service— At Your Service.* Washington, D.C.: U.S. Government Printing Office, 1967.

U.S. Civil Service Commission. *Investment for Tomorrow.* Report of the Presidential Task Force on Career Advancement. Washington, D.C.: U.S. Government Printing Office, 1967.

VAISON, ROBERT A. "Collective Bargaining in the Federal Public Service: The Achievement of a Milestone in Personnel Relations." *Canadian Public Administration.* vol. 12, no. 1 (Spring 1969), 108–122.

VAN RIPER, PAUL P., et al. *The Merit System: Foundation for*

Responsible Public Management. Chicago: Public Personnel Association, 1963.

VOSLOO, WILLIAM B. *Collective Bargaining in the United States Federal Civil Service.* Chicago: Public Personnel Association, 1966.

WAGNER, AUBREY J. "TVA Looks at Three Decades of Collective Bargaining." *Industrial and Labor Relations Review.* vol. 22, no. 1 (October 1968), 20–30.

WALTON, EUGENE. "Rooting Out Racism in Organizations." *The Bureaucrat,* vol. 2, no. 1 (Spring, 1973), 107–116.

WARNER, KENNETH O. *Collective Bargaining in the Public Service: Theory and Practice.* Chicago: Public Personnel Association, 1967.

WARNER, KENNETH. *Developments in Public Employee Relations: Legislative, Judicial, Administrative.* Chicago: Public Personnel Association, 1965.

WARNER, W. LLOYD, PAUL VAN RIPER, NORMAN MARTIN, and ORVIS COLLINS. *The American Federal Executive.* New Haven: Yale University Press, 1963.

WELLINGTON, HARRY H., and RALPH K. WINTER, JR. "The Limits of Collective Bargaining in Public Employment." *Yale Law Journal.* vol. 78, no. 1 (June 1969), 1107–1127.

WELLINGTON, HARRY H., and RALPH K. WINTER, JR. *The Unions and the Cities,* Washington, D.C.: Brookings, 1971.

"Women in the Public Service." Personnel Bibliography, *Public Personnel Review,* vol. 31, no. 1 (January 1970).

ZAGORIA, SAM. ed., *Public Workers and Public Unions.* Englewood Cliffs, N.J.: Prentice-Hall, Inc. 1972.

FIVE

CHANGING TRENDS IN THE BUDGETARY PROCESS

It is generally assumed that the control of financial affairs is tantamount to the effective management and coordination of the entire administrative process. Part Five deals with this critical aspect of administration by exploring the critical relationships between fiscal management, the administrative process, and the political system.

The budgetary process has traditionally been viewed simply as a means for allocating and controlling public expenditures. Through such allocation and control of money comes the ability to determine the nature and scope of governmental programs. Only in recent years has any concentrated effort been made to look at the budgetary process as an over-all systematic means to achieve more effective planning as well as management of the administrative system. It is now quite obvious that the budgetary process is the combination of many strategies aimed at determining not only proper fiscal management, but also the future course of administrative programs and policies.

A major step in the direction of linking budgetary management and program planning was the introduction of Planning-Programming-Budgeting Systems (PPBS) during the

John Kennedy administration of the early 1960s. This effort to link modern techniques of decision making and accountability to the traditional budgetary system began experimentally in the Department of Defense. President Johnson followed by expanding its use to a much greater number of federal departments and agencies. The application of PPBS continued into the Nixon administration although questions arose as to how effective PPBS was in meeting the expectations of its supporters given the apparent reluctance of both executive agencies and legislative leaders to embrace it.

Perhaps symbolic of the changing role of the fiscal process as a management tool is the President's Plan for Reorganization—the Bureau of the Budget is redesignated the Office of Management and Budget with responsibility for the effective management of fiscal resources and policies. The major thrust of OMB is to emphasize fiscal analysis, increase its capacities in program evaluation and coordination, improve executive branch organization, information, and management systems, and add to the development of executive talent.

Increased attention is given to the evaluation of program performances in assessing the extent to which programs achieve results and deliver services. This would supplement the program evaluating process which remains a function of the individual agencies. Additional emphasis is placed on interagency cooperation through the new office, as well as assistance in intergovernmental programs. Of further significance is the expected continuous review of the reorganizational structure and management processes of the executive branch and the projected proposals for needed change which would come from the office. Finally, the office is charged with developing career executive talent and advising the President on development of new programs to recruit, train, motivate, deploy, and evaluate men and women in the top ranks of the civil service.

According to Allen Schick, the above changes helped to hasten the effective decline of PPBS at the federal level. Schick, who has done extensive writing on PPBS, contends that this failure is due to the inability of budget reformers to successfully dispense the idea that budget analysis and policy outcomes are linked. The proponents of PPBS saw analysis used in conjunction with budgetary processes as a means to recast budgeting from a repetitive process of financing permanent bureaucracies into an instrument for deciding purposes and programs of government. The clear impact of these two elements, according to Schick, became a threat to the budgeters as well as an embarassment to the reformers.

PPBS cannot be viewed apart from the managerial and political realities among which it had to operate. Its emphasis on rationality appeared to evoke an image which seemed contrary to American values of debate and compromise in the political arena. Greater utilization of PPBS techniques appeared to be given to managerial roles in the budget process rather than the more controversial programmatic roles. The creation of The Office of Management and Budget (OMB) was a capstone in this process as it hardened the separation of management decisions from policy decisions, leaving the latter in the hands of the newly created Domestic Council.

OMB has the responsibility for coordinating federal programs. It has had some difficulty in doing so because the existence of many overlapping and different information systems among agencies and departments has made any centralized management difficult, if not impossible. Thus, OMB continues pretty much in the role of keeping track of detailed budgets and expenditures with efforts aimed primarily at improving traditional budget processes rather than using the budget for analytical and program purposes.

At the same time, Schick points out that Congress has a poor record of support for PPBS. He suggests that any Congressional support will tend to be tied to its ability to increase the extent of its power *vis-a-vis* the executive in fiscal areas. Influential persons in positions of power within Congress also tend to be wary of tampering with processes that have tended to be beneficial to the maintenance of that power.

Schnick concludes, however, that PPBS represents a meaningful effort to develop comprehensive planning and programming within the budgetary process. Although he speaks at length about the "demise" of PPBS, he suggests that it could return provided that methods are developed to maintain effective financial accountability and that the ability of agencies to receive funds from a variety of sources and under interchangeable funds is reduced or removed. When these problems of control are solved, perhaps the climate for reconsidering PPBS will be more hospitable.

A key link in the budgetary process is the means by which information is gathered by OMB from the many executive branch agencies. These inputs from the agencies provide basic data from which budgetary estimates and recommendations are made and ultimately submitted to Congress in the President's Budget Message. James W. Davis and Randall B. Ripley discuss this process of information collection. The student should be aware, however, that since 1971, the functions of the Bureau of the Budget, have been taken over by the Office of Management and Budget (OMB). However, the information gathering process remains essentially the same.

Davis and Ripley investigate the relationships between the Bureau (OMB) and selected agencies of the executive branch. The authors are concerned with identifying the bases for contacts between the Bureau and the executive agencies, the nature of the contacts made, the images agencies hold about the Bureau, and what considerations affect the agency-Bureau relationships. These relationships are instrumental in the clearinghouse function of accumulating, digesting, and producing program plans as well as managing the budgetary process.

The occasions for contact are many and varied—some formal, but most informal. For the agencies, the main link with the Bureau is through the budget examiners. Other links exist; their importance varies with the given agency. The most important consideration, according to Davis and Ripley, is to keep an open flow of information. As a general rule the atmosphere tends to be friendly. Whatever bargaining occurs does so in terms of the openness of the informational flow. If conflict arises, resolution may be had at a variety of levels—although only a few ever reach the top. In addition, the authors found that the avoidance of decision by the Bureau may, itself, constitute a means for conflict resolution.

An aspect of fiscal reform very closely linked to policy areas has recently appeared—revenue sharing. Revenue sharing constitutes a departure from the more traditional grant-in-aid program of the federal government in which monies were made available to states or localities on the basis of some matching formula and contingent upon the recipients meeting certain administrative as well as fiscal control standards. The last two selections in Part Five explain the philosophy and reality of revenue sharing and look at an existing revenue-sharing program in operation.

Edward Banfield describes the underlying philosophy behind revenue sharing and relates it to the reality of revenue sharing as he sees it. According to Banfield, the question is not necessarily one of financial need so much as the raising of services at the state and local level to a standing that state and local political realities will not permit. Within this perspective it can be seen that some programs of national importance and impact, although executed at state and local levels, may well need additional financial support from the national level. He questions, however, whether the federal government should finance inadequate programs or programs that are patently state and local rather than national.

Rather than being solely a financial device to share tax monies, Banfield says that revenue sharing is a basic part of "the new federalism," a movement to decentralize governmental power (away from the federal level and toward the state and local levels) and to restore balance between state and national government levels. Through general and special revenue-sharing programs, previous national grant-in-aid programs could be consolidated and streamlined. Within rather broad guidelines—usually of the fiscal accountability variety—state and local governments would be able to determine specific uses for revenue-sharing monies, choosing to allocate funds for a continuance of previous grant-in-aid programs or moving in different program areas.

The realities of the political process have much to say

about revenue sharing. Banfield points out that organized beneficiaries of grant programs would not welcome revenue-sharing programs since to do so might jeopardize their power, program, or job. Members of Congress might balk at such a change since it would take away much of their ability to take credit for programs initiated by them or their colleagues. In addition, there would be concern that the position of the executive might be enhanced at the expense of the legislative body by means of revenue sharing. Furthermore, Banfield points to the fact that Governors and Mayors would stand to gain decisional power due to the availability of resources at little or no direct risk of local taxpayer reaction.

Many questions still exist about the efficacy of revenue sharing. Apart from the questions about relative levels of power, there is real concern for the ability of state and local governmental units and officials to effectively and efficiently utilize revenue-sharing funds. Questions about adequate management techniques and effective control and accounting procedures remain. In addition, there are many skeptics who would contend that program decisions at the local and state levels would reflect political or personal preferences, rather than the real needs of the people.

Nevertheless, Banfield sees a continuing movement toward experimentation in revenue sharing. He cautions, however, that power will not really be shifted from the federal level. Rather, a different formula for dispensing federal power has been devised with much evaluation still left to be done.

Enough time has passed for some data to have been made available about revenue-sharing programs and upon which some tentative judgments can be made. Stanley Vanagunas discusses one such program, the Law Enforcement Revenue Sharing Act of 1971. He looks at the program in order to evaluate how well it has succeeded in meeting the goal of upgrading state and local criminal justice services as compared to its predecessor bill, the Safe Streets Assistance Program.

Vanagunas maintains that some obvious improvements have been made, especially in regard to removing the "matching" provisions of the previous grant-in-aid program. He suggests that the substitution of revenue sharing will also tend to increase the confidence of local officials that assistance will be of sufficient continuity and permanence so that they might be more willing to generate sound law enforcement improvement projects.

Some flaws are also noted by Vanagunas. The continuing requirement that the states file annual comprehensive law enforcement plans seems to be unrealistic and costly, mainly because the execution stage for "safe streets" tends to be local rather than state and any attempt by states to develop comprehensive plans to deal with hundreds of police jurisdictions seems fraught with problems of information and management. Also, Vanagunas points out that the revenue-sharing bill provides for a built-in bias toward using monies for law enforcement hardware.

Perhaps the most significant change deals with the removal of the requirement that states and local governments could not supplant their law enforcement funds with federal assistance monies. This deletion, according to Vanagunas, is detrimental to the improvement of criminal justice administration because it subsidizes other functions of state and local governments.

Other revenue-sharing problems are related to the "pass-through" provisions, by means of which states are directed to allocate revenue-sharing funds to local governmental units. State governments have tended to be reluctant to pass through sufficient funds to so-called "high crime" areas, namely cities.

Regardless of philosophy or reality, revenue sharing is with us for the foreseeable future. General revenue sharing, as opposed to special revenue sharing has been in effect for several years now and data of its utilization and effectiveness in permitting state and local governments to more adequately deal with their governmental problems will soon be available. Attention must surely be paid to the effect of revenue sharing upon governmental policies and programs, both those previously under grant-in-aid legislation and those newly emerging.

The full impact will not be clear until feedback is available from states and localities, from the political sector as well as the general public. In any case, events of the recent past demonstrate that fiscal policies and budgeting processes are very much a part of the political process and thus subject to its vagaries. One example of this is Congress' creating separate budget committees whose function will be to provide Congressional input of a character more consistent with the demands of budgeting problems. Future developments in the budgetary process will reflect the inputs of a changing governmental and private sector as well as the general public.

23

richard m. nixon

REORGANIZATION PLAN NO. 2 OF 1970—
MESSAGE FROM THE PRESIDENT

To the Congress of the United States:

We in government often are quick to call for reform in other institutions, but slow to reform ourselves. Yet nowhere today is modern management more needed than in government itself.

In 1939, President Franklin D. Roosevelt proposed and the Congress accepted a reorganization plan that laid the groundwork for providing managerial assistance for a modern Presidency.

The plan placed the Bureau of the Budget within the Executive Office of the President. It made available to the President direct access to important new management instruments. The purpose of the plan was to improve the administration of the Government—to ensure that the Government could perform "promptly, effectively, without waste or lost motion."

Fulfilling that purpose today is far more difficult—and more important—than it was 30 years ago.

Last April, I created a President's Advisory Council on Executive Organization and named to it a distinguished group of outstanding experts headed by Roy L. Ash. I gave the Council a broad charter to examine ways in which the Executive Branch could be better organized. I asked it to recommend specific organizational changes that would make the Executive Branch a more vigorous and more effective instrument for creating and carrying out the programs that are needed today. The Council quickly concluded that the place to begin was in the Executive Office of the President itself. I agree.

Richard M. Nixon, "Reorganization Plan No. 2 of 1970." *Congressional Record*, March 12, 1970, pp. S3579–3581.

The past 30 years have seen enormous changes in the size, structure, and functions of the Federal Government. The budget has grown from less than $10 billion to $200 billion. The number of civilian employees has risen from one million to more than two and a half million. Four new Cabinet departments have been created, along with more than a score of independent agencies. Domestic policy issues have become increasingly complex. The interrelationships among Government programs have become more intricate. Yet the organization of the President's policy and management arms has not kept pace.

Over three decades, the Executive Office of the President has mushroomed but not by conscious design. In many areas it does not provide the kind of staff assistance and support the President needs in order to deal with the problems of government in the 1970s. We confront the 1970s with a staff organization geared in large measure to the tasks of the 1940s and 1950s.

One result, over the years, has been a tendency to enlarge the immediate White House staff—that is, the President's personal staff, as distinct from the institutional structure—to assist with management functions for which the President is responsible. This has blurred the distinction between personal staff and management institutions; it has left key management functions to be performed only intermittently and some not at all. It has perpetuated outdated structures.

Another result has been, paradoxically, to inhibit the delegation of authority to Departments and agencies.

A President whose programs are carefully coordinated, whose information system keeps him adequately informed, and whose organizational assignments are plainly set out, can delegate authority with security and confidence. A President whose office is deficient in these respects will be inclined, instead, to retain control of operating responsibilities which he cannot and should not handle.

Improving the management processes of the President's own office, therefore, is a key element in improving the management of the entire Executive Branch, and in strengthening the authority of its Departments and agencies. By providing the tools that are needed to reduce duplication, to monitor performance and to promote greater efficiency throughout the Executive Branch, this also will enable us to give the country not only more effective but also more economical government—which it deserves.

To provide the management tools and policy mechanisms needed for the 1970s, I am today transmitting to the Congress Reorganization Plan No. 2 of 1970, prepared in accordance with Chapter 9 of Title 5 of the United States Code.

This plan draws not only on the work of the Ash Council itself, but also on the work of others that preceded—including the pioneering Brownlow Committee of 1936, the two Hoover Commissions, the Rockefeller Committee, and other Presidential task forces.

Essentially, the plan recognizes that two closely connected but basically separate functions both center in the President's office: policy determination and executive management. This involves 1) what government should do, and 2) how it goes about doing it.

My proposed reorganization creates a new entity to deal with each of these functions:

—It establishes a Domestic Council, to coordinate policy formulation in the domestic area. This Cabinet group would be provided with an institutional staff, and to a considerable degree would be a domestic counterpart to the National Security Council.

—It establishes an Office of Management and Budget, which would be the President's principal arm for the exercise of his managerial functions.

The Domestic Council will be primarily concerned with *what* we do; the Office of Management and Budget will be primarily concerned with *how* we do it, and *how well* we do it.

DOMESTIC COUNCIL

The past year's experience with the Council for Urban Affairs has shown how immensely valuable a Cabinet-level council can be as a forum for both discussion and action on policy matters that cut across departmental jurisdictions.

The Domestic Council will be chaired by the President. Under the plan, its membership will include the Vice President, and the Secretaries of the Treasury, Interior, Agriculture, Commerce, Labor, Health, Education and Welfare, Housing and Urban Development, and Transportation, and the Attorney General. I also intend to designate as members the Director of the Office of Economic Opportunity and, while he remains a member of the Cabinet, the Postmaster General. (Although I continue to hope that the Congress will adopt my proposal to create, in place of the Post Office Department, a self-sufficient postal authority.) The President could add other Executive Branch officials at his discretion.

The Council will be supported by a staff under an Executive Director who will also be one of the President's assistants. Like the National Security Council staff, this staff will work in close coordination with the President's personal staff but will have its own institutional identity. By being established on a permanent, institutional basis, it will be designed to develop and employ the "institutional memory" so essential if continuity is to be maintained, and if experience is to play its proper role in the policy-making process.

There does not now exist an organized, institutionally-staffed group charged with advising the President on the total range of domestic policy. The Domestic Council will fill that need. Under the President's direction, it will also be charged with integrating the various aspects of domestic policy into a consistent whole.

Among the specific policy functions in which I intend the Domestic Council to take the lead are these:

—Assessing national needs, collecting information and developing forecasts, for the purpose of defining national goals and objectives.

—Identifying alternative ways of achieving these objectives, and recommending consistent, integrated sets of policy choices.

—Providing rapid response to Presidential needs for policy advice on pressing domestic issues.

—Coordinating the establishment of national priorities for the allocation of available resources.

—Maintaining a continuous review of the conduct of on-going programs from a policy standpoint, and proposing reforms as needed.

Much of the Council's work will be accomplished by temporary, ad hoc project committees. These might take a variety of forms, such as task forces, planning groups, or advisory bodies. They can be established with varying degrees of formality, and can be set up to deal either with broad program areas or with specific problems. The committees will draw for staff support on Department and agency experts, supplemented by the Council's own staff and that of the Office of Management and Budget.

Establishment of the Domestic Council draws on the experience gained during the past year with the Council for Urban Affairs, the Cabinet Committee on the Environment and the Council for Rural Affairs. The principal key to the operation of these Councils has been the effective functioning of their various subcommittees. The Councils themselves will be consolidated into the Domestic Council; Urban, Rural and Environment subcommittees of the Domestic Council will be strengthened, using access to the Domestic Council staff.

Overall, the Domestic Council will provide the President with a streamlined, consolidated domestic policy arm, adequately staffed, and highly flexible in its operation. It also will provide a structure through which departmental initiatives can be more fully considered, and expert advice from the Departments and agencies more fully utilized.

OFFICE OF MANAGEMENT AND BUDGET

Under the reorganization plan, the technical and formal means by which the Office of Management and Budget is created is by re-designating the Bureau of the Budget as the Office of Management and Budget. The functions currently vested by law in the Bureau, or in its director, are transferred to the President, with the provision that he can then redelegate them.

As soon as the reorganization plan takes effect, I intend to dele-gate those statutory functions to the Director of the new Office of Management and Budget, including those under section 212 of the Budget and Accounting Act, 1921.

However, creation of the Office of Management and Budget represents far more than a mere change of name for the Bureau of the Budget. It represents a basic change in concept and emphasis, reflecting the broader management needs of the Office of the President.

The new Office will still perform the key function of assisting the President in the preparation of the annual Federal budget and overseeing its execution. It will draw upon the skills and experience of the extraordinarily able and dedicated career staff developed by the Bureau of the Budget. But preparation of the budget as such will no longer be its dominant, overriding concern.

While the budget function remains a vital tool of management, it will be strengthened by the greater emphasis the new Office will place on fiscal analysis. The budget function is only one of several important management tools that the President must now have. He must also have a substantially enhanced institutional staff capability in other areas of executive management—particularly in program evaluation and coordination, improvement of Executive Branch organization, information and management systems, and development of executive talent. Under this plan, strengthened capability in these areas will be provided partly through internal reorganization, and it will also require additional staff resources.

The new Office of Management and Budget will place much greater emphasis on the evaluation of program performance: on assessing the extent to which programs are actually achieving their intended results, and delivering the intended services to the intended recipients. This is needed on a continuing basis, not as a one-time effort. Program evaluation will remain a function of the individual agencies as it is today. However, a single agency cannot fairly be expected to judge overall effectiveness in programs that cross agency lines—and the difference between agency and Presidential perspectives requires a capacity in the Executive Office to evaluate program performance whenever appropriate.

The new Office will expand efforts to improve interagency cooperation in the field. Washington-based coordinators will help work out interagency problems at the operating level, and assist in developing efficient coordinating mechanisms throughout the country. The success of these efforts depends on the experience, persuasion, and understanding of an Office which will be an expediter and catalyst. The Office will also respond to requests from State and local governments for assistance on intergovernmental programs. It will work closely with the Vice President and the Office of Intergovernmental Relations.

Improvement of Government organization, information and management systems will be a major function of the Office of Management and Budget. It will maintain a continuous review of the organizational structures and management processes of the Executive Branch, and recommend needed changes. It will take the lead in developing new information systems to provide the President with the performance and other data that he needs but does not now get. When new programs are launched, it will seek to ensure that they are not simply forced into or grafted onto existing organizational structures that may not be appropriate. Resistance to organizational change is one of the chief obstacles to effective government; the new Office will seek to ensure that organization keeps abreast of program needs.

The new Office will also take the lead in devising programs for the development of career executive talent throughout the Government. Not the least of the President's needs as Chief Executive is direct capability in the Executive Office for insuring that talented executives are used to the full extent of their abilities. Effective, coordinated efforts for executive manpower development have been hampered by the lack of a system for forecasting the needs for executive talent and appraising leadership potential. Both are crucial to the success of an enterprise—whether private or public.

The Office of Management and Budget will be charged with advising the President on the development of new programs to recruit, train, motivate, deploy, and evaluate the men and women who make up the top ranks of the civil service, in the broadest sense of that term. It will not deal with individuals, but will rely on the talented professionals of the Civil Service Commission and the Departments and agencies themselves to administer these programs. Under the leadership of the Office of Management and Budget there will be joint efforts to see to it that all executive talent is well utilized wherever it may be needed throughout the Executive Branch, and to assure that executive training and motivation meet not only today's needs but those of the years ahead.

Finally, the new Office will continue the Legislative Reference functions now performed by the Bureau of the Budget, drawing together agency reactions on all proposed legislation, and helping develop legislation to carry out the President's program. It also will continue the Bureau's work of improving and coordinating Federal statistical services.

SIGNIFICANCE OF THE CHANGES

The people deserve a more responsive and more effective Government. The times require it. These changes will help provide it.

Each reorganization included in the plan which accompanies this message is necessary to accomplish one or more of the purposes set forth in Section 901 (a) of Title 5 of the United States Code. In particular, the plan is responsive to Section 901(a) (1), "to promote the better execution of the laws, the more effective management of the Executive Branch and of its agencies and functions, and the expeditious administration of the public business"; and Section 901(a) (3), "to increase the efficiency of the operations of the Government to the fullest extent practicable."

The reorganizations provided for in this plan make necessary the appointment and compensation of new officers, as specified in

Section 102(c) of the plan. The rates of compensation fixed for these officers are comparable to those fixed for other officers in the Executive Branch who have similar responsibilities.

While this plan will result in a modest increase in direct expenditures, its strengthening of the Executive Office of the President will bring significant indirect savings, and at the same time will help ensure that people actually receive the return they deserve for every dollar the Government spends. The savings will result from the improved efficiency these changes will provide throughout the Executive Branch—and also from curtailing the waste that results when programs simply fail to achieve their objectives. It is not practical, however, to itemize or aggregate these indirect expenditure reductions which will result from the reorganization.

I expect to follow with other reorganization plans, quite possibly including ones that will affect other activities of the Executive Office of the President. Our studies are continuing. But this by itself is a reorganization of major significance, and a key to the more effective functioning of the entire Executive Branch.

These changes would provide an improved system of policy making and coordination, a strengthened capacity to perform those functions that are now the central concerns of the Bureau of the Budget, and a more effective set of management tools for the performance of other functions that have been rapidly increasing in importance.

The reorganization will not only improve the staff resources available to the President, but will also strengthen the advisory roles of those members of the Cabinet principally concerned with domestic affairs. By providing a means of formulating integrated and systematic recommendations on major domestic policy issues, the plan serves not only the needs of the President, but also the interests of the Congress.

This reorganization plan is of major importance to the functioning of modern government. The national interest requires it. I urge that the Congress allow it to become effective.

24

allen schick

A DEATH IN THE BUREAUCRACY: THE
DEMISE OF FEDERAL PPB

> Agencies are no longer required to submit with their budget
> submissions the multi-year program and financing plans, pro-
> gram memoranda and special analytical studies . . . or the sched-
> ules . . . that reconcile information classified according to their
> program and appropriation structures.

By these words, PPB became an unthing. No publicity or press release; only an erasure from the administrative record. The death
notice was conveyed on June 21, 1971, in a memorandum accompanying Circular A-11, the Office of Management and Budget's (OMB)
annual ritual for the preparation and submission of agency budget
requests. No mention was made in the memo of three initials which
had dazzled the world of budgeting five years earlier, nor was there
any admission of failure or disappointment. The memorandum depicted the termination of PPB as part "of continuing OMB efforts to
simplify budget submission requirements."[1]

What died and what remains? The name is gone and so too are
the burdensome routines that came to be the end products of budget
innovation. But there survive cadres of committed and skilled analysts, a growing supply of analytic studies and data, and perhaps most
significantly, a spreading consensus (among budgeters, program administrators, and congressmen) that the inherited budget practices

Reprinted from the *Public Administration Review,* Journal of the American Society for Public Administration, vol. 33, no. 2 (March–April, 1972).
Copyright 1972 by the American Society for Public Administration. Reprinted by permission.

are in need of improvement. Among those who believe that analysis always has been "the heart and soul of PPB"[2] it has become fashionable to interpret the abandonment of PPB as evidence of the new sophistication of reformers who after much sorrow have learned to distinguish the product from the package. Many analysts long have regarded the system and its bundle of techniques—in particular the program structure and the long-range plans—only as the necessary price for projecting analysis into federal decision making. When the price became too high and the technique got in the way of analysis, the deadwood was cut away without impairing the analytic core. Thus they see the stripping away of PPB's mechanistic apparatus as evidence of the strength and durability of their analytic efforts.[3]

THE MEANING OF FAILURE

With those who believe that the spirit—if not the essence—of PPB lives, I have no quarrel. But I believe that they err in regarding analysis as the central concern of PPB. What PPB tried to do, and the measure by which it must be judged, was to recast federal budgeting from a repetitive process for financing permanent bureaucracies into an instrument for deciding the purposes and programs of government. Analysis was to be a change agent; it would reorient budgeting by serving it. The linkup of analysis and budgeting was to close and direct, through plans, cost-effectiveness studies, and the other informational channels opened by PPB. Analysis was not valued for its own sake or structured to operate independently of the budget process. Rather, PPB—as its initials attest—was designed with budget outcomes in mind. That is why it required an overlay of forms and routines.

Budgeting is the routinization of public choice by means of standard procedures, timetables, classifications, and rules. PPB failed because it did not penetrate the vital routines of putting together and justifying a budget. Always separate but never equal, the analysts had little influence over the form or content of the budget.

It can be argued that a fundamental change in budgeting was beyond the reach of PPB, that its techniques were inappropriate for this task, and that analysis should not have been tied to the budget process. Because of its historical development and the diverse functions it must serve, budgeting is encumbered by traditions and practices which cannot be easily uprooted. Elsewhere I have identified several alternatives to PPB which do not depend for fruition on the entrenched routines of budgeting. These include the use of analysis for developing new program legislation and long-range planning separated from current policy issues.[4] But once its lot was cast with budgeting, PPB could not succeed or survive unless it had a measurable impact on budget allocation. Viewed from this perspective, the termination of PPB ended attempts to overhaul federal budgeting. Though some agencies continued their own PPB-type operations, the withdrawal of OMB meant that there could be no governmentwide change.[5]

From the very start, PPB's effectiveness was impaired by the failure of many analysts to comprehend the connection between their work and budgeting. Because they came to PPB with little administrative or budgetary experience, they did not recognize that in a PPB system the fate of analysis hinges on its use in budgeting. Those who view the cancellation of PPB as a boon to policy analysis still have not learned the place of budgeting and its techniques in the allocation of federal resources.

Where PPB succeeded, it had an impact on budget decisions. The most notable success, of course, though one that is frequently misinterpreted, was in the Defense Department where PPB was used by the Secretary to make major program and spending decisions. It was used, as Enthoven and Smith suggest in the title of their book, for determining "How Much is Enough?"[6] While the pioneering analytic accomplishments of the RAND Corporation in the 1950's provided the logical foundations for what was implemented a decade later, it was only after McNamara gave the analysts command over the central programming and budgeting systems that PPB became a working reality. Before 1961, analysis was divorced from Defense budgeting, much as it would be from civilian budgeting under PPB.[7] Undoubtedly, the status and influence of Defense analysts depended on sustained support from the top, but this is likely to be the case under any system that tries to unite the disparate budgeting and analytic processes. Other factors that worked to meld PPB and Defense budgeting were the organizational changes made in DOD during the 1950's[8] and the suitability of systems analysis for major procurement decisions. Where these conditions are weak or absent, it takes more than the good intentions and talents of analysts to make a dent in budget policy.

The use of PPB in civilian departments never reached the status it attained in Defense. The main problem was that unlike McNamara, whose initiative enabled him to forge his own PPB system, civilian department heads were ordered to graft an alien, standardized system onto their regular budget processes. In formulating a government-wide PPB system, the Bureau of the Budget gave little consideration to the preferences or problems of individual departments. It adopted the Defense system, including most of its procedures and terminology, and directed the civilian departments to fall into line. From the vantage point of the departments, PPB was something manufactured by and for the use of the Budget Bureau. The departments did not have an opportunity to design their own systems or procedures, nor were they able to relate PPB to their established budgetary practices. In fact, several departments were compelled to abandon or revamp analytic efforts and budget improvements launched prior to the introduction of PPB. Mosher and Harr expertly chronicle the "everyone loses" struggle between the State Department and the Budget Bureau in which State fought for its own Comprehensive Country Programming System (CCPS) and Budget insisted that PPBS be adopted. It is not important which side was right; a logical case can be made for either approach. What is important and beyond doubt was the effect of a foreign system on departmental receptivity.[9] Faced with an imposed system which they neither designed nor understood, many departments reacted by divorcing the PPB system from budgeting. This separatist tendency was reinforced by the Budget Bureau's insistence that new analytic staffs be organized.[10] The net result was that little analysis was pumped into the budget stream.

Yet it would be wrong to conclude that PPB died because of departmental subversion. Indifference and confusion took their toll, but most departments, at least in the first years, gave PPB a try. They went through the motions and submitted the required documents, organized their analytic staffs, and fashioned program structures. Only after they perceived that the Budget Bureau itself was not committed to budget change did the departments cut their losses. For all its preaching about an integrated planning and budgeting system, the Budget Bureau steadfastly kept the two apart, quarantining its tiny PPB operation from the powerful examinations and budget review staffs, and promulgating separate PPB and budget instructions.[11] The departments could not accomplish for themselves what the Budget Bureau refused (or was unable) to do for itself.

The difference between civilian and Defense PPB is well illustrated by a comparison of the Draft Presidential Memorandums (DPM) used in Defense with the Program Memorandums (PM) mandated by the Budget Bureau. The DPMs were prepared by the Office of Systems Analysis for the Secretary, circulated among the services and the Joint Chiefs for comment, and in final form used by the Secretary for transmitting his program and budget recommendations to the President. As described by Enthoven and Smith, each DPM "combined strategy, force requirements, and financial considerations" and "spelled out concisely the assumptions, rationale, and supporting analysis" of the recommended course of action. Most importantly, the DPMs "became the means by which the Secretary of Defense submitted his recommendations to the President and . . . the means by which he made his decisions and policies known throughout the Defense Department."[12]

Though modeled after the DPM, the Program Memorandum was a pale shadow of the original. In its first PPB bulletin, the Budget specified that the PMs, one for each program category, should describe program objectives, make explicit the assumptions and criteria which support recommended programs, and compare the cost and effectiveness of alternative objectives and programs.[13] Only on paper does this resemble what happened in Defense. The critical difference is that the DPM was sent to the President, while the Program Memorandums went to the Budget Bureau. In effect BOB was telling the agencies: "Expose to us the internal process leading to your major program and budget recommendations, including the alternatives which you rejected. Then we will review your analysis and recommendations and make our own decisions." The DPM was a decisional document; the PM only an intermediate step in the long process of budgeting. Other differences flowed from these: The DPM was prepared by systems analysts to reflect McNamara's views; the PM was composed by analysts removed from the centers of power. The DPM used concepts and terms developed for Defense; the same language was foreign and confusing when transplanted to the domestic arena.

Because the initial PMs were overloaded with descriptive wordage, BOB modified the guidelines to require submissions only when a major program issue was involved. But the fatal defect in the PMs was beyond remedy; they were the Budget Bureau's idea, and one which BOB itself isolated from the main business of budgeting.[14] The agencies protected themselves in a variety of ways: many used the memoranda to bolster their budget justifications, and ignored Budget's demands for analytic content; some submitted unsigned memorandums, thereby indicating that the documents represented the views of analysts and not agency policy; others ceased submitting any memorandums when they realized the futility of the whole process.

Long before it was officially terminated, PPB was a threat to budgeters and an embarassment to reformers. PPB reminded budgeters of the inadequacies of their process and reformers of their inability to deliver promised improvements. PPB's name and procedures were in disrepute and there was no prospect of salvaging it from a "living death," breached in letter and spirit, but kept on the books. The best hope was to start anew and to allow individual departments to process according to their own wills.

A TANGLE OF FAILURES

PPB died of multiple causes, any of which was sufficient. PPB died because of the manner in which it was introduced, across-the-board and without much preparation. PPB died because new men of power were arrogantly insensitive to budgetary traditions, institutional loyalties, and personal relationships. PPB died because of inadequate support and leadership with meager resources invested in its behalf. At its peak, the BOB staff charged with monitoring and promoting the governmentwide effort numbered fewer than a dozen professionals.[15] PPB died because good analysts and data were in short supply and it takes a great deal of time to make up the deficit. The causes of PPB's demise are as varied and numerous as the perspectives of those who have studied the debacle.[16]

One line of reasoning, first developed by Lindblom and Wildavsky, but now widely held by political scientists, is that PPB failed because it ran roughshod over some important American political values.[17] The argument is that the bargaining-incremental mode of budgeting gives expression and representation to diverse political interests which might be neglected if budget choice were centralized in the hands of analysts. In shrillest form, the argument has been employed by Victor Thompson to explain what went wrong in Vietnam: "The war in Indochina illustrates the problem of PPB. The actions of the United States in that war were informed by this kind of decision making."[18] To uphold this point of view requires the caricaturing of PPB as zero-base budgeting, comprehensive and consistent reordering of national priorities, government by planners, and the gathering of all decisional authority in a single power center. It is much too late and sterile to resume the PPB versus politics debate, but one might wonder how a paper tiger such as PPB could possibly wreck the entrenched values defended by the armies of interest groups which patrol the budget scene. Besides, even those who question the value of PPB generally welcome more policy analysis.[19] Wildavsky proposes the rescue of policy analysis from PPB; what is really needed, given the recent history of budget innovation, is to rescue policy analysis from budgeting.

For all the reasons and all the failures lead to budgeting as the prime factor. PPB failed to penetrate because the budgeters didn't let it in and the PPB'ers didn't know how to break down the resistence. But even if the leadership, data, analytic capability, resources and support, interpersonal and institutional sensitivity, and all the factors which worked against PPB had been favorable, there still would have been the anti-analytic thrust of the budget process to contend with. This does not mean that no level of PPB effort can crack the budget process—successful implementations in a few states show that an investment which is commensurate with the difficulties can have some impact[20]—only that it is a formidable and uncertain chore.

BUDGETING AS CONFLICT-SUPPRESSION

There are many reasons why budgeting and analysis do not readily fit together. The one which I will discuss here derives from budgeting's abhorrence of protracted or intensive conflict. Budgetary warfare brings challenges to those interests which are advantaged in the budget; it invites political and administrative disruption; and it may mean payless paydays, program cuts, reduction-in-force, and even agency terminations. It is no small accomplishment that 250 billion of potential conflicts are negotiated with minimal strife each year. While the process is not free of conflict—it couldn't be with so much at stake—it has available many devices and strategies for regulating and containing discord. In recent years, as pressures on the budget have mounted, additional conflict-abatement mechanisms have been devised or put to increased use, including a stretching of the time allowed for completing action on appropriations, continuing resolutions, informal understandings between congressional committees and agencies, and a widening of the gap between authorizations and appropriations.

If PPB were successfully implemented, it would have an impact on the conflict-resolving capabilities of the budget process. PPB would escalate conflict by pushing for greater consistency in program objectives (recent budgets, for example, have spent money to promote tobacco growing and to discourage tobacco smoking); it would seek more explicit understandings on program purposes (all that the budget now requires is agreement on dollars and activities); it would advocate the termination of some low-yield programs (nowadays it is hard to exercise anything from the budget); it would expand the range of alternatives the budget process considers (generally, the only alternative now considered is the one advocated by the agency). Probably its most significant effect would result from the unveiling of some of the costs and benefits of federal programs, thereby arming historically weak budget claimants with greater capability to alter the outcomes.[21] In sum, PPB would take some of the comfort out of the incrementalism that now dominates budgeting.

There are two ways to accommodate this greater load on the budget. One is to increase the uncommitted funds available in the budget; the other to raise the tolerance for diversiveness and contention. If additional funds above the requirements of incremental growth were available, it would be feasible to satisfy new claims without contesting past decisions, and PPB energies could then be channeled into the analysis of new program proposals. This is what happened in Defense in the early 1960's when new money was channeled into strategic forces and conventional war capability.[22] When PPB was inaugurated in 1965, it appeared that there would be an ample fiscal dividend to finance major program expansions. But the situation changed almost overnight as the available funds were consumed by Vietnam escalation, the built-in cost spiral of Great Society programs, inflation, tax cuts, and flagging economy. By the time PPB got off the ground, the issue no longer was whose ox should be fattened, but whose ox should be gored.

To come to grips with new program demands when all funds are encumbered requires that budgeting have the stomach for conflict. It may be that the costs of settling the budget quietly often are too high (the suppression of urgent new claims; overprotection of the budget base; and the retardation of change) and that more conflict would be a good thing, but until this view is more widely held, PPB does not stand much of a chance of affecting budget outcomes.

The prospects for bolstering governmental tolerance of prolonged budgetary impasses are not bright. An essential mission of all budgeting is to keep agencies and their activities in business. Consequently, unresolved disputes which threaten the continuation of agencies and programs are avoided. Safety valves such as continuing resolutions are valued because they expand government's capacity for conflict without bringing spending and operations to a halt. While budgeting often is labeled as action forcing, in fact it is a process which has action forced upon it. If governments possessed some device to keep going even in the absence of annual spending decisions, the shape of budgeting would be markedly different and the potential of PPB would be boosted. Perhaps a lengthier budget cycle—with a three- or five-year decision frame—is a prerequisite for freeing budgeting from its compulsion for conflict avoidance.

BACK TO MANAGEMENT

Those who pioneered the PPB movement came to budgeting from backgrounds to economics, systems analysis, and allied disciplines. They knew little about public administration or about the readiness of budgeting for the vast changes they undertook. But when PPB arrived, federal administration—at the top and in the departments—was going through a difficult period. The Budget Bureau had slipped in prominence and capability. It lost the lead in program development to the White House and it no longer gave central guidance to administrative management.[23] The separate management and budget staffs within BOB had little contact with one another. The informational bases for budgeting were much in need of overhaul and it was increasingly difficult for the Bureau to keep track of federal programs and spending. Computerization of the Bureau's information systems lagged substantially behind that of the individual departments. It no longer was possible for the examiner to stay on top of things by dint of hard work, long hours, and inquisitiveness. As programs became more interdepartmental and intergovernmental, the Bureau's traditional lines of communication and control became outmoded.

Things also were in disrepair in the main domestic departments. The Great Society piled new programs alongside old in a tangle of separate grant categories, program requirements, administrative channels, and delivery mechanisms. Many departments found it difficult to ascertain what they were purchasing or accomplishing with the funds they distributed. Program coordination in Washington and in the field was inadequate. It was difficult to coordinate related activities when they were managed by separate organizations.

In 1967 President Johnson was told by his Task Force on Government Organization (headed by Ben Heineman) that the Great Society domestic programs were failing because of administrative shortcomings. The task force recommended that program management be strengthened at the top levels of the federal government, with new functions and capabilities assigned to the White House, the Budget

Bureau, and department heads. In line with PPB concepts, the Budget Bureau would have the lead role in policy analysis. The President failed to act on these recommendations; presumably he preferred programmatic solutions (model cities, concentrated employment program, neighborhood service centers) or weak coordinating devices (interagency committees, task forces, lead and convenor authority) to major administrative changes.

The 1969 election brought to office a President whose domestic initiatives have tended to be managerial rather than programmatic. President Nixon has acted to realign the regional structures of domestic agencies, to simplify and decentralize the processing of categorical grants, to consolidate grants into broad program groupings, and to reorganize the domestic departments and his Executive Office. Taken as a whole, these actions signify the ascendency of management in the highest circles of government. They also represent divergences from the aims of PPB.

The Executive Office

Nixon's first management decisions revamped the Executive Office of the President, an institution that had undergone few significant changes since its establishment in 1939.[24] This priority was dictated by the President's conviction that programs could not be coordinated below if they were pulled apart at the top. Reorganization of the Executive Office was fashioned by the President's Advisory Council on Executive Reorganization (the Ash Council), comprised mostly of men with backgrounds in business management. In accord with the Ash Council's recommendations, the Domestic Council was established as a new Executive Office unit and the Budget Bureau was transformed into the Office of Management and Budget. Reversing the formula proposed three years earlier by the Heineman task force, the Ash Council gave the Domestic Council responsibility for new program development and OMB the job of coordinating federal programs. Thus, programming was to be split off from the budget process, and budgeting was to be treated as one of a number of related management processes. The downfall of PPB was to be hardened into organizational patterns.

Viewed from the White House, PPB never was a particularly useful instrument. It was targeted to a budget process which constrains presidential discretion and is operated by career officials through time-consuming and policy-obscuring routines. The Domestic Council promised to give the President a policy-analysis capability stripped of PPB-type techniques and associations with the budget process. Budgeting, however, would be put to work as a process for improving program management. In the overdrawn language of the President's reorganization message, "The Domestic Council will be primarily concerned with *what* we do; the Office of Management and Budget will be primarily concerned with *how* we do it and how *well* we do it."[25] Budgeting would operate alongside program coordination, management information systems, and other administrative functions. It would not be the central process for shaping the President's program and analyzing policy alternatives.

This division of organizational authority suffered from a key ambivalence. The Domestic Council would concentrate policy formation in a White House staff, but the President also was on record in favor of governmental decentralization and giving the departments a larger role in executive decision making. On paper, the ambivalence was resolved by awarding the major domestic agencies representation on the Domestic Council; in practice, it has been handled by giving the Domestic Council a lower profile and a somewhat smaller staff than was originally planned. The Domestic Council does not yet match in size or prominence Henry Kissinger's National Security Council.

The downgrading of the budget function has gone according to script, but the relationship between the budget and management sides of OMB is weak. There now are two additional administrative layers between the President and the examinations levels, and the amount of presidential time allocated to budget making has dropped in recent years, with most presidential time invested on macroeconomic issues rather than on departmental programs. In budget matters, the Director of OMB generally has the final say, and few appeals are taken to the President. With political men now stationed in OMB and with constant intervention by White House operators, the ordinary budget examiner has less involvement in presidential policy making than he once had. In effect, the examiners and their process have been demoted.

However, the budgeters and management specialists continue to have little contact with one another, though OMB is trying to bring them together through the Spring Preview. It bears remembering that this is the same point at which analysis and budgeting were supposed to be conjoined in the PPB system. Budgeting may prove to be as resistent to invasion by managers as it was to invasion by analysts.

Department Reorganization

PPB and departmental reorganization can be regarded as partial substitutes for one another. When PPB was flourishing in the Defense
Department, it was utilized to accomplish many of the objectives that
had been sought in earlier reorganization attempts. Even though each
of the military services retained its separate organizational identity, it
was possible for the Secretary of Defense to make cross-cutting decisions by means of the mission-oriented program budget. Air Force
had charge over Minuteman and Navy over Polaris, but both were
lodged in the strategic forces program. In this way, it was possible to
overcome internal organizational constraints within DOD without
having to engage in what probably would have been a futile battle to
abolish the tri-service structure.

Governmentwide PPB, however, did not have the same effect
on organizational boundaries. It proved much more difficult to
"crossover" between departments than to reconcile organizational
problems within the same agency. Under the PPB system mandated
by the Budget Bureau, each department had its own program structure and it would have taken an enormous concentration of power in
the Budget Director (making him, some department officials feared,
the McNamara of domestic policy) to integrate programs that crossed
departmental lines. Short of the President, no one had reasonably full
authority over domestic programs.

In 1971 President Nixon proposed the abolition of seven domestic departments (retaining the two staff departments, Justice and
Treasury), and the creation of four new departments: Community
Development, Human Resources, Natural Resources, and Economic
Affairs. Reorganization would attempt to accomplish what PPB
proved unable to do: to structure the decision-making apparatus of
the federal government along program lines. The logic was that for
departments to budget according to objectives they first had to be
organized according to objectives. This theme was sounded in the
President's message to Congress in support of his reorganization:

> We must rebuild the executive branch according to a new un-
> derstanding of how government can best be organized to per-
> form effectively. The key to that new understanding is the con-
> cept that the executive branch of the government should be
> organized around basic goals. Instead of grouping activities by
> narrow subject or by limited constituencies, we should organize
> them around the great purposes of government in modern soci-
> ety.[26]

The four new departments would be organized around four major systems: spatial, social, environmental, and economic. Client-oriented departments (such as Labor and Agriculture) and means-oriented departments (such as Transportation) would have their functions distributed among the new departments. The most radical dismemberment was proposed for Agriculture: its units would be distributed among all four new departments. Rural electrification would go to Community Development: food stamps to Human Resources; Forest Service to Natural Resources; and Commodity Credit programs to Economic Affairs. A governmentwide program structure probably would not have looked very different than the new departmental setup. But judging from initial reaction in Congress, reorganization will be no easier to achieve than PPB. Under pressure, the President has withdrawn much of his proposal concerning the Department of Agriculture; in the end he will settle for far less than he wanted.[27]

Information Systems

In trying to impose an informational structure suitable for planning and analysis, PPB ignored the many other informational requirements of the budget process. It also assumed that there is a unique configuration of governmental objectives—the "program structure"—serving all analytic purposes. In fact, however, there are as many ways to classify information as there are analytic perspectives. Unable to satisfy all uses or users, the program structure turned out to be an additional layer of classifications, not very different in many agencies from older functional categories. Moreover, it was not possible in most cases to recast the established budget and appropriation accounts, and these had to be "crosswalked" to the program structure.

A 1969 consultant's report proposed that the program budget be integrated into the Budget Bureau's informational systems by means of "entity programs," basic accounting units comparable to cost or responsibility centers.[28] Each entity program would be suitable for aggregation into an organizational, functional, or program budget. Not much progress has been made, however, and the various informational structures continue to be separate. One problem is that during the 1960's most major federal agencies invested heavily in the installation of their own management information systems, and these are not always compatible with the structures used by the central budgetary apparatus. A related problem is the clash between managerial and analytic perspectives, with the core categories appropriate for one purpose quite different from those helpful for the other.

Still another problem is the cost and technical difficulty of meshing the various structures for the government as a whole. Burned by the PPB experience and uncertain as to the direction it should take, OMB has been reluctant to commit itself fully to a new and costly approach. This reluctance has brought it into conflict with the Joint Committee on Congressional Operations which is monitoring implementation of the Legislative Reorganization Act of 1970. Section 202 of that Act directed OMB to work with the Treasury and GAO to "develop, establish, and maintain standard classifications of programs, activities, receipts, and expenditures of Federal agencies in order to meet the needs of the various branches of the Government." OMB's initial approach was very cautious:

> The evolution of the decisionmaking processes over time has created constituents for conflicting classification approaches. . . . Consequently, the transition from existing structures to any new concept will pose real challenge. A trend or movement to standardization must be "within reason."[29]

OMB set up four task forces with a handful of part-time staff persons to identify appropriate organization and fund codes, program structures, and supplementary classification systems. In effect, OMB merely continued the low-level information work it had commenced some years earlier.

The Joint Committee found these efforts "not reassuring," for they failed to take into account the informational needs of Congress or to move effectively toward the design of new standardized information systems. Under prodding by the Joint Committee, OMB finally admitted:

> that the scope of the system development effort as anticipated by the Congress is substantially greater than previously incorporated in our plans. . . . It is apparent that the limited part time involvement of staff . . . is grossly inadequate.[30]

OMB now estimates that over the next decade total development costs might reach $500 million and require 50 to 100 additional OMB personnel.

The clash between OMB and the Joint Committee arose in part from two old issues which plagued the installation of PPB. One has been OMB's reluctance to expand the kinds of budgetary and program information routinely available to Congress; another is OMB's reluctance to become the informational czar of the federal government. Until these are resolved, it is doubtful that congressional pressure will suffice to overcome OMB recalcitrance.

For OMB the main priority is to do something about the basic budget accounts and the methods for preparing the detailed budget and keeping track of expenditures. OMB finally has welcomed the computer into its chambers, though it has a long way to go before the computer is fully hitched to the routines of budgeting. OMB is aiming for a Rolling Budget System which would enable it to update the budget whenever changes occur as a consequence of departmental, presidential, or congressional action.

There is a significant difference between the informational ferment that was associated with PPB and that which now dominates OMB. Unlike PPB, current informational reforms are designed to improve the traditional budget process, to convert manual routines into computerized operations, to improve the accuracy of budget details, and to obtain current data on the status of all accounts. OMB has decided that the modernization of its core budget process must take precedence over the use of the budget for analytic purposes.

Performance Budgeting

PPB came on the scene before the aims of a previous reform—performance budgeting—had been realized. One of the chief purposes of performance budgeting was the use of work and cost measures in the preparation and execution of the budget. Cost and production goals would be established when the budget was formulated and these measures would be compared to actual performance. With only a few exceptions, performance budgeting failed in reaching these objectives. Consequently when PPB arrived, most agencies lacked adequate work and cost reporting systems. The demise of PPB has spurred renewal of the performance budgeting efforts suspended in the mid 1960's.

OMB has been pilot testing a Performance Measurement System which combines features of performance budgeting and PPB. The system calls for pinpointing managerial responsibility and requires the manager to specify performance targets for his program. A reporting system shows variances from planned performance and enables program managers and OMB to take corrective action when variances exceed tolerance levels. Whether this system becomes a basis for a renewed PPB drive depends on at least two design features: the utility of the individual program as building blocks for larger aggregations, and the types of output measures used.

The likelihood, however, is that this system will not mature into a PPB-type operation but will conform rather closely to the performance budgeting models which were in vogue during the 1950's. In testimony before the Joint Committee on Congressional Operations, an OMB spokesman described the system as based on "very fundamental, old-fashioned principles":

> Really, all we are trying to do is get a very explicit statement of exactly what it is he [a program manager] plans to accomplish, the time period for attaining specified results, and then let him prepare his own report card on how well he is doing in working toward the specified results.[31]

In sum, the performance measurement system is aimed at program managers rather than at top-level officials, and is oriented to work targets rather than to program objectives.

ON THE HILL

PPB was conceived almost exclusively from an executive perspective, as if Congress does not exist and that all it takes to make a budget is to review agency requests within an administrative setting. Moreover, PPB was engineered in a way that enabled the Bureau of the Budget to bypass Congress. The appropriation accounts were not restructured nor were significant alterations made in the budget submissions to Congress. The special PPB plans and analyses were destined for executive use and were not incorporated into the flow of data to Congress.

For its part, Congress generally preferred to continue in its accustomed ways, and the appropriations committee took little note of efforts to change the budget process. As a general rule, the closer a committee was to the appropriations process and to substantive power over spending, the less interest it showed in PPB. The only important PPB hearings were held by advisory committees, the Joint Economic Committee, and a Subcommittee of the Senate Government Operations Committee. On occasion, however, congressmen were piqued over the refusal of executive agencies to reveal the analytic and planning products of PPB. When it suits their purposes, congressmen want access to long-range cost projections and analytic studies. But they seem to have little interest in the overall PPB system.

Any inquiry into legislative attitudes toward PPB must reckon with Congress as an institution and with the division of labor and power among its members. To the extent that PPB would require Congress to trade away its control over the executive in favor of a larger policy role, it will be difficult to find many enthusiasts on Capitol Hill. However, if policy analysis can be fashioned into an instrument of legislative control over executive spending, the prospects become more favorable. For this reason there is bound to be a great disparity between executive and legislative uses of PPB. The President and program officials normally are willing to disclose the outcomes of their analyses and plans—that is, the programs and policies to be funded in the budget—but they are reluctant to reveal the alternatives which were considered and rejected, the analytic calculations which undergird their policy decisions, or the future costs of their policies. Congress, however, is as much interested in the alternatives as in the policies, and it looks to the analyses and projections as a means of challenging the executive's budget and program recommendations.

This tug of war explains recent congressional interest in budget innovation. Congress took the lead in the Legislative Reorganization Act of 1970. In addition to calling for a restructuring of budget classifications, that Act mandates five-year cost estimates for new programs and directs the Comptroller General "to review and analyze the results of Government programs and activities carried on under existing law, including the making of cost benefit studies," and it gives the GAO the go-ahead to recruit persons "who are expert in analyzing and conducting cost benefit studies of Government programs."

These requirements now written into law strive for the very objectives that executive PPB failed to accomplish. The parallel is strikingly complete because the federal PPB system that failed also gave top priority to a new program classification, multi-year plans, and program analysis. Knowledgeable persons do not expect the recent exuberance in Congress to transform federal budgeting or executive relations at once.

After all, GAO has had a broad mandate to evaluate administrative programs since its creation in 1921, but it has taken on this posture slowly and reluctantly. And the call for multi-year projections brings back memories of Public Law 84-801 enacted in 1956 which also prescribed long-range cost estimates, but has been honored infinitely more in the breach than in the practice. It will take much more than legislation to breathe vitality into program evaluation, but the 1970 Reorganization Act reflects the mood of Congress at this period in executive-legislative relations.

There is evidence that at least some congressmen or committee intend to take their new role seriously. The Family Planning Service and Population Research Act of 1970 delineates the types of information that Congress now wants. Section 5 might have been written for an executive's PPB system: it calls for a five-year plan specifying the number of individuals to be served, along with program goals and costs, as well as annual reports which compare results achieved during the preceding fiscal year with the objectives established under the plan and which indicate steps being taken to achieve the objectives of the plan.

It remains to be demonstrated whether Congress can accomplish via legislation that which PPB failed to accomplish by administrative order. However, the test of legislative successes must be the same that I have applied to the executive; that is whether the central processes of budgeting are any different because of the availability of new analytic devices.

A RETURN TO PPB?

The failure of PPB in the federal government was not inevitable, though the traditions of budgeting and the manner of implementation made it likely. The few states which have achieved substantial budgetary renovation give evidence of what can be accomplished when resources are marshaled intelligently and forcefully. With so much of the business of PPB undone, it is probable that under a different label and with somewhat different approaches and techniques there eventually will be a return to the aims of PPB.

However, it is possible that the next wave of budget reform on the federal level will be directed toward one of the oldest issues of modern budgeting—the maintenance of financial control and accountability.[32] Contemporary issues of control fall into two categories. First is the reappearance of a very old problem—the ability of the government to control total spending. In current form, the problem is not of holding agencies to the spending limits established in law, but of "uncontrollable" forces that push total federal spending well above the figures estimated in the budget. A second cluster of issues pertains to the use of resources in instances where the normal internal controls are not effective. This situation prevails in intergovernmental fiscal relations and whenever there is a divorcement between spending authority and program delivery. As the granting government, the United States clearly has less effective control over the fiscal practices of recipient states and localities than it has over its own agencies.

A related problem is known as multi-pocket budgeting. When a spending agency (or government) receives funds from a variety of sources and the funds are interchangeable, it may be able to evade financial controls by shifting funds from one pocket to another. The spread of government by contract and the growing entanglement of public and private funding and activities also diminish the force of internal controls. Outside contractors and private agencies often are not subject to the stringent administrative and financial controls applicable to regular governmental institutions, and they rarely have fully internalized the norms and rules practiced by public agencies. In fact, one of the reasons why governments turn to contractors and private parties is to escape the administrative controls to which they are subject. But in so doing, they open the possibility of fiscal impropriety and a loss of accountability for the use of public funds. The opportunity for mischief seems to multiply when government agencies are in a position to determine the eligibility (or entitlement) of private parties for public benefits. Even where corruption is under control, impropriety flourishes when governments award valued subsidies to private beneficiaries.

All these are classical control problems in the sense that they pertain to the proper use of public resources. But their urgency derives from the enormous growth of government and the formation of new administrative institutions and relationships. The return of PPB will have to await the resolution of these problems, for control always is the first business of any budget process.

ENDNOTES

1. Office of Management and Budget Transmittal Memorandum No. 38, June 21, 1971.
2. The term is Alice Rivlin's, though she may not agree to the interpretation to which it has been put here. See Alice Rivlin, "The Planning, Programming, and Budgeting System in the Department of Health, Education, and Welfare: Some Lessons from Experience," in U.S. Congress Joint Economic Committee, *The Analysis and Evaluation of Public Expenditures: The PPB System*, p. 915. In this article, "analysis" is meant to cover planning as well.

3. This was the view of a panel of PPB practitioners who gathered in Washington on March 2, 1972, under the auspices of the Association for Public Program Analysis to discuss "Is PPB Dead?"

4. See Allen Schick, "Systems for Analysis: PPB and its Alternatives," in Joint Economic Committee, *op. cit.*, pp. 817–834.

5. One report suggests that in preparation of the 1973 HEW budget, a productive relationship was forged between the budgeters and the analysts. The analysts took the lead in formulating a revised program strategy which gave priority to "reduction in human dependency." While it is not clear whether this shift means only the momentary ascendency of certain participants or a more profound reorientation, an examination of HEW's 1973 budget figures does not give evidence of a marked change in priorities. Secretary Richardson took a realistic view of what was accomplished. "In terms of the gross department budget, the definable impact of the strategies is relatively small. But the strategies are significant in imparting a direction. They reflect a cutting edge of the department's future direction." See John K. Iglehart, "Budget Report/HEW Department, Largest Federal Spender, Seeks to Funnel More Money to the Poor," *National Journey*, January 29, 1972, pp. 168–180.

6. Alain C. Enthoven and K. Wayne Smith, *How Much is Enough?* (New York: Harper & Row, 1971).

7. For an insightful study of the relationship between planning and budgeting in the Defense Department during the early 1950's, see Frederick C. Mosher, *Program Budgeting: Theory and Practice* (Chicago: Public Administration Service, 1954).

8. Although Enthoven and Smith acknowledge that "between 1947 and 1961 substantial progress was made in improving the organization and legal structure of the U.S. Defense establishment" (p. 8), they do not recognize that the PPB developments in the 1960's would not have been possible without the organizational reforms of the 1960's.

9. See Frederick C. Mosher and John E. Harr, *Programming Systems and Foreign Affairs Leadership* (New York: Oxford University Press, 1970).

10. The first PPB guidance, Bulletin 66-3 (October 12, 1965) provided: "Specialized staff assistance is also essential in all but the smallest agencies. . . . Each agency will, therefore, establish an adequate central staff or staffs for analysis, planning and programming."

11. Thus, PPB instructions were contained in special bulletins, while budget instructions were issued in the regular Circular A-11. PPB references were introduced into Circular A-11 in 1968 and 1969, but no attempt was made to revamp the instructions in accord with PPB doctrines.

12. Enthoven and Smith, *op. cit.*, pp. 56–58.

13. Bulletin 66-3, *op. cit.*

14. The main PPB documents—the program and financial plans and the program memorandums were targeted for the Spring Preview while Circular A-11 was dominant during the fall Budget Review when hard decisions were made.

15. William Gorham recently compared the amount of money spent on housing research—$60 million per year—with the sums spent on other programs: defense spends 14,000 per cent more; space, 4,300 per cent

higher; atomic energy 790 per cent more; agriculture 340 per cent more. See The Urban Institute, *Search* (January-February 1972), p. 2.

16. See Peter C. Sarant, *Is PPBS Dead?* mimeo, U.S. Civil Service Commission, December 1971.

17. See Aaron Wildavsky, "The Political Economy of Efficiency: Cost-Benefit Analysis, Systems Analysis, and Program Budgeting," *Public Administration Review* (December 1966), pp. 292-310.

18. Victor A. Thompson, "Decision Theory, Pure and Applied," General Learning Press, 1971, p. 16.

19. See Aaron Wildavsky, "Rescuing Policy Analysis from PPBS," in Joint Economic Committee, *op. cit.*, pp. 835-852.

20. See Allen Schick, *Budget Innovation in the States* (Washington, D.C.: The Brookings Institution, 1971).

21. For one of the first comprehensive attempts to show the distribution of budgetary benefits, see U.S. Congress Joint Economic Committee, *The Economics of Federal Subsidy Programs*, January 1972.

22. During the later Eisenhower years, Defense spending was held relatively constant; the level of spending was boosted $5 billion between 1962 and 1963.

23. See Allen Schick, "The Budget Bureau that Was: Thoughts on the Rise, Decline, and Future of a Presidential Agency," *Law and Contemporary Problems* (Summer 1970), pp. 519-539.

24. Most of the changes in the Executive Office since 1939 were the addition of new units—such as the Central Intelligence Agency and the Office of Emergency Preparedness—rather than a shift in the functions of the existing units.

25. Reorganization Message of President Richard M. Nixon to Congress, March 12, 1970.

26. Message of President Richard M. Nixon to Congress, March 25, 1971.

27. On the difficulty of achieving departmental reorganization, see U.S. Congress, House Committee on Government Operations, *Executive Reorganization: A Summary Analysis*, March 15, 1972, p. 53.

28. An entity program was defined as "a self-contained operating program managed by a single agency, and, within the agency, by a responsible line manager. It consumes resources (stated in appropriation account terms) to produce outputs aimed at specific objectives (stated in PPB terms)." McKinsey & Co., *Strengthening Planning, Programming, and Budgeting, and Budgeting in the Bureau of the Budget*, June, 1969.

29. U.S. Congress, Joint Committee on Congressional Operations, Hearings on *Fiscal and Budgetary Information for the Congress*, 92nd Congress, 2nd Session, 1972, p. 163.

30. *Ibid.*, p. 63.

31. *Ibid.*, p. 31.

32. See Allen Schick, "The Road to PPB The Stages of Budget Reform," *Public Administration Review* (December 1966), pp. 243-258.

25

james w. davis
randall b. ripley

THE BUREAU OF THE BUDGET AND
EXECUTIVE BRANCH AGENCIES: NOTES ON
THEIR INTERACTION*

INTRODUCTION

This article analyzes data obtained in interviews on contracts and relations between personnel in the U.S. Bureau of the Budget and personnel in other Executive Branch agencies. Although there has been a fair amount written on the Bureau of the Budget as an institution, much of the available material only describes the various aspects of the Bureau's job.[1] A recent analysis of the politics of the budgetary process discusses relations between the Bureau and operating agencies in the context of budgetary calculations and strategies.[2] This is only one aspect of the Bureau-agency relationship, however. The Bureau of the Budget and Executive Branch agencies are also jointly concerned with program planning, management, and organization structure. This paper focuses on several questions: What is the range of issues or problems that brings the Bureau into contact with Executive Branch agencies? How is contact maintained? What image do agencies have of the Bureau of the Budget? What considerations affect the relationship between the agency and the Bureau of the Budget?

James W. Davis and Randall B. Ripley, "The Bureau of the Budget and Executive Branch Agencies: Notes on Their Interaction." *The Journal of Politics*. vol. 29 (November 1967), pp. 749-769. Reprinted by permission.

In the summer of 1965 we conducted 61 interviews on the subject of Bureau-agency relations in which we asked these questions. Each respondent was promised both personal and, except for the Bureau, agency anonymity. Nineteen of the interviews were with officials in the Bureau of the Budget. These men varied greatly in length of service and held a variety of jobs. The remaining 42 interviews were held with officials in three cabinet departments and two large independent agencies. All of these five agencies operate primarily in the domestic area. Twenty-six of the interviews were at the top management levels of the agencies. These men presumably had the viewpoint of their secretary or agency head in mind. Sixteen of the agency interviews were with bureau chiefs and other bureau officials. Most agency officials with whom we talked were relatively senior, although they held a variety of jobs.

We did not select the respondents with any thought of randomness or representativeness. Rather we picked men reputed to have a great deal of knowledge about Bureau-agency relations. We chose the five agencies in part to obtain a mixture of those thought to have "good" relations with the Bureau and those thought to have "bad" relations with the Bureau. In the Bureau itself we talked both to persons directly responsible for the five agencies and to persons with broader policy or staff responsibilities.

The interviews were open-ended. A number of subjects were probed in every interview, but the order and wording of the questions followed no fixed pattern. We were seeking the peculiar experience of every respondent and so, within broad guidelines, we let his interests dictate the subject matter of the interview. We sought to discuss the whole context of Bureau-operating agency relationships. Typical questions focused on the number and frequency of contacts, content of contacts, initiation of contacts, personnel involved, understanding or lack of understanding in the relationship, instances of particularly satisfactory relations and the reasons for them, instances of particularly strained relations and the reasons for them, the role of the department in relation to the operating bureaus and the Bureau of the Budget, and suggestions for change. The interviews lasted between one hour and two and a half hours. The average interview lasted about an hour and a half.

The discussion that follows first describes the occasions for contact between the Bureau and the operating agencies. Second, it analyzes the points of contact. Third, it considers the agencies' images of the Budget Bureau. Finally, it discusses conditions that affect the relationship between the agencies and the Bureau of the Budget.

THE OCCASIONS FOR CONTACT

There are six general occasions for contact between the Bureau of the Budget and an operating agency. In most agencies the occasions arise throughout the year on virtually a daily basis. Some of the occasions, such as the formal preparation of the budget for the coming fiscal year, are regular and predictable. Most of them are not.

First, if an agency wants to submit proposed legislation to Congress it must come into contact with the Bureau of the Budget.[3] The more that an agency relies on legislation for its growth, the more it must rely on the Bureau of the Budget for support for its legislative ideas. One of the respondents in an operating agency said, "This is a legislating agency. We go to the legislative trough constantly. We are thus involved with the Bureau of the Budget constantly." A respondent in another agency said, "Legislation is the area in which I get in touch with the Bureau of the Budget. We have 200 or 300 bills a year which apply to us." Another agency respondent indicated the frequency of contact with the Bureau: "I have several contacts a day with the Bureau of the Budget on program matters. Under the law we develop a work program and then must go to the Congress through the President, which means the Bureau of the Budget."

Second, agencies are necessarily in close contact with the Bureau each year as they prepare their budget for the following year.[4] The Bureau must take the individual agency requests and through a long and grueling process produce the President's budget for submission to Congress. The "budget cycle" inexorably pushes operating agencies and the Bureau together closely for a number of months each year.

Third, as the operating agencies spend money during the course of a fiscal year, they come into contact with the Bureau because the Bureau has specific duties in relation to what might best be called the execution of the budget. Apportionment and requests for supplemental appropriations are the two major instances in which contact is necessary. But the Bureau, through its examiner for each agency or cluster of agencies, is interested in the whole range of activities carried on by the agencies and what they are doing with the funds that Congress has appropriated. Said a budget officer in one of the five operating agencies: "Either I myself or my staff are in constant contact with someone over there, really on a daily basis. Seldom a day goes by without one or two calls; or we see someone for a lunch or a meeting. It may be a matter of getting guidance from them, or a matter of fighting or arguing with them." A respondent from another agency said, "Our department has an enormous number of contacts with the Bureau of the Budget. We are a fast growing and dynamic agency. We have appropriations all the time. We have a batch of supplementals over at the Bureau this week as a matter of fact."

Fourth, operating agencies and the Bureau have contact with each other on a number of specialized problems involving, for example, questions of management and organization, statistics, and automatic data processing. The Bureau's interest in management and organization problems manifests itself in budgetary or program contacts. But this is also a continuing separate concern of the Bureau. Personnel questions, such as average grade and average salary of employees in an agency, create agency-Bureau contact. The Bureau has a special concern with the purchase and utilization of automatic data processing equipment by the federal government. The current presidential drive for cost reduction in the agencies is, in part, a question of management that brings the Bureau into frequent contact with many agencies. The problem of maintaining comparable statistics in various government agencies is another specialized problem demanding Bureau-agency contact.

Fifth, in addition to its need for specific information from the agencies in order to oversee the legislative program, the preparation and execution of the budget, and elements of management and organization, the Bureau of the Budget has a general information-gathering role to perform for the President. When the President wants to know what is happening with respect to almost anything in some part of the Executive Branch he is likely to turn first to the Bureau of the Budget to report the relevant information to him. Thus the Bureau is constantly requesting various facts, figures and less "hard" information from the operating agencies. Likewise the agencies must often turn to the Bureau for information. What does this directive mean? How should this Executive Order be interpreted? What priority should be attached to the latest cluster of directives?

Sixth, there is also a general learning and teaching contact between the operating agencies and the Bureau. The agencies try to educate the Bureau on the purpose and value of their programs. The Bureau tries to educate the agencies on the will of the President and on the nature of the Bureau itself as a staff arm to the President.

A number of our respondents in the agencies commented on their effort to educate the Bureau of the Budget. Said one, "The training of a new Bureau of the Budget examiner is a major point of contact. He will suggest some field trips for himself and we will also draw up many itineraries for him." Said another, "I do a lot of stuff to be sure that people at the Bureau of the Budget understand what we are trying to do here. My opinion, based on experience, suggests that within reasonable limits you can deal with philosophical hostility, but you can't deal with ignorance or misunderstanding. Thus we try to promote the flow of information."[5] A respondent in the Bureau of the Budget indicated that he was likewise eager to have the examiners for whom he was responsible learn rapidly as much as possible about the agencies with which they were working: "When I take on an examiner I have him set up meetings with agency people to get acquainted with them and their programs."

THE POINTS OF CONTACT

What parts of the agencies and of the Bureau are involved in important contacts with one another? The answer, broadly stated, is that almost everyone in the Bureau will at some time come into contact with operating agencies and that almost everyone in the middle management grades and higher in the operating agencies is likely to have important business with the Bureau. Lower-grade program personnel may also have contacts, but these are less predictable.

THE BUREAU OF THE BUDGET

Within the Bureau of the Budget, the formal organization has an impact on determining who talks to the agencies and on what matters. The Director and Deputy Director are appointed by the President and generally come into contact with the agencies only on a budget decision of some magnitude or perhaps on a sticky interagency problem. The statutory Assistant Directors are appointed by the Director with the approval of the President and serve as line or staff officers as the Director may assign work to them, often on an *ad hoc* basis. Thus their contacts cover the entire spectrum of the agencies. The Executive Assistant Director and Special Assistant to the Director also become involved with operating agencies only on important, non-routine matters. The budget review, legislative reference, statistical standards, and management and organization staffs, headed by career Assistant Directors, have contact with the agencies on the special topics suggested by their titles. This may involve a great deal of contact with some agencies and less with others. The primary point of continuing intensive contact with agencies is in the seven divisions that oversee the budgets of Executive Branch agencies and assign examiners to each of the agencies. Thus consideration of the contact between the Bureau and agencies must begin with the examiners assigned to these seven divisions.[6]

The budget examiner is the main link between the Bureau and most agencies, particularly the smaller, less visible ones. Examiners get involved to some extent with almost everything an agency does. An examiner's contact with the agency is likely to be daily and will cover questions involving program, personnel, management, and legislation. As one examiner commented:

> I feel as if I have had a free hand in covering the waterfront of issues with my agencies. I spend about 40–45 percent of time on budget and related matters, about 30 percent of my time on legislation, and 25–30 percent of my time on management and organization, including some personnel matters by choice and others have forced themselves on me. I get into management matters more than most examiners. I have a public administration background. I get into this one when I have time.

Another examiner reported, "I get involved with my agencies on almost everything. The most glamorous and important things are program issues. I also get heavily involved in organizational questions. I spend a good deal of time on legislation too. The proportion of time spent on these various segments varies radically from agency to agency and year to year. My major interest is program development and operations." Comments from personnel in the operating agencies made it clear that the examiners do, in fact, range broadly.

The variety of an examiner's interests and responsibilities suggests that he must use a variety of contacts and sources of information. The examiner is the primary intelligence agent for the Bureau and thus must collect information where he can find it. An important source of information for him is, of course, the agency budget office. But examiners do not generally find agency budget officers sufficiently program-oriented. Thus they turn to agency members with direct program responsibility. In some agencies they deal with the budget office only when technical details of budget preparation are in question. One examiner, for example, noted that he went to the budget office in the agency only when he "needed numbers." Clearly, most Bureau examiners will try to go to any source in an agency that they think will yield the needed information.

The examiners' superiors in the Bureau—branch chiefs and division chiefs—are also in contact with the agencies, ordinarily on a higher level. A branch chief said, "I will have contact with the budget office and with the assistant secretary for administration and on occasion with other assistant secretaries. I am also in rather frequent contact with the under secretary." It is unusual for an examiner to have extensive contacts this high in the departmental structure, although examiners do have extensive contacts with bureau chiefs.

When do the examiner's superiors become involved in questions involving a single agency? One examiner summarized his experience:

> The legislative system forces legislative matters to go to the Office of Legislative Reference. In other areas we make a weekly report to the division chief and then a consolidated report goes to the Director. Any major program changes immediately go to the division chief. Almost anything that involves much time comes to the attention of the branch chief or the division chief. The Bureau is very fluid in terms of responsibilities. There are very few things that I do alone. An important part of my job is keeping my boss informed.

Another examiner indicated he brought matters to the attention of the branch chief and then the division chief only "if I can't solve the problem." Still another examiner indicated that the personality of the agency representatives with whom he was dealing helped determine what would go higher in the Bureau. Some agency personnel predictably appealed a great many of his decisions and positions, and thus forced matters higher in the Bureau themselves.

Division chiefs tended to view their role as one of solving as many problems and ending as many arguments as possible when they were brought to them by the examiners or by the agencies. Only those that they could not resolve went higher in the Bureau. Said one division chief, "I can get involved in anything if it is important enough or controversial enough." Another division chief viewed his own involvement somewhat more narrowly:

> I deal with agencies on matters that the Director asks me to handle and occasionally an examiner may bring a problem to me. Or in presentation at a review I may see a question that should be taken to an assistant secretary or the under secretary and then I get involved. My examiners have a good deal of leeway. We recruit on the understanding that a man will take responsibility. I expect them to use their own discretion in bringing things to my attention. Usually an examiner would go through one of the assistant division chiefs and the assistant division chief would see me.

Operating agencies also have contacts with the non-divisional parts of the Bureau of the Budget. On cost reduction matters, for example, the Office of Management and Organization may be involved with the operating agencies. On legislative programs, the Office of Legislative Reference would be involved. On matters relating to the preparation of a budget, the agencies may contact the Office of Budget Review. On occasion, when important issues are at stake, a senior agency official may be in contact with an Assistant Director in the Bureau, or the Bureau official may initiate the contact.

In these contacts between agencies and the non-divisional parts of the Bureau of the Budget, the examiner is not left out, however. As the budget officer in one department noted, "Legislation winds up with examiners and they are the ones I have contact with. As a matter of fact these examiners tend to become liaison men on lots of items. They pass the word along from the other divisions of the Bureau." Respondents in the Bureau confirmed the important place of the examiner in virtually every matter. For example, the Office of Legislative Reference is small—with only ten professional staff members—and thus must rely on examiners for many of the legislative recommendations.

The Operating Agencies

The variation between departments and agencies on the range of points of contact with the Bureau is great. Some departments and agencies officially encourage widespread contact with the Bureau, feeling that this will increase the chances for developing sympathy in the Bureau for their programs and for their particular problems.

Other departments and agencies are extremely conscious of "channels" and insist that the Bureau make its requests of the agency only through its budget officer. This position may be unpopular with both operators and Bureau examiners. A bureau chief in a department may feel that he can get a more sympathetic response from the Bureau of the Budget without going through his own department's budget office. A Bureau examiner may feel that the information received through the budget office is at least partially distorted and the truth is partially concealed. From his point of view the only way to get at the truth may be to ignore channels and talk directly with the operating personnel involved, either in Washington or in the field.

A number of Bureau of the Budget personnel interviewed discussed the problem of contacts both in and out of channels. One examiner commented, "In working with this department our major and normal channel should be the Budget Office. But we have mixed success in working with them. Their examiners are unlike ours; they don't deal with policy. They are only accountants. So I go directly to the bureau personnel. I try to keep the department informed of what I am doing." Speaking of the same department, another Bureau of the Budget examiner described direct contacts with the operating bureaus:

> We may not go through the department budget office if we are just seeking a piece of information or if we want to clear up a technical matter. But if there is a difference between the Budget Bureau and the department we will go through the department. On any matter that the secretary's office should know about we go through the department office. Basic policy issues relating to financing of programs go through the department budget office. And if the department and one of its bureaus differ—then we go through the department.

Still another examiner said:

> A lot of my relationship bypasses the department budget office. The tendency in this branch is to have us work through the department budget office, but each examiner finds that this is not entirely satisfactory either from a time standpoint or from a clarity standpoint. As you go through the department office there is some filtering out. If I am in a hurry I go direct to the bureau and inform the department office. I'd say the department tried to hold the bureaus in line, but I don't know with what success.

The problems of time and clarity (or honesty) that this examiner identifies also appeared in Bureau relations with other departments. Examiners generally noted that to go through the department often wasted time and might produce distorted answers. To avoid both problems, examiners are often moved to go directly to the operating personnel. Sometimes this works smoothly; other times it increases friction between the Bureau and the department, or even the Bureau and the departmental bureau.

Departmental officials have varying positions on the question of using channels in communications with the Bureau of the Budget. The natural departmental position is to limit extra-channel communications in some way. A department may want to control what the Bureau finds out so that it can present a united front to the Bureau and not be undercut by its own operating bureaus. It certainly wants to know what the Bureau does find out. Departmental personnel are often frustrated by knowing less about the operations of their own programs than Bureau of the Budget personnel.

But some departments feel more comfortable with direct contact than do others. One bureau chief said, "The Bureau of the Budget representative sits in on all regional directors' meetings. He hears the bad as well as the good. The Bureau of the Budget comes to all of our major meetings. They observe us in action all the time. The Bureau has unlimited access to us. Even when we have staff parties we always invite Bureau people too." In the same department, an assistant bureau chief of a different bureau noted, "We have a great deal of direct contact. Examiners from the Bureau of the Budget don't only go through channels. They come here directly for the facts. Of course, on policy matters we go through the department. But there is much direct contact."

Even in this relatively open department, a department official said, "We have to run the place so there is free communication between constituent units and the Bureau of the Budget, but we have to be careful on the kinds of contacts. On some things there can be direct contact between the Bureau of the Budget and our constituent parts and on other things no. We have had problems here. And there is no way to solve it completely. We want to be in on the major policy questions."

Not all operating agencies agree that free communication between constituent units and the Bureau of the Budget should be allowed. Some demand that all communication flow through the department office and at least one requires a detailed memorandum from any employee who has contact with anyone from the Bureau of the Budget.

What causes differences in agency practices? Their calculations of how best to get the support of the Bureau of the Budget or at least how to avoid fatal opposition or non-support are important in making this decision. A Bureau examiner summed up the difference from his perspective: "Some agencies think the more you know the more you can hurt them. Others think the more you know the more you can help them."[7]

Freedom of communication varies with the support and sympathy that the agency thinks it obtains from the Bureau. If a department views the Bureau as supportive and relatively generous, communication is likely to be freer than if the image of the Bureau held by the department is negative. Freedom of communication or lack of it also is conditioned by the understanding of the role of the Bureau of the

Budget held by the department. One budget officer in a department took the view that the Bureau represented the boss (the President) and thus had the right to go anywhere and look at anything. He required that the constituent members of the department inform him of contact with the Bureau, but he did not require the Bureau to go through him. In contrast, the budget officer in another department tended to view any direct contact between the Bureau of the Budget and a constituent unit as an attempt of the examiner to circumvent him unfairly. To him the Bureau was just another outside agency—with special powers, perhaps, but with no special mandate to collect information of which he was not aware.

THE IMAGE OF THE BUREAU OF THE BUDGET

It is clear that operating agency personnel have daily contact with Bureau of the Budget personnel and have many opportunities to observe, evaluate, and form impressions of the performance of Bureau examiners in particular and the Bureau of the Budget in general. These impressions are important since they affect the relationship between the agency and the Bureau.

Given the significance of the examiner's role in agency-Bureau relations, it is legitimate first to ask how the agencies view their examiners. The answer clearly is that there is no single view. Examiners are a widely varying group. This means that a large department with several examiners assigned to it may feel that some are treating it well and others not so well. It also means that a small agency or a bureau within a department with only one examiner may, from its viewpoint, be either blessed or afflicted by the Bureau of the Budget because of the personality and abilities of the one man with whom they deal.[8]

The comments of operating personnel highlight the great variation in examiners from their point of view. An assistant secretary in a large department said that, "Some have maturity and understand the purposes of our programs. They seek the same objectives we do and there is no problem. Then there are the brash young fellows. And then there are the nit-pickers, the trivia-oriented." Reports from other operators also showed the variation. Some were happy: "We have had excellent understanding of our work plans from the Bureau of the Budget, because we have had excellent examiners." "We have examiners who understand us much better than perhaps we have a right to expect. We have been very fortunate." "To be fair to the Bureau of the Budget I must admit that I have never dealt with a representative of the Bureau where I wasn't impressed by his intelligence. There are no nuts, kooks, or bureaucrats over there. And you can't run over them. They are savvy people. They pick up any mistakes I make quickly and this is proper." But others were unhappy. As one noted, "We have an examiner over here that we would just as soon have replaced. He is unreasonable, opinionated, and academic. But I suppose a new one might even be worse."

Agencies tend to place the attitude of their examiner toward their programs in one of three categories: advocacy, neutrality, or hostility. Neutrality appears to be the normal stance of the examiners, as seen by the agencies. This is certainly the attitude for which the Bureau of the Budget strives. But agencies have also perceived examiners as being either hostile non-supporters or advocates for their programs within the Bureau. One agency respondent said, "All the junior examiners, *once educated*, have become our staunch friends." But most did not feel that examiners became advocates. Said one, "I've never sensed any real advocacy by our examiners perhaps, but I have never seen any fundamental dislike either." A Bureau respondent noted, "By and large most of our examiners are in the middle. They resist the normal tendency to get co-opted."

Agencies view not only their individual examiners as hostile, neutral, or inclined to advocacy; they also view the Bureau of the Budget as an institution in these terms. Again the range of viewpoints is wide.

Perhaps the most favorable statement made by a high-level department official (a bureau chief, in this instance) was that "The sincerity and knowledge of the Bureau of the Budget is impressive at every phase. The Bureau of the Budget understands the social nature of our mission and is sympathetic to it. They have given us a reasonable deal all along the line. I would be happy to put the monetary fate of this agency completely in the hands of the Bureau of the Budget."

Several other departmental respondents also felt that the Bureau played a basically supportive role.

> We have fundamental respect for the role the Bureau plays. We have a relationship of frankness. We deal with them on an open-handed basis. We don't hide our problems. Generally, when the Bureau complains, we say, "if you know of a better way to do it, please tell us."

> We deal with a great deal of candor with the Bureau of the Budget. We're proud of what we are doing and we try to do a good job. We tackle problems forthrightly and tell them about

them, try to get their help. Some organizations treat the Bureau of the Budget as an adversary; we don't believe in that. There is a temptation, of course, to say that we can't run our own programs. But I think we're better off to have the Bureau of the Budget. It is a bridge between us and the White House. It is very useful to have it. We can find out what the White House thinks and it can explain us to the White House.

But not all operating officials took such a sanguine view of Bureau of the Budget influence on their program. Some viewed the Bureau as some form of the enemy, if not the devil:

> Our main problem with the Bureau has been an inability on our part to convey the social character of our programs or an inability on their part to grasp the social character and implications of what is too often described as just a credit program.
>
> The Bureau of the Budget is instinctively on the other side of everything we propose. They play the devil's advocate. They don't tip their hand; they certainly never urge us to do anything new.[9]
>
> The Bureau of the Budget doesn't agree with our objectives. They are not in sympathy with the idea of our clientele being treated as a special class.
>
> The main problem with all of the central agencies and personnel is that they have an attitude of suspicion or distrust as they approach operating people.[10]

Several complaints about the Bureau in the interviews suggest the specific images that agency personnel have of the Bureau of the Budget. One respondent complained that the Bureau of the Budget is politically naive:

> Sticky problems arise because of the political isolation of the Bureau of the Budget. The Bureau does not have good comprehension of what is in the minds of key congressional committee chairmen and members we have to deal with. They find incomprehensible the political problems we try to explain to them. They see us as being more responsive to Congress than to the President. There may be an element of truth here but they don't understand Congress.[11]

Respondents in other agencies made the same point. Said one, "The Bureau ought to acknowledge that it doesn't understand the appropriations process or it ought to force itself to understand the process." Said another, "When we are legislating we are in contact often. In part we try to find out their views and in part we tell them to keep their mouths shut before they lose what the President wants." These men felt that the Bureau followed too literally the President's admonition to leave politics to him.

Some Bureau personnel agreed in part with the agency respondents. They felt that the Bureau does sometimes reach decisions that make little sense politically or have little chance of success. But most of the Bureau respondents indicated that they did not feel that their job extended to the realm of politics. "The President has told us to leave political judgments to him; our job is to inform him on the merits," said one Bureau official. Some Bureau respondents also felt that some agencies are attuned *only* to political answers and are not willing to examine propositions on their merits.

A second persistent criticism was that the Bureau does not give positive help in developing agency programs. Said one agency official, "They have never been helpful in an inventive way. They have only given me a few germs of small ideas now and then." Some indicated that a few constructive suggestions had come from the Bureau, especially on legislative matters.

Bureau officials consider policy oversight and direction and program development to be their main tasks—particularly when the President encourages the Bureau to perform them. They were quite proud of their record here, especially under Presidents Kennedy and Johnson, and thought that the agencies would be aware of their leadership. In fact, however, in the agencies we studied, the message had come through only partially. Agency staff were not able to view the Bureau as a positive force, but thought of it largely in negative terms.[12]

Another comment made repeatedly by personnel from the agencies was that the Bureau was indecisive. Said one respondent, "I have the feeling at times that there is an avoidance of decisions on the part of the Bureau—they will say things need further study, they need more evidence." Others made the same point. "Around here some people call the Bureau of the Budget the House of Wax. You have to light a fire under it to get it to move." "The Bureau of the Budget never takes a position on its own. They force you into taking a position." "In its coordinating roles the Bureau of the Budget rarely takes a firm position." "It is hard to know what the Bureau position on some questions is."

Some of the agency respondents also made complaints that the Bureau intruded into management responsibilities. From their perspective, they felt that the Bureau treated all agencies alike, regardless of the job being done by the agency's management. Thus it engaged in an overly-detailed review of the operations of the agency, lumping good managers and poor managers together in the same category. One manager, for example, said that the Bureau applied the latest "management fad" to all government agencies without discriminating between those doing well already and those doing poorly:

> Each successive fad is believed during the period of its popularity to be capable of solving all of the problems of the federal government. The nature of the work that we do here tends to produce a highly pragmatic attitude. From our standpoint, management is successful accommodation to all elements so that we keep moving ahead. The fads originate from real problems and real solutions, but the Bureau pounces on something that has worked somewhere and extrapolates universal principles. Now the Bureau is in a lather about cost benefit analysis. It is nonsense. We're wasting hundreds of thousands of man hours going through the motions of applying cost benefit analysis where it is useless, and it is going to get worse before it gets better.

CONDITIONS AFFECTING THE RELATIONSHIP

A number of different considerations, some of them obvious and others not so obvious, affect the relations between the Bureau of the Budget and Executive Branch agencies. Wildavsky makes one of the critical points: "The dominant role of the Bureau of the Budget, in form and in fact, is to help the President carry out his purposes. The orientation of the Bureau depends, therefore, on that of the President."[13] What the President takes an interest in, wants to support, has sympathy for, is likely to be viewed favorably by the Bureau. A cooperative relationship is likely if an agency's view of its programs is congruent with the presidential view and the Bureau of the Budget view. If there is divergence of views there is likely to be conflict. If the Bureau thinks that an agency can be depended on to perform in a manner consistent with presidential objectives, the degree of supervision diminishes. This is likely to result in the agency's holding a positive view of the Bureau of the Budget.[14]

Relations between the Bureau of the Budget and operating agencies are also affected, of course, by the budgetary decisions that the Bureau makes. According to one examiner, "Strained relations are most likely to occur because of budgeting pressures which force us to make decisions contrary to those that interested people in the agencies, in Congress, and the private groups want." The point was made more succinctly by another examiner. "There will be conflict over chintzy allowances." Another examiner made an observation that is relevant: "The type of program that an agency has may affect how it gets along with us. If an agency has a dynamic, fast moving program it may bridle at restraint."

The relationship between operating agencies and the Bureau of the Budget is also affected by the need that the agency feels for the support of the Bureau of the Budget. This can be illustrated in a number of ways. According to one respondent, "Agencies with the most muscle are the least afraid of the Bureau." Another respondent, speaking of an independent agency, remarked that it did not have cabinet status and its Hill ties "are not that good. The BOB is more important to them. They could get us to do some things that they were not able to do themselves." This remark emphasizes that an agency's relations with the Bureau of the Budget are affected by its relations with other participants in the political process. To paraphrase one respondent, one agency may make end runs to the President, another may run to the Hill, yet another may have to depend on (and thus have to get along with) the Bureau of the Budget. But it is important to remember that agencies are not unchanging. According to one Bureau of the Budget respondent, "Cooperation with the Bureau of the Budget is a very uneven thing among the agencies. You can't say that one department is a foregone loss and another is not. Under one regime it may be impossible to get agreement and then the regime may change—and the relationship changes."

The relationship between a cabinet department and its constituent bureaus (is the department in control or not?) may have an effect on the relationship between the Bureau of the Budget and the department and its bureaus. According to one division chief,

> We have a good relationship with the department of x and with the bureaus. Here in x the secretary runs the department and we have a good relationship. In y the operation of the department is quite different than in x. The bureaus there have more autonomy and this presents more of a problem. The department is a problem for the secretary and if the secretary has problems with the bureaus this affects our relationship with department and bureaus.

Another member of the Bureau of the Budget made the same point:

> X department has a good budget shop—and this affects the relations. Consider y—there is a very real problem here. The bureaus are going off in 40 different directions and there is no strong department budget office. The stuff that comes in from

> the bureaus varies—some is good, some bad. This is not true in x. All material that comes here is cleared by the department budget office and if it is unsatisfactory it is sent back before we ever see it; and the budget officer has the support of the Secretary.

The effect that the quality of an agency's submissions may have on the agency-Bureau relationship can be illustrated in another way. If an agency can develop quantitative measures of its work load, if it can measure quantitatively its productivity, if it can develop quantitative measures of benefits in relation to costs, then its relations with the Bureau of the Budget are likely to be relatively smooth. If an agency can remove the justification of its requests from the realm of speculation and instead quantify its justifications there may be less argument with the Bureau of the Budget. A possible consequence of this is that those agencies that find it difficult or impossible to describe their programs quantitatively may in the near future have a relatively rocky relationship with the Bureau.

Personal relations also affect the relations between agencies and the Bureau of the Budget. Respondents in both the Bureau and in the agencies stressed the importance of personality. One abrasive or difficult person on either side can affect how the organizations get along and view each other. Conversely, a sympathetic or supportive person can also affect the relationship. The following comments are illustrative:

> When I began work here I was green. You have to learn how to operate. There is a lot of gamesmanship you have to pick up. Personal relationships are very important. The budget officer in one bureau later told me that he had tried to test me when I first came on the job. He would try to scare me by saying, "I think we should see the Administrator on this problem." I was quaking in my boots, but bravely replied, "O.K., let's see the Administrator."

> You rapidly get to know which agencies are going to be cooperative and which are not. This depends on both personalities and institutional positions.

> So much depends on personality. Some people are just anti-Budget Bureau.

> Disagreement is not so much a matter of issues as personality. With some people you can depend on a fight no matter what you say and others you can count on to be reasonable.

> A good 80 percent of what gets done is based on personality.

Much of the contact between the Bureau and operating agencies is maintained by men of roughly equivalent rank and position.

But it is also maintained by junior examiners in the Bureau and senior personnel in the agencies. (The reverse is not true—only senior personnel in the departments and bureaus maintain contact with senior Bureau of the Budget personnel.) In other words, in the contact between Bureau of the Budget examiners and agency personnel the condition of status incongruence exists.[15] This condition, which is marked by relatively junior civil servants (Bureau of the Budget examiners) appearing to exercise authority and influence over relatively senior civil servants (agency personnel), may well affect the behavior of the persons in contact with one another and by extension the relations between the organizations represented. High level department and agency personnel interviewed were aware of the disparity of status and some seemed to resent it. In some instances it was a source of ill-will toward the Bureau of the Budget. It was also a source of strain for junior examiners. Contact between the Bureau and the agencies would probably be smoother if examiners were not so often junior.

CONCLUSION

The material here presented suggests four broad conclusions. First, the relationship between the Bureau of the Budget and any given operating agency is not predictably hostile. There are many subtle variations and gradations between the poles of complete agreement and complete antagonism. Bureau of the Budget oversight and interference do not produce only tension and conflicts. They can also produce agency gratitude, cooperation, or dependence. It is clearly inaccurate to assume that the Bureau and the operating agencies are natural enemies bound to do battle on almost every important issue that they view differently. Almost every agency has enough power to bargain with the Bureau on contested matters. As long as the bargaining channels are not closed completely, the possibility of reconciliation short of a fiat from the Bureau is present.

Second, access to and control over information appear to be the most important internal factors affecting the bargaining process between the Bureau and the operating agencies. Some agencies are concerned with controlling the flow of information about themselves. They want the Bureau of the Budget to find out only what they think it should know. Other agencies do not worry about controlling or restraining the Bureau's quest for information. Some agencies are anxious to present a consistent image to the Bureau; others are not bothered by inconsistency. Bureau examiners search their environment constantly for timely and accurate information. The upper echelons of the Bureau rely on what their juniors tell them.

Third, resolution of conflict between the Bureau of the Budget and an agency, when necessary, can come at a variety of levels. Disagreements may be settled at the lowest level, that is, by the examiner. But some conflicts escalate. Each higher level in the Bureau may try its hand at conflict resolution. Conflicts, of course, are also escalated in the agencies. They may go from a staff member in the budget office of an operating bureau, to the budget officer himself, to the bureau chief, and then on to the departmental hierarchy. Each hierarchical level in both the Bureau and the agencies may be viewed as a syphon that takes off some conflicts. Only a few reach the top—the Director of the Bureau of the Budget and a departmental secretary or independent agency head—and only some of these reach the President. In some interagency conflicts the Bureau may act only as a mediator, but successively higher levels of the Bureau and the quarreling agencies may still become involved.

Fourth, delay and the avoidance of decision on the part of the Bureau may be a tactic in conflict resolution. Stalling in endless conferences and repeated requests for more information are ways to postpone, if not prevent, conflict. Indecision is one way to deal with complex situations. If decisions are not made, someone else may make them, or the demand for a decision may gradually disappear, or one decision (the *only* decision) may become clear, inescapable, and justifiable.

ENDNOTES

1. See, for example, Arthur A. Maass, "In Accord with the Program of the President?" *Public Policy* (1953), pp. 77–93; Fritz Morstein Marx, "The Bureau of the Budget: Its Evolution and Present Role," *American Political Science Review,* vol. 39 (August, October, 1945), pp. 653–684, 869–898; Richard E. Neustadt, "Presidency and Legislation: The Growth of Central Clearance," *American Political Science Review,* vol. 48 (September 1954), pp. 641–671 and "Presidency & Legislation: Planning the President's Program," vol. 49 (December 1955), pp. 980–1021; and Arthur Smithies, *The Budgetary Process in the United States* (New York: McGraw-Hill, 1955).
2. Aaron Wildavsky, *The Politics of the Budgetary Process* (Boston: Little Brown, 1964).
3. For discussion of contact in this area see Neustadt's article, "Presidency and Legislation: The Growth of Central Clearance."
4. See Wildavsky, *op. cit.*

5. Wildavsky, p. 39, suggests there is a tendency to push information at the examiners.

6. See the section on the Bureau of the Budget in the current edition of the *United States Government Organization Manual*. The Bureau reorganized in late 1967, thus some of the details in the text are no longer accurate. But the reorganization does not change the central importance of the examiner.

7. This dichotomy seems to contrast with Wildavsky's observation, "More and more, however, there is a tendency to actually push information at the examiners all the time and not merely when asked." p. 39.

8. The significance of the budget examiner is commented on by Wildavsky: "The role adopted by its budget examiners is important to an agency even if the general orientation of the Budget Bureau is different." p. 36.

9. This comment may be coupled with Wildavsky's observation: "The Budget Bureau is expected to cut partly because it has an interest in protecting the President's program and partly because it believes the agency likely to pad." p. 23.

10. Again Wildavsky provides a useful addition: "Yet the Budget Bureau ordinarily does not give as much weight to advocating Presidential programs as to seeing that they do not go beyond bounds, because everyone expects the agencies to perform the functions of advocacy." pp. 35–36.

11. The view from the Hill is apparently similar. "Congressmen sometimes find the Bureau insensitive to considerations of practical politics both in relation to their constituency demands and to their requirements as members of a legislative social system who have to get along with their colleagues." Wildavsky, p. 38.

12. A comment from Neustadt, "Presidency & Legislation: The Growth of Central Clearance" (p. 661), is of some interest. "In 1948, the Bureau also embarked on a wholly new approach to the coordinative aspects of its clearance tasks, subordinating negative protection of President and agencies to positive development and drafting of administration measures." Would Neustadt have seen the positive approach if he had been formerly employed in a department, rather than in the Bureau of the Budget?

13. Wildavsky, p. 35.

14. The transmittal of Bureau attitudes occurs constantly. For example, Wildavsky comments on the importance of an agency's experience in day to day dealings with the Budget Bureau staff. "Their attitudes, nuances of behavior, may speak more eloquently than any public statement as to the Administration's intentions." p. 25.

15. For a discussion of status incongruence see George Homans, *Social Behavior: Its Elementary Forms* (London: Routledge and Kegan Paul, 1961), pp. 248–251.

*We wish to record our gratitude to the interview respondents who provided the raw material for this study. We were also aided by advice and financial support from an informal steering committee in Washington, the members of which wish to remain anonymous.

26

edward c. banfield

REVENUE SHARING IN THEORY AND PRACTICE

How one evaluates revenue sharing will depend upon what one takes the central issues to be. Oddly enough, what must appear to many people to be *the issue*—namely, how to keep the cities and states from going bankrupt—is not properly speaking an issue at all.

Mayor Lindsay has long tried to give the impression that catastrophe lies just ahead unless the federal government provides "massive" additional financial support. Recently other political leaders have been saying the same thing. "Countless cities across the nation," Mayor Gibson of Newark told the press recently, are "rapidly approaching bankruptcy." Governor Rockefeller, after having been informed of the Administration's latest plans, remarked that the federal government must do even more to prevent the states and cities from "virtually falling to pieces." Meanwhile Governor Cahill of New Jersey was telling a joint session of his legislature that "the sovereign states of this nation can no longer supply the funds to meet urgent and necessary needs of our citizens, and institutions and our cities." A day or two later Senator Humphrey in a single sentence made two of the most outstanding rhetorical contributions. The cities, he said, are "mortally sick and getting sicker" and the states "are in a state of chronic fiscal crisis."

In fact, the revenue-sharing idea was, at its inception, the product of exactly such forebodings. Back in 1964, when Walter Heller and Joseph Pechman proposed it, many well-informed people expected that state and local governments would soon be in serious

Reprinted with permission from *The Public Interest*, No. 23, (Spring 1971), pp. 33–45, Copyright © 1971 by National Affairs, Inc.

financial difficulties while at the same time the federal government would be enjoying a large and rapidly growing surplus. The war in Vietnam was expected to end soon and, if federal income tax levels remained unchanged, the normal growth of the economy and the increase of population would yield large increases in revenue year after year. Thus, while the federal government fattened, the state and local governments would grow leaner and leaner. Because of rising birthrates and population movements, the demands made upon states and localities for all sorts of services, but especially schools, would increase much more rapidly than would their ability to raise revenue. Whereas the federal government depends largely upon the personal income tax, the yield of which increases automatically with incomes, state and local governments depend mainly upon sales and property taxes, which are inelastic. This being the outlook, it seemed sensible to make up the expected deficit of the state and local governments from the expected surplus of the federal government. Heller and Pechman proposed to do this by giving the states a claim on a fixed percentage of federal taxable income, subject to the requirement that a fair amount "pass through" the states directly to the cities. The idea quickly won wide acceptance. Both political parties adopted revenue-sharing planks, and in 1968 some 90 revenue-sharing bills were introduced in Congress.

What happened, however, was not what was expected. Federal expenditures rose unexpectedly (defense spending was cut, but increases in the numbers of persons eligible for social security together with higher payment levels and unexpectedly high costs for Medicaid took up the slack) and, because of the recession, tax collections fell off. Instead of a surplus the federal government faced a deficit. State and local governments meanwhile fared better than expected. Legislatures and electorates were surprisingly ready to approve new taxes and higher rates. In 1967, for example, the states increased their tax collections by 15 per cent, and in 1968 they increased them by another 15 per cent. Cities also found it possible to raise more revenue than they had expected. Between 1948 and 1969 state-local expenditures increased in real terms from 6.7 per cent of Gross National Product to about 10 per cent. For some time they have been the fastest growing sector of the economy. The credit rating of the cities has improved, not worsened. With respect to the 50 largest cities, only three (New York, Boston, and Baltimore) received lower ratings from Moody's Investment Service in 1971 than in 1940 and many (including Chicago, Los Angeles, and Cleveland) received higher ones.

Dangerous as even short-run predictions in these matters have proved to be, it therefore seems safe to say that no "fiscal crisis" looms for most states and cities. In 1975, according to an estimate cited in a recent article by Richard Musgrave and A. Mitchell Polinsky, state and local expenditures will reach $119 billion. Assuming that federal aid increases at no more than the normal rate of recent years, this will leave a short-fall of $17 billion. Eleven billion of this will be made up from normal borrowing. The remaining deficit of $5 billion, Musgrave and Polinsky say, "could be met by a 5 per cent increase in tax rates at the state-local level, an increase which seems well within the reach of state-local governments. . . ." As more and more state governments adopt income tax laws, their revenues will be less dependent upon the vagaries of legislatures and electorates. Moreover, thanks to the recent decline in the birthrate, the principal item of state-local expense—schooling—will for at least a decade be considerably less than had been expected.

INABILITY OR UNWILLINGNESS?

The "fiscal crisis" issue is spurious if defined as the inability (economic, organizational, legal or even political) of the states—and therefore in a sense of the cities, which are their legal creatures—to support public services at high and rising levels. It is real, however, if defined as their unwillingness to support many of these services at what most reformers deem minimum-adequate levels. Presumably what Governor Cahill meant to tell the New Jersey legislature was something like this: "Any proposal to raise state and local taxes to what everyone would consider satisfactory levels would surely be voted down." The issue, then, has to do with using federal revenue to raise the level of services above the level that, given the realities of state and local politics, would otherwise exist. In other words, it concerns the amount and kind of income redistribution that the federal government should undertake.

That the federal government, and not state-local ones, should be primarily responsible for any income redistribution has long been generally accepted. In recent decades this principle has been used to justify giving federal aid to states and localities in spectacularly increasing amounts. As John M. DeGrove has pointed out, the increase was ten-fold in the last 20 years, four-fold in the last 10, and two-fold in the last five. In 1970 federal aid to states and cities reached an all-time peak of over $24 billion. The question therefore is not *whether* they should be aided but (a) by how much and (b) on what principle of distribution.

In considering what is involved in this, it is necessary to distinguish those state-local needs that are in some sense national from those that are not. That millions of poor rural people have moved to the cities is not something that the taxpayers of the cities should bear the entire financial responsibility for; apart from fairness, there is another consideration—presumably the nation as a whole will be injured if these millions do not receive adequate school, health, police, and other services that only state and local governments can provide. This is one argument that may justify large additional federal support for the states even though they could—if they would—raise the necessary money themselves. Some state-local needs, however, are in no sense national. Most pollution control and much highway construction is in this category. Why, one may ask, should the people of New York be taxed to pay for cleaning up a river in Vermont? As Dick Netzer has remarked in his excellent *Economics and Urban Problems*, ideally such non-national needs should be met by the development of regional governmental agencies, interstate in some cases and metropolitan in others, that can collect taxes and distribute benefits with a view to whatever public is affected—and to that public only. Unfortunately, such jurisdictions do not exist and it is politically impossible to create them. There is, however, as Netzer points out, a substitute for them—namely, the state governments. So when mayors and governors demand *federal* aid for non-national purposes, they do not have a persuasive case. Not only is it unfair to shift the cost of essentially state-local benefits to the national public; it is also very wasteful, for when someone else is to pay the bill, the natural tendency is to be prodigal. (Since Uncle Sam is to pay, why not build the bridge or sewerage system twice as big and four times as costly as necessary?)

Still, there unquestionably do exist truly national needs which urgently require increases in federal aid. But aid to whom? Revenue sharing is not a self-evident proposition. In dealing with the redistribution problem, the Nixon Administration itself has consistently put the emphasis on aiding individuals rather than governments. Shortly after taking office it exempted persons below the poverty line from paying federal income taxes. In its first two years its main effort was to bring into being the Family Assistance Plan, the effect of which would be to reduce those income inequalities that in large part constitute the "crisis of the cities."

Looking at revenue sharing from this standpoint, there is much to be said against it. Compared to the existing federal grant-in-aid programs, it would be much less redistributive.[1] The existing programs are redistributive because grants are generally awarded on the basis of some criteria of need. The shared revenue, on the other hand, would be distributed to states and cities on the basis of population and tax effort. This means that the wealthier states (in terms of per capita income) would benefit; the poorer states would not. Moreover, it is not likely that all of the money that went to the richer states would end up in the pockets of its neediest citizens. Such features of revenue sharing make for complications.

Under the present grant programs, for example, New Yorkers pay in taxes much more to the federal government than they get back in grants from it. In 1967, the per capita personal income tax paid from New York state to the federal government was $433 whereas the grants received in 1968 amounted to only $120 per capita. In North Dakota it was the other way around; there the per capita personal income tax payment was $177 and per capita grants were $357. On the basis of these figures, a New York politician (say Senator Javits) might decide that revenue sharing is a big improvement over the grant system. After all, under the Administration's proposed plan, New York state, which accounts for 10.98 per cent of the national income, would get 10.68 per cent of the shared ('general') revenue, whereas under the present grant system it gets only (the figure is for 1968) 8.6 per cent. On the other hand, an Arkansas politician (say Wilbur Mills, Chairman of the House Ways and Means Committee) might conclude that revenue sharing is a very bad idea. Arkansas, which accounts for .67 per cent of the national income and gets (1968) 1.46 per cent of the federal grants would, under revenue sharing, get only .86 per cent of the $5 billion.

In the last decade or so, the movement of poor people from the country to the city has made income redistribution an intra-city, or rather intra-metropolitan area, problem, as well as an interstate one. Of the $17 billion granted in the fiscal year 1968, $10 billion went to metropolitan areas. Some of the largest grant programs—especially OEO, Model Cities, and Title I of the Elementary and Secondary Education Act of 1965—put money mainly or entirely in so-called poverty areas. From the standpoint of the people who live in these areas, revenue sharing is subject to exactly the same objection that it is subject to in Arkansas: i.e., that it will give these areas less than they would get if the same amount were distributed under the existing grant programs. As Governor Sargent of Massachusetts has pointed out, the wealthy suburb of Newton would get $1,527,668 of the $5 billion that the Administration proposes to share, whereas Fall River, a city that is really poor, would get $827,760. One way to meet this objection, at least in part, would be to declare small cities, most of which are well-off suburbs, ineligible to share in the fund. Two years ago, the Intergovernmental Relations Advisory Commission suggested limiting eligibility to cities of 50,000 or more but it has since been realized that this would leave more than 40 per cent of all cities without an incentive to support the plan. The small suburbs are disproportionately Republican, of course, and this must also be taken into account by the Nixon Administration.

That a state like Arkansas or a city like Fall River would rather have $5 billion distributed under the existing grant programs than under revenue sharing is quite irrelevant if, as some observers claim, Congress could not possibly be persuaded to increase the total of grants by any such sum. Those who think that the Administration must "come up with something new" if it is to have any chance of getting "massive" new money for the cities will presumably conclude that $5 billion in revenue sharing is preferable to, at best, a few hundred million more in grants.

Of course the choice need not be between revenue sharing and grants. These are indications that Congress might be willing to assume the costs of certain social programs, especially welfare. Insofar as the object is to redistribute income, it would certainly make more sense to allot the $5 billion to welfare than to revenue sharing. This has been the Administration's position all along. Family assistance, not revenue sharing, was, and presumably still is, its first love.

A "NEW FEDERALISM"?

From the standpoint of the Administration, the central issue is neither the alleged "fiscal crisis" nor the problem of income redistribution. Rather it is the direction in which the federal system is to develop. From his first statement on the subject (August 13, 1969), the President has emphasized the need to create what he calls a New Federalism. Revenue sharing, he said when he first proposed it, would "mark a turning point in federal-state relations, the beginning of the decentralization of governmental power, and the restoration of a rightful balance between state capitals and the national capital." By the end of the decade, he predicted, "the political landscape of America will be visibly altered, and state and cities will have a far greater share of power and responsibility for solving their own problems." In his recent State of the Union Message, he went even farther. He was proposing, he said, a New American Revolution.

> . . . a peaceful revolution in which power will be turned back to the people—in which government at all levels will be refreshed,

renewed, and made truly responsive. This can be a revolution as profound, as far reaching, as exciting, as that first revolution almost 200 years ago.

One of the things that caused the President to think along these lines was the rapid and continuing growth that has been—and still is—taking place in the number of federal grant-in-aid programs. As he pointed out in his 1969 message, this growth has been 'near explosive'; between 1962 and 1966, he said, the number of categorical grant programs increased from 160 to 349. There was no reason to think that the rate of increase would slow down, much less stop, of its own accord; but unless it *did* slow down, categorical programs would soon number in the thousands. Revenue sharing was one of the means by which the Administration hoped to slow it down. Instead of creating more categorical programs, Congress would be asked to give the money to the states and cities "with no strings attached." Along with revenue sharing, the President asked for authority to order consolidations of categorical programs, provided that Congress did not within 60 days disapprove his orders. He also proposed a Manpower Training Act which (among other things) would have permitted the consolidation of about 20 more or less competing manpower programs and would have given the governors of the states a good deal of control over the consolidated program.

All of these measures had a common rationale—to simplify the structure of federal aid to the states and cities in order to bring it under control and reduce waste. With hundreds of grant programs, each with its own laws and regulations, no central direction is possible. Cabinet officers cannot keep track of—let alone exercise policy direction over—the many and varied programs for which they are responsible. Governors cannot find out what federal money is coming into their states or what is being done with it. The largest cities employ practitioners of the new art of "grantsmanship," in some instances with great success; many small cities, however, finding that they must apply to scores, or even hundreds, of programs, each with its own special requirements and each administered by a different bureaucracy, have more or less given up any hope of getting much help. The system, if it can be called that, is as wasteful as it is frustrating. A state or local government cannot trade a project that is low on its priority list for one that is high. Perhaps it can get $20 million for an expressway that it does not want but not $200,000 for a drug addiction project that it wants desperately. This involves a double waste: first in what is taken (local authorities can rarely refuse money

that is "free") and second in the foregone benefits of desirable projects for which grants are unavailable.

The proposals in the State of the Union Message represent
elaborations of those put forward in 1969. "General" revenue sharing
differs from the revenue sharing then proposed only in amount and in
the percentage (now 48) to be "passed through" to the cities. "Special" revenue sharing is (despite the confusing terminology) nothing
but consolidation of categorical programs on an all-at-once, comprehensive basis rather than on a piecemeal one. As everybody presumably knows by now, a few categorical programs would be eliminated
and most of the others grouped into six super-categories (urban community development, rural community development, education,
manpower training, law enforcement, and transportation) each under
a cabinet officer. Under "special" revenue sharing, grants-in-aid
would be distributed among states and local governments on the basis
of need as in the past, but the distribution would be according to an
agreed-upon formula (or rather formulae because each super-cate-
gory would have its own) rather than as the result of (among other
things) grantsmanship, endurance, "clout," and chicanery—criteria
that cannot be excluded at present. Under the plans so far announced
(in the nature of the case these are incomplete and somewhat tentative) some interests are bound to gain and others to lose. Mayor
Hatcher of Gary, Indiana, for example, has complained that his city
would lose about one-fourth of the $150 million a year that it now
receives. To such complaints the Administration has replied that it
will hold in reserve a fund from which to make up any losses that
local governments may suffer because of changes in distribution formulae.

ORGANIZED BENEFICIARIES

There is no doubt that state and local officials enthusiastically favor
consolidating and simplifying the grant system and giving them (the
officials) wide discretion in deciding the uses to which federal aid
should be put. Congressmen, too, are well aware of the faults of the
present system, and many have spoken out against it. Nevertheless,
there is reason to think that proposals to change the system fundamentally will not prove acceptable now or later, no matter who proposes them or what their merits.

It must be remembered that every one of the categorical programs (the most recent estimate is 550) has its organized beneficiar-

ies—not only those who receive grants but also those who are paid salaries for administering them. These beneficiaries have a much livlier interest in maintaining and enlarging their special benefits than the generality of taxpayers—unorganized, of course—has in curtailing them. If there happens to be a grant program for re-training teachers in secondary schools having high drop-out rates, it is safe to say that there exists an organization that will exert itself vigorously to prevent the consolidation of that program with others. It is safe to say, too, that no organization exists to put in a good word for the consolidation of the teacher-retraining program with other manpower programs.

From the standpoint of organized interests, dealing with Congress and the Washington bureaucracies (a few key Congressmen and administrators are usually all that matter to any particular interest) is vastly easier and more likely to succeed than is dealing with the legislatures and governors of 50 states, not to mention the officials of countless cities, counties, and special districts. This consideration alone might well be decisive from the standpoint of organized labor, which knows just where to go and whom to see in Washington, even if the political complexions of the state and local governments were exactly the same as that of the national government. In fact, of course, they are not; some interests that are well received and can make themselves heard in Washington—organized labor, minority groups, the poor—would be ignored in certain state capitols and city halls.

Interest groups will not be the only, or probably the most important, defenders of the grant system, however. Congressmen—especially those on important committees—are fond of categorical programs for at least two reasons. One is that they constitute answers to the perennial question: What have you done for me lately? A narrowly defined category is ideal from this standpoint. It is custommade to suit the requirements of some key group of constituents and the Congressman can plainly label it "from me to you." Revenue sharing, whether "general" or "special," altogether lacks this advantage. It gives benefits not to constituents directly but in wholesale lots to state and local politicians who will package them for retail distribution under their own labels, taking all of the credit.

Congressmen also like categorical programs because of the opportunities they afford to interfere in administration and thus to secure special treatment, or at least the appearance of it, for constituents among whom, as Jerome T. Murphy shows in his case study of the politics of educational reform (*Harvard Educational Review*, February 1971) state and local as well as federal agencies sometimes figure prominently. These opportunities are plentiful because the Congressmen see to it that "ifs," "ands," and "buts" are written into the legislation in the right places, and because administrators are well aware that every year they must respond in public to whatever questions may be asked in appropriations and other hearings. Wanting to stay on the right side of those members of Congress with whom they must deal, administrators frequently ask them for "advice." Perhaps it is not too much to say that the categorical system constitutes a last line of defense against what many Congressmen regard as the usurpation of their function by the executive branch.

As this implies, the present coldness of Congress to President Nixon's revenue-sharing proposals is not to be explained solely or perhaps even mainly on the ground that he is Republican and Congress is Democratic. The crucial fact is that his proposals would involve a large-scale shift of power from Congress to the White House. *No* Congress would like that, although sooner or later one may feel compelled to accept it.

Revenue sharing would also shift power to governors and mayors. To hear some of them talk, one might think that they would like to have the federal government dismantled and the pieces turned over to them. In fact, most of them are likely to find excuses for not accepting powers that may be politically awkward—and what ones may not?

In his valuable book, *The American System*, the late Morton Grodzins provides some evidence on this point. He tells at some length the story of the Joint Federal-State Action Committee, which President Eisenhower created in 1957 after a flight of oratory (" . . . those who would be free must stand eternal watch against excessive concentration of power in government . . .") to designate federal functions that might be developed to the states along with revenue to support them. The Committee was a very high level one; it included three members of the Cabinet, the Director of the Bureau of the Budget, and a dozen governors. After laboring for two years, it found only two programs that the federal government would give up and that the states would accept—vocational education and municipal waste treatment plants. As Grodzins explains, the difficulty was not so much that the federal agencies could not be persuaded to give up functions as that the governors would not accept them. They would not take the school lunch program, for example, because doing so would involve a fuss about parochial schools, and they would not take Old Age Assistance because they knew that the old people's lobby would not like having it transferred to the states. Modest as the

Committee's two proposals were and strongly as President Eisenhower backed them, Congress turned them down.

Whether state and local governments would make good use of the federal funds if given them "with no strings attached" is much doubted by career civil servants in Washington and by what may be called the good government movement. State and city governments, it is frequently said, are in general grossly inefficient and in many instances corrupt as well. The charge is certainly plausible—one wonders whether New York City, for example, has the capacity to use wisely the large amounts that it would receive. The fact is, however, that no one really knows what the state and local governments are capable of. And even if their capacity should prove to be as little as the pessimists say it is, may it not even so be superior to that of the present system *as it will be in another decade or two?*

Administrators in Washington generally assume that the management capacity of state and local governments can be much improved by provision of special grants to strengthen the staffs of the chief executives and by teaching the techniques and advantages of comprehensive planning. The lessons of the last 10 years give little support to this assumption, but the Administration is nevertheless proposing a fund of $100 million for more such efforts. In my judgment the results are bound to be disappointing. It is the necessity of working out compromises among the numerous holders of bits and pieces of power on the state-local scene that is the main cause, not only of "inefficiency," but of corruption as well. Giving governors and mayors authority over the spending of federal funds would, by strengthening their political positions, reduce the amount of compromising that they must do and the amount of corruption that they must pretend not to see if they are to get anything done. In this way it would contribute more than anything else to increasing the coherence (to use the word that is favored among planners) of state-local programs. The $100 million in management assistance that the federal government proposes would probably work in the very opposite direction. In practice if not in theory, giving "technical assistance" usually means maintaining and extending the influence of the federal agencies.

THE PROSPECT BEFORE US

Insofar as there would be a real devolution of power to governors and mayors—and therefore, as the President said, to the people who elect them—the Administration's proposals could bring the federal system closer to what the Founding Fathers intended it to be. In my opinion, this is a consummation devoutly to be desired. There is no denying, however, that the short-run effect of decentralization of power would be to take a great deal of pressure off those states and local regimes, of which there may be many, that have no disposition to provide essential public services on an equitable basis or at what reasonable people would regard as adequate levels. This is a powerful objection. It may, however, only be a temporary one. Within a very few years, the political arithmetic of every sizable city and every industrial state will be such as to give politicians strong incentives to take very full account of the needs and wishes of those elements of the electorate that have been, and in some places still are, neglected.

Still, given the political realities that I have mentioned—a public opinion that favors income redistribution but is divided as to how far it should go and how costs and benefits should be apportioned; tax boundary lines inappropriately drawn but not susceptible to being redrawn; hundreds of federal agencies having programs to protect; interest groups even more numerous and with more at stake in the status quo; interstate and intra-metropolitan area differences of interest; Congressmen loath to see their powers diminished; governors and mayors equally loath to accept responsibilities that can be avoided—it is not to be expected that any quick or clear-cut settlement will be found for the issues that revenue sharing raises.

I expect that the federal government will continue to play a larger role in raising revenue for all sorts of purposes. As Julius Margolis has pointed out, the larger and more diverse the "package" of expenditure (or other) items that a government presents to its voters, the harder it is for the people to make their decisions on the basis of self-interest as opposed to ideology. This being the case, those who want to win acceptance for proposals that would not be accepted if self-interest were the criterion always try to include them in packages that are sufficiently large. That is, they prefer to have decisions made on a city-wide rather than a neighborhood basis, on a state-wide rather than a city-wide one, and on a national rather than a state one. It seems to me that the changing class character of the population reinforces this tendency. As we become more heavily upper-middle class, we are increasingly disposed to regard general principles (or ideology, as Margolis calls it), not self-interest, as the proper criterion.

If the federal government will have an ever-larger part in raising revenue, it is not likely to have an ever-smaller one in spending it. He who pays the piper calls the tune. To be sure, he may choose to permit, or even to require, others to do some calling when the number of tunes to be called is inconveniently large, and by so doing he may make everyone better off. The essential fact is, however, that the state governments can be what Governor Cahill called them—sovereign—only if they do what he says they cannot do—supply the funds to meet the urgent and necessary needs of their people. I myself am strongly in favor of the reforms that the President has proposed because I think they represent the largest improvement over the present situation that it is reasonable to hope for. I do not, however, share his expectation that these reforms will bring about "a historic and massive reversal of the flow of power in America." Indeed, in the event—unlikely, I am afraid—that his proposals are accepted and carried into effect, I would be very surprised if first Mississippi and then New York did not discover that they are ruled as much as ever by national public opinion, acting through national institutions—the Presidency, Congress, the Supreme Court—and that this opinion and these institutions, the White House most of all perhaps, will in the years ahead assert conceptions of the national interest more vigorously than ever.

ENDNOTE

1. What is under discussion at this point is the so-called "general" revenue-sharing proposal: that is, the $5 billion, to start with, that would go to states and cities with "no strings attached." This is to be distinguished from "special" revenue sharing, which is the grant system much reorganized and with $1 billion in "new" money added to it.

27

stanley vanagunas

SHARING CRIME CONTROL FUNDS

On March 2, 1971, President Nixon sent to Congress the Law Enforcement Revenue Sharing Act of 1971. This bill is in the form of an
amendment to Title I of the Omnibus Crime Control and Safe Streets
Act of 1968. The Law Enforcement Revenue Sharing Act was the
first of six special revenue-sharing proposals that the President introduced in this session of the national legislature. Since the Safe Streets
Act is a bloc grant program whereby the role of state governments in
the distribution of federal aid is already a substantial one, its use by
the Administration as an ice-breaker for other revenue-sharing
schemes made sound political sense. Attorney General Mitchell said
as much. In his address before the National Sheriff's Association in
June 1971, he referred to the Safe Streets program as "a forerunner
of revenue sharing.[1]

On the other hand, a disadvantage of using law enforcement
assistance as one test case of congressional attitudes on revenue sharing has been that major political issues involved tended to override
the essence of the problem at hand—how can the national government best assist state and local governments to upgrade their law
enforcement capabilities.

This key consideration has been obscured by influential opposition to the overall concept of revenue sharing; opposition which has
caused all special revenue-sharing proposals to lie dormant on the
agendas of the various congressional committees. It appears inevita-

Reprinted with permission from the *Public Administration Review,* journal of the American Society for Public Administration, Vol. 32, No. 2 (March-
April, 1972). Copyright 1972 by the American Society for Public Administration.

ble, however, that if the Nixon Administration is victorious in the 1972 election, it will, with even greater vigor, pursue revenue sharing as a major policy goal. Consequently, before the clouds of partisan rhetoric rise again, now is the time to analyze law enforcement revenue sharing solely from the perspective of a delivery system of federal dollars for upgrading state and local criminal justice services, and to compare this approach to its predecessor, the safe streets assistance program with which the criminal justice community has had more than three years of experience.

The Law Enforcement Revenue Sharing Act of 1971,[2] originally intended to take effect on January 1, 1972, comes before the Congress as a list of White House-proposed amendments to the Omnibus Crime Control and Safe Streets Act.[3] The latter statute served to establish the first major federal bloc grant assistance program in the nation. At the time of the passage of the Safe Streets Act in 1968, it was acclaimed as a major innovation in federal-state fiscal relationships, for it attempted to correct the problems encountered with the categorical grant-in-aid programs previously prevalent. (For an indepth analysis of the bloc grant concept with specific reference to the Safe Streets Act, see B. Douglas Harman, "The Bloc Grant: Readings from a First Experiment," in the March/April 1970 *Public Administration Review.*)

The Safe Streets Act established the Law Enforcement Assistance Administration (LEAA) within the Department of Justice and vested it with the power to implement the safe streets assistance program. It further provides for the establishment of state planning agencies with the responsibilities to administer federal law enforcement assistance on the state level. It also calls for each state to prepare comprehensive law enforcement improvement plans which must be approved by LEAA as a condition for release of safe streets grant funds to each state. The Act enumerates the categories of law enforcement improvement programs eligible for assistance and provides grants up to 75 per cent of their cost. Part C of Title I is the key section of the safe streets statute which establishes the bloc grant system. It provides that from the appropriations for any given year, 85 per cent shall be allocated to the states according to population and 15 per cent to LEAA to award at its discretion. The states, in turn, must make available not less than 75 per cent of their bloc grant to units of local government.

President Nixon's proposed Law Enforcement Revenue Sharing Act of 1971 maintains these essential characteristics of Title I of the Safe Streets Act while providing for the following major changes:

Comprehensive Planning—The present requirement that the states annually revise and submit to the Law Enforcement Assistance Administration a comprehensive criminal justice improvement plan is not changed. However, prior plan approval by LEAA to release federal funds to each state is not required. LEAA would merely review and comment on each plan.

Special Revenue-Sharing Payments—Revenue-sharing payments would replace bloc grants to states. The extent of such payments to each state would be determined according to their relative population—the existent procedure under the safe streets bloc grant.

Allocation of Revenue-Sharing Payments to Units of Local Government—Effective July 1972, the states are required to allocate revenue-sharing payment to their units of local government in proportion to state/local law enforcement expenditure experience in the year preceding.

Matching Requirements—The local matching requirements are eliminated and federal funds can be used to cover 100 per cent of law enforcement improvement project cost.

Maintenance of Effort—The current requirement that safe streets assistance funds cannot serve to supplant state and local funds allocated for law enforcement purposes is eliminated.

The above summary highlights the major changes to the existent legislation; important amendments which will be discussed below in detail. The revenue-sharing bill provides for several other modifications which merely change the emphasis of already applicable provisions in the safe streets statute. For example, Title VI of the Civil Rights Act of 1964 which prohibits discrimination in federally funded programs is made specifically applicable to special revenue-sharing. The President is requesting a sum of $425 million to cover law enforcement revenue-sharing payments for FY 1972. This compares with $340 million allocated to the states for FY 1971 under the safe streets bloc grant.

COMPREHENSIVE PLANNING

On the surface, the proposal that prior plan approval by LEAA is not required to initiate the annual flow of assistance funds to states appears to be a major change to existent safe streets legislation and a serious diminution of federal control over law enforcement assistance funds. The implication is that under revenue sharing states may spend federal funds as they choose, providing that law enforcement or some other aspect of the criminal justice system are the beneficiaries. In reality this is not a very substantial change. The revenue-sharing bill provides that LEAA will have the responsibility to review and comment on each state comprehensive plan. Conceivably, and highly likely, if such LEAA comment points to legitimate flaws in a given plan, such as the lack of adequate support to one area of criminal justice, say the courts, it can exert sufficient suasion to cause the abusing state to make appropriate amends in its subsequent plan, as the latter must be updated, revised, and filed annually. Review and comment power by LEAA can be formidable when properly applied, even if it occurs after the annual assistance funds have flown the federal treasury coop.

What is perhaps most surprising about the revenue-sharing bill's amendments as they pertain to comprehensive planning under the Safe Streets Act is that so little change has been proposed in the first instance. There are serious problems with state comprehensive criminal justice improvement planning, and these had three planning periods to surface: 1969, 1970, and 1971.

Part B of Title I of the Safe Streets Act provides the basic statutory guidance for the planning operation at the state level. Briefly, Part B provides funds to set up state planning agencies which shall be representative of law enforcement agencies, units of general local government, and public agencies maintaining programs to reduce and control crime. Such an agency shall be under the jurisdiction of the chief executive of the state. The state planning agencies are charged with the responsibility of preparing and annually revising a statewide plan for improving their systems of criminal justice administration. Part B further provides that at least 40 per cent of the annual planning grant shall be subgranted by the state to units of local government for law enforcement planning. The statutory language has since been elaborated by a series of LEAA guidelines to the states. By January 1970 the essence of the comprehensive plan format had emerged and, except for some minor alterations, is in effect today.[4]

The basic format calls for two main sections to the plan. The first, commonly referred to as the "annual action plan," requires the states to list the programs they intend to fund during the planning year for which funds have already been appropriated by Congress and allocated to the states in accordance with their population. The law enforcement improvement programs to be included in the annual action plan are left to the discretion of each state subject to LEAA approval. Each program description, however, must be titled, its objectives stated, and its means of implementation specifically laid out. The programs require a forecast of federal funds allocated for their implementation. The total of such a forecast is then equal to the bloc grant for which the state is eligible.

The second main section of the state comprehensive plan is "the multi-year plan." Referred to by LEAA as the "critical element of the state plan," it requires the states to structure law enforcement improvement programs for five years, including a projection of future federal assistance required for program implementation. The annual action plan serves as the first year of the multi-year plan.

From the start, state comprehensive law enforcement plans, as called for by LEAA, have been largely meaningless as any kind of real blueprints for the systematic improvement of the criminal justice systems of the states. The fault cannot be entirely attributable to problems of state administration, initiative, or lack of skills; reasons, for example, extended by the Urban Coalition in its critical report on state law enforcement planning.[5] The fault stems from the inherent lack of viability in the planning concept as promulgated by LEAA.

According to LEAA guidelines, the states are asked to structure their five-year plans, 1971 through 1975 for example, on an "ideal" law enforcement system concept with a regard to normal anticipated constraints, such as manpower, but without regard to fund sources. Two problems became immediately apparent when planning under such requirements. In the first instance, since the annual action plan was the first year of the multi-year plan, and since the annual action plan was totally constrained to meet the sum of the available federal bloc grant, while the other four years in the multi-year plan have no constraint as to source of revenue for improvement, the document becomes unrealistic. In the second case, the multi-year plan is not true to the planning principle, since it is used by LEAA as a propaganda document to badger Congress into ever-increasing appropriations for the Safe Streets Act. LEAA guidelines themselves face this issue without equivocation, pointing out that the multi-year plan "may have a substantial impact upon determination of the nature and amount of future federal funding."[6]

The essential consideration that the LEAA comprehensive planning guidelines do not face up to, except for a brief and passing reference, is that in the cases of all states, safe streets assistance funds represent a relatively small fraction of state and local funds that are devoted to criminal justice services. In Wisconsin, for example, better than $120 million of state and local tax source funds will have been spent in 1971 for the police, the judicial system, and corrections. During the same year, Wisconsin received approximately $8 million in safe streets assistance. Until such time when state law enforcement improvement plans take into account such realities, they cannot be considered "comprehensive plans."

The route to meaningful comprehensive law enforcement planning may not be entirely attainable. The reason lies in the fact that the law enforcement system in the United States is largely a local government function. There are a great many autonomous police agencies and courts of independent jurisdiction. Since the process of planning also implies ability of the planning agent to have some impact on the realization of the plan, this is made exceedingly difficult under the local law enforcement concept. Wisconsin alone, a state that represents a median in many things, has over 440 local police agencies and 98 trial courts, without considering their branches.

The statutory requirement that at least 40 per cent of the annual planning grant given to the states be passed through to local government for regional planning is not, by far, an adequate solution. Regional law enforcement planning is subject to essentially the same pitfalls as state planning. Vast sums must be expended to produce adequate regional criminal justice improvement plans.

One empathized with Ramsey Clark who, in giving his testimony on the Safe Streets Act before the House Committee on the Judiciary, felt compelled to pose this rhetorical question: "Is there one state plan which can really be called a planning instrument with a comprehensive analysis of status, commitments, priorities, goals, and measured progress, or are we creating shipping lists?"[7] Considering that in FY 1971 alone, $26 million was allocated by Congress for law enforcement planning, this question requires careful consideration indeed.

A feasible alternative is to maintain the funding of state planning agencies but perhaps under a new generic name, such as "State Criminal Justice Improvement Councils," which would have memberships broadly representative of law enforcement, local government, and general citizenry. The functions of such councils would be to look probingly into the entire spectrum of criminal justice administration in their respective states and to propose select programs, not unimplementable "comprehensive plans," for the resolution of priority problems. The Councils would view law enforcement fund sources as a totality and treat federal assistance funds as merely ancillary to the total pool of revenue available for criminal justice improvement.

SPECIAL REVENUE-SHARING PAYMENTS

If one measure of the effectiveness of a federal assistance program is the confidence by its recipients that such aid may have reasonable continuity to implement a project whose duration may be several years, then, in this respect, the Safe Streets Act has not been successful. Through no fault of its own, but rather due to the vagaries of many predecessor federal grant-in-aid programs, LEAA's law enforcement assistance efforts have not as yet attained widespread credibility, particularly with local law enforcement. A ship in the night, here-today-gone-tomorrow attitude on the part of a large segment of the criminal justice community prevails. Such a lack of confidence has been harmful to the improvement of law enforcement.

As a result, local agencies have favored submission of project applications for "one-shot deals" like purchase of police equipment, elaborate communications facilities, and short-lived training sessions. Established local criminal justice agencies have held off from submitting assistance requests to their state planning agencies for sound projects that involve employment of new personnel for fear that the federal government would soon leave their parent local governments holding the tax bag. On the other hand, applications to fund projects of dubious criminal justice improvement quality are not lacking.

Such project proposals stem primarily from two sources. Private groups of an ad hoc nature, rising to the occasion of suddenly available federal dollars, offer projects such as summer camping trips for problematic children, hastily organized half-way houses for offenders, and various community crime prevention schemes. Another group of agencies, more established and generally characterized by their previous access of federal funding, seek safe streets assistance for ongoing projects which have only a remote connection to the system of criminal justice administration. Educational institutions, private social service organizations, and various community action agencies, faced by decreasing revenue opportunities since the Republicans cut back on many aid programs inherited from the Johnson Administration, file requests for safe streets assistance. Their project applications present painfully strained cases for their anticipated contribution to crime prevention and to the improvement of criminal justice administration.

Some project proposals originating from the above sources reflect genuine creativity, particularly in the delinquency prevention area. These should be assisted. However, while it is important to recognize that there is great correlation between crime rates and, for example, poverty, urban blight, lack of educational opportunity, and similar manifestations in our society, serious attempts to eradicate such causes of crime are beyond the fiscal means of the Safe Streets Act. The answers to these issues lie in the totality of effort that all levels of government put in to eradicate social ills. Safe streets funds should be used for the upgrading of police services, the judicial system, and the correctional and rehabilitative process. In terms of crime prevention, it is in the criminal justice system that the maximum benefit per federal dollar spent will be found. During 1968-69, for example, the Institute for the Study of Crime and Delinquency undertook a research project to develop a model community correctional program. San Joaquin County, California, was chosen as the sample. A major result of this study was "that given the most pessimistic outlook about the ability of the correctional client to change, there is clearly a great deal that can be done to help the system do what it is now doing more efficiently, less expensively, more humanely and probably more effectively."[8]

It is consequently of great importance that the criminal justice community look upon federal attempts to upgrade law enforcement as not a passing attempt, but one that will continue until the problem is largely resolved—until the streets are safer. Such confidence must exist, otherwise the skills and initiative that are locked up in the local law enforcement system will not rise to generate projects for genuine improvement in the administration of justice.

Law enforcement revenue sharing as a concept contrasted to a grant may promote greater confidence on the part of the criminal justice profession and local government in the longevity of federal assistance. Just from the semantical viewpoint, "revenue sharing" implies a vested interest by the "sharer" in the funds to be shared and connotes their greater permanency over time than a "grant," a manifestation of federal largess to be given or taken away at bureaucratic whim.

ALLOCATION OF REVENUE-SHARING PAYMENTS TO UNITS OF LOCAL GOVERNMENT

As indicated previously, the Law Enforcement Revenue Sharing Act proposes that effective July 1, 1972, the states be required to allocate revenue-sharing payments to their units of local government in proportion to state/local law enforcement expenditure experience in the year preceding. Until July 1, 1972, at least 75 per cent of the total revenue-sharing payment to a given state must be passed through to local government. The Act also calls for assurance by the states, presumably expressed in their comprehensive plans, that an adequate share of their revenue-sharing payments are allocated to deal with law enforcement problems in high crime areas, meaning the cities.

All of the above provisions pertaining to the pass through of funds to localities are essentially those as contained in the Safe Streets Act. It is noteworthy that the Nixon Administration does not prescribe for the states any formula for pass through of revenue-sharing funds to the individual units of local government. The requirement that at least that proportion of funds should be made available to localities as represented by their dollar inputs into the annual state law enforcement expenditure pool is expressed in aggregate terms. Neither the proposed Act nor the existent safe streets statute calls for across-the-board sharing by the states with their units of local government of federal law enforcement improvement monies. Except for the requirement to fund "high crime" areas, the state governments are given substantial say as to the allocation of law enforcement payments to their local jurisdictions.

A major recurring criticism of the safe streets program has been that the states are not passing through sufficient federal funds to the cities. The "high crime areas" amendment to the Safe Streets Act and its continuation in the revenue-sharing bill is in direct response to such criticism. The vocal critics have been the National League of Cities and the U.S. Conference of Mayors. In February 1970, for example, these organizations put out a joint report strongly critical of the state role under the safe streets bloc grant and called for direct federal aid to the cities.[9] The states, through the National Governors Conference, rebutted, citing a study of the Advisory Commission on Intergovernmental Relations which showed that 75.3 per cent of FY 1969 safe streets bloc grant funds have been passed through by state governments to cities and counties over 50,000 population. These 411 cities represented less than 40 per cent of the nation's population, and approximately 65 per cent of the crime.[10] In terms of hard conclusions as to the issue involved, both parties have been largely premature. Their arguments must wait for firm LEAA data on the pattern of state expenditures for 1970 and 1971. It should be kept in mind that not only the states, but also their cities, need time to structure law enforcement improvement projects. In the latter case, the cities, despite the immediacy of their crime problem, were not more prepared than the states for the Safe Streets Act.

Clearly, neither the Safe Streets Act nor the proposed Law Enforcement Revenue Sharing Act can be construed as effective unless the crime problems of the major cities are alleviated. The revenue-sharing bill appears to include sufficient statutory safeguards to assure adequate aid to city law enforcement. Moreover, the proposition that states have traditionally ignored big city problems and will continue to do so is arguable. In the first place, "one man one vote" holdings by the courts have substantially changed the composition of many statehouses. State capitols are more conscious than ever of their role in urban improvement, as evidenced by the creation of cabinet-level "urban-local affairs" departments in many states. It is generally true that as crime in the cities rose to its present shocking levels, as city police service became a second-rate, underpaid profession, and as metropolitan courts staggered under unconscionable backlogs, the states, in their characteristically impecunious situations, sat back, treating crime as a local problem. It is no less true, however, that as crime in the cities rose and as their law enforcement systems began to break down, the federal government, not unlike the states, also took only a passive interest in their plight. The main difference was that the national government, in comparison to the states, has been virtually rolling in money since the Internal Revenue Act of 1913.

The states have a role to play in improving law enforcement services. Certain areas of criminal justice, such as corrections and the higher, appellate courts, are basically state government functions. In the smaller states the same is true even of police services. Local law enforcement agencies do not exist in isolation, but intertwine, in many respects, with the entire criminal justice system of their parent state. As a result, the state governments are closer to the crime and criminal justice problems of their localities than the federal authorities, and can play the role of a more intelligent arbitrator in the dispensing of law enforcement assistance funds.

As was mentioned previously, both the existent Safe Streets Act and the proposed revenue-sharing bill provide for such a state government role. Under the revenue-sharing measure, an interesting problem in terms of its ultimate consequences may arise in the state governmental processes as a result of the latitude that the states have for allocating federal law enforcement assistance funds to localities. Under the current Safe Streets Act provisions, the state planning agency boards with a representative membership of law enforcement, other public crime control agencies, and local government are empowered, with the chief executive's concurrence, to make subgrants from bloc grant funds. Under the revenue-sharing bill this power is unaltered. Up to now the state legislatures have been conditioned to sit back and not generally interfere with the machinations of federal grant-in-aid programs. Under the revenue sharing, with its implications of local proprietary rights to federal funds, the state legislators may increasingly resent the exercising of their inalienable prerogative, the control of the state purse strings, by pseudo-legislative bodies such as the law enforcement state planning agencies.

MATCHING REQUIREMENTS

Perhaps the greatest readily observable boon to the criminal justice community of the proposed Law Enforcement Revenue Sharing Act is its elimination of the state/local matching requirements. Under the amended Safe Streets Act, two matching formulas are in effect. Construction of law enforcement facilities calls for a 50-50 match. All other law enforcement programs are subject to a 75 per cent federal to 25 per cent state/local formula.

Local matching can take two forms: cash or in-kind. The latter prevails. It is commonplace in the federal grantsmanship game to hear the observation that an in-kind match is no match at all. This has also tended to be the experience under the Safe Streets Act. Where an "in-kind match" cannot be adequately mustered by a local law enforcement agency, the application for assistance funds, and often for potentially meritorious projects, is not generated. Frequently, raising the local match can be as onerous to local government as coming up with the entire fund to cover the cost of the contemplated project.

The argument that 100 per cent funding will discourage local striving for law enforcement improvement is no more valid than the proposition that public assistance to the needy will discourage personal initiative. As in the case of most family budgets, local and state government criminal justice administration budgets are at the end of their tax tether where significant improvements in their law enforcement operations are not achievable unless an alternative source of revenue can be found.

MAINTENANCE OF EFFORT

The amendment to the Safe Streets Act contained in the President's law enforcement revenue-sharing bill, proposing that federal funds no longer need to supplement state and local funds presently devoted to law enforcement purposes, is of highly dubious value in terms of improving criminal justice administration. The amendment would allow the state or local government to use revenue-sharing payments to supplant their own source funds budgeted for criminal justice and, consequently, divert them to uses other than law enforcement.

It was emphasized in the previous section discussing local matching that such should not be required, as characteristically the current state and local law enforcement budgets are already strained just to meet day-to-day operations. It is not inconsistent to apply the same argument against supplanting: the goal is to improve rather than to maintain criminal justice services. The central issue of the Law Enforcement Revenue Sharing Act of 1971, insofar as the criminal justice community is concerned, is the marginal impact of federal funds on improvement of law enforcement, not tax relief or improvement of some other state/local governmental function. Supplanting will tend to maintain the status quo in the quality and quantity of law enforcement services. These, as evidenced by the need for the proposed law enforcement revenue-sharing measure itself, are inadequate and in need of much improvement.

Another undesirable feature of the revenue-sharing proposal is its failure to seek the repeal of the current safe streets requirement that not more than one-third of the annual federal assistance given to a state be spent for the compensation of police and other regular law enforcement personnel. Its original intent was to encourage states and localities to undertake new, and hopefully innovative, law enforcement improvement projects.

This intent was not yet realized to any significant extent. On the contrary, the one-third personnel limitation built in a bias for law enforcement hardware in the Safe Streets Act. If states are prevented by statute from spending funds for personnel, they will spend them on construction or equipment. Hardware is obviously not the answer to criminal justice improvement—people are. The critics of the Safe Streets Act who loudly pointed to police hardware grants by states as signs of ineffectiveness of the bloc grant program invariably failed to consider the one-third personnel limitation nuance in the statute.[11]

In summary, the President's Law Enforcement Revenue Sharing Act of 1971, as a piece of legislation designed to upgrade criminal justice administration, is a potential mixed blessing.

Some of its provisions are an obvious improvement over the existent safe streets program, such as the elimination of local matching share requirements. Also, substitution of "revenue sharing" for "grants-in-aid" will, most likely, serve to increase the confidence of local government that assistance will be of sufficient continuity and permanency to motivate states and localities to general sound law enforcement improvement projects.

In several ways the bill proposed by Mr. Nixon does not go far enough to correct some obvious flaws in the safe streets program. Continuation of the requirement that the states file an annual comprehensive law enforcement plan is extending support to a costly and doubtful venture. Failure of the Revenue-Sharing Act to seek the repeal of the "one-third personnel limitation" clause detracts from the proposed bill as it maintains this built-in bias for law enforcement hardware.

Lastly, the deletion of the current requirement under the Safe Streets Act that states and local governments cannot supplant their funds expended for law enforcement purposes with federal assistance monies is the most significant change to the safe streets statute proposed in the Law Enforcement Revenue Sharing Act of 1971. This provision may be very detrimental to the very purpose of the assistance program—improvement of criminal justice administration. To allow supplanting is, in effect, to subsidize other functions of state and local government. While such may be desirable in principle, from the point of view of law enforcement improvement, it clearly is not.

ENDNOTES

1. Press release, U. S. Department of Justice, June 21, 1971.
2. Press release, The White House, March 2, 1971. As of July 1, 1971, the Law Enforcement Revenue Sharing Act of 1971 was before the House and the Senate Judiciary Committees (91st Congress) as HR-S408 and S-1037, respectively.
3. Title I of Public Laws 90-351 and 91-644.
4. *Guidelines for Fiscal 1971 Comprehensive State Law Enforcement Plans*, Law Enforcement Assistance Administration, U.S. Department of Justice, September 1970.
5. *Law and Disorder State Planning Under the Safe Streets Act*, The Urban Coalition and Urban America Inc., 1969.
6. LEAA guidelines, *op. cit.*, p. 51.
7. Transcript of a statement by Ramsey Clark before Subcommittee No. 5 of the Committee on Judiciary, U.S. House of Representatives, February 18, 1970.
8. *Model Community Correctional Program* (Sacramento, Calif.: Institute for the Study of Crime and Delinquency, 1969).
9. *Street Crime and the Safe Streets Act: What is the Impact*, (Washington, D.C.: National League of Cities and U.S Conference of Mayors, February 1970).

10. *The States and Omnibus Crime Control Program: Two Years After the Signing of the Act* (Washington, D.C.: National Governors' Conference, June 19, 1970).

11. See, for example: L. Velie, "Case of the Purloined Crime Law," *Reader's Digest* (November 1970), and J.C. Goulden, "Cops Hit the Jackpot." *The Nation* (November 23, 1970).

FURTHER READINGS

BEHAN, R.W. "The PPBS Controversy: A Conflict of Ideologies." *Midwest Review of Public Administration,* vol. 4, no. 1 (Feb., 1970), 3–16.

CHARTRAND, ROBERT L., KENNETH JANDA, and MICHAEL JUGO. *Information Support, Program Budgeting and the Congress.* New York: Spartan Books, 1968.

Committee for Economic Development. *A Fiscal Program for a Balanced Federalism.* New York: The Committee, 1967.

Committee for Economic Development. *Budgeting for National Objectives.* New York: The Committee, 1966.

DAVIS, JAMES W., JR. *Politics, Programs, and Budgets: A Reader in Government Budgeting.* Englewood Cliffs: Prentice-Hall, Inc, 1969.

DAVIS, OTTO, M.A. DEMPSTER, and AARON WILDAVSKY. "A Theory of the Budgetary Process." *American Political Science Review.* vol. 60, no. 3 (September, 1966), 529–547.

FENNO, RICHARD F., JR. *The Power of the Purse: Appropriations Politics in Congress.* Boston: Little, Brown, 1966.

FENNO, RICHARD F., JR. *The Public Purse.* Boston: Little, Brown and Company, 1966.

Financial Management in the Federal Government. 92nd Congress, 1st Session, Senate Document No. 92–50, Washington, D.C.: Government Printing Office, 1971.

FISCHER, G. H. *The World of Program Budgeting.* Santa Monica: The RAND Corporation, 1966.

FISHER, LOUIS. "Funds Impounded by the President: The Constitutional Issue." *George Washington Law Review.* vol. 38, no. 5 (July, 1970).

FISHER, LOUIS. "The Politics of Impounded Funds." *Administrative Science Quarterly.* vol. 15, no. 3 (September 1970).

GERWIN, DONALD. "Towards a Theory of Public Budgetary Decision-Making." *Administrative Science Quarterly.* vol. 14, no. 1 (March 1969), 33–46.

GOLEMBIEWSKI, ROBERT T. *Public Budgeting and Finance: Readings in Theory and Practice.* Itasca, Illinois: F.E. Peacock Publishers, Inc., 1968.

HAVEMAN, ROBERT and JULIUS MARGOLIS. eds. *Public Expenditures and Policy Analysis.* Chicago: Markham Publishing Co., 1970.

HELLER, WALTER W. ed. *Revenue-Sharing and the City.* Baltimore: Johns Hopkins University Press, 1968.

HORN, STEPHEN, *Unused Power, The Work of the Senate Committee on Appropriations.* Washington, D.C.: Brookings, 1970.

JERNBERG, JAMES E. "Information Change and Congressional Behavior: A Caveat for PPB Reformers." *Journal of Politics.* vol. 31, no. 3 (August 1969), 722–740.

KIMMELMAN, WILLIAM M. "Revenue Sharing in Theory and in Practice." *Governmental Finance.* III, #1 (February, 1974), 18–22.

LYDEN, FREMONT J., and ERNEST G. MILLER. *Planning-Programming-Budgeting: A Systems Approach to Management.* Chicago: Markham Publishing Co., 1967.

MAYO, ROBERT P. "Federal Budget Policy and Coordination." *Municipal Finance.* vol. 43, no. 1 (August 1969), 10–16.

MCCLURE, CHARLES E., JR. "Revenue-Sharing: Alternative to Rational Fiscal Federalism." *Public Policy.* vol. 19, no. 3 (Summer, 1971), 457–478.

MEREWITZ, LEONARD and STEPHEN SOSNICK. *The Budget's New Clothes.* Chicago: Markham Publishing Co., 1972.

MOSHER, FREDERICK C., and JOHN E. HARR. *Programming Systems and Foreign Affairs Leadership, An Attempted Innovation.* New York: Oxford University Press, 1970.

NOVICK, DAVID. *Program Budgeting: Program Analysis and the Federal Budget.* Cambridge: Harvard University Press, 1965.

OTT, DAVID J. and ATTIAT F. OTT. *Federal Budget Policy.* Washington: The Brookings Institution, 1969.

PADGETT, EDWARD R. "Programming-Planning-Budgeting: Some Reflections Upon the American Experience with PPBS." *International Review of Administrative Science,* vol. 37, no. 3 (1971), 353–362.

PORTER, DAVID O. and TEDDIE WOOD PORTER. "Social Equity and Fiscal Federalism." *Public Administration Review,* vol. 34, no. 1 (Jan.-Feb., 1974), 36–43.

REAGAN, MICHAEL. *The New Federalism.* New York: Oxford University Press, 1972.

REUSS, HENRY S. *Revenue Sharing: Crutch or Catalyst for State and Local Governments?* New York: Praeger, 1970.

SCHICK, ALLEN. "The Budget Bureau That Was: Thoughts on the Rise, Decline and Future of a Presidential Agency." *Law and Contemporary Problems.* vol. 25, (1970), 519–539.

SENATE SUBCOMMITTEE on SEPARATION of POWERS. *Executive Impoundment of Appropriated Funds.* 92nd Cong., 1st Sess., Washington: Government Printing Office, 1971.

SHARKANSKY, IRA. "Agency Requests, Gubernatorial Support, and Budget Success in State Legislatures." *American Political Science Review,* vol. 62, no. 4 (Dec., 1968), 1220–1231.

SHARKANSKY, IRA. "Four Agencies and an Appropriations Committee: A Comparative Study of Budget Strategies." *Midwest Journal of Political Science.* vol. 9, no. 3 (August, 1965), 254–281.

SYMPOSIUM. "Planning-Programming-Budgeting Symposium." *Public Administration Review.* vol. 26, no. 4 (December, 1966), 243–319.

THOMPSON, RICHARD E. *Revenue Sharing: A New Era in Federalism.* Washington: Revenue Sharing Advisory Service, 1973.

TURNBULL, AUGUST B. *Government Budgeting and PPBS: A Programmed Introduction.* Reading, Mass.: Addison-Wesley, 1970.

WILDAVSKY, AARON. *The Politics of the Budgetary Process.* Boston: Little, Brown & Co., 1964.

WRIGHT, DEIL S. *Federal Grants In Aid: Perspectives and Alternatives.* Washington: American Enterprise Institute for Policy Research, 1968.

SIX

THE PROBLEMS AND PROSPECTS OF ADMINISTRATIVE RESPONSIBILITY

Perhaps the most critical measure of the success or failure of a democratic administrative process is the ability to keep the administration responsible and accountable. Part Six explores several dimensions of public accountability as they presently exist and may exist in the near future.

Administrative accountability has, until recently, been normatively concerned. Although an awareness of the structured relationships between the administrator, his superiors, Congress, and the courts exist, the basic measure of accountability has been efficiency. However, a greater understanding of the behavior and attitudes of people toward administrative actions, fostered by the empirical and behavioral approaches to administration, has expanded the traditional definition for efficiency. No longer can efficiency mean only "the greatest output from the least input," but also efficiency must relate to the satisfactory accomplishment of given program goals as attested to by the persons affected by said programs.

Within a democratic political system, the government is ultimately responsible to the people. However, a multitude of channels exist through which this responsibility may be tested. This part looks closely at legal, political, and social processes of accountability. Is there a "public interest" which administration seeks to serve? If so, how is responsibility defined for this dimension? What roles, if any, are to be played by administrative agencies, Congress, or individuals in the process of accountability? And, what of the demands for the future? If administration does not meet the desired demands for accountability, what kinds of adaptation are needed? These questions and others shall be pursued in the following selections.

It is widely assumed that the goals of public administration are to execute policies in behalf of the "public interest." Michael M. Harmon's selection attempts to analyze the many meanings of the term "public interest" and to suggest an operational definition derived from fundamental assumptions about democracy. He argues that "the fundamental premise underlying democracy is that the ethical or moral "correctness" of political and social values, and of resultant policy, is not subject to proof.

Harmon compares four sets of conflicting values regarding the public interest. From this comparison he defines the public interest as "the continually changing outcome of political activity among individuals and groups within a democratic political system." For him the public interest is seen through the operation or process of administration rather than the substance.

He constructs a policy formulation grid based on his definition under which he describes styles of administration relating to policy formulation. The two dimensions of the grid represent "responsiveness" or "advocacy." Responsiveness in behavior most closely represents that which is accountable to the democratic process while advocative behavior is active support by administrators for the adoption of policies.

Of the five styles he suggests—survival, rationalist, reactive, prescriptive, and proactive—Harmon prefers the proactive as most closely achieving the maximum degree of responsiveness by the administrator to the democratic process and those to whom he is responsible. In this style he predicts the greatest likelihood of the fusion of advocacy and responsiveness.

Independent regulatory agencies perhaps best reflect the efforts of the democratic system to provide governmental instruments for the protection of the public interest. The degree to which they have succeeded in advancing the public interest is discussed in the following two selections.

Most recent writers seem to agree that the regulatory agencies have failed to meet the expectations of those who see them as protectors of the public interest against encroachment by mass organizations, public or private. However, this failure must to some extent also rest upon other inadequacies in the political system. Greater responsibility for monitoring the regulatory process must be assumed by Congress, the media, and the many competing interest groups who at present seem content to vie for power regardless of the effect on the public.

Richard Leone identifies the relatively closed nature of the regulatory process and suggests that a remedy for this might be found in the "public service advocate" who sets out to redress the imbalances between government and corporate legal resources and those available to the private citizen. He sees these efforts directed toward criticizing and reforming both the regulators and the regulated.

According to Leone, the advocates argue that the due process safeguards have failed to provide adequate access for private citizens or adequate protection for the public interest. By identifying issues, making them generally understandable, and increasing public scrutiny of the public decision-makers, they hope to bring a greater impact for the public good to the regulatory process. Publicity, then, is a major tool for the public interest advocate.

Taken as a whole, the public interest advocacy movement represents a wave of reform activity which may significantly affect the political process. Only time will tell whether actual political outcomes will be affected or if it is simply a passing fad.

James Q. Wilson takes a somewhat different approach. He suggests that the basic problem of the regulatory process is related to the nature of the tasks given to the agencies as well as their method of carrying out those responsibilities.

Rather than developing general rules and reasonable standards applicable to all parties which permit the affected parties to conduct themselves free from the fear of capricious governmental action, the regulatory agencies carry out an *ad hoc,* particularistic process, affected but not determined by policy habit or inclination. In fact, Wilson contends that the agencies go to some effort to avoid such general rules because: 1) the greater the codification of substantive policy, the less power the agency can wield over any client in any particular case and 2) the agency and its staff wish to be able to achieve particular goals in particular cases.

What then of the future for regulation in the public interest? Wilson contends that neither industry nor the agencies need fear major reforms which would reduce the item-by-item regulation which currently exists. He suggests that a greater trend toward increased regulation, discretion, and challenges to corporate practices will emerge regardless of the cost to the public consumer. Efforts will increase, according to Wilson, for the regulatory agencies to protect the consumer by setting the price he pays or forbidding him to buy dangerous known products. In sum, trends in public interest protection in the regulatory process do not look favorable.

Earlier in this text (Part Four) public personnel processes were discussed from the perspective of efforts to make personnel selection processes more reflective of the general population. Arthur D. Larson summarizes the theory behind the concept of representative bureaucracy. In addition, he cites some deficiencies in the rationale for representativeness. But most importantly he focuses on the relationships between the public and the bureaucracy, especially in regard to the formulation of administrative policy which responds to the people's demands for policy change by taking into account group and local concerns as well as situational differences.

Larson attacks the assumption that individuals who are like other people with respect to their values, attitudes, beliefs, and interests will act alike in similar circumstances. He cites multi-group memberships and societal pluralism as forces which would reduce the likelihood of this happening. He further suggests that policies and programs based on this concept would, by definition, not provide a base for serving all groups equally and/or equitably.

Larson agrees that the time is here for correcting serious deficiencies in the selection process in regard to women and minorities. This is a matter of rights. Secondly, he places more emphasis in training programs which enhances knowledge about political, social, and economic forces at work in the society. He does not support representation simply on the basis of population match-ups. Finally, he suggests that the greatest chance of success for a truly representative bureaucracy rests in the external (legislative, executive, or judicial bodies) controls for enforcing responsibility rather than in allowing public administrators to make their own rules.

Does what Larson sees as happening have any meaning in reality? John Strange and Gary English look at two administrative programs which include provisions for citizen participation in the administrative process, namely the Community Action Programs (CAP) and Model Cities. They each look at the nature of these programs and evaluate their success in providing for effective representation in the administrative decision-making process.

John Strange shows that citizen participation is quite well entrenched in the political history of this nation. However, he suggests that recent developments in the mass society have generated an interest in participation by groups who have previously tended to be less likely to participate, such as the poor and the minorities. Two significant federal programs were created to extend the participatory process to these groups: Community Action Programs (which tended to advocate full participation of the poor and minorities); and Model Cities (which limited citizen participation and guaranteed government and business participation.)

Strange indicates that differences exist in the working definition of "who is to participate, in what way, and to what extent," when both programs are compared. He shows how techniques of implementation affect the participatory process and also indicates how administrative processes and procedures tend to place restrictions on the ability of groups and individuals to participate. Furthermore, he found variances in definition, implementation, and administrative practices from community to community.

The impact of participation in these programs has been varied. With regard to the participants, Strange suggests that greater activity took place among low income and minority groups through these programs and their general knowledge about governmental activities and operations increased. In program areas the conclusions of observers tend to be unclear. Some indicate a correlation between participation and significant policy changes; others claim either no significant changes have occurred or that the effect has been negative rather than positive. Strange hints that perhaps the most significant effect in the sphere of policy is the development of channels into the decisional process which may be extended in time. Similar conclusions are reached about the effect of participation in the community. Some semblance of management and control by minorities at the local level has taken place along with an increase in symbolic meaning for the groups. Nevertheless, Strange is quick to conclude, that, overall radical changes in the distribution of power, influence, services, rewards, or other benefits have not come about.

Where do we go from here? Strange offers some suggestions. First, he suggests that the failure to succeed in reducing poverty was more from a lack of national commitment than the failure of citizen participation. Secondly, citizen participation must be seen as only one objective among many aimed at increasing the ability of the poor and minorities to affect programs which bear directly upon their lives. To that extent, the programs were somewhat successful and justified since participation benefits society by increasing stability, providing for new ideas and concerns, and decreasing dissatisfaction with government.

In another vein, Gary English examines citizen participation from the perspective of the administrator and the ability of the administrative organization to accomodate this unique and promising social innovation. He admits that problems exist in implementing citizen participation, especially in regard to conflicts in American social values. But, his main concern is with problems that exist in the operational mechanisms of the CAP bureaucracy and that make effective participation difficult.

English identifies the CAP Board as the key unit for implementing citizen participation. He describes problems in recruitment, time, and leadership, not to mention the political realities within which the Board is set and must operate. He furthermore points out the weakness of the staff arm which he contends is the result of the insecurity of CAP positions moreso than poor salary or knowledge. Of vital importance in keeping an effective staff is the stability of the CAP Director whose position, he suggests, is often untenable due to conflict within the CAP agency and between CAPs and the other governmental and private sector agencies. Finally, English maintains that the paper jungle which exists between the CAPs and the state and federal offices is unmanageable.

What can be done to remedy these problems to enable more effective citizen participation through a better organized bureaucracy? English suggests: 1) Congress needs to clearly decide whether or not it wants the CAPs and, if so, needs to adequately finance them; 2) state agencies must take a more positive role by being more constructive and supportive rather than taking their usual watchdog, do-nothing stance; 3) more adequate personnel must be found through better training which should include extensive social science backgrounds, especially in poverty behavior and management as well as the more technical and legal skills; and 4) efforts should be made to improve the membership on the CAP Boards which provide a vital link for effective communication of representative views into the policy process.

Thus, in English's opinion, participation of the poor and minorities alone will not make administrative programs more responsive or representative of the community. What is also needed is an effective and trained leadership and staff along with the financial and political support of all governmental levels

In view of the changing nature of the public sector, what does the future hold for the public administrator? Professors Chapman and Cleaveland attempt to answer this question. They identify four major trends and challenges to the public service in the next decade: 1) pressures for centralization and decentralization; 2) unionization of the public service; 3) increased citizen involvement; and 4) the impact of technological change.

These challenges should affect public administration in the following ways according to Richard L. Chapman and Frederic N. Cleaveland. Public organizations will become flatter, greater use will be made of *ad hoc* special groups, and more long-range planning will become a necessity. At the same time, control and accountability will become more difficult to ascertain. The public work force will be characterized by increased levels of training and specialization, along with a greater opportunity for self-expression and self-actualization. Mobility both within and among agencies will increase as the extent of agency loyalty tends to decrease. In addition, they see a continued increase in the pressure for greater politicization of the public service.

Chapman and Cleaveland see two somewhat conflictual trends in organizational dynamics. A trend toward greater flexibility is seen in the organizational context while at the same time greater rigidity is seen as a result of the increase in moves toward unionization and politicization. The interfacing of these two trends will add to the complexity of the public organization and will call for the development of new standards for effectiveness and accountability. Although the administrative process will operate more openly, they also point out that the ability of the public service to deliver services will tend to decline in the light of increased conflictual and contradictory demands.

Regarding the public administrator, the authors state that he will become more of a facilitator and coordinator, a bargainer and politician, as well as an agent for change. He will be much more visible and available and less tied to organizational or personal relationships which might preclude change.

He will have to be able to contend with challenges to his profession which will be evidenced by a decline in the public service ethic, the erosion of organizational loyalties, and greater political activism on the part of public employees. Although the challenges are great, Chapman and Cleaveland conclude that they can be successfully met provided the proper training and leadership is available.

The point that must be made clear in this final part is that public administration is a dynamic rather than a static process, undergoing pressures for adaptation and change much like any other public institution. Either administration will be responsible or responsive to the demands of the participants in the democratic process or the forces in the society will either bypass the administrative apparatus or cripple it. This is valid whether we speak of the legislative representative function or of the efforts to make administration more representative. The real challenge for the future is whether or not administrators and administration can successfully synthesize the changing demands for technical proficiency and representation within the context of an open and legitimate process. Nothing less will suffice.

28

michael m. harmon

ADMINISTRATIVE POLICY FORMULATION AND THE PUBLIC INTEREST

Among students of public adminstration the concept of "public interest" has occasioned considerable debate, yet little consensus. Ironically, the lack of consensus in the academic community seems equalled only by the certainty with which official pronouncements are
uttered in the name of public interest, a circumstance leading many
scholars to abandon the concept altogether. While it is tempting to
follow suit, such a collective quietude will in the long haul relegate
the public interest to an innocuous position in the conventional wisdom shared by The Essential Brotherhood of Man and The American
Way. In the hope that it is still a viable concept, an operational
definition derived from a fundamental assumption about democracy
will be offered, followed by a consideration within that context of
styles of administrative behavior in formulating public policy.

While unanimous agreement on the matter is not anticipated,
the argument is advanced that the fundamental premise underlying
democracy is that the ethical or moral "correctness" of political and
social values, and of resultant policy, is not subject to proof.[1] Freedom to propose change, or indeed to defend the status quo, is simply
assumed because the legitimate limitation of such activity requires
proof of an alternative position. Freedom's traditional democratic
counterpart, equality, is justified on similar grounds. We need not
contend that "all men are created equal"; rather, since no one can

Michael M. Harmon, "Administrative Policy Formulation and the Public
Interest," *Public Administration Review*, September/October 1969, pp.
483–491. Reprinted by permission.

prove that his values or policy preferences are correct (unequal), the assumption of equality is all that remains. The burden of proof rests with the advocate of elitism. Since inequality cannot be proved, preferences are presumed to be of equal validity until subjected to appropriate tests of disproof.

This position, which defines democracy as essentially a null hypothesis, admittedly has little rhetorical appeal; but it is useful as a point of departure for redefining public interest and for addressing some normative issues relating to the role of administrators in formulating public policy.

SOME DIMENSIONS OF PUBLIC INTEREST THEORY

Academic discourse on the public interest reveals some dimensions under which conflicting views about the concept may be usefully summarized. The public interest is asserted to be either: (1) unitary or individualistic, (2) prescriptive or descriptive, (3) substantive or procedural, and (4) ultimate (static) or dynamic.

Unitary Versus Individualistic Conceptions of the Public Interest

A *unitary* conception of the public interest, as described by Meyerson and Banfield, is one in which "the 'whole' may be conceived as a single set of ends which pertain equality to all members of the public. . . . The plurality is an entity or body politic which entertains ends in a corporate capacity; these may be different from those entertained by any of the individuals who comprise the public."[2] Individualistic conceptions, according to these authors, assume that:

> . . . the ends of the plurality do not comprise a single system, either one which pertains to the plurality as an entity or one which is common to individuals. The relevant ends are those of individuals, whether shared or unshared. The ends of the plurality "as a whole" are simply the aggregate of ends entertained by individuals, and that decision is in the public interest which is consistent with as large a part of the "whole" as possible.[3]

An eloquent proponent of a unitary public interest is Walter Lippmann, who differentiated public from private interests.

> Living adults share, we must believe, the same public interest. For them, however, the public interest is mixed with, and is

often at odds with, their private and special interests. Put this way, we can say, I suggest, that the public interest may be presumed to be what men would choose if they saw clearly, thought rationally, acted disinterestedly and benevolently.[4]

The difficulty with Lippmann's view is that he assumes that the "correctness" of public policies, and of the values on which they are based, is in some way knowable. The only clue to aid in the enunciation of policies in the public interest is his admonition that men should act disinterestedly and benevolently. Disinterest, however, is at best a rare commodity in politics; and given even the purest of motives, there is no certainty that one can act in such a manner. Moreover, the curious array of political activities undertaken in the name of benevolence marks Lippmann's unitary version of the public interest as one of dubious utility. Possessing neither guarantees of disinterest and benevolence, nor (more importantly) objective "proofs" for making judgments about policy, a unitary public interest is rendered untenable. An individualistic public interest (based on the axiom of self-interest), on the other hand, is not bound by the constraints inherent in unitary versions. Specifically, proof becomes an issue when an advocate of a law or policy assumes the exclusive prerogative of making judgments for others. Since self-interest makes no necessary claim about the appropriateness of individual preferences for others, it does not violate the premise of unprovability. Choices made and preferences states in this context are existential; proof is not an issue.

Prescriptive Versus Descriptive Conceptions

Our inability to prove the correctness of substantive goals and policies places additional constraints on what may be considered an appropriate definition of the public interest. While judgments may be made about what the public interest should be in regard to political issues, the absence of "ultimate" criteria for verifying such claims forces us to reject prescriptive interpretations. Since prescriptions about its substance are inherently tentative and uncertain, the public interest may be viewed more usefully as a descriptive concept. That is, it describes the result of political activity, rather than prescribing what that result ought to be. A descriptive interpretation does not, certainly, preclude advocacy of change as a legitimate political or adminstrative act. It is simply a reminder of the tentativeness with which policy proposals must be advanced in a democratic system.

Substantive Versus Procedural Conceptions

If we accept the position that the public interest is a descriptive concept, we may regard attention to the policy *process* as being an equally legitimate responsibility as our traditional concern with its *substance*. The former, in fact, is really the prior issue. In evaluating policy, emphasis must initially, at least, be shifted from its substance to the process by which it is created. Because of the tentativeness of criteria for evaluating substantive policies, attention is focused on the degree to which arbitrary constraints exist in political systems which tend to deny articulation of policy preferences and expenditure of political resources. It is the elimination of such constraints which allows (fully, in theory) latent values and resources to become manifest, permitting a more accurate identification or description of the public interest. The accuracy of its identification depends on the degree to which latent values, interests, and policy preferences are not prohibited from becoming manifest. It is in this sense that the elementary proposition that democracy is a process rather than a philosophy has meaning.

In supporting a procedural view of the public interest we are unable to infer a definitive blueprint of appropriate political and administrative machinery. From our initial premise that the correctness of policy preferences is ultimately unprovable we can infer only that procedures which limit the articulation of such preferences are unacceptable.

Static Versus Dynamic Conceptions

Since the public mood is in a continual state of flux, it is axiomatic that the public interest must be viewed as changing also, rather than static or constant. And if the public interest changes, the development of a political system which can respond effectively to those changes is imperative. Students of large-scale organizations have lamented that traditional criteria for evaluating organizational performance (such as production and profits) are inadequate because they are static indicators and do not account for changes in organizational goals. Warren Bennis[5] has argued that a "healthy" organization is, in part, one which can successfully respond on a continuing basis to changing demands from its environment. There appears to be a logical corollary here between the concept of "organizational health," at one level, and a procedurally based definition of the public interest, at the political level. Each idea in effect suggests that political and organizational systems are effective to the degree they are responsive to environmental demands. A healthy organization is a democratic one; a democratic political system is "healthy."

THE PUBLIC INTEREST REDEFINED

To summarize, the public interest, to be consistent with our initial premise, must be viewed as (1) individualistic rather than unitary, (2) descriptive rather than prescriptive, (3) procedural rather than substantive, and (4) dynamic rather than static. Put another way, *the public interest is the continually changing outcome of political activity among individuals and groups within a democratic political system.*[6] By stressing process rather than substance, this definition has important implications regarding the appropriateness of styles of administration in the formulation of policy in public organizations.

THE POLICY FORMULATION GRID

While administrators may possess little conscious knowledge of public interest theory, the manner in which they conduct their activities as advocates and/or implementors of policy reflects certain assumptions about the concept. A high degree of certainty about the correctness of a given policy, for example, may indicate an administrator's implicit commitment to a fundamentally substantive and prescriptive view of the public interest. Static interpretations of the concept are evident in administrators having a consuming concern with the value of efficiency.

In an attempt to relate the public interest concept to the ways in which administrators perform their functions in the policy arena, a typology of administrative styles is depicted on a two-dimensional grid similar to the Managerial Grid of Robert Blake.[7] *The Policy Formulation Grid* describes styles of administration relating to policy formulation in public organizations. *Responsiveness,* a central issue deriving from the foregoing discussion of the public interest, is depicted on the vertical axis of the grid; the horizontal axis indicates the extent of policy *advocacy* of administrators. The number 1 depicts minimal activity, while 9 indicates maximum activity. In the lower-left corner, the 1,1 style describes administrative activity which is both nonadvocative and unresponsive. The upper-left corner describes the 1,9 style in which the administrator is highly responsive, but minimally advocative. The 9,1 style in the lower-right corner depicts a high degree of policy advocacy accompanied by low responsiveness to political system demands. The 5,5 style, at the midpoint, is a compromise between responsiveness and advocative behavior, which are assumed by the administrator to be antithetical. A maximization of both of the grid's dimensions (i.e., high advocative *and* responsive behavior) is described by the 9,9 style in the upper-right corner. The terms *responsive* and *advocative* are intentionally defined broadly to accommodate their varying interpretations implicit in the five styles shown on the grid. While specific assumptions are made about their meaning in each of the styles, suffice it to say generally that *responsive behavior* is that which is accountable in some way to the democratic process, whether by voting, mutual adjustment, or some other method by which public demands are, or might be, legitimately translated into policy. *Advocative behavior* is defined as the active support by administrators for the adoption of policies.

Survival Style (1,1)

In his discussion of metropolitan special districts, John Bollens has argued that the limited scope of such agencies has often resulted in their becoming isolated from agencies and problems related to their special purpose. While in some cases they are barred by district laws and political pressure from expanding and coordinating their functions with other levels of government, ". . . districts of limited purpose have shown their inclination to seek authorization for additional services."[8] A case in point has been described by Edward T. Chase, who criticized the Port of New York Authority for ignoring problems of mass transit in order to promote the "efficiency" of its own operations. While the PA's revenues rose steadily and impressively over the years, the problem of traffic congestion continually worsened.

> . . . on its own terms the PA is doing a grand job. But those terms, today, are cockeyed. The world has changed but the PA stubbornly refuses to cope with the new problems.
>
> It cheerfully reports one achievement after another. Yet at the same time, mass transportation serving New York is faltering and the city is foundering under the weight and pollution of traffic.[9]

FIGURE 1. Policy formulation grid

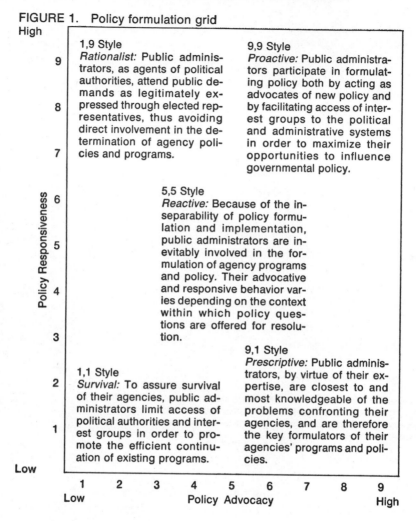

Because the Port Authority has established a reputation as an efficient agency providing vital services to the New York-New Jersey metropolitan area, its ultimate survival was seldom questioned. Yet, at the writing of the Chase article, the PA reflected essentially a style of administrative survival (1,1). Given almost unlimited discretion to formulate policy to promote "the improvement of transportation and terminal facilities," the PA chose to interpret its mandate narrowly. In the context of the Policy Formulation Grid, its advocative activity was minimal in that little effort was made to effect major policy changes. Effectiveness was seen in terms of the efficiency with which the Port Authority could executive existing policies. Further, by its refusal to respond to public demands to expand its responsibilities into the area of mass transit, its responsiveness was negligible.

Rationalist Style (1,9)

The rationalist style is in a broad sense a restatement of rationalist public interest theory described by Glendon Schubert.[10] Its primary assumptions have been stated by Norton Long.

> The legitimacy of the will, like the concept of sovereignty, provides the basis for a logical deductive system moving from the first principle—be it the will of the people via Congress, or the will of the people via Congress through President, or the will of the people via President. In any event, the prime problem of administration is to give effect to this will.[11]

Thus provided a presumably value-free premise for public administration, Herbert Simon, the leading modern advocate of administrative rationalism, concludes that problems of administration are reducible to problems of engineering. His statement provides an illustration of the 1,9 position on the grid.

> The theory of administration is concerned with how an organization should be constructed and operated in order to accomplish its work efficiently. A fundamental principle of administration, which follows almost immediately from the rational character of "good" administration, is that among several alternatives involving the same expenditure the one should always be selected which leads to the greatest accomplishment of administrative objectives: and among several alternatives that lead to the same accomplishment the one should be selected which involves the least expenditure.[12]

In attacking the utility of rationalist theory, Long presents a two-fold critique:

> The view of administration as sheerly instrumental, or even largely instrumental, must be rejected as empirically untenable and ethically unwarranted. The rejection will entail abandonment, on the one hand, of Herbert Simon's quest for a value-free administration and, on the other, of the over-simplified dogma of an overloaded legislative supremacy of his logical comrade in arms, Charles Hyneman. These two views fit like hand in glove. Legislative supremacy provides Simon with value prem-

> ises, which can then permit a value-free science of administra-
> tion the esthetic delight of unique and verifiably determinate
> problem solutions through the application of the value premises
> to the fact premises. . . . But, alas, we know this institutional
> divorce, however requisite for a value-free science of adminis-
> tration, does not exist.[13]

Not only do the rationalists err in assuming that policy formulation and implementation are separable, but they also assume that all
legitimate values relevant to policy formulation are expressed
through voting or elected representatives. Since most issues facing
public administrators relate only to limited segments of the total
population, the formal processes of voting and legislative representation are incapable of coping with demands of individuals and interest
groups on a day-to-day basis. Administrators, therefore, are left with
the responsibility not only of implementing policy handed down from
their political superiors, but they must also confront the prior problem of constructing and maintaining a system through which demands
can initially be articulated. The rationalists' failure to deal effectively
with this issue renders their behavior as responsive only in a passive
and highly formal sense. Regarding the dimension of advocacy, it
goes almost without saying that the doctrine of legislative supremacy
which the rationalists accept precludes them from advocating substantive policy.

Because total avoidance of policy advocacy and formulation is
unlikely, the rationalist style in its purest sense is not descriptive of
the dominant behavior of many administrators. Nonetheless, it has
had considerable importance as an administrative ethic as illustrated
by the consolidation in 1964 of the Los Angeles City and County
health departments.[14] After more than 50 years of debate of the
question, the City of Los Angeles decided to abolish its health function by taking advantage of state enabling legislation which allowed
cities operating independent health departments to transfer, at no
cost to them, that function to the county. In terms of money spent on
public health services and numbers of people affected by the move,
the city's action was the largest of its kind in the nation's history. Its
incentive to transfer the health function was a legitimate one—to
alleviate tax inequities suffered by city residents who paid taxes to
support two health departments, the city's and the county's, while
receiving direct benefits only from the city health department.

Because of City Council apathy about public health policy, City
and County Health Department administrators were given almost
total discretion in defining the future policies of the newly consoli-

dated county department. Interestingly, during the dispute administrators and health officials voiced strong commitment to the ethical neutrality of administration in policy matters, a commitment due largely to the professionalization of Los Angeles governmental bureaucracies. The ethic of administrative neutrality conflicted sharply, however, with the finding that administrators were deeply involved in making important policy decisions regarding the transfer of the City Health Department to the county. This is not to say that the administrators were hypocritical; rather, their perceptions of what constituted policy decisions, as opposed to purely technical ones, were weighted heavily toward the latter. These perceptions were reinforced by their political superiors who delegated highly important decisions to the chief administrative officers and health department officials on the assumption that those decisions were mainly technical.

At the same time that public health policy relating to the consolidation was being made, professional and community action groups in the City of Los Angeles, which were generally vehemently opposed to the move, were given in most instances only pro forma consideration of their demands. Their limited avenues of real influence illustrate some of the pitfalls for responsiveness when the rationalist style is assumed to be descriptive of administrative activity where there are questions of policy formulation.

Prescriptive Style (9,1)

Although rationalist and prescriptive styles appear at opposite corners of the grid, a distinction between the two in practice is frequently difficult to discern. As already noted, perceptions of what constitute policy questions, as opposed to technical questions, vary among government officials. To the extent that generally accepted criteria for making such distinctions are lacking, distinguishing between rationalist and prescriptive administrators becomes complicated.

The prescriptive style of administration predominates institutions either where wide latitude for statutory interpretation by administrators is allowed or where the technical complexity of issues requires expertise peculiar to a very limited number of personnel within an agency. In the latter case, whether administrative neutrality exists in matters of substantive policy is often open to serious question. Administrative strategy reflecting elements of both 1,9 and 9,1 styles is evident in what Sayre and Kaufman call the "doctrine of neutral competence."[15] Their argument is that administrators, to further their discretion over issues of substantive policy, make what are essentially policy decisions under the guise of technical expertise, i.e., they exhibit 9,1 behavior in the guise of a 1,9 style. In the Los Angeles health dispute, however, administrators decided important questions of policy, not because they were intent on increasing their discretion in such matters, but because the responsibility for making such decisions was delegated to them by their political superiors.

The subtle distinctions between the conclusions of Sayre and Kaufman and the health consolidation study illustrate the complexities surrounding the question of what determines administrative style in policy formulation. While personality and professional values undoubtedly are key determinants, administrative style is affected by a broad range of factors. A partial list of these would include: role expectations of superiors, subordinates, and peers; the political volatility of the agency; the number and diversity of client groups served by the agency; the specificity of the agency's statutory mandate; the apparent effectiveness of current operations; and the nature of agency-legislative relationships.

Reactive Style (5,5)

The difficulty in drawing clear distinctions between policy formulation and implementation requires administrative reactivists to operate in both areas, although they regard separation of the two as an ethically desirable yet unattainable norm. Lepawsky has described their dilemma:

> Perhaps the most promising way of continuing a healthy separation between politics and administration, while entertaining a growing concern about the need for tying them together, is to refine the relation of the administrator or managerial expert to policies or political questions. Administrators at all levels of responsibility are being constantly thrown into the area of decision-making, and their decisions inevitably add up to major policies in the subsequent course of events. . . .
>
> As a matter of governmental evolution, therefore, the administrator cannot avoid some policy making responsibility. However, he can more accurately define his role with relation to policy. Specifically, administrators should (1) constantly gather facts and prepare findings that may lead to changes in policy or to policy decisions; (2) inform their chief, and with his approval inform the policy-making body or (3) recommend and inititate policies but advocate them only with superior consent.[16]

The conclusion one is forced to draw from this statement is that without the most stringent prescription of the administrator's role, responsive and advocative behavior are inevitably compromised. The complications generated by Lepawsky's advice force the reactive administrator ultimately to conclude that to the extent he is advocative, he is unresponsive; conversely, responsive behavior is nonadvocative. Despite the good intent of Lepawsky and others in attempting to specify the appropriate limits of administrative advocacy, their suggestions frequently seem remote from the "real world" of the administrator. In a state of ethical confusion and with few clear guides for behavior, the reactivist relies primarily on the hard lessons of experience. An awareness of where power is located and how it is used provides him with little control *over* his environment, but enables him generally to cope successfully *within* it. His ability to anticipate the potential exercise of influence by others often makes him an effective tactician of the type described in Edward Banfield's case studies of Chicago politics.[17] Since the nature and amount of responsive and advocative behavior in the reactive style are governed by context rather than conscience, personal risk taking is minimized and policy changes are, at most, incremental.

A common thread running through the prescriptive, rationalist, and reactive styles is the assumption that the freedom of administrators to advocate policy and their requirement to be responsive to public demands are popular norms. The issue is least troublesome to prescriptive administrators whose monopoly of technical knowledge justifies to their satisfaction their exclusive privilege not only of advocating policy, but of having the final say in its determination. Their Weberian and Taylorian heritage frees them from the uncertainties clouding normative controversies external to their immediate areas of concern. When pressed on the matter of responsiveness they may, often legitimately, reply that their policies are implicitly responsive. A conscious effort to test such assumptions, however, is not generally evident.

Rationalist administrators, whose historical antecedents can be traced to the American era of reform, confront the issue more directly, yet are left convinced of the essential polarity of responsiveness and advocacy. Accepting unequivocally the doctrine of legislative supremacy, they are certain of the rightness of their ethic, but are unsure of its workability under conditions of uncertainty and flux.

In achieving a balance between the conflicting norms of the rationalist and prescriptive styles, administrative reactivists avoid confronting the ethical problem directly by allowing the outcome of issues to be governed by the situation. Lacking a coherent philosophy of administration, they rationalize their position by arguing that they are at the mercy of forces over which they have only minimal control.

Proactive Style (9,9) [18]

The dispute over whether advocacy and responsiveness are ultimately incompatible can be confronted more directly when reduced to a more basic level. To assume their incompatibility is fundamentally to make the commonly held assumption that individual freedom and social responsibility are incompatible. Robert P. Biller has argued that to assume this is to draw an unwarranted inference. "Since we 'know' the meaning of each in only proximate ways, data about their apparent present or past incompatibility is useful only in determining the degree of confidence with which we would undertake risks involved in their fusion." [19] By initially remaining neutral on the issue, it is possible to gather data about conditions under which fusion or incompatibility may be predicted.

The literature of humanistic psychology leaves room for considerable optimism about the potentiality of their fusion. Abraham Maslow, whose discussion of *synergy* is somewhat representative of the humanistic or existential psychologists' views on the freedom-responsibility issue, contends that mentally healthy people, more often than less healthy people, make choices which are essentially synergistic, i.e., choices which satisfy selfish needs and at the same time satisfy those of others. [20] Becoming free involves making choices and taking risks to achieve one's potential, for which a high degree of self-awareness is a precondition. Acting responsibly entails a recognition of situational elements which either constrain behavior or make apparent new choices or directions. In this sense freedom and responsibility are congruent for the healthy person. The prime test of mental health occurs in the making of choices and taking of risks which force confrontation between "selfish" and environmental needs.

In the formulation of policy, the proactive administrator is responsible only secondarily in a political sense; primarily he is a responsible person and citizen. His sense of responsibility is derived not from prescriptions external to his life experience (as implied by strict adherence to the doctrine of legislative supremacy), but is mainly a function of his high degree of mental health. As the hippies would say, he knows "where he is at."

In contrast to rationalist administration, responsiveness in the proactive style is highly active. While recognizing legitimate legislative and legal constraints on his agency and himself, the proactive administrator is actively involved both in removing arbitrary barriers to interest articulation and in facilitating access of client groups (actual and potential) to the decision process. Responsible free choice is characterized by his advocacy of policies which are always subject to negotiation with his environment. In determining policy, proactive behavior implies reciprocal influence between the administrator and those to whom he is responsible, rather than passive acceptance and implementation only of those policies directed to him by his superiors.

Although situations will exist when the policies he advocates will be at odds with the demands of his constituents, the proactive administrator is less often forced into the position of making a clear choice between the two alternatives. By continually testing his own policy preferences against those of his clientele he is more likely to emerge with what Mary Parker Follett called a "creative synthesis"[21] than with the often dramatic but initially unpopular decisions of the type described by President Kennedy in his *Profiles in Courage.*[22] Although the fusion of advocacy and responsiveness cannot be guaranteed in every instance, the proactive style at least increases its probability.

CONCLUSION

No theory of public interest can realistically offer clear answers to the hard choices with which administrators and political leaders are confronted; nor does the theory presented here presume to do so. In fairness, all that can be reasonably demanded of such a theory is that it provide a framework within which administrative behavior may be tentatively, but productively, evaluated. In each of the styles on the Policy Formulation Grid are assumptions about the public interest, some of which are simply illogical and others destructive of democratic values. In behaving consistently with the theory of public interest offered here the proactive administrator is not assured correct answers. Perhaps it is not too presumptuous to suggest, however, that he will be aided in asking more of the right questions.

ENDNOTES

1. Thomas Landon Thorson, *The Logic of Democracy* (New York: Holt, Rinehart, and Winston, 1962), pp. 138-139.

2. Martin Meyerson and Edward C. Banfield, *Politics, Planning and the Public Interest* (New York: The Free Press of Glencoe, 1955), p. 323.

3. *Ibid.*, p. 324.

4. Walter Lippmann, *The Public Philosophy* (Boston: Little, Brown and Company, 1955), pp. 41–42.

5. Warren G. Bennis, *Changing Organizations* (New York: McGraw-Hill, 1966).

6. While important normative questions about policy are clearly left unanswered by this definition, it avoids what might be labeled the General Bullmoose Syndrome of public interest theory characteristic of unitary and prescriptive interpretations.

7. Robert R. Blake and Jane S. Mouton, *The Managerial Grid* (Houston: Gulf Publishing Company, 1964).

8. John C. Bollens, *Special District Governments in the United States* (Berkeley: University of California Press, 1957), p. 91.

9. Edward T. Chase, "How to Rescue New York from Its Port Authority," *Harper's Magazine*, June 1960. p. 58.

10. Glendon Schubert, *The Public Interest* (Glencoe, Ill.: The Free Press of Glencoe, 1960).

11. Norton Long, "Power and Administration," *Public Administration Review*, Vol. IX (1949), pp. 24–25.

12. Herbert A. Simon, *Administrative Behavior* (New York: Macmillan, 1947), p. 38.

13. Long, *op. cit.*, p. 23.

14. Frank P. Sherwood, Michael M. Harmon, and Alexander Cloner, "The Inherited Decision: Health Consolidation in Metropolitan Los Angeles" (School of Public Administration, University of Southern California, October 1966), mimeographed.

15. Wallace Sayre and Herbert Kaufman, *Governing New York City* (New York: Russell Sage Foundation, 1960), p. 404.

16. Albert Lepawsky, *Administration* (New York: Alfred A. Knopf, 1949).

17. Edward C. Banfield, *Political Influence* (New York: The Free Press of Glencoe, 1961).

18. My first exposure to the word "proactive" was in an article by Hubert Bonner entitled "The Proactive Personality," in J. F. T. Bugental (ed.), *Challenges of Humanistic Psychology* (New York: McGraw-Hill, 1968), pp. 61–66. Some interesting insights into the psychology of proactive administration can be inferred from the essay. For an earlier and more comprehensive reference, see Bonner. *On Being Mindful of Man: Essay Toward a Proactive Psychology* (Boston: Houghton Mifflin, 1965).

19. Robert P. Biller, "Some Implications of Adaptation Capacity for Organizational and Political Development," paper prepared for the Minnowbrook Conference on the New Public Administration, Syracuse University, Syracuse New York, September 1968, p. 22. The Biller paper also includes some insightful comments on the null hypothesis interpretation of democracy mentioned earlier.

20. Abraham Maslow, *Eupsychian Management* (New York: Dorsey, 1966).

21. Henry C. Metcalf and L. Urwick (eds.), *Dynamic Administration, The Collected Papers of Mary Parker Follett* (New York: Harper & Bros., 1942).

22. John F. Kennedy, *Profiles in Courage* (New York: Harper, 1956).

29

richard c. leone

PUBLIC INTEREST ADVOCACY AND THE
REGULATORY PROCESS

Modern America is characterized by the expansion of government and corporate power. To monitor and condition these concentrations of power, particularly in the private sector, we have created a complex of public regulatory mechanisms. These organizations for administrative regulation are, one would hope, the foremost institutionalized advocates of the public interest. They are the watchdogs we have set on an economic system we have difficulty controlling and sometimes even understanding.

Many regulatory agencies are expected to ensure that in vital areas of private activity, the interest of the public is not overridden by private considerations of economic gain. Other agencies monitor the use of scarce resources, some of which are, by their nature, public. And still other aspects of administrative regulation affect the workings of governments themselves at all levels. Most of the areas in which regulatory agencies are involved—pure foods, safe water, transportation, product safety, protection against deceptive advertising, safe working conditions, and the like—are of great potential significance for most people most of the time. In this sense, regulatory agencies fill one of the most immediately vital and sympathetic roles of government. The policy decisions they make and the way in which they are implemented can have a direct impact on the quality and safety of people's lives. Delay or failure to act can have an equally important consequence.

Reprinted from *The Annals*, Vol. 400 (March, 1972). Copyright 1972 by The Academy of Political and Social Science. Reprinted by permission.

Yet, no one could claim that the regulatory agencies are among the cherished institutions in our society. They have been subjected to sharp criticism throughout their history. The agencies involved, in theory, should have responded to these criticisms as translated by various checks on the regulatory process, including the Congress, the courts, the press, and the political parties. Each of these groups, in theory, provides a mechanism for bringing individual grievances, public opinion, and widely shared community values to bear on the regulatory process. Perhaps out of disenchantment with these mechanisms, as much as with the regulatory agencies themselves, a new group of activists have established themselves in recent years as persistent and unyielding critics of administrative regulation.

The public interest advocates, as they frequently are called, have set out to watch the watchdogs. In conception and approach, their leader is Ralph Nader. He has given the movement inspiration, even a name, "Naderism." The term *public interest advocate* lumps together a variety of groups and individuals who have emerged in recent years as critics of government and corporate activity. Some are directly imitative of Nader's across-the-board gadfly approach; others confine their activities to discrete areas, such as civil liberties and environmental protection.

More specialized in their approach but basically of the same genre are the public interest law firms, such as the Center for Law and Social Policy in Washington, D.C. These groups hope to redress some of the imbalance between the legal resources available to the government and private corporations and those available to private citizens attempting to promote the public interest. They probably are a direct outgrowth of poverty law programs and the general movement within the legal profession toward greater relevancy to pressing social problems. They also are a response to the conclusion—not unreasonable, given the history of the last twenty years—that one major way to bring about social change is through the courts.[1]

With regard to administrative regulation generally, public interest advocates, lawyers or not, have one thing in common; they all seek the reform and reorientation of regulatory agencies. Although their methods differ, all of them tend to bring more scrutiny and publicity to bear on these agencies. Since most people agree that powerful government agencies should be subjected to a maximum amount of scrutiny, these efforts have been widely applauded—a reaction made all the more likely by the varying degrees of disrepute into which regulatory agencies have fallen. A look at almost any agency's history, for example, reveals a series of studies or commission reports indicting the agency for numerous failures and calling, typically, for sweeping reorganization. These indictments, in a sense, provide an ideal context for public interest advocates. In fact, few specific problems of administrative regulation were discovered by public interest advocates. They simply have given focus and substance to difficulties which long have been recognized by scholars as characteristic of the American regulatory experience.

The public interest advocacy movement is, in a sense, a second round of regulatory reform, following the New Deal era criticism which concentrated on achieving procedural safeguards and minimizing arbitrary actions. Its most important and obvious result was the Administrative Procedure Act. Before this act was passed in 1946, it was sometimes impossible to ascertain the basic procedural and substantive actions involved in a regulatory decision.

Current criticism, though it includes complaints about access to information, focuses on administrative apathy, abuse of discretionary authority, disregard for citizens' rights, bureaucratic stultification, and cozy relationships with special interests. These criticisms of the agencies, familiar to those who have thought about regulation, have shaped the development of public interest advocacy in this field. Perhaps more importantly, they may be crucial to the prospects for the long-term effectiveness of the movement.

ISOLATION OF THE REGULATORY PROCESS

One of the most common observations about the regulatory bodies is that they are somewhat isolated from the general political process or perhaps more precisely, that their relative independence means that only selective "political pressures" affect them. This is so partly by design; architects of the regulatory process intended to fashion a quasi-judicial system functioning above the rough-and-tumble of partisan conflict. But that inherent immunity has been reinforced by factors perhaps not foreseen by early regulatory proponents. Disincentives have emerged which discourage other public institutions from acting as monitors, critics, and reformers of the regulatory structure.

Legislators, chief executives, and press alike have been frustrated by the sheer size of the regulating bureaucracy. Once considered a daring and legally questionable application of the delegation of power, the regulatory apparatus has flourished and expanded until now the establishment of new agencies, endowed with sweeping discretionary powers, is a predictable response to any new technologies or professional services. No one can stay abreast of all the regulatory activity at any given level of government—federal, state, or large urban.

At the legislative level, only the members of the appropriate substantive committees have a chance to become genuinely familiar with the work of a major agency. As a result, other members of Congress or state legislatures rely heavily on these members to oversee and finance regulatory operations. And, knowing this, the affected economic interests attach highest priority to seeing that sympathetic officials are named to these key committees. Their efforts in this regard have been generally successful at the federal level, particularly in the House of Representatives, and spectacularly successful at the state level.

Chief executives are discouraged from attempts to reorient public agencies, in part because of the potentially high political costs of such efforts and the lack of offsetting public demands for change.

The printed press, which we expect to resist outside political influences, often has yielded to internal copy-room pressures. The vicious circle which overtakes many state newspapers finds news editors unable to free reporters for long-term investigative projects, while these same reporters, under relentless pressure to produce usable copy, become dependent on the daily press releases of regulatory agencies and increasingly reluctant to bite the hand that feeds them.

The courts have been so reluctant to second-guess agency decisions that an entire, course-length body of law has sprung up to describe the "standing" and "ripeness" required to sustain a complainant's petition for review. When regulatory decisions are overruled at the judicial level, it is almost always at the behest of an aggrieved company or trade group. They alone have the legal resources, the detailed knowledge of agency decisions, and the common interest necessary to launch a costly and extended litigation.

INDUSTRY INFLUENCE

The one group which does oversee agency activities with a keen, critical eye is the regulated industry. It expends considerable effort in lobbying agencies and Congress to make its position known and to see that it is accepted. Industries have the resources to assign someone to cover agency rule-making on a full-time basis. Over time, they develop channels for obtaining preferential access to the early stages of decision-making, when it is usually easier to affect outcomes. Their pressure tactics are refined, focused, and effective. The long-term personal relationships they nurture with key regulatory personnel are likewise aids to successful lobbying.

Given the context in which most regulatory agencies operate, industry has other built-in advantages. On questions of rate regulation, for example, regulatory decisions frequently are made on the basis of industry figures and forecasts. Indeed, most state departments of insurance, to pick an obvious case, have far too few staff members even to review adequately the figures provided by the large and expert staffs of the underwriters' associations. In the area of product-testing, regulators must depend heavily on the results of industry tests. In fact, given the magnitude of the tasks assigned to them, many agencies must depend on the good will and good intentions of industry—which presumably are expressed through voluntary compliance—in order to accomplish the missions assigned to them by legislative bodies.

Many legislators, in turn, apply pressure to regulatory agencies on behalf of the special interests of powerful constituents. Until an alternative method for campaign financing is discovered and implemented, most office holders will have important relationships with industrialists and others with a direct interest in administrative regulation. In many cases, legislators themselves have business interests which impact directly on the actions of administrators. Since they are the source not only of agency authority but also of financing, legislators are highly effective in getting their points across.

By contrast, the group which is least represented in this system is the private citizenry. Because of the nature of many of the industries regulated—food, consumer products of all kinds, health services, and the like—policy decisions and the efficiency and fairness with which they are implemented are of tremendous concern to the private citizen. Yet, for most citizens most of the time, no individual regulatory action seems important enough to cause reorganization of their lives and reordering of personal priorities in order to monitor and pressure the agency involved. Recent attempts, such as Common Cause, have tried to pool citizen concern and thus create the possibility of a citizens' lobby. Mass membership environmental groups are similar attempts to represent the affected citizen in the process. To be effective, such groups must educate the public about the extent to which their interests are involved in administrative decisions.

Among the obstacles to organizing citizens is lack of knowledge.

Agencies are reluctant to disseminate information, and comprehensive press coverage of regulatory affairs does not exist. The day-to-day operations of most regulatory agencies are not very newsworthy; or, rather, they are newsworthy only to the specialized industry press. People, not surprisingly, fail to perceive the broader implications of specific grievances or how they relate to regulatory inaction or action. The regulatory process remains invisible for most citizens. Altered train schedules seldom are related to the Interstate Commerce Commission or a bad chicken to the Food and Drug Administration. And even if they are so inclined, most private citizens lack the training and time to monitor agency decisions of relevance to them. When a citizen does act, he soon discovers the procedural delays and complexity of rulemaking and hearings. Due process requires the intervention of a lawyer and that, in turn, requires expense.[2] And, the question of court standing has seriously hampered individual attempts to force agencies to be responsive to particular needs.

In the absence of coherent public pressure, administrative agencies are free to respond to their own internal pressures. Government bureaucracies, like any other large institutions, develop a life of their own with certain internal pressures and goals—pressures which often have little to do with protecting the interest of any other group. Large bureaucracies, after all, are designed to carry out—to prolong and extend—existing policies. They are meant to keep operating in the absence of outside interference. They build up their own internal systems of rewards and punishments and seek to reduce internal conflict. One of the ways such values are maximized is also to avoid unfavorable attention from outside. This means, in part, minimizing conflicts with special interests and powerful legislators.

Regarding publicity, industry enjoys another advantage over public interest advocates. The regulated industry seldom desires to damage the public image of the agency. It poses no threat to the bureaucracy—indeed, it shares an interest in low visibility and even secrecy. This common interest fits in well with the agency's bureaucratic imperative to minimize external pressures. True, the advocate may be pressing the same public interest which is the agency's presumed mission but, imprudently, advocates want "to make it all public."

Created and designed to preserve existing policies, agencies often are one of the last groups to respond to altered circumstances. Because of their internalized perspective, they frequently fail to see their role in terms of broader social goals, society at large, or even the government in general.

A ROLE FOR PUBLIC INTEREST ADVOCACY

In a system of balancing interests and pressures, a group incapable of articulating its needs and without significant organized power is seen as less important to satisfy than those like the industries, which effectively make their influence felt. One objective of public interest advocacy is to mitigate this imbalance by providing private citizens with the information and analysis needed to perceive common interests and, potentially, to organize common pressures. Public interest advocacy operates from the premise that the only way regulation will be more responsive is for more people to become aware of the extent to which their interests are bound up in regulatory decisions.

In this sense, the first task of public interest advocates is to educate. They must develop materials which break complex issues down into a form which is comprehensible to the public. They must discover, for example, what the operating policies of regulatory agencies are, what impact they have on the parties involved, who benefits, who gets hurt, which groups or individuals are most affected by these policies, how they are affected, who pays for them, who stands to lose or gain by proposed changes, how the decision-making process works, and how pressure is applied.

In this effort to make such complex questions understandable to the layman, there is clearly a danger of oversimplification; thus not infrequently, public interest advocates have been, in an absolute sense, unfair in an attempt to arouse public ire. They are likely to dramatize; there is a bit of "theatre" involved in arousing public indignation and even outrage.[3] On occasion, they hold up a mantle of righteous indignation which can be a mask for malice and carelessness. Advocates, on the other hand, should be blunt, even harsh, in their criticism, particularly when compared with political leaders. And in so doing, they can "run interference" for office holders or even a timid press.

Working properly, public interest advocacy goes beyond straight reporting to analysis of existing policies. It examines alternative approaches and assesses the likely public impact of variations in agency operation. Ideally, publication of studies will force legislative bodies and the press—"official" guardians of the public interest in the area—to take a more aggressive role.

In this context, an important role of a public interest advocate is to make the patterns of agency action clear. He can, in this way, provide something of a check on its arbitrary use or misuse of discretionary power. In attempting to fulfill this mission, he runs into the problem that much discretionary action is not rule-governed and, therefore, is not covered by the disclosure provisions of the Administrative Procedure Act and the Freedom of Information Act. Much of the difficulty encountered in any attempt at finding information involves learning the facts about decisions made in discretionary areas. In response, public interest advocates seek to have patterns of action, tacit principles, and policies made explicit. Thus, private citizens—indeed, the advocates themselves—have a chance to understand what is at stake and make choices about where to press for change. Publicity is the best available check on the misuse of discretionary powers.

The Administrative Procedure Act did not make agencies completely open in their operations, but it did make it possible for determined investigators and researchers to learn about major policy changes and procedures. Under section 3 of the act, "public information" agencies are required to make available statements on organization, procedure, and substantive rules. All matters of official record now should be available to concerned persons. Today, regulatory agencies spew forth an almost overwhelming amount of information and paper. One of the paradoxical consequences of the Freedom of Information Act is that the volume of information has in itself become an obstacle to citizen knowledge.[4] Most states have passed acts similar to the Administrative Procedure Act, although at the state level the information available is on a much smaller scale.

Public interest advocates today have contradictory feelings about the Administrative Procedure Act. On the one hand, it has failed to provide information in usable form to the public; but, on the other hand, without it and its state counterparts there might have been no Ralph Nader and no public interest advocacy.

NADER'S ROLE

Talking about advocacy as we know it today is tantamount to talking about Nader; he is universally regarded as the prototype of the public interest advocate. He provides, if not always the model, at least the inspiration for most other advocacy operations. Public interest groups frequently identify themselves as "Nader-type" organizations.

In addition to being the best known, Nader is of course the most respected and the most powerful. It may be overstating the case to say, as a *New York Times Magazine* reporter did, "He has become an institution, at least as formidable as General Motors."[5] But there is no denying that his access to media, his credibility, and his influence are enormous. Credited to his legislative account is the chief responsibility for passage of six major laws for protecting the public interest: the Natural Gas Pipeline Safety Act of 1968, the Radiation Control for Health and Safety Act of 1968, the Coal Mine Health and Safety Act of 1969, the 1970 Comprehensive Occupational Health Safety Act, the Motor Vehicle Safety Act of 1966, and the 1967 Wholesome Meat Act (portions of which were applied to poultry products in 1968).

On the administrative ledger, Nader's 1968 FTC study resulted in President Nixon commissioning an American Bar Association investigation, the findings of which produced top-level staff changes in the commission. His critique of FDA operations led to the ban of cyclamates from soft drinks and the discharge of three top agency officials. Nader regards such responses as mere "cosmetics." "We always fail," he says. "The whole thing is limiting the degree of failure."[6]

His own misgivings aside, Nader has had an undeniable impact on the regulatory process. He has created a presence, a feeling of scrutiny, under which all regulators now operate; and he has launched a movement which draws on his prestige for its form and respectability. Still, Nader is a unique phenomenon, and an extensive concentration on him as a model for other groups is misleading. He can do things that a less well-known and credible group could not, and perhaps should not, attempt. His enormous public support—a recent Harris poll reported that 69 percent of the American public think "it's good to have critics like Nader to keep industry on its toes"—allows him to speak from a base of limited information and be sure that his utterances will be taken seriously. His enormous skills at making and shaping news enable him to command media coverage of his comments on virtually any issue. He can step in and have an impact on an already well-developed controversy where an unsupported statement from another group would be lost in the dispute.

Without his special relationship with the press or his wide public credibility—or the good furtune to be tailed by a General Motors private investigator—other advocate groups are confronted with serious legal and practical limitations which Nader can and does ignore.

The aspect of Nader's day-to-day operation which is perhaps most envied by others involved in public interest advocacy is his apparent freedom from restraints, imposed either by collegiate decision-making or, more importantly, by non-profit tax status. Most public interest advocacy groups are non-profit organizations, tax-exempt under section 501 (c) (3) or the Internal Revenue Code. Maintenance of this status is imperative for foundation funding. The code specifically excludes from exemption as a non-profit group any organization that, as a substantial part of its activities, attempts to influence legislation. According to the Internal Revenue Service, any organization is attempting to influence legislation when it contacts or urges the public to contact members of a legislative body to support or oppose legislation or when it otherwise advocates the adoption or rejection of legislation. In effect, this means that such groups are prohibited from lobbying, endorsing, or recommending a particular piece of legislation or bill. A group can urge general reforms and regulations and it can appear as an advocate at a hearing as long as the appearance is in response to a specific written invitation to testify as an expert.

Several of Nader's operations are tax-exempt. The Center for the Study of Responsive Law, his "parent group," receives support from several foundations. On the other hand, his Public Interest Research Groups are not tax-exempt and are free to lobby. Recently, Nader has launched Ralph Nader, Public Citizen, Inc., a Common Cause-like mass membership organization to support his projects.[7] Nader himself makes no attempt to limit his personal lobbying, even calling senators and threatening to denounce them to the press if they fail to go his way.

The Nader experience notwithstanding, there is no question that the limitations imposed by the IRS regulations place public interest advocates so affected at a distinct disadvantage in affecting public decisions. Nonetheless, some groups are credited with having an impact and, even with the limitations of the IRC, they have played a major role in the shaping of certain policies and decisions.

LAWYERS PREDOMINATE

One of the conspicuous aspects of Nader's methodology is his reliance on attorneys. It is only a slight exaggeration to say that he believes that if three or four lawyers are brought together, they can solve almost any problem. He sees many of the basic questions confronting society as essentially legal in nature.

Nader's approach is, of course, responsive to the social and political history of the last twenty years, when the courts, the litigation process, and lawyers were the cutting edge of social change.

Nader's statements imply that since other parts of the political process have been generally unresponsive to those causes we hold dear, he will continue to depend heavily on the courts. Yet, Nader's own work is much more that of publicist, popularizer, and spokesman for causes than it is that of practicing lawyer, reflecting his own impatience with the limits of the law firm approach.

In many cases, particularly those involving regulatory agencies, it is difficult to find a client with standing to bring a suit to court, or with a grievance which involves the precise substantive issue the advocate wants to raise. It is difficult, for example, to make a court case on the basis of someone habitually not showing up for work—the kind of "no show" political jobs which are common in some state and local governments. But the advantage, and it is a big one, to the litigation approach, is that when a public interest lawyer can find a client and take on an issue, there will be a definite determination. If victorious, the advocates have a hard victory with a court action behind them. The great appeal of this approach is that there is no way for an agency to "slide off." The problem is getting jugular cases in the right form, in spite of the difficult problems of timing, standing, and jurisdiction which may block access to the courts.[8]

THE MUCKRAKING METHOD

The non-litigating advocate groups face a different set of problems. They need not hunt for a client or worry about timing. They can make a "case" on the basis of anything which will appeal to the public's sense of outrage. They, however, are almost totally dependent on the press to get their story across and to develop sufficient public awareness about problems. They rely on others for direct pressure group tactics on legislators. The importance of sympathetic press coverage to some extent determines both the issues dealt with and the research methods employed. Public interest research groups are dependent on shock techniques. For, if the newspapers run their story once and then drop it, they have lost most chances to be effective. Extra headlines are brought about only by controversy and response. The "muckraking" release, which is applauded by a patronizing local press but successfully ignored by the agencies or interests attacked, is considered an unqualified failure.

In New Jersey, a study of auto negligence cases which recommended no-fault insurance might have been brushed aside by a calm-

er legal community. Instead, it resulted in the trial lawyers' association hiring a public relations firm to present the lawyers' point of
view. The consequence of this act was a protracted public controversy about no-fault insurance which otherwise might have been carried out on a much lower key with much less publicity.

Unlike Nader, second-generation advocate groups are not in a
position simply to give journalists a report and rely on them to wade
through and interpret it. Groups like these in New Jersey, Ohio, and
Connecticut must educate the press about their story in order to
obtain acceptance and demonstrate a point. They frequently confront
the problem of making their message digestible without having it
become meaningless.

No advocate group boasts a 100 percent record in seeing its
recommendations adopted. When their impact seems insubstantial,
most of these groups find comfort in the tentative but widely held
proposition that publicity and continual scrutiny of public agencies is
a desirable end in itself. Nader puts it well, "In our polity, where the
ultimate power is said to rest with the people, a free and prompt flow
of information from government to people is essential to achieve the
reality of citizen access to a more just governmental process. It is
especially essential to provide this informational flow in the Washington regulatory agencies, which are essentially unaccountable to any
electorate or constituency."[9]

The exposure of over-all agency operations becomes a necessity
when, as in the present circumstances, public confidence in regulatory agencies is low and studies of their performance are highly critical. Ralph Nader, perhaps more than any other individual, has helped
to suggest the gap between the agencies' perceptions of themselves
and their actual operations. His studies show inefficiency, ineptness,
and willful failure to act, on the part of the federal agencies. The
Center for Analysis of Public Issues discovered similar problems with
such minor agencies as the New Jersey Office of Consumer Protection and Department of Agriculture. Indeed, when an agency is failing to do a good job in terms of its own goals, the possibility for
reform is obvious, for reform in this sense is little more than holding
an agency or group to account against its own standards. When these
standards or values are shared widely in the society, public support
for reform is possible and even easy to obtain.

This attempt to enforce accountability, a key notion for public
interest advocacy, is much easier in an area in which public expectations and regulatory standards are set. While policies are still in formation—a good current example is cable television—it is much more

difficult to identify deficiencies and place blame. The FCC has failed for more than a decade to develop a coherent policy on CATV, but only recently has the commission been subjected to criticism from public-interest oriented groups.

FUNDING AND THE FUTURE

Despite public acceptance of the "product" of public interest advocacy, few are willing to pay the costs of "production." The resource constraint ultimately will end the current round of public interest advocacy. Many groups, as indicated, are heavily dependent on foundation support—a short-term solution at best. Indeed, for each group which succeeds in obtaining the minimal support necessary to commence operations, many others are stillborn because of failure in the competition for scarce foundation resources—a competition made keener by the reluctance of the vast majority of foundations to support such potentially controversial activities as public interest advocacy.

Some groups, particularly in the environmental field, are finding an alternative—and sometimes one that, because of non-tax-exempt status, permits overt lobbying—in mass membership support. Clearly, this route offers the most promising hope for long-term assistance. A special case of this approach is the student-funded Public Interest Research Groups springing up from Nader-planted seeds in several states.

The contingent fee may answer some of the financial questions with regard to public interest law firms. The possibility of sharing, say, 25 percent of the settlement may induce attorneys to risk their own time and money on the suit in question. A cynic, however, would see most of this activity as a mere transient response to a trend. It's "in" to be for advocacy, as it was "in" a few years ago to work for civil rights or, later, the poverty program, the Peace Corps, or the anti-war movement. It is no accident, in this sense, that the movement is dominated by well-educated white middle-class advocates, or even that most of its concerns are white middle-class. The movement also is elitist, made up principally of top law school graduates, Ph.D.'s, and the like. The foundations, after all, have some of the most sensitive antennae to current trends in "do-goodism" in America.

One way to perceive the whole public interest advocacy movement, then, is simply as another manifestation of the cyclical surges of reform in America. At times, the activities of institutions and individuals, both public and private, become so much at variance with widely held community values that criticism receives ready acceptance and encouragement. When such a period includes a feeling of powerlessness and frustration, individual reformers come to symbolize the needs and anger of millions of unhappy citizens. Almost every American agrees that the trouble with our society is that "nothing works anymore." Products appear shoddy, institutions unresponsive. We are bombarded by media reports of our failures and our problems. We perceive government agencies as not living up to standards they themselves have set. We fear that our national goals and values are unrealistic or, perhaps worse yet, unfashionable.

It is little wonder that the personification of the current reform movement, Ralph Nader, has some of the aspects of an Old Testament prophet calling the people back from their idolatry. It is little wonder that when he is pushed to define how to bring about the changes he desires on the massive scale required, he incants an almost romantic vision of the future, complete with a new professionalism and a renewed code of self-enforced personal behavior.

> We're interested in the development of initiatory democracy and this is more fundamental than participatory or representative democracy. We need a fundamental change in our structure so that people can initiate actions to make sure public officials are acting responsibly. I'm talking about the rights and remedies, plus legal responsibilities, so it can be a citizen versus the ICC or the FDA. A civil servant should be forced to make the law work and, if he won't do it, he should be censured or expelled from the government.[10]

When, in 1902, *McClure's* magazine blossomed briefly as the consumer's advocate, it began a period of muckraking that set standards of investigative journalism in the public interest seldom equalled in the history of the American press. It also signaled a turning in the political reform movement of the times—Populism, the Progressive movement, trust-busting, the labor movement, and so on.

It is barely possible that "Naderism" will affect the present rapid evolution of the political process. We may be struggling toward a new alignment of parties and a new partisan agendum. Some candidates are groping for new "populist" themes. Perhaps this is saying no more than that they seek to share some of Nader's public magic. The pressures to take a strong line on administrative regulation and consumer protection are real. One suspects that, though the emphasis may fade, its effects will be real—in terms of both statutory results and political behavior.

At this stage it is impossible to fix with any certainty the place and significance of the current surge of public interest advocacy. Much of what it has accomplished is episodic, journalistic. Even in the area of litigation, the cases have more often been demonstrative of what can be done on a specific issue than precedent-setting in their consequences for administrative regulation.

In terms of the over-all political movement in this society, it is hard to identify the present period as a reform era. Rather, the country is lurching toward some new accommodation with a set of forces which have reacted to and rejected much of American life. These attitudes, and this movement, do not seem likely to blow over. There will probably be important changes in the way corporations and administrative agencies operate, but whether public interest advocacy groups become institutionalized and play a continuing role in this process or not is an unanswerable question.

Some radicals argue that instead of changing the system, public interest advocacy is tinkering. Indeed, they go further and claim that its marginal adjustments in the system tend to make the system more tolerable and tend to reduce the chances for real change. Even rejecting that argument—which logically requires that we let things get as bad as possible, or even help them along—one cannot say that much of what is being done by the advocates will bring about permanent change. Perhaps in another sense they are only responding to more limited goals, to the more limited world of the possible. Their fights, even when they are small ones, frequently are tangible. And perhaps this approach—more generally familiar as *incrementalism*—in time will bring about changes in the regulatory process. Although it is much too early to assess the impact of public interest advocacy, it is quite possible that, in a decade or two, the current period will be seen as a time of dramatic change in the regulatory process. We may then identify this era as marking a turning away from sole reliance on due process and similar safeguards toward more forceful, independent policy development in the public interest. If such changes occur, public interest advocates will have a strong claim to any credit or blame.

ENDNOTES

1. More specifically, the public interest lawyers are emerging in response to a perceived need for "public" legal counsel in the regulatory process. In the challenge filed by the United Church of Christ vs. FCC, for example, 359F2D. 944 (DC ct. app. 1966 at 1003-4), Warren E. Burger, then of the U.S. Court of Appeals for the District of Columbia,

concluded: "The theory that the Commission can always effectively represent the lesser interest . . . without the aid and participation of legitimate listener representatives fulfilling the role of private attorneys general, is one of those assumptions we collectively try to work with so long as they are reasonably adequate. When it becomes clear, as it does now, that it is no longer a valid assumption which stands up under the realities of actual reference, neither we nor the Commission can continue to rely on it. The gradual expansion and evolution of concepts of standing of administrative law attest that experience rather than logic or fixed rules have been accepted as the guide."

2. Yet due process safeguards are essential in the context of necessary agency discretion. Protection of this sort has other costs. Due process can be the enemy of public necessity, and it certainly is the father of large regulatory bureaucracies—bureaucracies which swallow individual complaints rather than respond to them.

3. One of Nader's investigators once complained about the caution of middle-level staff personnel in a regulatory agency. He emphasized their fear of reprisal from above. But what about their fear of Nader's approach—the need for a headline, the impetus to find the "dirt" which will expose the agency's failure or venality?

4. A sampling of materials made available before a recent FCC rulemaking revealed that several individuals could be kept busy for several weeks simply organizing it into usable form and discovering the points of particular interest to the public interest advocacy group involved.

5. *New York Times Magazine*, March 21, 1971.

6. Ibid.

7. Nader also is the founder of The Center for Auto Safety and The Professionals for Auto Safety. In addition, he is starter of the Project for Corporate Responsibility, which included "The Campaign to Make General Motors Responsible." While not directly related to Nader, the Center for Law and Social Policy handles much of the litigation which emerges from his work.

8. One of the best examples of the potential of class actions in the consumer area was the 1970 settlement of the *Virginia v. Charles R. Pfizer and Co.* suit. Under the agreement, Pfizer agreed to pay $100 million for pricefixing on the drug tetracycline, dating back to 1954. But state courts generally have been unsympathetic, and a specific violation of a federal standard is usually a prerequisite for bringing such a suit.

9. Ralph Nader, "Freedom from Information: The Act and the Agency," article adapted from a statement released publicly on August 26, 1969.

10. *New York Times Magazine*, March 21, 1971.

30

james q. wilson

THE DEAD HAND OF REGULATION

After decades of public and journalistic neglect, the government agencies that set prices, control entry, and regulate conduct in many of our most important industries have suddenly found themselves in the limelight. Owing to the efforts of Ralph Nader and other advocates of "consumerism," a considerable segment of attentive opinion has become convinced that the prosaic, often arcane decisions of these little understood commissions are not always in the public interest. Such a view is correct, and for dramatizing the fact we owe Nader and the others a debt of gratitude.

But dramatic confrontations between "raiders" and "bureaucrats," however useful in creating an issue, are not so useful in understanding the issue. Persons easily convinced that the government is not acting rightly tend to assume that it is because the government is not righteous; if industries are being regulated wrongly, then (in this view) it must be because bad people are doing the regulating. It would be unfortunate if the resolution of the regulatory issue were framed in terms of the moralistic premises that first gave rise to it.

It would be all the more unfortunate considering that a number of scholars, chiefly economists, have developed over the last ten years a substantial set of analytical tools and empirical findings which, taken together, constitute an impressive contribution to our knowledge of what happens when the government tries to intervene in the economy. Yet compared to the enormous influence of those economists who have developed ways of managing our tax, fiscal, and

Reprinted with permission from *The Public Interest*, No. 25 (Fall 1971), pp. 39–58, copyright © 1971 by National Affairs Inc., 1971.

monetary policies, the influence exercised by the regulatory economists has been negligible. About the only serious effort to move in the
direction suggested by their analyses was President Kennedy's 1962
transportation message calling for the abandonment of minimum-rate
regulation in the shipment of bulk commodities on trucks, trains, and
barges. The plan was buried in Congress, opposed by the truckers,
the barge operators, and the rate setters (in this case, the Interstate
Commerce Commission).

If the economists' success in getting their aggregate strategies
accepted reaffirmed what the invisible hand of the market could do
under proper guidance, their failure in getting government to accept
their critique of non-aggregate strategies testified to the enduring
strength of the dead hand of regulation. Paul W. MacAvoy of MIT in
The Crisis of the Regulatory Commissions (New York: Norton, 1970)
summarizes the most important analyses of regulatory economics as
an "accumulation of substantial quantitative findings" leading to the
general conclusion that "regulation has imposed considerable costs
on public utility company operations without providing compensating
benefits."

The problems of regulatory agencies go beyond price setting,
however, and involve issues ranging from allocation (e.g., deciding
who will get a television broadcast license) through the approval of
business practices (e.g., deciding which firms may merge and which
may not) to the control of what may or may not be broadcast (e.g.,
deciding whether radio stations will be allowed to editorialize or
whether television stations show too much violence or too many com-
mercials). In evaluating these and other kinds of government regulations, there are two standards one may employ—efficiency and equity. By "efficiency" I mean that a given regulatory policy achieves a
desirable objective at minimal cost; by "equity" I mean that the
regulatory policy, whether efficient or not, treats those subject to it
fairly—that is, treats like cases alike on the basis of rules known in
advance and applicable to all.

Until the end of the 1950s, the many criticisms of regulatory
commissions were generally based on rather narrow or truncated
versions of these two criteria. Those concerned with efficiency
tended to emphasize the problem of who would determine what the
desirable social objective should be and thus to whom regulatory
agencies would be accountable. This in general was the concern of
the Hoover Commission and of the political scientists who complained that the commissions were a "headless fourth branch" of

government and were being "captured" by the very industries they were supposed to regulate. Typical of the reform proposals of such commentators, most of whom accepted without much question the desirability of regulation, were suggestions that the commissions have "stronger leadership," "clearer mandates," "popular support," and "effective management." Rarely did any of these authors say to what concrete ends that leadership and popular support should be directed or what should be contained in the clear mandate. And as for industry influence over commissions, the best answer came from Louis Jaffe of the Harvard Law School: Whether a commission does or does not serve the ends of industry is much less important than whether it serves the correct ends, and these may or may not be what industry wants.

Critics concerned with equity, who on the whole were less favorably disposed to the idea of administrative regulation at all, concentrated their fire on the administrative procedures of the commissions, and sought by various legal and judicial remedies to insure that parties appearing before the commissions would receive ample notice, a fair hearing, an opportunity for review, and the other elements of due process as then conceived. The culmination of this movement was the passage of the Administrative Procedures Act of 1946. Though its proponents, mostly lawyers, hailed it as marking a new era in administrative law, the new era did not arrive. In the opinion of most observers, the influence of the act was marginal, and such effect as it did have was generally in the direction of making regulation slower and more costly rather than fairer.

Indeed, insofar as it sought to treat affected parties more justly, the act was doomed from the start, for it was based on a fundamental misconception of much of the regulatory process. Adjudication, as it occurs in a court of law, is (in the words of Lon Fuller) an "institutionally protected opportunity to present proofs and arguments" to support a claim of right deriving from some previously agreed to standard. This is what we do, for example, when we sue a person for failure to pay a debt. But most regulatory commissions do not have such standards, nor do most of their clients have a "right" to (for example) a vacant television license, an airline route, or a particular price for long-distance telephone calls. In deciding who shall receive the license or fly the route or what the price shall be, the agency has no single solution to which the affected parties can direct their arguments. Equity or justice in cases of this sort does not consist so much in providing the opportunities for court-like speeches as in enunciating and adhering to a reasonable standard, applicable to all, that will permit the affected parties to conduct themselves free of the fear of capricious governmental action.

THE EFFECTS OF REGULATION

The economists have cut through much (though as we shall see, not all) of the fuzzy rhetoric and empty reforms addressed to these issues and have asked instead the simple question, "What effect does a regulatory policy have and, given certain goals, how can that effect be improved?" The first thing to decide was whether regulatory policies, especially in the rate-fixing area, *had any effect at all*. Everyone, of course, assumed that they had. Why else would businessmen complain so much about these rates and an aroused public demand even lower ones? The landmark study on this issue has been the effort of George J. Stigler and Claire Friedland to determine whether or not state control over the prices that electric utilities could charge had any effect on what prices they did charge. They compared the rates charged by utilities in states with regulation to those charged in states without it during the period (before 1937) when there was a significant number of unregulated states. They did not compare the rates directly—for obviously many factors other than regulation will affect prices—but compared the "residual rates" after controlling for the effects of urbanization, the price of fuel and the incomes of consumers.[1] In calculations for various years from 1912 to 1937, the existence of regulation had no significant effect. Nor was there in unregulated as opposed to regulated states any evidence of greater price discrimination (between, for example, domestic and industrial consumers) or of differences in utility profit levels as measured by stockholder experience. Stigler and Friedland explain their findings by the absence of long-run monopoly power in the hands of electric companies (they face competition from other energy sources) and the inability of a regulatory body to determine what rates ought to be relative to costs, or even to learn what the costs are.

That the incompetence of the agency as much as the nature of the industry may make price regulation so chancy a phenomenon will suggest to some readers what it has suggested to several generations of reformers: the need to have "better" commissions, perhaps ones staffed with economists as able as Professor Stigler. After all, what is required is simply to set prices so as to provide a "reasonable return on investment." And there are some firms that are so nearly in the position of a natural monopoly that regulation is the only means short of public ownership to prevent them from charging monopoly prices. It remains only to determine what the investment or the production costs are, and then to set the price. But as Felix Frankfurter and Henry Hart pointed our over 35 years ago, a fair and defensible determination of the rate base is maddeningly hard to make. Initial capital investment obviously will not do, as the value of the plant has no doubt appreciated since it was built. Replacement cost seems a better alternative, until one realizes that estimating it for an electric light or telephone company requires a kind of economic science fiction almost impossible to justify. What is the cost of "replacing" a utility that grew with the surrounding community's growth from village to metropolis and now exists in such close interconnection with the people it serves that to "replace" it would require virtually replacing the community itself? And in any case, assessing the value of a company can take (and has taken) years, hardly an arrangement conducive to regular and flexible adjustments in rates to meet changing economic conditions. And as for using the costs of production as the basis for price fixing, what a firm chooses to term a cost (as opposed to an investment), how it chooses to allocate costs between the regulated and unregulated aspects of its business, and what service levels it is willing to provide to its customers under various cost conditions are all matters that, if knowable at all, are known only to an array of accountants prepared to conceal as much as they reveal. Furthermore, taking even knowable costs as the basis for price setting by a commission may eliminate much of the firm's incentive to reduce costs or adopt more efficient technological innovations. The intention of government price setting may be to protect the helpless consumer, but its effect may be to protect the incompetent producer.

Just because it is hard to fix rates does not mean that rates are not fixed. They are, and often with quite significant results to the consumer. This is perhaps best illustrated in the field of transportation. Anyone who buys an airplane ticket or ships his furniture to another city is paying a price that is affected by, and sometimes uniquely determined by, a government agency. Merton J. Peck of Yale has studied the results of this process for shippers and Richard E. Caves has studied it with respect to airlines. Both conclude that prices would be lower to the consumer if they were not regulated. Peck estimates that abolishing government-set minimum rates for rail, truck, and barge shipments of bulk and agricultural commodities would save the consumer in excess of $400 million annually *and* at the same time increase the profitability of the railroads. Caves offers no dollar estimates, but concludes that the airline industry is sufficiently competitive to insure good service without government control over either prices or the right of a new firm to enter the industry. (Maintaining safety standards would, of course, be required, but that can be done by inspecting and certifying aircraft and air crews and does not require economic regulation.)

EFFICIENCY

The inefficient use of economic resources in fields such as transportation does not result from the fact that stupid or corrupt men regulate these industries, but from the fact that well-meaning and reasonably intelligent men do. The Interstate Commerce Commission sought to prevent railroads from gouging farmers during the period when trains afforded almost the only way of shipping many farm products to market. I do not know how successfully the ICC protected the farmer when railroads had oligopoly positions, but today, when they do not, the ICC protects him very well. According to John Meyer, Merton Peck, John Stenason, and Charles Zwick,[2] rail revenues during the period 1939 to 1959 represented between 120 and 140 per cent of costs for agricultural products, while revenues for manufactured products have averaged between 165 and 203 per cent of costs. Nor do prices discriminate only among kinds of things shipped. Short-haul rail prices are a lower fraction of costs than long-haul prices, and many places are grouped for the purpose of calculating rates. Thus, the price to ship some things from California to Maine has been the same as from Idaho to Pennsylvania, even though the distances vary by as much as a thousand miles.

These and other anomalies result from the fact that the ICC has felt it necessary to set rates on an item-by-item, point-to-point basis, partly because it sought originally to protect the farmer (at the expense of the manufacturer) and partly because the railroads themselves practiced this form of price discrimination in the days before they had much competition. The ICC decided to strike a compromise between the interests of farmers and those of the railroaders by tinkering with existing prices rather than by starting all over. What began as tinkering wound up as a set of 75,000 separate rate schedules and an administrative procedure for handling (in 1962) over 173,000 proposed tariffs submitted by truck and barge as well as rail firms. Among the rates the ICC now "sets" are ones which distinguish, as Phillip Locklin has noted, between horses for slaughter and horses for draught, between sand used to make glass and sand used to make cement, and between lime used in industry and lime used in agriculture. Of course, no agency could "set" all these rates every year; the best it can do is look at a few, change any flagrant ones, and hope for the best.

The chief cumulative cost to society of ICC rate setting is not its administative confusion or intellectual untidiness, but the distortions it causes in the effort to create a balanced and efficient transportation system. When trucks came onto the scene, they did not seek out those routes for which they were the most efficient carriers (e.g., short-haul carriage of agricultural products) but, as Peck points out, those where they could make the most money even though they might be the least efficient (that is, long-haul carriage of manufacturing products for which the rates were kept artificially high in part by government action). The ICC responded, not by deregulating railroads so they could compete, but by regulating trucks so they could not. It did not quite succeed, however. The best it could do was to set truck and rail prices at the same level, but then the competition turned on quality of service (at which trucks had the advantage because they could go anywhere a road was to be found), and the railroads suffered anyway.

The Civil Aeronautics Board has been a better friend to the airlines than the ICC has been to the railroads. Prices on the high-density, big-city air routes are higher than they would be if competitively set. It costs less per mile, for example, to fly from Los Angeles to San Francisco (an intrastate route not subject to CAB regulation) than from New York to Washington, D.C. (an interstate route that is CAB-regulated). The CAB justifies this in part by requiring the airlines serving the high-density, over-priced routes also to serve low-density, unprofitable routes in order to insure that the nation has a complete airline system. Even assuming that it is in the national interest to guarantee that virtually any city can be reached by air, and that to do it a subsidy is required, it is not clear why the cost of that subsidy should be borne by passengers on the high-density routes rather than by the nation as a whole, or why the subsidy should be conferred covertly (by internal fare regulation) rather than openly (by cash payments). Or rather it *is* clear—it is politically easier to subsidize if it is done inconspicuously and in ways that do not appear to be a charge on the tax rate.

Nor are the economic inefficiencies limited to the transportation field. By a combination of policies administered by various agencies, we insure that the nation produces too much crude oil and too little natural gas. Restrictions ("quotas") on the importation of foreign oil guarantee that the price of oil in the United States will be higher than it need be (i.e., than the world price) and that there will be more drilling in scarce domestic oil reserves than is justified. At the same time, the Federal Power Commission until recently has set the field price of natural gas below the rate necessary to clear the market, and thus below the rate many think is necessary to encourage vigorous exploration for new sources of supply. This means that while present-day consumers of gas may have been benefited because prices have been kept low, future consumers may well have been harmed because of the shortages they will encounter (and to some extent, already are encountering).[3]

WHO HAS CAPTURED WHOM

Scholars as diverse as the radical historian Gabriel Kolko and the conservative economist George Stigler offer a simple explanation for the behavior of these and other regulatory agencies: They have been captured by, or were created to serve the interests of, the industries they are supposed to regulate. To Kolko, business regulation, like all other "reform" efforts in American government, has had the intended effect of making secure the control over wealth exercised by the dominant economic class. To Stigler, any industry with sufficient political influence will use the coercive power of the state to limit entry into the industry and thus to restrict competition; failing that, it will take the second-best strategy of obtaining cash subsidies from the government to help defray the cost of competition. ("Second best," because a cash subsidy, without entry control, would have to be shared with all new entrants into the industry, and the bigger the subsidy the more numerous the entrants.)

There are examples of regulation that seem to have no other explanations than those. The benefits given to the petroleum industry by import quotas and tax-depletion allowances represent an enormous subsidy (perhaps as much as $5 billion a year). The CAB has not allowed the formation of a new trunk airline since it was created in 1938. At one time the butter producers virtually suppressed the use of margarine by obtaining laws that forbade coloring margarine to look like butter. Plenty of other instances could no doubt be added.

But just as striking are the cases contrary to the theory of industry capture. The Federal Power Commission can hardly be called the tool of the natural gas producer interests; until recently it has set well-head prices below what the producers would like and indeed what the public interest probably requires. If the ICC was once dominated by the railroads, it is not today: So generous has that agency been to the chief rivals of the railroads, the truckers and barge lines, that today the rail industry favors deregulation altogether. Television broadcasters (such as WHDH in Boston) that have lost their license to a rival claimant because of the action of the Federal Communications Commission, or newspaper owners who face the possibility of having to divest themselves of television station ownership, or television networks that have had the amount of programming they could supply in prime viewing time reduced by a half-hour each day are not likely to think of themselves as playing the role of captor with respect to the FCC.

Indeed, there may well be as many industries that have been "captured" by their regulatory agency as agencies captured by the industry. But the term "capture" reflects a simplistic view of the politics of regulation. Though there have been very few good studies of agency politics, what probably happens is this: An agency is established, sometimes with industry support and sometimes over industry objections, and then gradually creates a regulatory climate that acquires a life of its own. Certain firms will be helped by some of the specific regulatory decisions making up this climate, others will be hurt. But the industry as a whole will adjust to the climate and decide that the costs of shifting from the known hazards of regulation to the unknown ones of competition are too great; it thus will come to defend the system. The agencies themselves will become preoccupied with the details of regulation and the minutiae of cases in whatever form they first inherit them, trying by the slow manipulation of details to achieve various particular effects that happen to commend themselves from time to time to various agency members. In a burst of academic masochism, Paul MacAvoy recently read all 1,041 pages in Volume 42 of the *Federal Power Commission Reports*, and concluded that it is hard to find any consistent policy preference concealed in their bureaucratic and ponderous language; hints appear here and there in the few important cases, but it would be hard to call them a "policy." The net effects of the FPC's actions often are clear, but whether they are intended, and if so on what grounds, is not clear.

Louis Jaffe has probably stated the political situation more accurately—the agencies are not so much industry-oriented or consumer-oriented as *regulation-oriented*. They are in the regulation business, and regulate they will, with or without a rationale. If the agencies have been "captured" by anybody, it is probably by their staffs who have mastered the arcane details of rate setting and license granting. Take the Anti-Trust Division of the Justice Department: No one supposes that this division is animated by any clear, consistent, and economically defensible theory of the impact of firm size on market performance, and indeed it is not. Some may suppose that in the absence of such a theory it will be guided instead by political pressures or White House inclinations; but despite the efforts of Nader's Raiders to find evidence of such influences, there is little to support this supposition. As far as anyone can tell, the Anti-Trust lawyers are guided chiefly by their trained habits to find a case that with available evidence and under prevailing court opinions can be made to stick. Any case.

In any event, most regulatory agencies have been doing pretty much what Congress has asked of them. Congress never intended that competition should govern in transportation, and the ICC has seen to it that it hasn't. The ICC was supposed to "co-ordinate" our transportation system, and though one may question (and I certainly question) whether co-ordination can be achieved by detailed regulation, the fact is that the ICC, supposedly "owned" by the railroads, has in the name of co-ordination been quite generous to the trucking and barge industries—so much so that now the railroads are in favor of deregulation. Indeed, if any agency has been "captured" by its clients, it has been, under certain presidents, the National Labor Relations Board; but again, this is exactly what Congress intended in the Wagner Act. (Curiously, academic criticism of business domination of regulatory agencies rarely extends to organized labor influence in the NLRB.) The Securities and Exchange Commission has had a running feud with much of Wall Street, just as Congress hoped it would. Indeed, if any single political force benefits from economic regulation, it is Congress—or more accurately, those key Congressional committee and subcommittee chairmen with a substantive interest in, or appropriations responsibilities over, the regulatory agencies. The FCC has been reluctant to make any change in its controls over cable communication without checking with key Senators, and the NLRB regularly hears from members of the House Education and Labor Committee about matters pending before it.

But even Congressional intervention, like industry control, is not in itself a problem; everything depends on the ends toward which such intervention or control is directed. The problem of efficiency, in short, is not wholly a problem of clientelism, political meddling, or agency incompetence; in substantial part it is a problem of the nature of the tasks which we have given the agencies. These tasks probably could not be performed well even in theory, and amid the practical realities of confused ends and ambiguous standards they are, through the fault of no one in particular, performed abominably.

EQUITY

The economic analyses thus far described have rather little to say explicitly about the problem of equity, though their criticism of piecemeal rate making has clear implications about the fairness with which (for example) shippers of similar products over similar distances are treated. The general question of equity is not raised by economists, and those who do raise it—chiefly business firms that feel unjustly treated—are often ignored on grounds, quite plausible in many cases, that they are engaged in special pleading.

But the issue remains, even if it is difficult to get people to take it seriously. Not that people are generally indifferent to considerations of justice and fair play; far from it. But they tend to limit their concern to victimized individuals and groups with whom they have sympathy. Those who publish books and articles rarely, if ever, argue that a person should be subject to arbitrary arrest, or that *ex post facto* laws should be tolerated, or that demonstrations should be allowed or forbidden at the pleasure of an administrator. Or do they? Consider the following statement, written by a man who was later to become a Justice of the United States Supreme Court:

> Unless the police officer has effective bargaining power, little can be expected. He must have sanctions or desired favors which he can trade for changes in behavior. . . . He may be asked to exercise his discretion, for example, to allow a certain demonstration to take place. Then, if the need of the demonstrators is sufficiently urgent, a trade may be consummated. In return for the favor of the police officer, the demonstrators may change their speeches and leaflets in accordance with the police officer's conception of equity and justice.

I venture that most readers would find this statement shocking and odious. The idea that the right to demonstrate should be subject to arbitrary powers and the content of the demonstration modified by the capacity of a policeman to bargain with the demonstrators seems the height of unfairness.

Now, I must confess that the Justice-to-be (Abe Fortas, as it turns out) did not exactly say this. Instead, Fortas was writing, in

1937, about how the staff of the SEC should behave. His exact words were as follows:

> Unless the administrator has effective bargaining power, little can be expected. He must have sanctions or desired favors which he can trade for changes in practices. . . . He may be asked to exercise his discretion, for example, to accelerate the effective date of registration [of a new security]. Then, if the need of the registrant is sufficiently urgent, a trade may be consummated. In return for the favor of the administrator, the registrant may amend his practices in accordance with the administrator's conception of equity and justice.

Most people, other than securities registrants, would find this statement at worst to be a candid but scarcely shocking glimpse into the real-life behavior of bureaucrats. Political scientists would probably cite this approvingly as an example of how the informal use of "necessary" administrative discretion can lead to the more "effective management" of the economy. I am perfectly aware, of course, that there are differences, perhaps decisive ones, between free speech and securities registration; but I think it behooves all who unhesitatingly condemn the first quotation and approve the second to think through rather carefully just what these differences may be and why speech should have near-absolute protection and commerce near-zero protection.

Whether or not we place the interests of the firm on the same plane as the interests of the writer or speaker, it seems clear (again, hardly anyone has examined the problem) that a person or corporation subject to regulation cannot in many cases know in advance where he stands, nor expect to be treated tomorrow by the same rule that governed his actions today. The theory of regulation advanced in the earlier part of this paper—that it tends to be an ad hoc, particularistic process, affected, but not determined, by a policy habit or inclination—suggests not only that agencies will not operate on the basis of general rules, but that they will go to some pains to avoid developing such rules.

There are two reasons for this. One is that the greater the codification of substantive policy, the less the power the agency can wield over any client in the particular case. As Michel Crozier has argued with respect to bureaucracy generally, power depends in part on uncertainty—I have power over you to the extent you cannot be sure in advance what my reactions to your behavior will be. If the agency could only apply known rules to corporate behavior, it would still constrain that behavior, but far less than if it improvised its action in each case. In a baseball game the umpire has power because he can call me out after three strikes; but his power over me would be much greater if every time I came to the plate he told me that how many strikes I would be allowed depended on how well I swung the bat, or maybe on how clean my uniform was.

The second reason for avoiding codification is related to the first: The agency and its staff wish to be able to achieve particular goals in particular cases. Though the goals may be ambiguous and the cases all different, the general desire to realize a particular state of affairs is more important to the agency than the desire simply to insure that the rules are followed. To continue the analogy, it is as if the baseball umpire desired not just to see that the game was played fairly, but also that a certain number of runs were scored (so the fans would be happy), a certain number of pitches thrown (so the pitcher would get a good workout), and a certain price charged by the owners (so they would be either happy or unhappy, depending on his intentions).[4]

REGULATING THE BROADCASTERS

Television and radio renewals display many of the attributes of a form of regulation deliberately without policy or rules. Each license must be renewed every three years, and the vast majority are in fact renewed almost automatically, or with only perfunctory review. But the power not to renew, and the actual shifting of licenses in some cases (technically, WHDH in Boston only had a "temporary" permit, not a regular three-year one) and the threatened shift in other cases, give to the FCC vast potential influence over the owners of stations and their conduct. To some extent that power is used to serve desirable objectives, such as that represented by the diversification rules. These are intended to encourage competition and specify that no applicant for a license may own more than one outlet in any one market area or more than seven outlets nationwide.

But increasingly, that power is used (or more accurately, its use is hinted at) to achieve a wide range of not very clear, not very consistent, and in many cases not very desirable social policies. Though the diversification rules are presumably intended to insure competition, the local ownership rules seem designed to prevent it. A radio or television stations is supposed to be locally owned by people who have past broadcast experience, a record of participation in civic affairs, a willingness to engage in "public service" (i.e., unsponsored but "worthwhile") broadcasting, a capacity to find out (by opinion surveys and other means) what their audience wants, and so on. In short, they are supposed to be "good guys," somehow defined, even if they run to a certain bland sameness.

Furthermore, the owners are supposed to be fair. They have, in the Commission's words, "an affirmative duty generally to encourage and implement the broadcast of all sides of controversial public issues over their facilities" and to "play a conscious and positive role to bring about the balanced presentation of opposing viewpoints." The fairness doctrine as interpreted by the FCC means that a station broadcasting a program in favor of fair employment practices must also broadcast a program opposed to it, that a station indicating opposition to the nuclear test ban treaty must find and put on the air a spokesman who favors it, and that a station discussing the nutritive value of vitamin pills and white bread must seek out persons with different views. These are actual cases; there are others.

In principle, no one is opposed to fairness and in practice many of us may welcome, as a last resort, the existence of the fairness doctrine as a weapon with which to challenge the most egregious examples of one-sided broadcasting by stations with monopoly positions in their communities. But by now we should have learned that the existence of a federal power stimulates a demand for its use, and thus what begins as an ultimate weapon for extreme cases becomes a ready weapon for every day cases. The United States Court of Appeals in Washington, D.C. has recently held that a station which shows a commercial for a high-powered automobile or leaded gasoline can be compelled to show programs, free of charge, about the dangers of air pollution. It is obvious that pollution is a problem and that cars contribute to it (many of us, we should recall, learned those facts from television!); but the implication of this decision is that showing anything (even a paid advertisement) about a controversial public issue creates an obligation to show something on the other side—free if necessary, and even if the other side has already expressed its views on other stations or in other media. If the purpose of the decision was to insure vigorous public debate, its effect, if it stands, is likely to be the opposite. Vigorous debate arises from boldness, while the decision is likely to inspire timidity.

Consider the necessary implications of the agency's position in this matter: Part of the government is empowered, on the basis of an inevitably vague standard, to control access to, and to influence (though not determine) the content of, an important medium of communication. No government agency has that power over newspapers, books, or magazines, and very few of us, I imagine, would want such an agency to exist.

Radio and television, of course, are supposed to be different from other media, but whether they really are is not clear. It surely is not because of their monopoly power—there are far more broadcast stations than newspapers serving most (perhaps all) American cities. And it cannot be because the public "owns" the airwaves; for the need to control their use (other than to prevent interference) does not follow from the fact of "ownership." But it is hard to see in what sense the airwaves are "owned" at all or, if they are somehow in the public domain, why they are any more so than the forests out of which newsprint is made or the public streets on which newspapers are sold. It may be that radio and television have a greater, perhaps even hypnotic effect on their audience, which thus must be protected. No one has shown this empirically to be the case[5], and in any event, no one suggested a Federal Motion Picture Commission when the movies were supposed to be the dominant (perhaps hypnotic) form of entertainment and persuasion. Perhaps it is because radio and TV are more directly available to children that we give them special treatment; but so are comic books, and the influence of either medium on young people is hard to assess.

I think that in fact we accept government regulation of broadcasting because we have it, we are used to it, and we all know of things we would like to see improved in radio and TV. If the First Amendment had never been added to the Constitution, and if it therefore had been possible to have a Federal Newspaper Commission, we probably would have one in some form and expect it to "improve" our daily reading matter, eliminate objectionable advertisements, reduce the violence portrayed on the printed page, and allow only "balanced" editorial viewpoints (which is to say, no editorial viewpoints at all other than trivial ones). We would especially accept this form of control if those who would make use of it were people with views similar to our own.

IS THE FCC TO BLAME?

The FCC is no more solely responsible for the bland sameness of TV than the ICC is for our unbalanced and excessively costly transportation system. The central facts about the broadcast medium, especially television, are: (1) It must attempt to secure the largest possible number of viewers; (2) there is a shortage of creative talent with which to satisfy all of those viewers all of the time and some of those viewers any of the time; (3) until the general advent of cable television or other technologies there will be a lack of channels with national linkages to serve specialized audiences.

But the FCC has helped in its own way to make matters worse. The local ownership rule eliminated the possibility of regional stations; the initial decision to favor VHF over UHF broadcasting kept down the number of available channels; the local and public service programming rules have helped insure that there will be some programs on the air that almost nobody wants to watch; the anti-network decisions have reduced the contribution of almost the only group with the capacity to attract the most expensive (and usually the most gifted) talent; the fairness doctrine has helped inhibit (though it has not prevented) the growth of editorializing and the showing of controversial programs; and the ban on the cable importation of distant signals into the largest markets has impeded the growth of cable television and thereby conferred a hidden subsidy to over-the-air broadcasting.

Perhaps more importantly, FCC discretionary power over licenses has been increasingly encouraging to anybody who wishes to "improve" radio and television and increasingly worrisome to those who run stations. Community groups, often aided by "public interest" law firms, can and will object to license renewals for any station that has offended them and may succeed in time in switching licenses to owners whom they are willing to approve. The attacks of Vice-President Spiro Agnew on newsmen are bound to have more of a chilling effect on an industry (such as TV) that knows its very existence depends on government approval than on one (such as newspapers) entirely independent of such authority. It is doubtful that the FCC will become the agent of Agnew's views, but nothing is more natural than for broadcasters to suspect it may have become so and to act accordingly. (If Agnew really wishes to change broadcasting, he might have his supporters hire a law firm of their own and challenge some offending stations at renewal time.)

The extent to which citizens' groups will be able to use renewal hearings as a means of controlling broadcasting is not yet clear, but the momentum is growing. In Des Moines a radio station is being challenged because it intends to stop playing "progressive rock," while a Syracuse station is being challenged because it has stopped playing classical music. In Los Angeles, a Mexican-American group has charged NBC–TV with portraying Mexicans in a demeaning manner on a long list of network programs and has demanded that NBC sign as agreement allowing the citizen organization to monitor all scripts and to veto any programs it considers "racist." Italian-American groups made sure long ago that most persons portrayed on television as gangsters will not have Italian names.

We can always hope, of course, that the FCC will reject any challenges that seem to inhibit free political communication, as they often have in the past. When a California FM radio station was challenged on the grounds that its programming was subversive and indecent, the FCC eventually cleared the station after an investigation. But why should there have been even the possibility that the station could thus have been put out of business? (If it had violated any proper law by its actions, there were civil and criminal remedies available to the regular law-enforcement agencies.)

One rejoinder to this criticism of the FCC is that we already have radio and television censorship, but it is practiced by network executives and station owners who are accountable to nobody. And to a considerable extent, this is true. While the degree of conscious control over television news by network executives is less than one might expect (their overriding concern is to find ways of creating visual entertainment and audience appeal out of roughly the same news stories everybody else is covering), it does exist: There seem to be cases of controversial documentaries being dropped or modified, of certain continuing stories (such as Vietnam) being covered from a particular perspective, and of views offensive to listeners or advertisers being tempered or quashed. But given the nature of the medium, that is almost inevitable. It is a *mass* medium supported by advertiser revenue, and TV executives would properly be judged incompetent if they aided their competitors by deliberately narrowing their appeal or reducing their revenues.

Those on the FCC who have attempted to create more diversity in television have acted as if they did not understand this and thus have adopted methods likely to make the problem worse. There is no way the FCC can regulate talent, diversity, or controversy *into* television; the best (or worst) it can do is to regulate *out* things it or someone else finds objectionable, and to otherwise keep the station owners on tenterhooks. The only way to free broadcast executives from the constraints under which they now operate is either to restructure the medium so that all or part of it is free from the need to advertise (as with pay television), or to create so many channels, nationally linked, that minority audiences with special tastes can be reached in sufficient numbers to warrant advertiser investment (as may perhaps be possible with cable television). No regulation can

ever be successful if it is based on an effort to thwart powerful motives of self-interest; regulation works when it harnesses self-interest
to public purposes.

The FCC has issued rule after rule apparently intended to require broadcasters to be better people with higher motives; but when
faced with requests for pay television, it has either refused them or
allowed only small experiments under conditions seemingly designed
to insure failure. And, for all practical purposes, cable has been kept
out of the one hundred largest markets, in which over 80 per cent of
all television receivers are to be found. (This limitation will probably
be partially lifted in the near future).

It is beyond the scope of this article to dwell on ways in which
the necessary allocation of broadcast frequencies can be made without asking an agency to assess the character of the would-be owners
or to monitor the content of their broadcasting. Ten years ago Ronald
H. Coase suggested in the *Journal of Law and Economics* that the
simplest means would be to auction off broadcast licenses, thereby
both insuring a non-political allocation process and recovering for the
public treasury some of the considerable value of the license. The
advent of cable television offers opportunities for so increasing the
number of TV channels available and so lowering the cost of origina-
tion that hardly anyone need be excluded from access on economic
grounds; it also may make possible a feasible pay-TV system using
one or more channels on a national scale. And there are other possibilities.

I doubt that anyone in the broadcast industry would favor either the auction or the cable, or that many would support any fundamental changes in the FCC's regulatory powers. On almost any decisive issue the broadcasters will support the Commission as it now
operates, not because business has "captured" it (many broadcasters
are deeply suspicious of the Commission and view its actions as
wrong or capricious), but because the regulatory climate created by
the Commission is what the industry knows and has more or less
learned to live with. Besides, however offended any individual broad-
caster may be by an FCC decision, the broadcasters' trade association
is hardly likely to curry FCC itll-will by a frontal attack.

THE UNLIKELIHOOD OF CHANGE

Neither industry nor the agencies have much need to fear major
reforms, or at least reforms that reduce the item-by-item discretion-

ary regulation that now exists. Quite the contrary. The reform impulse, except among economists who specialize in the problems of better use of regulated resources, is now of an entirely different sort—increased regulation, increased discretion, more numerous challenges to existing corporate practices. Commissioner Nicholas Johnson of the FCC has even published a book, *How To Talk Back To Your Television Set*, that is a manual of ways to challenge broadcasters; if its lessons were followed by a large number of citizen groups, the already considerable tendencies of broadcasters to provide programs that offend absolutely no one would be given a powerful impetus. What the pursuit of audience ratings has started, the law suits and renewal hearings would consummate. (In fairness it should be noted that Commissioner Johnson has also been an advocate of cable television and the greater diversity it promises.)

With respect to rate-fixing agencies, a move toward greater reliance on market forces in industries where competition is adequate is also unlikely. Not only would the agencies oppose it, but some groups will lose in the short run from any deregulated rate: Consumers might have to pay more for natural gas, oil companies might earn less from crude oil, and some shippers would pay more in rail and truck rates. Everyone who stands to pay more will naturally oppose deregulation, and those who will pay less (consumers, future generations, some firms) are typically not organized to seek such benefits— if, indeed, they are even aware of them.

But most importantly, the most articulate segment of public opinion has recently become aroused by the issue of "consumerism," and this almost surely will lead to demands for increasing the power and aggressiveness of the regulatory agencies. There is, of course, no necessary contradiction between a desire to protect the consumer and the desire to use scarce resources more efficiently; the efforts of the Federal Trade Commission or the Food and Drug Administration to insure that false and misleading claims are not made for products and that harmful substances are not sold to unwitting buyers are in principle unobjectionable. Indeed, one of the ironies of economic regulation is that it has generally existed with respect to those tasks it can do only poorly (such as setting rates and prices and controlling market entry) and has not existed, or has been indifferently managed, with respect to those tasks it could do well (such as controlling the effects of business activity on third parties or on the environment). Reducing the emission of noxious fumes or preventing the sale of a harmful drug is conceptually and perhaps administratively easier than deciding what allocation of television licenses will be in "the public interest" or what price levels are "reasonable"; yet until recently Congress has encouraged the agencies to do the latter but not the former. In so far as the contemporary concern for ecology and public health redresses this balance, it is all to the good.

But it is unlikely that the desire to improve and perfect human affairs will stop there. An effort will be made to "protect" the consumer by setting the price he can pay or forbidding him to buy certain products of whose dangers he is fully aware. Moreover, enhancing the powers or stimulating the activity of regulatory agencies for what ever reasons will lead the agencies themselves to enlarge their mandate and extend their influence. Consumer advocates, including as they do many of those most skeptical on other grounds of the manageability of large government organizations, should be the last to suppose that bigger consumer-protection agencies will work as intended; but of course, they are among the first to suppose it.

ENDNOTES

1. For the technically-minded reader, regulation-nonregulation was a dummy variable in a regression equation in which the dependent variable was the log of the average revenue per kilowatt hour and the predictor variables were the log values of the population in cities over 25,000, the cost of coal per BTU, the per capita income, and the proportion of power from hydroelectric sources.
2. *The Economics of Competition in the Transportation Industries* (Cambridge: Harvard University Press, 1964).
3. The extent to which there is or may be a shortage depends in part on estimates of the size of the natural gas reserves, and this is a hotly disputed issue; it may also be ultimately unanswerable. Whatever the size of the reserves, the issue remains as to whether wellhead rates are high enough to encourage exploration for new fields and whether there is enough competition to insure that market prices will not be monopoly prices. Studies by Paul MacAvoy suggest that field prices are (or without regulation, would be) competitive.
4. Some agencies have codified their policies; the NLRB is one. As Roger G. Noll has pointed out, the NLRB is almost unique in dealing with two influential, well-organized, and competitive interests—labor and management. It is, therefore, under steady pressure to define its policies, and its decisions are appealed to the courts much more frequently than those of any other agency.
5. For a discussion of one such effort to prove it, see my article, "Violence, Pornography, and Social Science," in *The Public Interest*, Winter, 1971, pp. 45-61.

31

arthur d. larson

REPRESENTATIVE BUREAUCRACY AND ADMINISTRATIVE RESPONSIBILITY: A REASSESSMENT

There is wide agreement among scholars, laymen, and government officials that the principal problems of the public bureaucracy today are not the traditional ones of securing competence and efficiency, but those of insuring responsibility.[1] It is frequently proposed that to meet these problems of responsibility, the bureaucracy be made *representative*—that is, that the composition of the personnel of the bureaucracy reflect the major socio-economic, geographic, and other groupings of the society. The assumption underlying this idea is that if all the major values, interests, and points of view in the society are present within the bureaucracy, then it will be responsible in the sense of serving the interests and needs of all the people, and not just those of a particular class, section, or group. The purpose of this paper is to review this "theory" of representative bureaucracy, examine some of its major deficiencies, assess its usefulness for enhancing administrative responsibility, and note other functions served by representativeness in the bureaucracy.[2]

The practice of representative bureaucracy is not new, of course, but only its formulation as an explicit theory of public administration. The public service during the Federalist period was composed largely of people drawn from the eastern classes which controlled the wealth and political power of the nation. As a result of

Reprinted by permission from the *Midwest Review of Public Administration*, Vol. 7, No. 2 (April 1973), pp. 79–89. Copyright 1973 by the Midwest Review of Public Administration, Inc.

strong opposition to an entrenched bureaucratic class and demands for more responsive government, the public service under the spoils system and the merit system which succeeded it was open to and became more representative of the people.[3] Norton Long and Paul Van Riper have suggested that the character of the American public service and its constitutional position are the result of its highly representative character. Long asserts that the bureaucracy is more representative of the overall composition and interest group structure of the larger society than Congress, and in fact compensates for grave deficiencies of that body with respect to representativeness, and is an important part of the working constitutional system.[4] Van Riper suggests that as a representative bureaucracy, the public service reflects an integration of two contrasting approaches to governmental administration—the ideal bureaucracy approach emphasizing purpose, rationality, and efficiency, and the free enterprise approach emphasizing a minimum of governmental administration and a maximum of private corporate endeavor—which is ideally suited to the pluralism and pragmatism of American society.[5]

The theory of representative bureaucracy, as contrasted with its practice, was not advanced until the early 1940s, however.[6] It grew out of a recognition of the deficiencies of constitutional and administrative theory for meeting the problem of responsibility posed by the role and power of the bureaucracy in the modern service state. Constitutionalism does not recognize bureaucracy as part of the constitutional system. At best, bureaucracy is seen as a tool, and an important function of the legislative is to control—indeed to dominate—the bureaucracy. With the growing recognition toward the end of the last century that administration was not just a necessary evil, but an indispensable part of government, three important principles were advanced which reconciled administration with constitutionalism and rationalized its role in the state: the separation of policy and administration, efficiency, and political neutrality. These principles became the central tenets of public administration doctrine, and were not seriously challenged for forty years. But the emergence of the modern service state in which the bureaucracy plays a central role made these principles untenable. Administrators are not simply neutral tools who efficiently carry out policies laid down by the legislature, but in fact are deeply involved in formulating policies, concerned as much with ultimate results as with efficiency, and, while perhaps officially neutral, are deeply committed to the programs they administer.

Proponents of representative bureaucracy maintain that because of the character, scope and power of modern bureaucracy, the traditional external controls enforced by the legislature, executive, and courts are inadequate by themselves to insure administrative responsibility, and may make the bureaucracy rigid and ineffective if carried too far. They assert that under these conditions, public officials will be responsible only if they want to be. According to their view, whether and to what extent the official is responsible depends ultimately on the values, attitudes, beliefs, and interests which underlie his administrative behavior as these are shaped by the socio-economic and other groups of which he is a member. Given this, it follows that a bureaucracy, the members of which are drawn predominantly from one particular grouping, will be more responsive to that grouping than to others in the society. To insure responsible bureaucracy, then, the personnel should be drawn from all important groupings so that it will be equally responsive to all.

This theory of representative bureaucracy is summed up in the following way by Donald Kingsley, its earliest proponent:

> . . . the essence of responsibility is psychological rather than mechanical. It is to be sought in an identity of aim and point of view, a common background of social prejudice, which leads the agent to act as though he were the principal. In the first instance, it is a matter of sentiment and understanding, rather than of institutional forms. This is not to say that the mechanics of responsibility are without importance; it is to say that their importance has been enormously over-rated. We have long understood this with respect to legislative bodies, but we have been less clear concerning its application to the executive. This is due, I think, to a persistent belief in the outmoded theory of the seperation of powers and to a failure to understand that the constitutional center of gravity has long since shifted to the executive branch in the matter of policy formation. It is due, also, to the traditional indifference of political theorists to administrative facts and to the existence of an historic body of constitutional doctrine which utterly ignores the role of bureaucracy.

Kingsley concludes that

> if the essence of responsibility is psychological, the degree to which all democratic institutions are representative is a matter of prime significance. No group can safely be entrusted with power who do not themselves mirror the dominant forces in society; for they will then act in an irresponsible manner or will be liable to corruption at the hands of dominant groups.[7]

What is the precise meaning of representativeness as the concept is employed in the theory of representative bureaucracy? To Kingsley and Donald Levitan, a representative bureaucracy is one which "mirrors" the "composition," the "dominant forces," or the "skill, class and personality background" of the society. It is clear from their discussion that representativeness in these respects is to be achieved by drawing the personnel of the bureaucracy proportionately from the major groupings of the society. Van Riper provides a definition of representative buraucracy which reflects these two aspects of its meaning:

> A representative bureaucracy is one in which there is a minimal distinction between the bureaucrats as a group and their administrative behavior and practices on the one hand, and the community or societal membership and its administrative behavior, practices, and expectations of government on the other. Or, to put it another way, the term representative bureaucracy is meant to suggest a body of officials which is broadly representative of the society in which it functions, and which in social ideals is as close as possible to the grass roots of the nation.[8]

In what Pitkin terms the "formalistic" interpretation of the word, all elected and appointed officials of government are representatives because they have been authorized to act for the represented by election or appointment, and because they are accountable for their actions to the represented.[9] The traditional external controls imposed on the bureaucracy by the legislature, executive, and courts are the mechanisms of authorization and accountability in this form of representativeness. Officials in the so-called clientele agencies are also representatives because of what they *do* to advance the interests of particular interest groups. But in the theory of representative bureaucracy, officials are representatives not only because of acts of authorization and accountability, or because of what they may do in the service of an interest group, but because of what they *are*, because they resemble or are like those they represent.)

In what ways does this form of representativeness enhance administrative responsibility? Gilbert points out that administrative responsibility is usually defined in terms of the procedural or substantive ends of the bureaucracy, or the institutional means by which these ends are pursued.[10] Administrative responsibility defined as procedural and substantive ends is "a complex of presumptively popular values" including responsiveness, flexibility, consistency, stability, leadership, probity, candor, competence, efficacy, prudence, due process, and accountability. In the theory of representative bureaucracy a responsible bureaucracy is one which serves the interests and needs of all of the people and groups in a society. The emphasis would therefore appear to be on the policy ends of responsiveness and effectiveness: in the formulation and administration of policy the representative bureaucracy responds to popular demands for policy changes and recognizes group and local concerns, and "situational differences."

DEFICIENCIES OF REPRESENTATIVE BUREAUCRACY

To summarize, the argument of the proponents of representative bureaucracy includes three major propositions: first, the bureaucracy is deeply involved in policymaking as well as policy implementation, and is large, complex, and powerful in its own right; second, traditional external controls are inadequate for achieving administrative responsibility in these circumstances; and third, administrative responsibility can be enhanced in these circumstances through representativeness. The first proposition is, of course, indisputable. At first glance, the second proposition also appears to be well established, although there has been little research in the area and perhaps the full potential of formal controls is not being realized. The concern here, however, is with the third proposition, which for convenience sake has been called the theory of representative bureaucracy. This theory has several important weaknesses, none of which seems to have received the critical attention of its proponents.

It would seem that the validity of the entire theory of representative bureaucracy rests on the assumption that an individual who resembles or is like other people with respect to his values, attitudes, beliefs, and interests, will act like they would in similar circumstances in the bureaucracy. There is little in the way of research to support this assumption, however, and it remains a very tentative one. Even if it should prove to be generally true, the question of which groups the individual is representative of remains. While the influence of the groups involved in socialization to adulthood certainly persists, the individual comes under the influence of many additional groups as an adult. If he is upwardly mobile, some of these groups will participate in the resocialization necessary to mobility, and will therefore be particularly influential.

One of the most important groups to which the individual belongs is the bureaucracy itself. Bureaucracy tends by its very nature to be unrepresentative of the larger society. It includes people who in terms of skill, health, age, and other more subtle characteristics, are unrepresentative of the general population, the degree of unrepresentativeness increasing from the lower to the higher levels. It brings strong influences to bear on the individual to mold him into a useful and responsive member, particularly if he is part of the administrative or professional cadre, and this organizational socialization will tend to dilute the influence of outside groups. Promotion of the individual from a lower to a higher level in the bureaucracy will not only increase the strength of these organizational influences, but may result in changes in his external group memberships—his socio-economic class membership, for example.

Related to the question of which groups the individual represents is the matter of which groups in the larger society should be represented. It is obvious that all groupings cannot be represented, but only those which are politically significant. In a highly structured society, the pattern of political significance among groups is well-established and stable, but in a pluralist society the pattern is never entirely clear at any point in time and changes over time. To maintain representativeness within all levels and subdivisions, the bureaucracy would have to make a continuing series of judgments about which groupings were to be represented and in what proportions. This would entail seriously compromising or abandoning the central principles of the merit bureaucracy. Recruitment, promotion, and other personnel decisions would have to be based in large measure on ascription rather than on merit, and on compulsion rather than on choice, and personnel policies and practices would necessarily be arbitrary and even capricious.

How would representativeness operate to enhance responsibility in the bureaucracy as reflected in its policies? One possibility is that the individuals representative of the various groups would work for the interests of their respective groups, the overall result being policies which served the interests of all groups. This raises the possibility of the paradox that the bureaucracy would be responsible in the aggregate in that it served the needs and interests of all because its members were individually irresponsible in pressing for the needs and interests of the particular groups of which they were representatives. A second possibility is more subtle: administrators would not be advocates for particular groups, but their administrative behavior would be guided at least in part by the values, attitudes, beliefs, and interests of the groups of which they were representative, the result again being policies which served the interests and needs of all people and groups in the society.

But in either case, while values, attitudes, beliefs, and interests representative of the larger society might prevent the pursuit of policies favoring some groups in the society over others, they would not provide a basis for the formulation and administration of policies which served all groups equally. Such policies would have to be based on a set of values and interests which was shared by all administrators, and which took precedence over their more parochial views. It seems unlikely, however, that groups which were the source of the diverse backgrounds of the administrators would also provide a transcendent set of values, attitudes, beliefs, and interest shared by them all. While representativeness might prevent the bureaucracy from favoring particular groups at the expense of others, it is not clear how it would insure by itself that the bureaucracy would serve the needs and interests of all groups equally. One response of bureaucracies to the diversity of outlooks introduced by greater representativeness might be to increase the strength of organizational influences to insure that all members acquired a common set of values, attitudes, beliefs, and interests. This raises the possibility that the long-run result of an increase in representativeness in terms of the origin or external group memberships of bureaucratic personnel might be to decrease representativeness with respect to the values which they hold.

The final question concerns the enforcement arrangements or mechanisms of representativeness as a means of securing responsibility. Under traditional external controls, the officials must fulfill the standards and ends established by the legislature, executive, and the courts, and account to them and be punished for any failure to do so. But whether the official is responsible in the manner anticipated by the theory of representative bureaucracy depends entirely on the individual himself, on his conscience, on his "sense of responsibility" as contrasted with his "duty of responsibility." There is no agency outside of the individual to which he must account and which can enforce directly on him the standards and ends which are to guide his behavior. To many, a dependence on the individual's conscience, sense of obligation, or morality to enforce administrative responsibility represents a step backward in the development of democratic government. Indeed, Herman Finer suggests that a reliance on the individual's "conscience" or "will" to enforce responsibility, rather than on an external agency, is characteristic of dictatorship.[11] To

Finer, the role and power of modern administrators means that traditional external controls must be tightened, and not that the task of enforcing their own responsibility should be placed in the hands of the administrators themselves.

CONCLUSIONS

The foregoing criticisms of representative bureaucracy rest on the assumption that "representativeness" means that the composition of the bureaucracy should be an accurate or precise reproduction of the composition of the general population. The proponents of the theory do not make themselves entirely clear on this point, however. Kingsley appears to attach a precise interpretation to representativeness in stating that the bureaucracy should "mirror the dominant forces in society."[12] Van Riper on the other hand, states that a representative bureaucracy is one which consists of "a reasonable cross-section of the body politic" and which is "in general tune with the ethos and attitudes of the society."[13]

If representativeness is interpreted in the sense of "reasonably representative," then many of the foregoing criticisms lose their force. But a "reasonably representative" bureaucracy will inevitably be in some respects an 'unrepresentative" one, and would therefore appear to be unacceptable under the theory. If reasonable representativeness is in fact what is meant, however, then the theory provides little more than a rationalization of existing practice. As noted earlier, one of the notable features of the Federal government bureaucracy is its compositional representativenss, achieved through what Van Riper calls the "opportunity system," based on "individual capacity" and "freedom and equality of opportunity." Data on the backgrounds of Federal executives collected by Van Riper and others suggest that the "representative" public service which is the result of the opportunity system is over-representative of the business and professional classes, males, and the college educated, at least at the executive levels.[14]

But whether representativeness is meant in the "precise" sense or in the "reasonable" sense makes no difference with respect to the question of whether it should or could serve as a basis for administrative responsibility. The deficiencies of representativeness would be present in either case, and it seems clear that these are so serious as to render it unworkable and unacceptable as a recognized means of meeting the problem of responsibility in the modern bureaucracy.

This does not mean that representativeness does not or should not play a role in enhancing responsibility. The variety of points of view introduced by the "broad representativeness" achieved through the opportunity system undoubtedly makes a significant contribution to the responsiveness of the bureaucracy. This contribution would be strengthened by correcting serious deficiencies in this pattern of representation—with respect to women and minority groups, for example. It could be enhanced further by two reforms proposed by Levitan.[15] The first would be to insure that the academic training of candidates for the public service, rather than emphasizing, "administrivia," be of a kind which will develop their understanding of the social, political, and economic forces and problems of the society with which the policies they formulate and implement must deal. The second reform would be to insure that members of the public service enjoyed the full rights of citizenship, not only because it is unjust to deny these rights to them, but also because they will be less inclined to recognize in ordinary citizens what they themselves are denied.

In addition to its contribution to responsibility, representativeness serves other purposes in the bureaucracy. As Frederick Mosher suggests, representativiness is a symbol of openness and equality of opportunity of the public service, two important traditional values of American society.[16] Perhaps more important from the historical point of view is Van Riper's assessment that because of its "broadly representative" character, the Federal bureaucracy has been able to steer a middle course between the "mechanistic rationalization" and "corporate anarchy" models of the state, both unsuited to a democratic, pluralistic society.

The question of meeting the problem of administrative responsibility posed by modern bureaucracy remains, of course. While the alternatives available for meeting the problem cannot be examined here, it should be noted in conclusion that the definition of the problem offered by the proponents of representative bureaucracy may be incorrect. As noted earlier, one of their arguments for representativeness is that traditional external controls are inadequate to enforce responsibility in the modern bureaucracy. It may be, however, that these controls can be made more effective—in fact, must be made more effective if democracy is to survive. As Finer states:

> [T]he servants of the public are not to decide their own course; they are to be responsible to the elected representatives of the public, and these are to determine the course of action of the public servants to the most minute degree that is technically

feasible. . . . This kind of responsibility is what democracy means; and though there may be other devices which provide 'good' government, I cannot yield on the cardinal issue of democratic government.[17]

ENDNOTES

1. A substantial body of literature on responsibility in government has developed since World War II. In addition to the material cited below in connection with the discussion, the following are pertinent: Arch Dotson, "Fundamental Approaches to Administrative Responsibility," *10 Western Political Quarterly* (September, 1957), pp. 701-727; Roland J. Pennock, "Responsiveness, Responsibility, and Majority Rule," *46 American Political Science Review* (September, 1952), pp. 790-807; Norman John Powell, *Responsible Public Bureaucracy in the United States* (Boston: Allyn and Bacon, 1967); and Herbert J. Spiro, *Responsibility in Government: Theory and Practice* (New York: Van Nostrand, 1969).

2. Space does not permit the review of the more general questions of the nature of administrative responsibility and the various approaches to enforcing it which would be an appropriate prelude to this examination of represenatative bureaucracy. For an earlier critical treatment of representative bureaucracy, see V. Subramanian, "Representative Bureaucracy: A Reassessment," *61 American Political Science Review* (December, 1967), pp. 1010-1019.

3. See Paul P. Van Riper, *History of the United States Civil Service* (Evanston: Row, Peterson, 1958); also Sidney H. Aronson, *Status and Kinship in the Higher Civil Service* (Cambridge: Harvard University Press, 1964).

4. Norton Long, "Bureaucracy and Constitutionalism," *46 American Political Science Review* (September, 1952), pp. 808-818.

5. Van Riper, *op. cit.,* pp. 4-7.

6. The discussion in this section is based on Donald J. Kingsley, *Representative Bureaucracy: An Interpretation of the British Civil Service* (Yellow Springs: Antioch Press, 1944); David M. Levitan "The Responsibility of Administrative Officials in a Democratic Society, *61 Political Science Quarterly* (December, 1946); Frederick C. Mosher, *Democracy and the Public Service* (New York: Oxford University Press, 1968); and Dwight Waldo, "Development of Theory of Democratic Administration," *46 American Political Science Review* (March, 1952), pp. 81-103.

7. Kingsley, *op. cit.,* pp. 282-283. The Marxian basis of Kingsley's analysis is noted by Waldo, and strongly so by Herman Finer. See Waldo, *op. cit.,* p. 91; and Herman Finer, *Theory and Practice of Modern Government* (New York: Holt, 1949), pp. 784-786. Regardless of one's ideological preferences, however, "[A]dministrative devices *are* relative to the economic and social composition and the ideological complexion of the societies in which they exist," as Waldo suggests.

8. Van Riper, *op. cit.,* p. 552. Italics in first sentence in original omitted.

9. The discussion in this paragraph is based on Hanna Fenichel Pitkin, *The Concept of Representation* (Berkeley: University of California Press, 1967).

10. Charles E. Gilbert, "The Framework of Administrative Responsibility," 21 *Journal of Politics* (August, 1959), pp. 373–407. Gilbert divides the institutional means into those which are "external" to the bureaucracy and those which are "internal" to it. External "formal" controls include those of legislatures and courts, and external "informal" controls those of interest groups; while internal "formal" controls include the administrative controls of the executive and bureaucracy itself, and internal "informal" controls the professional standards, codes of ethics, and social values possessed by individuals. Traditional controls of the bureaucracy are of the external formal type, while representativeness is an internal informal control based on social values.

11. Herman Finer, "Administrative Responsibility in Democratic Government," 1 *Public Administrative Review* (Summer, 1941), pp. 335–350. Finer's paper appears as a response to a paper by Carl J. Friedrich in which it is proposed that, to strengthen responsibility in the bureaucracy, traditional controls be supplemented by controls based on professional standards enforced by the individual. Friedrich's arguments supporting the necessity for such internal informal controls are the same as those of the advocates of representativeness. See Carl J. Friedrich, "Public Policy and the Nature of Administrative Responsibility," in Carl J. Friedrich and Edward S. Mason, eds., *Public Policy* (Cambridge: Harvard University Press, 1940), pp. 3–24.

12. Kingsley, *op. cit.*, pp. 282–283.

13. Van Riper, *op. cit.*, p. 552.

14. W. Lloyd Warner, Paul P. Van Riper, Norman H. Martin, and Orvis F. Collins, *The American Federal Executive: A Study of the Social and Personal Characteristics of the Civilian and Military Leaders of the United States Federal Government* (New Haven: Yale University Press, 1963), pp. 28–31 and pp. 177–179.

15. Levitan, *op. cit.*, pp. 583–589.

16. Mosher, *op. cit.*, pp. 13–14.

17. Finer, "Administrative Responsibility in Democratic Government," p. 336.

32

john h. strange

THE IMPACT OF CITIZEN PARTICIPATION ON PUBLIC ADMINISTRATION

Few pieces of domestic legislation have created as much controversy in recent years as has the mandate for "maximum feasible participation" of the poor in the Community Action Programs of the Office of Economic Opportunity and the attempts to insure "widespread citizen participation" in the Demonstration Cities Program (commonly referred to as the Model Cities Program, reputedly because of the negative political connotation of "demonstrations") of the Department of Housing and Urban Development. But citizen participation is not new to the politics of the United States. In fact, perhaps no other theme has so persistently dominated debate concerning American government.

THE TRADITION OF CITIZEN PARTICIPATION

Even prior to the Revolutionary War, great emphasis was placed on government *by the people*. Admittedly, participation in local public decisions was severely limited, by economic status, race, sex, and often education, but there was never great debate over the principle that ultimate governmental authority was to rest with the people. Citizen participation and control of government has been a widely

Reprinted with permission from the *Public Administration Review*, journal of the American Society for Public Administration, vol. 32, Special Edition, (Sept., 1972). Copyright © 1972 by the American Society for Public Administration.

accepted objective of our government from its inception. The translation of this general objective into institutional form occurred in many ways. Executives were limited in their appointive powers. Legislatures were restricted in the number of days they could meet and in the measures they could initiate and enact. The establishment of a decentralized federal system of government, as well as separation of governmental powers into separate institutions insured that not only government per se would be limited, but also that the role of the individual citizen would be enhanced.

The initial emphasis on the role of the citizen was furthered considerably with the rise of Jacksonian democracy. A renewed emphasis on decentralized decision making open to any person without regard to education or status greatly expanded the democratic nature of government in the United States.

Other institutional changes have led to a much broader role for citizens in political decision making. The expansion of suffrage rights to those without property, Negroes, women, immigrants, the poor and illiterate, and most recently to 18-year-olds are all evidence of the value attached to, and attempts to expand citizen participation. Of course it must be noted that even though the democratic creed is a participatory creed, our political institutions have not been opened to those previously excluded from decision making without considerable debate, opposition, and even turmoil.

Recent developments in our political history have multiplied the ways in which citizens participate in government. Interest groups such as labor unions, trade and farm associations, civil rights and protest organizations, and neighborhood groups have all been used as vehicles for expanding the role of citizens. Open primaries, recall and referendum procedures, and long ballots involving the election of "everyone from mayor to dog catcher" have all been advocated as methods of enhancing the role of the citizen in government, even though in practice these techniques have not entirely succeeded in this objective. We also have emphasized techniques to make governmental decision making as public and open as possible by limiting secret legislative actions, encouraging widespread press coverage, and making governmental information available to the public. These objectives are not fully met, but the underlying objective of enhancing the role of the citizen has been continuous.

Attention to and support for citizen participation has been especially evident on the local level in the United States. This includes both rural and populated areas. Recent concern with citizen participation has emphasized the participation of citizens on the local governmental level in urban areas. But much of our political history is studded with emphasis on participation in rural settings. Elkins and McKitrick have argued, in fact, that the events associated with conquering the frontier and settling new territories, at least outside the South, created conditions which not only fostered but *necessitated* citizen involvement.[1] Certainly there is ample evidence to indicate that one of the high points for citizen participation in and *control* of governmental functions has occurred in rural areas as a result of farm policies governing soil banks, crop allotment, and other agricultural legislation passed during the administration of Franklin Delano Roosevelt.

On both the state and local level, Herbert Kaufman has noted that the attempt to institutionalize participation has been one of three major goals of governmental reformers, and that it is currently the objective receiving the most emphasis. Robert Wood, in his provocative study of suburbia, argues that the desire for a highly participative democratic political system with considerable autonomy over governmental objectives deemed to be local has been a major attraction of the suburb. He identifies this overwhelming desire for participatory democracy and governmental autonomy as full consistent with and reflective of American political history. Although he decries the failure to develop a unique political theory for urban government, he acknowledges the extent to which Americans seek a chance to play a direct role in governmental decision making.

Thus we see that an emphasis on and a desire to enhance the role of the citizen has been a continuous objective of Americans and their government. Citizen participation as an objective is certainly not new to either our political thought or practice. Yet it has been a goal which has been elusive at times and which has varied in importance and in the intensity with which it has been pursued.

THE CURRENT EMPHASIS ON PARTICIPATION

The growth of small towns into huge cities and the development of mass transportation which separates work from residence and attachment to a single local government have reduced the ability of many to participate in local affairs. In addition, the reduction of local government to the administration of decisions in the absence of conflict which has sometimes occurred in homogeneous suburbs has resulted, as Robert Wood has said, in "grassroots government run by automation. Under these circumstances, the purest theory of democracy requires no democratic action or responsibility at all."[2] More important for our purposes is the fact that participation, although a generally accepted objective, has been limited to different groups at different times in our history. Only propertied, well-educated, white males have always been eligible to participate in our government processes, and it is only recently that full participation has become likely for the poor and black in America. It is because of this extension of the right to participate to new elements of our population that the concept of participation has recently been emphasized, denounced, sought, and demanded.

The current concern and fascination with citizen participation began with requirements that the federal urban renewal process be carried out with the advice and involvement of local citizens. But it did not become an important political issue until the passage of the Economic Opportunity Act, after the assassination of President Kennedy, which called for the administration of the Community Action Program, the major programmatic vehicle of that Act, with "maximum feasible participation" of the poor. This seemingly innocuous statement supporting an agreed-upon tenet of our political system was adopted with no debate and virtually no discussion. It emerged, however, as one of the most controversial phrases in any domestic legislation passed in the last decade. After its rise to prominence in 1964 and 1965, legislative drafters of the model cities legislation could not escape, whatever their desires, the necessity to pay obeisance to the tenet of participation, although they attempted to limit its emphasis on participation by the poor and the black by calling for the widespread participation of the business and organizational elements in a community rather than the "maximum feasible participation" of the poor. Recently the demands of blacks, the poor, and their spokesmen for participation has been extended to include the second part of the major objectives of local government identified by Wood: autonomy. These demands have taken the form of interest in and advocating of neighborhood control of governmental institutions, especially the schools and the police.

Our focus in this article will be on the Community Action Programs of OEO and the Model Cities activities of HUD. These are the two major federal programs in urban areas in which "participation" has been an issue. The administration of these two programs, especially the Community Action Program, further emphasized participation by the poor and the nonwhite. Not unexpectedly, this emphasis on the inclusion of new groups of citizens into participation in government has created considerable controversy. The Model Cities Program merits our special attention since it is an attempt to de-emphasize participation. Model Cities was to be a counter to OEO, which was becoming more and more identified as an advocate of participation of the poor.

Citizen Participation and Two Federal Programs

It is generally acknowledged that the phrase "maximum feasible participation" was included accidentally (or at least without serious consideration) in the OEO legislation. Adam Yarmolinsky notes that,

> At one point during the February 4 brainstorming session, when [Richard] Boone had used the phrase "maximum possible participation" several times, this writer recalls saying to him, "you have used that phrase four or five times now." "Yes, I know," he replied. "How many more times do I have to use it before it becomes part of the programs?" "Oh, a couple of times more," was the response. He did, and it did.[3]

Sar A. Levitan agrees when he says:

> It may be surprising that this language appeared in the first draft of the bill and was neither questioned nor commented upon. . . . Nor was it considered significant enough to be mentioned in the official summary of the bill which was released, as is customary. . . . To most of the task force participants, "maximum feasible participation" represented a nice sentiment and a means of giving the administrator of the program power to prevent segregation in community action programs.[4]

And none other than Daniel P. Moynihan indicates that the committee which drafted the legislation and the congressional committees which considered it paid little attention to the phrase, and certainly did not anticipate the emphasis which would be given to it.

It cannot be said, however, that the choice of the term "widespread participation" in the Model Cities legislation was not carefully considered. The choice was deliberate and came as a direct response to the belief of President Johnson and his White House advisors that entirely too much emphasis had been placed on maximizing the role of the poor and minority ethnic groups in the administration of the community action program. In addition, the White House (and OEO) was under pressure from Congresswoman Edith Green and others to provide local government, especially the mayors, with an urban program to assist the poor which the elected officials could control.

Because of the difficulty of changing OEO's approach once the Community Action Programs were established, it was decided to initiate a new urban program in a limited number of cities which would be administered by local governments with the widespread assistance of business groups, governmental agencies, and neighborhood residents. Thus two major departures from the community action approach to participation occurred in the Model Cities Program. First, local governments rather than private nonprofit agencies were given ultimate responsibility for the local administration and operation of the program. Second, participation of the poor (or neighborhood residents) was to be limited rather than maximized, and governmental and business participation was to be guaranteed.

MEANINGS OF "CITIZEN PARTICIPATION"

Whatever the intent of the framers of the legislation of these two federal programs, the meanings which have been attached to all of the terms—"maximum feasible," "widespread," "participation," "poor," "residents of the area"—have varied considerably. They have been different for different people. They have been different in the various regions of the country, and in rural and urban areas. They have been different at different times. Most of these terms have been interpreted differently by specific individuals at any given point in time depending upon the political needs of the person doing the interpreting. An OEO director puts a different meaning on "participation" or "the poor" depending on whether he is seeking additional financial support from OEO officials for a community action project or whether he is being confronted by an outraged group of citizens who feel their views or interests are being neglected by the agency. A Model Cities organizer interprets "widespread" differently depending on whether he is seeking to expand the influence of his "citizen group" *vis à vis* government officials or whether he is being faced with an attempt to oust him from his position by a group of residents not aligned with his citizens' organization. Thus the meanings of all these terms vary with people, over time, by region, and according to need.

Definitions

Three questions arise in considering both the OEO and Model Cities mandate for participation. First, what is meant by "widespread" or "maximum feasible?" How extensive is participation to be? What proportion of those active in either the OEO or the Model Cities Program were to be from the designated groups of citizens? Second, what is meant by "participation"? Does it mean giving advice, holding jobs, or making decisions? Third, what is the objective of participation? How meaningful is it to be? Fourth, what is meant by "the residents of the area involved," "the poor," or "citizen"? In other words, who is to participate, in what way, and to what extent?

Extent of Participation

Originally OEO merely attempted to make sure that some "representatives of the poor" were included on the boards of directors of the Community Action Agencies, and that these agencies hired poor people and members of ethnic minorities wherever possible. Soon, however, OEO program officials began insisting that at least one-third of the members of CAA boards must be "representatives of the poor." This requirement was often expressed in terms of a "three-legged stool"—the poor, the business and other organized aspects of a community, and the government sharing equally in the decision-making aspects of the program. Later Congress established the one-third provision as a minimum requirement, and still later altered it so that it was a precise proportion applicable to government, the poor, and other private organizations.

In the Model Cities Program no formula, such as one-third of all participants should be poor, has been required. Instead, regulations were developed which required that acceptable structures be developed through which neighborhood residents could participate, that provisions be established to insure that neighborhood representatives were *representative*, that sufficient information and necessary "interpretive" staff be supplied citizen groups, and that technical and financial assistance be provided to neighborhood participants. Thus Model Cities sought to insure a considerable but undefined level of neighborhood participation through the establishment of institutional structures in contrast to the mandated use of a percentage formula for participation of the poor by OEO.

What Constitutes "Participation"?

"Participation" was also open to considerable interpretation. The debate over the meaning had two aspects. First, where participation was mandated or required, in what aspect of the Community Action or Model Cities Program was it to take place? Several alternatives, none of which were mutually exclusive, were available. First, participation could be in the decision-making structure of the program. For private, nonprofit OEO programs the decision makers were the members of the board of directors of the Community Action Agency, or those who made the final program decisions. In Model Cities ultimate program responsibility was to rest with the mayor or some agency of local government. (As we will note later, some local governments delegated this ultimate program responsibility to community groups.) A second arena for participation was in advisory panels which could either be concerned with all of the activities of the program or a limited portion of the agency's program. If advisory groups had limited responsibilities, these limitations could be either geographic or substantive in nature.

Participation could also take place through staff employment. Both OEO and Model Cities have emphasized this approach, and on occasion particular agencies have been challenged in their hiring practices because of the belief that the poor, the residents, or other groups were inadequately represented on the program staff. In other words, participation has also meant jobs. Both Model Cities and Community Action Programs have also required "participation" by "residents" and the poor on the staffs (and on occasion governing bodies) of agencies, such as school systems or health boards, to which program responsibilities have been delegated.

Participation has at times been interpreted to mean the presence in the community of organizations of the poor or of neighborhood residents and the interaction of these organizations with the Model Cities and Community Action Agencies. In other words, participation is understood to be a process by which citizens organize into interest groups and lobby, bargain, and otherwise respond to the established program agencies. Some OEO activities have been designed to create such organizations. In some cases these organizations are a part of the Community Action Program. In others they have been independent of the CAA. To further complicate the picture, these organizations have been created in different ways. Some have been organized as groups of people who are recipients of a particular service, such as welfare mothers. Other organizations have been issue oriented (lobby groups for day care centers or better police service). Still others have been based on race, occupation, or residence. Some have been functional, nonprofit organizations, such as co-ops or credit unions. Finally, some have been organizations of organizations—coalitions or existing organizations combined to increase the effectiveness and impact of the respective member.

Who Is It That Is To Participate?

But who are the "citizens" to participate, whether that means the giving of advice or the exercise of control? This question has been much debated. First we note the different terms used in the various pieces of legislation and administrative memoranda: "residents of the area involved," "the poor and their representatives," "neighborhood residents," "citizen." This question of who is to participate has never been settled. As noted earlier, positions on this question change depending on whether one is seeking participation or is trying to resist it. By and large, however, these general statements can be made. In the South (except for the mountain areas) and in all cities, these various terms setting forth who it is that is to be encouraged to participate have meant, both to OEO and Model Cities, blacks or other members of minority ethnic groups (Orientals, Puerto-Ricans, Mexican-Americans, Indians) without regard to income level, and/or whites (in a relatively few cases) below some specified income level or at least generally recognized to be "poor." In the Model Cities Program these definitions are further restricted by requirements of residence within the "model cities area." In rural areas of the North and West, where few ethnic or racial minorities exist, those whose participation is mandated have been determined by economic criteria. In some cases, especially in some southern Community Action Programs, "representatives" of the poor have been acceptable participants. Often they represent groups such as the NAACP, the Southern Christian Leadership Conference, ministerial alliances, or other ethnic or minority organizations.

"Participation," "citizen," "poor," "maximum feasible," "widespread"—all are very imprecisely defined. They have been used and combined in countless different ways. They have varied by program, by cities, and over time. This wide variation in meaning of the central concept must be remembered constantly. Is it any wonder that much confusion and disagreement abound?

IMPLEMENTING CITIZEN PARTICIPATION

Citizen participation has been implemented differently in the Community Action Program and the Model Cities Program. The original legislative act establishing OEO, which was passed in 1964, required the "maximum feasible participation of residents of the area and members of the group served." In February 1965 OEO clarified the administrative meaning that was to be applied to the concept of participation. *OEO's CAP Guide* called for "the involvement of the poor themselves . . . in the planning, policy making and operation of the program." In addition it was suggested that the Community Action Agency should include "the population served" on "the policy making or governing body of the community action agency," or an advisory committee if the former were not feasible. OEO clearly intended, however, that the poor be included in the official decision-making process. This was made clear by field staff and program analysts. OEO also noted that "where appropriate," neighborhood groups might engage in the "conduct and administration of elements of neighborhood based programs." Encouragement was also given to the organization of community groups which might interact with the Community Action Agency as a "program operator, critic, supporter, or source for representatives."

In 1967 Congress passed legislation which required that one-third of community action boards be "representatives of the poor." Thus what was practice became official. CAP boards were to include *poor* people on them. Neighborhood organizations were also officially encouraged by the legislation. In February 1968 OEO mandated that for neighborhood (as opposed to community) boards "at least a majority of its members must be representative of the poor residing within the area," or where possible, they should be composed "predominantly, if not entirely of the neighborhood residents themselves." The memo further suggested that the success of CAA's could be measured by "the extent to which they entrust genuine policy making responsibility to neighborhood based organizations." In most cases this policy merely affirmed the practice of many medium- and large-size Community Action Agencies. On December 1, 1968, OEO issued a memorandum that noted that each "CAA is expected to recognize or help establish target area or neighborhood based organizations and to negotiate with them regarding their role in CAA sponsored programs." This was the high point of OEO encouragement of community organization and citizen participation.

After the establishment of Model Cities, OEO encouraged local CAA's to undertake activities which would "expand, increase and improve the quality of resident participation in the Model Cities planning process." Thus OEO encouraged maximization of citizen participation in its own programs as well as those of HUD!

TECHNIQUES OF IMPLEMENTATION IN OEO PROGRAMS

Four important points concerning the implementation of participation in OEO programs should be noted. First, and probably most importantly, citizen participation has taken place in private, nonprofit, nongovernmental agencies which were established to administer the Community Action Programs. OEO legislation provided that local governmental machinery would be bypassed if desired and the Community Action Agency could be operated outside of local government control. This is in fact the route that was taken in approximately 95 per cent of all Community Action Agencies in the country. The fact that the administration of the Community Action Program took place in a nongovernmental setting made considerable differences in the nature and extent of citizen participation and the controversy surrounding it.

Second, the original emphasis on citizen participation in OEO programs resulted from the activities of the civil rights movement. In situations where there were large numbers of minority ethnic group members, the terms "citizens" and "poor" came to mean members of ethnic group minorities. Thus, "citizen participation" and "participation of the poor" were interpreted as participation by ethnic group minorities.

Third, OEO emphasized that board memberships and staff positions, i.e., positions not just participatory in nature but decision-making or "control" positions, were to be filled by at least one-third poor people. As noted above, in some cases poor meant black.

Finally, despite the controversy surrounding the term maximum feasible participation, there have been only a very few instances in which participation has been maximized to such an extent that the poor or blacks have substantially controlled the community action programs.

Restrictions on Participation

It is often believed that OEO concentrated its attention on expanding participation and that it took no actions to limit participation. Although a popular view, it is incorrect. OEO engaged in many practices which severely restricted participation. One of the major restricting devices was the emphasis at the national level on national priority or national emphasis programs. A special division of the community action section of OEO was responsible for the development and implementation of programs created at the federal level. To the extent that program development occurred in Washington rather than at the local level, participation at the local level became relatively less important. Moreover, as OEO became an established program and as it began to have to answer annually to Congress when seeking appropriations, more and more priority setting was done at the national level and more package programs were developed nationally for use locally—thereby diminishing local programming. In this way an increasing number of decisions, especially program decisions, were removed from local control. This naturally affected the extent and importance of citizen participation on a local level.

Second, the funding procedures which OEO followed tended to restrict and weaken citizen participation as well. OEO, which originally was conceived as a program to be operated on an experimental basis in a limited number of cities, rapidly changed direction under the leadership of Sargent Shriver. Instead of a few experimental programs, Shriver sought, for very logical political reasons, to place a Community Action Agency in every congressional district in the country. As a result, some 1,000 Community Action Programs were established throughout the nation. With the presence of a large number of Community Action Agencies contending for a limited amount of funds, the appropriations available for any single Community Action Program were considerably reduced. In addition, the rapid escalation of American expenditures in Vietnam after the establishment of OEO and the shifting of funds away from domestic programs to support the Vietnamese War severely restricted the amount of money available to OEO. With limited funds to begin with and no increase in program monies, OEO was forced to limit growth of all Community Action Agencies. Most were forced to terminate programs; some entire agencies were closed. These restrictions on the size of local Community Action Agencies and the level of program operations which they could engage in also reduced the importance of citizen participation.

Third, OEO required a large number of documents to support program applications. These documents had to be tailored to the various groups which reviewed program requests at OEO: legal division, special projects, education, other substantive program areas, civil rights compliance, intergovernmental relations, and many others. Consequently, the time for program preparation was severely reduced at the local level and as a result program preparation and submission became a process in which, because of technical requirements and pressing deadlines, there could be little local participation by anyone—citizens, staff, or others.

Fourth, OEO itself reduced the amount of participation that was possible by constantly changing its regulations regarding participation and its definition of who constituted the "poor" or the "residents of the area involved." As a result of these changes and the different requirements which were promulgated by OEO, boards of directors were expanded and contracted at a rapid rate—sometimes doubling or tripling in membership from month to month. Consequently, those people who were on the board never knew how long they would be on, and those who were off always had a hope that they might be added soon. The effectiveness of participation was, of course, reduced by such indecision. The attitudes toward participation also varied among different people and over time at OEO. The purposes of participation, the methods to be used in trying to achieve participation, the meanings attached to the various phrases used in the legislation were constantly subjected to reinterpretation.

Fifth, because most of the Community Action Agencies were new in their community, much interagency rivalry existed. This rivalry diluted the amount of participation that was possible and also caused many people to avoid participation. Often OEO agencies had to restrict participation in order to survive in the highly competitive interagency politics.

Sixth, in many cases emphasis was placed on participation by the poor in staff positions. In some cases this severely reduced interest among the poor in the more important positions on boards of directors, since staff members were paid and board members were not. Many of the poor felt they would rather have the money resulting from jobs than the potential influence arising from being a member of the board of directors.

Seventh, in some cases professional standards were established for staff members, especially upper-level program positions, which severely restricted the opportunities for members of minority groups or people in poverty for participation through employment.

Eighth, OEO also failed to provide sufficient technical or financial support for participation. Although financial support was given through grants for community organizations, these grants were severely curtailed after 1967 and have been virtually eliminated during the Nixon Administration. At no time during the history of OEO has adequate technical and financial assistance been provided to local Community Action Agencies which would assist in the development of techniques to maximize the opportunities for citizen participation.

Since the inauguration of the Nixon Administration, OEO's emphasis on citizen participation has decreased. This has been evidenced by lack of concern with the extent of participation *prior to funding,* denial of funds for organizational activities, transfer of OEO programs to other agencies having less stringent participation requirements, increasing emphasis on research and planning as opposed to action, general reductions in level of funding, and general discouragement of citizen participation.

Citizen participation in Model Cities has taken a somewhat different form from that in Community Action Programs. As noted earlier, the Model Cities Program placed ultimate local responsibility with elected public officials. Section 103 of the Demonstration City and Metropolitan Development Act of 1966 indicates that in order for a Model Cities Program to be eligible for assistance there must be "widespread citizen participation in the program." This is only one of some 30 requirements for the acceptance of an application. In December 1967, Model Cities published a guidebook establishing standards for participation. It was provided that citizen participation structures "must have clear and direct access to the decision making process" and they must be provided with technical assistance to assure that they have "the technical capacity to make decisions." Nevertheless, private nonprofit organizations such as those which administered community action organizations were not allowed. This "return" of authority to local government, coupled with the emphasis on participation by business and government as well as by "citizens," was intended to drastically decrease the emphasis on and concern with citizen participation, especially when "citizen" was interpreted to mean the poor or ethnic minorities. There were several forces at work which attempted to limit these changes, however. First, many HUD and federal Model Cities employees sought to maximize the possibilities for citizen participation. Attempts were made to emphasize ethnic and economic minorities in defining "citizen"; institutionalize the mechanisms for participation by "the poor" through the provision of financial and technical assistance to community residents; further participation by citing the example of OEO; and, where possible, encourage local Community Action Agencies to support extensive citizen participation in the Model Cities Programs as well as their own. Attempts, a few of which were successful, were also made to allow local governments to delegate their ultimate program authority to citizens groups. This occurred in Cambridge, Massachusetts, and to a certain extent in Philadelphia, Boston, and Dayton, Ohio. After the election of President Nixon, such delegation agreements were officially discouraged and informally prohibited.

In other cities the Model Cities citizen participation structures, even though unsuccessful in gaining total control, did achieve control over a portion of the program development process. In a few cases they were able to control all program activities. The Nixon Administration has attempted to limit the powers of the neighborhood units to the exercise of a veto over programs, or preferably to the giving of advice. In May 1969 a Model Cities memo banned exclusive initiation of projects by citizens groups and required all Model City agencies to assure HUD that in no case would "the city's ability to take responsibility for developing the plan" be impeded. The message was clear: deemphasize participation. This is contrary to the explicit support of HUD officials during the Johnson Administration of *any* arrangement agreed upon locally and the implicit support of some HUD officials for programs which maximized the influence of neighborhood groups. Mel Moguloff warns, however, that "In some model cities, no matter what the new Federal policy, the character of the accommodation between black neighborhood leadership and city government will not permit a return to milder forms of citizen participation."[5]

In those instances where "citizen" participation was encouraged and where it was extensive, many of the same questions arose concerning who were the "citizens." Again, by and large, "citizens" was interpreted to mean ethnic group minorities or economically disadvantaged. Restrictions abounded, however, on participation in Model Cities. First there was the basic legislation emphasizing the role of local government and limiting the role of citizen participation. Although the technical and financial assistance to citizen groups provided by HUD was better planned and far more thorough than that provided by OEO, citizen groups still encountered major obstacles in their attempts to influence and/or control the Model Cities Programs. Advice giving, employment, organized support for the program, were all legitimate roles for citizens to play. But not control. That was to remain the province of the professionals and the elected politicians.

Another aspect of the Model Cities Program which decreased "citizen" participation was the emphasis on planning. The first two years of a local program was devoted to planning for the Model Cities effort. This emphasis on planning resulted in an increased importance of professional staff, thus reducing the potential impact of "citizens." Funding and application procedures also limited participation by imposing extremely tight deadlines.

IMPACT UPON PARTICIPANTS

The effect of the emphasis on participation can be examined by observing the impact on the participants, the program, and the community. In examining the impact upon participants we are immediately confronted with the dilemma that we really do not know what we are talking about. By participants do we mean employees, members of decision-making bodies, members of advisory groups, or members of pressure groups affecting the program? Furthermore, do we mean *all* the participants, or only those participants who were black, brown, or poor, or who, under other or previous conditions we would not expect to have been participants? Avoiding a direct answer to these questions, we can ask, who did participate in any or all of these ways? Why? Under what conditions? Over what period of time? What impact was there upon the attitudes of participants toward government, the Model Cities Program, the Community Action Program? What impact was there upon the participant's attitude toward himself? Many other questions are also possible. No firm answers can be made, even if we ignore the problem of not knowing precisely what we are talking about. We can, however, note several conclusions that have been set forth by various observers.

First, both the Model Cities and Community Action Programs hired more blacks and "low-income persons" than had previous federal programs, especially in program or management positions. Second, more blacks and low-income persons held positions on decision-making boards than in any previous government or governmental program. Third, of all the minority group members and persons with below-average incomes, those persons who participated were likely to have more education, a higher income, and generally higher "status" than those who did not participate. It is also very likely that the emphasis on "participation" and the actual involvement of new groups of citizens in these programs stimulated a desire to participate and increased hopes for more assistance from government and new political and economic benefits.

Participants also are likely to have learned about governmental activities and operations from their participation. Many may have been made aware of the complexities of government programs; others may have had their expectations expanded or hopes frustrated. Some participants in the program no doubt acquired control over additional resources (money contacts, office information, and status). This, most likely, altered their influence and status in their community.

IMPACT UPON PROGRAM

In trying to speculate about the impact of participation upon program we are again faced with the problem of an amorphous subject. We can say, however, that since participation was required, it became a matter for much debate and contention in both the Model Cities and

Community Action Programs. The debate about who should participate and when and where they should participate undoubtedly diverted energies that might have gone into other constructive activities. In addition, it created, in some places, animosities and difficulties within program staffs or decision-making bodies, or between these two groups. This in turn caused program delays, frequent shifts in policy, and consequent increased costs. In some situations limited resources were used to effectuate participation rather than to implement substantive programs. Some have suggested that the emphasis on minority group participation resulted in distrust of the programs on the part of lower-class whites, intense displeasure with the program on the part of local and national political officials, and an increase in racial polarization.

Important questions such as "what policy changes resulted from the emphasis on citizen participation in the Model Cities and Community Action Programs?" are especially difficult to answer. We lack evidence as to what policy changes resulted from the entire program, much less a specific aspect of the undertaking. It can be argued, nevertheless, that the emphasis on citizen participation did alter policy discussions in one way: it forced policy makers to deal with the problems of race. No longer could an explicit discriminatory position be taken; no longer could policy be made without considering the reactions and desires of racial minorities. There are also numerous examples available of housing projects altering their leasing and inspection policies, street repairs being made, stop lights being installed, garbage collection and street cleaning activities being increased, highways rerouted, and other alterations in services which are claimed to be the result of the emphasis on citizen participation. But the cause of such changes and their extent are impossible to document. Some studies have concluded the primary factor in bringing about policy changes and improved services was political pressure exerted through protest action. They go on to argue that a limited number of people actually engaged in and supported the protests, and that the protest leaders came from the most articulate and prosperous members of the black, poor, or minority community. Most of these activities are said to have taken place outside the Model Cities and Community Action Programs. Ralph Kramer takes this argument one step further and suggests that federal policy has been far more affected by riots than by more conventional participation of which we speak here.

An entirely different argument, which also negates the influence of citizen participation in causing program policy changes, suggests that program policy was altered primarily because new money was available for new programs which therefore had to be developed. In order to take advantage of newly available funds, program development and innovation occurred. In addition, it is argued, most institutional change resulted from negotiation and bargaining which took place in a setting where citizen participants could severely affect the compromises and agreements reached among the professionals.

Many observers claim that the emphasis on participation had a deleterious effect on planning. Citizens, not surprisingly, were not enthusiastic about planning, with its myriad possibilities for delay. What whey wanted was action, not further reviews of problems they were familiar with, promises they had heard before, and future attempts to secure the funds to respond. Many citizens believed planning to be a technique for the government and its agents to avoid clear and present problems. Others have argued that planning and coordination were victimized by the inordinate emphasis on and expenditure of resources to attain meaningful citizen participation.

In some places the claim to a right to participate did affect the program by undercutting restrictions on participation in decision making by certain groups. This was especially true where professional associations and requirements or civil service regulations effectively barred the introduction of new personnel and/or new standards of program effectiveness. Citizen participation in such instances proved to be a useful counter to exclusionary policies which limited program operation and evaluation to specific professional groups. As a result of the emphasis on participation, professionals and their programs were subjected to evaluation by new groups using different standards. The extent to which such changes occurred, and their ultimate impact on program policy and administration, is impossible to document.

Another impact of participation upon program activities occurred in the area of employment. Substantial evidence exists to support the conclusion that the employment of minority group members and the poor was significantly increased as a result of the emphasis on participation. Blacks, low-income residents, former welfare recipients were employed, many in responsible positions, in both the Model Cities and Community Action Programs. This pattern of employment, it can be argued, was the direct result of the emphasis on citizen participation. But it must also be acknowledged that the availability of positions which could be filled by minorities and others was the result of new program monies. Citizen participation did not result in the replacement of previously employed persons by minority group members or the poor. Only in areas of new employment did the emphasis on citizen participation affect employment patterns.

Two additional questions have been raised concerning the impact of citizen participation upon program: Did participation facilitate or hinder the achievement of particular goals by the program? Was a capacity for effecting institutional change developed as a result of participation? These questions are virtually impossible to answer given the difference of opinion as to what citizen participation is and what it means, and the absence of factual information.

One important development which has resulted from the emphasis on citizen participation has been the establishment of precedents for involvement of minority low-income groups in employment and program development. Moreover, regular channels of contact between government and citizens not normally consulted by government have been established. In addition, new institutions which are concerned with the needs and problems of minority groups and the poor have been established. These organizations are essential to the furtherence of the interests of these groups and to the protection of the rights and privileges to which they are entitled.

EFFECT UPON COMMUNITY

Another set of questions relates to the impact of participation upon the community. We mean by community the group from which citizens are drawn, as well as the broader political community. The questions include: Did participation develop new community leaders and/or new organizations? Was the distribution of political power affected by the emphasis on citizen participation? Did participation "radicalize" the community, unite it, or further divide it? Were the citizen leaders who emerged "representative" of their community? Did the emphasis on participation hinder or promote the use of violence as a political tactic? Did participation become symbolically important to the community?

Again we face great difficulties in attempting to answer these questions. For example, some students of citizen participation have argued that the "atmosphere and mood of the ghetto has improved" as a result of the emphasis on participation. This seems to me to be impossible to verify and very difficult to support. If the "mood of the ghetto" (whatever that may be) has improved, it is quite possible that it has occurred because of factors other than citizen participation. The existence of new programs and new jobs, the passage of the 1964 civil rights and voting acts, the increasing income levels for middle-class blacks, the hope resulting from promises to end poverty and overcome discrimination are all probably important to any explanation of an improved mood in the ghetto. But it also might be argued, as it has, that the mood of the ghetto has deteriorated as evidenced by the numerous riots in major urban areas, the increase in welfare cases and out-of-wedlock births, the escalation of crime, and the enormous increase in the use of drugs. Of course, all of this is speculation. We cannot discuss with any intelligence the impact of citizen participation on the "mood of the ghetto." And little useful speculation is possible.

What, then, can we say? It does seem possible to argue that minority groups have benefited from the emphasis on citizen participation. Considerable evidence indicates that their political role and influence has been enhanced. Minority group members have been provided access to governmental and community influentials. The act of participating has provided specific individuals with valuable political education, experience, and skills. The leadership structure of the minority community has been altered, primarily through the addition of younger and more militant spokesmen. This broadening of the leadership structure may have far-reaching consequences for the minority community which cannot be easily anticipated. Finally, minority group members have obtained some significant control over resources such as jobs, access to information and officials, access to mimeographs and other equipment providing opportunities for disseminating information, recognition, prestige, and money. All of these resources are vital to successful participation in the American political process. It is in the broadening of minority group leadership and the provision of training and resources for political action that the emphasis on citizen participation may have had its most important impact.

Certainly participation has had important symbolic meaning to minority group communities as well. In part, citizen participation has symbolized concern with minority rights, political influence for blacks and other groups alienated from the political system, and the problems of the poor. If you were "for" citizen participation you were "for blacks, Chicanos, Indians, and poor whites." To be opposed to citizen participation symbolized to many opposition to these same groups. It also symbolized an unwillingness to initiate or support significant change in governmental programs or policies. Of course the fact that citizen participation symbolized these beliefs does not mean that its supporters or opponents actually held the beliefs credited by the symbolic meaning. But people were classified into supporting or opposing camps on the basis of their attitudes toward the key symbol of citizen participation.

In terms of the impact on local government and other political institutions, two things can be said. First, emphasis on citizen participation (but *not* participation in the sense of control) has spread beyond the boundaries of the Model Cities and Community Action Programs. Colleges, health departments, YMCA's, United Funds, welfare boards, hospitals, have all been subjected to increased pressure to open up their staffs, boards, and services to those previously excluded, especially members of ethnic minorities. The extent to which these changes have occurred is not precisely measureable, but they have been widespread. And these changes have been the direct result, I would agree, of the legitimacy and attention given to the concept of and need for citizen participation and the general civil rights movement.

In other areas citizen participation has had minimal effect on local government. It has, no doubt, scared a number of sitting politicians, but few have lost their jobs because of the emphasis on citizen participation in Model Cities and Community Action Programs. Many mayors have lost a lot of sleep because of citizen participation, but few have lost significant political power. It is my belief that citizen participation was seen to be much more of a threat to local government than it actually has been. And much of the impact that it has had is because its impact was misperceived. No local government or "power structure" has fallen, or has even been seriously altered by the advent of citizen participation. In some cases the number of groups participating in the pluralistic contest for power and influence has been expanded, but no radical changes in the distribution of influence, power, services, rewards, or other benefits has occurred. To the extent that jobs, services, and other political outputs have been redistributed, middle-income interests have prevailed over low-income interests, and ethnicity has prevailed over poverty.

A PERSONAL STATEMENT

Much has been said and written about citizen participation. What does it all mean? Where do we go from here? Even though we hardly know the subject we are talking about, I nevertheless believe that there are some important conclusions to be reached as a result of an intensive look at citizen participation as practiced in the Model Cities and Community Action Programs.

Even though we concentrate our attention upon citizen participation, citizen participation was not the basic objective of either the

Model Cities or Community Action Program. Neither was established for the purpose of encouraging citizen participation. More sweeping goals were proclaimed, and probably, as is the nature of our society, expected. OEO, through its Community Action efforts, sought to abolish poverty in this country. HUD, through its Model Cities efforts, sought to demonstrate how the "quality of urban life" in all its aspects could be radically improved. I have no doubt that these goals were really the goals of both these agencies. I agree with the goals wholeheartedly. It is evident, however, and has been evident from the beginning, that neither of these agencies, no matter how hard they tried, no matter how much luck they had, no matter their political fortunes, no matter how creative their programming, would achieve or even approach its goals. The grandiose objectives of both projects were doomed from the start. The resources were just not made available to do the job. Some argue the funds were "diverted" to Vietnam, others argue they were lost due to "white backlash," excessive attention to problems of black poor, or inattention to political fence-mending. I disagree. It is my contention that this country and its leaders, despite the creation of these two programs with their lofty goals, never intended to accomplish the objectives set forth. Begin, yes. Attain them, no. We did not make the commitment then, and we have not since, to spend the money, redistribute political and economic power, and delay other "national priorities" which would result in the abolition of poverty in the United States and the radical improvement of the quality of urban life.

It is difficult to know the extent to which it became evident within the OEO and Model Cities Programs that their ultimate objectives would not and could not be attained. To a certain extent this did happen, however, and when it did, citizen participation became the primary objective to be attained. But even the attempts at the federal end to attain extensive and effective citizen participation "were erratic, piecemeal, misunderstood and possibly not really cared about."[6] But even in those cases where citizen participation was unreservedly accepted as the objective, it was insufficient as a substitute. It is not surprising that citizen participation replaced the more ephemeral goals of abolishing poverty and improving urban life. Citizen participation can be achieved, can be measured, and it is believed to be linked to the more unattainable goals noted. But to speak of citizen participation as an adequate replacement for, or even the only effective means of attaining quality and a radical improvement in the quality of our urban life is to delude ourselves.

Numerous students of the Model Cities and Community Action

Programs have reached this conclusion. The original and ultimate goals of the Community Action and Model Cities Programs will not be attained, without regard to citizen participation, unless the necessary fiscal resources are made available. Frances Piven notes that "sustained and effective participation" ultimately depends upon the "allocation to these communities of the social and economic benefits that are the resources for participation and influence in a complex society."[7] Ralph Kramer suggests that, "The community development process is no substitute for that massive commitment of national resources required to eliminate poverty by rebuilding the ghetto and restoring full citizenship to minorities."[8] Melvin Mogulof queries, "Can the most aggressive Federal policy towards citizen involvement be any substitute for a national policy failure to deliver adequate and appropriate resources to poor/black/brown people?"[9]

It is both irresponsible and incorrect to judge citizen participation by the extent to which poverty was abolished or life was made tolerable or even pleasant. Citizen participation is not an adequate technique for attaining these two goals of the OEO and Model Cities. The failure to attain these goals is the result of an insufficient commitment to the attainment of them. It is not a failure of citizen participation.

But what of citizen participation as a means of achieving some improvement in the quality of life and some lessening of poverty? Admittedly participation cannot achieve grand solutions to major problems in the face of the general indifference or opposition of society. But can it not play a role in the alleviation of poverty and the improvement of life? There are two answers to this question. The first is what I shall call the Moynihan position. It contends that participation in the political process (and that is what we are really talking about) by blacks and other minorities is not necessary for the attainment of economic, political, educational, and cultural benefits. Well-educated, compassionate liberals (or conservative Republicans who support a family assistance program in order to end "welfare") can achieve those ends, Moynihan argues, without being pressured into doing so. Admittedly the opportunities are not often present to accomplish such dramatic gains. But Moynihan contends that such an opportunity did exist shortly after the assassination of President Kennedy. He extends his argument beyond the contention that participation by a group is unnecessary to attain benefits for that group in two ways. First, he says we became confused about what our real objective was—participation or economic opportunity—and were diverted from passing the legislation and developing the programs (minimum family income, for example) that would abolish poverty. Second, he contends that the participation in the political process by blacks and other minorities, supported by federal funds, created political opposition which made it more difficult, rather than less, to achieve the desired results. Not only was citizen participation unnecessary and costly because it diverted our attention, Moynihan contends that it was positively costly.

The opposing position, and the one to which I adhere, is that no group ever gets significant benefits from the American political process unless it participates in that process and competes effectively for a limited supply of rewards and benefits. In other words, it will not do for the poor, the black, the brown, or the Indian to depend on the good will or the general liberal attitudes of the society and the political system. Acting alone or in concert, these groups must compete with others for the rewards of politics.

Which argument is correct? Is Moynihan right or am I? This is not the place to decide that question. I would suggest, however, that a careful reading of American history would clearly demonstrate that Moynihan is wrong. Good will has brought few radical social changes to this country. Such a reading might indicate that I, too, am wrong, or at least lead to a prediction that there is no combination of events that can reasonably be expected to occur which will lead to an abolition of poverty; or that, if such events occur, they will be the result of accidental or unplanned factors (technological development, for example). There is considerable evidence, however, to support my argument.

We have talked of the mistaken belief that participation was *the* objective of Model Cities and Community Action and of the debate concerning its usefulness as a means. But what about participation as *an* objective, one of many goals sought through these two federal programs? Mel Mogulof, among others, says,

> It is not that citizen participation helps us to get any place faster; although it may in fact do all the good things that have been claimed for it (e.g., decrease alienation, create a program constituency, calm would-be rioters, etc.). Rather we base the case for a broadly conceived Federal citizen participation policy on the argument that participation represents an unfulfilled goal in and of itself. It fits us well as a society. It is what the American experiment is about. And perhaps in the process of giving aggrieved groups influence over their resources and communal decision *because it is right* we will increase the life chances for all of us.[10]

I would support this position. What we are talking about is including blacks, the poor, and other minorities in the political process, rather than excluding them as in the past. There are all sorts of possibilities to achieve this. National voting registration standards, legal suits, revision of civil service requirements, mandatory representation in governmental bodies to qualify for aid, new states (New York City, Cleveland, Newark, or other areas with a good chance of electing minority senators, representatives, and other officials), massive training or minority groups in the law, federal "participation" standards along the lines of those developed in OEO and Model Cities—all are possible ways of expanding the role of blacks and other groups in the political process. But even if we accomplish these goals, it will be both not enough, and undesirable under certain conditions. Not enough because the ultimate objective, for me at least, must be the attainment of equality, not just effective participation. The ultimate goals must be the abolition of poverty and the creation of society which guarantees human dignity. Participation can only be *an* end, not *the* end. Moreover, participation in some cases may not be desirable. It may depend on the circumstances. Lewis Lipsitz has noted:

> To make judgments about the issues involved in matters of decentralization and participation, we have to know more about the polity we're talking about, and about the nature of the times. For example, if we knew that corporate economic power is abusive and cannot be controlled locally, we might opt for national regulation. . . . If we knew that libertarian principle were widespread, but opposed by elites, we might favor greater local law-making powers. If we knew that foreign policy commitments of a dubious sort were over-extending a society and leading to neglect of domestic needs, we might favor whatever measures were needed, central and/or local, to alter these priorities. If we knew that large numbers of people felt powerless and frustrated in their attempts to get government to respond to them, we might, if we were prudent, try to open more avenues for influence, and give such groups more power. In all such cases, various mixes of central-local initiative might be worked out, *depending on the circumstances.* . . . [Moreover] some policies must be immune from local decision-making, such as the notion of equal treatment itself.[11]

It seems to me that the confusion of whether participation is an end or means to an end has abounded in both the Model Cities Program and the Community Action Program. Too often participation has been overtly proclaimed as an end (or the end) while covertly it was seen as a means to other ends. The necessity, for political reasons, to be clandestine about participation as a means to other ends has led, I would argue, to confusion about whether it is a means or an end. We need therefore to recognize it as both. But we need to separate the two. It is an end because all people should have the right to participate at some stage in political decisions which affect their lives. Participating also benefits society, I would argue, by increasing stability, providing for new ideas and concerns, decreasing dissatisfaction with government. But participation is also a means to other objectives. Those objectives must be retained and must not be substituted for by participation. In addition we must understand what other actions will be necessary to attain those objectives. And we must expect opposition to participation *because it is an effective means (or is believed to be) of redistributing economic, social, and political power* Such a redistribution is not universally desired, or even widely desired, in this country today.

ENDNOTES

1. Stanley Elkins and Eric McKitrick, "A Meaning for Turner's Frontier," *Political Science Quarterly* (September-December 1954).
2. Robert C. Wood, *Suburbia* (Boston: Houghton-Mifflin, 1958), p. 197.
3. Adam Yarmolinsky, "The Beginnings of OEO," in James L. Sundquist (ed.), *On Fighting Poverty* (New York: Basic Books, 1969), fn. 2, p. 51.
4. Sar A. Levitan, *The Design of Federal Antipoverty Strategy* (Michigan: University of Michigan and Wayne State University, Institute of Labor and Industrial Relations, 1967), pp. 37–38.
5. Melvin B. Mogulof, *Citizen Participation: A Review and Commentary on Federal Policies and Practices* (Washington, D.C.: The Urban Institute, 1970), mimeo., Part I, p. 80.
6. *Ibid.*, Part II, p. 181.
7. Frances Fox Piven, "Participation of Residents in Neighborhood Community Action Programs," *Social Work*, Vol. 12, No. 1 (January 1966).
8. Ralph Kramer, *Participation of the Poor* (Englewood Cliffs, N.J.: Prentice-Hall, 1969), p. 273.
9. Mogulof, *op. cit.*, Part I, p. 93.
10. *Ibid.*, Part II, pp. 172–173.
11. Lewis Lipsitz, in H. George Frederickson (ed.) *Politics, Public Administration and Neighborhood Control* (San Francisco: Chandler, 1972).

33

gary english

THE TROUBLE WITH COMMUNITY
ACTION . . .

Community action programs all over the country are in trouble, but
then they always have been. The question as to whether the difficulties are the pimpled promise of adolescence or the rare rattle of a
dying federal program will soon be answered. Certainly by 1975,
when Richard Nixon will have been reelected or replaced, community action will be a mature, accepted part of the solution to poverty
or a memorable caveat. Community action programs (CAPs) operate
in a maelstrom of their own making as they attempt to bring together
the poor, the nonpoor, the black, the white, the private, the public,
the charitable, the funded, the local, the do-gooders, the carpetbaggers, the hostile, the selfish, the altruistic, the practical, the philosophic, the complex and technical, the uneducated and unsophisticated, the old, the young, the bold, the cautious, in a word, most of
the contentious forces in America today, into one problem-solving
instrumentality.

Yet, it is, paradoxically, this bringing together of the various
parts of American society in common cause that is the CAP's greatest
virtue and promise. It is this volatile mixture that contains DNA of
America's continuing evolution toward social progress and democracy. CAP is part, perhaps the best part, of the new American social
morality: the exchanging of the alms bowl for the bootstrap.

Like all social experiments, community action is fraught with
anxiety and stress, uncertain steps, hazy goals, and social friction.

Reprinted with permission from the *Public Administration Review*, journal of the American Society for Public Administration, Vol. 32, No. 3 (May-
June, 1972). Copyright © 1972 by the American Society for Public Administration.

Like all social innovation, community action draws tight the fabric of society and allows a glimpse of the patterns of strength, weakness, and superficial adornment that may otherwise be neglected or obscured. Social change, then, provided not only a means for the achievement of social goals, but an opportunity for observation of ourselves as social beings. And, if the developments are rapid enough to meet expectations and deliberate enough to keep the peace, society will not only be wiser, but stronger.

The exigencies of the community action result from two basic features of the program: the nature of the tree and the nature of the soil. In less poetic terms, the problems stem from the structure of the programmatic instrumentalities and the social and political factors of the operational environment.

A fundamental feature of the social context is the timocratic nature of man. People have always admired merit, and for Americans, indeed for western civilization, the criteria for merit have been largely material. It is a natural branch of the deeply rooted American legacy that the poor are held largely in contempt for lacking "what it takes," whether that be virtue or basic mental and physical equipment. This coloration of Social Darwinism is not compromised, but rather reinforced by the Christian ethic of helping the poor. The virtue of charity is in the giving, not in receiving. It is a quality of mercy behooving the more fortunate, not the dessert of the poor. Indeed, the less deserving the receiver, the more charitable the giver. Thus, it is not only to the shame of the poor that they are poor, but a compounded shame to receive help.

No matter how the social scientists and do-gooders may offer that the poor suffer from the "system" or various other structural repressions, there is still considerable suspicion that the poor are not quite capable or willing to help themselves. In the general population, of course, this skepticism toward the poor is a strong conviction. Otherwise, by positing that the poor suffer their condition through no fault of their own but rather of the systems of rewards and advantages in the society, one suggests that those who have garnered these material gains for themselves—from their own labors or those of their relatives—are not as deserving as they would like to think, and moreover, have participated in the exploitation of their fellow man. Now it can be argued that Americans have a masochistic streak and periodically indulge in an orgy of self-incrimination and contrition. But rarely has this indulgence taken the form of sharing the wealth except in the most grudging way.

The fact is that Americans, like other people, are neither inclined to denigrate their perceived achievements nor to part voluntarily with the profits thereof, unless, to repeat, there is something in it for themselves. The rendering of charity warms the heart; acceding to demands steams the collar.

An important dimension of poverty rooted in western culture in general and American culture in particular is that of white racism. This, together with minority responses, is a problem in itself. Whereas most of the poor are white, most of the nonwhites are poor. And it is the tendency of many to view aid to the poor as aid to whatever racial minority the local white majority believes to be the most threatening or troublesome. Whatever the prejudice stereotype, it generally includes "lazy" and "shiftless" and "they like it that way," with the possible exception of Orientals on the West Coast who are obviously not lazy, but rather "sneaky" and "devious." Because of the exceptional role of the poor and black in community action, this program has often met particular hostility.

The history of past efforts in dealing with the poor has made them skeptical and distrustful of present anti-poverty programs. The poor are quite sensitive to the attitudes of the persons with whom they must deal and they fail to develop an appreciation of the host of nonprogrammatic interests that invariably fascinate or dominate bureaucrats, public officials, and CAP board members. This, together with the poor's depreciated self-image, makes it difficult to establish an effective relationship between the needy and the programs. It is fairly well established, moreover, that there is an inverse relationship between the participation and benefit of people in the poverty programs and their need. There is haunting the poor a Spirit of Christmas Past which has given them mostly unfulfilled promises while academics, bureaucrats, and opportunists have enjoyed a windfall.

THE CAP BOARD

The governing body of a community action agency is the board of directors. Initially, this board was often comprised chiefly of the poor, and the results were often tragic for the poor people who, ill-prepared to govern such programs and allocate money by themselves, fell prey to carpetbaggers and mismanagement. In 1967 Congress passed the Green Amendment to the basic enabling legislation of community action, the Equal Opportunity Act of 1964, which provided, among other things, for a distribution of board membership of at least one-third low income, one-third public sector (appointed by the chief elected official in the political area), and the remainder from religious, industrial, educational, labor, and other such organizations in the private sector. But the private sector, although the smallest, is the primary source for Community Action Programs leadership. To chair a CAP board, for example, requires considerable time, personal financial resources, office services, and conversance with the operation of his CAP and the pecularities of the area of operation. The chairman, moreover, should have no demanding special interests. Since the poor rarely have the resources and the public officials the freedom from special interests, the leadership must come from the private sector which, being the smallest sector, may have few candidates. A CAP board chairman is an officer whose importance, in terms of program success, is equal to that of the executive director, the top paid community action agency (CAA) staff member. In addition to these requirements, the chairman needs considerable leadership qualities if he is to organize a board in accordance with the complexities of OEO guidelines and to move an uneasy combination of people along a constructive path. He must, moreover, do all this without benefit of any real sanctions.

CAP boards, rather than being bombarded with people interested in serving, often find membership recruitment difficult and suffer a significant attrition rate over the term period of one year. For one reason, a number of those who join the board seeking personal gain find that it is against the law for a board member or his immediate family to gain materially from board actions and therefore lose interest. Others, particularly those seeking jobs with the CAP staff, either are successful and must resign, or see that they have no chance and leave also. Many potentially good board members, such as medical people who would be quite valuable in areas of health services, are prevented from serving because of federal laws regarding conflicts of interest. A number of members who were the unenthusiastic appointments from the public sector simply do not come. Some members leave the geographic area, some quit in protest, some find other matters more pressing. For a host of reasons the attrition rate is high.

Serving on a CAP board is, after all, a voluntary thing. And, like all voluntary involvement, it suffers when the volunteers lose interest. There are in fact few creditable satisfactions to be gained serving on a CAP board. There seems to be little prestige derived from such membership and little opportunity to satisfy a constructive sense of power. The operations of the staff are often mysterious to board members, and the wishes of the board members must be channeled through the board, its leadership, and the staff hierarchy. All of this serves to chip away at the sense of direct involvement. The feeling of participating in a beneficial effort is often dissipated by the storm of complaints and criticisms often associated with community action programs. The constituencies, the staff, the governmental bureaucracies, and even board members always seem to find something about board decisions that they do not like.

Community action, like all organized efforts of any scale, must turn good intentions into effective technique. The relationship between the two is often obscured or hard to appreciate, especially when it is the techniques that continually confront the board members with problems about which they must make decisions. Problems of staffing, auditing, allocation of funds, critical public opinion, political in-fighting, and bureaucratic red tape constantly harass CAP boards. The CAPs themselves, particularly in the area of advocacy for the poor and legal aid services, often put board members, especially public officials but private sector, too, in the position of being the target of their CAP's actions. Although the turning aside of just that kind of thrust by the CAPs is the motivation of many members, they are not always successful. Such members can, however, bring the fight into the board, greatly adding to the confusion, heat, and stress of board participation.

For all this, board members must pay. There is absolutely no remuneration for board members, regardless of the time and effort they devote to the program—which may be considerable and crucial. (Guidelines provide that low-income members shall receive stipends, but CAPs have been prevented from doing this by OEO.) In the rural CAPs, a board member may travel an hour each way to attend a three-hour meeting, necessitating a meal out, a baby sitter, and other accompanying expenses. A board member is reimbursed for mileage, but except for those qualified as low-income, nothing else. For the average person, the responsibility, the work, the stress, the absence of dynamic results, topped by the financial outlay, takes a near debilitating toll in board membership and participation. As a result, it is proportionally harder to get and keep good board members than staff, especially good leadership.

When the operational area of a CAA is the same as a political entity, the chances of the agency's avoiding the power struggle for political control of the area are almost nil. On the other hand, when CAPs operate across political bounds, they pull to their bosoms many of the political contentions of the larger area. Vertically, and oftentimes among units of the same level, politics has a strong partisan coloration. The chances are quite good that between the pertinent precincts, cities, counties, states, and federal government (including representatives, senators, and presidential administration) there will be differences of partisan affiliation. Hence, CAPs are bound to get caught in struggles for city halls, courthouses, capitols, and federal offices. At each level there is considerable clout in the hands of incumbents—fiscal court letters of designation, and state and federal funding and administrative control. The states find that they must dance to the federal tune and the federal agencies find that the states' step do not fit the music. The bureaucracies receive frequent correspondence from members of Congress who, in response to constituents' letters, wonder what is going on—a perturbation often shared by the OEO bureaus who are supposed to know. The states find themselves opposed on various CAP matters because of partisanship differences, as a part of some programmatic disagreement, or because the CAPs have generated complaints which have found their way to the governors. Cities and precincts vie with one another for growth and development. Rural counties view each other with suspicion born of xenophobia. In the cities, the wards and neighborhoods act similarly to the various rural villages and Appalachian hollows in that their needs are immediate and demanding, for it is in these most local of entities that poverty lives.

At the most local levels, such as precincts, towns, and counties, the pressures of political potentates and hopefuls may not threaten with the same intimidation as the state and federal offices, but is more prevalent and incessant, and more likely to be built into the membership of board and staff either directly or through relatives or friends. Local officials find the problems of the CAPs less of a moral challenge than as a potential threat to their good standing with the electorate and, hence, a needless adventure. Indeed, the motivation of most local officials who participate on CAP boards is less to generate creative solutions than to keep a watchful eye on possible opposing partisan activity and "hanky-panky" by the inevitable demagogues and staff members.

STAFFING

While one may argue quite convincingly that is harder to get and keep good board members than good staff, it is still difficult to recruit and maintain good staff. One reason is that only a small portion of the steadily dwindling CAP funds may be used for staff, resulting in low salaries at a time when salaries are continually rising and good jobs have been easy to find. And, while most of the field staff of a CAP are recruited from low-income people, the central and professional staff, from the executive director down to the bookkeeper, must be of above average ability and training to have a good program. Community action programs require good administration because of their complexity and open-endedness. Equally necessary is a good political sense because of the contentious nature of community action and the environment in which it takes place. It is, as most everyone knows, difficult to find people who are good at either, much less both, and those who have these abilities find their services in high demand where the pressures are less and the financial rewards higher. The pool of good talent, so evident in the late 1960's, has been substantially depleted, although the current state of the economy may help somewhat.

It is doubtful, however, that salary levels have been the greatest hindrance to finding good staff. Probably a more significant factor has been the notorious insecurity of CAP positions, especially that of executive director. While there seems to be little in the way of hard data available, it would not be surprising to find that the average tenure of CAP directors is less than a year. The central focus of CAP activities is the director, assuming something approximating an adequate board, and it is upon his shoulders that the problems of the CAPs fall. The CAP director suffers from the lack of good available staff in an immediate and direct way: it affects his ability to carry out his functions. The political forces (used here in the general sense) find themselves either supporting or attacking the director's actions, with the latter often far outweighing the former. It is the CAP director who must tell government agencies that they have not been serving the poor, that is, doing their job. It is the director who is the central figure in achieving civil rights compliance with the banks, stores, and other local vendors with whom CAPs must deal and who, according to federal guidelines, must inform the board that certain actions they wish to take are illegal, unwise, or unfeasible. It is the CAP director who must force into federal compliance school boards (for Head Start) and other delegated agencies which are usually important political forces in their own right.

The CAP director must keep a board happy where the poor feel that he is moving too slowly and doing too little, the public sector that he is doing too much too fast, and the private groups who agree with both the poor and public sectors. All sectors seem convinced that the staff is incompetent, dishonest, or unfair, often with some justification. The CAP director's chair is kept very warm by the host of hands ready to yank it out from under him.

The removal of a CAP director hardly ameliorates a CAP's basic problematic inertia. The board views the new man with a hypercriticism that borders on hysteria, and his initial experience is less like that of a honeymooner than a lion tamer. While ineptitude has been the cause of many a director's downfall, the untenability of the position by anyone in a given CAP has frequently been the cause. As often as not, the removal of a CAP director is associated with the agency's being in a state of funding jeopardy. This means that the new director has not only the challenges of an ongoing program, but also the convoluted and entrenched problems that have led to the contemporary crisis. As for the former director, he will more than likely, because of disenchantment or a lack of good references, go into some other line of work.

CONFLICT

Government agencies, no matter how cordial their relations seem, are forever competitors. And the more related their fields, the keener the competition. This is true whether the agencies are quasi-government, that is, federally funded and supervised, such as community action agencies, or official arms of the government. The immediate prizes at stake may be status, personnel, clientele, or, more likely, funds. Yet, if interbureau competition is viewed in such simple, crass terms, a fundamental feature is missed: bureaus are more than programmatic instrumentalities; they are manifestations of policy, statements by society about what its values are and what it wants to do about them. Whenever such statements are in conflict, and they often are, then the agencies are also—fundamentally and fiercely.

Community action agencies, having fixed geographic bounds, are rarely in conflict with one another. They do, however, often find themselves bumping into welfare and other private and governmental social service agencies. The political contradictions that have been structured into CAP operations have been discussed above; the conflict among agencies is a part of this, too, but with certain aspects that call for a new category. Government agencies are political creatures whose umbilical cords are critically linked with Washington and/or the state houses, courthouses, or city halls. If an agency generates antagonisms at its political home base, unpleasant results may occur. Welfare agencies in particular may see themselves as unsung and poorly supported social heroes, but as they curse the dark, they also avoid the light in fear of heat it may bring.

CAPs, by their very nature, bring both light and heat. Because of their advocacy role or their poor reputations (whether putative or deserved), CAPs often find welfare agencies less than eager to cooperate. A given agency may be enjoying avoidance of civil rights compliance, an acquiescent clientele, the forbearance or support of politicos, and so forth. Community action, a significant social statement of the inadequacy of welfare agencies' effectiveness, may and should threaten all of this.

Agencies have definitions of problems and cherished ways of doing things that are jealously guarded. Each agency, moreover, has a vital link with various professional guilds, school systems for example, which strongly support the established bureaucratic values and procedures. Community action by activating the agency's clientele, often leads to an indictment of social, bureaucratic, and professional values. This is not to say that welfare agencies do not cooperate with community action agencies at all, but only that there are strong factors which have militated against the effective coordination of the CAP and other agency efforts.

Local church groups, and other private organizations who delve or dabble in social service, are also reluctant to link arms with community action agencies. Churchgoers in general tend to be the most conservative sector of society. A person who puts up with the unpleasantries of working in community action tends to have or develop attitudes somewhat different from those approved for the Methodist Youth Fellowship by the church leaders (read: local heavyweights). To give a dirty, smelly, and unlettered poor person a used suit of clothes or lecture on propriety is one thing; to sit down with a group of them as equals in a crowded room is quite another.

If a community action agency is able to avoid being caught playing politics, then it will hear little from the state office, the latter being satisfied merely to collect its own federal share and keep a partisan vigilance on the local CAPs. When a CAP reaches a state of crisis, however, and generally not before, the state agencies may step in to save it. Since the state government's own federal share is calculated on the number of CAPs within its domain, the states are reluctant to lose one. Revenue-sharing, of course, will eliminate this pressure for state protection.

An ominous sign for community action is the current effort by the Nixon Administration to turn block funds over to the states. The idea of such "revenue-sharing" is that the more local units will know better their own situations. As any astute observer of politics knows, the more local the politics, the less funds can be administered in a nonpolitical way. If the states can develop their economic opportunity offices into functional, constructive CAP support, then the program will be improved. If, on the other hand, the states deliver more of the same or even less, then community action will only receive more bleeding of its funds and more visits from state office people seeking to increase their travel reimbursement. There is, moreover, a real possibility that the states will exhibit outright hostility toward CAPs.

PAPER JUNGLE

The relationship between the CAPs and the Federal Regional Offices, on the other hand, is vastly different. It is to the Federal Regional Office that the CAPs must answer and from which they receive a blizzard of forms, regulations, guidelines, etc. In a very real and direct way the state of community action is a function of the federal OEO bureaucracy. This is good because without such federal support, community action would doubtlessly not exist at all; it is not so good because the federal bureaucracy has not done very well, for the rationality of forms and paperflow is rapidly replacing that of programmatic need and impact at the CAP level.

The labyrinthine jungle of "do's" and "don'ts" continually convoluted with eclectic additions by the Congress, Administration, regional offices, and individual bureaucrats confounds even the keenest of administrative minds. This jungle is a world of paper—forms, reports, and correspondence. And, while the pejorative "bureaucrat" finds comfort in the insularity and tangibility of shuffling papers, the more idealistic bureaucrat finds himself nonetheless in the morass. Unless a major overhaul is effected, the situation promises to get worse.

Regional OEO operations find themselves as canals for the ebb and flow of the paper tide between the local CAPs, their own auditing and evaluation staffs, and Washington. For the bureaucrats, there is little time and opportunity to do anything else. In fact, it is more than the operations staff can do just to keep the paper moving on schedule. This, of course, precludes any real help by the regional offices for the CAPs, and serves to exacerbate the problems of the CAPs, since without help they more easily drift into difficulty. The regional offices expend their nonpaperwork time and energy "putting out fires," which usually have developed from neglect when small problems are not addressed, and allowed to grow. The problem feeds upon itself.

The frequency of crisis (when asked how many of his CAPs were in trouble, one regional field representative replied: "All of them") means that the unending stream of normal paperwork begins to pile up. The results are the complication and aggravation of an already bad situation. A regional officer hand-delivered a letter to a board chairman in Atlanta, for example, and the chairman was back in Kentucky a full month before the carbons arrived. Contracts and money-transfer requests may sit in the regional office for months while the CAPs get wild-eyed with frustration. Separated by time, experience, and interest from the problems and dynamics of community action, federal bureaucrats peer anxiously down the narrow corridors of their paper worlds. Spellbound by the logic of their own procedures, the bureaucrats inflict their paper world upon the CAPs. Often this is done whimsically and rarely, if ever, with any input from the CAPs which do not seem to "understand" regional needs. More and more, the CAP staffs are pulled away from their programs to the ever-growing paper web of the regional bureaucracies, thereby making success in an already difficult job nearly impossible. The point here is not to belabor the regional offices, but to suggest that their support of the CAPs is not adequate to the need.

ADDRESSING PROBLEM AREAS

Many of the problems in community action are not susceptible to direct remedy; for example, the general attitudes of society and the poor, and the conflict that arises when the bounds of political territories are crossed. These will hopefully abate as the CAPs prove themselves strong, effective, and successful.

This can be done by immediately addressing on a broad front several specific problem areas. The power to cure lies in the hands of the federal government. First, the Congress needs to decide on whether it wants community action or not, and, if so, to support it with adequate funds. One of the problems with maintaining programs and good personnel has been the fluctuating appropriations. Most CAPs are operating programs that barely touch the vast need, especially in Appalachia with its poverty saturation. By funding these programs under a "continuing resolution" where no new monies are allowed, the effect is a reduction in funds. Given the state of community action agencies, however, increased funding should be allocated very carefully and in conjunction with the development of real and effective assistance to the CAPs. Increased funding without solving certain other problems would not be wise.

This leads to the second major problem, that is, the one of federal and state agencies. First, the state agencies must be developed to the point where they are constructive factors in community action and not merely a collection of do-nothings and political watchdogs. The regional offices simply cannot provide the technical assistance and guidance for all the local CAPs. Only the states can do this. The federal government can, however, put pressure on the state offices to earn their federal share by developing a staff and operation which will lead and support the CAPs in certain specific ways; for example, in program design and evaluations, administrative procedure, personnel, and the like. The fact that states do not in general favor community action means that the federal government will need critically to link funds the states seek in other areas—such as urban renewal, education, health, and mental health grants—with community action, so that keeping out the poor will keep out the money.

A third major problem area is the current dearth of qualified personnel at all levels—federal, state and CAA. This is not to say that there are not good men in the programs now, or that altered bureaucratic and political factors would suddenly unbind a well-qualified person, for neither is true. It is to suggest, however, that those working in these programs may not be the most promising, as previous crises have taken their toll, or sufficiently prepared for their tasks. There is, granted, some training going on in the programs, but few people, except perhaps those who are awarded training contracts, argue that the training meets the needs of CAPs in substance, direction, or amount.

Needed are a number of training schools or institutes strategically located around the country for persons engaged in the poverty programs, at all levels, to be educated and trained for their responsibilities. The curriculum should include the social sciences, especially in the areas of poverty behavior and management, as well as technically specific instruction such as how to properly fill out a CAP Form 81 or how to interpret OEO Instruction 6005-1. These schools should be given the same kind of financial support as the law enforcement educational programs.

A curriculum of this sort would contribute to the community action programs in several important ways. First, the behavioral approach to the study of people in poverty would give those concerned a frame of operational reference other than that of administrative technique, ideological name-calling, or mere do-goodism. Thus, the poor would be plugged into the program as human beings rather than as subjects or abstractions. Second, by maximizing the exposure of operatives to the same kind and quality of management theory and practice that big business enjoys, although adapted for the peculiar·ities of anti-poverty efforts, the generally muddled state of adminis-tration that exists throughout would have a better chance of being improved. Third, the technically specific curriculum would amelio-rate the "diversity of interpretation" problem that is so prevalent with guidelines and regulations and that needlessly consumes enor-mous amounts of man-hours. Indeed, it can justifiably be said that the bulk of anti-poverty effort is spent in the attempt to determine proper interpretations of the rules and in properly filling and filing the myr-iad of forms involved.

Finally, the curriculum should provide the federal, state and CAP people an opportunity simply to meet and discuss common problems and expectations, to reap insights and pet peeves, and, gen-erally, to appreciate more the nature of the other parties in the enter-prise. Currently each level of operation believes that it understands the other, but these tend to be less true understandings than highly negative stereotypes. There needs to be, therefore, an opportunity and common ground for reassessing mutual relationships.

A related effort that should be pursued jointly by the various levels is a talent bank of professional staff. Granted, the inflated fed-eral salaries would tend to preclude anyone's leaving that service to join a state or CAP staff. Transfers of personnel in all other directions, however, are quite feasible and highly desirable. It would be good, for example, for a capable staff person to join the state office and vice versa, because he would bring with him certain knowledge and in-sights not otherwise available. The talent bank would be a clearing-house for available personnel of desired quality and could be linked with the educational program to help assure the maintenance of cer-tain minimum standards.

To repeat, it is extremely hard for the CAP agencies to get good staff and almost impossible to get their more promising staff improved through training. And, while they will not admit it, this is also largely true of the federal and state agencies. Almost any effort in staff edu-cation, training, and recruiting that is reasonably on target and com-prehensive will be an improvement. Until such steps are taken on a systematic and all-inclusive basis, however, staffing problems will continue to be a major weakness in the war on poverty.

Improving staff qualifications and operations is only half of the built-in inadequacies of CAPs. What must be improved also are the governing boards. A better staff will, of course, improve board opera-tion, but the major problem with the boards will continue to be incentives for board members to maintain their involvement in the face of staffing, programmatic, political, and bureaucratic discouragement. First, all board members should be offered a stipend of, say, $25.00 a month, for two business meetings. For a 30-member board, this would amount to only $9,000 a program year, which would be negligible for a CAP with a total grant of, say, $500,000. Another inducement would be to pay for the meals necessitated by CAP business for all board members, not just those of low-income.

A meal on the house, any more than a small monthly stipend, would not really pay a board member for his time. But it would ease the discomfort of missing a favorite television show or an evening with the family. It would also give a nominal, but tangible, sign of appreciation for services rendered. Grant funds should allow for certain other niceties, such as certificates of appreciation for outstanding or retiring members, an annual banquet, or a personalized gavel for the board chairman. These items may seem trivial, but they may provide the symbols or guideposts of meaningful participation and achievement which are so elusive to board members and so telling in board operations.

Community action is a grand idea and one of the most noble of this nation's experiments. It is an encouraging part of the continuing American revolution in the best sense of that term. Equal opportunity, helping people help themselves—that is the American way. Successful participation of the poor in their own improvement will not only help the poor themselves, but help the nation as a whole by decreasing the social burden and improving the prevailing attitudes toward the less fortunate.

Community action agencies are delicate plants indeed, struggling desperately to survive and bear fruit in a difficult social and political environment. Yet, by giving the poor the opportunity to gain some control over their own destinies, community action offers the best, if not only, promise for breaking down the debilitating "psychology of poverty" which seems to afflict the poor. Thus, community action must and can be improved.

The record of community action to date, however, is a serious indictment of America's reputed "know-how." The experiment has reached a point where reappraisal, not discouragement or discontinuance, is in order. The problems of the CAPs are now somewhat obvious and specific, as are the remedies. The Congress and the Administration must act, and, trite but true, the time for action is now.

34

richard l. chapman
frederic n. cleaveland

THE CHANGING CHARACTER OF THE PUBLIC SERVICE AND THE ADMINISTRATOR OF THE 1980's

In 1971 the National Academy of Public Administration conducted a Delphi exercise on developments affecting the public service, 1971–1980. It was sponsored by a Ford Foundation grant, and its purpose was to bring together the collective views of a group (approximately 100) of well-informed leaders in public affairs regarding the changing character of the public service in the United States over the next decade. The results were expected to be helpful to both practitioners and educators, and to constitute an important element in the Academy's study of programs to prepare people for careers in public administration.[1]

The discussion which follows is based upon an analysis of the results of the Academy's Delphi exercise, conducted in three rounds from September to December 1971. Frederic N. Cleaveland directed the study and conducted the analysis jointly with Richard L. Chapman.

FORCES OF CHANGE AFFECTING THE PUBLIC SERVICE

Four major trends are seen as challenges to the public service today, and as important determinants of the public service in the next dec-

Reprinted with permission from the *Public Administration Review,* journal of the American Society for Public Administration, Vol. 33, No. 4 (July–August, 1973). Copyright © 1973 bv the American Society for Public Administration.

ade: (1) pressures for centralization *and* for decentralization; (2) unionization of the public service; (3) increased citizen involvement; and (4) the impact of technological change.

Pressures for Centralization and Decentralization

The pressure for greater centralization is fueled by the demands for national solutions to complex public problems, for national policy determination built upon uniform standards, and the demand for effective control. Widespread citizen interest in such issues as consumer rights, environmental protection and improvement, economic well-being, and access to medical care will strengthen the trend to seek national, centralized solutions. The pace of citizen intervention in public decision making, especially in local government, adds to pressures for centralization in those policy areas where intractable local conflicts seem to require transfer of the locus of decision to a more distant regional, state, or national level if a decision—any decision—is to become politically feasible.

The thrust of technology and the kinds of changes in government induced by technological development also strengthen centralizing forces. As effective performance in managerial and decision-making roles calls for greater scientific and technical competence and for adopting a systems perspective, the responsibility and authority for design and performance of public programs tend to move to higher levels of government closer to the chief executive. The complex technology required for information and control functions and the use of temporary problem-solving groups which require sophisticated direction and coordination (and which are less accessible to local political forces) further centralization. In similar fashion, the press for greater uniformity to insure equality in the way government deals with people, the expansion of legislative oversight over administrative actions, and the tendency toward judicialization of administrative decision making as a by-product of citizen intervention all encourage centralization.

What of the countervailing trend toward decentralization, toward returning governmental functions to government which is closer to the people? These pressures toward decentralization are reinforced by a number of trends, some of which contribute to centralization as well. For example, the move toward revenue sharing to help finance state and local government operations will stimulate further decentralization. Increasing experimentation with ways to organize regionally to cope with the problems of the complex metropolitan areas and the emergence of regional political processes and regional political leadership contribute to the growing interest in decentralization.

Greater emphasis on local control is not totally incompatible with the trend toward centralization. Efforts to decentralize have been concentrated in the areas of the delivery of services and the collection and analysis of information (including citizen advice and opinion). Both forces can be accommodated by redefining the role of the higher level of government as: (1) determining broad policy, (2) defining uniform national standards and program guidelines, and (3) evaluating information generated at the level of program execution and service delivery. By contrast, the local government would be engaged directly in managing the delivery of services for a unique local area with all the principles of decentralization met by: (1) regular feedback from those receiving the service, (2) opportunity to develop appropriate neighborhood delivery units and (3) emphasis on fitting quality of service to recipient needs—recognizing the value of diversity in program, policy, and even objectives.

Unionization in the Public Service

A second major trend is the spread of employee unionism in the public sector. Within the next 10 years a large majority of clerical and blue collar employees in government probably will be members of unions, and many, if not a majority, of those in middle management will be active in labor organizations. Without question this trend will have a significant impact upon the functioning of the public service.

In some places a professional association rather than an existing trade union has organized employees within an agency and is representing them in discussions with agency management. This suggests that the character of unions and union activity within the public service is likely to vary at least as widely as it does among labor organizations in the private sector. Some unions of public servants undoubtedly will manifest the values, objectives, and patterns of behavior characteristic of militant craft-type unions seeking to limit freedom of managerial decision, control entry into the trade or profession, and press for more emphasis upon seniority and compliance with formal union rules in hiring, promotion, and dismissal. Larger, more militant employee unions will reinforce the movement toward centralization noted above. Just as organization for collective bargaining in the private sector has been a centralizing force increasing the power of top union leadership and its industrial counterpart, so union activity in the public service may lead to greater concentration of authority.

The parallel growth of unionism among government employees and citizen participation in the processes of public decision making poses a double threat to the traditional power and authority of agency managers. If employee union leaders, representatives of the clients whom the agency is intended to serve, and militant public interest groups are all pressing the administrator simultaneously for some action (or inaction), the inevitable result will be to slow down the administrative processes and to force a retreat into more formal rule making. The potential competition for employee loyalty should also be noted. Whereas the public service in the United States has prided itself on the dedication of public employees to the public interest, the prospect for the 1970s and beyond is for a public servant who must respond to pulls and tugs in at least three directions:

1. Union pressures will be directed toward serving the special needs of its members and extending its influence.

2. Professional pressure will be exerted upon the public servant to encourage that behavior which will enhance the stature of the profession and extend its control over vital work processes.

3. The agency will continue its efforts to build a loyal and dedicated work force committed to the public service ethic and to *its* view of the public interest.

Increasing Citizen Involvement

The involved citizen is the ideal of a democratic society, and, according to democratic political theory, is the *sine qua non* of a working democratic political system. Yet the thrust of citizen participation today goes will beyond the well-informed, voting citizen. Now citizens regularly are challenging government decision makers about denial of equal rights in employment, about failure to consider all environmental impacts before locating a public facility, and so on. The growth of consumer power put together through the challenges to government and to large-scale private interests by the public interest lobby, as symbolized by Ralph Nader, has added alternatives of citizen participation and built a whole range of new norms and behavior patterns into the conception of citizen activism.

The mutually reinforcing thrusts of unionism among public employees and activism among citizens who are clients of public agencies will further politicize the administrative process. Agency managers will become more vulnerable to pressures, both from outside and from within. A further judicialization of administrative processes will result since the legal process continues to offer an appropriate weapon to both disaffected agency employees and disgruntled citizens among those affected by its proposed actions. As the process of government decision making becomes further politicized and judicialized, the role of professionals in the public service will be subtly altered. Citizen activism may affect the nature of the public service both by modifying the nature of the administrative process and by altering the reward structure, making it more difficult to attract and retain competent people in the public service.

The Impact of Technological Change

The pervasive influence of past technological developments can be observed readily in the creations of new professions or career fields—for example, in the area of computer science and automatic data processing, or in the emergence of systems analysis as essential to adequate perspective. Systems analysis appears especially relevant in the public service since so many contemporary issues in American politics involve trying to understand the relationships among parts of what is assumed to be a complex, yet single entity. Technology works first on the nature of the tasks to be performed and then on the requisite training, experience, and orientation of public servants, affecting their capacity to perform these tasks. Increased emphasis will be placed upon a public manager having the capability to use the product of quantitative analysis and upon managers whose backgrounds are interdisciplinary in character.

Developing technology has reinforced trends to loosen hierarchical organizations, making them more flexible, open systems. The very structure and operating style of some agencies have proved conductive to innovation and an open, experimental approach. Working groups have been organized around clearly defined tasks but given only a temporary life, to be broken up and regrouped once the task is performed.

The effect of new technology upon the mix of, and the boundaries between, public and private sector roles in American society is another important consideration. There is ample evidence that the distinctions between private and public sector are disappearing or becoming blurred. Private corporations, both profit and not-for-profit, are engaged in performing public functions. The implications for the nature of the public service—mobility between private and public sector, and potential areas of competition—are relevant issues for exploration.

THE PUBLIC SERVICE OF THE 1980S

The foregoing trends are viewed as affecting four important components of the public service of the future: the organization of executive functions, the work force of the public service, the administrative process, and the administrator.

Organization of Executive Functions

First, one can expect flatter organizations with shorter chains of authority but a broader network for providing information and advice. More employees at all levels of government will be engaged in sophisticated data collection and analysis, program evaluation, and similar decision-supporting or participating tasks.

Second, greater use will be made of temporary groups which pull together a team of specially qualified people to do a job, and who, upon completion of the task, return to their parent organizations or become members of new temporary groups. Such assignments will stimulate creativity and provide a sense of participation and accomplishment. But such assignments also will cause anxiety about future assignments, requiring employees constantly to upgrade their knowledge and skills. Managing an organization of such teams presents challenging balancing and control problems to the agency leadership.

Third, the trends toward decentralization and wider participation make the control of public programs more difficult and more complex for top management. The agency director becomes more dependent upon a wider variety of people for information and analysis and faces more points of potential intervention by those outside of the agency (e.g., citizen activists using the courts). There is greater potential for vetoes by citizen groups—or at least delay—but project organization and more structured, rapid systems of communication promise the potential of quicker response once decision is reached. In terms of authority and control, the political executive may be the loser unless he can use citizen intervention as a lever within the bureaucracy. The power of the professional, who will have to be very knowledgeable about the system, can be enhanced considerably.

Conversely, there will also be influences at work associated with increasing politicization which can weaken the influence of professionals.

Fourth, greater attention will be given to planning. This will include long-range planning and the more systematic use of forecasting. Closer operating relationships will develop between those responsible for planning and those responsible for program execution.

Fifth, accountability will become more difficult because of the larger number of actors in the advisory-decision process (even though there may be fewer actual decision points) and because of the progressive blurring of the public and private sectors in the planning and conduct of public programs.

The Public Service Work Force

The term "work force" designates the people—generally career civilians—who constitute the public service. They include the classified civil service, wage boards, and members of special systems outside civilian classified service such as public school teachers and administrators, foreign service officers, Public Health Service physicians and nurses, and police and firemen.

An important result of trends described above will be much greater emphasis upon the development of new skills and knowledge by public employees at all levels. The need for post-entry training and a changing emphasis on the content of pre-entry education is evident. Increased participation by both citizens and the work force, more centralization in control and information but decentralization in the delivery of services, together call for administrators with considerably improved interpersonal, intergroup, and leadership skills. The increased use of systems analysis and quantitative measurement will require more employees with these skills or with the ability to use the product of such analyses. Both technical and organizational changes will place greater importance on the continuing nature of education—no longer can one complete a degree program with the comforting assumption that it will be sufficient to see one through a decade, much less a full career.

Public employees will have greater opportunity for self-expression and self-actualization with fewer restrictions in their roles as public servants. Wider participation is opening the public service to currents of opinion and ideas that used to be ignored or considered inappropriate. The public service is beginning to be more representative of the heterogeneity of American society. The use of project teams and more temporary types of organizations, and better education, broaden the opportunities for members of the work force.

There will be greater mobility in the public service, both within levels of government and between levels. More specific transferable skills and the use of temporary team groups will facilitate movement among agencies or sub-elements within agencies. The increasingly federated nature of public programs, where control and policy are centralized but services are decentralized, will require closer ties among federal, state, and local governments. In order to upgrade state and local capabilities, there will have to be more joint efforts to tap resources for education.

Employees will pay less obeisance to their agency. A better educated work force will not automatically follow agency policy if it is seen as in error, unjust, or unresponsive to the needs of the time. To the extent that "rebellion" hinges on strictly personal predispositions or on narrow, perhaps professional, self-interest, it can be seriously destructive of the public service by undermining political executives, the legislative process, and public confidence in the ability of the public service to serve the public interest. A decline in the public service ethic can be expected if classical unionization sweeps the work force or if professional and peer loyalties grow stronger than the larger sense of the public interest. Such a decline probably will carry with it a noticeable reduction in effectiveness.

Pressures toward politicizing the public service will have a direct impact on the work force. Citizen intervention in the administrative process will encourage employees to become active advocates for or against particular policies or programs. Strong unionization or professional associations may have the same effect, reducing the neutrality of the employee in the discharge of his program responsibilities. This can lead to considerable friction within an organization and to action against programs or individuals by legislators and political executives. Politicization will lead to greater conflict, more anxiety, less continuity, and less action.

The Administrative Process

Three tendencies clearly are identifiable—the first two of which are directly at odds: increasing flexibility and increasing rigidity. A number of trends reinforce increasing flexibility: (1) the increase in temporary organizations with better ability to shift resources to meet changing needs; (2) more reliance on state and local governments with greater attention to diversity; (3) greater use of private enterprise in performing public services, providing more options for the delivery of services; (4) more emphasis on a systems perspective, stimulating consideration of more options; and (5) the greater involvement of citizens and more intense focus upon local problems, promoting closer responsiveness to citizen-defined needs.

On the other hand, there are a number of developments which tend to promote rigidity more than flexibility. For example, although citizen participation (or intervention) in the administrative process can force a new look at old premises, it can also politicize the process, bring the intervention of the courts and the legislatures, and surround the process with a quasi-judicial context—ultimately more rigid and less responsive to change. Militant industrial unionism will tend to debase whatever flexibility now exists in the personnel system and erode management flexibility as well. Where employee dissent or citizen intervention reaches a pathological state, the administrative process will be forced into highly structured channels in order to act at all.

A third significant influence is that of increasing complexity in the administrative process. There will be more participants and a heavier representation of those who have played lesser roles in the past: consumers, conservationists, welfare recipients—even prison inmates—plus legislative committees and the courts. The use of sophisticated analyses in program evaluation and planning will demand systematic procedures incorporating a wider variety of skilled people. Greater attention to state and local problems, but from a national perspective and using national resources, will give an intergovernmental cast to more public programs, requiring better liaison and coordination. The blurring of the distinction between private and public enterprise, and the greater use of contractual services to perform public functions also will contribute to the complexity of the administrative process.

Four changes can be expected to have significant effects upon the future administrative processes. First, new standards for effectiveness and for accountability will be developed. "Least cost" was disposed of some time ago as the more important criterion for measuring program success. Even "most services for the money" is considered less than adequate. There is increasing concern about related or secondary impacts of services delivered and the nature of their delivery, as well as the process by which public program decisions are reached.

Second, the administrative process will be much more open— available for observation or participation by a wider variety of people, groups, and institutions. Decision points should be more easily identified. But there will be a tendency for the process to slow down as the number of observers or intervenors increases. As is the case now, it will be easier to block action than to push it through. The processes of participation and intervention will have to be structured carefully in order to preserve their purpose, yet permit timely action.

Third, where complex public issues involve many groups and strongly diverse opinion, there will be a decline in the ability of the public service to deliver. This will be the price of wider access by both citizens and the work force in the administrative process. The likely intervention of the courts will force administrators into the habit, perhaps unconsciously, of developing a record which can be used in judicial proceedings.

Fourth, there will be a significant expansion in the planning function, which will be tied more closely to, and with more emphasis upon, program evaluation and assessment, program execution, and attention to program purposes. There will be greater emphasis upon comprehensiveness, responsiveness to and integration with both the management and political considerations that are part and parcel of program operations.

THE PUBLIC ADMINISTRATOR OF THE 1980S

The cumulative effect of these trends is most important in terms of how they affect the administrator, the man who as agency head, program director, or branch chief must make organizations perform. His role has been the traditional focus of public administration. The individual administrator will face considerable change in: (1) how he leads and directs his agency; (2) how he handles relations with other organizations, other levels of government, the public, the legislature, the judiciary, and his executive superiors; (3) maintaining his own competence and some sense of direction without being submerged in change; and (4) the personal and ethical challenges to him as a professional administrator.

Coordinator and Facilitator

The administrator of the future will be more of a moral leader, broker, and coordinator than he will be an issuer of orders. Several factors will force more of a leadership and collegial role upon the administrator. Hierarchical authority already has been on the decline for several decades, as authority based upon position has become less synonymous with the requisite skills or knowledge needed for decision and leadership. Contributing further to this change will be the improved education of the work force, tied closely to increased specialization and the rise of authority based upon knowledge or skill.

Another factor facilitating this change in roles will be the increased interdependency within the administrator's organization. Increased applications of technology, greater use of temporary organizations, and more complex organizations to deal with the variety of interrelated programs combine to require an improved capability for meshing specialists in a productive fashion. The fact that specialists will be vital to the agency's operations, that employees or their organization representatives will exercise more authority within the organization, and that a wide collection of diverse people (frequently without any substantial loyalty to the agency itself) must be orchestrated in order for programs to function, all demand this change in role of the administrator.

Bargainer and Politican

The public administrator of the 1980s will be subject to vastly increased political pressures. The institutionalization of citizen intervention in the administrative process will make the administrator more visible publicly, and he will be pressed to adopt an advocacy role by citizen and political activists. In a simpler time the administrator could concern himself with accountability principally to one or two congressional committees and a few well-recognized clientele groups. In the future he is more likely to face competing groups of citizens working at cross purposes. Competing interests will stimulate increased attention from legislators and their committees, as well as from the judiciary, when competing interests seek court intervention to block or stimulate action.

Administrators in the future will work with a much greater array of organizations than has been true in the past. Increasingly, programs cut across levels of government so that an administrator must work effectively, not only with sister organizations, but with counterpart organizations at federal, state, local, or regional levels. Revenue sharing and other forces of decentralization (as well as the trends toward centralization) will tend to blur what once were considered clear lines of authority and responsibility, so that programs must be cooperative in nature—strengthening the demand for administrative roles of a bargaining and political nature.

An Agent of Change

The pace of change, the increased complexity of institutional arrangements, and the demise of traditional hierarchy will require the public administrator of the future to be adaptable, knowledgeable about changing trends and new developments, and perceptive in his judgment about which trends to exploit and which to resist or ignore. Personal and organizational relationships will be less permanent, making it necessary for administrators to adapt to constantly changing organizations and shifting personnel. The administrator will be able to reap substantial benefits, as can his subordinates, through increased mobility and the opportunity to learn new skills through new job assignments. There will be greater need for advanced planning, forecasting of trends, and evaluation of future alternatives. Both technical and social change will force the administrator constantly to upgrade his own skills, as well as to provide means for developing the skills of his staff. Education will be viewed as a continuing process involving informal, personal, and graduate refresher education as an integral part of keeping fit for the job.

Personal Challenges

Among the changes which will mold the public service are several which will challenge the public administrator personally as a professional: (1) a decline in the public service ethic, (2) erosion of loyalty to an employee's organization, and (3) greater political activism by employees, directed at policy changes. In the face of rapid change, increased complexity, and mounting pressure to produce results, these challenges weaken an administrator's ability to meet, responsibly, more substantive problems by diverting his time and attention.

As part of the Delphi exercise, participants were asked to assess changes in key attributes of the public service from 1961 to 1971. The results reflect a current pessimism about the adequacy of public institutions and public leadership to deal effectively with major problems (See Table 1). The same attitudes were revealed by the recent study *Hopes and Fears of the American People*.[2]

Of 12 attributes rated, eight were judged to have improved since 1961. When viewed as a composite, the change was positive (and statistically significant). But the four attributes rated as most important in 1961 declined:

- "honesty and impartiality in the conduct of assigned responsibilities,"

TABLE 1   Attributes of the Public Service: Their Relative
Attainment, 1961–1971

(using a 10 point scale, 0 = completely failed to attain,
10 = completely attained)

Respondents were given 12 attributes significant in judging the quality of
the public service. They were asked to select the 6 most important and to
assess where the U.S. public service was in 1971 and where it was a decade
earlier on each attribute.

		Means		
		1961	1971	Calculated t
1.	Honesty and impartiality in the conduct of assigned responsibilities.	6.70	6.60	− .59
2.	Cognizant of, and responsive to, the desires and wishes of the public.	5.22	6.19	+3.23*
3.	Encouraging organizational innovations and experimentation with new ways of conducting the public business.	4.26	4.95	+2.62*
4.	Emphasizing value and worth of individuals, both in government and outside, and need to respect dignity and worth.	5.08	6.08	+3.65*
5.	Employing a reward and incentive system that attracts the highest quality personnel and retains them for long careers.	4.97	5.81	+2.77*
6.	Public confidence in the capacity and integrity of the public service.	5.90	4.50	−5.83*
7.	Committed to merit principles in appointments and promotions throughout the system.	6.72	6.33	−1.00
8.	Maintaining strong, progressive manpower planning and career development programs.	4.37	5.59	+5.55*
9.	Responsive to changing needs and sufficiently flexible to move in new directions rapidly.	4.62	5.05	+1.65
10.	Fully responsive to political leadership established by the electorate.	6.05	6.02	− .18
11.	Able to adapt to technological change and take maximum advantage of technological innovation.	5.00	5.95	+3.65*
12.	At all administrative levels, broadly representative of the heterogeneity of American society as a whole.	3.57	4.39	+2.73*

*Calculated t is significant at the .05 level using the repeated measures formula.

	Means		
	1961	1971	Calculated t
Composite of the 12 attributes	5.18	5.53	+2.58*

- "public confidence in the capacity and integrity of the public service,"
- "committed to merit principles in appointment and promotions," and
- "fully responsive to political leadership established by the electorate."

At the very time when one can foresee the need for professional leadership in the public service, the base upon which it and a professional public service must rest appears to be weakening. The public administrator of tomorrow will be sorely tested.

The future promises to be extraordinarily challenging to those who pursue careers in the public service over the next decade. In many respects, public administrators will have to be more adaptable, knowledgeable, patient, tenacious, and perceptive than ever before. Yet they will have new tools of management, analysis, information, and control. Managing public programs will be even more demanding than it is today, but those challenges can be met if today's administrators take the lead in anticipating the future and preparing to meet it.

ENDNOTES

1. See Richard L. Chapman and Frederic N. Cleaveland, *Meeting the Needs of Tomorrow's Public Service: Guidelines for Professional Education in Public Administration* (Washington, D.C.: National Academy of Public Administration, 1973).
2. Albert H. Cantril and Charles W. Roll, Jr., *Hopes and Fears of the American People* (Washington, D.C.: Potomoc Associates, 1971).

FURTHER READINGS

ABERBACH, JOEL D. and JACK L. WALKER. "Citizen Desires, Policy Outcomes, and Community Control." *Urban Affairs Quarterly,* vol. 8, no. 1 (Sept., 1972), 55–74.

ALFORD, ROBERT R. *Bureaucracy and Participation: Political Cultures in Four Wisconsin Cities.* Chicago: Rand McNally, 1969.

ALTSHULER, ALAN. *Community Control: The Black Demand for Participation in Large American Cities.* New York: Pegasus, 1970.

ANDERSON, STANLEY V. ed. *Ombudsmen for American Government?* Englewood Cliffs: Prentice-Hall, Inc., 1968.

ANDERSON, STANLEY V. *Ombudsman Papers: American Experience and Proposals,* Berkeley, Calif.: Institute of Governmental Studies, University of California, 1969.

BAILEY, STEPHEN K. "Ethics and the Public Service." *Public Administration Review.* vol. 24 (December 1964), pp. 234–243.

BERGER, RAOUL. "Administrative Arbitrariness: A Synthesis." *The Yale Law Journal.* vol. 78, no. 6 (May, 1969), pp. 965–1006.

BERNSTEIN, MARVER. "Understanding the Political Economy of Public Regulation," *Polity.* vol. 4, no. 4 (Summer, 1972), 549–556.

BOESEL, DAVID, RICHARD BERK, W. EUGENE GROVES, BETTYE EIDSON, and PETER W. ROSSI. "White Institutions and Black Rage." *Trans-Action.* vol. 6, no. 5 (March 1968), pp. 24–31.

BOONE, RICHARD W. "Reflections on Citizen Participation and the Economic Opportunity Act." *Public Administration Review.* Special Issue (Sept., 1972), 444–456.

BOYER, WILLIAM. *Bureaucracy on Trial.* Indianapolis: The Bobbs-Merrill Co., Inc., 1964.

CARY, WILLIAM L. *Politics and the Regulatory Agencies.* New York: McGraw-Hill Book Company, 1967.

COX, EDWARD F., *et al. Nader's Raiders.* New York: Grove Press, 1969.

CUNNINGHAM, JAMES. "Citizen Participation in Public Affairs." *Public Administration Review.* Special Issue (October, 1972), 589–602.

CURRAN, CHARLES E. "Public Administration Forum-Employment of the Hard-Core Poor: Whose Responsibility?" *Midwest Review of Public Administration.* vol. 30, no. 1 (February 1969), pp. 20–36.

DAVIS, KENNETH C. *Administrative Law in Government.* St. Paul: West Publishing Co., 1960.

DAVIS, KENNETH C. *Discretionary Justice: A Preliminary Inquiry.* Baton Rouge: Louisiana State University Press, 1969.

ELDEN JAMES N. "Public Administration and the Anti-Administrative Rebellion: Manifestations, Causes, and Implications." Paper delivered at the 65th annual meeting of the American Political Science Association, New York, September 2–6, 1969.

FANTINI, MARIO and MARILYN GITTELL. *Decentralization: Achieving Reform.* New York: Praeger Publications, Inc., 1973.

FAURI, DAVID. "Citizen Participation and the Rationale for Program Participation in Social Service Organizations." *Midwest Review of Public Administration.* VIII, #1 (January 1974), 42–51.

"The Federal Communications Commission and the Bell System: Abdication of Regulatory Responsibility." *Indiana Law Journal.* vol. 44, no. 3 (Spring 1969), pp. 459–477.

FREEMAN, J. LEIPER. *The Political Process: Executive Bureau-Legislative Committee Relations.* New York: Random House, Inc., 1955.

FRIEDMAN, ROBERT S., BERNARD W. KLEIN, and JOHN H. ROMANI. "Administrative Agencies and the Publics They Serve." *Public Administration Review.* vol. 26, no. 3 (September 1966), pp. 192–204.

FRITSCHLER, A. LEE. *Smoking and Politics: Policy Making and the Federal Bureaucracy.* 2nd. ed. Englewood Cliffs; Prentice Hall, Inc., 1975.

FUCHS, RALPH F. "The New Administrative State: Judicial Sanction for Agency Self-Determination in the Regulation of Industry." *Columbia Law Review.* vol. 69, no. 2 (February 1969), pp. 216–245.

GELLHORN, WALTER. *Ombudsmen and Other Citizens' Protectors in Nine Countries.* Cambridge: Harvard University Press, 1966.

HALL, ROBERT H. "Judicial Rule-Making Is Alive But Ailing." *American Bar Association Journal.* vol. 55 (June 1969), pp. 637–640.

HARRIS, JOSEPH P. *Congressional Control of Administration.* Washington, D.C.: The Brookings Institution, 1964.

HENDERSON, THOMAS A. *Congressional Oversight of Executive Agencies: A Study of the House Committee on Government Operations.* Gainesville: University of Florida Press 1970.

House Subcommittee on Government Operations. *The Block Grant Programs of the Law Enforcement Assistance Administration* (Parts 1 and 2), 92nd Congress, 1st Session, Washington, D.C.: Government Printing Office, 1971.

HERRING, E. PENDLETON. *Public Administration and the Public Interest.* New York: McGraw-Hill Book Company, 1936.

KREFETZ, SHARON PERLMAN and ALLAN E. GOODMAN. "Participation for What and for Whom." *Journal of Comparative Administration.* vol. 5, no. 3 (November 1973), 367–380.

KRISLOV, SAMUEL, and LLOYD D. MUSOLF. eds. *The Politics of Regulation.* Boston: Houghton Mifflin Company, 1964.

LANDIS, JAMES M. *The Administrative Process.* New Haven: Yale University Press, 1966.

LIPSKY, MICHAEL. *Protest in City Politics: Rent Strikes, Housing and the Power of the Poor.* Chicago: Rand McNally, 1970.

LORCH, ROBERT S. *Democratic Process and Administrative Law.* Detroit: Wayne State University Press, 1969.

MOYNIHAN, DANIEL P. *Maximum Feasible Misunderstanding: Community Action in the War on Poverty.* New York: The Free Press 1969.

MUSOLF, LLOYD. "American Mixed Enterprise and Governmental Responsibility." *Western Political Quarterly.* vol. 24, no. 4 (Dec., 1971), 789–806.

"OEO: Making Citizen Participation Work." *Public Management.* vol. 51, no. 7 (July 1969), pp. 21–22.

PEEL, ROY V. *The Ombudsman or Citizen's Defender: A Modern Institution.* Philadelphia: The American Academy of Political and Social Science, May 1968.

PIPE, G. RUSSELL. "Congressional Liaison: The Executive Branch Consolidates Its Relations with Congress." *Public Administration Review.* vol. 26, no. 1 (March 1966), pp. 14–24.

POWELL, NORMAN J. *Responsible Public Bureaucracy in the United States.* Boston: Allyn and Bacon, Inc., 1967.

ROWAT DONALD C. ed. *The Ombudsman: Citizen's Defender.* 2nd ed. Toronto: University of Toronto Press, 1968.

ROWAT, DONALD C. *The Ombudsman Plan.* Toronto: McClelland and Stewart, 1973.

SCHNETTINGER, ROBERT. "Bureaucracy and Representative Government: A Review Analysis." *Midwest Review of Public Administration.* vol. 7, no. 1 (April, 1973), 17–22.

SCHUBERT, GLENDON. *The Public Interest: A Critique of the Theory of a Political Concept.* New York: The Free Press, 1960.

SHAPIRO, MARTIN. *The Supreme Court and Administrative Agencies.* New York: Free Press, 1969.

SHARKANSKY, IRA. "An Appropriations Subcommittee and Its Client Agencies: A Comparative Study of Supervision and Control." *American Political Science Review.* vol. 59 (September 1965), pp. 622–628.

SMITH, MICHAEL. "Alienation and Bureaucracy: The Role of Participatory Administration." *Public Administration Review.* vol. 31, no. 6 (Nov.–Dec., 1971), 658–666.

Special Issue, "Citizens Action in Model Cities and CAP Programs: Case Studies and Evaluation." *Public Administration Review.* 32 (September 1972).

"Curriculum Essays on Citizens, Politics, and Administration in Urban Neighborhoods," *Public Administration Review,* Special Issue. 32 (October 1972).

STENBERG, CARL W. "Citizens and the Administrative State: From Participation to Power." *Public Administration Review.* vol. 32, no. 3 (May-June, 1972), 190–198.

THOMAS, NORMAN C. *Rule Nine: Politics, Administration, and Civil Rights.* New York: Random House, Inc., 1966.

WARREN, KENNETH F. "The Search for Administrative Responsibility." *Public Administration Review.* vol. 34, no. 2 (March–April, 1974), 176–182.

WEISS, CAROL H. *Evaluating Action Programs: Readings in Social Action and Education.* Boston: Allyn and Bacon, 1972.

WOLL, PETER. *Administrative Law: The Informal Process.* Berkeley: University of California Press. 1963.

WYNER, ALAN J. Lieutenant Governors as Political Ombudsmen. Berkeley, Calif.: Institute of Governmental Studies, University of California, *Public Affairs Report.* vol. 12, no. 6 (December 1971).

96780

350
U   96780

Uveges.
The dimension of public
administration.

350
U
                                     96780

AUTHOR

Uveges.

TITLE **The dimension of public
administration.**

DATE DUE	BORROWER'S NAME
AP 30 '83	Elmonda Forde